World Trade and Payments

The HarperCollins Series in Economics

Allen
Managerial Economics

Binger/Hoffman
Microeconomics With Calculus

Bowles/Edwards
Understanding Capitalism

Branson
Macroeconomic Theory and Policy

Browning/Browning
Microeconomic Theory and Applications

Byrns/Stone
Economics

Caniglia
Statistics for Economics

Carlton/Perloff
Modern Industrial Organization

Cooter/Ulen
Law and Economics

Ehrenberg/Smith
Modern Labor Economics

Ekelund/Tollison
Economics

Flanagan/Kahn/Smith/Ehrenberg
The Economics of the Employment Relationship

Fusfeld
The Age of the Economist

Gordon
Macroeconomics

Gregory
Essentials of Economics

Gregory/Ruffin
Basic Economics

Gregory/Stuart
Soviet Economic Structure and Performance

Hamermesh/Rees
The Economics of Work and Pay

Hartwick/Olewiler
The Economics of Natural Resource Use

Hogendorn
Economic Development

Hughes
American Economic History

Hunt
History of Economic Thought

Hunt/Sherman
Economics: An Introduction to Traditional and Radical Views

Husted/Melvin
International Economics

Krugman/Obstfeld
International Economics: Theory and Policy

Kwoka/White
The Antitrust Revolution

Laidler
The Demand For Money

Lardaro
Applied Econometrics

Lipsey/Steiner/Purvis/Courant
Economics

McCafferty
Macroeconomic Theory

McCarty
Dollars and Sense

Melvin
International Money and Finance

Miller
Economics Today

Miller/Benjamin/North
The Economics of Public Issues

Mills/Hamilton
Urban Economics

Mishkin
The Economics of Money, Banking, and Financial Markets

Petersen
Business and Government

Phelps
Health Economics

Ritter/Silber
Principles of Money, Banking, and Financial Markets

Ruffin
Intermediate Microeconomics

Ruffin/Gregory
Principles of Economics

Salvatore
Microeconomics

Sargent
Rational Expectations and Inflation

Studenmund
Using Econometrics

Tietenberg
Environmental and Natural Resource Economics

Waud
Macroeconomics
Microeconomics

Sixth Edition

World Trade and Payments
An Introduction

Richard E. Caves
Harvard University

Jeffrey A. Frankel
University of California, Berkeley

Ronald W. Jones
University of Rochester

HarperCollins*CollegePublishers*

Acquisitions Editor: John Greenman
Developmental Editor: Barbara Conover
Project Coordination: Donna DeBenedictis
Project Editor: Arlene Grodkiewicz
Design Supervisor: Wendy Ann Fredericks
Cover Design: Wendy Ann Fredericks
Cover Photo Montage: Roseanne Lufrano. Photos: Brooklyn
   Bridge, New York © Mark Romine/SuperStock; Tower
   Bridge, London © Paul Steel/The Stock Market
Production Administrator: Jeffrey Taub
Compositors: Syntax International/Better Graphics, Inc.
Printer and Binder: R. R. Donnelley & Sons Company
Cover Printer: The Lehigh Press, Inc.

World Trade and Payments: An Introduction, Sixth Edition

Copyright © 1993 by Richard E. Caves, Jeffrey A. Frankel, and Ronald W. Jones

Library of Congress Cataloging-in-Publication Data

Caves, Richard E.
   World trade and payments : an introduction / Richard E. Caves,
Jeffrey A. Frankel, Ronald W. Jones.—6th ed.
      p.   cm. — (The HarperCollins series in economics)
   Includes bibliographical references and index.
   ISBN 0-673-52274-1
   1. International trade. 2. Balance of payments. 3. Commercial
policy. I. Frankel, Jeffrey A. II. Jones, Ronald Winthrop, 1931–
III. Title. IV. Series.
HF1379.C38 1992
382—dc20   92-24764
                                                            CIP

92 93 94 95 9 8 7 6 5 4 3 2 1

CONTENTS

I

The Basic Trade Model   9

4 APPLICATIONS OF THE BASIC TRADE MODEL   52

II

International Trade Patterns and Income Distribution   *73*

5 TECHNOLOGY AND THE RICARDIAN TRADE MODEL   75

9 TRADE IN PRODUCERS' GOODS   158

10 INTERNATIONAL FACTOR MOVEMENTS AND MULTINATIONAL COMPANIES   176

III

The Theory and Practice of Commercial Policy   197

11 TARIFFS AND THE NATIONAL WELFARE   199

IV

Money, Income, and the Balance of Payments   303

V

International Financial Markets and Their Macroeconomic Implications   *445*

VI

The Determination of Exchange Rates in International Asset Markets   *563*

PREFACE

The sixth edition of *World Trade and Payments* arrives in a world filled with uncertainties about international commerce and the policies that affect it. The former centrally planned economies of Eastern Europe are groping toward the creation of market economies. That transformation will tend to restore major trading links with Western Europe that were severed by the central planning process and the Cold War. The Western European countries have completed a year that was marked by the removal of hundreds of types of administrative barriers to trade among members of the European Community. The Community economies now face the prospect of adjusting to the opportunities and competitive threats opened by those changes at the same time that major changes loom in trade with Eastern Europe.

The same pattern holds in the Americas. The United States and Mexico have been negotiating a free-trade arrangement at the same time that various South American nations have pondered seeking parallel arrangements. A U.S.-Canada free-trade arrangement was ratified in 1989, but the two countries have been caught up in several divisive policy disputes over particular trade issues.

In the trading world at large, negotiations over the Uruguay Round of trade liberalizations under the General Agreement on Tariffs and Trade staggered to an unpromising end. Many proponents of a liberal international trading regime view liberalization like a bicycle that must stay in motion to avoid a reversionary tumble into a retaliatory tangle of controls. The threat of entanglement seems close at hand for the United States as the general public fixes on Japan as the trading enemy, and major U.S. industrial sectors continue to obtain special protection from international competition.

As to the resolution of these uncertainties we claim no clairvoyance. We do, however, believe that students can be prepared to understand and interpret these structural changes and policy issues in the international economy along with others yet to come.

WHAT'S NEW IN THIS EDITION

Through this and previous editions of *World Trade and Payments* we have sought to combine a clear exposition of the proven and longlasting basic theories and analytical constructs of international trade and finance with applications that illustrate their uses. We have incorporated new theoretical developments as they came on stream and adjusted the emphasis given to those—new or old—that seem particularly helpful to the student seeking to understand the currently high-profile issues. At the same time we have kept a place for analyses speaking to issues currently shaded from popular attention but likely to burst forth in the future into the light of public discourse.

This general objective guides the changes that were made in this sixth edition— which are numerous. In Parts I and II we sought to lighten the tone of the basic theory without diminishing its content. In Chapter 2 a nation's gains from trade are related to the effect of its switching from one trading bloc to another. In Chapter 9 we clarified and further developed the analysis of comparative and absolute advantage. Chapter 10 contains a fuller analysis of the effects of immigration on wages and employment in the United States.

In Part III a major change was to transpose Chapters 13 and 14 in the fifth edition. The treatment of imperfect competition in international trade is now joined with the general-equilibrium analysis of trade controls (Chapters 11 and 12) and provides background for the political economy of trade (Chapter 14). Chapter 15 has been extensively rewritten to pick up recent developments in preferential trading arrangements and to organize what we know about trade and resource allocation in the centrally planned economies as background for anticipating the transition process.

Parts IV and V were completely rewritten in the previous edition to reflect the importance of international macroeconomics and finance in the 1990s. They have undergone significant compression and polishing. Attention is given to many recent and prospective developments including the liberalization of Japanese financial markets and the internationalization of the yen, economic shock therapy in Poland and the monetary unification of Germany, and the European Community's agreement on a European Monetary Union.

PEDAGOGY

Pedagogical features from previous editions of this book are retained and strengthened. Each chapter ends with a series of problems and discussion questions, as well as a list of suggestions for further readings. These readings represent either fundamental contributions or elaborations and applications that might prove useful to both student and instructor. The accompanying *Student Workbook* by Carsten Kowalczyk and Linda Tesar, also revised, provides extensive review of key concepts and contains numerous problem sets.

ADAPTING THE COURSE

World Trade and Payments is adaptable to various tracking styles. Some chapters are followed by one or more appendixes that explain specialized points or analytical constructions that some instructors might want to emphasize. Omitting any appendix, however, will not lessen comprehension of the chapter. For instructors wanting a more advanced approach we have retained, at the back of the text, the mathematical supplements presented in previous editions.

The book covers a conventional full line of topics, and with some additional material can serve as the basis for a full-year course at the undergraduate level or for separate semester (quarter) courses on the real and financial aspects of international trade. We have paid specific attention, however, to the needs of one-semester courses. The chapters in Parts I and Chapters 17, 18, and 22 provide the nucleus of a one-semester course that covers both the core of the real theory (with applications) and elements of open-economy macroeconomics and balance-of-payments adjustment. Many of the chapters outside this core are at least somewhat independent of one another, so that instructors can round out the course with selections from them. A course in international macroeconomics might include Chapters 16 to 19 and 21 to 24, also emphasizing Chapters 21 and 25 if the orientation is one toward finance, or Chapters 19 and 20 if it is toward less-developed countries.

ACKNOWLEDGMENTS

As authors of a textbook in its fifth revision, we have acquired a string of debts to colleagues, students, and various helpers that stretches the bounds of memory, let alone explicit acknowledgment. We confine ourselves to thanking those who helped with the sixth edition. Suggestions for revision were received from Janice Boucher, Bradley B. Billings, Colleen M. Callahan, Vandana Chandra, John Cuddington, Michael Ellis, Stephen Golub, Louis C. Green, Arvind Jaggi, William F. Maloney, Jaime Marquez, Usman A. Qureshi, Federico Sturzenegger, and Xavier de Vanssay. For clerical and related assistance or data, we thank Ann Flack, Lorie Wolfanger, Erik Evenhouse, Shang-jin Wei, Benjamin Chu, Marilyn Skiles, and Peter Hooper.

RICHARD E. CAVES
JEFFREY A. FRANKEL
RONALD W. JONES

1

INTRODUCTION

Unique among the concerns of economics, international trade has always carried a note of romance—the lure of the exotic, the hint of danger. Traders' dreams of bartering for the riches of the Orient spurred the European voyages of discovery that began in the fifteenth century. Today, supertankers move hundreds of thousands of tons of crude oil at a time from producing to consuming lands at strikingly low cost—except when the breakup of a tanker at sea pollutes hundreds of miles of shoreline.

The romance of international commerce surges through its contact with public policy. British restrictions on colonial trade helped to fuel the American Revolution. After World War II the nations of Western Europe, sickened by the recurrent wars spawned by modern nationalism, sought permanent reconciliation and peace through a trade treaty that removed barriers to commerce through the European Community.

This book promotes an understanding of the economic causes and consequences of international exchange. Any branch of economics rests on theoretical concepts and models. The scholar's job is to bring systematic observation and explanation to the chaotic diversity of the world. The Census Bureau records data on about 14,000 classifications of commodities entering into the foreign trade of the United States—4,000 for exports and 10,000 for imports. Are 14,000 explanations for these trade flows truly necessary? Could one explanation possibly cover every bundle of merchandise? Our quest is for the simplest model, or the smallest family of models, capable of answering the important questions about trade patterns and how public policy should deal with them.

The foreign commerce of nations, one of the oldest branches of economics, has drawn the attention of some of history's greatest economists. Indeed, many of the ideas in this book can boast of famous ancestors. Modern economics owes much of its understanding of money in international trade to the philosopher David Hume (Chapter 19). One principal model of international trade and production derives from David Ricardo (Chapter 5), an English stockbroker with a powerful analytical mind. Still, much of present-day international economics is quite new. A fruitful model relating trade to factors of production comes from two twentieth-century Swedish economists, Eli F. Heckscher and Bertil Ohlin (Chapter 7). As well, our understanding of how trade relates to employment, and how policy can deal properly with both, is in part a late fallout of the Keynesian Revolution of the late 1930s (Chapter 18).

1.1 THE SUBJECT OF INTERNATIONAL ECONOMICS

International economics is somewhat curiously related to the other conventional branches of economics. Public finance, money and banking, and labor economics select a neatly distinguished group of transactors or markets in the economy for special study. "But," you may ask, "doesn't international economics similarly deal with international markets?" It does, and these markets are capable of exact *legal* definition. Sovereign states are ubiquitous; therefore, we always can tell whether the two parties to a transaction are citizens of different countries.

Still, are international transactions economically unique and readily separated from transactions within nations? Do Kansas wheat farmers know or care whether the bushels of wheat they sell will be exported? When you buy a handkerchief, do you inspect it closely for a label indicating manufacture abroad? International transactions are indeed interrelated with domestic markets. Ultimately our explanation of international trade must be part of an explanation of each national market.

This intertwining of international and national markets runs throughout international economics. If India decides to train more physicians, the supply of physicians in Britain is apt to increase (through immigration). If the United States raises government spending to increase employment, employment in Canada is almost sure to increase. Clearly then, international economics can easily (and usefully) be viewed as "international aspects of supply and demand," "international aspects of money and finance," or "international aspects of taxation." Nonetheless, international trade and payments must be treated—for many good reasons—as a separate field of study. Following are two of the most important reasons for such treatment.

The Power of International Economic Theory

The most useful models for explaining international trade are those that are simple, strong, and general. They not only explain international trade patterns, they also tell much about patterns of production, income distribution, and so on within countries.

What, indeed, is the simplest possible way to model the international economy? The central questions about international trade deal solely with *exchange* between traders in two national markets. This book will argue that the sparest and clearest explanation of trade between nations, and of the gains nations derive from trade, requires only a description of the exchange of fixed endowments of goods. Such simplification, by concentrating first on exchange, stems from putting aside the details of how goods are produced. We then can explain, for example, what happened in 1973 when the exporting nations quadrupled the price of oil. Having set the essentials, the basic model of trade can be expanded to explore details of how bundles of goods are produced.

Why should economists employ separate models to explain international trade and domestic trade? The traditional answer holds that factors of production—labor and capital—in the long run move freely within the national economy, but are immobile between countries. Presumably, labor and capital move freely between New York and California, whenever workers or lenders feel that such a shift will improve their real incomes. If that assumption is correct, the goods traded between the two states and the effect of that trade on their "native" factor endowments will be less interesting. On the other hand, if little movement of labor and capital occurs between, for example, Mexico and France, the commodities they trade and their benefits from the exchange become both interesting and important.

The assumption that factors of production are perfectly mobile within countries and perfectly immobile between them is not completely correct. Consider the international migrations of the nineteenth century, the outflow of capital to the developing countries in the 1970s, and the immobility of low-paid labor in America's Appalachia or Italy's Mezzogiorno! However, probably no assumption used by economists is completely accurate. Economists start out by supposing that the assumption is correct but then relax it in two ways. They introduce a form of immobility in the domestic economy by assuming that one factor of production used by each industry is tied to that industry and cannot find employment elsewhere, no matter what happens to its wage. They also relax the assumption that factors are immobile between countries; after learning how trade affects the incentive for factors to migrate internationally, they can show more easily what happens when some factors seize the opportunity.

The same power belongs to models of the macroeconomy. A quarter of a century ago, American macroeconomists mostly used (and taught) models of national income and employment that ignored international transactions. Events in the international economy then forced economists to change their tactics. For example, international capital flows play an important macroeconomic role by representing a difference between domestic saving and investment. Any major disturbance to domestic saving or investment decisions—for instance, when the government decides to run a large budget deficit—triggers a large change in international capital flows and other important macroeconomic variables.

The Importance of Nationhood for Policy   +Trade pattern & public policy

The other factor that distinguishes international economics is rooted in policy-making, especially in the context of policies toward international trade and payments. Trade occurs between sovereign nations, between us and them. Two governments, with potentially clashing objectives, can apply their policies to the flow of trade between them, and against each other's interests. More profoundly, the fear and suspicion of outsiders, felt by even the most saintly mortal, repeatedly prompt the debate over whether or not the nation benefits from trading with foreigners. No one asks whether Vermont gains from trading with New Hampshire, or Minneapolis with St. Paul. The proposition that the United States and France both gain from trading with each other might not, however, win a majority vote—in either country. Rich countries fear they will suffer from importing the products of low-wage foreign labor; poor countries dread imports created by foreign high-level technology.

This universal xenophobia contributes to the often bitter and protracted nature of countries' international economic policy disputes. For example, a major issue in a 1988 Canadian election was approval of a free-trade agreement to end restrictions on trade flows between the United States and Canada. Widespread consensus among economists suggested that the arrangement would add at least several percentage points to Canada's national income. However, many Canadians considered the arrangement an invasion of their sovereignty and nationhood. This debate was dramatic but by no means unusual. Such disputes over international policy are often bitter not only because some parties gain and some lose, but also because dollars-and-cents issues become emotionally charged.

Conflicts over international economic policy can divide two or more nations, usually in proportion to the intensity of feelings about the policies within each nation. Once again, concerns for economic welfare often give way to concerns for perceived fair treatment and national honor. For example, a large excess of U.S. imports from Japan over U.S. exports to Japan has deeply bothered Americans. In 1988 this concern led the U.S. Congress to pass legislation urging the president to retaliate against any country maintaining "unfair" trade barriers against American exports, although analysis suggests that a country's bilateral trade balance with any single trading partner has no particular significance (the *overall* balance does). Furthermore, the complex institutional factors that limit Japan's imports of manufactured goods (from all sources, not just the United States) result primarily in increased cost to Japanese consumers, not in lower incomes for the foreign suppliers. Clearly, the motive behind the American enthusiasm for retaliation lies in something other than a detached calculation of national economic benefits.

The Japanese challenge has also stirred great concern about the "competitiveness" of the U.S. economy. Economists point out that competitiveness is a treacherous concept when applied to the national economy as a whole. The worthy result of concern over competitiveness, they generally agree, is to focus attention on cost-effective ways to increase the productivity of our national factor endowment. Paradoxically, if such remedies can be found, the case for adopting them in no way depends on whether other national economies are more or less competitive.

How, then, does international economics pick its way through this minefield of nationalistic attitudes and controversies? A critical role for the theory of international trade is to identify the gains from trade and their indications for economic policy. Hence, the spare, clear explanation of trade through a simple model of exchange is particularly useful for determining the gains from trade.

After the gains are determined, the next focus is the division of gains among the trading nations. International economics takes a flexible approach to this question. Following the tradition of general economics, international economics often concentrates on maximizing the welfare—the real income—of a single country's citizens. However, economic analysis also identifies policies maximizing global welfare, which often differ with a particular national interest. Many policies that raise the welfare of one trading nation lower the global welfare and perforce the welfare levels of other trading nations. Identifying the clashes and harmonies between national and world welfare is an important task of this book. In addition, the welfare of groups of countries (such as the European Community) and of groups of income recipients within a country must be considered. Changes in the international economy or in trade policies almost always change the distribution of a country's income as well as its level. Only by understanding the relation between trade and income distribution can we discover why American labor has opposed foreign investment by U.S. companies or why the South once opposed but now favors high tariffs.

Issues of international conflict and harmony also arise over short-run macroeconomic policies and their implications for employment and inflation. From 1983 to 1985, the United States and Japan pursued macroeconomic policies that kept the price of the dollar high and the yen low. Japanese goods became cheap for American buyers, and Japan's resulting bilateral trade surplus provoked complaints from competing American industries and, ultimately, the cries for retaliation previously noted. Even though the policies in question were not serving either nation's interests particularly well, in principle these policies certainly could have been coordinated to the betterment of both countries. In macroeconomic policy as well, international economics can affect why conflicts may arise among national policies and how conflicts can be turned into mutual gain by coordinating those policies.

In short, international economics seeks to cast light through the dark waters of contention over economic policy by (1) showing how international exchange and improvements in economic policies can result in gains; (2) identifying the bases for conflict over international economic policy, both within nations (between interest groups) and among them; and (3) pointing to ways in which conflicting groups or nations can resolve their differences for mutual benefit.

(margin handwritten note: gains / conflict / mutual benefit)

1.2 THE ORGANIZATION OF THIS BOOK

International economics builds models to explain the links between national economic systems and to show how nations' policies can yield maximum welfare and stability. The purpose of this book is to explain these models simply but comprehensively and to show how they can be used. We shall apply those models liberally to present-day issues of international economic policy—not from a delusion that those problems will look the same tomorrow as they do today, but because they provide a handy proving ground to turn theoretical concepts and models into an "active vocabulary" for understanding new issues as they arise.

We have promised to begin with the simplest model of trade between nations, and that is the focus of Part I. Chapter 2 investigates exchange between the citizens of two countries who hold arbitrary stocks of goods that they can barter with one another. Chapter 3 examines the nation's productive apparatus to show how the production capabilities of trading countries affect their international trade. Chapter 4 illustrates some uses of this basic apparatus for analyzing changes in the terms of trade, the growth of productive capacity (can our economy's growth make us worse off?), and flows of capital from one country to another.

(margin handwritten note: (1-4) simple)

Part II builds into this simple model various explanations of the nation's production apparatus. We first describe production processes in the fashion of David Ricardo, with a unit of each output requiring inputs of only a certain number of labor-hours (Chapter 5). Another scenario assumes each output requires labor plus units of a factor of production used only in that sector (Chapter 6). In a third scenario, each output requires both capital and labor, but in different proportions (Chapters 7 and 8). These chapters contain models of the way trade interacts with the domestic pattern of production and affects the distribution of income. Chapter 9 shifts focus from

(margin handwritten note: (5-8) types of production)

international trade in final goods to international trade in intermediate goods, and Chapter 10 discusses factors of production. Movements of footloose intermediate stages of production among countries and the underlying factors of production are important to any understanding of international exchange.

Controls

Part III considers tariffs and other controls on trade, identifying their effects and asking in what circumstances they might be desirable from the controlling nation's point of view. A major clash of interests exists in that the welfare of all countries together generally would be raised by removing all restrictions on international trade, but one country acting alone sometimes can improve its own welfare by maintaining or increasing restrictions. Chapters 11 and 12 present the theory of controls on trade, and Chapters 13, 14, and 15 apply this theory to present-day trade policies. Chapter 13 analyzes special problems posed by imperfectly competitive markets, in which nations attempt to exert monopoly power in international trade or to combat similar efforts by other countries. Chapter 14 examines types of trade restrictions in actual use and various nations' efforts to reduce restrictions through international cooperation. Chapter 15 explores special types of preferential trading arrangements, such as the European Community and the Canada-U.S. free-trade arrangement, which seek to eliminate trade restrictions among members while maintaining them against outsiders.

Financial Movements

Part IV presents models of short-run disequilibrium and adjustment in order to understand what happens when income and expenditure are not equal, or when money prices are sticky. The analysis begins with simple models, then allows additional factors to vary. Chapter 16 explains the balance of payments accounts. Chapter 17 introduces the influence of the exchange rate on the balance of trade. Chapter 18 allows for variations in income (or employment) and the rate of interest. Chapter 19 discusses the influence of the money price level. Chapter 20 focuses on adjustment in a special but important case—the "small, open economy" that takes as given the prices of all the goods it buys and sells on the world market, but that contains a sector producing goods and services that are not traded internationally.

Capital Movements

While Part IV addresses international movements of money and holdings of foreign-currency reserves, Part V examines international capital movements. Chapter 21 provides background on the international financial markets—trends and major innovations, plus the liberalization and internationalization that has increasingly integrated national financial markets. Chapter 22 develops the implications of financial-market integration for the domestic macroeconomy, in particular for the operation of fiscal and monetary policy. Chapter 23 applies this analysis to the international interdependence of policies, while also introducing the role of inelastic supplies of output as an influence on price levels and inflation.

Part VI considers exchange rates' determinants. Chapter 24 develops the role of expectations when determining the foreign-exchange rate. Lastly, Chapter 25 discusses the problem of exchange-rate forecasting and the role of risk in determining international asset portfolios and prices.

Following the final chapter is a group of supplements to the principal theoretical chapters of the book. To satisfy readers who seek a more formal approach, we have added these supplements, which demand some mathematical sophistication—a basic knowledge of differential calculus. The supplements are designed to be read with the text, but the text is, of course, independent of the supplements. The text is completely free of any formal mathematics other than a sprinkling of high-school algebra, drawing instead upon simple diagrams and verbal reasoning.

SUGGESTIONS FOR FURTHER READING

Following each chapter is a brief list of suggestions for further reading, which is provided principally for the instructor who wishes to assign fuller accounts of some points developed in the chapter and the student who seeks either further enlightenment or a term-paper topic. Sometimes we refer to classic expositions of important ideas in the chapter. In other cases we mention fuller contemporary accounts. Many references deal with applications of international economics to empirical explanation and policy-making. To each reference we have added an explanation of its content. Following is a list of volumes of readings or collected material relevant to many aspects of international economics.

Baldwin, Robert E., and J. David Richardson, eds. *International Trade and Finance: Readings*, 3rd ed. (Boston: Little, Brown and Co., 1986). Many readings useful to undergraduate students.

Bhagwati, Jagdish N., ed. *International Trade: Selected Readings*, 2nd ed. (Cambridge, MA: M.I.T. Press, 1987). A collection of recent scholarly papers.

Bhandari, Jagdeep S., and Bluford H. Putnam, eds. *Economic Interdependence and Flexible Exchange Rates* (Cambridge, MA: M.I.T. Press, 1983). Collection of scholarly papers.

Caves, Richard E., and Harry G. Johnson, eds. *Readings in International Economics* (Homewood, IL: Richard D. Irwin, 1968). A collection of classic articles, mostly on the theory of international economics.

Cooper, R. N., ed. *International Finance: Selected Readings* (Harmondsworth, UK: Penguin, 1969). Another collection of classics.

Dornbusch, Rudiger, and Jacob A. Frenkel, eds. *International Economic Policy: Theory and Evidence* (Baltimore: Johns Hopkins University Press, 1979). Papers surveying the major aspects of international economic policy; some are addressed to the professional economist; some are less technical.

Fieleke, Norman S. *The International Economy under Stress* (Cambridge, MA: Ballinger, 1988). Essays on current policy questions.

King, Philip. *International Economics and International Economic Policy: A Reader* (New York: McGraw-Hill, 1990). Current readings useful to students.

Letiche, John M., ed. *International Economic Policies and Their Theoretical Foundations: A Sourcebook*, 2d ed. (New York: Academic Press, 1992). A wide-ranging collection of analytical papers related to international economic policy.

Ohlin, Bertil, Per-Ove Hesselborn, and Per Magnus Wijkman, eds. *The International Allocation of Economic Activity: Proceedings of a Nobel Symposium Held at Stockholm* (London: Macmillan, 1977). Reflections of leading scholars on the current state of international economics.

Spence, A. Michael, and Heather A. Hazard, eds. *International Competitiveness* (Cambridge, MA: Ballinger, 1988). Papers on current issues of international economic policy.

I

The Basic Trade Model

2

THE INTERNATIONAL EXCHANGE OF COMMODITIES

Some trade patterns need little explanation. If you live in the United States and like coffee, you have your coffee imported from Brazil or some other coffee-growing country because it is not produced at home. If you live in Germany or Italy, you depend on foreign sources to supply fuel and lubricants for your sports car. If such imports were cut off, your level of well-being or "real income" would surely be reduced. If all trade were of this kind—with each country producing commodities desired by all countries but available only locally—there would be little need for the economist either to expound on the virtues of trade or to explain trade patterns. These would be almost self-evident. Indeed, billions of dollars in world trade are spent each year on coffee, chromium, copper, tea, oil, sugar, and other items that nature has placed in some communities but not in others.

Many items that are exchanged on world markets, however, could be produced in a number of locations. Cost comparisons dictate that some countries produce and export transistor radios, steel, and textiles to other countries that find it advantageous to concentrate on agricultural or mineral products. Countries differ from each other in their technologies, climates, and skill levels, as well as in their relative supplies of primary factors such as land and labor; these differences all bear upon production costs and trade patterns. Some productive activities require a large scale of output to bring costs down, so these occur in relatively large countries. Historical experience has conditioned labor forces in different countries to acquire different skills, thus imparting an advantage in the production of particular commodities and not in others.

In order to describe the fundamental forces that determine trade, this opening part of the book considers a simple model in which two countries engage in trade and in which each country is capable of producing two commodities (food and clothing). Labor and any other inputs in the production process are trapped within national boundaries, and international trade provides each country the opportunity only to consume food and clothing in proportions different from those produced locally. If the basis for mutual gains from trade can be established in such a simple, stripped-down model ("the basic trade model"), there is even more reason to expect flourishing trade in a world of many countries and many commodities.

The present chapter simplifies matters even further by ignoring cost considerations. Commodities only exist in nature. It is impossible to identify the costs of producing commodities and thus to connect trade patterns to underlying cost differentials. Each country is endowed with certain amounts of food and clothing, and there is no way in which the quantities in the "endowment bundle" can be varied in response to changes in price. The motivation in making such a patently unrealistic assumption is twofold: (1) Such a simple trading world is easier to describe than one in which resources can be pulled out of one sector and attracted to another by a rise in price. (2) The ultimate rationale for mutually beneficial trade can be seen to rest on deeper considerations than the existence of cost differentials between countries.

The "endowment" model of commodity exchange is actually less restrictive than this description suggests. International differences in supplies of commodities are important. Indeed, trade patterns will depend upon these supply differences as well as upon differences in taste patterns. What is momentarily kept at bay is information as to cost comparisons between countries and how they reflect technologies, skill levels, and factor supplies. Even with commodities in strictly inelastic supply, there can arise mutual gains from international trade. The next two chapters explore how more obvious sources of trade gains—being able to reallocate resources to those activities one does best—serve to enhance and enrich the description of the possibilities for gain already established in this chapter's austere model of commodity exchange.

2.1 THE GAINS FROM TRADE

This section establishes a result that is absolutely basic:

> If relative commodity prices differ between countries in the absence of trade, both (all) countries can gain by exchanging commodities at any intermediate price ratio.

To understand this proposition we review some concepts perhaps familiar from previous study: budget lines and indifference curves.

Relative Prices and the Budget Constraint

The concept of "relative" price arises naturally in this simplified two-commodity trading world. Clothing's relative price is the amount of food that must be surrendered in a market exchange for one unit of clothing. You are more used to prices being quoted in money terms—dollars in the United States, escudos in Portugal, and yen in Japan. If you know money prices, you can compute relative prices; if clothing costs $5 a yard and food $10 a bushel, the relative price of clothing is $\frac{1}{2}$, measured in bushels (of food) per yard (of clothing).

The reason we wish to concentrate on relative prices instead of absolute (currency) prices is that we are making an extremely simple assumption about the link between people's expenditures and the "incomes" represented by their endowments of clothing and food: Individuals (and therefore nations as well) spend exactly the value of their incomes. In general, an individual often manages a close balance between current spending and current income, with discrepancies met by net cash outflows or inflows or by changes in other assets and/or liabilities. Here we assume an exact balance.

Such an assumption, which we refer to as the "classical" form of budget constraint, greatly eases our task in the first half of this book because it allows us to postpone (until Part IV) those issues dealing with exchange rate crises, the international monetary system, and a nation's balance-of-payments adjustment problems. This does not mean we are describing a barter economy. Instead, we take for granted the advantages that a monetary system conveys in easing transactions. We only require that any market purchase of food be matched exactly by a sale of clothing of equivalent value. Because of this restriction on spending behavior, it becomes important to pierce the "monetary veil" of currency prices to know how much clothing must be exchanged per unit of food or how much food must be surrendered to purchase one clothing unit.

Figure 2.1 illustrates the consumption choices available to an individual who possesses endowment bundle E (OG units of clothing and OF units of food) but who is capable of trading food for clothing (or vice versa) at some specified market prices. Given these prices, the individual can compute all the combinations of food and clothing that have the *same value* as does this endowment point, E. These combinations are shown in Figure 2.1 by a downward-sloping line through E, the budget constraint line *BEA*. For example, suppose the individual wishes to consume the

---

FIGURE 2.1   The Budget Constraint

The slope of the budget line *BEA* is HJ/JE. It shows the relative price of clothing. Its inverse, JE/HJ, is the relative price of food.

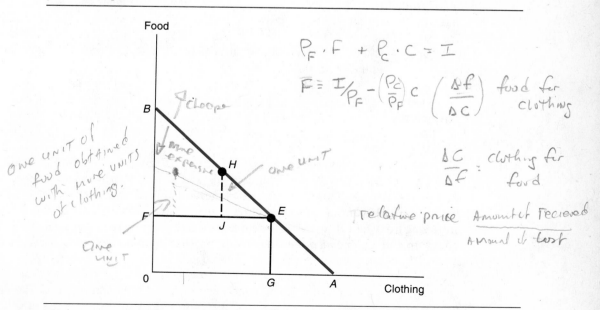

commodity bundle shown by point H on this line. Let food and clothing prices be denoted by p_F and p_C, respectively. If H is to have the same value as endowment point E, the value of purchases of food (p_F times amount HJ) must equal the value of clothing given up in exchange (p_C times amount JE). That is, clothing's relative price, p_C/p_F, is shown by the absolute value of the *slope* of the budget line HJ/JE.

The slope of the budget line indicates how much of one commodity must be given up to obtain one unit of the other. If commodity prices change but the individual's endowment point (E in Figure 2.1) does not, the budget line changes slope but still must pass through the endowment point. Suppose that food's relative price rises. Would this be shown by rotating budget line BEA around point E in a clockwise or counterclockwise direction? This is a simple question, but experience reveals that it is well worth thinking through. A higher relative food price than is shown by line BEA in Figure 2.1 would be shown by a *flatter* line through E—more clothing would have to be given up in exchange for one unit of food.

The budget line through the endowment point shows only what food and clothing bundles *could* be purchased; it does not specify which point *would* be demanded. To determine consumption choices, we must have information about taste patterns or preferences, as well as about endowments and relative prices.

Indifference Curves

Indifference curves, expressing our individual preferences or tastes concerning food and clothing, are illustrated in Figure 2.2. Start by considering the bundle of food and clothing shown by point E (quantity OD of clothing and OF of food). As long as both commodities yield satisfaction, any consumption bundle northeast of E, such as H, must be preferred to E, and any bundle with less of both commodities than E, such as I, must be less desirable than E. To proceed, suppose one unit of clothing is added to the consumption basket at E, which leads to the higher level of satisfaction that would be obtained from bundle J. Then ask how much food must be taken away from the individual so that welfare is restored exactly to what it was at E. Suppose this quantity is JB. If so, the individual is indifferent to the choice of consuming bundle E or bundle B. E and B lie on the same indifference curve, labeled y_0 in Figure 2.2. (Throughout the book the symbol "y" indicates "real income," "utility," or "satisfaction.")

The foregoing remarks establish that indifference curves are negatively sloped: A sacrifice in the quantity of one commodity consumed must be balanced by an appropriate increment in the quantity of the other commodity. The indifference curves in Figure 2.2 also are bowed in toward the origin, reflecting the common assumption that the marginal rate at which individuals are willing to substitute more of one commodity for less of another changes along an indifference curve. The ratio JB to EJ in Figure 2.2 shows the *marginal rate of substitution* between food and clothing in moving from E to B. The ratio KC to BK is smaller (the curve gets flatter in moving from E to B to C), showing that the further sacrifice of food involved in moving from B to C (C has one more unit of clothing than B does) can be smaller while still keeping the individual on indifference curve y_0. As the consumer has less and less food, each unit provides greater value, whereas each additional unit increment of clothing will raise satisfaction less the more clothing the consumer possesses. The marginal rate

FIGURE 2.2   Indifference Curves

The bowed-in shape reflects diminishing marginal rates of substitution. All points on indifference curve y_1 are preferred to any point on indifference curve y_0.

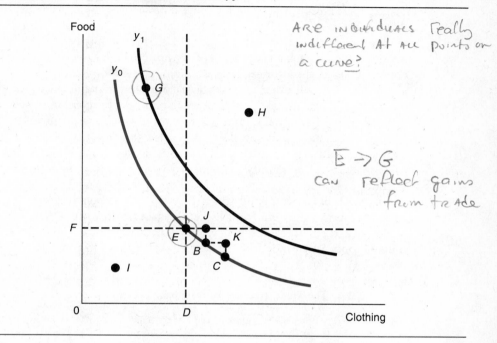

of substitution is indicated by the slope of the indifference curve. It diminishes along the curve y_0 as more clothing is substituted for food.

The indifference curve y_0 is one of many that could be drawn. Indeed, the "commodity space" is filled with these curves. Another is curve y_1, which is farther out from the origin and therefore indicates a higher level of real income than does curve y_0. For example, point G is preferred to point E. If the individual initially possessed the bundle of food and clothing indicated by point E and then was able to exchange some clothing for food to allow consumption of point G, the individual's well-being would clearly be improved. As we shall illustrate, trade can bring about precisely this kind of gain.

Trade Benefits Both Countries

We now make a bold assumption—that the indifference curve apparatus illustrated in Figure 2.2 can be used to show levels of *country* welfare, with E as the aggregate bundle of food and clothing available to that community in the absence of any possibility of exchanging goods with other nations.[1] With no such international trade

---

[1] Some of the problems involved in aggregating indifference curves of individuals in order to talk about the welfare of the community are discussed in Section 2.5. The basic reference to the issue of drawing indifference curves for a community is P. A. Samuelson, "Social Indifference Curves," *Quarterly Journal of Economics*, 70 (February 1956): 1–22.

allowed, the slope of the community's indifference curve at E must reflect relative
commodity prices prevailing in this no-trade state of "autarky." Prices in the home
market reflect the trade-off between food and clothing in consumer tastes. These
indifference curves, along with endowment point E, are redrawn in Figure 2.3. Two
budget lines are drawn through E: line CED and line AEB. They each represent a
different set of relative prices, with food relatively cheaper (and thus clothing relatively
more expensive) along CED than along AEB. For each relative price (and associated
budget line) there is a most preferred consumption point if the community can exchange
commodities at those prices. For example, point F is the best consumption point
along line CED; all other points would lie on lower indifference curves than curve
y_1. Note that consumption could not reach point F if the community were not allowed
to trade with other nations, for it would then be forced to consume food and clothing
precisely in the amounts locally available (as shown by E). The slope of line AEB
shows the relative price of clothing that must exist if trade is disallowed. At no other
price would the community be content to consume food and clothing in the proportions indicated by point E.

Line CED in Figure 2.3 illustrates the possibilities open to this community to trade
at relative prices different from those prevailing before trade. The community then
could offer to export GE units of clothing, which have the same market value as FG
units of food. Such trade would allow the community to consume the bundle, F, on

---

FIGURE 2.3   The Trade Triangle for the Home Country

The home country originally consumes its endowment bundle, E, at relative prices shown by line AB. If
it could trade at prices shown by line CD, it could export GE units of clothing to obtain FG units of
food, thus consuming the bundle shown by F and improving its real income to the level indicated by
the y_1 indifference curve.

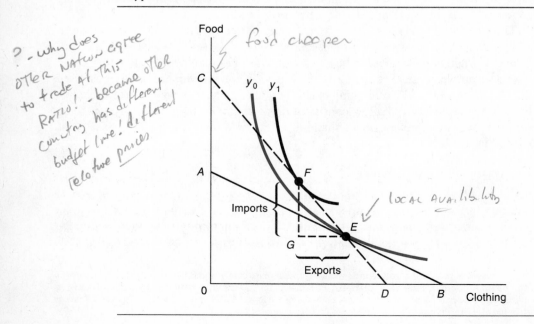

FIGURE 2.4   The Trade Triangle for the Foreign Country

The foreign country originally consumes its endowment bundle, E^*, at relative prices shown by line A^*B^*. If it could trade at prices shown by line C^*D^*, it could export E^*G^* units of food to obtain G^*F^* units of clothing, thus consuming the bundle shown by F^* and improving its real income to the level shown by the y_1^* indifference curve.

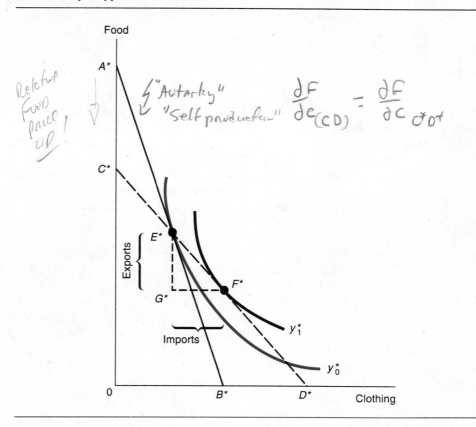

the indifference curve y_1. This indifference curve is higher than the original curve, y_0, passing through the endowment bundle. In such a manner we can prove that the opportunity to trade at relative prices different from those in isolation at home must improve real incomes at home.[2]

But is such trade feasible? Could the home country obtain the desired food imports from abroad? Figure 2.4 illustrates a case in which the foreign country would be willing to export, at the same price ratio as shown by line CED in Figure 2.3, amount FG of food to the home country. In Figure 2.4 the foreign country's endowment point is E^*, and through that point line $C^*E^*D^*$ is drawn with the same slope as line CED

---

[2] Here we only consider the case in which the relative price of food offered to the home country is lower than the price shown by AEB. However, the symmetry of the case should convince you that if the home country were offered a relative clothing price lower than line AEB (shown by a line through E flatter than AEB), it also could reach a higher indifference curve than y_0.

in Figure 2.3, thereby showing the same relative commodity prices. Along budget line $C^*E^*D^*$ the foreign country's most desired consumption point is F^*. It would be willing to export E^*G^* of food (equal to FG in Figure 2.3) in exchange for G^*F^* imports of clothing. Note that if the foreign country could not engage in trade, it would evaluate food and clothing by its marginal rate of substitution at E^*, shown by the slope of line $A^*E^*B^*$. But this slope is different from the slope of AEB in Figure 2.3. The relative price of food and clothing that is illustrated in Figure 2.3 by CED and in Figure 2.4 by line $C^*E^*D^*$ lies intermediate between the low price of clothing in the home country before trade (shown by the slope of AEB in Figure 2.3) and the high price of clothing in the pretrade situation in the foreign country (shown by the slope of $A^*E^*B^*$ in Figure 2.4). This justifies the basic result stated at the beginning of this section: A divergence in the relative price of commodities in the two countries before trade indicates a mutual potential gain from trade for both countries at a common intermediate price ratio. It is important to note that no "exploitation" is involved. Although world total supplies of food and clothing are unaltered throughout (by the fixed-endowment assumption), a redistribution of each commodity from the country in which it is cheaper to the country in which it is valued more highly increases the welfare of both countries.

Example: A P.O.W. Camp

Shortly after World War II, R. A. Radford, an Allied prisoner of war in Italian and German prison camps for several years, published an account of the manner in which markets developed among prisoners in order to exchange endowments originating primarily in fairly even allocations of Red Cross parcels.[3] Of course, taste differences stimulated active trade flows. An item such as cigarettes, found regularly in the parcels, would be in heavy demand by some and would offer virtually zero value for others— except as a medium of exchange. Of special note for our purposes is Radford's observation that different national groups supported different relative prices. Any individual with access to more than one such group could make great gains via arbitraging among the price differences. (Radford describes a priest who started with a tin of cheese and five cigarettes and converted them into a sizable hoard by this activity.) Coffee was relatively more expensive in French camps, tea in English and Canadian ones. If these camps were connected by a common price system, all would gain. If the camps were kept separate, some of the potential gains would accrue to arbitragers. As Radford emphasized, this was an exchange economy in which production virtually did not exist. Gains from trade derived from differences in individual evaluations of initial endowments.

2.2 FREE-TRADE EQUILIBRIUM

The common price ratio allowing mutually beneficial trade in Figures 2.3 and 2.4 is an example of a *free-trade equilibrium*. Can prices be found that guarantee such a balance between exports and imports? The most basic tools in economics, demand

---

[3] R. A. Radford, "The Economic Organization of a P.O.W. Camp," *Economica*, 12 (November 1945): 189–201.

what causes balance of value for
Exports and imports

FIGURE 2.5 World Demand and Supply

The terms of trade, OT, are determined by the equilibrium between the world's demand for food $(D_F + D_F^*)$ and the supply of food $(S_F + S_F^*)$.

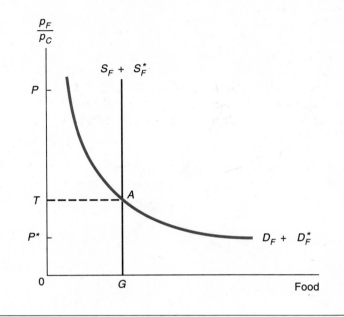

and supply curves, can be used to establish that such an equilibrium generally can be obtained.

Consider each country in turn. The home country's demand and supply response to price changes can be deduced from Figure 2.3. Supply is easy, since the quantities of food (and clothing) the home country can produce are fixed at point E; its supply curve would be vertical (no change in quantity as price varies). Demand, however, does depend on price. Figure 2.3 illustrates an increase in the quantity of food demanded at home from the level that would be consumed at home in autarky (measured vertically to point E) to the greater quantity (measured vertically to point F) of food demanded at the lower relative world price of food depicted by line CFD. Foreign supply remains fixed at point E^* in Figure 2.4, while it is possible to trace out the response of the foreign demand for food to changes in prices.

The responses of consumers and producers in the two countries can be brought together in Figure 2.5, since free trade implies that there is one world market in which a common price is established. Figure 2.5 shows that at relative price for food, OT, the world market is cleared. This price corresponds to the parallel lines CED (Figure 2.3) and $C^*E^*D^*$ (Figure 2.4).[4] In Figure 2.5 two other relative food prices are indicated

---

[4] As will be discussed in Chapter 3, the world supply curve would normally be positively sloped when commodities are produced, whereas the demand curve may, for high prices, become positively sloped. These complications are ignored here.

FIGURE 2.6   Excess Demand and Supply

Equilibrium quantity OA shows free-trade imports of food by the home country at the equilibrium price ratio, OT.

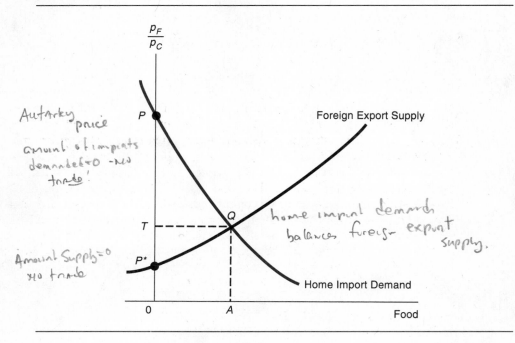

Handwritten annotations:
Autarky price
amount of imports
demanded=0 - NO
trade!

Amount Supply=0
no trade

home import demand
balances foreign export
supply.

on the vertical axis: (1) The high price OP at which the home market would be cleared if the home country could not trade is shown by line AEB in Figure 2.3. (2) By contrast, the food price that would rule in isolation abroad is lower, OP^* (corresponding to line $A^*E^*B^*$ in Figure 2.4). Of course, with world demand and supply for food equated at OT, so must world demand and supply for clothing be matched.[5]

Thinking of the world as a single market in which total world demands and supplies are compared provides us with one way of illustrating free-trade equilibrium. An alternative technique is to consider the *net* response of consumers and producers at home in one curve and compare it with the *net* reaction abroad, shown by a different curve. Concentrate on the market for food. Figure 2.6 shows a downward-sloping home import demand curve for food together with an upward-sloping foreign export supply curve for food. The relative food price OP corresponds to the autarky price ratio for the home country illustrated in Figure 2.3 by line AEB. For higher prices of food the home country would attempt to export food, while for lower prices its demand for food exceeds the quantity available in its endowment bundle. The foreign country's demand for food is brought into balance with its own supplies at the lower

---

[5] This follows since each country is assumed to spend on both commodities the same amount as the total of its endowments. (See Chapter Problem 6.)

price ratio, OP^*. Higher prices bring forth excess supplies for export. At the free-trade equilibrium price ratio, OT, home import demand balances foreign export supply.[6]

2.3 PRODUCT VARIETY AND INTRA-INDUSTRY TRADE

The preceding discussion of mutual gains from the international exchange of commodities assumed that the "food" and "clothing" available in one country are exactly the same as those available in the other. We now propose a detour by supposing, instead, that the kind of commodity classified in one industrial category has somewhat different characteristics in one country from those it has in the other. In such a case opening a country's markets to international trade could result in simultaneous exports and imports in each category, a phenomenon referred to as *intra-industry trade*.

Two main types of taste patterns are singled out to account for such two-way trade. Most obvious, some individuals prefer one type of food to another, whereas other individuals would reverse this ranking of preferences. All it takes to support two-way trade is that each country contain individuals of both types. Lovers of sports cars and of no-nonsense basic automobiles may reside both in Italy and in Germany. International trade then would involve each nation's cars being exported to the other. Alternatively, any single individual may be like any other, but each may display a love for variety in product types. Being able to consume two or more kinds of "food" (e.g., brie and cheddar) may be preferred to being restricted to either national type alone. Thus trade could once again exhibit a pattern whereby products in the same industrial category are both imported and exported.

The phenomenon of intra-industry trade forces us to make a distinction between gross trade flows and net trade flows. If food is a homogeneous commodity, a country's imports represent the net balance between total consumption and local production. By contrast, if food is heterogeneous, with the type of food product available in each country somewhat different, even a balance in aggregate consumption and production in each country could mask substantial trade flows. Net trade could be close to zero, but gross trade could be large as consumers in each country partake of the fare available abroad as well as at home.

To consider a particularly simple example, suppose that two countries have identical tastes for and endowments of aggregate food and clothing. If each commodity is strictly identical (homogeneous) in its characteristics in the two countries, there will be zero trade and no benefit from trade. However, if food and clothing are not the same in each country, mutual gains can be had from each country shipping some of its produce abroad and obtaining, by trade, a diversified mixture of food and clothing types. Such a case of *pure* intra-industry trade could be illustrated by Figure 2.7. In autarky each country consumes what it produces, at point E, yielding real income level, y_0. After trade each country consumes the same aggregate bundles, but these are made up of mixtures of two types of food and clothing. Point E after trade lies on indifference curve y_1, representing a higher level of satisfaction than y_0. Although

---

[6] Economists frequently illustrate free-trade equilibrium with yet another diagram showing "offer curves." This is discussed in the appendix to Chapter 3. Also analyzed in Chapter 3 (and the appendix) is the possibility that the foreign export supply curve becomes backward-bending at a sufficiently high price.

FIGURE 2.7   Pure Intra-Industry Trade

Each country has the same taste pattern and can produce OC units of clothing and OF units of food. After trade relative prices are the same, point E still reflects the aggregate consumption bundle in each country, but trade in different varieties has caused the indifference map to move in; intra-industry trade allows E to reflect the higher real income level, y_1.

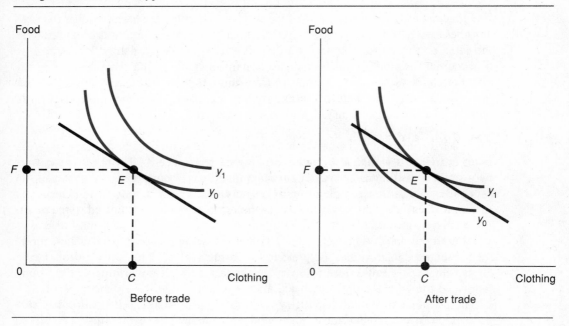

consumption bundles are the same, international trade allows the *composition* of OC and OF to be broadened by trade. Relative prices of food and clothing aggregates may be the same as before trade in each country, but benefits accrue from the increase in variety available to consumers.[7]

In a more general context certain questions would have to be raised concerning intra-industry trade. Why do countries produce different varieties of a product? Are multiple varieties available in one country or region before trade as well? Does the profusion in product types depend on the nature of costs or on market imperfections? We postpone consideration of these questions. Clearly, however, the existence of variety in tastes or love of variety per se among consumers in each country can support flourishing two-way trade in any industrial group if real or perceived international differences in product quality exist. End of detour.

2.4   THE BASIC ARGUMENT FOR FREE TRADE

We are now in a position to present a basic plank in the free-trade case: Free trade leads to a world distribution of consumption that cannot be altered in any way so as to improve the welfare of *all* trading participants. In this sense, free trade is *efficient*.

---

[7] We ignore here the possibility that the shape of indifference curves changes with trade. More formally stated, we assume that the possibility of consuming a wider variety of each type of commodity with trade causes the set of indifference curves to shift in uniformly toward the origin.

Before turning to a diagram, let us consider the logic of the argument. If all possible artificial barriers to exports and imports, such as tariffs or quotas, are dismantled, and if we ignore real-world costs of transporting commodities between countries, individuals in both countries face the same commodity prices with free trade. Each individual picks the most preferred point on its budget line, and (as Figures 2.3 and 2.4 illustrate) at such point the marginal rate of substitution is equated to the commodity price ratio—the same price ratio faced by all other individuals. Thus, with free trade each individual faces the same "trade-off" at the margin between food and clothing as does every other. Section 2.1 established the mutual gains from trade that are available if marginal rates of substitution (or price ratios) differ between countries. The matching up of price ratios between countries with free trade signals that all such mutual gains have already been achieved.

The Box Diagram and the Contract Curve

Economists devised the "box diagram" to illustrate welfare propositions in those cases in which the distribution between participants of fixed total bundles of commodities is at issue. This illustration matches the assumption in this chapter that each country's commodity endowment bundle is fixed.[8] These fixed total supplies provide the dimensions of the box.

In Figure 2.8 any point within the box can represent a division of the fixed world totals of two nations, where these commodities are now assumed identical between countries. For example, point E (E^*) shows the original endowment allocation. Measure quantities belonging to the home country with respect to the southwest "O" origin and those belonging to the foreign country with respect to the northeast "O^*" origin. A pair of indifference curves is drawn through endowment point E (E^*). The curve y_0 for the home country illustrates that a consumption bundle such as A would be valued exactly as highly by the home country as would endowment point E. The shape of the foreign indifference curve y_0^* through E^* is explained by the measurement of foreign clothing consumption leftward from O^* and foreign food consumption downward from O^*. Point A^* means as much to foreigners as does endowment point E^* because they both lie on curve y_0^*. Note that any redistribution of the world totals between countries that lies in the shaded area between curves y_0 and y_0^* represents an improvement in welfare for both. *Free trade leads to one such point of mutual welfare gains.*

The CC' curve is the locus of all distributions that equate marginal rates of substitution between countries. That is, move along any indifference curve for the home country (for example, y_0) until you find a point where a foreign indifference curve is tangent to it (point A has foreign curve y_2^* tangent to home curve y_0). This point is especially significant: It shows the redistribution that obtains the maximum welfare abroad that is possible without altering welfare at home. The *contract curve*, CC', collects all such points. From any point off the contract curve (for example, E) it would be possible to redistribute commodities and improve welfare in both countries. (Anywhere in the shaded area would do.) From any point on the contract curve it is

---

[8] One reason for studying a model of fixed endowments first is that it reveals the basic nature of the gains from trade independent of any additional gains that can be obtained if trade causes resources to be reallocated to increase world outputs.

FIGURE 2.8   The Box Diagram and the Contract Curve

The CC' curve is the contract curve, which is the locus of all points where an indifference curve of the home country is tangent to an indifference curve of the foreign country. Point Q represents free-trade equilibrium.

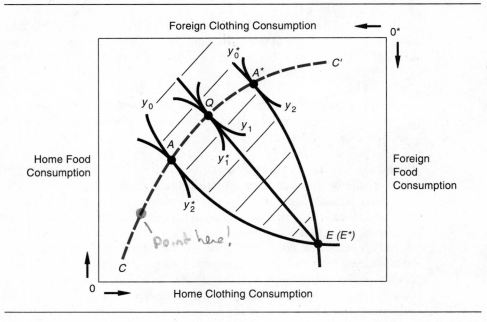

still possible to make one country better off, but not without inflicting harm on the other. All points on the contract curve thus pass the "efficiency" test.

Free trade leads to a world consumption point at which marginal rates of substitution in each country are equated to a common price ratio, shown by the slope of line QE in Figure 2.8. The free-trade point is on the contract curve. Free trade raises the welfare of both participants and leaves the world at a point from which further mutual gains are not possible.

Granted that free trade leads to an efficient point on the contract curve, is it the best such point? Countries obviously will disagree over this issue, since other points involve a gain for one country (but a loss to the other). A more pertinent question is whether either country might be tempted to try, and perhaps to succeed in, improving its level of well-being beyond that obtainable at free trade. Later discussions of the application of tariffs, quotas, and other instruments of commercial policy explore this issue. Even in the stripped-down illustration of free trade represented by point Q in Figure 2.8, however, two points can be made: (1) Any measures taken by one country that cause its welfare level to rise above the free-trade level must harm the other country. (2) Any such measure will prove inefficient from a world standpoint if it pushes the equilibrium point off the contract curve. Most devices employed by countries attempting to maneuver to a better position than that obtainable with free trade introduce price distortions that push the trading point away from the contract curve.

2.5 DISAGREEMENTS OVER FREE TRADE

Although free trade has its vocal adherents, arrayed against them are "protectionists" of various types who argue that it is in someone's interest (a local group, a nation, a group of nations) to cut back the volume of trade by tariffs, quotas, or other devices. Without delving too deeply into these questions at this stage, it is possible to suggest why individuals may be hurt by free trade and why a country may not wish to accept the trading patterns implied by a free-trade equilibrium.

The Individual in International Trade

Do individuals gain from trade? In some broad sense of the word the answer must be yes, unless existence as a jack-of-all-trades is deemed superior to the degree of specialization and division of labor indulged in by most. In addition, international trade may make available new products not producible at home. However, within the austere confines of the two-commodity food-and-clothing model presented in this chapter, does international trade benefit the individual?

If a community is not made up of identical individuals, opening up the country to international trade may hurt some people. Perhaps images come to mind of skilled American artisans undercut by cheaper foreign labor or nineteenth-century British landlords seeing their rents suffer as low-cost sources of food are opened up abroad. An examination of the impact of trade on wages, rents, and other factor returns must be postponed until Part II, but the point that some individuals may be hurt by trade can be made at this time.

Take a close look at what happens in most communities before they engage in trade with other countries: Individuals at home will be trading with each other. Some equilibrium price ratio will be established at which all those net sellers of clothing find purchasers who are willing to give up an equivalent value of food in exchange. Now suppose the community has an opportunity to trade in food and clothing with the outside world, and suppose that food is relatively cheap abroad (and clothing relatively expensive). Not everyone at home need gain by this new trading opportunity. Indeed, the potential losers are easy to identify—all the individuals who were net sellers of food at home before world trade is opened up.

The situation for one of these individuals is shown in Figure 2.9. Owning the bundle of food and clothing shown by E, the individual "exports" EA units of food (to fellow citizens) in order to purchase AG units of clothing. International trade lowers the relative price of food; the individual's budget line rotates from "1" to "2" (around the endowment point E). Consumption is reduced from G to H, and the individual is unquestionably worse off.

If some individuals gain from opening up their country to international trade while others lose, what can be said about the community as a whole? This is an issue typically faced in the political realm, where decisions (here trade policy) almost always entail some groups being hurt and others gaining. Although the typical result in such cases is that some groups *do* get hurt while others gain, the economist is tempted to ask about the possibility of compensation so that all parties can gain by the move.

FIGURE 2.9   International Trade Can Hurt

This individual is a net seller of food (amount *EA*) at home, with home prices shown by line 1. With food relatively cheaper on world markets (line 2), The individual's consumption is reduced from *G* to *H*. The individual is hurt by international trade.

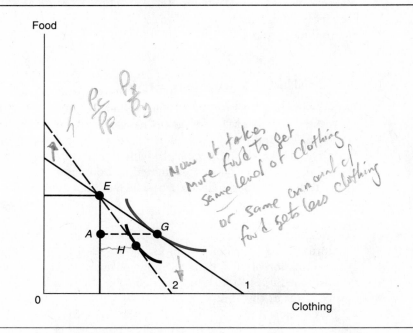

A Compensation Scheme

This line of argument is worth pursuing because it *is* possible to design a scheme whereby all individuals who would lose by a move from no international trade to free international trade can be compensated by those individuals who stand to gain by such a move, with the original gainers still better off after paying the compensation. The redistribution scheme involves switching the original endowment point for each individual to the consumption point that would be chosen when internal trade (but not international trade) is allowed. Thus in Figure 2.9 the individual is compensated by an addition of *AG* units of clothing, while a sacrifice of *AE* units of food is made, thus switching the "endowment" point from *E* to *G*. Are there enough supplies of food and clothing to go around? Yes, because the local market was originally cleared. Now open the community to international trade. With prices different in the world market, every individual can gain by a move from that person's new, "compensated" endowment point. Free trade, with compensation, benefits everyone.[9]

---

[9] For the individual in Figure 2.9, the budget line appropriate to world prices now passes through *G*, with the same slope as line 2. Trade now will clearly benefit such a person. Of course, those who were originally clothing exporters do not gain as much as they would if there were no compensation, but they still gain to some extent.

To summarize, everyone stands to gain from trade as such, even in this simple model that ignores more obvious sources of gain (being able to consume goods not available locally or being able to reallocate productive resources). The move from local trade to more extended international trade also can be defended if one ignores the local redistribution of income or makes appropriate compensations. However, it is precisely this redistribution that often causes such controversy over new initiatives in the trade area. We seldom witness a country debating whether to engage at all in trade with other countries (nineteenth-century Japan aside), but we have witnessed Britain's agony in deciding whether to enter the European Community and special interest groups lobbying in the U.S. Congress for protection from imports. Even sharp changes in international prices that are described in "crisis" terms are not harmful to all. How should an American shareholder in a major oil company have felt about the energy crisis as it erupted in the 1970s? Would such views be shared by a non-stockholding neighbor?

The Free-Trade Issue: Canada in 1988

The Canadian parliamentary election held in 1988 was one of the most animated and hard fought in recent history. One issue dominated, and it split the electorate: free trade. Explicitly, the question was, "Should Canada proceed to ratify an agreement with its large southern neighbor whereby remaining tariff barriers to goods traveling between the United States and Canada would be gradually abolished over the next ten years?" The agreement, already passed through the U.S. Congress, awaited only Canadian approval. The anti–free-trade forces seemed to tap a raw nerve in the Canadian electorate when they predicted that such a move would endanger Canadian sovereignty and interfere with Canada's ability to follow its own social programs and maintain its own cultural identity. The election returns in Canada's three-party system provided a parliamentary majority for the Progressive Conservative party, which had negotiated the agreement, despite the fact that less than 50 percent of those voting seemed to favor the proposal. The issue of free trade proved enormously divisive.[10] And the question lingers on, with the possibility of a wider North American free-trade pact that includes Mexico.

Changing Trading Blocs

Does this chapter's basic message concerning the gains from trade apply when a country leaves one trading bloc to join another? Not necessarily. The recent disintegration of the Soviet Bloc emphasizes this point. Clearly, vast changes can be expected to emerge as institutions reflective of central planning get replaced by market mechanisms. But other issues are at stake. A country such as Poland traded with other Eastern European countries and the Soviet Union at one set of prices before the 1990s and is now faced with a rather different set of trading opportunities in Western Europe and the world at large. Clearly there are losers as well as gainers

---

[10] Details of the Canadian-American Agreement are discussed in Chapter 15.

within Poland. On balance, however, the question remains whether the new "terms of trade" will prove to have shifted in Poland's favor. The move from one trading bloc to another does not guarantee that greater gains will accrue.

Self-Sufficiency Versus International Dependence

Severe swings in the relative prices of some internationally traded commodities have characterized recent years. Changes in the prices of oil and related energy products caused the greatest concern, and in the United States many voices suggested that the country was "too dependent" on imports of oil from abroad.

The basic explanation of the gains from trade given earlier in this chapter was not qualified by the extent of the volume of trade. A country gains from trade if its pattern of consumption is allowed to differ from its pattern of production. To remain self-sufficient in every item is to throw away the benefits that are associated with international trade.

However, governments often seem concerned with the extent to which international trade establishes a dependence on foreign sources of supply. An increase in the relative price of an imported commodity hurts, so why not avoid that hurt by ceasing to import the commodity? The reason is that such a move to self-sufficiency would serve to raise the price of the formerly imported items, thus bringing about the very damage it was intended to avoid.

A defense for a policy of limiting trade can be mounted, however, by considering the costs of adjusting to sudden changes in prices and/or foreign supplies. No nation wishes to be completely dependent on others for foodstuffs, military equipment, or other items deemed essential for survival, because critical time may be required to establish local sources of supply. This issue, of course, raises questions beyond the framework of this chapter's model of commodity exchange; but it may help to explain why the search for gains from trade is moderated by the realization that changes in the terms on which trade is conducted can cause severe changes in welfare for an economy heavily dependent on trade.

CHAPTER PROBLEMS

1. With reference to the home country's trade triangle illustrated in Figure 2.3, suppose the world relative price of clothing stays at the slope shown by line CFD. How would the home country's volume of imports and exports be altered if (a) a fire destroyed 10 percent of its clothing endowment or (b) a bumper harvest expanded its food production by 10 percent?

2. Referring to the previous exercise, if a fire destroys quantity GE of clothing in Figure 2.3, will the home country cease to trade if the world relative price of clothing is shown (again) by the slope of line CFD?

3. In a pair of diagrams such as Figures 2.3 and 2.4, illustrate the mutual gains from trade if (a) tastes are similar between countries but endowments differ and (b) tastes are different but endowments are the same.

4. In Figure 2.6, a positively sloped curve is drawn to show the foreign supply of exports of food rising as the price of food rises. How can this response be reconciled with the assumption that each nation's endowment supply of commodities is fixed with respect to price?

5. The individual whose tastes are shown by the indifference curves in Figure 2.9 is a net seller of food at autarky home prices shown by line 1. This individual loses if trade with the rest of the world is allowed and food prices are lower there, shown by line 2. Show how this same individual might gain if the world price of food is even much lower than that shown by line 2.

6. The relative price that clears the world's food market is shown by *OT* in Figures 2.5 and 2.6. Using the assumed balance in each country between total expenditures and total income, prove that the world's clothing market must be cleared as well. Would this mutual clearing of markets take place if one country tried to "live beyond its means"?

7. For the individual portrayed in Figure 2.9, describe the trade pattern after the compensation scheme is in effect. How does this compare with the trade pattern of others in the country?

SUGGESTION FOR FURTHER READING

Meade, James. *The Stationary Economy* (London: Allen and Unwin, 1965). Chapters 1–4 present the exchange model.

3

PRODUCTION AND EXPANDED GAINS FROM TRADE

A full understanding of how countries benefit from trading in international markets requires us to consider production changes and resource reallocations stimulated by new trading opportunities. Two new sources of gain are added to those described in the preceding account of commodity exchange: (1) Trade encourages nations to concentrate productive efforts in those activities that each performs relatively well. This is the famous doctrine of *comparative advantage*. (2) In addition, exposing producers in each country to a wider world market may encourage a reorganization of productive activities; such reorganization may lead to gains from expanded production runs and larger scales of output than are possible in a smaller national market. In the concluding section we bring together supply and demand behavior to consider the ways in which a country's demand for imports is sensitive to the terms of trade.

3.1 THE PRODUCTION-POSSIBILITIES SCHEDULE AND AUTARKY EQUILIBRIUM

Economics would become superfluous, and therefore totally uninteresting, if a community could produce all the goods and services it desired. That it cannot do so reflects both the basic limitation of resources, natural and manufactured, and the quality of technological knowledge that guides the transformation of resources into final commodities. The production-possibilities schedule (or "transformation" schedule) shows the maximum amount of one commodity that can be produced given the quantities of all other commodities produced. An illustration of such a schedule is the TT' curve, in Figure 3.1, for a simple economy capable of producing only two commodities—again, food and clothing. For example, if clothing output is distance OG, the maximum amount of food that can be produced is AG.

Figure 3.1 illustrates several properties of production. First, some points of production (e.g., D) are beyond the productive capacity of this community. If the resource

FIGURE 3.1 The Production-Possibilities Schedule

The bowed-out curve TT' shows the maximum amount of food that can be produced for each amount of clothing, subject to the constraints of technological knowledge and a fixed resource base. The slope shows the opportunity costs of producing clothing, which increase as more clothing is produced.

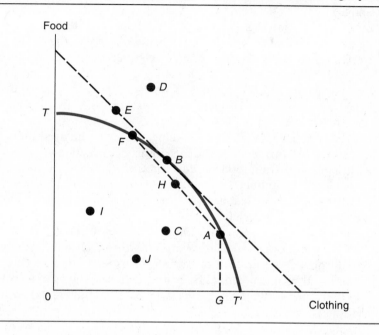

base expands with time, or if better production techniques are developed, then point D eventually could be produced. Second, and closely related, is the negative slope of the TT' schedule. To produce more food than indicated by point A, some current production of clothing must be sacrificed to release resources from clothing into the food industry. Third, note that the community can produce at point C. Such a point, of course, would be inefficient in that, as the TT' schedule shows, more of both commodities can be produced than at C. If the community does not use all of its available resources, a point such as C is quite possible. For example, during the depression of the 1930s, most industrial countries faced severe unemployment of labor and capital equipment. Perhaps less obvious is the possibility of the combination of production shown by C even with full employment of all resources. Point C might represent the outcome of an arbitrary across-the-board decision to employ exactly 68 percent of every factor of production in the clothing industry, with the remaining 32 percent producing food. Such a decision would not take into account the fact that some resources are especially productive in one sector and not in the other, or, more generally, the fact that techniques of producing clothing are qualitatively different from those of producing food. An economic answer lurks behind the question of allocating the community's resources most efficiently, and one of the strong arguments in favor of competition is that society's production of commodities will be efficient, lying along the production-possibilities curve.

The TT' schedule bows out from the origin, reflecting the so-called law of increasing costs. That is, this shape embodies the assumption that the opportunity costs of obtaining an additional unit of a commodity increase as more of that commodity is produced. Consider clothing production, as shown initially at point F. The slope of the TT' curve at F shows the sacrifice in food production required to produce an additional unit of clothing. This is clothing's opportunity cost, that is, the cost of an extra unit of clothing, not in dollars, labor, or material costs, but in terms of the quantity of the other desired final commodity, food, that must be forgone in order to release the resources required by the unit expansion in the clothing industry. Note how this opportunity cost of producing clothing rises when production of clothing expands to the level shown at B. That is, TT' at B is steeper than at F.

What accounts for this general relationship whereby the opportunity cost of any commodity rises as its output increases? Some factors, such as highly skilled labor especially trained to produce clothing, may be employed already in clothing production at F; a further expansion in clothing production will rely on less-skilled labor as it is released from food production. Conversely, when increasing food output at the expense of clothing, the supply of the best grade of fertile land may be used up by the time B is reached, necessitating the use of poorer land for food production in moving to F. Elements of this phenomenon—the variability in the aptitude of factors in each occupation—are almost always present in the real world to help account for increasing costs. (A particularly simple case in which some resources cannot be transferred from one occupation to another forms the setting for Chapter 6.) Even if each factor has the same potential skills in one occupation as in another, the fact that the two industries may require inputs such as labor and capital in different proportions is sufficient to generate increasing costs. (This more subtle point is picked up in Chapter 7.) Appendix A to this chapter describes how increasing opportunity costs, as reflected in the bowed-out shape of the transformation schedule, result even if average production costs in each industry stay constant instead of rising with scale of output.

Some productive processes may, at least for a range of outputs, exhibit what is known as increasing returns to scale (or decreasing costs). That is, costs per unit produced may fall as output expands. Section 3.3 pursues this possibility. Here we emphasize that even if such scale economies prevail, they may not be sufficiently strong to overcome the tendency for opportunity costs to increase brought about by industries requiring different factor proportions and/or the variability of factors' aptitudes in different occupations. Indeed, we continue to assume that the transformation curve for the economy is bowed out.

Autarky Equilibrium

Our description of equilibrium before international trade is similar to that in Chapter 2, except consumers now have pretrade choices. If an economy cannot engage in international trade, the production-possibilities curve in Figure 3.1 also serves as a "consumption-possibilities" schedule; the community only can consume what it produces. Figure 3.2 again shows the production-possibilities curve TT', as well as a pair of indifference curves for the community. Of all points available to the country (without trade), point A maximizes satisfaction. Although food and clothing in combination

---

FIGURE 3.2   The Optimal Production Point for a Closed Economy

An economy not engaged in trade can produce and consume anywhere along TT'. Point A, where an indifference curve is tangent to the transformation curve, represents a higher level of welfare than any other point (e.g., B). The slope of the common tangent at A shows the relative price of clothing.

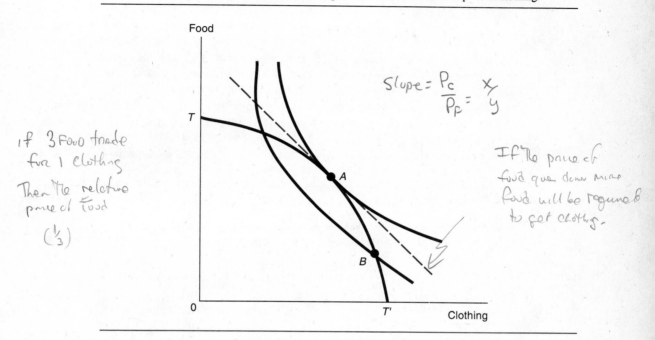

[handwritten notes surrounding figure:]

Slope $= \dfrac{P_c}{P_F} = \dfrac{x}{y}$

if 3 Food trade for 1 clothing Then the relative price of Food

($\frac{1}{3}$)

IF the price of food goes down more Food will be required to get clothing.

B can be produced, point A is preferred. The slope of the dashed line tangent to the indifference curve at A shows the relative price of clothing (to food) that would lead consumers to demand these items in the proportions shown by point A. This line also is tangent to the production-possibilities schedule. Competitive producers respond to price incentives by equating price to marginal cost. The slope of the transformation curve, reflecting the sacrifice of food output to obtain an extra unit of clothing, precisely measures the marginal cost of producing a further clothing unit. This cost is measured now not in dollars or labor-hours, but in forgone food output. In autarky the community produces and consumes at A at prices reflected in the common slope of the indifference curve and transformation schedule tangent at A.

[handwritten note at right margin:] VERY WEAK?

[handwritten note in text:] Price comes out of them!

3.2 TRADE AND COMPARATIVE ADVANTAGE

Patterns of production in all countries are significantly affected by international trade. Some countries take advantage of trade to pour a relatively large volume of resources into activities for which there is little local demand—Zambian copper, Saudi Arabian oil, Greek shipping services. Other countries, such as the United States, have a more balanced productive base, yet certain sectors depend heavily on the export trade. Japan relies heavily on its exports of automobiles, TV sets, and a wide range of consumer durables to finance its heavy reliance on world markets for oil and other raw materials.

The gains alluded to in these examples suggest that international trade allows each country to break out of the constraint imposed by producing only for the local market and so channel its resources into lines more appropriate at world market prices. The following discussion of possible production gains begins by returning to the two-commodity, food-and-clothing example illustrated in Chapter 2, with the discussion first focusing on how a country can augment the gains to consumers by reallocating resources along its production-possibilities schedule. The next section explores an alternative route whereby trading in a world market can benefit a country: The production-possibilities schedule itself may expand with trade.

Consider Figure 3.3, which shows the consequence of trade for the home country. If the home country is not allowed to engage in international trade, its consumption possibilities are restricted to points on its transformation schedule, TT', and of these the best is shown by point E, where indifference curve y_0 is tangent to TT'. The

---

FIGURE 3.3   The Trade Triangle in the Home Country

With free-trade prices shown by the slope of the line 2, production at home takes place at A and consumption at B. BDA is the trade triangle. The community exports DA units of clothing in exchange for imports of BD units of food.

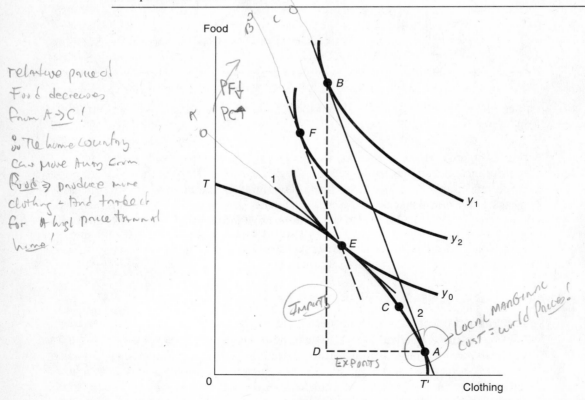

[Handwritten marginal notes:]
relative price of Food decreases from A → C!

So The home country can move away from Food → produce more clothing + And trade it for A high price than at home!

PF↓ PC↑

Imports

Exports

Local marginal cust = world price!

pretrade relative price of clothing that clears the local market is shown by the slope of line 1. Suppose that, with the opening of trade, world prices are shown by the slope of line 2. Because clothing is relatively expensive abroad, free trade encourages resources to flow from food production into the clothing industry until local marginal costs equal world prices (at point A). Line 2 shows the new expanded locus of consumption possibilities, and the most desired consumption bundle is point B. At these prices the community desires to export DA of its clothing output in exchange for BD imports of food. BDA represents the trade triangle.

The gains from trade are shown by the increase in real income, moving from curve y_0 to the higher curve, y_1. If resources were frozen into their occupations at point E, the country still would gain from trade—the consumption point moving from E on curve y_0 to F on curve y_2. The movement in consumption from F on y_2 to B on y_1 shows the extra gains provided by trade when production is allowed to change from E to A.

World prices are determined by supply and demand in both countries. In a free-trade equilibrium the home country's import demand for food must be matched by the foreign country's willingness to export the same quantity of food. If the price line 2 in Figure 3.3 is to reflect an *equilibrium* price ratio, the trade triangle, BDA, must find its mirror image in the foreign country. That is, production and consumption decisions abroad must show matching amounts, as in Figure 3.4. The foreign country also gains from trade—the movement from E* to B* entailing a rise in real incomes abroad from level y_0^* to y_1^*. Foreign exports of A^*D^* of food match home imports of BD. The slope of A^*B^* is, of course, the same as the slope of BA in Figure 3.3.

As in Chapter 2, there are several alternative but equivalent ways of determining what price ratio clears world markets. For example, countries may be grouped together to illustrate world demand separately from world supply. In this case, the appropriate diagram will differ from that in Figure 2.5 in that each country's responsiveness of production to changes in commodity prices leads to an upward-sloping world-supply curve. For any given price ratio, each country's competitive production response is found at the point of tangency of the production-possibilities schedule and a line whose slope reflects that price ratio. Furthermore, such a line is the budget line for that country, and the "best" consumption point is where an indifference curve is tangent to the budget line. Thus, for any price ratio common to both countries, each nation's production and consumption patterns are determined, and world demand and supply curves can be constructed. This information can alternatively be portrayed as in Figure 2.6, focusing on each country's net excess demand or supply for one of the commodities. Appendix B to this chapter describes how "offer curves" can represent this market information even more concisely.

Comparative Advantage

A glance at Figures 3.3 and 3.4 reveals the strong bias in the transformation schedules—the home country's curve has been drawn flatter than the foreign country's. This (arbitrary) assumption allows us to speak of a production bias toward the home country's *comparative advantage* in producing clothing, in that it exhibits a lower relative autarky price for clothing that does the foreign country. Note the double "comparison" involved. It is the pretrade cost *ratio* (p_C/p_F) in one country as opposed

FIGURE 3.4   The Trade Triangle in the Foreign Country

The slope of line 2 is the same as in Figure 3.3. Trade is balanced as the foreign country's trade triangle, $A^*D^*B^*$, matches the home country's BDA in Figure 3.3.

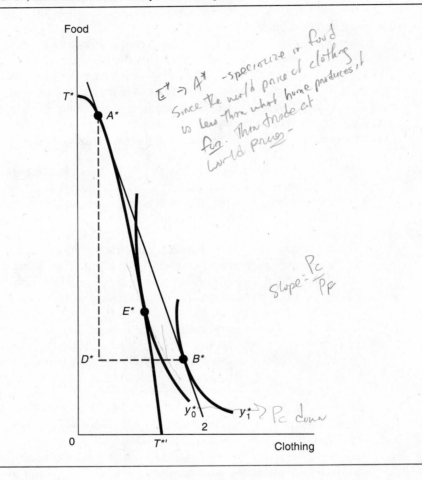

to another that is the object of comparison in determining comparative advantage. Figure 3.5 illustrates the production bias found in Figures 3.3 and 3.4.

At this stage of the discussion, relative country size is not a material consideration in affecting relative costs, so Figure 3.5 concentrates on the composition of demand and production by showing how *ratios* of food to clothing respond to relative prices. Figure 3.5 shows that for any price ratio faced in common by both countries—e.g., free-trade price ratio T—the foreign country would, in a competitive market, produce relatively more food (at G^*) than the home country (at G). Alternatively, if both countries attempt to produce goods in the same proportion, the relative cost of producing food abroad (at A^*) would be lower than at home (at A). Figure 3.5 simplifies on the demand side by assuming tastes are identical in the two countries, shown by the downward-sloping relative demand curve passing through points B and B^*. Thus,

---

FIGURE 3.5 Comparative Advantage

The pair of relative supply curves illustrates the production bias in favor of the foreign country possessing a comparative advantage in producing food. If tastes are comparable (autarky at B and B*), positions of comparative advantage and the trade pattern (foreign country exports food) are consistent with the production bias.

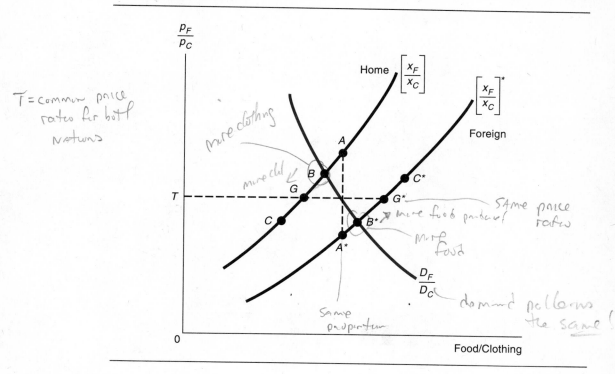

(handwritten annotations: "T = common price ratio for both Nations", "more clothing", "more cl", "more food produced", "same price ratio", "more food", "Same proportion", "demand patterns the same!")

---

the autarky comparisons of relative prices and outputs are more moderate than the extremes shown by a vertical or horizontal comparison. The foreign country's comparative advantage in producing food would, at B*, be reflected in a lower relative price for food in autarky and a greater relative production than is the case for the home country at B.

What causes this production bias between countries? Part II develops the rationale along two different lines: The foreign country possesses relatively superior technical knowledge required to produce food, and/or the foreign country is relatively well endowed with those productive factors that are especially well suited for food production.

Biases in Tastes

Need a country with a production bias favoring clothing necessarily possess a comparative advantage in clothing and thus become a clothing exporter? No. Taste differences between countries also influence the trade pattern. Indeed, Figure 3.6 illustrates a free-trade equilibrium in which foreign production at A* reveals a strong

FIGURE 3.6   **Strong Taste Biases**

The foreign country has a production bias favoring food. Tastes may be biased even more strongly, however, leading the foreign country to import food (B^*D^*) in a free-trade equilibrium. World prices are shown by lines 1 and 1*.

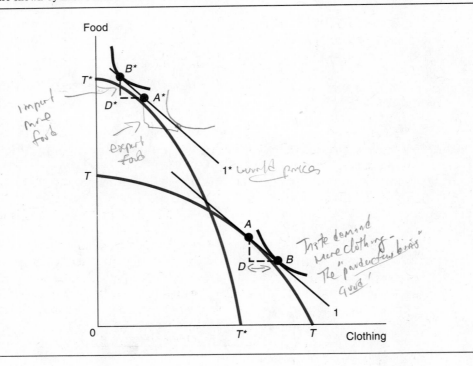

production bias in favor of food compared with home production at A, with both countries facing the same world prices. Despite such a production bias, taste differences are illustrated as even more striking, leading to balanced trade triangles ABD and $A^*B^*D^*$. With tastes in the home country so strongly biased toward the commodity it produces in relative abundance, clothing, the home country takes advantage of trade opportunities to import clothing. A comparison between autarky price ratios would reveal that food is relatively cheap at home before trade. (This corresponds to separate country relative demand curves intersecting national supply curves at points C and C^* in Figure 3.5.) In this extreme case, comparative advantage is affected more by dissimilarities in tastes than by conditions of production.

Need every country have a comparative advantage in something? Yes, except for the accidental possibility of a tie. Becoming *relatively* worse at some activity establishes that the country becomes *relatively* better at other activities. This is a point frequently misunderstood. For example, Lutz Hoffmann, president of the German Institute of

Economic Research, in lamenting the recent rise in labor costs in eastern Germany, states that "East Germany is rapidly losing its comparative advantage as a low-wage economy and has no other advantage with which to compensate for this."[1]

3.3 SCALE ECONOMIES AND WORLD TRADE

Even before David Ricardo (1817) explained the advantages of international trade, advantages based on each nation's having a certain range of commodities in which it has a comparative advantage, Adam Smith expounded on the benefits that accrue from an enlarged scale of operations and the division of labor. Steel, automobiles, many types of manufacturing activity, and production of agricultural commodities all display at least some initial cost-reduction features attributed to larger volumes of production. Countries with large internal markets may exhaust most of these "economies of scale" even without the opportunity to produce for the world market, whereas smaller countries may find that international trade allows for an expansion of the scale of output of a particular variety of commodity significantly beyond the limits of their national markets. According to Adam Smith, the division of labor is limited by the extent of the market. When comparing production possibilities available to a self-sufficient country with those possible in a world market, it is unrealistic to ignore the influence of scale economies.

In Chapter 2 we discussed the possibility that the kind of clothing found in one country differed from that found in another, and consumers gained by the increase in variety available through trade. Now we expand this scenario by assuming there is a range of types in each industry aggregate produced and consumed within each country before trade. For example, to produce each variety certain setup costs or fixed costs may be required as well as costs incurred per quantity produced. Therefore, expansion of the scale of operations for each variety could entail a reduction in average costs per unit output. This scenario presupposes a type of competition (*monopolistic competition*) that we discuss in more detail in Chapter 8. Here it suffices to note that the number of different varieties of clothing (or food) produced and consumed in autarky depends on a balance between consumers' interests in having a wide selection from which to choose and the cost savings that accrue to producing larger volumes of only a few varieties.

How does the ability to trade in world markets alter the situation for consumers and producers within any given country? Producers now face competition from abroad, but they expand their sales opportunities by finding customers in world markets. Consumers find varieties available abroad that are not produced locally. Indeed, it is assumed that each producer's choice of variety is influenced by the desire to offer a specialty that differs from those of competitors at home and abroad. Of course, how much each country produces of each type depends in part on the extent to which resources are reallocated between the two broad aggregates, and differences between countries encourage each to concentrate on that aggregate in which it has a comparative advantage.

---

[1] As reported in the *International Herald Tribune*, March 22, 1991.

Focus now on the disposition of a given bundle of resources to a particular aggregate. The extra competition and opportunities provided by international trade encourage a reduction in the number of varieties produced by any country, matched by a greater volume of output for each variety. Consumers everywhere find a greater total range of items available on world markets, although the spread produced locally is narrowed. As described earlier, a basic property of international trade is that consumption possibilities are freed from local production patterns, and the general effect of trade is to enlarge consumption possibilities while encouraging concentration and greater specialization in production.

The changes in production brought about by opening the economy to trade are represented by drawing the nation's transformation schedule linking the two industry aggregates. Figure 3.7 illustrates that the move from autarky to free trade shifts the transformation schedule for these aggregates. To see why this occurs, suppose that quantities of different varieties within each industry are added to obtain an aggregate industry total. For a given bundle of resources, the country with trade produces fewer varieties, each with a longer production run. The outcome is a larger total production

---

FIGURE 3.7   Trade Shifts the Transformation Schedule

If clothing and food are aggregates of a range of types produced locally and the average cost of producing each type diminishes with scale of output, opening the country to a wider world market can increase the aggregate index of all clothing and food that can be produced from any allocation of given resources. The number of varieties produced nationally decreases, while consumers enjoy a wider selection of types in the world market.

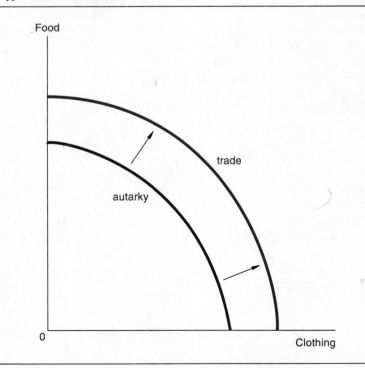

for each aggregate. This description glosses over details that will be covered in Chapter 8 but should suffice to suggest that international trade, by making markets more competitive for a nation's producers, allows greater aggregate outputs from a given resource bundle.

When European countries lowered tariff barriers among themselves as members of the Common Market in the 1960s, observers expected that some industries in each country would be driven to the wall by the extra competition from their neighbors. Given this expectation, they were surprised at the outcome. The pattern resembled what we have sketched previously: Firms in each country producing different varieties from those of their neighbors could expand into foreign markets. The pattern was one of interpenetration and intra-industry trade.

What Was Left Out

Other considerations also suggest that once a nation participates in a free-trade world market, its production-possibilities schedule may lie outside its autarky schedule.

1. Trade may expand information regarding technology. If the move from autarky to free trade involves a country's gaining access to new ways of combining its own resources, the locus of possible production points with this new information is superior to the autarky transformation curve.

2. Trade may enable a country to purchase raw materials and intermediate products not available locally. In the present discussion, trade is restricted to final commodities, but Chapter 9 explores further gains available when international markets exist for some inputs into the production process. Indeed, some countries rely heavily on such trade: Norway is a materials exporter, Japan a heavy resource importer. Gains accrue both by allowing alterations in the composition of a nation's input supplies and by allowing net trades of resources for final commodities.

3.4 SOURCES OF GAINS FROM TRADE: A RECAPITULATION

The different sources through which a nation gains from trade are additive. Figure 3.8 helps tabulate the results.

1. The level of income shown by indifference curve y_0 corresponds to that of autarky; consumption of food and clothing is limited to the quantities of aggregate food and clothing produced and the varieties of each type produced nationally before trade.

2. Being able to trade at different (world) prices leads to the choice of aggregate bundle A', if production were to remain frozen at point A. These exchange gains from trade include consumers' ability to spread their consumption purchases over an increased variety of food and clothing. As was described in Chapter 2, the benefits of such intra-industry trade can be captured by relabeling the indifference curve map (not done here) so that each bundle of diversified food and clothing represents a higher level of utility than would a less diversified bundle available in autarky with the same industry totals.[2]

---

[2] We once again simplify by assuming that the move to free trade shifts the indifference curves uniformly toward the origin so that their shapes are not altered.

FIGURE 3.8   Sources of Gains from Trade

Autarky consumption and production are shown by point *A*. International trade brings about an outward shift in the transformation schedule and allows resources to be reallocated according to comparative advantage. Optimal production is at point *C*, allowing consumption at *C′*. Further gains to consumers follow from the wider variety of food and clothing available at *C′*, compared with autarky bundle *A*.

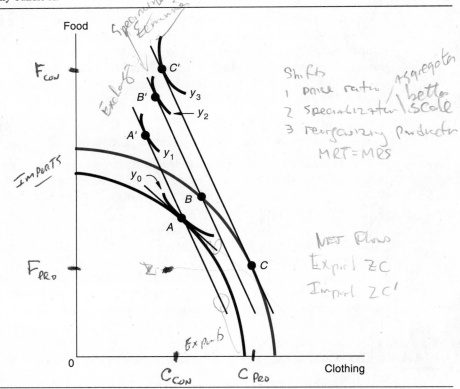

3. If resources are kept roughly channeled to the two commodity groups (food and clothing) as in autarky but a greater aggregate volume of production is possible because a narrower range of varieties produced is combined with decreasing average cost of producing any variety, the transformation schedule shifts out. Production at *B* could support the aggregate consumption bundle at *B′*.

4. Relative to the rest of the world (as reflected in world prices), the country shown in Figure 3.8 has a comparative advantage in producing clothing. The shift of resources from *B* to *C* allows further consumption gains to point *C′* on indifference curve y_3.

Figure 3.8 does not explicitly reveal the details of the changes in the range of goods produced and consumed within each aggregate. The outward shift in the transformation schedule shows that trade allows a concentration in production to fewer different varieties within each aggregate group. Similarly, shifting the indifference map inward indicates that trade allows increased diversification for consumers because the world market contains many more varieties than are available at home in autarky.

A shortcut procedure is to note that free-trade aggregate consumption bundle C' corresponds to a higher welfare level than it would if the number of varieties in each consumption bundle were limited to those available in autarky. The trade triangle connecting points C and C' (not drawn) would illustrate an export of clothing in exchange for imports of food. But these are only net flows of industry totals. In addition, there may be a considerable volume of gross trade flows within each industrial group. In the real world such flows are seen in the relatively large volumes of intra-industry trade among major industrial countries.

Market structure is also an important characteristic of this description. Consumers are acting competitively as "price-takers," as revealed by the tangency between price lines and indifference curves. If pure competition characterized producer behavior, with relative prices accurately measuring marginal opportunity costs, the kind of tangency indicated by point C also would be appropriate. But the presence of activities with fixed costs suggests a type of market structure known as monopolistic competition. Departures from competitive behavior, in particular a lack of correspondence between marginal costs and prices, imply that the economy does not achieve the full gains from trade pictured in Figure 3.8. This problem and various other issues concerning international trade and the structure of markets will be discussed later.

3.5 FREE TRADE AND THE BEHAVIOR OF IMPORT DEMAND

Once a country is embedded in a world trading system, with production taking place on the appropriately enlarged transformation schedule and resources reallocated according to comparative advantage, it becomes appropriate to ask how sensitive import and export volumes are to disturbances in the terms of trade.

The extent of the response in production depends on all those factors determining the degree to which the transformation schedule is bowed out. Similarly, the consumption response depends in part on the shape of indifference curves. If these are sharply bowed in, any given rise in food's price causes the consumer to purchase less food, but little movement along an indifference curve is required to bring the marginal rate of substitution (slope of the indifference curve) in line with the new price. But more is involved, and this is the tricky part: Any price change affects the real income of a trading community and, through this effect, the demand for all commodities. When analyzing the effect of price changes on demand, it is important to isolate the *substitution effect* (movements along a given indifference curve) from the *income effect* (movements from one indifference curve to another).

Substitution and Income Effects in Consumption

There are two important aspects of the income effect on demand when price changes: (1) determining how real income is affected by the price change and (2) determining what the impact of a given change in real income is on demand for importables. The latter reflects only the consumer-preference pattern. Revert, for the moment, to the practice of quoting incomes and prices in dollar units. If incomes rise by $100 and spending on food (the good being imported) rises by $40, by definition the *marginal propensity to import* (food) is 0.4. The answer to (1) depends greatly on the extent of trade. The greater the quantity of food currently imported, the more severely will real incomes be hit by a rise in food's relative price.

These points are illustrated in Figure 3.9. Suppose that production is fixed at point *E* and that initially the home country imports food at the price ratio shown by line 1, consuming at *A*. Now let the terms of trade improve. The price reduction for imports is shown by the slope of a steeper line (2 or 3, which are parallel). With the budget line rotating around the production point (*E*), consumption of food rises (from *A* to *B*). This demand change can be broken down into two parts: (1) The move from *A* to *C*: This is the *substitution effect*, that is, the change in demand if consumption is restricted to the same indifference curve. (2) The move from *C* to *B*: This is the *income effect*. A fall in import prices raises real income (from curve y_1 to curve y_2). The income effect shows how such an increase in real income at constant prices spills into increased demand for both commodities.

Remember that the income effect is strongly influenced by the extent (and direction) of trade. Now consider the following exercise. In Figure 3.9 suppose the production point is *G* instead of point *E*. That is, suppose imports of food initially are roughly twice the amount illustrated (distance *AG* is roughly twice the distance *AE*). Then show, by drawing the new budget line through *G*, that the drop in food price raises real income by more than previously shown (indeed, by roughly twice as much).

FIGURE 3.9   Substitution and Income Effects

With point *E* the production point, consumption is initially at *A* at terms of trade shown by line 1. A fall in food's import price is shown by steeper lines, 2 or 3. The substitution effect is the move from *A* to *C* along the initial indifference curve. The income effect is the move from *C* to *B*.

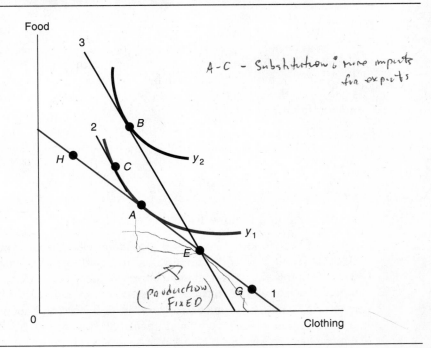

This discussion illustrates an important general point: For a country engaged in trade, any price change affects real income. If the price of a commodity rises, real income at home goes up if that commodity is exported and falls if it is imported. Furthermore,

> the extent of the impact of a change in the terms of trade on real income is proportional both to the extent of the price change and to the volume of trade.

These basic points find many applications throughout this book.

Import Demand Elasticity and the Supply of Exports

If the price of imports falls (i.e., the terms of trade improve), we now can present the three ingredients that contribute to an increase in import demand: (1) a substitution effect in consumption—more of the importables will be demanded (along an indifference curve); (2) an income effect—the fall in the price of imports raises real incomes (pushes the consumer onto a higher indifference curve) and thus raises import demand; and (3) the production effect—the fall in import price serves to attract resources to other industries. Production of importables falls along the production-possibilities schedule.

The *elasticity* of import demand relates the relative extent of import expansion to the initiating price fall. Suppose food import prices fall by 10 percent. By how much will these ingredients conspire to raise import demand? If the answer is greater than 10 percent, import demand is said to be *elastic;* if the answer is less than 10 percent, import demand is *inelastic.* These are purely matters of definition, but the distinction between elastic import demand and inelastic import demand is intimately connected to the aggregate volume of exports supplied.

Take the elastic case first. Suppose a 10 percent fall in import price causes an expansion of 15 percent in the quantity of imports demanded. Is more or less being paid for imports? Per unit, less, which is what price reflects. But payment equals price times quantity, and in the case of elastic import demand the quantity rises relatively more than price falls. Therefore, payments rise as price falls. But how are payments expressed? Recall the budget constraint: Exports must pay for imports. The volume of exports must rise as the relative price of imports falls if the demand for imports is elastic.

The case of inelastic demand for imports reverses this conclusion. If the relative price of food imports falls by 10 percent and the quantity of imports demanded rises by only 5 percent, the country faces a lower overall import bill. That is, the volume of exports required to finance imports at the lower price falls.

You may notice something odd about the behavior of export supply for an economy in which import demand in inelastic. For example, an inelastic import demand for clothing in the foreign country implies that a fall in clothing's relative price lowers the quantity of food that country must supply as exports. Stating this in terms of food's relative price, the foreign supply of food exports falls as the relative price of food rises. In Figure 2.6 this would be shown by a stretch of the foreign export supply function that is negatively sloped (or backward-bending).

Just as with import demand, a three-part analysis can be used to reveal how export supply from abroad changes with price: (1) A rise in food's relative price shifts resources

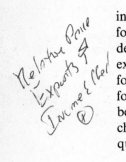

into food production abroad, which by itself would tend to raise foreign exports of food. (2) The substitution effect in consumption abroad encourages reduced foreign demand for food as food becomes more expensive; this effect supports a rise in food exports from abroad as well. (3) The income effect abroad runs counter to these two forces and must outweigh them if foreign import demand for clothing is inelastic. As food's relative price rises, foreigners as a group find their real incomes increased because their nation exports food. Part of the increase in real income would be channeled into extra food consumption, and this by itself would tend to lower the quantity of food available for export.

This concern with demand behavior on the part of *exporters* of a commodity is, in a sense, unique to international trade theory. Usually when students are first introduced to demand theory, the question is posed as follows: Suppose the price of apples rises—what happens to the quantity of apples demanded, assuming all other prices are constant and money income remains constant? In effect, questions about demand behavior are asked in the context in which individuals are always net buyers (of apples or whatever commodity is being discussed), so a price rise reduces real income. In such a case, substitution and income effects go hand in hand to reduce quantity demanded whenever price rises.

When the price of oil increased dramatically in the 1970s, what happened to the demand for gasoline by oil-exporting countries? Traffic jams in Caracas, Lagos, and Tehran increased. Perhaps Venezuela, Nigeria, and Iran seem special because they benefited from the rise in oil prices. But this stance—as an exporter of a commodity that has gone up in price—is one generally shared by half the market! The volume of purchases must be matched by the volume of sales. When demand behavior in a context of international trade is studied, it is inappropriate to disregard the fact that any price rise makes exporters better off even if it worsens the lot of importers.[3]

The Case of Multiple Exports

Suppose we relax the assumption that only two commodities (food and clothing) are involved in trade. Instead, suppose that a country exports many commodities and that the price of one of them rises. What happens to other export sectors whose prices do not rise? They are squeezed. They probably lose resources to the sector that benefits from a rise in price. With home real incomes improved, increased home demand would cut into supplies available for export from these other sectors as well. This kind of general interdependence among export sectors, sometimes labeled the "Dutch Disease," will be explored more fully in Part II. The key point here is that an aggregate

---

[3] The field of labor economics provides another example in which income effects might dominate substitution effects for exporters. If the wage rate rises, will more or less labor be supplied by households? Hours of labor worked represent exports of individuals with a given stock (24 hours per day) and an alternative usage, leisure. An increase in the wage rate implies both a substitution effect (less higher-priced leisure purchased) and an income effect (workers are better off at a higher wage and thus consume more leisure). If the income effect dominates, less labor is supplied (exported) at the higher wage. Countries such as Malawi and Lesotho typically export large quantities of workers to Zambia and South Africa. Perhaps fewer laborers would work in foreign mines if wage rates were higher.

index of export volume in a many-commodity world might shrink when an index of export prices rises, even though the volume of the particular export that has increased in price may expand.[4]

3.6 SUMMARY

Both this chapter and the preceding one were designed primarily to identify the sources of gain from engaging in trade. A simple model—the *basic trade model*—was developed to illustrate the nature of the gains from trade and how these gains are enhanced if a nation's production patterns also can be realigned to take advantage of trading opportunities. We argued that gains accrue when resources are reallocated in the direction indicated by comparative advantage, and that further gains may well be harnessed if producers take advantage of wider world markets to concentrate on fewer types of commodities and spread fixed costs over larger volumes. In Part II we explore in more detail the possible patterns of trade that are encouraged by variations among countries in technology, resource endowments, and the degree of scale economies.

We also examined more carefully the ways in which a trading economy responds to a change in the terms of trade. In particular, price changes cause production to respond along the production-possibilities curve and consumers to substitute for commodities that have risen in price. It is the essence of any trading situation that price changes reallocate real incomes, causing incomes to fall in the country importing the commodity that has risen in price and to rise in the exporting country. Both of these income changes feed back to affect demand for importables and exportables.

CHAPTER PROBLEMS

1. The home country in Figure 3.3 responds to the trading opportunities shown by line 2 by increasing production of clothing for export (from E to A) and actually reducing the quantity of clothing consumed. Show why:
   a. For a country in which production cannot change (e.g., the home country in Figure 2.3), trade *must* result in a drop in consumption of the good exported.
   b. If production can respond to new world prices, the quantity of clothing consumed at home could rise.
   c. In Figure 3.3 a reduction in clothing consumption results in an increase in well-being compared with taking advantage of trade to consume more of both commodities.
2. Some consumers have quite rigid taste patterns. Suppose the indifference curves for a community are strictly right-angled, and the corners of ever-higher indifference curves lie on a ray from the origin. To be precise, suppose that whatever the prices prevailing in the market, two units of food are demanded for each unit of clothing demanded. Furthermore, suppose the transformation schedule shows considerable flexibility in production, so much so that it is a downward-sloping straight line with vertical food intercept of 20 units and horizontal clothing intercept of 40 units.

---

[4] The distinction between aggregate export behavior and individual export performance is discussed in R. W. Jones and E. Berglas, "Import Demand and Export Supply: An Aggregation Theorem," *American Economic Review* (March 1977).

a. If the country cannot engage in trade, how much of each commodity does it consume and produce?

b. In the no-trade (autarky) state, what is the relative price of food?

c. Suppose world trade is now opened up and the relative price of clothing is double what it was in autarky. Describe what happens to consumption and production.

d. Is the country better off with trade? Is there a sense in which it is twice as well off in trade?

3. Suppose that in autarky the decomposition of food and clothing aggregates reveals ten varieties of each produced, each variety requiring 200 units of resources for setup costs, regardless of scale of output. In addition, each unit of food of any variety produced requires one unit of resources, and each unit of clothing requires two units of resources. The autarky output levels are 400 units of each variety of clothing and 200 units of each variety of food. With trade, competition from the world market narrows the number of varieties produced in each (food, clothing) industry to four. If resources are allocated to food and clothing industries exactly as in autarky, by how much has trade allowed each industry aggregate to expand? Why did the number of varieties produced not get cut back to four in each industry before trade?

4. (Answer this problem after reading Appendix A.) In showing why the production-possibilities curve in Figure 3.1 bows out, we assumed that techniques used at F to produce food differed from those used at A to produce food. Similarly, we assumed techniques differed in clothing production between F and A. Now suppose this is not so. Suppose only one all-purpose input is required to produce either food or clothing and that two units of this input are required per unit of food produced regardless of the scale of output, and four units are required to produce a unit of clothing. If the community possesses 400 units of this all-purpose input, draw its production-possibilities schedule. How sensitive to demand are prices if the country cannot trade? (Your answer will be useful in Chapter 5.)

SUGGESTIONS FOR FURTHER READING

Krugman, P. "Increasing Returns, Monopolistic Competition and International Trade," *Journal of International Economics*, 9 (4) (November 1979): 469–479. An early treatment of the benefits of variety and a simple analysis of increasing returns.

Leontief, Wassily. "The Use of Indifference Curves in the Analysis of Foreign Trade," *Quarterly Journal of Economics*, 47 (May 1933): 493–503, reprinted in American Economic Association, *Readings in the Theory of International Trade* (Philadelphia: Blakiston, 1949), Chapter 10. An early exposition showing how to combine transformation schedules and indifference curves to illustrate equilibrium with trade.

Meade, James. *The Stationary Economy* (London: Allen and Unwin, 1965). Chapter 4 gives some simple exercises.

APPENDIX A:
CONSTANT RETURNS TO SCALE
AND INCREASING OPPORTUNITY COSTS

A simple argument shows that a nation's production-possibilities schedule bows out from the origin even if food and clothing production each separately exhibit constant returns to scale. Consider all the inputs required to produce a unit of clothing.[5] If the quantities of all these inputs are expanded by the same proportional amount, constant returns to scale are said to prevail if clothing output also expands by precisely the same proportional amount.

Figure 3.1 is used to illustrate the argument. At point F a certain bundle of resources is used to produce food and the remainder of the economy's resources is employed in clothing production. Point I is halfway to the origin relative to F, so the food and clothing output bundle at I could be produced with exactly half the economy's resources. Now consider point A. This output combination also uses all the economy's resources, and point J, halfway to the origin, would require exactly half the economy's resources to produce (again, the reason is that both food and clothing exhibit constant returns to scale). Suppose half the economy's resources are used to produce J and the other half to produce I. The resultant production bundle is shown by point H, which lies exactly halfway along the chord connecting points F and A.

This argument does not demonstrate that the transformation schedule is flat between F and A. Rather, it shows that any point on chord FA *could* be produced. However, if techniques used in producing clothing at F differ from those used at A (and similarly for techniques used to produce food at F and A), such a mixture (I, J) entails producing clothing simultaneously with two different techniques. It never pays to do this. There is a single technique that is best.[6] The upshot: A point such as H can be improved on. The production-possibilities schedule bows out.[7]

APPENDIX B:
THE OFFER-CURVE DIAGRAM

All the diagrams used to show free-trade equilibrium and the pattern of trade have illustrated directly how quantities demanded and supplied respond to relative prices. An alternative diagrammatic apparatus, in use in the literature in international trade for more than a century,[8] contrasts directly the quantity of one commodity a country wishes to import against the quantity of the commodity offered in exchange as exports. Retaining the assumption that the home country is an exporter of clothing in a free-trade equilibrium, Figure 3.A.1 illustrates the *offer curves* for the two countries.

---

[5] There may be many input bundles that accomplish this task. Part II covers these details. Here we consider any such bundle.

[6] In the parlance of Chapter 6, this follows if isoquants are strictly bowed in to the origin.

[7] It also follows that if production exhibits slightly increasing returns, the production-possibilities schedule would still be bowed out (except near the axes).

[8] Offer curves, or "reciprocal demand and supply" curves, were extensively used by Alfred Marshall in his *Pure Theory of Foreign Trade*, London School of Economics and Political Science, 1930, first published in 1879.

FIGURE 3.A.1   Offer Curves

Free-trade equilibrium is shown by point Q, with the equilibrium terms of trade equal to the slope of ray OQ.

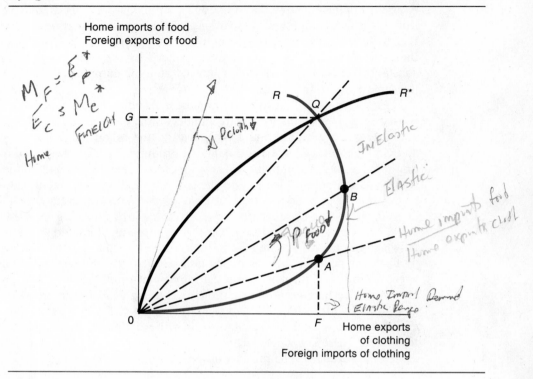

Since quantities are shown along the axes, relative prices are indicated in this diagram by the slopes of rays from the origin. Consider the home country's response to the world relative price of clothing shown by the slope of ray OA. At this relative price the home country chooses to demand quantity AF of food over and above its local production. In order to obtain this by imports, it must be prepared to export OF units of clothing, which have equivalent value. Should the relative price of food fall to the level shown by ray OB, home demand for imports of food rises. In this range home import demand is elastic because the quantity of clothing exports it is willing to give up increases from A to B; a rise in total revenue spent on a product when its price falls indicates an elastic demand. By contrast, a further reduction in food's relative price to the ray OQ shows a reduction in clothing exports. More food imports are demanded at Q than at B, but the fall in food's relative price is more severe than the increase in quantity demanded so that total outlay (as measured by clothing exports) has fallen. This inelasticity in import demand reflects a behind-the-scenes conflict between greater production of clothing at Q than at B (because clothing's relative price has risen) and lower local demand for clothing via the substitution effect, on the one hand, and a stimulus to local demand for clothing via the income effect on the other. (The rise in clothing's relative price from B to Q raises real incomes for the home clothing-exporting country.) This conflict is won by the income effect in the move from B to Q and by the substitution effects in production and consumption in the move from A to B.

The foreign offer curve (OR^*) has been drawn as elastic throughout. Decreases in the relative price of the commodity imported abroad (clothing) correspond to steadily rising import demand and export supply as clockwise-moving rays from the origin sweep the curve OR^*. Equilibrium is attained at a price ratio (shown by ray OQ) at which home demand for imports of food matches foreign supply. This equilibrium point, Q, also reveals that foreign demand for clothing imports matches home export supply.

Trade volumes and terms of trade in the offer-curve diagram can be related to our earlier graphs. Thus, with reference to Figure 2.6, the quantity of food entering trade (OG in Figure 3.A.1) would correspond to OA, while the quantity of clothing imported abroad (GQ in Figure 3.A.1) would be shown in Figure 2.6 by the *area OTQA*. With reference to Figure 3.3, home clothing exports (DA in Figure 3.3) are shown by GQ in Figure 3.A.1, while the slope of OQ in the offer-curve diagram, the equilibrium relative price of clothing, is shown in Figure 3.3 by the (absolute value of) the slope of line AB.

4

Applications of the Basic Trade Model

If Brazil has a bumper coffee crop, what happens to the world price of coffee? To real incomes in France? To welfare in Brazil? If oil supplies from the Middle East are restricted, how does the impact on Japan compare with that on the United States? If a country discovers new mineral deposits, how does this affect its current balance of trade? These are examples of questions that can be applied to the basic trade model outlined in Chapters 2 and 3.

4.1 DISTURBANCES FROM ABROAD

Europeans used to remark that if America sneezed, Europeans caught pneumonia—a reference to the effect of a recession in the United States on employment levels in other countries. That particular phenomenon, the international transmission of business cycles, is out of bounds in the present discussion, which assumes flexible prices and full employment. However, when countries are linked via a network of commodity trade, disturbances abroad have real effects at home. The discussion here covers two such types of disturbance.

A Rise in Foreign Demand

Suppose foreign tastes change so that foreigners demand more of the kind of commodities produced by our export industries. How does this effect our terms of trade, our welfare, and, indeed, our volume of trade? The basic trade model provides answers to these questions.

Figure 4.1 illustrates clothing market equilibrium in a world consisting of home and foreign countries by adapting the use of home export supply curves (of clothing) and foreign import demand curves suggested in Figure 2.6. Initial free-trade equilibrium price and quantity of clothing traded are shown by point Q where our export supply curve, X_1, intersects the foreign import demand curve, M^*. This equilibrium now is disturbed by a change of tastes abroad that serves to shift foreign demand for our clothing outward from M^* to curve $M^{*\prime}$. Equilibrium price and quantity of clothing exported both rise along the X_1 supply curve to new point A.

FIGURE 4.1   An Outward Shift in Foreign Demand

An outward shift in foreign demand for home exports of clothing raises clothing's price, but may or may not increase home exports of clothing.

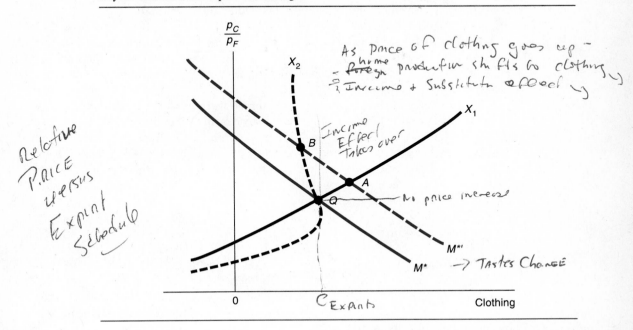

Figure 4.1 shows an alternative export supply function for home clothing producers, the X_2 curve. With either the X_1 curve or the X_2 curve, the initial equilibrium position is shown by point Q. When foreign demand for home clothing exports shifts outward from curve M^* to curve $M^{*\prime}$, the relative price of clothing is driven upward, either to point A or to point B, depending on home supply response. If home exports respond positively to price, as with curve X_1, the increase in foreign demand for clothing results in greater foreign imports of clothing (point A). However, the rise in the price of our clothing exports (i.e., the improvement in our terms of trade) causes real incomes at home to increase, and this, by itself, encourages increased home consumption of clothing, the export commodity. Of course, the increased price of clothing triggers substitution effects in demand (less clothing and more food consumed) and in production (more clothing and less food produced), but the X_2 supply curve illustrates the possibility that the income effect in demand can outweigh these substitution effects. If so, actual exports would fall from point Q to point B, despite the fact that the market was disturbed by a rise in foreign demand.

Supply Shocks

Changes in commodity supplies can dramatically affect world prices and incomes. The mose severe fluctuations seem to characterize markets in natural resources. Few commodity markets have changed as much or have received as much attention as the market in oil (and related energy sources). The rapid growth in world demand for energy in the late 1960s and early 1970s caused some tightening of oil prices even before the politically inspired decision of Arab oil producers to cut production and raise prices. The price rise was dramatic. For a complete decade (1960–1970) the posted price of Arabian light crude oil remained a constant $1.80 per barrel. (Actual prices differed a little from the posted price.) By October 1, 1973, this price had increased to $3.01, but a scarce three months later the posted price increased almost fourfold (to $11.65 per barrel).[1] Although in the succeeding four years the nominal price of oil rose, in real terms (i.e., relative to other prices) it fell slightly until the next round of sizable increases in 1979.

Some estimates of the magnitude of the terms-of-trade effect on real incomes can be made. U.S. imports of petroleum products rose from $7.6 billion in 1973 to a figure of $24.3 billion in 1974, the value more than tripling. Quantity figures remained roughly constant (imports of crude products were up slightly, refined products were down by around 10 percent), so that as a first approximation the rise in oil prices entailed a real income loss of roughly $16.7 billion (the increased cost of purchasing the same quantity of imports).

American dependence on oil imports steadily increased until 1974 (around 35 percent of U.S. requirements were imported in 1973, with this figure approaching 50 percent at the decade's end). Japan depends even more heavily on foreign sources, importing more than 99 percent of the crude oil it consumes. Between 1973 and 1974 the quantity of imports (of crude and partly refined petroleum) dropped by around 4 percent but the value of imports rose by an estimated $12.9 billion.[2] Relative to income and size, the terms-of-trade impact on Japan was more severe than the impact on the United States.

Of course, the prices of other traded goods also were changing during this period. Suppose the "unit value of imports" (a price index) to the United States had a value of 100 in 1973. Then one year later, this jumped to 150, but the unit value of export prices also rose somewhat, to 127. Thus, the terms of trade (the ratio of export to import prices) deteriorated for the United States from 1973 to 1974 from an index of 100 to 85. Four years later (1978), inflationary forces increased both import and export prices, but left the terms of trade virtually unchanged. However, the further price increases in the energy field in 1979 drove the U.S. terms of trade down to around 79.[3] By contrast, Japan's terms of trade fell from 100 in 1973 to 74 in 1974. The strengthening value of the yen in subsequent years helped keep import prices down so that by 1978 the terms of trade stood at 81. However, the rise in oil prices and Japan's heavy dependence on imports helped push this figure down almost 10 points one year later.[4]

Changes in export prices also can severely affect a nation's terms of trade. For example, Sweden is almost completely dependent on imports of oil. On the export side, though, wood, pulp, and paper are important, and these products were rising

---

[1] These figures are cited in *Energy and Prices* 1960–73, prepared by Foster Assoc. (Cambridge, MA: Ballinger, 1974.)

[2] Bank of Japan, *Economic Statistics Monthly*.

[3] These figures are calculated from the U.S. *Survey of Current Business*.

[4] See the Bank of Japan, *Economic Statistics Monthly*.

in price at the same time oil prices were rising. Sweden's terms of trade in 1971 and 1972, before the oil crisis, were not much different from those in 1975 and 1976. Indeed, in spite of the second round of oil price rises in 1979, Sweden's terms of trade improved by around 35 percent from 1978 to 1982.[5]

4.2 GOVERNMENT REGULATION OF PRODUCTION AND TRADE

The doctrine of comparative advantage reveals the gains a country can obtain if it allows resources to be reallocated toward their best use given world prices. Thus, in Figure 4.2 the country can do no better than to produce at A if world relative prices are shown by the slope of line 1, allowing consumption at point E. At point A prices reflect marginal costs, a hallmark of competitive behavior. Is there any rationale for the government to step in and to interfere in resource allocation—in effect to "command" a different production combination, such as point B or point C?

Such interference in market outcomes could well be promoted by special interests. For example, suppliers of agricultural equipment may realize greater gains when food output is raised from A to B. As we describe in more detail in Chapter 12, special interest groups frequently do lobby the government to interfere in free markets in order to further their own ends—with such interference not only being opposed to the national interest but also wasting resources in the lobbying effort, resources which might otherwise have been used to produce commodities.

Putting aside these pressures, is there an argument for government interference for the national benefit? Perhaps. The key is the possibility that government action can alter prevailing world prices. *[handwritten: LARGE Country can alter prices!]*

Consider the two alternative production bundles in Figure 4.2—B and C. If government measures cause production to move from A to C, what would happen to the country's terms of trade? If this country represents only a small portion of the world market, prices would remain pretty much the same, and a budget line drawn through C with the same slope as line 1 would be inferior to that drawn through A. However, if alterations in outputs at home can affect world market prices, which way will they change? The move from A to C reflects a greater volume of clothing exports offered to the world market, and therefore the country's terms of trade would deteriorate. Not a smart move. But changing production patterns from A to B—promoting a resource reallocation toward the country's import-competing food industry—would serve to improve the country's terms of trade. If the relative world price of clothing rises by as much as is shown by the slope of line 2, the country could reach a higher indifference curve than it attained (at E) when there was no government interference.

If the country can gain by restricting clothing exports, why don't clothing producers realize this and do it on their own? If all clothing production were controlled by one

---

[5] See the United Nations, *Yearbook of International Trade Statistics*, 1980, 1981 (New York: United Nations); and *International Financial Statistics*, International Monetary Fund, 36 (10) (October 1983). For an example of more violent ups and downs in the terms of trade consider the case of Zambia. When oil prices rose from 1973 to 1974, the unit value of imports (price index) rose 30 percent, but the rise in world copper prices raised the unit value of exports by 20 percent. The following year (1975), import prices continued to rise, but copper prices crashed. With 1973 as a base year of 100, Zambia's terms of trade deteriorated to only 92 in 1974, but fell to 47 one year later. (These figures are computed from the International Monetary Fund, *International Financial Statistics*.)

FIGURE 4.2   Restriction on Exportables Production

If free-trade world prices are indicated by the slopes of lines 1 and 2, the home country might benefit by lowering clothing output from *A* to *B*, if such a policy could raise world clothing prices to those indicated by line 2.

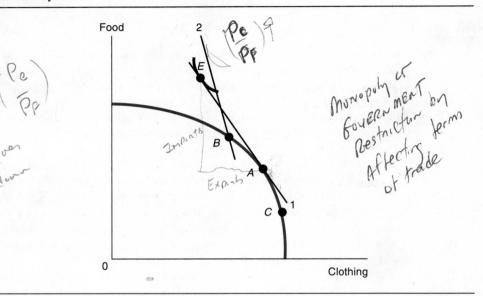

firm, such a (local) monopolist might be expected to do precisely that—monopolists typically restrict output in order to raise prices.[6] But if the clothing industry is competitive—i.e., characterized by a large number of producers unable to organize and individually not important enough to influence price—output restriction is not in any firm's individual interest. Hence a role for government.

This argument serves as the opening wedge in the case for protection of a nation's import-competing sector. If means can be found to divert resources from clothing exportables to the food import-competing sector, such a deliberate market interference could benefit the home country overall by improving the terms of trade. Part III will explore this question in more detail. Still, many issues are raised, even in this crude example: What controls are available to reduce output of clothing—output quotas, export quotas, subsidies to food producers, tariffs on food imports? Are some controls better than others? What about home consumers? Should their consumption of clothing be taxed or encouraged?[7]

A country's ability to change its terms of trade by interfering in home production patterns may make possible gains superior to those achieved by allocating resources according to comparative advantage. However, world output consequently suffers; if

---

[6] Of course, the situation gets somewhat more complicated if the monopolist faces competition from foreign producers. Chapter 14 delves more deeply into the interplay between trade and market structure.

[7] Appeals are often heard for government interference to *subsidize* exporters. Typically the setting is one in which large export firms are heavily engaged in competition with foreign firms, such as in the aircraft industry.

Inelastic   *Elastic*

the home country gains, other countries lose. In addition, as will be discussed later, foreigners may retaliate with protective measures of their own. Much can be achieved by international coordination and agreements to eschew policies that favor one country but beggar its neighbors.

4.3 GROWTH AND TRADE

Brazil And Coffee

→ Growth concentrated in export sector
→ demand elasticities low - inelastic

↑% P↓
-↓
5% Q↑

Does a community necessarily gain by producing more? The wary reader may wonder about the quality of life as it is affected by the extra production. Is growth beneficial if it leads to increased congestion, pollution, and crime in urban areas? In a different vein, is aggregate growth desirable if it reflects a population explosion that threatens to lower per capita income? These arguments against growth are both popular and easily understood, but there is a less obvious question: Can an outward shift of a country's production-possibility schedule with a constant population—with food and clothing "goods" instead of "bads"—ever lead to a lowering of real incomes at home? If a country is engaged in foreign trade, the answer is "perhaps."

P | demand not sensitive to price | Q

If demand is inelastic

The preceding discussion of the way in which changing the composition of output can alter the terms of trade and real income serves as the key to the possibility that these terms-of-trade changes might even outweigh the directly beneficial effect of growth. Consider Brazil, heavily committed to an export crop, coffee, for which world demand is highly inelastic. Suppose it is a good season, or for some other reason Brazil's transformation schedule shifts out primarily in the direction of coffee production. The world price of coffee might fall so much that Brazil loses real income as a consequence of the good crop. The argument also is valid for groups within a country. Agriculture provides the prime example. Many nations attempt, on behalf of their farmers, to encourage crop-restriction programs—the opposite of growth— to keep farm prices from falling in the face of inelasticity in demand.

The possibility that growth could lower real incomes by being concentrated in a nation's export sector and by significantly worsening the country's terms of trade is illustrated in Figure 4.3. This is known as a case of *immiserizing growth*. Initially, the terms of trade are given by the slope of line 1, with the home country's production at A and consumption at B. Growth in some form that favors the nation's export industry, clothing, shifts the transformation schedule outward from TT to $T'T'$. As a consequence, it is assumed that the relative price of clothing in world markets drops to the level shown by the slope of line 2. The home country adjusts its production to point C and, at the new terms of trade, maximizes its real income by consuming at point D. However, its real income after growth, as indicated by the y_1 indifference curve, is lower than the original real income shown by indifference curve y_0. Economic growth has hurt the country.

Two basic factors contribute to produce this result: (1) Growth primarily increases capacity and output in a nation's export industries. (2) Demand elasticities throughout the world for the country's export commodity are quite low. The first factor ensures that the major effect of growth in world markets is the increased supply of the nation's exports, whereas the second suggests that the terms of trade must deteriorate sharply to raise world demand enough to clear commodity markets. Figure 4.4 illustrates these two factors. The home country experiences growth, and at initial prices (OA)

2 Factors

FIGURE 4.3   Immiserizing Growth

Growth biased toward the nation's export industry (clothing) can reduce real income by so worsening the terms of trade (from line 1 to line 2) that consumption (at *D*) ends up on a lower indifference curve than initially (at *B*).

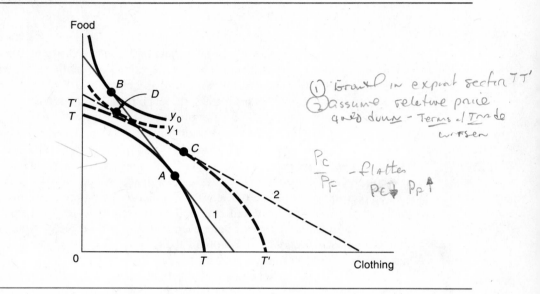

this growth is concentrated in its clothing export sector. This is shown by the rightward shift in the world supply schedule. The world demand curve also shifts to the right because at home a fraction of the extra incomes earned in the clothing sector spills over into extra clothing demand. The relative price of clothing is driven down to *OB*, and such a drop is more severe the less elastic are world demand and supply. Such inelasticities are feared by many agricultural communities.

This discussion perhaps casts too pessimistic a pall over the prospects of growth for a country engaged in trade. For a small country, little change in world prices can be expected as a consequence of growth, so the feedback on home real incomes through a terms-of-trade effect can safely be ignored. For a larger country, growth can improve the terms of trade if it is concentrated in a country's import-competing sector. Clearly, the assumed composition of output changes affects the terms of trade. However, is it possible to isolate the effect of growth per se on real income in a trading economy? Yes, by considering the following case.

Suppose a country experiences neutral growth in the sense that at initial world prices home output of every commodity increases by, say, 15 percent and consumption of all commodities rises by the same 15 percent. If other countries do not grow, world markets are thrown out of line. The reason: the country's supply of exports has also risen 15 percent, as has its demand for imports, and pressure is set up for the home

---

FIGURE 4.4 Output Growth and Terms-of-Trade Deterioration

Growth concentrated in the home country's clothing export sector shifts the world supply curve to the right by more than the world demand curve. The deterioration in the terms of trade (*OA* to *OB*) is more severe the less elastic are world demand and world supply.

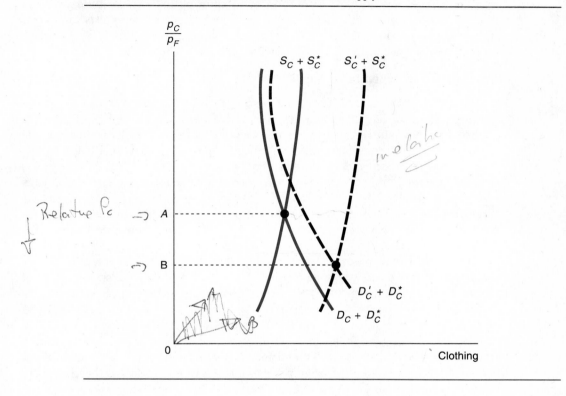

country's terms of trade to deteriorate. *The sheer act of growing more than other countries increases the demand for imports and thus induces a deterioration in the terms of trade that to some extent may erode the gains from growth.*[8]

This argument reveals the strong links that international trade forges among national real income levels. However, there is a bright side. Suppose your country is growing less rapidly than others. If such growth is of this "neutral" variety, your country's terms of trade are apt to improve. Growth anywhere in the world benefits the trading community as a whole, but whether all participants share in the gains depends not only on the initial allocation of growth among nations, but also on the succeeding adjustments in world prices.

---

[8] You may wonder if in this case of neutral growth the terms of trade could deteriorate to such an extent that growth becomes immiserizing. This is possible if elasticities are sufficiently low. The supplement provides the details.

4.4 THE TRANSFER PROBLEM | Monday?

Once countries are linked by commodity trade, any change in world prices hurts some (those who import commodities that have risen in price) and yields benefits to others (those who export these commodities). These terms-of-trade changes serve to transfer real income between importing and exporting nations. Historically more direct forms of transfer have been important as well, leading economists to analyze the resulting welfare consequences for open economies once secondary transfers, represented by price changes, are considered together with the initial direct transfer.

The Transfer Problem: Purchasing Power

Consider the following case. The home country is obligated to make a gift or reparations payment to the foreign country. The home country could be France after the Franco-Prussian War in 1870–1871 or Germany after World War I. To broaden the possible categories, consider a different kind of "gift," the Marshall Plan, whereby the United States sent aid to Europe after World War II. For analytic purposes international lending and borrowing will also be included, but the future problems of repaying loans (a reverse transfer) will be ignored. A recent example concerns the "recycling" of surpluses earned by oil-exporting countries into loans to Western Europe. All these cases have something in common: One country transfers purchasing power to another.

The easiest way to prepare the basic trade model to handle this problem is to let the home country cut the aggregate value of its spending below the current value of its produced income by precisely the same amount as the foreign country expands its spending above its current aggregate production level. (Only in this way can world expenditure balance world production.) This amount is called the *transfer*.

How does such a transfer affect the terms of trade? This can be answered by asking what the transfer does to world demand and supply for one of the traded commodities (e.g., food). A transfer of purchasing power would leave the world supply schedule in place but might cause the world demand curve to shift. At any given price ratio, the home, or transferring, country can be expected to cut back its spending on all normal commodities such as food. Abroad, the receipts of the transfer are disbursed in general over all commodities, including food. Therefore, the home demand curve for food shifts leftward while the foreign curve shifts rightward; depending on the differences in the two countries' taste patterns, the world demand curve could shift in either direction.

The first conclusion, then, is that transfer can move the terms of trade in either direction. To probe more formally, let m and m^* denote home and foreign *marginal propensities to import*. These propensities indicate, for each country, the fraction of a unit extra total spending that would be allocated to the consumption of importables at initial prices. Thus, if T denotes the transfer, the home country, at initial prices, cuts its spending on food by $m \cdot T$. The foreign country imports clothing, so it allocates $(1 - m^*)$ times the transfer to extra food consumption. Thus, the world demand curve for food shifts to the right if and only if $(1 - m^*) \cdot T$ exceeds the home cut, $m \cdot T$. That is, the terms of trade turn against the transferor (food's relative price rises when the home country makes a transfer) if and only if the sum of the two countries' marginal propensities to import falls short of unity.

If the sum of the marginal propensities to import does fall short of unity, economists speak of the "secondary burden" of the transfer in acknowledgment of the fact that price changes create an international redistribution of income additional to the initial loan or grant. Between the two world wars, a number of eminent economists were concerned with the practical importance of this issue. John Maynard Keynes eloquently argued that the reparations payments imposed by the Allies on Germany after World War I underestimated the true payment that Germany would have to make.[9] According to Keynes, Germany's export prices would have to fall considerably, coupled perhaps with a rise in its import prices, in order for Germany to create the export surplus that would comprise the counterpart of the financial transfer. In reply to Keynes, Bertil Ohlin proposed that the transfer itself, by lowering spending in Germany and raising spending in the recipient country, could bring about the required export surplus without imposing a change in the terms of trade. Ohlin's reasoning is closer to the analysis here, which suggests that it is not necessary for the terms of trade to change one way or the other.[10] In any event, tracing the adjustments that the German reparations required is difficult, for this period was characterized by an additional reverse transfer in the form of private loans and capital movements from the United States to Europe.

Is It Better to Give or to Receive?

The transfer criterion tells us that the terms of trade move in favor of the country making the transfer if the sum of import propensities exceeds unity. How favorable can the terms of trade become? The discussion of the possibility of immiserizing growth in Section 4.3 makes clear the analogous possibility that the home country, by giving away purchasing power, might so improve its terms of trade that it ends up with improved welfare. This, however, cannot happen in this two-country setting, for "it is never better to give than to receive." Figure 4.5 helps explain the limits to any "secondary blessing" of the transfer.

The initial world equilibrium in the food market is shown by a relative price of food, OA, and quantities produced and consumed, OF. If the home country makes a transfer, its real income is reduced. On the other hand, if its terms of trade improve (the price of food falls), this loss will not be so severe. Let price OB represent exactly the improvement in terms of trade (compared with OA) required to compensate the home country for the transfer. That is, if the price of food falls to level OB, neither country's welfare will be altered from its pretransfer level. The question boils down to the following: Can the transfer shift world demand to the left sufficiently to reduce food's price to OB or lower? It cannot, because after the transfer if the price were OB, world demand for food would have to exceed its initial value, OF. The reason follows from looking at income and substitution effects. By assumption, net real income

[9] John Maynard Keynes, *The Economic Consequences of the Peace* (New York: Harcourt, Brace and Howe, 1920).

[10] See the exchange between Keynes and Ohlin: Keynes, "The German Transfer Problem," *Economic Journal*, 39 (March 1929): 1–7, and B. Ohlin, "The Reparation Problem: A Discussion," *Economic Journal* (June 1929): 172–73. Both are reprinted in American Economic Association, *Readings in the Theory of International Trade*. A discussion of the effect of a transfer on the balance of payments appears in Chapter 17.

FIGURE 4.5   Transfer and the Terms of Trade

A transfer may improve the terms of trade of the transferor, as shown by the drop in food's relative price from OA to OG when the home country (the importer of food) makes a transfer. OB represents such an improvement in the home country's terms of trade that its real income would be unaffected by the payment. Therefore, at price OB world demand must exceed world supply, because only substitution effects are involved in demand.

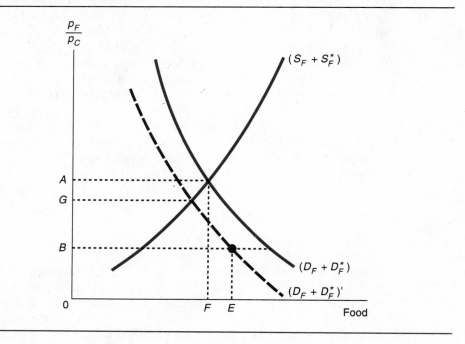

in both countries is unchanged if the price of food falls to OB; therefore, there is no income effect.[11] Substitution effects in both countries call for greater food demand at a lower price. Therefore, even if the transfer shifts the world demand schedule to the left, it must be to some position such as $(D_F + D_F^*)'$, with a new relative price for food (OG) above OB.

Brazil might improve its position by burning part of a bumper coffee crop. It cannot improve its position by giving that coffee away. Growth (or the reverse) shifts the world supply curve; a transfer of purchasing power does not. Without a change in supply, price changes in this two-country world do not outweigh the direct effect of the transfer.

---

[11] Price OB is the price that leaves the home transferor's real income unaltered, by assumption. But the transfer itself cannot create or destroy real income in the world, so at OB foreign real income also is undisturbed. However, this conclusion needs some modification if more than two distinct countries are engaged in trade. At price OB there then could be a redistribution of income among other countries even if home income is constant, and such a redistribution could create excess world supply at OB. In this case, the transferor would (paradoxically) gain.

The Transfer Problem: Real Resources

A transfer in the form of a gift, a loan, or reparations often involves more than a redistribution of purchasing power. Real resources may be moved from one country to another. This movement may be direct, as in the stripping of German capital equipment at the end of World War II and its relocation in Eastern Europe and the Soviet Union. The process also may be more indirect: Canada, for example, may borrow on the New York market, causing a greater investment in new capital equipment in Canada and perhaps less new capital equipment in the United States. This section investigates the possible repercussion on the terms of trade and real incomes that follow a transfer of real capital from one country to another.

Analyzing the effect of such a real transfer on the terms of trade means reconsidering the logic used in the previous section. In a stable market the relative price of a commodity rises only if the transfer creates an excess world demand for that commodity at the original price. The world supply schedule in our previous analysis was unaffected by transfer. However, if productive resources are involved in the transfer, the world supply curve, as well as the demand curve, may shift.

How much might world supply change? Obviously, much depends on how the resources are used in each country. At one extreme the pattern of output reduction in the transferor might exactly match the output expansion made possible in the receiving country. In such a case no changes in world output take place; it is as if only purchasing power were transferred. At the other extreme the output changes in each country might involve completely different commodities. For example, each country might produce only one commodity and exchange it in trade for the other country's commodity. The home country transfers resources out of clothing (its only produced commodity in this example) and into the foreign country, where they are devoted to food production. Such extreme output changes lead to definite conclusions as to movements in the terms of trade: The transferor's real income loss is partly mitigated by a terms-of-trade improvement. The transfer increased world food output (and lowered clothing output) and lowered food's relative price.[12]

4.5 THE BASIC TRADE MODEL: A BROAD INTERPRETATION

The discussion of the advantages that countries gain from engaging in international trade and the ways in which they adjust to changes in world market conditions has been confined thus far to a rather restricted setting: Two countries trade a pair of final commodities with each other, with each nation's imports from the other balanced in value by its current exports. Such a stripped-down setting allows a simple presentation of the details of the argument, but does not do justice to the rich array of trading opportunities available to nations once the possibility of engaging in world markets frees up the composition of consumption from that of local current production. A wider interpretation of world markets reveals the following possibilities.

1. *Many Final Commodities.* It has already been shown that the food and clothing categories can be thought of as aggregates, each masking a bundle of varieties. Thus,

---

[12] The transferor actually could have its real income increased by such a supply change.

trade enlarges the menu of types available to a nation's consumers. Trade likewise expands the number of other commodity types found on world markets and allows a nation to concentrate its resources on the production of those aggregates in which it possesses a comparative advantage while also producing fewer varieties within each aggregate, to take advantage of division of labor and economies of scale. By freeing up the necessity to produce what is consumed, international trade allows a country to obtain a consumption basket comprising a vast array of commodities relative to what is produced at home. Countries typically produce fewer commodities than are consumed.

2. *Many Countries and the Issue of Bilateral Balance.* In the real world countries exchange commodities with many other countries. Once this fact is recognized, it is not necessary for a nation to balance its trade accounts with any particular country in isolation. The United States can run a trade deficit with Japan and trade surpluses with Latin America or European countries. Overall trade balance does not imply, or even suggest as desirable, restricting bilateral balances with each other trading country. Furthermore, even if the home country currently is importing a greater value of goods and services than it is exporting and wishes to cut back on its imports, it is not necessary for the home country to focus on that type of imported commodity produced by a country that has an overall export surplus with the home country. These points are often overlooked in the heated debate about imbalances in the trade account between the United States and individual countries such as Japan. In a free-trade world it would be natural to find bilateral deficits or surpluses between any pair of countries.

3. *Trade in Intermediate Goods and Raw Materials.* Countries such as Japan and Canada often are portrayed as opposites in their trading patterns. Japan is starved for oil, coal, rubber, and many raw materials required for its booming manufacturing sector, while Canada possesses an abundance of many primary products and energy, which it can trade for automobiles, television sets, and word processors. Chapter 9 surveys the possibilities for gains by countries that are able to rely on world markets to match imbalances in final goods trade with opposite imbalances in raw materials and intermediate goods. The sheer volume of world trade in nonconsumer goods is impressive—over three-quarters of the world's exports are categorized as producer goods, raw materials, or intermediate goods, and this fraction is increasing as the world's production facilities become ever more integrated.

4. *Intertemporal Trade.* Thus far it has been assumed that each nation balances its current production and consumption, or its current exports and imports. Individuals and nations look to the future as well, however. A young person may plan to spend now in excess of current earnings, to be made up later when earnings are expected to rise. In similar fashion, the aggregate of individual decisions within a country may call for a deficit or surplus in current spending plans, with borrowing or lending in world markets allowing intertemporal smoothing of consumption and production plans. Goods today and goods tomorrow are different. Comparative advantage, taste patterns, and productive potential can vary over time, just as they do over commodity types, and can suggest optimal patterns of net trade over time as well as net trade in autos or computers.

To consider a simple example, suppose a nation initially balanced in exporting a variety of commodities that match in value its current imports discovers new coal deposits, which take time to develop. In future years it can confidently expect outputs to rise significantly over current levels. Assuming it does not expect prices to be much affected by these discoveries (i.e., ruling out the specter of immiserizing growth), how might its trading pattern be affected? Its current level of wealth has increased because of its expectations of greater production in the future. It probably would be best to spread the benefits of this wealth over time, and such consumption smoothing would entail running current deficits (an excess of imports over exports), to be made up later when production expands by planned trade surpluses (an excess of future exports over imports).

Such intertemporal trade requires using assets with internationally recognized value, just as exchanges of commodities within any time period are aided by using money to avoid the transaction costs required by barter. More will be said later about such assets and the problems encountered when using different currencies. One obvious problem with intertemporal trade is the possibility of changes over time in exchange rates linking currency values in various countries. Here the emphasis is on a different set of prices: interest rates. Countries that tend to discount future consumption relatively heavily may be encouraged by the opportunity to borrow on world markets at interest rates that seem low by national standards. The world pattern of interest rates, and of commodity prices, reflects the diversity among countries in tastes and production plans. Just as it is not necessary for a country's trade in any commodity category or with any group of countries to balance, so it is not necessary to balance overall payments within any given time period. This merely reflects the gains from trade over all commodities, present and future, when world markets supplement or replace the requirement for item-by-item balance found in autarky.

A simple illustration of intertemporal trade is provided in Figure 4.6, which uses only the ingredients developed in Chapter 2's model of commodity exchange. Suppose point E is the endowment point, reflecting a "brighter" future in which next year more of a composite good will be owned than is the case this year. Furthermore, suppose world interest rates are shown by the slope of line EA. More particularly, the slope of this line is $(1 + r)$, where r is the rate of interest. The "trade triangle" is EGA, where the country runs a deficit (excess of consumption this year over production this year) of GA, paid for by a promise to pay back EG next year. EG exceeds GA. (Their ratio is 1 plus the interest rate, so that trade is balanced intertemporally.) The slope of the home indifference curve at E reflects the higher rate of time preference in autarky for the home country. As this example illustrates, intertemporal trade yields standard gains from trade if autarky prices differ from those on world markets.

A country such as the United States may be running a current account deficit, as it has in recent years, but this may not necessarily represent a disequilibrium position in dire need of policy correctives. Although views regarding the urgency of the need to combat such deficits vary widely, the argument sketched here is that this deficit represents an imbalance in one time period that can be offset by opposite imbalances in the future. Intertemporal trade can yield gains to all participants.

5. *"Intra-Asset" Trade.* The types of bonds, stocks, and financial assets, not to mention currency, found in one country may differ from those found in others. Even

---

FIGURE 4.6   Intertemporal Trade

The home country expects a larger endowment of goods next year than it has this year. It gains by giving up more next year (*EG*) than it borrows for extra consumption this year (*GA*).

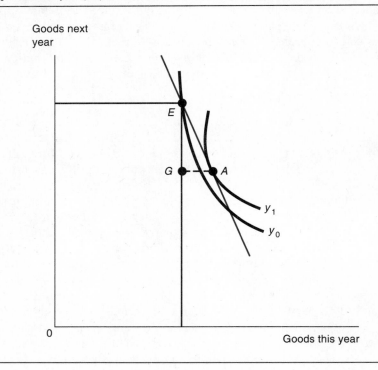

if a country plans to spend currently no more or less on commodities than the aggregate value of its production, it may wish to diversify its portfolio holdings by exchanging assets with other countries. This, on the asset side, is analogous to the intra-industry trade among varieties in any commodity group. Changes in interest rates, exchange rates, and commodity prices could well lead to a reshuffling of these asset holdings, whether or not accompanied by "new trades" between assets and consumable commodities (i.e., intertemporal trade).

   6. *Trade and Market Structure.* When concentrating on the gains that accrue when a country exchanges goods and services in a world market, we downplay one potentially significant role for trade. Widening the market affects the nature of competition. The presumption is that trade will produce procompetitive effects. National monopolies may find rivals in other countries, and competition from other sources may affect the structure of the market locally. As will be described in Part III, the structure of the market may be so altered that trade results in an actual lowering locally of the relative price of the commodity that a country exports, or perhaps stimulates local production of a commodity that will be imported. On occasion the opportunity to trade encourages the formation of cartels or allows an increase in the control held by a monopolist or set of oligopolistic firms. Our stance is to assume relatively

competitive behavior, and a significant feature of free trade is that such an assumption generally is more feasible in wider markets. In other words, one consequence of a move toward protectionism in trading relationships could be to encourage local monopoly power stemming from the fragmentation of markets.

This sketch of the manner in which the basic trade model can be given an interpretation broader than that of two countries producing and trading two commodities in the current time period should be extended in another way: Productive factors such as labor, capital, and management services may to some extent be capable of moving from country to country. Multinational enterprises may facilitate such mobility of factors. As well, any nation may find its level of technological knowledge enhanced by its trading contacts with other nations. (Chapter 10 pursues these topics.)

The fundamental principle of trade underlying all these remarks is that international trade frees up the lockstep connection between patterns of consumption and production that characterizes a state of autarky. Severing the umbilical cord connecting local demand and supply in general allows a wider choice for consumers and encourages a concentration of resources in production. These themes will reappear as we go on to analyze in more depth the details of how technology, relative factor endowments, scale economies, and the possibility of trade in nonfinal commodities shape trading patterns and the distribution of income.

4.6 SUMMARY

Part I of this book was devoted to developing what we call "the basic trade model." Chapter 4 showed how that model can be applied to the following issues that characterize the world trading community.

1. Any source of disturbance abroad that causes world markets to settle at new prices affects the home country. A change in foreign tastes or in foreign supplies involves a terms-of-trade impact for the home country, which may be sizable, as our discussion of the oil crisis suggests.

2. A country with sufficient volume of trade to influence world prices can, by interfering with its competitive production pattern, engineer an improvement in its terms of trade. (We defer until Part III an examination of the significance of this observation in understanding noncompetitive behavior in trade and its relevance in the analysis of commercial policy.)

3. A growing community finds that repercussions of its growth are reflected in its terms of trade. We argued that on balance the benefits of growth in one country would spill over favorably to affect other countries through cheapening the growing country's exports. We even considered extreme cases in which growth might leave a country in a worse position. Agriculture supplies many examples in which crop restriction (the opposite of growth) might benefit farmers.

4. Some disturbances may affect both countries in opposite directions. The transfer process, wherein a gift or loan is made between countries, provides the classic example. If only purchasing power is transferred, the crucial consideration involves how tastes differ between payer and receiver. Any required price adjustment involves a "secondary" transfer of real income.

5. The basic trade model is broadly applicable to settings in which many countries produce and exchange a wide range of goods and services. The requirements of overall balance do not imply a necessary bilateral balance between any pair of countries. Furthermore, countries may exchange assets with each other and may take advantage of trading contacts to rearrange aggregate consumption and production over time. International net borrowing and lending may represent an equilibrium outcome by which interest rates help balance national dissimilarities in time preference and expected changes in resources and wealth.

"Every exit is an extrance to another stage." This survey of the basic trade model prepares the way for a more detailed investigation of what lies behind a nation's production possibilities in Part II. Although these chapters will focus on different issues—the effect of trade on the distribution of income and the influence of technology and factor endowments on the pattern of trade—the models we develop there represent more detailed variations of the basic model discussed in Part I while remaining consistent with it. Can an expansion in an open economy's supply of capital bring about actual harm? Once we know how such growth affects the nation's output pattern, the discussion in this chapter will help expose the elements that determine the fate of the nation's real income.

CHAPTER PROBLEMS

1. Figure 4.3 illustrates the phenomenon of immiserizing growth when the country's growth is strongly biased toward its export industry (clothing). Construct a diagram that illustrates the possibility that a country will suffer a welfare loss when growth (at initial terms of trade) results in a balanced (proportional) increase in food and clothing outputs. Can such immiserization accompany growth that is concentrated in food (the import-competing sector)?

2. If imports of food represent 20 percent of a country's national income and the relative price of food rises by 10 percent, by approximately how much is national income reduced?

3. Suppose that home and foreign countries' taste patterns differ but that each is inflexible: The home country consumes food to clothing in proportions 2:1 (at any prices), while the foreign food to clothing consumption ratio is always 1:1. The two countries have identical bowed-out transformation schedules. What happens to the home country's terms of trade if it makes a consumption loan to the foreign country? Is there a secondary "burden" of the loan?

4. Draw a diagram to illustrate the case of uniform growth—the transformation schedule shifts out radially from the origin by 30 percent. How might such growth affect the country's terms of trade? Now suppose a country receives as transfer a quantity of resources from its trading partner and suppose this has the effect of causing its transformation schedule to shift out 10 percent and the giving country's schedule to shift uniformly in by 10 percent. Would the giving country suffer a secondary burden or blessing? How is the growth case related to the transfer exercise?

5. Suppose that only two countries engage in trade and that initially trade is balanced in the current period. If the home country discovers a new process that will raise productivity in its export sector in the next period, how would the current balance of trade be affected? Would your answer be modified if both countries also expect that the discovery will worsen the home country's terms of trade during the following period? (*Hint:* Could the foreign country's real net "wealth" be increased by more than the home country's as a consequence of the expected terms-of-trade change?)

SUGGESTIONS FOR FURTHER READING

Bhagwati, Jagdish. "Immiserizing Growth: A Geometrical Note," *Review of Economic Studies*, 25 (3) (June 1958): 201–205. A treatment of the possibility that growth can harm a country.

Samuelson, Paul A. "The Transfer Problem and Transport Costs: The Terms of Trade When Impediments Are Absent," *Economic Journal*, 62 (June 1952): 278–304. A thorough analysis of classical transfer theory.

APPENDIX:
THE STABILITY ISSUE

Chapter 4 illustrated world market equilibrium in Figures 4.1, 4.4, and 4.5. Each of these figures shows a unique stable equilibrium in which stability is guaranteed by two features: (1) Supply and demand curves are drawn so that at prices above equilibrium world supply exceeds world demand, while at prices below equilibrium world demand exceeds world supply. (2) It is assumed that price is driven up if, and only if, excess world market demand exists.

Competitive markets that are not so well behaved can be illustrated. For example, the counterpart to Figure 4.1's illustration of a stable free-trade equilibrium is Figure 4.A.1's depiction of multiple possible free-trade equilibria. Point C in Figure 4.A.1a shows world demand and supply for food in balance, but the equilibrium point is unstable. If the price of food were slightly higher, at (2), world demand for food would exceed world supply by distance AB. Such an excess demand would drive food's price upward, away from point C. [Similarly, for a price of food lower than (1), world excess supply would drive food's price lower, toward stable equilibrium point E.]

Figure 4.A.1b illustrates this instability in an offer-curve diagram. At disequilibrium terms of trade (2), TV indicates the excess of the home country's import demand for food (given by point W along home offer curve $OIWQHR$) over foreign export supplies (given by point V along foreign offer curve $OHQVIR^*$). Food's price will rise, rotating price line (2) clockwise toward stable intersection point I and away from unstable point Q. Point Q in 4.A.1b corresponds to point C in 4.A.1a.

Each diagram helps reveal the ingredients that conspire to make an equilibrium unstable. As point Q in the lower panel indicates, instability requires a high degree of inelasticity in both countries' offer curves.[13] The upper panel shows that for instability the aggregate world demand curve in the neighborhood of equilibrium must be positively sloped and even flatter than the world supply curve.

Can the world demand curve be positively sloped? Yes, if at least one country's demand curve has a positive slope in the neighborhood of a free-trade equilibrium. Consider first the importer of food, the home country. As food's price rises from (1), substitution effects suggest less food is demanded. Furthermore, real income falls, so assuming food is a "normal" commodity, both income and substitution effects conspire to reduce the home country's demand for food. Thus, instability must stem from the demand behavior of the exporter. For foreign exporters of food, income and substitution effects run counter to each other. As the price of food rises, so does foreign real income, and this tends to make the foreign demand curve for food positively sloped. In order for the world's demand curve to be positively sloped, the exporter's income effect must outweigh the income effect of the importer as well as both countries'

---

[13] As the supplement to Chapter 4 proves, the criterion for stability is that the sum of the two countries' elasticities of demand for imports exceeds unity, the so-called *Marshall-Lerner condition*.

FIGURE 4.A.1   Multiple Equilibria

There may be multiple free-trade equilibria. The middle equilibrium point (C in a, or Q in b) is unstable, flanked by a pair of stable equilibria.

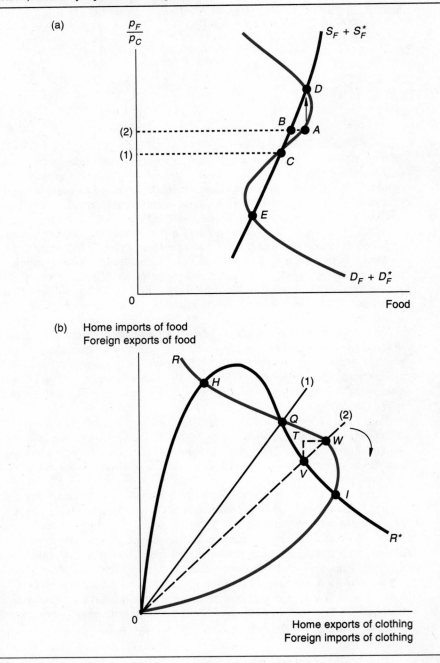

(a)

(b)   Home imports of food
       Foreign exports of food

Home exports of clothing
Foreign imports of clothing

substitution effects. In order for the market to be unstable, the exporter's income effect must in addition outweigh any positive production response of food producers at home and abroad.

Nothing automatically guarantees market stability in the relationship between income and substitution effects. Therefore, an additional assumption that the market is stable must be made. Little interest attaches to equilibria that are unstable because prices will tend to run away from such equilibria. The applications of the basic trade model considered in Chapter 4 involve comparing one equilibrium with another, under the assumption that prices do approach the second equilibrium after the market is disturbed (by growth, taste changes, or transfers). Such a procedure makes sense only if the market is assumed stable. The supplement to Chapter 4 probes more deeply into the analytics of this issue.

II

International Trade Patterns and Income Distribution

5

TECHNOLOGY AND THE RICARDIAN TRADE MODEL

What characteristics of production help to explain patterns of world trade? And what are the repercussions of international trade on workers' wages? On returns to land or capital? Countries differ from each other in technology, climate, the skill levels of factors of production, the composition of the factor endowment base, and size. Some countries are abundant in natural resources and land, whereas others possess relatively plentiful supplies of labor but are poorly endowed with accumulated capital. International trade can have a profound effect in realigning the functional distribution of income within as well as between countries. The models presented in Part II will help reveal why various groups within a nation hold such strong views about trade policy.

The role of technology in explaining trade patterns is the focus of this chapter. Technology is constantly in the news these days—do Japanese firms now possess technology that is superior to that mastered by American entrepreneurs? Can advanced techniques in West Germany be successfully transferred to the East? It is perhaps ironic that the earliest model of trade (1817), that associated with the name of David Ricardo, can be used to discuss technology as a source of trade.[1] Chapter 2 already demonstrated the basic result concerning gains from trade: Countries can mutually benefit from trade if the relative prices of commodities differ between countries in the absence of trade. Ricardo is credited with establishing this result in a simple model in which a country's relative prices must reflect the ratio of labor costs of production. Thus, the trade pattern in a Ricardian world is determined by differences in labor productivities among countries.

5.1 BEFORE TRADE

Ricardo adopted the "labor theory of value" in describing the ratio in which commodities are exchanged for each other in an economy closed to the possibility of foreign trade. According to a strict version of the labor theory of value:

---

[1] A recent edition is David Ricardo, *The Principles of Political Economy and Taxation* (Cambridge, UK: Cambridge University Press, 1981), Chapter 7. The work was first published in 1817.

1. Labor is the only factor of production that receives remuneration.
2. All labor is homogeneous and all occupations pay the same wage.
3. In any occupation the number of labor-hours required per unit of output neither rises nor falls as output expands. Real cost per unit remains constant.

Although our account begins in the simplified world of two commodities (food and clothing), the Ricardian model can easily be expanded to cover more realistic cases in which many commodities are consumed and traded. With only one factor (labor) required in the production process, the country's technology is completely described in our two-commodity setting by a pair of numbers: the amount of labor required to produce one unit of food (a_{LF}) and one unit of clothing (a_{LC}). The reciprocals of these numbers are sometimes used instead; labor's productivity in producing food is shown by $1/a_{LF}$, the output of food obtainable from one hour's labor. If all costs are absorbed by labor, the only productive input in a competitive market, then commodities exchange for each other in a ratio that reflects labor inputs. If twice as many hours are needed to produce a unit of food as to produce a unit of clothing, food's price is double that of clothing.

These productivity figures combine information as to technology—in the sense of blueprints available to guide the transformation of labor services into food and clothing—and as to skills of labor. Higher education levels or more appropriate attitudes toward discipline in the work place show up in higher output per unit of labor just as would superior technology. Improvements in labor productivity are created in both the classroom and the research labs.

Suppose a country's supply of labor available for employment (L) is fixed. A production-possibilities schedule can then be drawn. However, in the Ricardian model it will not exhibit the bowed-out shape familiar from the basic trade model of Chapters 3 and 4. Instead, it is a downward-sloping straight line. To see this, consider the total labor demanded by either sector: This is the product of the scale of output, x_i, and the intensity with which labor is required for each unit of output in that sector, a_{Li}. Thus, the clothing sector demands $a_{LC}x_C$ units of labor, and food employs $a_{LF}x_F$ units of labor. Add these together. If full employment prevails, as assumed, these sum to the total labor supply L:

$$a_{LC}x_C + a_{LF}x_F = L \tag{5.1}$$

Because input/output requirements (a_{LC}, a_{LF}) are constant, invariant to the scale of output, the full-employment relationship (Equation 5.1) restricts output levels to the straight-line transformation schedule illustrated in Figure 5.1. The endpoints show the maximum quantity of each commodity that could be produced if that activity absorbed the entire labor force.[2] The slope is easily calculated to be (minus) the constant ratio, a_{LC}/a_{LF}. How much extra food could be produced if clothing output is reduced by one unit? This reduction would release a_{LC} units of labor. Because a_{LF} hours are required per food unit, a_{LC}/a_{LF} extra food units are produced. In a closed economy, this figure represents the relative price of clothing—measured in units of food that must be surrendered to purchase one unit of clothing.

---

[2] Suppose it takes a worker 20 hours to produce a unit of food and 10 hours per unit of clothing. An economy that possessed 1,000 hours of labor supply could produce a maximum of 50 units of food or 100 units of clothing, or any linear combination of the two.

FIGURE 5.1   The Ricardian Production-Possibilities Schedule

The opportunity cost of producing clothing is shown by the slope of the straight-line transformation schedule, which is the ratio of labor coefficients a_{LC}/a_{LF}. Before international trade, the country produces and consumes at A, with welfare levels shown by the indifference curve, y_0.

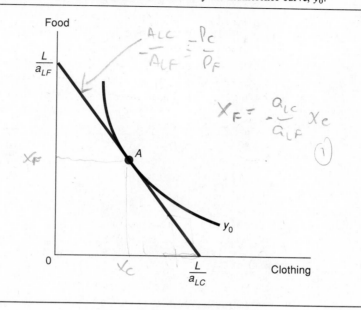

A closed economy must rely on its own production to satisfy its consumption needs. Therefore, relative prices in such an economy are shown by the constant slope of the transformation schedule. The pretrade consumption (and production) pattern would be illustrated in Figure 5.1 by the point (A) at which an indifference curve (y_0) is tangent to the straight-line transformation schedule. These remarks easily generalize to a closed economy with any number of commodities. Relative prices are all technologically determined by the invariant labor productivities. As will soon become clear, this view of the determinants of prices no longer is applicable once the economy is opened to trade.

5.2 ABSOLUTE AND COMPARATIVE COSTS AND THE PATTERN OF TRADE

Part I's message was that trade patterns reflect a comparison of *relative* prices between countries in the pretrade state. This is also the case in our Ricardian world. Once again it is useful to consider diagrams in which relative outputs are related to relative prices. The relative supply curve in a Ricardian world is horizontal: If both food and clothing are to be produced, the relative price of food must reflect the (constant) ratio of labor costs in food to labor costs in clothing. The straight-line transformation schedule of Figure 5.1 implies the horizontal relative supply curve of Figure 5.2. Demand therefore has no role in determining pretrade prices, a phenomenon peculiar

FIGURE 5.2   Relative Demand and Supply in a Ricardian Model

The Ricardian relative supply curve is horizontal. The pretrade relative price of food is the invariant labor cost ratio, a_{LF}/a_{LC}.

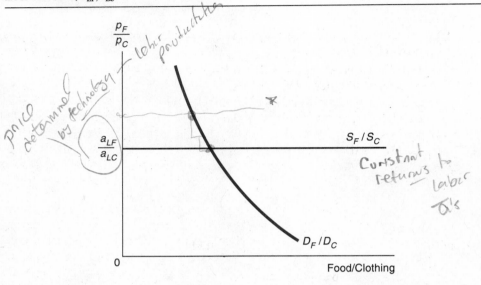

to the Ricardian model. Instead, technology is all-important. The pattern of trade is determined completely by the technological differences between countries. The foreign country emerges as a food exporter if, and only if, its relative supply curve is lower than the home country's. Put more formally, *the foreign country has a comparative advantage in food (and exports food) only if*

$$\frac{a_{LF}^*}{a_{LC}^*} < \frac{a_{LF}}{a_{LC}} \tag{5.2}$$

Throughout we shall retain this assumption that the cost of producing food is relatively lower abroad. The Ricardian model is the extreme case in which trade patterns are determined solely by differences in relative costs and these cost differences are independent of the production pattern.[3] Hence the home country will always be a clothing exporter.

So far no comparison has been made of the *levels* of technology in the two countries. Indeed, Ricardo discussed his theory of comparative costs in the context of a numerical example in which one country (England in his case) had higher labor costs per unit of production than the other country (Portugal) in both commodities. That is, Portugal was assumed to possess an *absolute advantage* in all commodities—a

_____

[3] Compare this with the case of vertical relative supply curves, which is the model of exchange introduced in Chapter 2. In that case pretrade price ratios are determined by supply and demand (as in the general case), but demand has no influence on quantities produced. The exchange model and the Ricardian model represent two extreme cases.

productivity edge over England in all activities. This being the case, why should Portugal import anything from England? Because, although English labor was at an absolute disadvantage in both wine and cloth, its disadvantage was assumed by Ricardo to be relatively less in one of the goods (cloth). The criterion shown by Inequality 5.2 illustrates that *comparative* costs provide the key to trade patterns. As will be seen in Section 5.4, if Portuguese labor is more productive in both goods, the wage rate must be higher in Portugal than in England. Thus, once trade takes place, the total cost of producing cloth in Portugal will not be lower than in England—the high Portuguese wage serves to offset the superior Portuguese labor productivity.

If this Portuguese advantage is a consequence of superior Portuguese technology (or, in the case of wine, superior climate) instead of superior inherent or acquired labor skills, English labor might be tempted to migrate south. Ricardo assumed that national borders kept labor (or any other productive factor) at home. Trade in commodities is then a substitute for international mobility of factors. Final commodities enjoy a world market, but factors of production compete with each other only within national boundaries.

This asymmetric assumption has typically characterized simple models of international trade and will be maintained in this and the succeeding three chapters. But in modern times it does some violence to the facts of trade—the extensive commerce in intermediate inputs, capital goods, and raw materials, as well as some international mobility of labor. Therefore, in Chapters 9 and 10 we shall take the opportunity to examine trade patterns when some inputs are mobile—a setting in which absolute advantages in technology play a more important role. But Ricardo's assumptions still have much relevance in a world in which national differences in languages, customs, and laws severely inhibit permanent international relocation of productive factors.

5.3 NATIONAL AND WORLD GAINS FROM TRADE

We have assumed, in Inequality 5.2, that comparative cost ratios differ between countries. This implies that, in the Ricardian model, once free trade is established the common relative price cannot equal the cost ratio in both countries, because these cost ratios stay a constant distance apart. Indeed, in the typical classical representation of such a case, international prices were distinctly different from the cost ratio in *either* country. This conclusion caused an obvious problem for Ricardo's successors, for it suggested that the labor theory of value, whereby prices reflected labor costs, must come to grief in a world of international trade.

The problem with asserting that relative prices reflect relative (labor) costs is that a country may be forced by international competition to abandon some line of production. If so, it is precisely because the international price of some commodity falls short of the costs per unit required to produce the commodity at home that no local production can take place. Figure 5.3 illustrates a free-trade equilibrium in which the home country specializes in the production of clothing, in which it has (by virtue of Inequality 5.2) a comparative advantage, and the foreign country's labor force is entirely devoted to food production. A market-clearing free-trade price ratio is established—the same ratio for each country (dashed line BE has the same slope as E^*B^*)—with home exports of clothing (CE) matched by foreign imports of clothing (C^*B^*). The rationale for the gains from trade is similar to that described for the

FIGURE 5.3   Free-Trade Equilibrium

Pretrade equilibrium at home is shown by point *A* in the upper diagram, abroad it is shown by *A** in the lower diagram. Equilibrium terms of trade are illustrated by the slope of the dashed line for each country. The home country produces at *E* and consumes at *B*; the foreign country produces at *E** and consumes at *B**. Each country gains from trade.

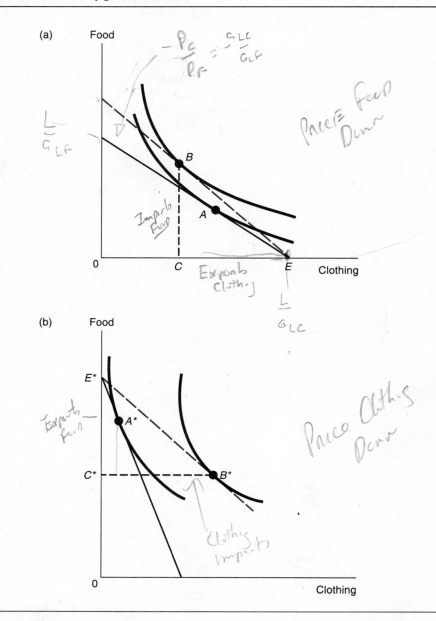

basic trade model in Part I. What is special about the Ricardian model is the potentially drastic consequence of trade for patterns of production. In each country not only are some resources attracted to the export sector but all resources flow there. Clearly this reflects the assumption of constant opportunity costs as opposed to increasing opportunity costs (along a bowed-out production-possibilities curve). Each country gains from trade, with free-trade consumption points (B and B*) lying on higher indifference curves than do pretrade consumption bundles (A and A*).

Country Size

Does the assumption of constant (labor) costs necessarily require each country to be completely specialized with trade? No. The international terms of trade must lie somewhere between the cost ratios in each country, but not necessarily strictly between. For example, if one country is much larger than the other, the world terms of trade could settle at the cost ratio of the large country. If the world were made up of the United States and Costa Rica, it would be impossible for Costa Rica, with a presumed comparative advantage in sugar, to supply the entire American market. In such a case, world prices would have to reflect American costs, so some American sugar production also would take place.

World Production Gains

The possibility that some country may not be completely specialized is shown more generally in a diagram designed primarily to show the trade gains from a world point of view, that is, gains from the reallocation of labor resources that are over and above the consumption gains described in the model of exchange in Chapter 2. Recall that in Chapter 2 both parties could gain even though world production remained constant. Figure 5.4 illustrates the extra gains that arise when trade encourages larger world production.

The concept of a transformation schedule, or production-possibilities schedule, is familiar as applied to an individual country. What is proposed here is to add the two countries' transformation curves to show the production possibilities with free trade for the world as a whole. This is shown by the solid line in Figure 5.4, ABC, with the stretch AB depicting the home country's transformation schedule and BC showing the foreign country's transformation schedule. To trace out the world production-possibilities locus, consider all conceivable world terms of trade. For very high food prices, both countries would specialize in food. Thus, OA in Figure 5.4 is the sum of the two countries' vertical intercepts in Figure 5.3. Starting from this point (A), consider how world outputs respond to changes in the price ratio: As p_F/p_C is reduced, it eventually reaches the home country's cost ratio, given by a_{LF}/a_{LC}. For such a price ratio the foreign country must remain specialized in food, but the home country can produce anywhere along its own transformation schedule. In Figure 5.4 point B represents the world output combination when the home country specializes in clothing and the foreign country in food. World production would be fixed at point B for any lower values for p_F/p_C until this price ratio reaches the cost ratio for the foreign country, a_{LF}^*/a_{LC}^*. At such a price ratio the foreign country can begin to produce

FIGURE 5.4   The World Transformation Schedule

The locus *ABC* shows world output possibilities with free trade. Free trade generally enlarges world outputs over autarky (e.g., the move from *G* to *B*).

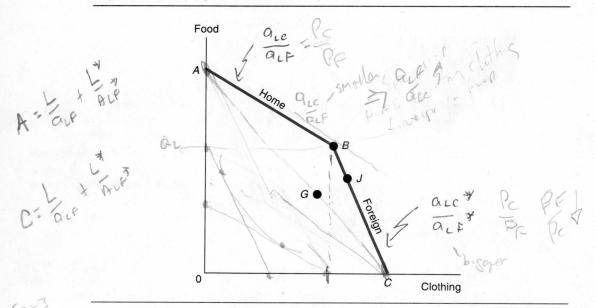

clothing. The distance *OC* in Figure 5.4 corresponds to maximum world production of clothing.

Point *B* in Figure 5.4 shows world output when each country specializes completely in producing the commodity in which it has a comparative advantage. Point *B* will in fact represent production if demand conditions yield a free-trade equilibrium price ratio strictly between the cost ratios in each country, but this need not be the outcome. Fairly strong world demand for clothing could result in point *J* as the world production point, with clothing's relative price driven up to the relative labor cost (for clothing) in the foreign country. As was already hinted, such a result is more likely if the foreign country is substantially larger than the home country (so that line segment *AB* is much shorter than *BC*). Whether free-trade world output settles at a point such as *J* or *B*, it will represent world gains in production relative to autarky consumption and production point *G*.

The World Market

The interplay of demand and supply in free trade can be seen in the depiction of the world food market in Figure 5.5. The supply curve is derived from the world transformation schedule in Figure 5.4. Distance *OA* in Figure 5.5 represents the maximum output of food in the foreign country, and length *AB* shows how much food could be produced at home if all labor were devoted to raising food. The kind of equilibrium illustrated earlier in Figure 5.3, in which world prices settled strictly between the cost

FIGURE 5.5   The World Market for Food

The world supply curve is composed of two horizontal steps, each at the price corresponding to a country's relative labor cost of food, and the vertical sections at outputs A and B.

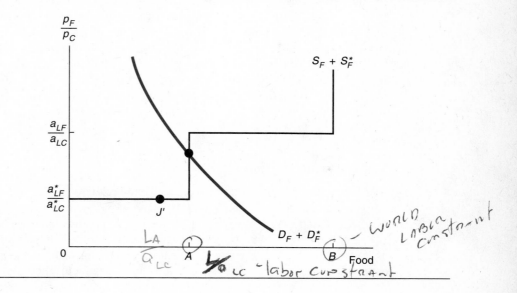

ratios in each country (with the home country specialized in clothing and the foreign country in food), also is shown in Figure 5.5; the world demand curve cuts the world supply curve at an intermediate price. To construct the world demand curve, just add, for each price, the optimal consumption of food for each country separately along the country's budget line. Clearly, a different set of tastes could lead to an equilibrium world output of food greater than OA or less than OA (as at point J in Figure 5.4, in which case the world demand curve in Figure 5.5 would intersect the supply curve at J'). It must be the case, however, that at least one country is completely specialized.

5.4 INTERNATIONAL WAGE COMPARISONS AND PRODUCTIVITIES

Although commodities move freely from country to country with trade, it is assumed that labor does not. There is no reason why home wages should match up with foreign wages. What determines the wage rate in a Ricardian model, and how does the comparison between home and foreign wages reflect the comparison of technologies? Are the commodity terms of trade also of relevance in wage comparisons?

In any economy, wage rates are closely linked to productivity (the reciprocal of the unit labor input requirements). This relationship is exact in a model that assumes that competition exists. Begin the argument by considering the general relationship between costs and prices in the home country. In a competitive *equilibrium* the unit costs of producing any commodity cannot fall short of that commodity's market price.

The reason is simple: If unit costs in food production were less than the price of food, the consequent profits would signal new entrants into the food industry. Enlarging food output would drive down the price of food; increasing the demand for labor would cause the wage rate to be bid up. This process, whereby new firms are attracted to the food industry, would continue until unit costs were raised enough to equal price. Unit costs can, however, exceed price, even in a competitive equilibrium. You may wonder why an entrepreneur would continue producing food if it is priced lower than the labor costs of production. In this competitive model the answer is "none would." Therefore, local food production would be zero. For an economy engaged in trade, food can be obtained from abroad instead of being produced at home. Indeed, in many of the illustrations in this chapter world terms of trade are established at which the home country is forced out of food production and the foreign country produces no clothing.

The Competitive Profit Conditions

The term "price" usually carries the meaning "relative price"—the quantity of one commodity that must be given up in exchange for one unit of the other. In analyzing production and factor returns it is frequently more convenient to refer to absolute prices in terms of a common unit of account or money. For example, the wage rate at home will be referred to as w, meaning dollars, for example, per labor-hour. An expression such as w/p_F would eliminate the nominal currency unit of account and denote food units per hours worth of work. With this in mind consider the *competitive profit conditions* shown in Inequalities 5.3 and 5.4:

$$a_{LC}w \geq p_C \tag{5.3}$$

$$a_{LF}w \geq p_F \tag{5.4}$$

These inequalities formally express the argument in the preceding paragraph. A competitive equilibrium must be characterized by an equality between unit cost and price if production is carried on in that equilibrium. Unit cost never can be less than price in a competitive equilibrium. Unit costs may exceed price, but only if all producers leave the industry. A similar set of conditions would, of course, apply to the foreign country, except that the wage rate abroad, denoted by w^*, need not be the same as at home, although with trade the price of either commodity will be identical in the two countries.

Productivity and Wages

Labor's physical "productivity" is measured in each industry by the inverse of the labor coefficient. For example, $1/a_{LC}$ is the number of units of clothing that can be produced with an input of one hour of labor.[4] If this is multiplied by the price of clothing, to obtain $p_C \cdot 1/a_{LC}$, a measure is derived of the "value" of labor's productivity in clothing. Thus, Inequalities 5.3 and 5.4 can be reinterpreted as meaning that the wage rate must equal the value of labor's productivity in any industry in which labor

---

[4] Because the input coefficients, a_{LC} and a_{LF}, are assumed to be constant, $1/a_{LC}$ denotes both labor's "average product" and its "marginal product."

is employed and must equal or exceed the value of its productivity in any industry that must shut down.

These remarks suggest that wage rates are linked to commodity prices as well as to physical productivities. To see what is entailed we once again adopt the procedure of asking what production patterns will be observed at various prices. First, suppose a free-trade equilibrium is attained at terms of trade lying strictly between the cost ratios of the two countries so that the home country specializes in clothing production and the foreign country in food. Then at home,

$$a_{LC}w = p_C$$

while abroad,

$$a_{LC}^* w^* = p_F$$

Dividing these two gives Equation 5.5:

$$\frac{w}{w^*} = \frac{(1/a_{LC})}{(1/a_{LF}^*)} \cdot \frac{p_C}{p_F} \tag{5.5}$$

The ratio of home to foreign wage rates (the factorial terms of trade) depends both on the ratio of home to foreign labor productivities in the single commodity produced by that country—clothing at home and food abroad—and on the relative prices of these two commodities. The basic trade model in Part I illustrated that home real incomes would rise (and foreign real incomes fall) if the relative price of home exports improved. With labor the only recipient of a nation's income, the same kind of result must link home and foreign wage rates—w/w^* must rise as p_C/p_F goes up. Note that without consulting commodity prices there is no way of comparing home productivity in clothing $(1/a_{LC})$ with foreign productivity in food $(1/a_{LF}^*)$.

If the comparison of wage rates internationally depends on commodity prices as well as productivities, are there any upper or lower limits to the ratio w/w^*? Yes. The extreme cases are those in which either the home or foreign country can produce both commodities, as shown by the flat stretches in the world transformation schedule in Figure 5.4. If world demand for clothing grows sufficiently, the relative price of clothing will reach such a level that the foreign country (which has a comparative disadvantage in clothing production) will be able to produce clothing as well as food. However, with both countries producing clothing, their wage rates are tied solely to their labor productivities in clothing. More formally, with clothing priced high enough that both countries produce clothing,

$$a_{LC}w = p_C$$

and

$$a_{LC}^* w^* = p_C$$

Dividing shows that

$$\frac{w}{w^*} = \frac{1/a_{LC}}{1/a_{LC}^*} \tag{5.6}$$

If the home country's labor is twice as efficient as foreign labor in clothing production, home wages could be double the foreign wage rate, though that is the maximum. The lower limit is provided by a comparison between home and foreign labor productivity in food.

This general relationship among productivities, relative wage rates, and the commodity terms of trade is summarized for our two-commodity, two-country world in Figure 5.6. If countries produce a commodity in common, their wage comparison is dictated by their workers' efficiencies in producing this commodity. If, instead, they specialize on different goods, relative wages move proportionally with the commodity price comparison. The home wage rate cannot exceed (a^*_{LC}/a_{LC}) times the foreign wage, for if it did, the foreign country's costs would be lower than those at home even in the commodity (clothing) in which the home country has a comparative advantage. Similarly, the home country's wage level cannot fall below (a^*_{LF}/a_{LF}) times the foreign wage, or else the foreign country would be undercut even in producing food, in which it has a comparative advantage. Note that in Figure 5.6 horizontal lines have been drawn at these crucial productivity comparisons. If these two countries are the only countries in the world, the equilibrium terms of trade must be between a_{LC}/a_{LF} and a^*_{LC}/a^*_{LF}, inclusive of the endpoints. But if these two countries are embedded in a larger trading world, the terms of trade could easily lie outside these boundaries. Indeed, the horizontal lines then come into their own in revealing the wage comparison for these two countries, which would share a common trading pattern.

FIGURE 5.6   Relative Wages and the Terms of Trade

If the terms of trade lie strictly between the cost ratios in the two countries, an improvement in the home terms of trade has a proportionally favorable effect on the home relative wage. If the terms of trade allow both countries to produce the same commodity, relative wages reflect labor's productivity in this commodity.

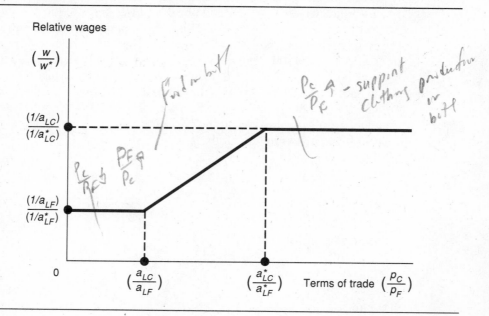

If each country has an absolute advantage in one commodity (say a_{LC} is lower than a_{LC}^*, but a_{LF} is higher than a_{LF}^*), it is not at all surprising that with trade each country should concentrate production (perhaps exclusively) in the activity in which it excels. It was Ricardo's contribution to demonstrate that mutually profitable trade depends only on *relative* cost differences. Suppose the home country is more efficient than the foreign country in every line, although relatively even more efficient in clothing than in food (Inequality 5.2). With trade the home country then imports food from abroad. Does this mean residents at home are purchasing food from a (foreign) source that is more expensive than food locally available? No. Despite the fact that a_{LF}^* is (by assumption) higher than a_{LF}, this is compensated for by the fact that foreign wages must be lower than those at home. This discussion of the limits to the wage rate comparison shows that if one country's labor has an absolute advantage in every occupation, it must receive a higher wage rate.

Viewed from the high-wage country, what can be made of the argument that cheap foreign labor threatens to undermine our competitive position in a wide array of industries? This argument is not valid if such a wage comparison is solidly grounded in absolute productivity differentials. Nonetheless, this so-called "pauper-labor" argument keeps surfacing in debates about commercial policy.

5.5   MANY COMMODITIES AND MANY COUNTRIES

The Ricardian model of trade is simple enough to allow us to take a big step toward the more realistic setting of world trade with many countries and many commodities.[5] Consider, first, the position of some small country previously isolated from an already flourishing world economy. This small country has relied on its own technology, as summarized by a set of labor input coefficients for all the commodities it consumes. Following Ricardo's model, it is assumed that the country's technology is determined by local conditions and need bear no resemblance to technology and labor skills found in other countries. It is also assumed the country is "small," so that once this nation is allowed to trade, preexisting world prices are not disturbed. The small country is a "price-taker," much like an individual or firm in a competitive market.

What Does a Country Produce?

What will this country produce and trade when contact is made with the world economy? Suppose the new trading country adopts the same currency as the rest of the world.[6] How do local costs of production compare with world prices? Given local technology, everything depends on the wage rate. If the wage rate is ridiculously low, the new country might find it could produce all, or almost all, commodities at a cost lower than the world price. This could not represent an equilibrium, for the wage rate would be bid up. Suppose the wage rate is so high that costs locally exceed world

[5] More details on this subject can be found in the supplement to Chapter 5.

[6] This is not the place to launch into a discussion of different currencies and the exchange rates that link them together (see Part IV). It will become clear, however, that a country can change its exchange rate as it pleases so long as the wage rate is changed proportionately.

prices for all commodities. This clearly would not represent equilibrium either. Would it be correct to split the difference and argue that the wage rate probably will settle at a level allowing the country an edge in monetary costs in, for example, half the commodities, while for the other half world prices are below local costs? No. If local technology is really unrelated to that in the rest of the world, this small country likely will produce only *one* commodity, and its wage rate will be determined by labor productivity in the single commodity in which this country has the greatest comparative advantage.

To see why this must be, calculate for each commodity i, the ratio between the world price p_i and the technical labor-hours required in this country to produce one unit of commodity i, a_{Li}. This ratio, p_i/a_{Li}, shows the quantity of dollars obtainable per labor-hour if labor is used to produce i and the output is sold at world prices. Clearly, the commodity with the highest p_i/a_{Li} ratio is the most attractive. The forces of competition ensure that this ratio is precisely the wage rate. If the wage were lower than this, entrepreneurs would rush to employ all the labor they could to produce i, which would yield a positive profit over and above payments to labor. Such competition would drive up the wage. Could the wage be higher than the highest p_i/a_{Li}? No, because then to produce any i would involve losses. If the wage exactly equals the highest p_i/a_{Li}, it would exceed (barring ties) such a ratio for any other commodity. The only exception would be a tie, where, accidentally, the country's technology has the ratio between a_{Li} and the labor cost figure for some other commodity, a_{Lj}, exactly equal to the world price ratio, p_i/p_j.

All this assumes the country is "small." But suppose, instead, it is large enough that its entrance into the world's trading arena has an effect on world prices. Being relatively large, the country may well end up producing more than one tradable item, with world prices now adjusting to reflect the country's own technology for producing these goods. We now turn to a scenario in which the world is comprised of two large countries and in which new discoveries result in improved technology, with repercussions on prices, trading patterns, and relative wages.

5.6 PRODUCTIVITY SHOCKS AND TECHNOLOGICAL SPILLOVERS

Technical progress in our world has always proceeded unevenly. Typically, an innovation is introduced in producing some commodity in some locale, and only with the passage of time will there be imitation and spread to other countries (or to other commodities that may make use of this innovation). How this process of transfer of technology takes place is a question of immense interest and current scrutiny—and we postpone discussing this issue until Chapter 10. But we are in a position now to ask about another feature concerning the spillover of localized technical progress: How does the existence of trading relationships among countries shape the manner in which the benefits of such technical progress get spread? In particular, do all countries tend to benefit when one country experiences progress? Or might trading relationships cause progress to backfire for the originating country? The starkly simple productive structure of the Ricardian model makes it ideal for analyzing this issue.

To set the stage we assume that there are, say, five different commodities, with the home country producing goods 1, 2, and 3 and the foreign country producing two others (4, 5).[7] Initial free-trade prices for commodities 1, 2, and 3 then must be in the same proportion as home labor costs (a_{L1}, a_{L2}, and a_{L3}). Similarly, the relative price of commodity 4 compared with commodity 5 would be shown by a_{L4}^*/a_{L5}^*. But what determines the price link between the two bundles? The answer is found in the requirement that prices clear markets—a requirement already given for the two-commodity case in which the home country was specialized in clothing and the foreign country in food (illustrated in Figure 5.3), with the *value* of aggregate import demands in the two countries being in balance. Thus, if home demand for commodity 4 (produced abroad) were to rise by a small amount (at the expense of commodity 2 produced at home), the foreign wage rate and therefore the prices of 4 and 5 would increase relative to the home wage rate and the prices of commodities 1, 2, and 3.[8]

We focus now on productivity shocks (instead of taste changes). Assume that a breakthrough in home technology in producing commodity 1 reduces labor costs, a_{L1}, but not by enough to alter the pattern of production (the home country remains specialized in the first three commodities). Competition among potential home producers ensures that 1's market price drops relative to the other pair of commodities produced locally (2 and 3) by exactly the same (relative) amount as the real cost reduction. To pin things down, suppose p_1 falls while p_2 and p_3 remain constant. What about the prices of commodities produced abroad? Although linked to each other, both p_4 and p_5 may fall, stay the same, or rise. These are the possibilities:

1. *Foreign Prices Remain Unchanged.* World demands may be sufficiently balanced that world commodity markets for foreign goods 4 and 5 continue to clear with $p_2, \ldots, p_5$ at their initial values. (Such a result is more likely to happen if, before the disturbance, the foreign country also produced commodity 3. With the two countries' cost structures thus locked together, only p_1 is changed. This result is possible even if the foreign country does not produce 3.) If foreign prices remain unchanged, both countries share in the gains represented by technical progress. Both wage rates would be unaltered, so the gains take the form of a lower price for the first commodity. Each nation gains an amount proportional to its consumption of the commodity that has gone down in price.

2. *Foreign Prices Rise.* This outcome would ensue if throughout the world substitution effects in demand are quite low. The reason: The price of one home-produced good has fallen, attracting world demand away from foreign goods because of substitution effects. However, world income has risen, raising demand for all goods, including foreign goods. If propensities to consume foreign-produced commodities are high, prices of commodities 4 and 5 could rise. Indeed, they may rise by so much

[7] To be explicit, it is assumed that a_{L1}/a_{L1}^* is smaller than a_{L2}/a_{L2}^*, and so on, up to the highest ratio, a_{L5}/a_{L5}^*. That is, commodities are numbered in descending order of comparative advantage for the home country.

[8] If home demand for commodity 4 rises sufficiently, the increase in foreign w^* relative to home w may allow home producers of commodity 4 to help supply the home market. Thus, in general, the dividing line between those goods produced in one country and those produced in another depends on the pattern of demand in both countries.

that the home country actually loses. This would represent the case of *immiserizing growth* discussed in Chapter 4.[9]

3. *Foreign Prices Fall.* Commodity 1 may, by contrast to the preceding case, be a very good substitute for foreign goods 4 and 5 both at home and abroad. If so, the reduction in 1's price at home may so divert demand away from foreign goods that both p_4 and p_5 may fall. Indeed, such a price fall in all of the foreigner's export markets may more than offset the initial reduction in the price of one of its imports. That is, sufficiently high demand elasticities could cause foreign real incomes to fall when the home country lowers the cost of one of its exports.

A significant fall in the costs of producing commodity 1 at home might so attract demand that home labor is completely pulled away from producing good 3—leaving the now lower-wage foreign country to produce 3 instead. Alternatively, low demand elasticities for good 1 (as in case 2) and the freed-up labor induced by the technical improvement could so lower the home relative wage that the home country can successfully compete in producing commodity 4.

The Ricardian model shows how a nation's technology binds together the relative prices of all the commodities it produces, while leaving sufficient room for world demand characteristics to help determine the relationship between that country's price levels and those in another country. The world gains from an improvement in technology that is focused on one commodity in one country, and this gain in productivity may benefit all. But if demands are either highly elastic or highly inelastic, the distribution of gains may prove to be skewed either in favor of the home growing country (demands highly elastic) or in favor of the foreign country (demands very inelastic).

5.7 NON-TRADED COMMODITIES

Thus far the model has neglected the costs involved in transporting commodities from one location to another as well as artificial impediments (tariffs, quotas) to international trade. Realistically, no commodity can be freely shipped from one country to another. Theory abstracts from many aspects of reality, however, and trade theory often neglects the costs of transport and the discrepancies they create between prices of traded commodities in different locales. For some purposes, however, it is convenient to consider those commodities for which transport costs are so high that no international trade can take place. The Ricardian model's production structure is so simple that introducing commodities whose markets are purely local is a relatively easy task.

Consider again the case of a country too small to be able to influence world prices. If these world prices do not reflect the small country's own technology, that country will pick the best of the traded goods to produce, the one with the highest p_j/a_{Lj} ratio. As was discussed already, the wage rate will be set equal to this maximum figure for dollars per labor-hour in producing tradables. Suppose there is also some commodity (call it N) that cannot be obtained from the rest of the world (for example,

---

[9] If substitution effects are completely absent, such immiserization *must* be the fate of the home country. A simple proof is found in R. W. Jones, "Demand Behavior and the Theory of International Trade," Chapter 17 of J. Chipman and C. Kindleberger, eds., *Flexible Exchange Rates and the Balance of Payments*, (Amsterdam: North-Holland, 1980).

personal services supplied by local labor—lawyers, physicians, etc.), but for which there is local demand. Let a_{LN} represent the (constant) labor cost of obtaining one unit of the non-traded commodity. Then N must be priced so that

$$p_N = a_{LN}w \qquad (5.7)$$

That is, the price of the non-traded good is determined by local technology and prices of traded goods (that determine the wage rate).

A Composite Traded Commodity

Suppose world prices for all the commodities that can enter trade are fixed. It is then possible to think of a composite traded commodity, an aggregate of all the individual traded commodities. The demand for such a composite behaves in the same regular way as the demand for any single commodity. Because all tradables are assumed to have a fixed price relationship with each other, any arbitrary unit of "output" of the composite can be adopted. In particular the dollar value can be considered a unit. Consider the transformation schedule, FAG, in Figure 5.7. Distance OF measures the maximum dollar value of tradables that can be produced if all labor is devoted to producing the tradable item, call it j, that maximizes the number of dollars that can be earned per hour's worth of labor. If, instead, the entire labor force produced the non-tradable commodity, quantity OG (in natural physical units) of commodity N

FIGURE 5.7   Non-Tradables and Tradables

A composite traded good can be formed if world prices of tradables are constant. Equilibrium production and consumption response for non-tradables can be shown by the tangency of transformation schedules and indifference curves.

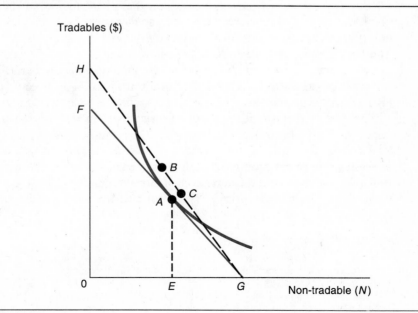

could be produced. With Ricardian technology, the transformation schedule must be a straight line whose slope is the dollar price of the non-tradable.[10] Figure 5.7 also shows an indifference curve tangent to FAG at point A. Point A represents the free-trade equilibrium for this small country.

A word of warning: Figure 5.7's depiction of an equilibrium where an indifference curve is tangent to the transformation curve may remind you of the way in which equilibrium for a closed economy is described. The reason for this is that the details of the composition of trade are suppressed in the diagram. Distance OE represents the quantity of non-tradables, N, that is produced. It also shows how much N is consumed in equilibrium. These must balance. Distance AE shows two things: It shows the dollar value of *production* of tradable commodity j, the good reflecting the optimal use of labor among the set of all tradables. It also shows the aggregate value of *consumption* of all tradables. Hidden from view is the allocation of this amount over all the commodities purchasable on world markets. Figure 5.7 does not deny trade; instead, point A shows a position of balanced trade. It shows that the aggregate value of consumption of all tradables (spread out over many commodities) equals the aggregate value of production of all tradables (concentrated on one product, commodity j).

Technical Change

Suppose, now, that conditions of production at home change, with no change in world prices. In particular, suppose that some new process is discovered whereby the quantity of labor required to produce a unit of commodity i is reduced, so much so that p_i/a_{Li} now exceeds p_j/a_{Lj}. With Ricardian-type technology, the impact on this economy is simple but drastic. It is drastic in the sense that local production of commodity j is wiped out. The new method of producing commodity i establishes it as the new best way of earning dollars on the world market, at the expense of the previous best-traded industry, j. However, an asymmetry now becomes apparent: The non-tradable sector is not competed away. In Figure 5.7 the change in technology leads to the new schedule $HBCG$. If all labor were devoted to tradables, around 20 percent greater value could be produced in i than in j. The wage rate is driven up by this amount, as is the dollar price of non-tradables. The N sector can pass on its higher costs to consumers; the j sector, competing at given world prices for j, cannot.

The rise in p_N may cause consumption and production of non-tradables to fall, such as the move from A to B in Figure 5.7. This, indeed, would be the case if demand for tradables as a group were elastic. The new indifference curve, however, could be tangent at C; substitution effects might be weak and newly created incomes might spill over primarily in the direction of non-tradables. That is, despite the wage-provoked increase in the price of non-tradables, this sector of the economy actually may expand.

---

[10] The relative price of non-tradables to tradables, shown by the slope of line FAG in Figure 5.7, is sometimes referred to as the *real exchange rate*, as distinct from a *nominal exchange rate*, which is the relative price of two currencies. For further discussion of this concept see Part IV.

The kind of reaction described here, in which progress in one tradable sector spells trouble for another, may be caused by changes in world prices instead of technical progress.[11] Chapter 6 will return to this kind of question in a model in which nonlabor resources also are required for production.

5.8 SUMMARY

The Ricardian model is both the oldest and the simplest model of trade in which the details of production are fully incorporated. In summarizing its content, its special features will be pointed out. These will serve to highlight some truths about world trade, but may require some modifications in Chapters 6 through 8.

1. The pattern of trade is dictated solely by the "supply side." In particular, in the two-commodity case the home country must export clothing and import food if the invariant labor productivity in clothing in the home country is relatively higher than that abroad. This assumption was embodied in Inequality 5.2. In more general models, both supply and demand differences contribute to the relationship between pretrade commodity price ratios in the two countries and therefore to the pattern of trade. (In an extended Ricardian model, with many countries and commodities, demand does play a role in determining trade patterns. The supplement provides details.)

2. If the world terms of trade lie strictly between the cost ratios in the two countries, each will specialize completely in the production of one commodity (clothing in the home country and food abroad). This severe shift of resources is not characteristic of the models of trade to be considered next, in which a country might engage in trade while supporting an import-competing industry.

3. The Ricardian model places extreme emphasis on differences in technology between countries, without explaining why methods of production should differ. Subsequent models incorporate the influence of nonlabor factors of production affecting labor productivities and allow a distinction between similarity in technical knowledge and similarity in techniques of production actually adopted. (Rice may be grown differently in Thailand and in Louisiana, even though no technological secrets may be guarded.)

4. The spillover effects of technical change in one country on real incomes at home and abroad are simple to analyze in a Ricardian model because within a country technology firmly binds relative costs. Progress in one country may benefit all. Alternatively, the home country may lose (the case of immiserizing growth) or foreigners may lose (if the markets for their products are strongly disrupted by the reduction of costs at home).

5. Some commodities do not enter international trade because of high transport costs. In a world in which technology and/or prices for some traded commodities

---

[11] Such a case also could be analyzed, but care must be taken with the concept of a composite tradable because consumers are faced with a relative price change within the composite.

change, non-traded commodities are not subject to as intense competitive pressure as tradables. In the Ricardian model for a small country, progress in one tradable sector may completely wipe out another. These extremes are moderated in models that will be examined in subsequent chapters.

6. Finally, note that the Ricardian model is not wedded to a theory of labor productivity. Rather, it is a model of production that severely aggregates all of a nation's productive factors into a single "lump," presumed to be of the same quality and composition for each industry. The trade models to be examined in the next two chapters were developed primarily to relax this assumption and to reveal how differences in the composition of countries' resource endowments affect the trade pattern and how trade causes an uneven reaction on local distribution of income among factors.

CHAPTER PROBLEMS

1. Figure 5.4 shows the array of world outputs that free trade allows; it is the best possible menu of outputs that can be produced. Obviously the worst involves huge unemployment in each country, but suppose all labor is fully employed. Then draw the set of possible world outputs before trade is allowed. What is the menu of the worst combinations of outputs? Could countries end up on the best locus, *ABC*, even in the absence of trade?

2. In the discussion of Section 5.6 suppose both home and foreign countries produce commodity 3. What can be said about the distribution of income between countries if home demand switches a small amount from commodity 2 to commodity 4? If home technology for producing commodity 1 improves?

3. Suppose costs of production depend only on labor costs and that to produce a unit of each commodity in each country takes the number of labor-hours shown.

	Commodity A	Commodity B	Commodity C
Home	10	10	10
Foreign	3	5	7

a. In which commodity does the home country possess the greatest comparative advantage?
b. If the foreign wage rate is $1 per labor-hour and a free-trade equilibrium is reached, what is the most that the home wage rate can be? Why?
c. If the foreign wage rate is $1 per labor-hour, what would a possible home wage rate be so that the home country can produce only one commodity? Which commodity would it be?

4. In a Ricardian world with labor the only factor of production being paid, the following table gives, for countries α and β, the constant labor costs per unit of producing different commodities.

	Wheat	Cars	Tankers	Atomic Reactors	Tractors
α	10	10	10	10	10
β	5	8	10	12	14

a. In which goods does country α have an absolute advantage? Why?
b. In which goods does country β have a comparative advantage? Why?
c. Which country would export tankers? Explain.

5. Consider the world to consist of two countries (home and foreign) made up of individuals with identical (and "homothetic") taste patterns. Portray these by a set of smoothly bowed-in indifference curves. Suppose the home country requires two labor-hours per unit of food and only one labor-hour per unit of clothing, whereas the foreign country's figures for food and clothing are just the opposite. The foreign country's labor force consists of 1 million labor-hours. Illustrate how:
a. If the home country is small relative to the foreign country, one of the countries will produce both goods. Which country? What will be food's relative price?
b. If the home country is large relative to the foreign country, one of the countries will produce both goods. Which country? What will be food's relative price?
Illustrate these two cases in a diagram such as Figure 5.5.

SUGGESTIONS FOR FURTHER READING

Elliott, G. A. "The Theory of International Values," *Journal of Political Economy*, 58 (February 1950): 16–29. Discusses the two-country, many-commodity case.

Graham, Frank. *The Theory of International Values* (Princeton: Princeton University Press, 1948). Many numerical examples of the many-commodity Ricardian case.

Jones, Ronald W. "Comparative Advantage and the Theory of Tariffs: A Multi-Country, Multi-Commodity Model," *Review of Economic Studies*, 28 (June 1961): 161–175. The extension of Ricardian theory to higher dimensional cases.

———. "Technical Progress and Real Incomes in a Ricardian Trade Model," Chapter 17 in *International Trade: Essays in Theory* (Amsterdam: North-Holland, 1979).

Ricardo, David. *The Principles of Political Economy and Taxation* (New York: Penguin, 1971). Chapter 7 is the classic source, with the examples of England and Portugal producing wine and cloth cited in most textbooks.

APPENDIX:
RICARDO AND "THE MISSING LINK"

In the Ricardian model the entire labor force in each country is strikingly different in its productive ability from that in any other country. Such a situation is consistent either with each country possessing different technological knowledge or with special skills embodied in each type of labor. In the latter interpretation it is possible to ask how trading patterns are explained if each country possesses a mix of several labor types. That is, suppose now that

---

FIGURE 5.A.1   "Missing Link" Trade Patterns

Type-*A* labor possesses a comparative advantage in producing clothing, and the home country possesses relatively large supplies of type-*A* labor. If tastes are similar, the home country produces *E*, consumes at *G*, and exports clothing. This model provides the "missing link" between Ricardian models and Heckscher-Ohlin models of trade stressing factor-endowment differences as the explanation of trade patterns.

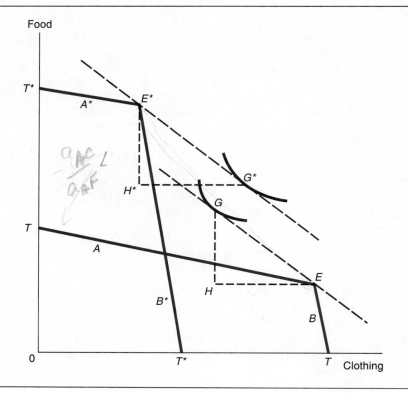

there are two types of labor (*A* and *B*), and the fraction of the world's total of type-*A* labor residing in the home country differs from the fraction of type-*B* labor employed at home. Thus, technological differences are properties not of nations but of individual laborers, and the pattern of trade obviously depends not only on these differences but also on the relative factor endowment differences between countries. Such an interpretation produces "the missing link" between Ricardian trade theories and subsequent theories (Chapters 6 through 8), stressing differences in factor endowments as the key determinant of trade patterns.[12]

Figure 5.A.1 illustrates a possible pattern of consumption, production, and trade in such a world. Type-*A* labor throughout the world is relatively good at producing clothing in the sense

---

[12] This interpretation is credited to Roy Ruffin. See his "The Missing Link: The Ricardian Approach to the Factor Endowments Theory of Trade," *American Economic Review* (September 1988): 759–7,72.

that

$$\frac{a_{AC}}{a_{AF}} < \frac{a_{BC}}{a_{BF}}$$

which is the analogue, for labor-types A and B, of Inequality 5.2 in the text. The home country is assumed to possess relatively greater amounts of type-A labor than the foreign country does.[13] This difference in relative factor endowments is reflected in production points E and E^* if trade takes place at world prices indicated by the slopes of budget lines GE and E^*G^*. To highlight the consequence for trade patterns of different endowment positions, it is assumed that countries share a common pattern of tastes. Free-trade consumption at home is G (and abroad is G^*), with trade triangle GHE matching foreign triangle $E^*H^*G^*$. Each country exports the commodity that is produced by the labor type found in relative abundance in that country.

Note how each country's production-possibilities locus is a broken line that essentially mirrors the world transformation schedule shown in Figure 5.4. This is the basic feature of the "missing link" model. Each country possesses a variety of labor types, with each type of labor assigned to produce the commodity in which it possesses a comparative advantage. Countries differ from each other only in the supplies of each labor type that are locally present, but this difference accounts for the production bias supporting the pattern of trade. As well, if each labor type throughout the world possesses the same set of skills, its wage rate will be the same in every country if they all face free-trade prices for commodities. As will be seen in Chapters 7 and 8, such a result, whereby free trade in goods equalizes the rewards to the same factor in various countries, is a more delicate property in the model of production and trade most often discussed in the literature—the Heckscher-Ohlin model.

[13] As drawn, Figure 5.A.1 shows the home country with an absolute greater supply of type-A labor and the foreign country with an absolute greater supply of type-B labor.

6

Increasing Costs, Specific Factors, and Trade

International trade allows and encourages countries to concentrate their resources to produce fewer types of goods than they consume. The Ricardian model of Chapter 5 carried specialization to extremes. By contrast, often a country will import large quantities of particular commodities without entirely giving up its local production of these items. For years Britain has been extremely dependent on other countries for supplies of foodstuffs, yet it has retained some local agriculture. Unit costs can depend on the scale of production, and countries may be able to produce small outputs at a reasonable price whereas larger volumes might drive up costs of obtaining particular inputs relatively scarce in supply.

Reliance on the one-factor Ricardian model also serves to hide the reasons for the strong internal disagreements within a nation that often accompany trade policies. Explicitly allowing for more productive factors helps to reveal how changes in the terms of trade create real gains for some income groups and real losses for others. In this chapter it is assumed that to produce foodstuffs the economy must combine labor with land, while to produce clothing the services of capital must be combined with labor.

In what proportions should land and/or capital be combined with labor in the production process? The chapter begins with this question, from the point of view of a competitive firm reacting to market prices for factors and goods. The discussion then traces out production possibilities for an economy made up of many competitive firms in two different industries. For the economy as a whole the available supplies of labor, land, and capital help determine the factor prices ultimately faced by individual firms, as well as production patterns once the economy engages in international trade. By describing the way in which factor endowments and technology interact in contributing to increasing costs of production, Chapters 6 and 7 fill in the details on the production side of Part I's basic trade model.

6.1 CHOICE OF TECHNIQUE FOR A COMPETITIVE FIRM

Elements of choice are basic in economics. Chapter 2 reviewed the decision problem faced by a typical consumer when facing a set of commodity prices. Now the focus is on a competitive firm that must decide, among other things, how best to combine inputs in order to produce commodities. Just as tastes guide consumption choices, so does technology influence the proportions in which factors are combined.

For a typical clothing producer assume technology exhibits *constant returns to scale* to the use of two inputs, capital and labor. That is, if the firm hires 50 percent more capital and labor, the quantity of clothing it produces would expand by exactly 50 percent. This characteristic of technology is incorporated in the set of clothing *isoquants* portrayed in Figure 6.1. The isoquant labeled X'_C displays all the combinations of capital and labor that could be employed to produce amount X'_C of clothing. Point C on isoquant X''_C represents a 50 percent greater use of both labor and capital than does point A on isoquant X'_C; X''_C must therefore depict an output level half again as great as X'_C.

FIGURE 6.1 Isoquants and the Choice of Techniques

An isoquant is the collection of input combinations that yield the same level of output. Isoquant X''_C is a 50 percent radial blowup of isoquant X'_C and represents a 50 percent expansion in output. The α-line, whose slope is the wage rental ratio, shows unit costs of producing X'_C being minimized by choosing technique A.

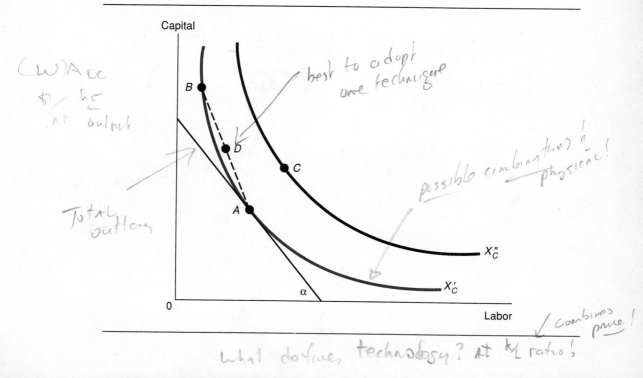

Isoquants are drawn with a bowed-in shape, much like indifference curves described in Chapter 2. To see what this means consider the two input bundles A and B, each of which could support output of clothing in amount X'_C. By the constant-returns-to-scale property just described, half the input bundle shown by B could produce exactly half of X'_C, and half the input bundle at A could also produce half of X'_C. Add these input halves together to get input bundle D. Drawing the isoquants bowed in toward the origin is tantamount to assuming that a point such as D could produce a clothing output larger than X'_C. That is, it never pays a firm to adopt two different techniques to produce a given level of output. The bowed-in shape reflects diminishing marginal rates of substitution between inputs in the same fashion that diminishing marginal rates of substitution between commodities characterize consumer indifference curves.

The line labeled α in Figure 6.1 is an *iso-cost line*, all points along which represent the same total outlay on labor and capital by the firm. The slope of the iso-cost line depicts the trade-off between labor and capital costs, that is, the ratio of wages to rentals. (The rationale is analogous to the slope of a budget line for consumers in Chapter 2 reflecting the ratio of commodity prices.)

Parallel iso-cost lines drawn farther out—for example, passing through point B—would represent a greater total outlay on labor and capital at the same wage rate and rental. Therefore, the factor proportions represented by point A on X'_C show the least-cost methods of producing given (X'_C) clothing output for the factor prices indicated by the slope of the α-line. Alternatively, if costs are fixed by the α-line, X'_C represents the maximum clothing output the firm could produce. The constant-returns-to-scale property of the technology also guarantees that if the firm wishes to expand output by 50 percent, at the same factor prices, the factor bundle chosen (along X''_C) would be point C; point C is on the ray from the origin that runs through point A and 50 percent farther from the origin than point A.[1]

Prices, Wages, and Rents

The discussion of the Ricardian model introduced the competitive profit conditions. They are applicable here as well. For a clothing producer facing a given wage and rental, how do average (and marginal) costs compare with the price of clothing? If the price of clothing is less than unit cost, the firm (and others like it) would be dissuaded from active production; equilibrium output would be zero. Of course, the firm would be delighted to receive a price for clothing exceeding unit costs (including the return to the entrepreneur), but so would other potential entrants with access to the same technology. The forces of competition would encourage ever greater output until the price of clothing is bid down and/or wages and rentals are bid up. *Competitive equilibrium requires that price not exceed unit costs.*

Constant returns to scale plus competitive pricing lead to a fundamental result:

If factor prices change, the percentage change in the commodity price must lie between the percentage changes in factor returns.

---

[1] With technology exhibiting constant returns to scale, isoquants are *homothetic*. That is, all isoquants are radial blowups (or contractions) of the isoquant showing a unit level of output (the unit isoquant). Therefore, the slopes of all isoquants along a ray from the origin are all the same.

Suppose both wages and rents rise 10 percent. As was previously shown, techniques do not change and unit cost also rises 10 percent; in competitive markets price also will rise by the same amount. Similarly, if both wages and rents rise 20 percent, so must price. Now suppose wages rise 10 percent but rentals go up 20 percent. Unit costs must go up by more than 10 percent, but cannot rise by a full 20 percent; the commodity price change is trapped between the changes in factor prices. Sometimes this result is stated more formally—the relative price change for a commodity is a positive weighted average of the relative changes in input prices. This proposition will be referred to several times in this chapter and Chapter 7 because it provides the basis for some fundamental relationships between the terms of trade and the internal distribution of income for productive factors to open economies.[2]

Diminishing Returns

If the economy also produces food, similar decisions as to choice of technique must be faced by firms in the food sector. Suppose (in this chapter) that such firms require the use of land but not capital. Such firms can be viewed as hiring land at market-determined land rentals (as well as hiring labor in open labor markets), and precisely the same analysis of the choice of technique in producing food can be made as that used to describe a typical firm in the clothing sector. Now consider the decisions made by a firm that owns a parcel of land but cannot obtain any more (or dispose of what is possessed). Figure 6.2 illustrates the total quantity of food output increasing as more labor is employed on this fixed unit of land. The *law of diminishing returns* is evident: As more and more labor is hired, food output goes up, but at a diminishing rate. In Figure 6.2(a) this is shown by the ever-flatter curve relating output of food to labor input assuming the quantity of land utilized is kept constant. In Figure 6.2(b) the same phenomenon is reflected in the declining curve that shows the marginal physical product of labor (MPP_L^F) getting smaller as more labor crowds onto a fixed parcel of land.

The concepts of constant returns to scale and diminishing returns to increases in a single factor should be clearly distinguished. The assumption that returns to scale are constant ensures that a 10 percent rise in inputs of labor *and* land would cause food production to rise in proportion; if, instead, only labor's employment rises (as in Figure 6.2), food output rises but not in proportion. This reflects diminishing returns.

Suppose such a firm faces a wage rate, w, and market price of food, p_F, whose ratio is shown in Figure 6.2(b). The firm's optimal hiring strategy is to employ L_0 units of labor and thus to equate the value of labor's marginal physical product to the prevailing wage rate. (The slope of the total product curve at B in the upper panel also shows labor's marginal physical product.) To stop short of L_0 in hiring labor is to forgo the product of an extra unit of labor that has a greater value than the wage.[3]

---

[2] The supplement to this chapter discusses the "weights" to be used in averaging input price changes. They are the "distributive factor shares." For example, labor's distributive share in producing clothing is the fraction of the total revenue generated by clothing sales that is paid out as wages.

[3] As described in price theory texts, in equilibrium the return to the other input, land, is shown by the shaded area in Figure 6.2(b), that part of total product not going to pay the wage bill.

FIGURE 6.2   Total and Marginal Physical Product

Output of food expands, but at a diminishing rate, as more labor is applied to a fixed unit of land. If the wage rate (in units of food) is w/p_F, L_0 units of labor will be employed.

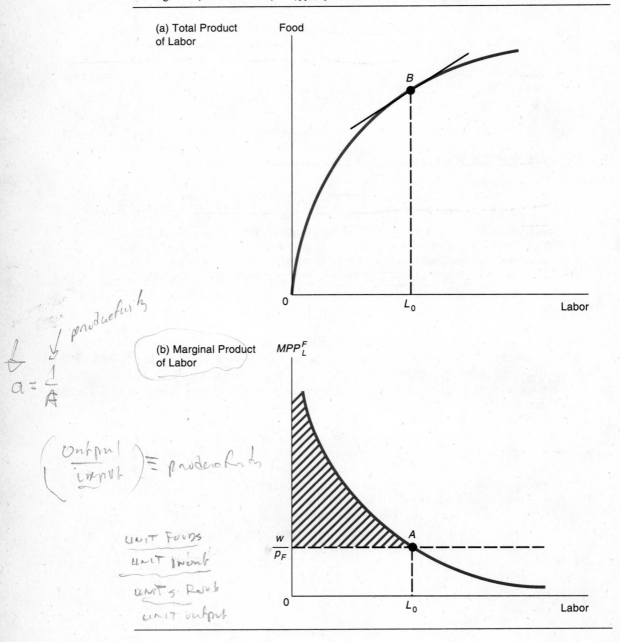

(a) Total Product of Labor

Food

B

0   L_0 Labor

(b) Marginal Product of Labor

MPP_L^F

$\dfrac{w}{p_F}$

A

0   L_0 Labor

6.2 SPECIFIC FACTORS AND ECONOMY-WIDE PRODUCTION POSSIBILITIES

These concepts now can be assembled to describe an economy possessing fixed overall amounts of three distinct productive factors: labor, land, and capital. Labor is used to produce both food and clothing; land is used only in food; and capital is specific to the clothing sector. These assumptions suffice to rule out the phenomenon associated with Chapter 5's Ricardian model, whereby an industry could expand by hiring more labor without driving up unit costs. Instead, production possibilities reflect increasing costs.

The bowed-out production possibilities curve is displayed in quadrant I of Figure 6.3, using the relationships drawn in quadrants II, III, and IV. Note especially:

1. Quadrant III shows a downward-sloping 45° line to illustrate the full employment of the economy's total (fixed) labor resources either to produce food (shown leftward from the origin) or to produce clothing (measured downward from the origin).

FIGURE 6.3   Production Possibilities with Diminishing Returns and Increasing Opportunity Costs

The production-possibilities curve in quadrant I is derived by picking a labor allocation along the full-employment line (quadrant III) and displaying the outputs of food (quadrant II) and clothing (quadrant IV) obtainable in quadrant I. Diminishing returns lead to increasing opportunity costs.

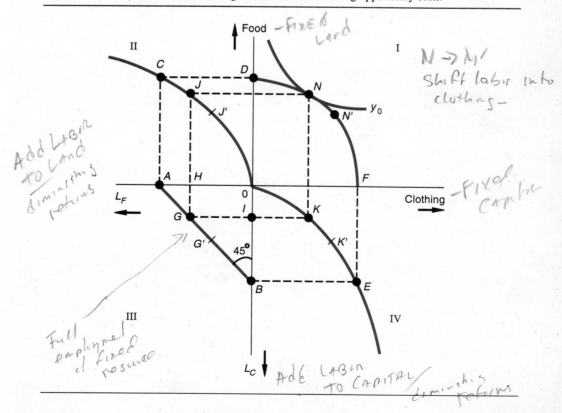

2. The curves showing total labor productivity for the two industries (quadrants II and IV) illustrate diminishing returns to labor as more is applied to the fixed amount of the cooperating factor (land in food and capital in clothing). This is the same kind of relationship as shown in Figure 6.2(a).

The production-possibilities schedule in quadrant I reflects increasing opportunity costs. Endpoint D shows the maximum amount of food that could be produced if all the economy's labor force were employed in food. (OD also is shown by AC in quadrant II.) Similarly, endpoint F is the maximum clothing output, obtainable if labor force OB is used to produce BE units of clothing (quadrant IV). Any intermediate labor allocation, such as G in quadrant III, results in food output (HJ, quadrant II) and in clothing output (IK, quadrant IV) which is shown as point N on the transformation schedule (quadrant I). Other points can be derived in similar fashion (e.g., labor allocation G' yields output bundle N' by completing the rectangle). Consider the movement from N to N' that accompanies the labor reallocation from G to G'. As extra labor is poured into the clothing sector, diminishing returns decrease labor's productivity (in clothing) at the margin. Meanwhile, the departure of labor from the food industry serves to raise the productivity of remaining workers in food. On both counts the relative cost of producing clothing rises (the transformation schedule becomes steeper). The transformation schedule bows out because labor is subject to diminishing returns in each sector, and the cooperating inputs (land in food, capital in clothing) are fixed in supply.

6.3 THE DISTRIBUTION OF INCOME IN A CLOSED ECONOMY

As a prelude to considering how international trade affects factor returns, consider a country in autarky. It must produce for itself what it wishes to consume. The resulting pattern of production determines the demand for each factor's services and the equilibrium wages and rentals that clear factor markets.

Figure 6.3 shows the closed-economy equilibrium at point N in quadrant I where indifference curve y_0 is tangent to transformation schedule DNF. The allocation of labor between sectors is shown by point G in quadrant III. What can be said about equilibrium factor prices? The wage rate must, in equilibrium, reflect the value of labor's marginal productivity in each sector. The marginal physical productivities are shown by slopes at J (quadrant II of Figure 6.3) for the food industry and at K (quadrant IV) for the clothing sector. Relative commodity prices are shown by the transformation schedule's slope at N (quadrant I).

We now turn to a different but extremely useful diagram—one that highlights the role of commodity prices and factor supplies in helping to determine labor's marginal productivities and thus the wage rate. This is Figure 6.4. Because it is relative prices that count, fix the price of food at some arbitrary level and let the VMP_L^F curve (literally the curve showing the value of the marginal product of labor in producing food) describe how the value of the additional output of food produced by one more laborer declines as more labor is added to the food sector, measuring rightward from origin O_F in Figure 6.4. This, of course, matches the shape of the curve in panel (b) of Figure 6.2, because the value of labor's marginal product is the given price of food times labor's marginal physical product. A similar schedule can be drawn for the

FIGURE 6.4 Wage Rate Determination

Equilibrium wages (at A) equate the values of the marginal product of labor in the two sectors by labor allocation at G. If free trade raises clothing's price, labor shifts out of food into clothing (from G to G'). The wage rate rises, but not as much as clothing's price.

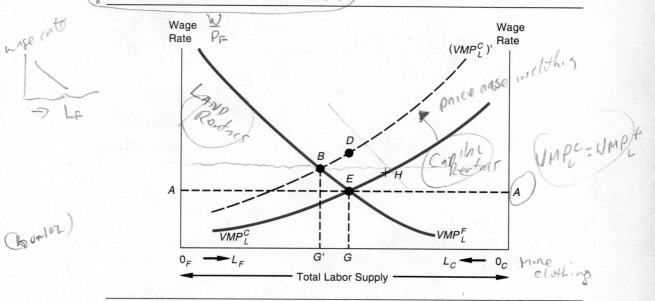

value of labor's marginal product in producing clothing (multiply labor's marginal product by the price of clothing reflected by the slope at N in Figure 6.3). Figure 6.4 depicts such a VMP_L^C schedule reading from right to left from origin O_C. It is possible to bring these curves together as shown because the total labor supply (the horizontal distance separating O_F from O_C) is fixed and is fully employed. Equilibrium labor allocation is at point G (both in Figure 6.4 and Figure 6.3).[4] Height A in Figure 6.4 depicts the equilibrium wage rate. Each of the specific factors, land and capital, receives the total revenue in the sector that employs that factor, over and above the wage payment (e.g., land receives the shaded area in Figure 6.2).

6.4 FREE TRADE AND INCOME DISTRIBUTION

When this economy is opened up to trade, which factor of production benefits? Which loses? Is it possible to identify unambiguously each group? We make use of Figures 6.3 and 6.4 in tracing through, step by step, the impact on an economy initially producing at point N in Figure 6.3 (with labor allocation shown by point G in quadrant III of Figure 6.3 or by G also in Figure 6.4). Suppose clothing is relatively

---

[4] Thus, at equilibrium point G the price of clothing times labor's marginal physical product in clothing equals the price of food times labor's marginal physical product in producing food. Therefore, the slope of the transformation schedule (at N in Figure 6.3), which is the closed-economy relative price of clothing, must be the ratio of labor's marginal product in food divided by its marginal product in clothing.

expensive on world markets, so that output responds as shown by the movement from N to N' in Figure 6.3—clothing output expands. In Figure 6.4 we have illustrated this country's emergence into the world market by (arbitrarily) keeping the price of food constant (and thus the VMP_L^F schedule) and raising the price of clothing. If clothing's price is, say, 40 percent higher in world markets, the VMP_L^C schedule shifts upward by exactly 40 percent. The reason: Any given labor input into clothing (e.g., initial level O_CG) and the fixed background quantity of capital yield the same marginal *physical* product of labor, but at a price increase of 40 percent this implies a 40 percent higher marginal *value* product of labor. As we see, this serves to raise the wage rate, at least in nominal terms. The wage is driven up as workers leave the food sector, attracted by higher wages in clothing until the wage rate is equalized in both sectors at point B in Figure 6.4.

How do land, capital, and labor react to the move to free trade?

1. Owners of capital are delighted by the new prices. As workers move into the clothing sector, the marginal physical product of capital rises. Add to this the price rise for clothing (40 percent), and the return to capital is twice blessed—it rises by more than 40 percent.

2. Landlords are at the other end of scale. Stuck in the food sector, whose relative price is now lower, they are forced by the market to pay more for labor. The reason for this is that as workers decamp for the clothing sector, less labor is available per unit of land and the marginal physical product of land therefore falls. The consequence: Land rentals fall relative to the price of food and even more so compared with the higher price of clothing. Landlords unambiguously lose. Their self-interest would be served by opposing free trade.

3. The fate of workers is less extreme. As just seen, the land/labor ratio in producing food rises as labor leaves the agricultural sector, so wages rise in terms of food. But the price of clothing has increased more than the wage rate. Look at Figure 6.4. The price of clothing has risen by 40 percent, the ratio DE/EG. Wages have risen in the move from E to B, but by less than 40 percent. This confirms point 1 above, that the return to capitalists rises by more than 40 percent, and point 2 above, that landlords' return falls, relative to the given price of food, since nominal wages have gone up. In each industry the price (and unit cost) change must be flanked by the relative changes in factor rewards for inputs used in that sector.

Trade Policy Can Alter the Distribution of Income

The preceding arguments show that changes in commodity prices have an uneven impact on the incomes of various categories of productive factors. Those factors of production (labor in this model) that have opportunities for employment in all sectors of the economy and are highly mobile may find their real position not significantly altered by changes in the terms of trade. However, specific factors (land and capital in this model) are severely affected. Specific factors used only in the industries suffering from a fall in relative price have no other outlet for employment. Their low mobility ensures that real rentals fall. By contrast, those specific factors in the favored industry (owners of capital in the clothing industry) find their rentals unambiguously raised. They are sheltered from increased competition from similar factors in other industries (no textile machines are available in the food industry) and benefit from the arrival of newly attracted other factors (labor) that serve to raise productivity.

Any government policy (for example, a tariff change) that serves to affect relative commodity prices will be viewed differently by various factor groups. Factors used only in the favored sector would strongly support the proposed measure. Factors used only in the rest of the economy would unambiguously lose. In the model there is a third category—those factors (such as labor) that are not affected much one way or the other by such a policy. Indeed, political scientists would find such a model useful in explaining why some sectors of the population do not bother voting on certain issues whereas others care deeply. Very few policies that impact primarily on commodity prices can be expected to gain widespread approval.

When speaking of the effect of trade policies on the distribution of income, other interpretations of our "specific factors" categories must be considered, especially the special labor skills factor. Tariff protection might be contemplated for an industry using labor with special skills (call it "human capital") that are not particularly useful in the rest of the economy. Such protection could unambiguously raise the real return to such skills even if the general level of wages does not change by much. Generally speaking, many labor types feel better trained in particular occupations, that is, those in which they are engaged, and thus feel their returns are closely linked to the fate of industries in which they are employed.

6.5 FACTOR SUPPLY CHANGES IN A SMALL TRADING COMMUNITY

A nation's resource base need not remain static. Over time one might expect the capital stock to rise, and perhaps more (or less) land to be brought into productive use. Population may grow, but this might be offset by shortening of the work week or, in the opposite direction, by increased participation of both spouses in the marketplace. As well, foreign investment may encourage capital accumulation or immigration might expand supplies of unskilled and skilled labor. Here we ask how changes of this type alter production choices and factor returns in an economy too small to have these supply changes affect world prices. This is in keeping with our procedure of analyzing one issue at a time and also serves as a prelude to our subsequent discussion of the connection between patterns of trade and the composition of countries' factor supplies.

Suppose, first, that growth is confined to one of the specific factors. To be precise consider for this small trading community the consequence of a 50 percent increase in the quantity of land available. The primary impact of such a change is to increase labor's productivity in producing food. At constant commodity prices this will entail a shift of labor resources and will bring in its wake a change in all factor returns and an outward shift in the community's production-possibilities curve. The four-quadrant graph introduced in Figure 6.3 comes into its own in explaining details of this change in land supplies.

Figure 6.5 reproduces labor's productivity in food schedule from quadrant II of Figure 6.3. The new dashed curve shows the impact on labor's productivity of a 50 percent increase in the quantity of land available for producing food. Suppose that initially OH units of labor are employed, with output HJ. With more land available

FIGURE 6.5   An Increase in Land Shifts Labor's Productivity Curve

An increase of land by 50 percent shifts labor's productivity curve radially outward by 50 percent (QJ is 50 percent of OJ). The slopes at J and Q are the same.

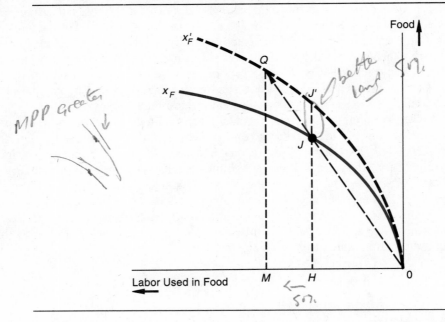

this given quantity of labor could produce a greater output—HJ' instead of HJ. Furthermore, the slope at J' must be greater than at J, for a higher land/labor ratio pushes up labor's marginal physical product. This is a signal for labor to be attracted from the clothing sector. Has labor's productivity, however, increased by 50 percent (in the sense of $J'J$ representing 50 percent of HJ)? No. Constant returns to *scale* ensure that food output would increase by 50 percent if land *and labor* inputs each rose by 50 percent. Let MH be 50 percent of HO. Then output MQ will be 50 percent higher than JH. In short, a 50 percent increase in land's endowment shifts labor's productivity schedule *radially* outward from the origin by 50 percent.

This shift in the labor productivity schedule in quadrant II translates into an outward shift in quadrant I's production-possibilities curve. Clearly, for any given labor allocation the quantity of clothing produced would remain the same, but the quantity of food produced would increase (e.g., HJ' instead of HJ for allocation OH of labor to food in Figure 6.5). The new production-possibilities curve is shown by the dashed curve in Figure 6.6. Consider its properties.

1. The new schedule lies everywhere outside the old curve except for point D, which shows complete specialization in clothing.

2. If point A represents the initial point on the old transformation schedule, then the point (B) on the new one at which the slope is the same as at A lies northwest of A.

FIGURE 6.6 An Increase of Land Shifts the Production-Possibilities Schedule Upward

An increase in land, used only in food, causes more food (and less clothing) to be produced at given terms of trade.

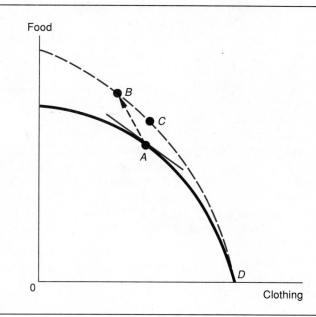

To understand this latter point, consider the effect of a 50 percent increase in land availability on the value of the marginal product of labor in food schedule in Figure 6.4. With commodity prices unchanged (to match the slope at B with that at A in Figure 6.6), the increase in land shifts the VMP_L^F curve in Figure 6.4 *rightward* by 50 percent. (Recall the constant-returns-to-scale argument: If labor and land both increase by 50 percent, labor's marginal productivity remains the same.) Although not drawn in Figure 6.4, the new schedule for labor's marginal product in food would cut the clothing schedule at H. Wage rates are driven up and labor is attracted from the clothing sector, where output must, as a consequence, fall.

This shows that growth in one factor in a small community facing given terms of trade leads to a radical change in the composition of outputs. Clothing output must actually decline. With more land, the community will opt to produce more food. It will do so in part by taking some labor away from the clothing sector, which must, as a consequence, decline.

Labor growth leads to a more balanced expansion of both outputs because the use of labor is not confined to any one sector of the economy. Figure 6.3 is once again useful in detecting the effect of this kind of change. The 45° line in quadrant III shifts to the southwest, and the construction clearly shows that this would shift the production-possibilities curve outward. The outward shift need not be uniform, however, for much depends on the relative shapes of the labor productivity curves in the two sectors (quadrants II and IV). More specifically, the rate at which labor's marginal product falls in each sector as more labor is added helps determine which sector attracts more labor. In any case, both sectors expand to some extent.[5]

Even though the terms of trade are kept constant for this small community, factor growth unevenly affects the distribution of income. Not surprisingly, in the case in which the quantity of productive land expands by 50 percent, land rents per acre are driven down. (The labor/land ratio declines, driving down land's marginal product.) Also, as was previously shown, labor must benefit. With both commodity prices constant, the real wage unambiguously rises with the expansion in land.

How about capitalists? It may come as a surprise that one can be quite definite about the impact of land growth on the return to capital: It must fall. Capitalists do not benefit at all from the greater availability of the other specific resource (land). The reason? With the wage rate bid up and with a fixed price of clothing, capitalists are squeezed because less is available as a return to capital.

The same kind of distributional story results from capital growth unaccompanied by labor or land endowment changes. Workers would benefit, at the expense of both landlords and capitalists. But these roles do get reversed in the case of population (labor) growth unmatched by expansion in capital or land. As has already been seen, both sectors would expand. Labor is used more intensively everywhere, driving down the wage. At constant commodity prices the drop in wages increases returns to both landlords and capitalists.

Potential Political Alliances

These remarks, coupled with the analysis of terms-of-trade changes in the previous section, lead to the following generalizations.

1. If commodity prices remain constant but factor endowments change, the fortunes of the specific factors (land and capital) rise or fall together and are opposed to those of the mobile factor (labor).

2. If endowments remain constant but commodity price ratios change, the returns to the specific factors are driven widely apart, whereas the return to mobile labor is relatively unaffected. If the relative price of clothing rises, capitalists unambiguously gain and landlords lose.

These are important properties of this model, which will be used in subsequent policy discussions. Consider, here, some basic political considerations. The first generality suggests a natural political alliance between landlords and capitalists in small but growing communities immersed in a world market for sales and purchases. One would expect a mutual interest of landlords and capitalists in legislation designed to encourage immigration of labor, whereas workers already in the country might oppose immigration. In the 1920s the United States imposed tight immigration restrictions, largely because of pressure from unions. In Australia more liberal immigration policy is supported both by capitalists and by landholders, although trade unions find it in their interests to control such inflows. As Europe boomed in the decades after World War II, the American labor movement was often outspoken in its criticism of U.S. capital flows lured by the burgeoning European markets.

[5] Details are provided in the supplement to Chapter 6.

The second generality suggests that if the legislation under consideration concerns relative commodity prices, landlords and capitalists would be diametrically opposed. The Corn Laws in nineteenth-century Britain provide an important example. Parliamentary overrepresentation of the landed gentry allowed laws that prevented the importation of cheap grains. After 1832 and the Reform Bill, parliamentary representation of industrialists (and labor) expanded. By 1846 the movement to freer trade was in full swing. The interests of capitalists were clear: Lower food prices would drive workers off the land and serve to lower the industrial wage, thus leading to greater profits.[6] A twentieth-century analogy is found in present-day Japan, which has been highly restrictive in its tolerance of agricultural imports. (Japanese rice is over four times as expensive as that found in the world market.) The United States, ever anxious to improve its bilateral trade balance with Japan, has loudly denounced these agricultural trade restrictions. But perhaps American manufacturers competing with Japanese exporters would not be pleased if restrictions were loosened, allowing workers in Japan to receive nominal pay cuts while enjoying higher real wages as food prices fall. In addition, larger agricultural imports into Japan lead to greater Japanese exports of manufactures. Japanese landlords and industrialists are at odds over these trade restrictions, and, as in the case of nineteenth-century Britain, major changes may require political reforms to dilute the power of rural areas.

6.6   THE PATTERN OF TRADE

The preceding discussion of the impact of factor growth on a small trading country's productive structure is directly relevant to a different question: What determines the pattern of trade? The reason these two issues are linked is that trade patterns depend on supply and demand differences between countries, and differences in factor endowments are key determinants of supply. As was already discussed, trade patterns are discernible from an international comparison of pretrade commodity price ratios and these are determined by each country's equality of *relative* demand and *relative* supply. Figure 6.7 illustrates how the pretrade relative price of clothing at home, *OP*, is determined. Note that the relative supply curve slopes upward, consistent with a production-possibilities curve showing increasing costs.

Figure 6.7 shows the pretrade situation at home. With this as a reference point, how can the situation abroad be different?

1. Foreign tastes may differ. Compared with home demand, foreigners may, for comparable price ratios, consume a larger ratio of clothing to food. If so, this by itself would tend to make clothing more expensive abroad and, with the opening of trade, lead foreigners to import clothing.

2. Foreign technology may differ. This was the source of trade in the Ricardian model. Suppose both countries were to produce clothing and food in identical proportions. The height of the relative supply curve would indicate marginal cost ratios of clothing to food in each country. This ratio could be higher abroad because the home country has a *relative* technological superiority in producing clothing.

---

[6] The wage would not fall as much as the price of food.

FIGURE 6.7   Relative Demand and Supply

Pretrade price ratio, *OP*, is determined by relative demands and supplies. The supply schedule lies farther to the right the greater the community's capital endowment and/or the smaller its land base.

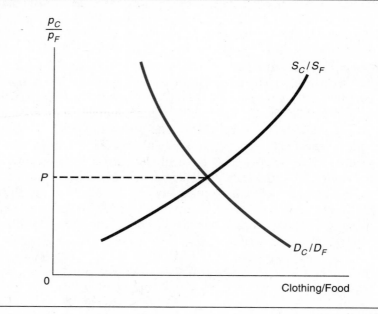

3. Factor endowment proportions could be different abroad. This is the feature highlighted here. Suppose, first, that foreigners have a roughly comparable labor force and land supplies but much more capital. With capital used only in the clothing sector (by assumption), the capital-rich foreign country would have an advantage in producing clothing. Its relative supply curve would lie to the right of the home country's. Indeed, the discussion of supply changes in the previous section reveals that at comparable prices the foreign country (with more capital) would produce more clothing and less food than the home country. If, instead, foreigners differed only in having more land, the foreign relative supply curve of clothing would lie to the left of the home curve, tending to support an eventual trade pattern in which foreigners import clothing. Finally, if foreign and home endowments of capital and land are each roughly comparable, but the foreign country has a larger labor force, the consequence for the trade pattern is less clear. Foreigners will have a comparative advantage in either food or clothing, depending on the shapes of labor productivity schedules (in quadrants II and IV of Figure 6.3). What is clear is that wages will tend to be lower in the labor-abundant foreign community.

6.7 THE "DUTCH DISEASE"

The energy crisis of the 1970s and early 1980s and associated wide swings in the prices of some world-traded products and resources have led to radical internal stresses for those economic sectors producing commodities whose world prices have not experienced such wide ups and downs. In Europe this kind of phenomenon came to be called the "Dutch Disease." The name referred specifically to the rapid development in the Netherlands of the sector producing natural gas and the resulting squeeze put on other traditional export sectors of the Dutch economy. Similarly, in Norway and Great Britain rapid exploration of North Sea oil deposits created severe hardships for these countries' manufacturing sectors that compete in world markets. Much less disruption is brought about in those economic sectors servicing purely local markets— the "non-traded" sector.[7]

The simple model developed in this chapter can be utilized to reveal strategic features of this phenomenon. Suppose a number of industries are producing for the world market, and in each one of these labor is drawn from a common pool (labor is the "mobile" factor) and combined with another factor specific to that sector and in fixed supply. Previously the broad categories "land" and "capital" were used for specific factors. Now let each sector have its own supply of capital equipment (and managerial expertise) that is uniquely designed for use just in that sector; some time would have to elapse before such capital could be transferred to other sectors (through depreciation and replacement, for example).

Now let the world price of the output in one of these sectors rise. The main features of the food-clothing model generalize readily to this multisector case.[8] In particular, returns to factors specifically used in the favored (booming) traded sector rise by more than price. More crucially, the wage rate is bid up, and this increase in wages squeezes all the other traded sectors that have not experienced a rise in price. In a Ricardian model with fixed labor coefficients (Chapter 5), a wage rise would cause the complete collapse of any traded sector facing fixed world prices. Here the industry may survive, but only as long as lower returns are accepted by specific factors. Higher wage rates triggered by the rise in price in the booming sector put the squeeze on "profits" (or return to specific capital and management) in any other traded sector.

Figure 6.8 illustrates the case of the Dutch Disease. A typical traditional export sector facing a constant price, $\bar{P}$, on world markets has an upward-sloping supply curve, S, as increases in output are achieved by combining more labor with a fixed quantity of capital. The presumed boom in another export sector pushes up the wage rate and, through this connection, affects costs throughout the rest of the economy. For this traditional export sector the supply curve shifts up to S', the returns to the specific factor are squeezed, and output is lowered from OA to OD if the sector does not benefit from a rise in price.

The Fate of the Non-Traded Sector

The discussion of the Ricardian model concluded with the introduction of the concept of a non-traded sector, an industry producing a commodity that can be neither exported nor imported because of high costs of transport. Suppose such a sector is added here. When one export sector expands, pushing up wage rates, the non-traded

---

[7] An analytic treatment of some aspects of this issue is found in W. M. Corden and J. Peter Neary, "Booming Sector and De-Industrialisation in a Small Open Economy," *Economic Journal* (December 1982): 825–848.

[8] Formal extensions are found in R. W. Jones, "Income Distribution and Effective Protection in a Multi-Commodity Trade Model," *Journal of Economic Theory* (August 1975): 1–15.

FIGURE 6.8   The "Dutch Disease"

A boom in a new export sector raises wages, which shifts costs upward for a traditional export sector. Returns to capital are squeezed and output falls.

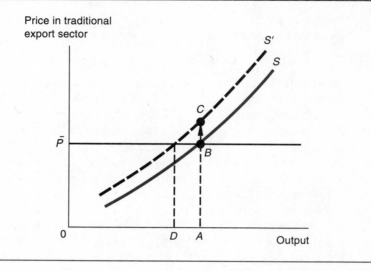

sector also experiences a rise in costs. However, the price to consumers can be raised. Figure 6.9 illustrates the supply curve for non-tradables pushed upward from S_N to S'_N by the wage rise. If there were no shift in demand, these cost increases could partially be passed on to consumers, with output and price changing from A to C. In this fashion the feedback effect on non-traded sectors of the economy when an export sector experiences boom conditions is less adverse than for other traded sectors tied into world markets and thus unable to pass on costs to consumers. To alleviate the situation further for non-tradables, the demand curve may shift to the right. With an export boom caused by a price rise, the community's real income expands with the favorable movement in the terms of trade. This will partly spill over to increase demand in the non-tradable sector. In addition, local demand might increase as a consequence of a direct substitution effect away from the exportable that has risen in price toward other markets. Figure 6.9 shows an extreme case in which the shift from D_N to D'_N is sufficient to raise price (from OB to OD) by more than the original cost push (distance AF). In such a case output actually would expand and the return to the factors specific to non-tradables also would expand.

Much the same story can be told if, instead of a price rise in one traded goods sector, there is technical progress (as illustrated in Chapter 5 for the Ricardian model), or there are new discoveries (such as North Sea oil).

The role of the doctrine of *comparative advantage* is crucial in understanding the phenomenon of the Dutch Disease. A country exports those commodities in which it possesses a comparative advantage. It may lose such an advantage in some commodities even if its technology is unchanged if, in other sectors, its technology (or price) improves. In the present model the route through which traditional sectors get

---

FIGURE 6.9   Cost and Price Changes for Non-Traded Goods

A boom in a new export sector raises wages, which shifts costs upward for the non-traded sector. But price can rise to some extent, perhaps significantly if the increase in real incomes shifts demand from D_N to D_N'.

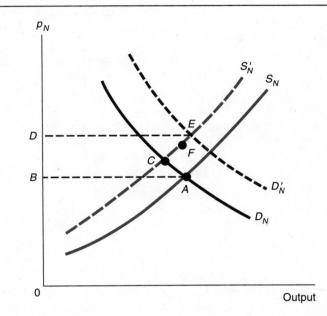

squeezed is a rise in the wage rate. Although the model is not explicitly geared to handle the phenomenon at this stage, another avenue through which traditional traded sectors can be affected is the exchange rate. British manufacturers of commodities enjoying an export market were hit at the end of the 1970s by a strengthening of the British pound, caused in part by anticipation of future oil revenues from North Sea discoveries.

6.8 SUMMARY

This chapter presents one of the classic models of production—a model in which diminishing returns describe the attempt of any sector to increase output by applying more labor to a fixed quantity of another factor specific to that sector. Commodities thus differ in their factor demands (clothing makes no use of land and food does not require capital), and factors of production differ in their degree of mobility (labor is costlessly transferable from sector to sector at a common wage whereas land and capital are each specific).

This description of an economy is rich in its conclusions for a community engaged in trade.

1. The internal distribution of income is vitally affected by any change in relative commodity prices. A productive factor specifically tied to some occupation (e.g., land

in the production of food) unambiguously gains by an increase in the relative price of the commodity in whose production it is employed. This price rise will cause other specific factor(s) to lose in real terms. The mobile factor, labor, is less affected by these commodity price changes because it can move from sector to sector. This feature of the model by itself predicts that any political decision within a community that threatens to affect commodity prices (such as tariff legislation—see Part III) will arouse ardent support on the part of some and strong opposition from others, as well as fairly widespread apathy from groups not vitally affected. This discrepancy in interests can be read in the historical record of almost any significant move toward, or away from, free trade. Changes in trade policy are apt to prove divisive, and this chapter traces the lines of division along the characteristics that distinguish one productive factor from another.

2. Income distribution also is affected by growth. Not surprisingly, greater supplies of a factor tend to depress its return. If commodity prices are largely determined by world markets, there is a natural alliance among specific factors (landlords and capitalists) to raise their own returns by encouraging immigration of nonspecific labor.

3. The composition of outputs is quite sensitive to changes in a community's underlying factor endowment base. This is especially true for changes in specific factors. A community relatively heavily endowed with land (capital) will tend to have a comparative advantage in producing land-using food (capital-intensive clothing). The pattern of world trade is closely linked to wide differences in resource endowments.

4. Trade encourages resources to move into sectors in which an economy enjoys a comparative advantage. Unlike the Ricardian model of Chapter 5, a country may nonetheless still support import-competing industries. The law of diminishing returns helps explain how a small amount of production may prove competitive even though the community relies on imports to provide the bulk of its consumption of some items.

5. All the essential features of the two-commodity model remain for economies characterized by a wide variety of productive activities if, in each, use is made of some factor of production available in nationwide markets (e.g., labor) as well as other productive factors specifically tied to each industry. In particular, any change in relative prices of traded commodities, or changes in technology, or discoveries of new resources, are apt to have radical repercussions in various sectors of the economy. The "Dutch Disease" describes how a favorable change in conditions affecting one tradable sector can adversely affect other tradable sectors by squeezing their profits (or returns to specific factors). For a small open economy, cost increases may successfully be passed on to consumers in sectors protected from foreign competition by high costs of transport, even though such relief is not available in traditional export- or import-competing sectors.

CHAPTER PROBLEMS

1. The discussion of the Ricardian model in Chapter 5 introduced the concept of an input-output coefficient, a_{Lj}. The reciprocal of this ($1/a_{LF}$ in the food sector, for example) referred to the average product of labor. In Figure 6.2 the top curve shows the total product of labor

in food and the bottom curve shows the marginal product. Draw in the average product of labor schedule. Use such a diagram to show how land rents as well as total wages can be illustrated.

2. With reference to Figure 6.4 it was suggested that a 10 percent increase in the price of food would shift the VMP_L^F curve upward by 10 percent while a 10 percent increase in the supply of land would (at constant food and clothing prices) shift the VMP_L^F curve rightward by 10 percent. Do these have equivalent effects on the wage rate? Which kind of change would workers prefer? Which would capitalists prefer?

3. Explain why Australian capitalists and landlords probably favor the same policy toward immigration. Given the traditional export position of Australian wool in world markets, how might owners of sheep stations be expected to react to an increase in domestic prices of manufactures brought about by a tariff? Through what mechanism might land rents be disturbed?

4. Contrast the effect on land rents of an increase in a nation's supply of land coupled simultaneously with a reduction in its supply of capital if:
   a. The country cannot engage in world trade.
   b. The country does trade freely with a much larger world market.
   Answer the same two-part question if the nation's supply of land remains constant while its supply of capital rises.

SUGGESTIONS FOR FURTHER READING

Jones, Ronald W. "A Three Factor Model in Theory, Trade, and History," Chapter 1 in Bhagwati, Jones, Mundell, and Vanek, eds., *Trade, Balance of Payments and Growth* (Amsterdam: North-Holland, 1971), reprinted in R. W. Jones, *International Trade: Essays in Theory* (Amsterdam: North-Holland, 1979). Sets out the basic model and explores some applications to trade and economic theory.

Mayer, Wolfgang. "Short-Run and Long-Run Equilibrium for a Small Open Economy," *Journal of Political Economy*, 82 (September/October 1974): 955–968. Interpretation of the specific-factors model as a short-run version of the Heckscher-Ohlin model in Chapter 7.

O.E.C.D. Economic Surveys. *Netherlands.* The March 1979 issue surveys developments in the Netherlands and fills in the details on the rise in wages and the exchange rate along with the huge expansion in the natural gas sector.

7

FACTOR ENDOWMENTS AND 2 × 2 HECKSCHER-OHLIN THEORY

[handwritten: Ricardo's Model / Specific Factors / H.O — factor intensity distinguishes Industrys]

A theory of international trade that highlights the variations among countries of supplies of broad categories of productive factors (labor, capital, and land, none of which may be specific to any one sector) was developed earlier in this century by two Swedish economists, Eli Heckscher and Bertil Ohlin.[1] Their model subsequently has been extended in scores of articles and treatises. Some of the new results were startling: Two countries that share the same general technology but differ in their endowments of the basic factors of production may nonetheless find that free trade in commodities forces wage rates in the two countries into absolute equality. Advocates of protection find support in another proposition: Even a broad-based factor such as labor may unambiguously gain by the imposition of tariffs.

Most of these propositions were carefully proven and were adequately qualified primarily in a simple form of the theory—the "two-by-two" model, so called because it analyzed an economy producing two commodities with the use of only two productive factors. This model has proved to be immensely popular not only in the area of international trade but also in fields such as public finance and economic growth. The strategy in this chapter is to expose the key production and pricing relationships in the 2 × 2 model before turning to the twin themes regarding trade for a 2 × 2 economy: (1) What determines the pattern of trade, and (2) what are the consequences of trade for the domestic rewards to labor and capital? Chapter 8 continues with a

---

[1] E. Heckscher, "The Effect of Foreign Trade on the Distribution of Income," *Ekonomisk Tidskrift*, 21 (1919): 497–512, retranslated in H. Flam and M. J. Flanders, eds., *Heckscher-Ohlin Trade Theory* (Cambridge, MA: M.I.T. Press, 1991), B. Ohlin, *Interregional and International Trade* (Cambridge, MA: Harvard University Press, 1933). In 1977 Ohlin shared the Nobel Prize in economics for his early work in trade theory.

discussion of trade in a more realistic setting in which many countries are linked by trade, many commodities are produced and consumed, and markets may not be perfectly competitive.

7.1 OUTPUTS AND FACTOR REWARDS IN A CLOSED ECONOMY

Once again the two commodities are food and clothing, but the underlying production structure differs somewhat from that described in Chapter 5's Ricardian model or Chapter 6's specific-factors model. It shares with these chapters the view that production takes place in a competitive setting in which the technology linking inputs and outputs exhibits constant returns to scale: Doubling all factor inputs exactly doubles output. However, there is an important difference: No longer (as in Chapter 6) does each commodity use an input not required by the other commodity. Instead, both industries compete for the same pair of productive factors, labor and capital. The crucial feature that distinguishes production of food from that of clothing is the *factor intensity* that each requires; the ratio of capital to labor used in food differs from that adopted by the clothing sector.

Factor Intensities

Figure 7.1 reveals the basic assumption concerning least-cost techniques used in these two industries: Food is capital-intensive relative to clothing in the sense that when optimal techniques are adopted, food production requires more capital per worker than is necessary in the clothing sector. Recall the discussion of the choices of techniques for a typical firm in Figure 6.1. To minimize costs when the ratio of wages to rents is shown by the slope of the parallel lines in Figure 7.1, both clothing firms and food firms select capital and labor combinations at points of tangency of cost lines and isoquants. It is assumed that such choices always favor a higher capital/labor ratio chosen by food firms; A in food lies on a steeper ray from the origin than does point B in clothing.[2] Saying that food is produced by relatively capital-intensive techniques compared to clothing is not to deny the possibility that clothing *could* use a higher capital/labor ratio than food—compare points C and A in Figure 7.1. But our assumption is that clothing *would not* use a higher capital/labor ratio if techniques are always chosen so as to minimize costs—compare points B and A.

Outputs and Factor Endowments

The significance of industries adopting different factor intensities can be understood by considering a question raised in a small-country setting in the previous chapter: How do production of clothing and food respond to a change in factor endowments? The way to simplify is to pick some numbers and suppose techniques in each sector are fixed:

[2] Section 7.3 discusses the possibility that such a capital/labor ranking in one country might be reversed in the other country.

FIGURE 7.1   Factor-Intensity Comparison

Food is presumed to be produced by capital-intensive techniques compared with clothing. When both industries face the same set of factor prices, the least-cost capital/labor ratio for food (at *A*) exceeds that chosen for clothing (at *B*).

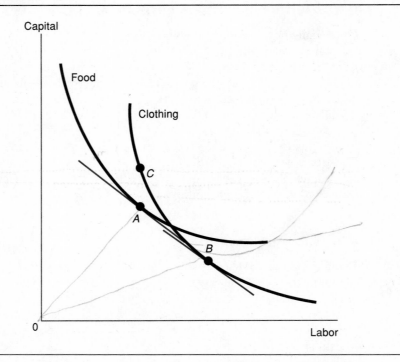

Factor Requirements per Unit Output

	Labor	*Capital*
Clothing	3	1
Food	1	1

Thus the capital/labor ratio in food (1/1) exceeds that in clothing (1/3). If initially the economy possesses 200 units of productive labor and 100 units of capital, the only combination of outputs that will fully employ both labor and capital is a clothing output of 50 units and a food output of 50 units. That is, if x_C and x_F denote clothing and food outputs, respectively, full employment implies that

$$3x_C + x_F = 200 \qquad \text{(for labor)}$$
$$x_C + x_F = 100 \qquad \text{(for capital)}$$

or that x_C and x_F each equal 50 units.

How, then, must the composition of outputs adjust if the endowment of labor expands by 10 percent, from 200 units to 220 units, with no change in the economy's

Rybczynski

supply of capital? The required change may come as a surprise: Adjustment of outputs to maintain full employment as the labor force expands requires an actual *contraction* in the sector that is capital-intensive.[3] A reworking of the balance equations reveals that clothing output expands by 10 units (from 50 to 60), while food output contracts (from 50 to 40). Note that clothing output in percentage terms rises by 20 percent, which is greater than the initiating increase in the labor force of only 10 percent. The labor-intensive clothing sector absorbs all of the economy's increase in labor (20 units), but it also absorbs factors from the food industry. Because there has been no increase in capital endowment, clothing output can rise only if it takes some capital from the food sector. At given techniques, this implies that clothing takes extra labor from the food sector as well. In the new equilibrium, in which all the economy's endowments of labor and capital are fully employed, the clothing sector raises its employment of labor by the 20 units representing the economy's overall increase plus 10 units released by the food industry and raises its demand for capital by 10 units.

Figure 7.2 illustrates the change in the composition of outputs. Each line depicts the constraint on outputs represented by full employment of one type of factor. Initial overall full-employment outputs at *A* must be adjusted in order to absorb an increase in the economy's labor supply. The new equilibrium at *B* shows labor-intensive clothing's output rising (by a magnified percentage of the labor growth) and food's output falling.

The Production Box

The concept of a consumption-box diagram was described in Chapter 2. The analogy that now proves useful is that of the production-box diagram shown in Figure 7.3. The dimensions of the box are the home country's fixed total endowments of capital and labor. Any point inside the box represents a possible allocation of capital and labor to the food sector (whose origin is the lower-left corner of the box) and to clothing (whose origin is the upper-right corner). Of course, not all possible allocations are efficient. Figure 7.1 illustrated that when food and clothing firms face the same wages for labor (and pay the same rentals on capital), they each adopt techniques such that isoquant slopes are equal to wage/rental ratios. This implies, however, that isoquant slopes are equal to each other. The *contract curve* $O_F ABO_C$ shows all capital and labor allocations for which such equalities hold. Points *A* and *B* are two such allocations; at each there is a food isoquant tangent to a clothing isoquant. Points along the contract curve are efficient—e.g., for given output X_F^A of food, the allocation that maximizes clothing output is shown by *A*. Each point on the contract curve not only shows (efficient) allocations of capital and labor to each sector, it shows total food and clothing outputs (by the values of the two isoquants tangent at that point). Thus, the points on the contract curve map into the outputs along the country's production-possibilities schedule. That is, each point on the home country's transformation schedule corresponds to an allocation of labor and capital to the two

---

[3] This relationship is known in the literature as the *Rybczynski Theorem*. See T. M. Rybczynski, "Factor Endowment and Relative Commodity Prices," *Economica*, N. S. 22 (November 1955): 336–341. See also R. W. Jones, "Factor Proportions and the Heckscher-Ohlin Theorem," *Review of Economic Studies*, 24 (October 1956): 1–10, reprinted in R. W. Jones, *International Trade: Essays in Theory* (Amsterdam: North-Holland, 1979).

FIGURE 7.2   Output Change with Labor Growth

At given techniques (3 units of labor and 1 unit of capital per unit clothing output; 1 unit each of labor and capital per unit output of food), full employment of both factors when overall L equals 200 units and K equals 100 units requires an output of 50 units each of clothing and food. Growth in the labor force causes labor-intensive clothing to expand and food production actually to contract from A to B.

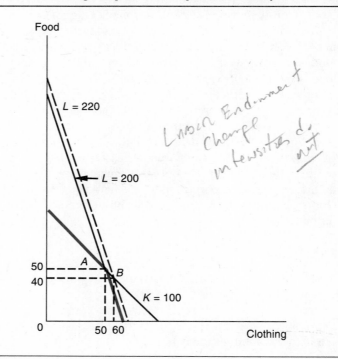

industries shown by a particular point on the contract curve in Figure 7.3's production box.

Points A and B in Figures 7.2 and 7.3 both indicate changes in the composition of outputs, but the settings are entirely different. In Figure 7.2 the labor endowment changed but intensities did not—the move from A to B showed how outputs must therefore adjust to preserve full employment. In Figure 7.3 endowments of labor and capital are held constant, but factor intensities adjust as the composition of outputs changes. Movements along the contract curve in Figure 7.3 require alterations in factor prices and the capital/labor ratios adopted in each industry.

To pursue this issue, consider the background adjustments in factor proportions and income distribution that would accompany a move from point A to point B in Figure 7.3, which corresponds to an increase in food production and a reduction in the quantity of clothing produced along the production-possibilities schedule. The diagram shows (by the slopes of rays from each origin to A and B) that such a move lowers the capital/labor ratios used in *both* industries. To see why, suppose that, as food output expands, firms in the food industry try to increase output by using the same capital/labor ratio selected initially, shown by ray $O_F A$. The firms must obtain capital and labor from the other sector, clothing, which cannot release factors in such

---

FIGURE 7.3   The Production-Box Diagram

Points on the contract curve $O_F ABO_C$ show efficient, competitive allocations of the economy's fixed overall endowments of labor and capital.

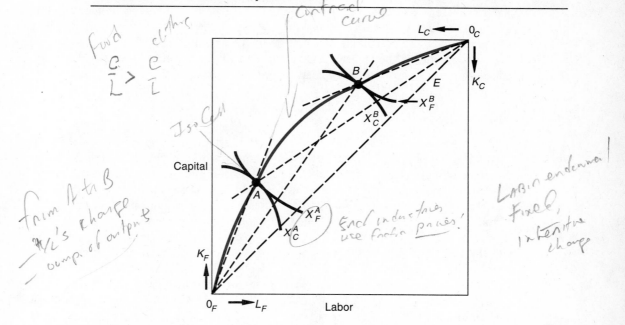

a high proportion of capital to labor, as clothing is relatively labor-intensive. The consequence is that as firms in the food industry expand, they drive up the ratio of rentals to wages. Such a relative cheapening of labor encourages firms in *both* sectors to adopt more labor-intensive techniques. Thus, at *B* food is produced with a lower capital/labor ratio than at *A*; likewise, clothing producers at *B* use a lower capital/labor ratio than at *A*. At *B* the pair of tangent isoquants are flatter than at *A*, the lower slope reflecting a lower wage/rental ratio.

How can both sectors change factor intensities in the same direction if the economy's overall factor supplies remain unchanged? By changing the composition of output. At *A* both industries adopt a *higher* capital/labor ratio than at *B*, but this is made possible by *lowering* the output of capital-intensive food relative to clothing.[4]

Increasing Costs

The same reasoning can be used to show why the expansion in food's output from *A* to *B* in Figure 7.3 must drive up the relative cost of producing food. Because techniques differ between industries, the attempt to expand capital-intensive food

---

[4] Suppose you have taken two exams and received a 70 on one and a 90 on the other—with an announced average of 80. You know that your professor is somewhat of a wimp and susceptible to pressure, and by complaining you might raise these two grades to a 74 and a 93. However, your wimpy professor may have the last word and keep your average at 80—by raising the weight that your first test score receives.

production must drive up rentals relative to wages. Why? Because otherwise the expansion in capital-intensive food would create excess demand for capital and a soft labor market. Such a change in factor prices then serves to drive up costs in food relative to those in clothing precisely because capital, the factor that has risen in price, is more intensively used in food than in clothing. Thus, the factor-intensity ranking between industries performs double duty: It explains why the rent/wage ratio rises as food expands, and it explains why that rise drives up costs of food relative to clothing. As a consequence the transformation curve exhibits a normal bowed-out shape reflecting increasing opportunity costs of producing food as food output rises.

Factor Prices

As these remarks indicate, the expansion in food production represented by the move from *A* to *B* in Figure 7.3 would be less welcome to workers than to capitalists because wages have fallen relative to rents. To be more precise: *Real* wages have unambiguously fallen and the *real* return to capital has risen. In each sector the increase in the labor/capital ratio (in moving from *A* to *B*) raises capital's marginal product and lowers labor's. To use the logic introduced in Chapter 6, the change in unit costs (and therefore price) in producing food must be trapped between the change in rentals and the change in the wage rate. Similarly, clothing's price change must lie between changes in the separate wage and rental components of cost. The conclusion: As food's output expands, rentals rise not only relative to wages, but relative to both commodity prices. Wages fall not only relative to rentals, but relative to both commodity prices. Changes in commodity prices, which cause changes in outputs along the transformation schedule, have pronounced (magnified) effects on the factoral distribution of income.

7.2 INTERNATIONAL TRADE IN THE 2 × 2 MODEL

Countries can differ from each other in a number of ways, with such differences leaving their mark on the pattern of commodity trade that becomes established between them. The Heckscher-Ohlin model of trade concentrates on one type of difference—that between the relative supplies of basic factors, labor and capital, in each nation's factor endowment bundle. This difference is highlighted if in other respects countries are assumed to be similar. We begin, therefore, by assuming that relative taste patterns are the same in the two countries and that the technology of producing either food or clothing is also common to home and foreign firms.

Factor Abundance and the Trade Pattern

You have already encountered one concept which compares ratios of factors—that of the *factor-intensity* ranking between industries. Heckscher-Ohlin trade theory is based as well on another—that of *relative factor abundance*. Thus we assume that the home country is *relatively labor abundant*: The ratio of home overall labor supply to that of capital exceeds the labor/capital ratio of endowments abroad. This intercountry difference in composition of factor supplies, when coupled with the assumption that the shared technology requires clothing to be produced always by relatively labor-intensive techniques compared with food, leads directly to the basic statement concerning the pattern of trade in the 2 × 2 Heckscher-Ohlin model: *The relatively labor-abundant country exports the relatively labor-intensive commodity.* That is, each country exports the commodity that requires relatively intensive use of the factor of production found locally in relative abundance. The labor-abundant home country exports clothing and imports food. This statement is known as the *Heckscher-Ohlin Theorem.*

Such a trade pattern rests on differences in production patterns between countries because we have assumed taste differences are nonexistent. Suppose wages and rents are the same in the two countries. (It soon will be shown how trade may bring about this intercountry equalization; here it is merely assumed.) Because they share a common technology, firms in the food sector in each country adopt comparable techniques (for example, the capital/labor ratio at *A* in Figure 7.1), as do clothing firms (for example, at *B* in Figure 7.1). With both techniques actually chosen and factor prices the same between countries, the unit cost of producing a unit of food (and, as well, the cost of clothing) must also be the same. The relative abundance in home labor supplies would, in these circumstances, be reflected not in prices or wages, but in the only remaining way—in a relatively large output of labor-intensive clothing.

Figures 7.4 and 7.5 illustrate this in two different ways. The labor-abundant home country's transformation curve in Figure 7.4 is drawn flatter than that of the foreign country for any common ray from the origin. Alternatively, the home country's relative supply curve in Figure 7.5 lies to the right of the foreign country's curve. In either

---

FIGURE 7.4   Transformation Schedules Reflect Endowments

The home country is assumed to be relatively labor-abundant. This implies that at similar commodity prices (e.g., the slopes at *A* and *B*), the clothing/food output ratio is higher at home. Points *A* and *B* above correspond to Figure 7.2's special case in which only the size of the labor force differs.

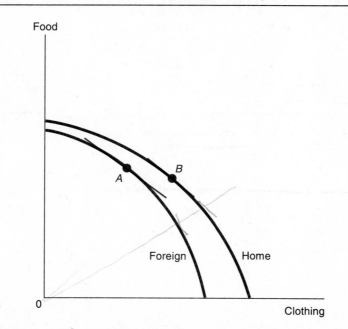

case the ratio of clothing to food produced is higher at home for comparable price ratios.

The earlier example (see Figure 7.2), in which home labor growth at constant techniques was examined, helps to establish this relationship between outputs in the two countries at similar prices. Suppose home and foreign supplies of labor and capital are initially identical; their relative supply curves in Figure 7.5 would then lie on top of each other. If just the home labor endowment expands, how does this shift the home supply curve at a given ratio of costs (and techniques)? The extra labor must be employed somewhere, and the labor-intensive clothing sector is the prime candidate. At given techniques this labor requires capital as well, and the only place this capital can be obtained is from the capital-intensive food sector. The upshot: At home the extra labor force is employed by increasing clothing production and reducing food production. (In Figure 7.4 point *B* must lie southeast of point *A*.)

The Role of Demand

The bias in production patterns imparted by the intercountry difference in relative endowments of labor and capital is sufficient in Figure 7.5 to ensure that before trade, when each country must balance its own demands and supplies, clothing is relatively

---

FIGURE 7.5   Relative Demands and Supplies

The labor-abundant home country's relative supply curve for labor-intensive clothing lies below and to the right of the foreign country's supply curve. If tastes are identical between countries, pretrade clothing prices are shown by point *A* at home and by *B* abroad.

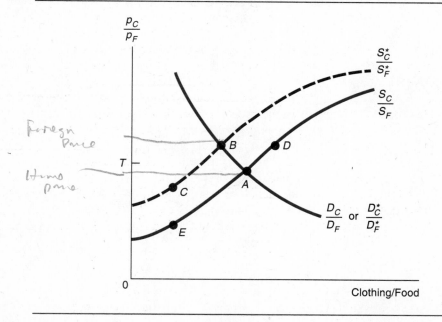

cheap at home. (Compare prices at *A* and *B*.) The assumption that the relative demand pattern is similar between countries is thus crucial. By contrast, suppose foreign tastes for clothing are comparatively weak, so that the foreign relative demand curve cuts at *C* instead of *B*. In such a case the trade pattern is reversed and the foreign country exports clothing.[5] The curves show that if the home country produced clothing and food in the same proportions at *E* as the foreign country does at *C*, relative costs of labor-intensive clothing would be lower in the labor-abundant home country. If relative demand for clothing is much higher at home, however, leading to autarky price *A*, home clothing costs would be driven up so much that the home country would, with trade, end up importing clothing from abroad. If tastes are similar between countries, however, factor endowment differences account for the trade pattern.

Income Distribution in the Move from Autarky to Free Trade

It is now possible to trace the consequences of moving from autarky to free trade for each country. Figure 7.5 shows by *OT* a relative price of clothing intermediate between price ratio *A* at home before trade and price ratio *B* abroad. International trade brings about such intermediate terms of trade. At home, production of clothing expands (and food contracts) along the production-possibilities schedule. This could be shown by the move from *B* to *A* in Figure 7.3's production-box diagram, with the attendant effect on wages and rentals such a move entails. Expansion of labor-intensive clothing at home raises wages and lowers rentals. Abroad the opposite changes are introduced by trade. As clothing becomes relatively cheaper, both labor and capital leave the clothing sector for the food industry. This move to capital-intensive food production drives up foreign rentals and lowers foreign wages.

Before trade, labor-intensive clothing was relatively inexpensive in the labor-abundant home country, and this reflected the relatively low wage at home. By contrast, the relative scarcity of labor abroad leads to high wages in autarky there and the high price for clothing shown by point *B* in Figure 7.5. International trade allows each country's demand to be freed from its production pattern, which permits home labor *indirectly* to be exported (via clothing exports) and relieves the pressure on scarce foreign labor. As observed, trade consequently raises wages (and lowers rentals) at home and lowers wages (and raises rentals) abroad. That is, international trade brings wages and rentals in the two countries closer together. If countries share the same technology, a remarkable feature of free trade is revealed: Wages and rentals are actually equalized between countries, despite the fact that labor and capital are assumed to be trapped within their own national boundaries.

This result was, in a sense, already revealed in our earlier argument. Recall that if technologies are the same, actual techniques used in the same industry in the two countries will also be the same if, and only if, their factor prices are the same. This implies that unit costs also would be identical internationally, with equal factor prices and equal commodity prices going hand in hand.

---

[5] The role of taste biases in providing an alternative basis for comparative advantages was discussed in Chapter 3. Compare, for example, Figures 3.5 and 7.5. Figure 3.6 could be used to illustrate how the trade pattern might be influenced more by taste dissimilarities than by differences in factor endowments.

In this 2 × 2 Heckscher-Ohlin model a given technology thus implies a strong relationship between prices of commodities (which enter trade) and returns to productive factors (which do not). Figure 7.6 shows this relationship, common to both countries if each produces both food and clothing. Because clothing is labor-intensive, an increase in wages relative to rents must raise clothing's price relative to that of food. Note, however, the magnified effect of a commodity price rise on factor prices: A 10 percent rise in clothing's relative price would raise the wage/rent ratio by more than 10 percent. Once again, as was discussed in Chapter 6, this reflects the necessary pricing relationship when two factors produce a single product: The change in the product price (which equals unit costs) must be trapped between the changes in the components of cost (wages and rentals). When trade raises the home clothing price from OP to OT, labor benefits in real terms, with relative wages rising from OA to OB. Trade equalizes factor prices because the initial high foreign relative wage, OA^*, is reduced to OB when clothing's price falls from OP^* to OT abroad.

These observations concerning the effect of trade on the distribution of income support the following two principal results of 2 × 2 Heckscher-Ohlin theory.

1. *The Factor-Price Equalization Theorem.* Free trade that equalizes commodity prices between countries sharing the same technology and producing the same two commodities must equate wages and rents in the home country with those abroad.

FIGURE 7.6   Factor Prices and Commodity Prices

The Heckscher-Ohlin theory determines that an increase in the relative price of labor-intensive clothing has a magnified effect on the wage/rent ratio. If countries share the same technology, and if before trade the home country is the low-wage country (OA versus OA^* abroad), clothing must be relatively cheap at home (OP versus OP^*). With free trade the home country exports clothing, and factor prices are equalized at OB if terms of trade settle at OT.

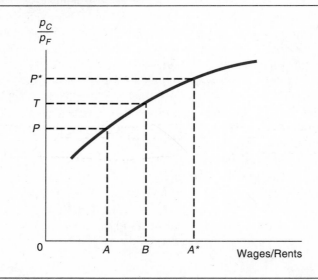

2. *The Stolper-Samuelson Theorem.*[6] Any interference with trade that drives up the local import price must unambiguously benefit the productive factor used intensively in producing the import-competing good.

It is important to note that whereas the assumption that countries share identical technologies is crucial for the factor-price equalization result, it is not necessary for the Stolper-Samuelson theorem. The latter reveals that regardless of the technology used at home, if the capital-abundant foreign country protects its labor-intensive clothing imports, it must succeed in raising real wages. This contrasts sharply with the effects described in Chapter 6, whereby a rise in either commodity price produces a more moderate effect on the wage rate: It rises in terms of one good but falls in terms of the commodity that has gone up in price. In the setting described in Chapter 6, labor was the only mobile factor, and specific factor returns (land and capital rentals) moved in a more extreme fashion when the relative commodity price changed. In the Heckscher-Ohlin model, both capital and labor are mobile, and changes in commodity prices produce magnified effects on both wages and rentals. The appendix and the supplement to this chapter discuss the factor price patterns in these two models in more detail.

7.3 THE HECKSCHER-OHLIN THEOREM AND EMPIRICAL TRADE PATTERNS

A strong attraction of the Heckscher-Ohlin theory is its numerous predictions about the relationships among actual trade patterns, factor endowments, and factor prices. Nonetheless, this theory has caused considerable frustration for empirical researchers seeking to test it formally. Consider the factor-price equalization theorem. Casual observation immediately suggests that wages are not equalized among countries. But are the wage levels seen those of "comparable" labor? The rewards to capital appear much more nearly equalized among countries, but then capital (contrary to the theory's assumption) is rather mobile among countries (see Chapter 10), and that mobility tends to equalize prices among nations without any reference to the effect of commodity trade. Certainly a given industry does not use the same mixture of factor inputs in different countries, as it would if factor prices were equalized.[7]

The Heckscher-Ohlin theorem, however, provides a tempting target for empirical testing. It links a country's relative factor endowment and the factor content of its trade flows, and these are magnitudes that should be observable. W. W. Leontief began this line of research with the following empirical version of the Heckscher-Ohlin theorem: Shortly after World War II, the United States reigned as the most capital-rich of the industrial countries, so U.S. exports should have been more capital-

[6] This relationship is known as the *Stolper-Samuelson theorem*, from its initial use in describing the impact of tariff protection if imports are labor-intensive. See W. F. Stolper and Paul A. Samuelson, "Protection and Real Wages," *Review of Economic Studies*, 9 (November 1941): 58–73, reprinted in American Economic Association, *Readings in the Theory of International Trade* (Philadelphia: Blakiston, 1949), Chapter 15.

[7] David Dollar, Edward J. Wolff, and William J. Baumol, "The Factor-Price Equalization Model and Industry Labor Productivity," in R. C. Feenstra, ed. *Empirical Methods for International Trade* (Cambridge, MA: M.I.T. Press, 1988) pp. 23–47.

TABLE 7.1   Domestic Capital Required per Labor Year per Million Dollars of U.S. Exports and Competitive Import Replacements, 1947 to 1972

Year	Exports	Competitive Imports	Ratio of Imports to Exports
1. U.S. production structure in 1947 and average composition of trade in 1947	$14,010	$18,180	1.30
2. U.S. production structure in 1947 and average composition of trade in 1951	12,977	13,726	1.06
3. U.S. production structure in 1958 and average composition of trade in 1962	14,200	18,000	1.27
4. U.S. production structure and average composition of trade in 1972	14,989	14,218	0.95

Sources: W. W. Leontief, "Factor Proportions and the Structure of American Trade: Further Theoretical and Empirical Analysis," *Review of Economics and Statistics*, 38 (November 1956): 392, 397; Robert E. Baldwin, "Determinants of the Commodity Structure of U.S. Trade," *American Economic Review*, 61 (March 1971): 134; Robert M. Stern and Keith E. Maskus, "Determinants of the Structure of U.S. Foreign Trade, 1958–76," *Journal of International Economics*, 11 (May 1981): 218.

intensive than the goods it produced in close competition with its imports. To perform this test, Leontief calculated the capital and labor required to produce $1 million worth of U.S. exports and $1 million worth of goods directly competitive with U.S. imports. For each industry, such as automobiles, he measured the capital and labor required per unit of output, not just in the auto assembly process itself, but also in the steel, rubber, glass, and other industries that supply inputs to the automobile industry. Noting the average composition of U.S. exports in 1947, he then computed the capital and labor needed to produce a million-dollar bundle of typical exportable goods. From the composition of U.S. imports that year (excluding items not produced in the country, such as coffee and bananas), he estimated the capital and labor required to produce $1 million worth of replacements for these imports at home.

He expected, from the Heckscher-Ohlin theorem, that U.S. exports would require more capital per worker than U.S. import-competing goods would require. His figures, however, showed that import replacements demand 30 percent more capital per worker than exports. The U.S. trade pattern is that of a labor-rich country![8] (His results appear in Table 7.1.) Concerned that his findings might stem simply from trade patterns distorted by World War II and its aftermath, he repeated the calculation using the average composition of exports and imports in 1951. As section 2 of the table shows, the greater capital-intensity of import-competing goods over exports, even though reduced substantially, still remained. A repeat of the test for 1962 (section 3 of the table) again yielded the paradoxical result, almost as strong as ever, although Maskus and Stern found it reversed in 1972. Applications of Leontief's test to other countries produced more paradoxes. Japan then seemed a labor-rich industrial country, yet its exports proved more capital-intensive than its import replacements. India's exports

[8] W. W. Leontief, "Domestic Production and Foreign Trade: The American Capital Position Re-examined," *Economia Internazionale*, 7 (February 1954): 3–32, reprinted in American Economic Association, *Readings in International Economics* (Homewood, IL: Richard D. Irwin, 1968), Chapter 30.

to the world at large happily proved relatively labor-intensive, as the country's labor abundance would suggest; however, India's exports to the United States proved more capital-intensive than goods competing with imports from America.

Explanations and Qualifications

Such contrary findings stirred up a concerted effort among researchers either to explain the result or to revise the method of the test. Ultimately, it turned out that Leontief's paradox had resulted mainly from a subtle but important error in specifying his test. A great deal can be learned, however, from the research and debate that preceded that anticlimactic conclusion.

The Heckscher-Ohlin theory was embraced so enthusiastically by international economists that their initial reaction was that the theory must be right and Leontief's test must be wrong, not vice versa. Consider some of the reconciliations that were offered.

1. *Effectiveness of U.S. Labor.* Leontief himself conjectured that his assumption of a capital-rich U.S. factor endowment was at fault. The typical U.S. worker might utilize more capital than, for example, the typical Italian worker, but were these workers themselves comparable? Leontief suggested that U.S. workers might be three times as productive as workers abroad, making the effective U.S. labor force triple the number of workers actually employed—a suggestion more plausible four decades ago than today. Leontief proposed that superior American entrepreneurship and economic organization increased labor's effectiveness. Even at the time his explanation found few takers. If American entrepreneurship did excel, why should organizational superiority make labor alone more effective and not capital as well?

2. *Labor Skills and Human Capital.* Perhaps, critics reasoned, Leontief erred in assuming that labor can be regarded as a homogeneous factor of production. Perhaps it is necessary to distinguish between skilled and unskilled labor: The United States might well be rich in skilled relative to unskilled labor, and therefore export goods demanding high levels of skill and import those produced in the United States mainly by unskilled labor. Alternatively, labor skills may represent an uncounted component of the U.S. capital stock: U.S. capital is invested not only in physical capital but also in education and training for the work force. Revising Leontief's test along either of these lines proved sufficient to remove the paradox.[9]

3. *Research and Development.* Somewhat related to the role of skilled labor is the influence of research and development on U.S. exports. Research activities themselves and the production of innovative goods typically require much skilled labor, and the comparative advantage of the United States was known to lie in research-intensive products. The U.S. aptitude for industrial research, therefore, might explain why U.S. exports are (skilled) labor-intensive, even though the United States is not in any sense labor-rich.[10]

[9] See Peter B. Kenen, "Nature, Capital, and Trade," *Journal of Political Economy*, 73 (October 1965): 437–460; William H. Branson and Nikolaos Monoyios, "Factor Inputs in U.S. Trade," *Journal of International Economics*, 7 (May 1977): 111–131.

[10] Donald Keesing, "The Impact of Research and Development on United States Trade," in P. B. Kenen and R. Lawrence eds., *The Open Economy: Essays on International Trade* (New York: Columbia University Press, 1968), pp. 175–189.

4. *Natural Resources.* Natural resources posed a problem similar to that raised by labor skills for Leontief's initial test. Resources are part of a nation's capital, but a gift of nature rather than an asset stored up through human effort. The United States, once resources-rich, has become a heavy importer of raw materials. The country's imports are primarily goods that are intensive in natural resources, which it pays for with exports of relatively abundant capital and labor. This pattern could account for the paradox if the extraction and processing of resources demands more capital (relative to labor) than activities that make light use of natural resources. U.S. import replacements then might exhibit higher capital/labor ratios than exports because they are dominated by resource-using activities.

5. *Tariffs.* Some critics argued that Leontief's findings were distorted by the presence of U.S. and perhaps foreign tariffs. Recall that Leontief calculated his typical bundle of import-competing products by taking the actual composition of U.S. imports and using these percentages to assign importance to the individual lines of import-competing production. Suppose that U.S. tariffs were systematically designed to protect domestic industries using large quantities of unskilled labor (as shown in Chapter 14). High tariff rates would curtail imports of such goods, so labor-intensive industries would carry very small weights in determining the average capital/labor proportions of import-competing production.

6. *Factor-Intensity of Demand.* For the Heckscher-Ohlin theorem to hold, countries' tastes must not differ too greatly. America might be well endowed with capital, but if American tastes are slanted heavily enough toward capital-intensive commodities, the country still will export labor-intensive goods in order to obtain imports that satisfy its capital-intensive cravings.[11]

7. *Factor-Intensity Reversals.* The Heckscher-Ohlin theorem requires that the factor-intensity rankings of goods hold for every possible set of factor prices. This assumption (illustrated in Figure 7.1) might not hold. Suppose, for example, that capital and labor can readily be substituted for each other in food production (the United States produces rice with elaborate machinery, while Asian countries rely mostly on hand labor), while clothing production requires about the same proportions of workers and machines regardless of factor prices. Food production, then (in the absence of factor-price equalization), could be capital-intensive in the capital-rich country and labor-intensive in the labor-rich country. A Leontief paradox, in this situation, would have to result for one country, if these two made up the trading world. If the United States exports clothing to Indonesia in exchange for food, and a factor-intensity reversal occurs, then each country is exporting the commodity that is labor-intensive in production at home, and one (the United States, on this assumption) must show a paradox.[12]

[11] Large differences exist in national consumption patterns associated with differences in incomes per capita, and these differences themselves can account for a lot of world trade. See Linda C. Hunter and James R. Markusen, "Per-Capita Income as a Determinant of Trade," in R. C. Feenstra, ed., *Empirical Methods for International Trade*, (Cambridge, MA: M.I.T. Press, 1988), pp. 90–109.

[12] The logic of this argument is spelled out in Ronald Jones, "Factor Proportions and the Heckscher-Ohlin Theorem," *Review of Economic Studies*, 24 (October 1956): 1–10. For evidence confirming factor-intensity reversals, see Michael Hodd, "An Empirical Investigation of the Heckscher-Ohlin Theory," *Economica*, 34 (February 1967): 20–29; Seiji Naya, "Natural Resources, Factor Mix, and Factor Reversal in International Trade," *American Economic Review*, 57 (May 1967): 561–570.

Not every one of these qualifying factors was shown empirically to help unscramble the paradox, but most of them appeared to contribute. Certainly the United States' exports are intensive in skilled labor, reflecting both U.S. abundance and America's affinity for research and innovation. Imports, therefore, tend to be capital-intensive because they are intensive in natural resources, and the production of many resource-intensive goods seems to require a high ratio of capital to labor.

Respecifying the Test

A critic of research on the Leontief paradox, Edward Leamer, argued for an entirely different approach to testing the Heckscher-Ohlin theorem. In order to test the hypothesis on one country, information is needed at the start about its factor endowment. It might be safe to guess that the United States is capital-rich, Bangladesh labor-rich, and Australia rich in natural resources. But what about the many countries that are not outliers in the distribution of the world's productive resources? Leamer proposed to test the Heckscher-Ohlin theorem by considering many countries at the same time and actually measuring their relative factor endowments (rather than guessing about the position of a particular country). His test requires measuring each country's share of the world's endowment of a factor, so that the United States can be called capital-rich only after determining that it holds a larger share of the world's capital stock than of other factors of production. Specifically, his test took this form.

> A country endowed with a relatively large proportion of the world's stock of a factor of production should make large net exports of products intensive in that factor.[13]

This test agrees nicely with the implications of the theory set forth earlier in this chapter: Trading nations' endowments of all the factors of production must be considered when determining their trade patterns.

Leamer's applications of this approach tended to dissolve Leontief's paradox, although Leamer's conclusions are not simple to summarize. Countries with particularly large shares of the world's capital stock do tend to be net exporters of capital-intensive goods, but their relative abundance of natural resources and variously skilled categories of labor also must be taken into account. The flavor of Leamer's results closely matches that of previous researchers who criticized Leontief for taking an insufficiently comprehensive view of the U.S. factor endowment.

This winding trail of tests of the Heckscher-Ohlin theorem may not yield neat, concise conclusions. It does, however, assign a considerable explanatory power to the model, especially when one takes a sufficiently complex view of nations' endowments of factors of production.

---

[13] Edward E. Leamer, *Sources of International Comparative Advantage: Theory and Evidence* (Cambridge, MA: M.I.T. Press, 1984). Leamer also found a misspecification of the form of Leontief's test (too complex to explain briefly) for the United States itself. When he performed Leontief's original experiment in a revised form, the data appeared consistent with the United States being a capital-rich country after all.

7.4 SUMMARY

This chapter builds on some propositions of the basic Heckscher-Ohlin theory for a trading world consisting of only two countries, two commodities, and two completely mobile productive factors. As contrasted to the discussion in Chapter 6 of production in which output in each sector is obtained by combining labor drawn from a national market with a factor specifically tied to that industry, the Heckscher-Ohlin theory assumes no factor is specific. Labor and capital are costlessly transferable from sector to sector.

Some of the Heckscher-Ohlin properties are similar to those encountered in Chapter 6:

1. Output in any industry cannot expand without driving up relative costs. Costs are bid up because the return to the factor used relatively intensively in that industry is bid up by a magnified amount.

2. Any change in a country's terms of trade is accompanied by a relatively more profound redistribution of factor incomes. Even a broad-based factor such as labor unambiguously gains if the relative price of labor-intensive goods rises. This particular result contrasts with the conclusion in Chapter 6 that a mobile factor such as labor cannot significantly alter its real wage through changes in commodity prices, although specific factors definitely could. The Heckscher-Ohlin model is less applicable to questions of short-run impact of policy changes on income distribution than is the specific-factors model of Chapter 6.

3. Differences in factor endowments influence the direction of trade. A relatively ample endowment of capital leads to exports that intensively require capital.

Perhaps the most striking conclusion of the simple Heckscher-Ohlin model is one not shared by the specific-factors model: Free trade in commodities can completely substitute for international mobility of capital and labor in the sense of driving wages and rents to equality for countries sharing the same technology. The sharp contrast between this factor-price equalization result and observed international comparisons of wage rates and returns to capital has contributed much to discredit Heckscher-Ohlin propositions as a whole. In defense of the Heckscher-Ohlin theory, the following can be pointed out:

1. If countries differ in technological knowledge (or climate and other influences on the relationship between inputs and outputs), any presumption that free trade brings about absolute factor-price equalization disappears.

2. Even if countries differ in technological knowledge, many propositions of the Heckscher-Ohlin theory are unaffected. For example, the impact of a tariff on real wages at home depends only on home technology and not at all on how commodities are produced abroad.

3. As will be argued in Chapter 8, when viewed in a multicountry, multicommodity setting, factor-price equalization is less likely to occur even between countries sharing the same technology. Instead, any significant difference between countries in basic capital/labor endowment proportions would be reflected in countries producing different sets of commodities. If they were to produce a commodity in common, the

capital-rich country would be likely to adopt more capital-intensive techniques precisely because its labor force was more productive and better paid.

In a famous empirical test of the Heckscher-Ohlin theorem, Leontief investigated whether the exports of the United States—a capital-rich country—embody more capital relative to labor than do the goods that the United States produces in competition with imports. To everyone's surprise, he found that U.S. exports were labor-intensive compared to import-competing goods. Subsequent research has partly resolved this paradox by showing that U.S. exports are intensive in human capital, and that the capital-intensity of import-competing goods is associated with the prevalence of raw materials. Empirical tests of the theorem have shifted recently to a global level. Countries rich in a particular factor generally have been found to make net exports of goods requiring that factor intensively.

CHAPTER PROBLEMS

1. In Figure 7.3's production-box diagram show that a country with given endowments of capital and labor could not produce food by capital-intensive techniques at one set of outputs, while switching to labor-intensive techniques at another (*Hint:* Show the inconsistency involved if the contract curve crosses the diagonal.) (Your answer should be compared with the discussion of factor-intensity reversal and the Leontief paradox.)

2. The text describes an example in which a country with the same capital endowment as another but a greater endowment of labor must actually produce less of one good if they both face the same terms of trade (this is the *Rybczynski theorem*). Establish this result by superimposing the box diagrams of the two countries so that they share a common food origin (lower-left corner). How do the two contract curves compare?

3. Although the discussion of the Heckscher-Ohlin model presupposes a fair degree of substitutability between capital and labor (as shown by the smoothly bowed-in isoquants in Figure 7.1), this is not necessary. Suppose there is only one technique that can be used in clothing production: To produce a unit of clothing requires four labor-hours and one unit of capital. Similarly, in food production each unit requires a single labor-hour and one unit of capital. At an initial equilibrium suppose the wage rate and the capital rental are each valued at $2. If both goods are produced, what must be their prices? Now keep the price of food constant and raise the price of clothing to $15. Trace through the effects on the distribution of income. Rank the relative changes in the wage rate, the price of clothing, the price of food (unchanged by assumption), and the rental on capital. Relate your results to the *Stolper-Samuelson theorem*.

4. Retain the assumptions about technology in Problem 3:

$$a_{LC} = 4 \qquad a_{KC} = 1 \qquad a_{LF} = 1 \qquad a_{KF} = 1$$

Draw a diagram with capital on the vertical axis and labor on the horizontal. Draw a ray through the origin with slope unity and show how outputs of food can be measured along this ray. Draw a flatter ray, with slope 1/4, and show how outputs of clothing can be measured along this ray. Suppose the economy possesses 1,000 units of labor.

a. Find the full employment levels of output of each good if the capital stock is 500 units.
b. Find the lowest and highest capital stocks that still allow full employment of both factors.
c. Draw the transformation schedule for each of the cases in 4a and 4b.

SUGGESTIONS FOR FURTHER READING

Heckscher, Eli. "The Effect of Foreign Trade on the Distribution of Income." A new translation is provided by Flam and Flanders, eds., *Heckscher-Ohlin Trade Theory* (Cambridge, MA: M.I.T. Press, 1991). This article originally appeared in Swedish: *Ekonomisk Tidskerift*, 21 (1919): 497–512. It discusses the effect of trade on factor prices in a nonmathematical format.

Johnson, Harry G. "Factor Endowments, International Trade and Factor Prices," *The Manchester School of Economic and Social Studies*, 25 (September 1957): 270–283, reprinted in *International Trade and Economic Growth* (Cambridge, MA: Harvard University Press, 1958). Chapter 1 discusses the Heckscher-Ohlin model.

Jones, Ronald W. "Factor Proportions and the Heckscher-Ohlin Theorem," *Review of Economic Studies*, 24 (October 1956): 1–10, reprinted as Chapter 1 in *International Trade: Essays in Theory* (Amsterdam: North-Holland, 1979). Emphasizes alternative definitions of factor abundance and comments on the meaning of the Heckscher-Ohlin theorem and the consequences of factor-intensity reversals.

Ohlin, Bertil. *Interregional and International Trade* (Cambridge, MA: Harvard University Press, 1933). Together with the Heckscher article this book forms the basis for the modern theory of trade.

Rybczynski, T. M. "Factor Endowment and Relative Commodity Prices," *Economica*, N.S. 22 (November 1955): 336–341. A statement and proof of the Rybczynski theorem, using production-box diagrams.

Samuelson, Paul A. "International Factor-Price Equalization Once Again," *Economic Journal*, 59 (June 1949): 181–197, reprinted in Stiglitz, ed., *The Collected Scientific Papers of Paul A. Samuelson*, Vol. 2 (Cambridge, MA: M.I.T. Press, 1966), Chapter 68. A restatement of Samuelson's factor-price equalization theorem.

Stolper, W. F., and P. A. Samuelson. "Protection and Real Wages," *Review of Economic Studies*, 9 (November 1941): 58–73, reprinted in Stiglitz, ed., *The Collected Scientific Papers of Paul A. Samuelson*, Vol. 2 (Cambridge, MA: M.I.T. Press, 1966), Chapter 66. The original statement of the Stolper-Samuelson theorem.

APPENDIX:
HECKSCHER-OHLIN AND SECTOR-SPECIFIC MODELS:
A TEMPORAL RELATIONSHIP

The two-sector Heckscher-Ohlin model has often been called a long-run model because of its assumption that both productive factors are mobile between occupations and earn the same return in each. By contrast, the sector-specific model described in Chapter 6 assigns to each industry a factor of production used nowhere else in the economy, although each industry also draws labor from a common pool. One interpretation of the specific-factor model considers that each industry uses labor and a type of capital equipment that is fixed in supply to that sector in the short run, but over time can be converted into the kind of capital used in the other sector. (This process can perhaps be visualized more easily if capital in one sector is allowed to depreciate and not be replaced and new capital is directed toward the other sector.)

Figure 7.A.1 brings together two previously used diagrams. The upper panel is the production-box diagram and the lower panel, similar to Figure 6.4, is a diagram whose curves show the value of labor's marginal physical product for given prices of food and clothing and given allocations of capital. Initially full short- and long-run equilibrium is at point *A* in the upper panel. The horizontal line through *A* indicates the initial division of the economy's capital stock between sectors. In the lower panel the L_F curve shows the value of labor's marginal product in producing food for the given initial capital assignment to the food sector. For a given price of food and capital stock, labor's marginal product is driven downward by any increase in labor use. The L_C curve shows the value of labor's marginal product in the clothing sector, where inputs of labor are measured leftward from the O_C origin. Intersection point D shows the original wage rate and the original equilibrium allocation of labor between sectors, which is the same allocation as that shown in the upper panel by point A.

Suppose the price of food rises by around one-third and the price of clothing remains constant. This price rise acts as a stimulus to the sector producing food, but in the short run it is assumed that only labor can be attracted to the food sector. The lower panel shows how the value of labor's marginal product is shifted upward to L'_F, uniformly by about one-third. That is, distance DE is approximately one-third of the existing wage rate. The wage rate, however, does not rise by this amount. Instead, higher potential wages in the food sector attract labor from the clothing sector; short-run equilibrium is restored at point G. The wage rate rises, but by less, relatively, than the price of food. Point C in the upper panel lies directly above point G and thus shows the new short-run labor allocation together with the fixed (in the short run) allocation of capital.

Figure 7.A.1 also traces through the process of adjustment over time as capital as well as labor becomes mobile. In the short-run situation at C the return to capital in the food sector was driven up by the price rise and the greater labor/capital ratio adopted at C. (That is, the rental on capital went up relatively more than the price of food.) By contrast, point C reveals that less labor is used per unit of capital in clothing, thus lowering the return to capital in the clothing industry. This discrepancy in rates of return provides the incentive for a reallocation of capital over time to the food sector. In the top panel this reallocation (of capital *and* additional labor) is shown by the path from C to B. At point B the rates of return are brought back to equality with each other in the new long-run equilibrium. In the lower panel the value of the marginal product of labor schedule in the food sector shifts proportionately to the right as the capital supply in food expands (in the movement from C to B in the upper panel). That is, the L'_F curve shifts to the L''_F position. In the clothing sector the loss of capital shifts the value of labor's marginal product curve in from L_C to L''_C. The intersection point, H, shows a labor allocation that corresponds to point B in the upper panel.

Note the reversal of labor's fortunes in moving from the short-run equilibrium at C (upper panel) to the long-run equilibrium at B. The wage rate has fallen from G to H (lower panel). Although the rise in food's price in the short run was shared to some extent by a rise in wages (the move from D to G), the subsequent movement of resources to the capital-intensive food sector serves to depress the wage rate. In addition, the wage rate must fall below its initial long-run value at D; in the Heckscher-Ohlin model a rise in the price of the capital-intensive commodity (food) must lower the wage rate.

Figure 7.A.2 relates the transformation schedule, TT, that is supported in the long run by points on the contract curve to the series of short-run transformation schedules that correspond to a fixed allocation of capital.[14] Point A' corresponds to initial full equilibrium at point A in Figure 7.A.1. The short-run transformation schedule, $t_A t_A$, shows maximal output combinations

[14] This construction is described in W. Mayer, "Short-Run and Long-Run Equilibrium for a Small Open Economy," *Journal of Political Economy* (September/October 1974): 955–968. The adjustment process from short run to long run is described also in M. Mussa, "Tariffs and the Distribution of Income: the Importance of Factor Specificity, Substitutability, and Intensity in the Short and Long Run," *Journal of Political Economy* (December 1974): 1191–1204, and R. W. Jones, "Income Distribution and Effective Protection in a Multi-Commodity Trade Model," *Journal of Economic Theory* (August 1975): 1–15. The diagrammatic linkage between the production box diagram and the value of labor's marginal product curves, Figure 7.A.1, is presented in J. P. Neary, "Short-Run Capital Specificity and the Pure Theory of International Trade," *Economic Journal* (September 1978): 1–23.

FIGURE 7.A.1 Short-Run and Long-Run Response to Price Changes

A rise in food's price attracts labor but no capital can move in the short run—from A to C. Long-run adjustment is from C to B. The bottom diagram has wages rise in the short run (from D to G), but fall in the long run (to H).

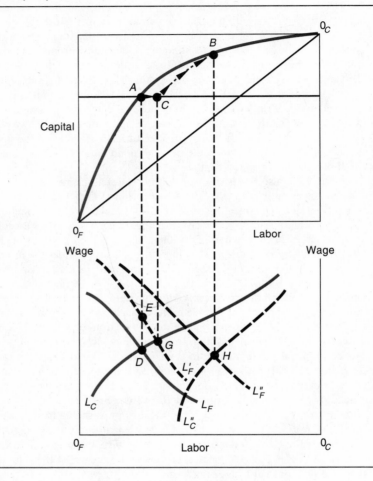

when the capital stock is kept allocated in the same manner, as shown by the horizontal line through A and C in Figure 7.A.1. Only point A along this line is a point on the contract curve. All other points must thus lead to output combinations along Figure 7.A.2's t_At_A curve that are inferior to some points on the long-run TT locus. The rise in food's price that moves labor's allocation in Figure 7.A.1 from A to C in the short run is captured in Figure 7.A.2 by the move from A' to C'. The transition to the new long-run equilibrium at these prices involves a reallocation of capital and a shift to a new short-run locus. Final equilibrium is reached at point B in Figure 7.A.1, corresponding to point B' in Figure 7.A.2. The short-run transformation curve t_Bt_B has a fixed capital allocation appropriate to point B on the contract curve. The slope of TT at B' equals the slope of t_At_A at C', the movement of capital (and labor) from C to B in Figure 7.A.1 is undertaken at constant prices in response to a (short-run) differential in rates of return to capital in the two sectors.

FIGURE 7.A.2   Short-Run and Long-Run Transformation Curves

The long-run transformation curve, TT, is the outer envelope of short-run transformation curves, such as $t_A t_A$ and $t_B t_B$. The allocation of capital between sectors is fixed along a short-run curve.

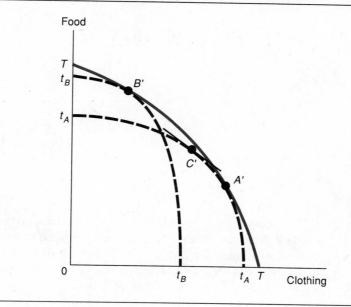

8

MULTICOMMODITY TRADE

Pickup fair
page 40 -
scales

A vast array of commodities is produced, consumed, and traded throughout the world. This rich pattern often reveals that commodities produced in one country may differ from those produced in another. An explanation of trading patterns in such a world can be based either on a multicommodity extension of the previous chapter's account of the 2 × 2 Heckscher-Ohlin model or on elements of scale economies and imperfect competition leading to what Chapters 2 and 3 referred to as intra-industry trade. Indeed, there is room for both sets of explanations in making sense of patterns of world trade.

/ Given Technology
/ fixed supply factors

To extend the Heckscher-Ohlin framework the strategy in this chapter parallels the one used in discussing many-commodity trade and production patterns in a Ricardian world. We ask how a small country with a given technology and fixed factor supplies reacts when trade is made possible with an outside world that produces many commodities but does not necessarily share the same technology. We then proceed to ask how this country's production and trade patterns would differ from those of another small country that shares an identical technology but has a higher relative endowment of capital.[1] This cross-sectional comparison between countries can be reinterpreted as an examination of how one country's production pattern can develop with growth—over time the country loses its comparative advantage in traditional goods while gaining a comparative advantage in more capital-intensive commodities. Subsequently, we examine intra-industry trade, fitting this discussion into a Heckscher-Ohlin framework.

8.1 TRADE PATTERNS: WHICH GOODS TO PRODUCE

Trade and production patterns for a small country facing a set of world prices depend on several ingredients: (1) *technology*, as reflected in sets of isoquants showing combinations of labor and capital that can produce a given quantity of each commodity

---

[1] The first section rests heavily on the discussion in R. W. Jones, "The Small Country in a Many-Commodity World," *Australian Economic Papers* (December 1974): 225–236, reprinted in R. W. Jones, *International Trade: Essays in Theory* (Amsterdam: North Holland, 1979).

in the small country; (2) *world prices* for all these commodities; and (3) *factor endowments* available in the small country. A description of the interaction of these various ingredients follows.

Unit-Value Isoquants

Figure 8.1 shows *unit-value* isoquants for a set of five possible commodities. Each unit-value isoquant illustrates all combinations of capital and labor that can produce $1 worth of output of that particular good. The shape of each unit-value isoquant should be familiar, for at a given world price for the commodity, the quantity of the commodity that yields exactly $1 on world markets is a given constant. However, the position of the curve obviously depends on world prices: A doubling of commodity 3's price, for example, would contract the unit-value isoquant for commodity 3 uniformly halfway toward the origin. Exactly half the bundles of inputs that produced $1 worth of x_3 before can now yield $1, since p_3 has doubled. Thus the shapes of the unit-value isoquants reflect the country's technology and the position of the unit-value isoquants depends as well on world prices.

Figure 8.1 reveals the following information about possible production patterns for this small country:

FIGURE 8.1   Unit-Value Isoquants

With given world prices, the home country's technology determines for each commodity the quantities of labor and capital that produce $1 worth of output. Production takes place on the inner frontier *ABCDEF* (extended).

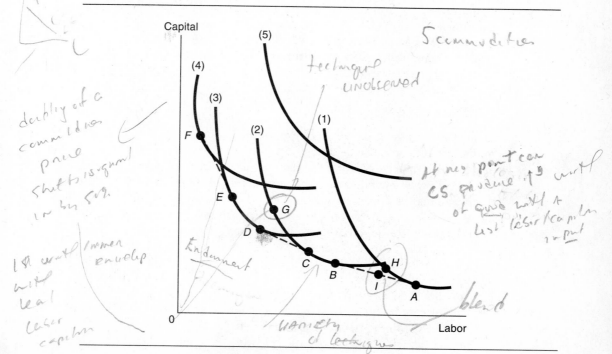

inferior isoquant

1. Some commodities will never be produced by this country because its technology in these commodities is inferior to that prevailing somewhere in the rest of the world. This is illustrated by commodity 5. No matter how the small country might choose to produce the fifth commodity, there are better uses for its labor and capital—"better" in the sense that production of some other commodity could earn $1 on world markets with less labor and less capital. Commodity 5 in this sense is "dominated" by the group of other commodities.

inefficient techniques

2. Certain techniques for producing some commodities will never be observed, regardless of the community's endowment base. Consider point G, showing the bundle of capital and labor that, if used to produce commodity 2, would yield output worth $1 on world markets. The country would be better served by producing commodity 3 with techniques shown, for example, by point D. A dollar earned this way would cost less in inputs of labor and capital.

blended commodities

3. What is less obvious is that other techniques of production (input bundle H to produce commodity 1, for example) may never be observed *despite* the fact that there is no single unit-value isoquant lying closer to the origin than H. This point is crucial. Although H is not dominated by some other single production point (as was G by D), it *is* dominated by a *blend* of production of commodities 1 and 2. Consider point I, lying, for example, 60 percent of the way from B to A. Suppose the community produces the first commodity by using the factor proportions shown by A, but with only 60 percent of the scale indicated by A. In addition, suppose the economy devotes capital and labor to producing the second commodity by using the proportions at B, but with only 40 percent of the scale shown by B. This output combination (60 cents worth of the first commodity and 40 cents worth of the second) uses a total bundle of inputs shown by point I, the point 60 percent of the way to A on the chord joining B and A. In a similar fashion, it is necessary to draw in the tangent chords CD and EF. Curve ABCDEF (extended at each end to follow isoquants 1 and 4) shows the best assortment of inputs of capital and labor that will allow this country to produce and sell exactly $1 worth of output(s) at world market prices.

The Factor Endowment Base

So far the discussion has been concerned only with the possibilities of production. Actual production patterns depend on further information: What are factor endowments? With respect to Figure 8.1, there is, of course, no reason why the community's factor-endowment bundle will lie *on* the inner locus ABCDEF (extended). That would only mean that the total national product would add up to exactly $1. What is relevant for our argument now is not scale but proportions. For example, suppose the ray from the origin whose slope shows the economy's endowment capital/labor ratio cuts this locus between points D and E. With trade, then, this community would devote all its resources to producing commodity 3 and would export this good to satisfy its demands for all other commodities. On the other hand, if the economy had a slightly higher endowment proportion of capital, so that a ray from the origin to the endowment point cuts the locus on the dashed line between E and F, the country would produce both commodities 3 and 4, although it would not produce any of commodities 1, 2, and 5. The pattern of production depends very much on factor endowments.

Factor Prices

Turn, now, to the question of factor prices. How does Figure 8.1 illustrate the wage/rental ratio that would correspond to any factor-endowment proportions? The factor-price ratio is shown by the *slope* of the inner locus *ABCDEF* (extended) at the point where it crosses the factor-endowment ray. Figure 8.2 traces out the relationship between factor endowments and factor prices for the assumed set of given world commodity prices. Start by having the country so labor-abundant that wages are extremely low (the wage/rent ratio shown by slopes along the first unit-value isoquant to the right of *A* in Figure 8.1). Specialization in the first commodity would be complete. The country could not successfully compete in any other commodity because capital requirements for that other commodity would be too severe in relation to the relatively high premium that capital earns at home. If this country's capital/labor endowment ratio steadily grows, it eventually produces both commodities 2 and 1 (for example, in proportions shown by point *I*). For local variations of the capital/labor ratio near this production point, the country remains incompletely specialized in 2 and 1, and factor prices are frozen at the level shown by the slope of chord *AB*. This is the kind of result shown earlier in the two-commodity example, in which a country produced both food and clothing and the wage/rent ratio was locked into the world commodity price ratio.

Figure 8.2 shows this pattern of alternately being completely specialized and then being incompletely specialized as greater capital/labor endowment ratios are considered. For example, point *I* in Figure 8.1 corresponds to point *I* in Figure 8.2. A country with this factor-endowment ratio would be incompletely specialized.

FIGURE 8.2 Factor Endowments and Factor Prices

Generally, the greater the capital/labor endowment ratio, the higher the wage/rent ratio for countries facing fixed world commodity prices. There are, however, plateaus of incomplete specialization where factor prices are uniquely determined by world commodity prices.

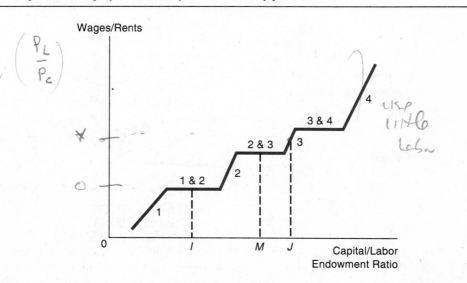

A Two-Country Comparison

Now consider two small countries facing the same set of world prices and sharing the same technological knowledge. Must their wage rates be the same? Their capital rentals? Not necessarily. Obviously, much depends on factor endowments. Suppose the home country is labor-abundant compared with the other country sharing its technology. For example, let OI at home and OJ in the other country (Figure 8.2) depict factor-endowment proportions. With free trade the wage rate is higher abroad. Even if the other country's endowment proportions allow it to be incompletely specialized (for example, its ratio is now OM, with both countries producing commodity 2 in common), foreign abundance in capital still will be reflected in a higher wage rate abroad.

The factor-price equalization theorem that free trade brings different nations' factor prices into equality is a strong result not apparently supported by the evidence. Even casual observation reveals that U.S. wages exceed those in Korea or Brazil. If countries do not share the same technological knowledge, then any presumption of factor-price equalization disappears, just as in a Ricardian world. As Figure 8.2 illustrates, even with the assumption that two countries have access to the same technology, factor prices need not be equalized. In a world of many commodities, the factor-endowment proportions must be rather similar between countries in order to equalize factor prices. (Countries would have to lie on the same plateau in Figure 8.2.) Techniques of production also can differ between countries even when they share the same technological knowledge. If the home country's endowment proportions are OI in Figure 8.2 and a foreign country's are OM, they both produce commodity 2. The foreign country, however, adopts more capital-intensive techniques of production than the home country does. Why? Because foreign wage rates are relatively higher as a consequence of a greater capital endowment per individual. In this broader context of many commodities, the Heckscher-Ohlin theory does not impose the assumption that techniques of production must be identical throughout the world. Instead, it explains *why* techniques and productivities *differ* systematically between countries. They do so in part because countries differ in their supplies of productive factors.

The Trade Pattern

Trade patterns in this many-commodity world reflect the tendency of countries to concentrate production rather severely. Returning to Figure 8.2, consider the trading pattern of a country with some "intermediate" capital/labor endowment ratio, OM, for example. The country produces only commodities 2 and 3. It may export either good 2 or good 3 or both. Look at its imports, however. This country relies on the rest of the world for commodity 1 (more labor-intensive than either of the goods it might export) and commodity 4 (more capital-intensive than either 2 or 3), as well as for commodity 5 (which, by assumption in Figure 8.1, it cannot produce competitively because of inferior technology, even though 5's capital/labor requirements are close to those of 2 and 3).

The trade pattern revealed by this example suggests that a country may not export all commodities with a capital/labor ratio higher than some crucial value and, in turn, import all commodities with lower capital/labor ratios. Such a view of trading patterns is inappropriate for a world that consists of many countries and many commodities. Trade allows countries to concentrate their productive activities exclusively on a few traded commodities whose factor requirements closely mirror the particular capital/labor proportions found locally, and to satisfy their demands by importing a variety of commodities whose factor requirements (if they were to be produced at home) would range the entire spectrum from very low to very high capital/labor ratios.

8.2 ECONOMIC GROWTH AND CHANGING COMPARATIVE ADVANTAGE

Growth experience in today's world varies widely from country to country. In North America and Europe relatively moderate growth rates (2 or 3 percent) alternate with periods of much slower growth. In many parts of Africa and Latin America the situation appears more grim, with periods of positive growth often being outweighed by years of decline. In the past two decades the success stories are to be found primarily in Asia. Japan, of course, comes readily to mind, but even more rapid rates of growth are being experienced by the so-called "tigers" of Southeast Asia: South Korea, Taiwan, Hong Kong, and Singapore, all exceeding 6 percent annual rates as an *average* over the past twenty years. These countries are being joined by Thailand, Malaysia, Indonesia, and, especially in its coastal areas, Mainland China.

All these countries are "outward-looking," with export activity fueling the growth process. But more is involved, and Figures 8.1 and 8.2 help tell the story. Growth is accompanied by large rates of capital accumulation, both physical capital and education (human capital). [According to the *Economist* (Nov. 16, 1991), Taiwan currently accounts for a full 25 percent of doctorates in engineering at American universities.] Such capital accumulation raises wage rates, and during this process a country's comparative advantage shifts away from more labor-intensive activities. Thus, years ago Japan saw its shipbuilding and textile industry lost to South Korea and Taiwan. As these NICs (Newly Industrializing Countries) grow, they in turn lose their comparative advantage to more labor-abundant countries further behind in the growth process. Taiwan is currently losing its grip as the world's leader in umbrellas as well as its established position in shoes and textiles. The very success of industries like these in raising wage rates in Taiwan now supports a shift toward higher technology and capital-intensive sectors. Taiwanese businessmen eye wage rates in Mainland China that are less than 10 percent of those prevailing in Taipei's tight labor market. As the next couple of chapters spell out in more detail, one characteristic of modern trade patterns is the great increase in trade in intermediate products, natural resources, and producer goods, facilitating a fragmentation of production processes whereby more labor-intensive activities get placed in low-wage areas. (The Chinese province of Guangdong with 13 percent yearly growth rate in the 1980s, those parts of Indonesia and Malaysia within 30 miles of Singapore, and the strip of Mexico below the Rio Grande have all experienced rapid growth in labor-intensive manufacturing activities.)

This pattern, wherein growth leads to higher real wages, entailing shifts in comparative advantage and actual declines in previously active labor-intensive industries, is often accompanied by rapid technological progress and quality upgrading of exports, and sometimes it is American commercial policy that encourages these moves. In the

1980s the United States urged the use of VERs (Voluntary Export Restraints) in Japan to stem the flow of Japanese exports of automobiles to the American market. With such quantity restraints in operation, the Japanese response was to raise quality, and whole new lines of more luxurious automobiles posed a threat to Detroit's more expensive models.

8.3 CONCENTRATION IN PRODUCTION

Although our discussion of competitive pressures in the multicommodity model predicts that trade will enforce a high degree of concentration in a country's productive activities, a glance at actual production patterns suggests that this conclusion is partially blunted in practice. Consider some of the reasons.

Transportation Costs ⇒ protective umbrella

Commodities cannot be moved from one location to another without incurring costs of transport, such as shipping charges, insurance costs, and the real costs involved in time required to transport goods. The impact of transport costs on patterns of trade is that they provide a natural protective umbrella for local production. For some items transport costs bulk large relative to production costs; thus most localities produce their own bricks and pour their own cement. The introduction of refrigeration in trains and ships allowed much greater worldwide concentration in meat packing, vegetable farming, and related areas of commerce.

If transport costs are greater than the cost spread between countries, that commodity does not enter trade. In this case economists speak of _non-traded goods_. The distinction between traded and non-traded goods is especially important for small trading communities. Local prices of non-traded goods are determined by local conditions affecting demand and supply. Local prices of traded goods (whether exportables or importables) are determined for this country by conditions in the rest of the world. Through policy changes, the home country can affect local prices of non-traded goods, but it cannot affect prices of traded goods.[2] In any case, a country produces all its non-traded goods, whatever exportables are suggested by comparative advantage, and importables that prove competitive with world prices augmented by the relevant transport costs.

Local policy affects prices of non-traded goods

Protection of Local Industries

While transport costs represent nature's way of providing protection for local industries, import duties and discriminatory taxes are artificial ways of achieving the same end. One consequence of protective policy is that a nation will engage in a wider variety of productive activities than could be sustained in the brisk climate of free trade. This leads to the obvious question: What costs (or benefits) does a nation incur by stimulating this wider productive base? Part III of our text picks up this theme.

duties taxes

---

[2] This distinction has been discussed in Chapter 5 and also is important in such questions as the effect of exchange-rate changes for a small country. See Part IV.

mobility

Specific Factors: Short Run and Long Run

The Heckscher-Ohlin account of trade often has been referred to as *long-run* theory.[3] It implicitly assumes that sufficient time is allowed for factors of production such as skilled labor, various kinds of capital goods, and entrepreneurs to avoid becoming trapped in depressed industries if possible returns elsewhere in the economy are superior, and that these factors cannot successfully beat off competition from new productive factors entering an industry with the required skills. Factors are mobile from industry to industry.

Dutch disease

Chapter 6 provides an illustration of *short-run* theory if what were referred to there as "capital" and "land" in reality represent productive factors that are specifically tied to their occupations in the short run but can be transformed to compete with each other in the long run. Examples abound of workers who can be retrained with new skills to enter new occupations only after a number of months or years, or of textile machines that must be scrapped or allowed to depreciate before they can figuratively be beaten into tractors or lathes.

Stolper

Consider the case of a textile manufacturer and mill owner who is offered a price increase (through tariff protection, for example). Suppose textiles are labor-intensive. Long-run Stolper-Samuelson theory suggests that if capital is mobile into and out of the textile industry, such an increase in textile prices will push real wages up and lower the return to capital. Should the textile manufacturer heed the implied advice to oppose such protection? Not if the manufacturer pays more attention to the possibility of considerable gain in the short run resulting from the magnified increase in returns (or rents) to the manufacturer and the mill as specific factors employing relatively mobile labor. Unless individuals are particularly longsighted, one could argue that the "short-run" type of model developed in Chapter 6 may be more relevant for policy questions (e.g., tariffs) concerned largely with changes in the distribution of income.

Natural resources

Both short- and long-run models function simultaneously in describing a nation's trade patterns. Some factors of production are genuinely specific, both in the short and long run; natural resources provide the obvious examples. (A nation's position can change over time, however, from net exporter to net importer as reserves or supplies become more scarce and local incomes and demands grow. Oil and iron ore were formerly exported from the United States.) Although the strict Heckscher-Ohlin setting, with mobile capital and labor, suggests only one or two traded goods produced (ignoring transport costs and tariff protection), a wider variety of production obviously can be supported by the existence of natural resources.

Aside from natural resources, there is another way in which the specific-factors model can help explain why a nation produces more traded goods than the small number suggested by the Heckscher-Ohlin theory. Return to Figure 8.1. Assume that the current capital/labor endowment ratio cuts the *ABCDE* (extended) inner locus between *E* and *D*, so that the Heckscher-Ohlin solution for this country would (in the absence of transport costs) suggest production of tradable good 3 only. Suppose,

---

[3] For example, see Wolfgang Mayer, "Short-Run and Long-Run Equilibrium for a Small Open Economy," *Journal of Political Economy*, 82 (September/October 1974): 955–968, and Michael Mussa, "Tariffs and the Distribution of Income: The Importance of Factor Specificity, Substitutability, and Intensity in the Short and Long Run," *Journal of Political Economy*, 82 (November/December 1974): 1191–1204.

however, that in the recent past the prices of both goods 2 and 4 had been somewhat higher (enough to have made them at one time the recipients of capital investment just as good 3 is currently the favored industry). If real capital literally were mobile, machines in industries 2 and 4 would have shifted into 3 as soon as prices of 2 and 4 fell. In reality, however, capital in 2 and 4 can be "trapped" in the short run, with production of goods 2 and 4 simultaneously carried on with 3. Something has to give—the rate of return to capital and entrepreneurs in industries 2 and 4. (The appendix to Chapter 7 discussed in geometrical terms the general relationship between short-run production patterns and Heckscher-Ohlin theory.)

A stylized picture emerges from this example. A factor such as capital is not instantaneously shiftable. At any time some traded activities earn higher returns to capital than others. Variations over time in world commodity prices and/or a country's own technology help account for the presence of production in sectors of the economy whose rationale for existence lies in the past. With the passage of time certain industries disappear from the scene, just as new ones emerge. The specificity of factors, such as capital in the short run, and the consequent possible variety in rates of return help blunt the stark long-run suggestion that only one or two traded industries can survive. Every period carries with it echoes of the past. However, the *range* of such activities in generally capital-rich countries should differ from that in countries abundant in unskilled labor.

Bilateral Trade Balances

When many countries engage in trade, variations among their factor endowments can explain not only the pattern of each country's trade with the rest of the world, but also characteristics of the bilateral trade pattern for single pairs of countries.

Figure 8.2 illustrates potential trade patterns for three countries with identical technologies whose capital/labor endowment ratios are shown by points I, M, and J. They all rely on other countries for consumption of commodities 4 and 5. Countries M and J are "closer" in their endowment proportions than are I and J. Thus, J may not export at all to M, but could export commodity 3 (the only commodity it produces) to country I. Similarly, J may import commodity 2 from M, but import more (commodities 1 and 2) from country I. The Heckscher-Ohlin view is that trade among countries reflects a disparity in their production patterns caused, in turn, by differences in the composition of endowments. The more disparate this composition is between any pair of countries, the more likely it is that bilateral trade between them could be substantial.[4]

The role of bilateral trade balances in revealing different sources for trade is emphasized even more strongly if factor inputs in addition to capital and labor are taken into account. Consider briefly a world with three trading regions, each with a different relative supply of labor, capital, and land. Suppose they are ranked as follows:

[4] In the next section it will be seen that another source of trade—the difference in *varieties* of goods produced with somewhat similar techniques by imperfectly competitive firms, can support more robust bilateral trade between countries with fairly *similar* endowment bases.

Relative Factor Supply	Region A	Region B	Region C
Ample	Labor	Land	Capital
Moderate	Land	Capital	Labor
Scarce	Capital	Labor	Land

Each region trades numerous commodities with the others under purely competitive conditions. These patterns of factor abundance imply something about bilateral trade balances among these countries. Region A is rich in labor but B is poor. Thus, B's demand for imports of the goods in which A specializes will be strong, the comparative disadvantage of their domestic production being great. However, the converse should not hold: A's maximum disadvantage lies in capital-intensive goods, but B is only moderately well endowed with capital. Therefore, other things being equal, A is likely to have a trade surplus with B. The situation for bilateral trade between A and C is the reverse: C's endowment is suitable for specialization in the capital-intensive goods that A is most likely to import, yet C is moderately well endowed with labor and thus may not be equally receptive to A's exports. A is likely to have a trade deficit with C. Note that A's predicted surplus with B and deficit with C are consistent with overall balance for A, its total exports equaling total imports. By the same reasoning, B is likely to run a surplus on bilateral trade with C, making it clear that this example also is consistent with overall trade balance for B and C as well.

Karl-Erik Hansson, who set forth this schema, proposed that it explains rather well the pattern of bilateral trade balances observed among major trading areas, up to World War I. Equate region A with the tropics, well suited to export resource-intensive products requiring unskilled labor but relatively little capital. Equate region B with the United States and the other temperate regions settled by European emigrants. Equate region C with the European countries. Trade balances between these regions were relatively stable and agreed closely with the theoretical prediction.[5]

8.4 PRODUCT VARIETY AND INTRA-INDUSTRY TRADE

The phenomenon of intra-industry trade was introduced in Chapters 2 and 3. A desire for variety in types of clothing, whether by each individual or as an aggregate over individuals with different tastes, could support simultaneous production of a range of quality types, with some varieties produced at home and others abroad. Recall from our earlier discussion that international trade patterns then could reflect an exchange of one country's varieties for those of the other country (intra-industry trade) and, as well, a net outflow or inflow of clothing, balanced by net trade in other

[5] Karl-Erik Hansson, "A General Theory of the System of Multilateral Trade," *American Economic Review*, 42 (March 1952): 58–68.

products, such as food (interindustry trade). Formal models designed to capture this mixed type of trade have been introduced in recent years, in a framework that makes use of the Heckscher-Ohlin model.[6]

Increasing Returns to Scale

Not included in the preliminary discussion of intra-industry trade in Chapters 2 and 3 is the mechanism by which the number of different varieties produced or consumed in any country is determined. If consumers value variety, why does the market not respond with a proliferation of countless products, each differing only slightly from competitors? The answer lies in cost reductions made possible by a larger scale of economic activity—the phenomenon of *increasing returns to scale*. This characteristic of technology refers to the possibility that a doubling of expenditure devoted to producing a commodity (at constant input prices) may result in a more than double consequent expansion of output, whereas the previous production models (Ricardo, specific-factor, and Heckscher-Ohlin) all assumed constant returns to scale.

Suppose now that in some productive activities an increase of 10 percent in labor and capital inputs would result in an expansion of output in excess of 10 percent. If variety is not valued per se, the existence of such increasing returns to scale would encourage the entire level of output to be organized in a single productive activity in a single firm. It is the joint presence of a desire for variety and increasing returns that leads to markets in which a large but finite number of differentiated products emerges, each product serving some segment of a national or world market.

In pursuing the formal details of such a trading world, it is extremely convenient to impose arbitrary but natural symmetry conditions, with regard to both technology and consumer taste patterns. More explicitly, assume that the technology describing how any variety of clothing is produced is identical to that of any other variety. For example, at comparable output levels the same capital/labor ratio would be used to produce blue blazers and tan sportcoats. Assume symmetry in taste patterns as well so that output levels are kept comparable: The demand curve facing the producer of one variety is assumed to be identical to that facing a producer of any other variety. As a consequence, any potential new entrant would consider producing only a variety that differs from those already on the market.

These symmetry assumptions allow us to describe a world in which increasing returns and factor endowments jointly determine output patterns in two aggregate industries: food and clothing. The food industry in each country consists of countless competitive firms, each producing a homogeneous product, with technology similar in both countries and characterized by constant returns to scale, as in the discussion in Chapters 5, 6, and 7. By contrast, the clothing sector consists of a number of differentiated varieties of clothing, each produced by a single firm. The discussion turns first to the description of the market for clothing varieties in a country closed to international trade, a market characterized by monopolistic competition. Then we describe production and trading patterns in a free-trade world.

---

[6] See especially E. Helpman, "International Trade in the Presence of Product Differentiation, Economies of Scale and Monopolistic Competition: A Chamberlin-Heckscher-Ohlin Approach," *Journal of International Economics* (1981) and the monograph by Helpman and Krugman, *Market Structure and Foreign Trade* (Cambridge, MA: M.I.T. Press, 1985).

Monopolistic Competition and Increasing Returns

Most intermediate theory texts describe markets with a high degree of competition—high enough to drive equilibrium profits to zero with free entry of firms—but with products of all firms distinguished from one another by the typical consumer. Demand for variety produced by any one firm is characterized by a slightly downward-sloping demand curve; if the firm were to raise the price of its variety while prices of competing varieties were held fixed, its sales would be drastically reduced, but not altogether eliminated.

Figure 8.3 describes the determinants of equilibrium output for a typical firm in this monopolistically competitive market. The demand curve facing the firm is downward-sloping (the AR or average revenue curve), implying that marginal revenue (MR) lies below average revenue. With the firm producing in the range of increasing returns, the average cost curve (AC) is declining. This, of course, implies that the marginal cost curve (MC) lies below the average cost curve. (A special case of increasing returns, although not the one illustrated in Figure 8.3, suggests that an element of fixed or setup costs is required before any production can take place, with subsequent additions to output achieved at constant marginal costs.) The typical firm seeks the output level at which its profits are maximized. This entails selecting the output for which marginal costs are equal to marginal revenue—level q_A in Figure 8.3. If, as assumed, new firms are free to enter the clothing sector, the resulting maximum profits are driven down

FIGURE 8.3   Monopolistic Competition

A firm in a monopolistically competitive equilibrium produces at q_A, with marginal revenue equal to marginal cost. Free entry wipes out all positive profits at price p_A, equal to average costs.

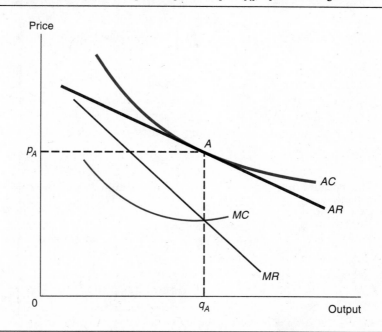

to zero. This is shown in Figure 8.3 by the tangency of the average cost and average revenue curves at point A. (If a temporary equilibrium revealed positive profits, entry of new firms would cause this firm's demand curve to shift downward or leftward until such a tangency is obtained.) Output q_A and price p_A represent the best the firm can do; any other output results in losses.

Firm Size and Product Variety in Autarky

Consider, now, how the autarky situation differs between countries with respect to the clothing sector. Consumers seek variety in product styles, but too much variety is costly because average costs are high if each firm produces a small amount. The requirement that marginal cost and revenue be equal on the one hand (profit maximization on the part of every firm) and that average cost equal average revenue on the other (entry forces a zero-profit equilibrium) helps to determine how many different varieties (one firm per variety) are produced and how large output is for any and all firms in a single country.

Figure 8.4 focuses on relationships between the number of clothing firms, n, and the size of any individual firm, x. Consider, first, the upward-sloping RC curve, common to both countries because they are assumed to share identical technologies and demand conditions everywhere are the same.[7] This curve shows, for a closed economy, possible combinations of firm size and number of varieties for the clothing industry in a monopolistically competitive equilibrium. The total size of the market is larger for points farther out along the RC curve; this suggests that any one firm will face stiffer competition as more brands are introduced. Assuming demand becomes more elastic and profits once again are squeezed out by the entry of new firms, as in the tangency solution of Figure 8.3, the size of a typical firm also expands. (That is, the tangency solution in Figure 8.3 slides farther down the average cost curve.) As a consequence, the number of varieties varies positively with the size of the representative firm. With the expansion in market size, any one brand faces closer substitutes and firms become larger.

The two points on the RC curve labeled H and F correspond to autarky positions at home and in the foreign country, assuming that the home autarky market for this industry is smaller. That is, if the two countries share a common technology, the smaller market will, in autarky, be served by a smaller number of firms, each similar in size to any other firm in that country but smaller in size relative to firms in the larger foreign market.

Consumers and Producers of Differentiated Products in a World Market

A common theme running through all the previous chapters is that the possibility of trading in world markets frees local consumers from a lockstep dependence on the output of national firms. Such a theme is especially relevant to countries producing differentiated products once the countries move from autarky to engage in world markets. The composition of trade, of course, depends on cost conditions and tastes for both the clothing and food sectors at home and abroad. Postpone, for the moment,

---

[7] A discussion of this curve is found in Helpman and Krugman, op. cit., pp. 153–157.

FIGURE 8.4 Size and Number of Firms

The *RC* curve shows how in each country (sharing a common technology) larger firm size goes hand in hand with the production of a greater number of varieties. In autarky, the smaller home market is served by firms (at *H*) that are fewer in number and smaller in size than in the larger foreign market (*F*). With trade, if the same resources are devoted to clothing as in autarky, producers concentrate (at *H'* and *F'*), all firms are the same (larger) size, and a larger number of varieties are available for consumers (at *W*).

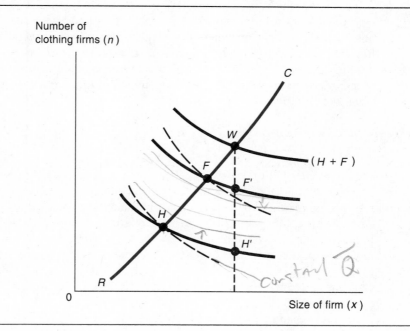

a full analysis of free-trade patterns by considering only how each country's consumers and producers of clothing respond to the possibilities of international trade if in each country the same commitment of total resources is made to the clothing industry. (It will then be asked how this allocation of resources can be altered by trade.)

Figure 8.4 illustrates a free-trade equilibrium for producers and consumers in both countries. Free trade creates a single world market for differentiated products. The strong symmetry assumptions made, coupled with this breakdown of the barriers to world trade, imply that the output of each and every firm anywhere in either country is the same, with each producing its own variety.

The curves *HH'* and *FF'* show, for home and foreign country, respectively, a given allocation of resources to the clothing sector—the same level as in autarky positions *H* and *F*. A move southeastward represents for each country a cutback in the number of varieties produced but an increase in the scale of operations in each variety. Now add these curves vertically to obtain the (*H + F*) locus, which cuts the *RC* curve at *W*. Point *W* depicts the situation for consumers in either country and shows how every consumer has a larger menu of varieties from which to select with trade. This expansion in consumption possibilities is especially large for the smaller home market.

Producers in each country feel the increased competition from producers abroad; greater elasticities of demand result in a smaller number of firms in each country, but each firm is of a larger scale. Given the (arbitrary) restraint on the allocation of expenditures to the clothing sector in each country, home supply response to trade is shown by point H' and the foreign response by point F'.

The dotted rectangular hyperbolas through points H and F show combinations of firm size and number of firms that yield the same aggregate clothing output (that is, points for which nx is a constant). The move by the home country from H to H' (and the foreign country from F to F') cuts higher and higher rectangular hyperbolas and thus shows that for a constant expenditure of resources in each, the move to higher-volume firms and fewer varieties allows each country to expand aggregate clothing production. This corresponds to Chapter 3's illustration of how the existence of increasing returns serves to shift a country's production-possibilities schedule with trade out from its autarky position.

8.5 FACTOR ENDOWMENTS AND INCREASING RETURNS IN WORLD TRADE

The Heckscher-Ohlin theory, with its explanation of trading patterns guided by factor-endowment differences, plays a role that is consistent with this scenario of increasing returns and monopolistically competitive markets in the clothing sector. Suppose all varieties of clothing are labor-intensive relative to homogeneous food and that the home country is relatively labor-abundant. With trade the home country diverts relatively more of its resources to the differentiated clothing sector than the relatively capital-abundant foreign country does. In Figure 8.4 home resource allocation to clothing exceeds levels shown by the HH' curve and, abroad, fewer foreign firms than at point F' produce clothing. (The position of world consumption, point W along the RC curve, depends on details of demand.)

Some varieties of clothing are produced in both countries with trade, and each firm's output is in part exported to consumers in the other country. This Heckscher-Ohlin framework simultaneously tolerates (1) intra-industry trade of varieties of clothing, with mutual interpenetration of markets, and (2) interindustry trade, with homogeneous capital-intensive food exported from the capital-abundant country in exchange for clothing. Although the home country is the primary clothing producer, firms in both countries operate, with similar-sized plants.

There is another way in which factor endowments and increasing returns interact in determining trade patterns. Product variety may not be just of the "horizontal" type discussed earlier, with techniques for producing any variety of clothing being the same as those for producing any other. Instead, products may differ in a "vertical" direction, with quality of product improving for types produced with higher capital/labor ratios. The "capital" used in this comparison includes "human" capital, and higher-quality product types may indirectly require higher capital/labor ratios via resources devoted to research and development. Clothing, automobiles, audio and video equipment, and machine tools provide examples. In automobiles some countries (e.g., South Korea and, earlier, Japan) produce lower-quality products—compared with Germany, the United States, or (later) Japan. Fixed costs, economies of scale, and a love for variety all conspire to explain intra-industry trade among countries producing roughly comparable quality products, but factor endowments, including human capital as well as produced technology, are crucial in explaining trade in low-, medium-, or high-quality products.

8.6 SUMMARY

The pattern of trade in a Heckscher-Ohlin world of many countries and many commodities shares much in common with a Ricardian world. Countries concentrate their productive activities around a few commodities whose demands for factors closely reflect total factor availability. More capital-abundant countries produce more capital-intensive commodities. If taste patterns are roughly comparable among nations, most will import commodities representing a wide dispersion in factor requirements (if produced at home) compared with those adopted in the export sectors. Factor intensities in a nation's aggregate output bundle reflect that country's factor-endowment proportions. Factor intensities in a nation's aggregate consumption bundle reflect average world factor endowments if countries have similar tastes. Trade flows represent the difference between output and consumption, so relatively capital-abundant countries on the average import relatively labor-intensive commodities. This is an *average* result however; the wide dispersion in imports still remains.

As countries grow over time, the range of goods produced for export changes systematically. Growth in physical and human capital leads to higher real wage rates, which systematically alter comparative advantage away from traditional labor-intensive commodities toward commodities reflecting higher capital/labor ratios and superior quality. This pattern is strongly reflected in the particularly high-growth economies of Southeast Asia.

Transport costs and tariffs serve to widen the range of productive activities that any one nation can enter. Resources specific to certain activities also convey a comparative advantage not captured solely by capital/labor rankings. In the short run, many types of capital (and perhaps skilled labor) are not mobile between sectors. This tends to lessen the concentration of production. The spirit of the Heckscher-Ohlin theory still remains to suggest that differences between countries in the endowment of broad classes of productive factors such as capital and labor will be reflected in differences in patterns of production and trade.

It often is the case that in industries in which consumers' tastes support a wide variety of qualities, markets are characterized by monopolistic competition. The demand curve facing the producer of any given variety is slightly downward-sloping, and in equilibrium such a firm will produce in the range in which average costs are declining (increasing returns to scale in the technology). If differences in technology among varieties is ignored, and if it is further supposed that demand is evenly balanced over all varieties produced, it is possible to model both autarky and free-trade positions in a Heckscher-Ohlin framework. Conclusions that emerge include:

1. In autarky, larger countries tend to produce more varieties of products than do smaller countries, and firms tend to be larger.

2. With free trade and a commonly shared technology, each country may produce a range of different product types as well as a homogeneous product that differs in

its required capital/labor ratio from that adopted by firms in the differentiated-products industry.

3. Firm size in each country will be larger with trade than under autarky and will be comparable among countries. Consumers everywhere enjoy a larger menu of varieties in a world market than with autarky, while producers face stiffer competition, encouraging longer production runs and a more limited range of varieties produced in any country.

4. Factor endowments affect the pattern of trade in Heckscher-Ohlin fashion. The relatively labor-abundant country, with output levels relatively higher in the labor-intensive industry, will tend to be a net exporter of that industry's output. If the industry is characterized by differentiated products, such a net export position reflects an underlying mutual interpenetration of the other country's markets by each firm.

5. Gross trade exceeds net trade. In such situations, in which some products are differentiated and some are homogeneous, both comparative advantage (as imparted by relative factor endowments) and increasing returns help explain nations' trading patterns.

CHAPTER PROBLEMS

1. Assume that input-output coefficients are fixed. The table shows capital requirements per unit output (a_{Kj}) and labor requirements per unit output (a_{Lj}) to produce one unit each of commodities 1 through 5.

Commodity:	1	2	3	4	5
a_{Kj}	4	2	1	1	1
a_{Lj}	1	1	1	2	4
Price	$16	$14	$10	$14	$16

Also shown are prevailing world prices for each commodity.
   a. If the economy has a labor/capital endowment ratio of 3:1, what does it produce? What are the wage rate and rental on capital?
   b. If the world price of commodity 1 should triple, would there be any change in this country's production pattern? Factor prices? Real income?
   c. At the initial prices shown in the table, how would factor prices differ in an economy with the same technology but a capital/labor endowment ratio of 3:1?
   d. For the economy with the original labor/capital endowment ratio of 3:1, how would production patterns and factor prices change if commodity 3's price on world markets should rise by 40 percent?
   e. Describe the pattern of trade for an economy with a capital/labor endowment ratio of 1:1.

2. Using Figures 8.1 and 8.2, show how an increase in the world price of commodity 2 would affect real wages in two countries sharing the same technology, both of them producing commodity 2, but the home country with endowment ratio OI (Figure 8.2) and the foreign country with endowment ratio OM.

3. In Figure 8.4 points H' and F' show each country devoting the same resources to the differentiated clothing sector as it did in autarky. Suppose that the home country is relatively

labor-abundant and clothing is labor-intensive relative to food. How would this alter the number of firms devoted to clothing in each country? Could the home country produce a wider variety of clothing with trade than the (larger) foreign country?

SUGGESTIONS FOR FURTHER READING

Helpman, Elhanan, and P. Krugman. *Market Structure and Foreign Trade* (Cambridge, MA: M.I.T. Press, 1985). A more advanced monograph; Chapter 7 describes trade in a setting of monopolistic competition.

Jones, Ronald W. "Heckscher-Ohlin Trade Theory," *The New Palgrave* (New York: Macmillan, 1987), pp. 620–627. A survey of the relationships among parts of Heckscher-Ohlin theory both in a 2 × 2 setting and in higher dimensions.

———. "The Small Country in a Many-Commodity World," *Australian Economic Papers* (December 1974): 225–236, reprinted in *International Trade: Essays in Theory* (Amsterdam: North-Holland, 1979) Chapter 2. A more general treatment of the material in Sections 8.1 and 8.2.

Krugman, Paul R. "Increasing Returns, Monopolistic Competition, and International Trade," *Journal of International Economics*, 9 (4) (November 1979): 469–479. An early discussion of trade with monopolistic competition and increasing returns.

Leamer, Edward E. *Sources of International Comparative Advantage: Theory and Evidence* (Cambridge, MA: M.I.T. Press, 1984). An interesting application of the Heckscher-Ohlin framework to a setting with three factors (land, labor, and capital). Traces the development of a number of countries.

9

TRADE IN PRODUCERS' GOODS

[handwritten margin notes: Absolute Advantages come in with mobility / inputs intermediates / expansion of prod. set]

Most items traded among countries do not represent final consumption items. Rather, they are typified by raw materials, such as coal, oil, or bauxite, or by producer goods or processed materials, such as steel, textiles, aluminium, or machinery. We estimate that in 1988 goods passing into consumption without significant further processing accounted for only 31 percent of the value of world exports. The strong distinction made by David Ricardo between those commodities (final consumer goods) that can be traded on world markets, and all productive inputs, which cannot, is at best an extremely qualified view of trade. As will be seen, the fundamental Ricardian concept of comparative advantage must increasingly be modified in a world where trade cuts ever more deeply into the production process.

Because the emphasis now shifts toward the empirical, this chapter begins by investigating actual features of international trade patterns before providing theoretical models that help to explain them.

9.1 RESOURCES AND MATERIALS IN INTERNATIONAL TRADE

Most final goods reach consumers after passing through a series of intermediate stages of production. For example, bauxite ore becomes alumina, then aluminum, then electrical wire, and finally a component of the house that is purchased. Often these successive conversions are performed by different industries, which may be located in different countries. The country with a cost advantage in aluminum wire may be poorly equipped to produce aluminium (an activity that is drawn to low-cost sources of electric power), in which case the aluminum enters into international trade. Nations should be thought of as specializing in activities or processing stages, not products.

Natural-Resource Endowments

One of the factors that governs the allocation of production processes among nations is the uneven distribution of natural resources. Saudia Arabia, richly endowed with petroleum, is apt to find most of its other factors drawn into the production of crude petroleum. Arabia may have no comparative advantage for producing petrochemicals, not to mention undertaking activities that require little or no crude petroleum as an input. Less obviously, natural-resource abundance can explain major changes in the long-run trade pattern of the United States. A century ago, the United States was, compared to its principal trading partners, rich in natural resources. Over the years some American natural resources, such as forests, metallic ores, petroleum, and natural gas, were partially depleted, and other nations were drawn into world trade to supply these primary products. Applying the Heckscher-Ohlin theorem of Chapter 7, we expect that "land" (natural resources in general), which was abundant, is now the scarce factor in the U.S. endowment, and that American trade switched from predominantly exporting resource-intensive products to principally importing them.

Some calculations by Jaroslav Vanek confirm this trend. The natural-resources content of trade flows cannot be measured directly. Agricultural land varies too much in topography, climate, and so on, to be measured by total acreage. The natural resources available to produce metals and minerals can only be tallied from the outputs themselves. Therefore, Vanek proceeded indirectly by measuring for various years the value of the products of natural resources embodied in U.S. exports and in the goods produced in the United States in competition with imports. As expected, the value of resource products in the typical bundle of U.S. exports fell from nearly twice that required (at home) for the production of goods competing with our imports, in 1870, to a level of about three-fourths of the requirements for imports in 1955.[1] The U.S. trade pattern obviously has changed toward the import of resource-intensive products and the export of products using other factors intensively.

Today most industrial countries share the U.S. position in drawing on other countries to supply many of their raw materials. They still differ a great deal, however, in the prevalence of final and intermediate goods in their international trade. Simple measures of these differences are hard to secure. Many manufactured goods can serve either intermediate or final uses. (Tires are sold either to automobile manufacturers or to the final buyer who suffered a blowout.) Some primary products pass immediately into consumption (fresh meat). Figure 9.1 provides a rough impression of the diverse situations in selected industrial countries. Plotted on the horizontal axis is a measure of these countries' exports of primary and intermediate goods as a percentage of total exports; the vertical axis records the same ratio for imports. Primary and intermediate goods are defined here as products of the agriculture, fishing, forestry, and mining sectors plus wood products and basic metals. Except for Norway the industrial countries are net importers of these goods, although for the United States and Canada the net-imports position is least strong. Japan is "off the chart" for importing primary and intermediate goods almost exclusively and exporting almost none of them. Economists have debated inconclusively whether Japan's position reflects simply that nation's lack of indigenous raw materials or some abnormal disinclination to purchase manufactured imports from other countries.[2]

The developing countries also are drawn increasingly into this network of intermediate and final goods trade. They have rapidly increased their exports of finished consumer goods to the industrial countries, buying mostly intermediate goods and

[1] Jaroslav Vanek, "The Natural Resource Content of Foreign Trade, 1870–1955, and the Relative Abundance of Natural Resources in the United States," *Review of Economics and Statistics*, 41 (May 1959): 146–153.

[2] See Edward J. Lincoln, *Japan's Unequal Trade* (Washington: Brookings Institution, 1990), especially Chapter 2.

FIGURE 9.1   Proportion of Primary and Intermediate Goods in Total Imports and Exports of Industrial Countries, 1988.

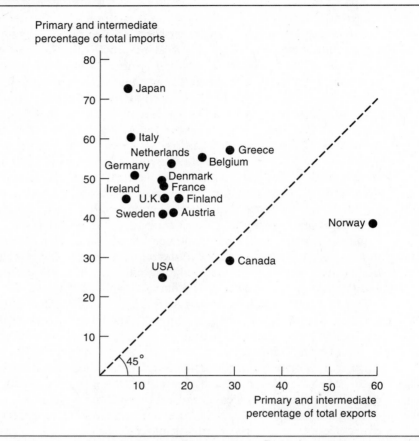

Source: Calculated from United Nations, *International Trade Statistics Yearbook, 1988* (New York, 1990), Vol. I.

finished capital goods in exchange. Between 1970 and 1980, the industrial countries increased their total imports of manufactures from the developing countries by a factor of 10.8 (normal value, not adjusted for inflation), but their imports of LDC (less-developed-country) manufactured consumer goods increased in nominal value by 14.6. (This development is examined more fully in Section 9.3.)

Scarce Natural Resources and the Terms of Trade

The terms of trade between intermediate and final goods have important effects on the welfare of trading nations. Consider a country such as Japan, which imports only intermediate goods, combining them with its own labor and capital into final goods. The resulting outputs provide both its own consumption and the exports that pay for its imports. If the prices of its imports rise relative to its exports (that is, if its terms of trade deteriorate), then the incomes of its factors of production are squeezed.

Every so often in the history of international commerce, a controversy arises over whether long-term trends affect these terms of trade and the relative incomes of countries that mainly export intermediate goods compared to those that mainly import and process them.

One of these controversies has surfaced over and over in the industrial countries, most recently at the end of World War II and in the 1970s following a major increase in the price of crude petroleum. The world's stock of nonrenewable natural resources—metals, energy sources, etc.—is a factor ultimately limiting the real incomes of those who consume them. The resources more readily available, those that require the application of the fewest other inputs, are utilized first. As these resources are exhausted, the margin of extraction moves to resources that are lower in quality, farther away, deeper in the earth, or otherwise more costly in terms of the resources needed to convert them into useful intermediate goods. The most recent expressions of concern, based on projections of the Club of Rome,[3] focused on the limit that would be reached as fossil energy sources grow scarcer to the point where securing another unit output of energy requires the input of just that much energy. At that point, no income would remain to allocate to other factors of production, resulting in the ultimate worsening of one's terms of trade. Most economists are not impressed by the Club of Rome's alarmist stance (and that of its earlier counterparts). It is not that they reject the assumption that nonrenewable resources hold this potential for shifting the terms of trade against other factors of production. Rather, they hold that the forecast neglects technological change, which over the course of history has shown a remarkable ability to cheapen the extraction of natural resources, make it easier to find previously undiscovered ones, and facilitate the substitution of other inputs for resources that have grown more expensive.[4]

A different theory concerning the terms of trade of materials fabricators was proposed in the 1950s and 1960s by Raul Prebisch.[5] He held that the terms of trade show a long-run tendency to turn against the countries that produce primary and intermediate goods. He thought these were primarily the less-developed countries, and he was not concerned with the Club of Rome's resource-scarcity argument. He did recognize that technological improvements affect the production of primary inputs as well as finished goods. He held, however, that the markets for primary products are typically competitive, whereas those for finished goods are oligopolistic. When productivity grows in primary products, competition drives down their prices in line with the reduction of their costs. Manufacturers, he asserted, keep their productivity gains in the form of higher profits because of their ability to maintain prices through oligopolistic agreements. Most economists greeted Prebisch's argument with no more enthusiasm than they did the Club of Rome's. Suppose his assumption that worldwide markets for finished goods are monopolistic is accepted. This means the primary producers' terms of trade at any one time are worse than they would be if finished

---

[3] D. H. Meadows et al., *The Limits to Growth* (New York: Universe Books, 1972).

[4] A century ago, when the horse was a principal source of motive power, concern arose over where enough land could be found to raise oats to feed all the horses required for transportation. The internal combustion engine, of course, spared us the need to raise oats in window boxes.

[5] Raul Prebisch, "Commercial Policy in the Underdeveloped Countries," *American Economic Review*, 49 (May 1959): 251–273; for a critique, see M. June Flanders, "Prebisch on Protectionism: An Evaluation," *Economic Journal*, 74 (June 1964): 305–326.

goods were sold competitively. This does not, however, imply any change in these terms over time. A monopolist charges the price that maximizes profits; if technological change lowers marginal cost, the profit-maximizing price also declines. Nonetheless, Prebisch's argument and the arguments of predecessors of the Club of Rome did bestir empirical research into the long-run course of the terms of trade between primary products and finished goods. No clear trend could be detected, given the difficulties, which include finding reasonable starting and ending points and adjusting for changes in the quality of goods.[6]

9.2 INTERMEDIATE GOODS TRADE AND PRODUCTION POSSIBILITIES

The international exchange of intermediate goods, raw materials, and other items involved in production opens up new sources by which countries gain from trade: A nation's production-possibilities curve expands for reasons that go beyond the possibility of increasing returns among product varieties described in Chapters 3 and 8. Trade in items used at earlier stages of the production process also facilitates new patterns of final goods being produced, combinations not achievable with the more limited range of resources available when there is no international trade.

A simple model suffices to reveal these new sources of gain. Suppose once again that food and clothing represent final consumer goods, and that they are produced with labor, perhaps some specific forms of (non-traded) capital or land, and two resources: fertilizer used to produce food and cotton used to produce clothing. To simplify matters assume that fertilizer and cotton require no extra labor or other resources to obtain; annual flows are available in fixed quantities, much as are food and clothing themselves in Chapter 2's model of commodity exchange. If fertilizer and cotton cannot be traded on world markets (the kind of assumption embodied in the paradigm of trade in final goods only that underlies our earlier chapters) the economy's production-possibilities curve could be shown in Figure 9.2 by the TT curve.

The shape of the TT curve suggests a relatively plentiful supply of fertilizer compared with cotton at home. Suppose now that both fertilizer and cotton can be traded on world markets at given world prices, and that these prices reflect a relative abundance of raw cotton in the rest of the world compared with home supplies. If some of the country's fertilizer can be exchanged for an equivalent value of cotton (at world prices), this exchange benefits the clothing sector at the expense of food production; the production-possibilities curve shifts to $T'T'$. Indeed, any number of transformation schedules, such as original TT or $T'T'$, can be drawn, each reflecting a different composition of the intermediate bundle (fertilizer, cotton), but all with the same value of these bundles at world prices. The $T''T''$ curve in Figure 9.2 represents the outer "envelope" of all these curves and is the production-possibilities schedule for the

[6] Robert E. Baldwin, "Secular Movements in the Terms of Trade," *American Economic Review*, 45 (May 1955): 259–269.

FIGURE 9.2   Trade in Inputs Expands the Transformation Curve

TT represents the home country's production-possibilities curve if intermediate inputs are barred from trade. The *T'T'* schedule reflects one possible balanced trade of fertilizer (used in food) for cotton (an input into clothing) at fixed world prices, while outer envelope *T"T"* shows production possibilities when cotton and fertilizer are optimally traded for each other with balance in intermediate exports and imports.

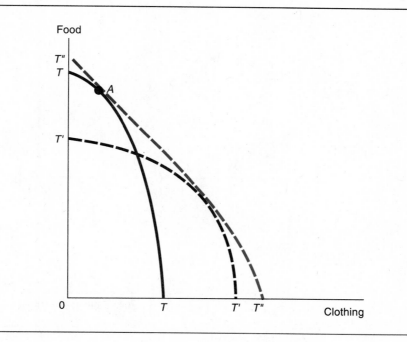

---

country, assuming balanced trade in intermediates at given world prices.[7] A country's pattern of production, and perhaps final goods trade, can thus be profoundly affected by the country's ability to trade intermediates and raw materials with other countries.[8]

Another argument also suggests how trade in intermediate goods could imply that the production possibilities with trade are improved over the menu possible in autarky. The argument runs parallel to that presented earlier (Chapter 2) in describing how consumers benefit by having a wider variety of commodities available through trade. In the production process the ability to use more specialized producer goods or materials facilitates the production of a greater output relative to a given outlay on

[7] Should world prices of intermediates change, so would the schedule. For example, the envelope would become much steeper if the world relative price of cotton were much higher. The construction of this envelope resembles the technique described in the appendix to Chapter 7, whereby the specific factor model in Chapter 6 converges over time to Chapter 7's Heckscher-Ohlin model as one type of specific capital is converted to another. This conversion takes place here through trade instead. A more general discussion of this phenomenon is contained in K. Sanyal and R. Jones, "The Theory of Trade in Middle Products," *American Economic Review*, 72 (March 1982): 16–31.

[8] As Lionel McKenzie observed in a classic article, nineteenth-century England would be unlikely to produce and export cotton textiles if it had to grow its own cotton. See L. W. McKenzie, "Specialisation and Efficiency in World Production," *Review of Economic Studies*, 21 (June 1954): 179.

FIGURE 9.3   The Marginal Value and Costs of Intermediates

World prices of final goods are fixed on world markets. The downward-sloping MV_I curve shows the marginal value (at these world prices) of another unit of intermediates (fertilizer or an equivalent value of cotton) in producing final food and clothing. At intermediate price p_I, optimal level of intermediate use is OT, which necessitates a deficit in resources trade for a country whose own value is OJ and a surplus for a country with intermediate endowment ON.

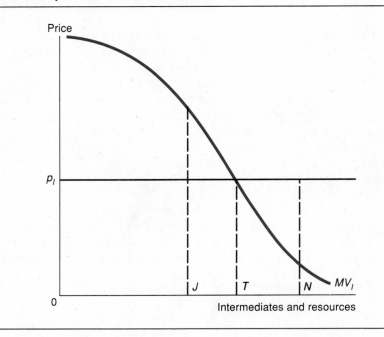

inputs. That is, the wider the range of potential inputs supplied by world markets, the greater the output attainable per given expenditure.[9]

Even *further* gains are obtainable if countries avail themselves of the possibility of unbalanced trade in intermediates. As Figure 9.1 points out, countries such as Japan rely on trade primarily to export final goods to obtain an excess of intermediates and resources over the levels found naturally at home. By contrast, Norway has a trade pattern involving exports of a variety of intermediates and materials, with the balance used to finance imports of final goods.

To pursue this possibility of unbalanced trade in intermediates, consider Figure 9.3, which shows a declining marginal value of intemediates schedule given a fixed underlying endowment of capital and labor (much as Figure 6.4 showed for labor's productivity in food or clothing, given fixed supplies of capital and land). Figure 9.3 contrasts in our model the marginal value of another unit of intermediates and resources with the price of such a bundle on world markets. For prevailing world prices of fertilizer and cotton, calculate the value of the country's own bundle of these

[9] This argument is presented in W. Ethier, "National and International Returns to Scale in the Modern Theory of International Trade," *American Economic Review*, 72 (June 1982): 389–405.

two resources and show this value on the horizontal axis. At given world prices of these final goods, by how much will the value of final food plus clothing production rise if another unit of resources (in whatever proportions desirable) is made available? For a country such as Japan, with the value of its own resources only OJ, the marginal value of obtaining another unit of intermediates and resources through international trade would exceed the world cost, p_I. By contrast, an original value of ON for a country such as Norway reveals that another unit of resources would increase net production of final goods (at world prices) by less than the cost of these resources. The implication is clear: Japan should purchase more intermediates and resources on world markets (to move from OJ to OT); Norway should sell off some of its bundle. As Figure 9.1 suggests, countries that lie near the 45° line on net conduct close to balanced trade in intermediates and resources (i.e., are already near point OT in Figure 9.3), although a healthy exchange of products with other countries within each category (final goods, resources, and intermediates) may well characterize these countries' trade patterns.

9.3 THE NEWLY INDUSTRIALIZING COUNTRIES AND FOOTLOOSE PRODUCTION PROCESSES

The rapid expansion of certain finished-good processes in the LDCs has significantly changed the structure of international trade during the past two decades. A small but important group of LDCs, often called Newly Industrializing Countries (NICs), enjoyed increases of threefold or more in the real values of their manufactured exports from 1973 to the end of the 1970s and by the mid-1980s seven of them were among the world's twenty largest exporters. The NICs include Hong Kong, Singapore, Taiwan, South Korea, Argentina, Brazil, and Mexico. (Some lists include several others.) The manufactures in question are mostly finished consumer goods: Clothing, footwear, and electronics predominate. The production processes typically involve the simple assembly of imported raw materials. Because no extensive or highly specialized capital goods or labor skills are required, these activities are easily expanded in any country where they prove profitable. By the same token, they are quickly contracted in a country where they prove unprofitable. They are sometimes referred to as "footloose." (The athletic-shoe industry is, happily, an example.) The growth of these activities led to rejoicing over the advances in real income enjoyed by the developing NICs, but these activities posed severe policy problems for the industrial countries, who found their own manufacturing industries being rapidly competed down.

NICs' Exports and the Heckscher-Ohlin Theorem

The Heckscher-Ohlin theorem proves valuable for explaining which production processes have gravitated to the NICs. Hal B. Lary proposed a simple way to flag the products most likely to appear among the expanding exports of the LDCs.[10] The lower an industry's value added per worker in the United States, the more likely are the developing countries to be its exporters. Value added per worker is the sum of

---

[10] Hal B. Lary, *Imports of Manufactures from Less-Developed Countries* (New York: National Bureau of Economic Research, 1968).

an industry's payments to all primary factors of production divided by its number of employees. Value added per worker can be high because the industry uses a large amount of physical capital or pays rents for the use of natural resources. It can be high because the industry's workers are highly paid. Among industries, differences in average pay are closely associated with the average amount of human capital and skills possessed by its employees. Value added per worker, therefore, is a respectable summary indicator of how much capital (of all sorts) the industry requires. Furthermore, if there are no factor-intensity reversals, an industry that is capital-intensive in the United States can only operate with relatively capital-intensive technology in other nations, even if all industrial technologies offer some possibilities for using relatively more labor in countries where wages are low.

Lary's investigations suggested that factor-intensity reversals are not an important problem among manufacturing industries. Later studies have confirmed Lary's conjecture about LDCs' factor endowments and export patterns. The less capital (both physical and human) a country possesses, the more labor-intensive are its exports (that is, the smaller is value added per worker in the corresponding industry in the United States).[11]

While labor-intensive manufactures prevail in the NICs' exports, differences appear among these countries in the capital and skill intensity of their exports. For countries on the lower fringes of the NICs, textiles and related goods are typically three-fifths or more of their manufactured exports; top-tier NICs, however, have lowered their concentration in textiles and clothing and export more consumer engineering goods and capital goods. Footloose activities using low-skill labor are shifting from countries such as Taiwan and Hong Kong to less-developed Asian nations. In fact, manufactured goods that the LDCs export to each other are typically more capital-intensive than their exports of manufactures to the industrial countries. Also, other LDCs receive a disproportionately large share of the capital goods that LDCs export. As expected, labor intensity is less fundamental to the LDCs' trade with each other than it is to their trade with the industrial countries.[12]

Pulls on Footloose Activities: *Maquiladoras* in Mexico

That simple, footloose processing activities gravitate to the NICs is consistent with the efficient use of the world's resources. Public policy, however, has exerted its own pull. One device used by the NICs to promote these activities is the *export processing zone*. About eighty of these zones existed in 1982, mostly in LDCs. A zone represents nothing more than a package of measures to make production costs lower than they would otherwise be for producers allowed into the zones. The zones are located to facilitate the assembly of imported components and their export as finished goods. No tariffs are levied on the imported inputs, and the government often subsidizes the zone's infrastructure costs. Administrative procedures are simplified, and various

---

[11] Bela Balassa, "The Changing Pattern of Comparative Advantage in Manufactured Goods," *Review of Economics and Statistics*, 61 (May 1979): 259–266; Mario I. Blejer, "Income Per Capita and the Structure of Industrial Exports: An Empirical Study," *Review of Economics and Statistics*, 60 (November 1978): 555–561. Blejer found that he had to sort out the natural resource–intensive industries to make his results stand out clearly, as we did in assessing the factor content of U.S. trade.

[12] Oli Havrylyshyn and Martin Wolf, "Recent Trends in Trade among Developing Countries," *European Economic Review*, 21 (June 1983): 333–362.

financial concessions and subsidies are offered. Specifically, "tax holidays" often excuse businesses (especially multinational companies based abroad) from paying taxes on their net incomes for a period of time (5 to 20 years). These zones cause the host country's factors of production to be reallocated toward activities permitted in them and away from other uses in the host countries. The favored activities typically employ low-skill labor and little capital, sell all or most of their output abroad, and employ labor that in LDCs may have quite low opportunity costs. From an international viewpoint, the zones allow countries to compete with each other in an effort to attract these processing activities. The competition may take the form of explicitly bidding for the processing business of multinational companies, which are highly flexible about where they locate these activities.[13]

Another policy affecting the location of these footloose industries is a provision in the tariff structures of the United States and other major industrial countries that allows companies to export materials for processing overseas and to reimport the finished products, paying tariffs only on the value added abroad (not the exported intermediates). This provision encourages enterprises in the industrial country to subcontract certain processing steps overseas. The ideal step to subcontract is labor-intensive. The labor intensity makes it worthwhile to transfer the production stage to the LDC, although the other stages may be efficiently carried on in the industrial country. Shipping costs for the subcontracted article must be low or the round-trip transportation cost (outbound intermediate good, inbound finished product) devours the production-cost savings. Cloth to be sewn into garments and semiconductor devices to be wired or assembled both satisfy these requirements. Empirical evidence shows that offshore processing of goods reimported to the United States is pulled toward countries with low wages, favorable government policies, and locations that are not too distant. Industries that make heavy use of the provision require little skilled labor but suffer from high wages in the United States. As expected, they have low shipping costs. Their production stages are divisible, a fact revealed by large amounts of trade in these same intermediate products among domestic firms.[14] No less than one-tenth of U.S. merchandise imports enter under these provisions for overseas processing.

An excellent illustration is the *maquiladoras* in northern Mexico—assembly plants controlled by multinational firms that process imported materials and components for export, mostly to the United States. The area is perfectly situated for footloose activities, is close to a major market, and has low unit labor costs for workers possessing the relatively simple skills required. These plants began operating under a 1966 treaty between the United States and Mexico that established specific export processing zones. The geographic restriction was lifted, however, and the plants have spread widely. As a consequence, the six Mexican states along the U.S. border now generate 22 percent of Mexico's gross national product, and the number of *maquiladoras* doubled (to 1,250) between 1982 and 1988.

[13] See D. Wall, "Export Processing Zones," *Journal of World Trade Law*, 10 (September 1976): 478–489; F. Fröbel, J. Heinrichs, and O. Kreye, *The New International Division of Labour* (Cambridge, UK: Cambridge University Press, 1980), Part III.

[14] Michael Sharpston, "International Sub-contracting," *Oxford Economic Papers*, 27 (March 1975): 94–135; J. Peter Jarrett, "Offshore Assembly and Production and the Internalization of International Trade Within the Multinational Corporation," Ph. D. dissertation (Harvard University, 1979), Chapters 7 and 8.

The Product Cycle: The Shrinking U.S. Lead in Innovation

Production processes also may be footloose in a long-run context. Economists have noticed that production of some final goods tends to migrate from country to country over a long period that stretches from their infancy as innovations to their decline as obsolete goods displaced by newer innovations. The course of their migration has an economic logic. Because innovations frequently create new opportunities to substitute capital for labor, either in production (electronic data processing) or consumption (dishwashing machines), they tend to arise in the high-income countries. These innovations are most valuable in high-income countries, where labor is most costly, and people thus devote the most effort to devising ways to economize on it. Innovative goods also are produced at the outset on a small scale by highly skilled labor, an operation well suited to the factor endowments of high-income countries. Once an innovation becomes established, it also finds markets abroad and becomes an export for the innovating country. When the good's technology becomes settled, producers start searching for ways to produce it on a large scale as cheaply as possible. Mass production with less-skilled labor becomes feasible, and production is pulled toward countries with lower labor costs (multinational companies may be involved in these transfers). The LDCs eventually may become significant producers, if the good's input requirements are suited to them, or the product simply may recede in importance as superior substitutes are introduced.[15]

The product cycle holds important implications for the structure of international trade. The exports of high-income countries that spend heavily on R&D (research and development), such as the United States, should show a prevalence of innovative goods, and their gains from trade should be augmented by the profits from innovations not yet imitated abroad. The evidence has long confirmed this hypothesis for the United States,[16] although it also suggests that America may be losing its margin of advantage. R&D spending has declined as a percentage of gross national product in the United States. Although the U.S. rate of R&D spending still exceeds the rates of most other industrial countries, many of theirs are increasing while the U.S. rate declines. Several forces may be speeding the diffusion of innovations. International transportation and communication have improved greatly, so the news about industrial innovations travels quickly around the globe. There is a rapidly growing international market in proprietary technology, whereby new industrial knowledge is licensed between independent firms or transferred administratively within multinational companies. Developing countries sometimes are eager to establish high-technology industries, even if these industries are not ideally suited to their production capabilities.

These factors suggest that U.S. international trade reflects a balance of dynamic factors: Innovations add to American exports and improve the terms of trade for American factors of production; the diffusion of innovations and resultant migration of processes abroad deteriorate those terms. Some recent evidence suggests that dif-

[15] Raymond Vernon, "International Investment and International Trade in the Product Cycle," *Quarterly Journal of Economics*, 80 (May 1966): 190–207; G. C. Hufbauer, *Synthetic Materials and the Theory of International Trade* (Cambridge, MA: Harvard University Press, 1966), Chapter 6.

[16] W. Gruber, D. Mehta, and R. Vernon, "The R&D Factor in International Trade and International Investment of United States Industries," *Journal of Political Economy*, 75 (February 1967): 20–37.

fusion processes are gaining in this race. This matter can be put to a specific test. Within the United States, outputs of the high-technology industries naturally have been growing faster than those of other manufacturing sectors. If the U.S. lead in innovation were widening, the U.S. high-technology sectors should not only be growing rapidly, but they also should be growing faster than their counterparts in other countries. The opposite, however, is the case. The higher an industry is in the technology scale (measured by R&D spending as a percentage of sales), the slower is U.S. output growing relative to output in the rest of the world. That pattern holds whether the United States is compared to the European Community, Japan, or various groups of developing nations.[17] The U.S. gains from trade in innovative goods thus may be slipping. It is not clear whether U.S. policy can or should do anything about this slippage; it may be simply that "all good things come to an end."

The Heckscher-Ohlin approach to international trade sheds some light on this accelerating diffusion of production processes. The relationship between the net exports of various U.S. manufacturing industries and their use of highly skilled labor and research inputs is becoming more pronounced over time.[18] That other industrial countries may be catching up as innovators does not mean the United States is dropping from the race as a net exporter of innovative goods. The competition confronting U.S. goods on world markets grows stronger partly because other industrial countries have been increasing their endowments of physical and human capital per worker faster than the United States, narrowing the factor-proportions basis for America's comparative advantage.[19]

9.4 FOOTLOOSE INPUTS: THE JOINT ROLE OF COMPARATIVE AND ABSOLUTE ADVANTAGE

The doctrine of comparative advantage points out that the absolute level of efficiency of inputs does not determine a nation's trade pattern. Poor climate and technology at home may contribute to less-efficient labor both in raising food and making clothing, but if such inefficiency is relatively less pronounced in the clothing sector, the home country exports clothing. This basic truth is thus strongly linked to the vision of trade offered in the classical paradigm: International markets are limited to final goods, while inputs are trapped within a nation's boundaries. Suppose, however, some productive inputs are footloose: They can be attracted to the country offering the highest return. In such a case, production and trade patterns internationally are determined by *absolute* advantage as well as *comparative* advantage.

To construct a model that can jointly handle the importance of absolute as well as comparative advantage, we adapt the Ricardian model of Chapter 5. Stick to the

[17] Thomas A. Pugel, "The Changing Position of U.S. Industries in the Global Pattern of International Production," *Special Study on Economic Change*, Vol. 9. *The International Economy: U.S. Role in a World Market*. U.S. Congress, Joint Economic Committee, Special Study on Economic Change (Washington: Government Printing Office, 1980).

[18] Keith E. Maskus, "Evidence on Shifts in the Determinants of the Structure of U.S. Manufacturing Foreign Trade, 1958–1976," *Review of Economics and Statistics*, 65 (August 1983): 415–422.

[19] Harry P. Bowen, "Changes in the International Distribution of Resources and Their Impact on U.S. Comparative Advantage," *Review of Economics and Statistics*, 65 (August 1983): 402–414. Direct measures of the size and quality of countries' technology stocks have become available to confirm this pattern (*New York Times*, May 28, 1991, pp. C1, C8).

two-commodity, food and clothing scenario, but now introduce an asymmetry in the way these two commodities are produced. As before, let food require labor only, with a_{LF} and a_{LF}^* denoting fixed unit requirements in the two countries. By contrast, clothing requires not only labor (a_{LC} and a_{LC}^*) but also the services of some internationally footloose factor, which we simply call A. To keep matters simple, suppose the pair of input coefficients (a_{LC} and a_{AC} at home, a_{LC}^* and a_{AC}^* abroad) is constant, but allow for intercountry differences not only in labor skills but also in the technology whereby A is used in clothing production. Input A is footloose in the sense that it is attracted to the country that can offer it the highest return (denoted by R_A, if at home, or R_A^* abroad).

Some of the lessons of the simple, competitive Ricardian model are applicable here as well. Each country must produce something in a free-trade equilibrium—food, clothing, or both. Competition ensures that unit cost equals price for any activity actually undertaken and does not fall below price (suggesting profitable opportunities that would be bid away in a competitive equilibrium) for activities not undertaken. Suppose world prices of food and clothing are determined in a large world market. Which of these two countries is in a better position to attract the services of footloose factor A? Here we restrict our attention only to these two countries as potential employers of A; later we ask whether A would be attracted to either of these countries if a larger world market exists. Technology for producing food in each country puts a floor on the wage rate. Thus, at home, Equation 9.1 reveals the minimum value for the home wage rate, w:

$$a_{LF}w = p_F \tag{9.1}$$

If the wage rate were higher, the home food sector would prove noncompetitive in world markets. For the home clothing sector, the prevailing world price of clothing, home technology, and this minimal level for home wages help determine the maximum amount, R_A, that the home country could bid to obtain the services of footloose factor A. These are formally related by Equation 9.2:

$$a_{LC}w + a_{AC}R_A = p_C \tag{9.2}$$

Now divide Equation 9.1 into Equation 9.2 to obtain:

$$\frac{a_{LC}}{a_{LF}} + a_{AC}\frac{R_A}{p_F} = \frac{p_C}{p_F} \tag{9.3}$$

This expression reveals, with given world commodity prices of food and clothing, the maximum amount that the home clothing industry could pay to obtain footloose input A. Of course, if the wage rate were even lower than the breakeven point for food production shown by Equation 9.1, more could be released to attract input A, but the existence of profitable activity in the food sector would bid up wages again.

Technology differs abroad, so that although foreign producers face the same prices for traded food and clothing, the maximum amount their clothing sector could pay to obtain A, without incurring losses, is R_A^*, shown in Equation 9.4:

$$\frac{a_{LC}^*}{a_{LF}^*} + a_{AC}^*\frac{R_A^*}{p_F} = \frac{p_C}{p_F} \tag{9.4}$$

A comparison of Equations 9.3 and 9.4 clearly reveals that the ability to attract the footloose input required to produce clothing depends both on potential *comparative* advantage in labor costs (a_{LC}/a_{LF} versus a^*_{LC}/a^*_{LF}) as well as an *absolute* superiority in the productivity of footloose input A (a_{AC} versus a^*_{AC}). In Figure 9.4 it is assumed that the home country possesses the absolute advantage in employing the footloose input (a_{AC} is smaller than a^*_{AC}), while comparative labor costs in producing clothing favor the foreign country. Relative world prices of clothing and food are shown on the vertical axis, and the maximum amount each country could pay to attract footloose input A is shown on the horizontal. The vertical intercepts of each line reveal comparative labor costs, while the slopes of the lines reflect absolute costs of the footloose input (A) in clothing production.

Armed with this apparatus, it is now possible to discuss several issues concerning trade and production patterns that arise when not all inputs have strictly national markets.

Who Produces What?

The answer to the question "Which country is better able to attract footloose factor A (and thus actively produce clothing)?" is "It depends." In particular it depends on whether clothing's price is relatively high, in which case the return to footloose factor

FIGURE 9.4   Comparative and Absolute Advantage

For relatively high world prices of clothing (above OD) the home country could outbid the foreign country to attract the internationally footloose input used to produce clothing. Below OD, relative labor costs become more important and production patterns switch so that the foreign country produces clothing.

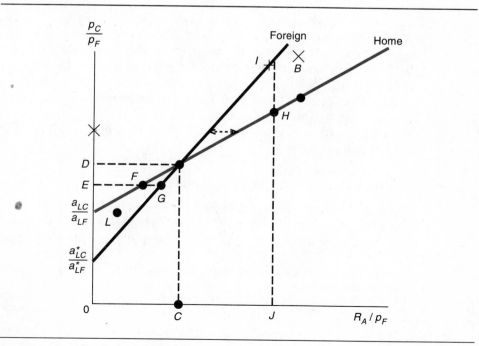

A is also high and, with such payments looming as important in the cost picture, the high-bidding country for A is the country with the superior technology for using A. In Figure 9.4, for any p_C/p_F exceeding OD, the home country can outbid the foreign country in attracting A. Conversely, low relative prices for clothing imply a low return for A, in which case relative labor costs loom as more important, just as in standard Ricardian theory. For example, at a clothing relative price given by OE, the foreign country can offer EG for use of A and still break even producing clothing, while the home country, with a comparative disadvantage in labor costs, could only offer EF for A. The vertical comparisons for any given value for R_A/p_F are also instructive. If the latter value in world markets is OJ, the foreign country's relative cost of producing clothing (JI) exceeds that at home (JH), and the home country would be the producer of clothing.

It is perhaps more instructive to imagine both home and foreign country embedded in a multicountry trading nexus in which the commodity prices *and* the rate of return to footloose input A are determined by world market forces. That is, these prices are shown by some point in Figure 9.4. Suppose this is point B. The foreign country cannot compete in the clothing sector. By contrast, the home country can successfully pay the going rate for input A and establish a competitive clothing industry. But point B lies above the home relative cost curve in Figure 9.4. This reveals that the home wage rate would be bid above the level that would allow home food production. In sum, at point B the home country is specialized in clothing, the foreign country in food. Should clothing and the return to footloose A become cheaper with the passage of time, moving to say, point L, clothing production would shift to the foreign low-wage country as relative labor costs became more important.[20]

The Product Cycle Once Again

Some aspects of the *product cycle* discussed in the preceding section can be illustrated here. The home country develops a new product (clothing) in which unskilled labor costs are relatively unimportant compared with high skilled labor (factor A, perhaps not footloose internationally) found locally in plentiful supply. During the development process, new techniques are developed and technology shifts toward relatively unskilled labor-intensive techniques. In Figure 9.4 imagine input requirements of the skilled input, a_{AC} and a_{AC}^*, dropping over time. The lines become flatter, point C drifts rightward, and production shifts toward countries with comparatively low (unskilled) labor costs.

National Tax Treatments and Absolute Advantage

The doctrine of comparative advantage recognizes that differences between countries that affect some industries in a *differential* fashion have an impact on trade patterns. This doctrine, however, denies the role of countries' characteristics that affect all local

---

[20] In the past 40 years the location of the American textile industry has shifted from the North to the South. Southern climate (especially high humidity and temperature) does not naturally favor textiles, but this advantage can be overcome by air-conditioning if electricity becomes cheap enough. In Figure 9.4 associate footloose input A with energy (or electricity) and the South, where higher energy inputs are required, with the foreign country.

sectors uniformly. Once international trade invades the markets for inputs into the production process, such a neglect of national characteristics is no longer appropriate.

For example, suppose tax rates on earned incomes are uniformly higher in one country than in another. If inputs are *not* internationally mobile, such a difference in national tax treatments does not affect production patterns. But if some inputs are footloose, their location will be influenced by taxes. Other things being equal, footloose inputs will be attracted to countries with low tax rates on earnings. Similarly, differences between governments in attitudes toward expropriation of firms or differences in overall levels of social overhead capital can steer footloose inputs toward some countries and away from others. Pollution controls provide another example. South Korea and Hong Kong have recently been under pressure to tighten up their controls over "dirty" industry. As a consequence, some of these processes have been shifted to countries like Thailand.[21]

Suppose, in Figure 9.4, the foreign country is uniformly a "better" place to work than the home country is in a sense that can be translated into an absolute lowering of all input requirements in all sectors. The vertical intercept of the foreign curve is unaffected; this reflects only *comparative* labor costs. The foreign schedule becomes flatter, however, and, if world commodity prices initially precluded foreign production of clothing, such a change in foreign national characteristics could alter its production pattern. That is, uniform tax reduction could serve to attract the footloose input to the clothing sector as the foreign country becomes a relatively more attractive locale.

Comparative Advantage and Dutch Disease

Finally, the enduring role of comparative advantage can be revealed in the following example. Suppose that the home country initially produces both goods and that a new innovation is introduced into the national food industry, serving to lower the labor requirement, a_{LF}. The home country's schedule in Figure 9.4 then shifts upward, possibly wiping out the home country's clothing sector. Despite the fact that no change has taken place in the production techniques for clothing or in the world prices of clothing and food, the country has developed a stronger *comparative* advantage in producing food. The wage rate rises, and footloose input A leaves the country for other parts of the world where wages have not risen. This is the Dutch Disease once again, with some inputs (A) now escaping the penalty of a shift in comparative advantage by possessing international mobility.

9.5 SUMMARY

Goods require as inputs not only capital and labor but also other goods, so that the production processes that give rise to a given finished product may be carried on in a number of countries. Nations differ in the roles of intermediate and finished goods in their exports and imports. Broadly speaking, the industrial countries are net importers of intermediate goods from the developing countries, but the industrial coun-

---

[21] *The Economist* of November 16, 1991, cites an increase from 25 percent to 55 percent of total applications for foreign investment "whose activities would produce significant amounts of hazardous wastes" in Thailand in the two-year period 1987 to 1989.

tries differ among themselves, and the developing countries have rapidly expanded their finished-good exports. Long-run trends in the terms of trade for finished goods relative to intermediates have long been a matter for debate, but neither clear historical trends nor persuasive predictions for the future can be found.

Balanced international trade in intermediate goods serves to expand a country's production-possibilities curve for final goods. This kind of trade thus allows gains to each country over and above those described in earlier chapters where final goods alone are traded on world markets. But countries such as Japan and Norway illustrate that yet further gains can be achieved by running an overall deficit (Japan) or surplus (Norway) in intermediate goods and resources trade.

The consumer goods exported by the NICs typically are produced by low-skill labor working with imported inputs. Such activities are "footloose" (easily relocated) and are well suited to developing countries according to the Heckscher-Ohlin theorem. Governments exploit this footloose property by policies that lower the input costs of businesses in these export-oriented activities. In a long-run context the product cycle describes the migration of production processes from the higher-income countries where they originate. United States exports are slanted toward new products, but the U.S. terms of trade may be suffering because of increased competition from innovators in other countries.

The existence of "footloose" inputs implies that world production patterns are affected by the *absolute* advantage each country possesses in employing such inputs, as well as by the *comparative* advantage imparted by labor or other factors trapped within national boundaries. Differences among countries in levels of taxation and provision of social overhead capital, as well as absolute levels of productive efficiency, become important determinants of the international location of productive activity when some inputs are internationally mobile, although such differences have little effect in a classical world in which only final consumer goods enter world trade.

CHAPTER PROBLEMS

1. A country such as the United Kingdom lies above the 45° line in Figure 9.1 because primary and intermediate imports represent a greater percentage of total imports than of total exports. Some of the countries listed, however, were running overall balance-of-trade surpluses or deficits. When adjustments are made for these imbalances, which countries had imports of primary and intermediate goods that exceeded exports of primary and intermediate goods?

2. In Figure 9.3 interpret the triangular region between the horizontal p_I line and the MV_I curve for the range from OJ to OT. What is the relationship between such an area and the gains from trade?

3. With reference to Figure 9.3 draw a transformation curve for country J and another for country N. For each country draw a budget line in the (food, clothing) space along which consumption takes place. How does the position of this budget line compare with a budget line that corresponds to trade when no trade in intermediate goods is allowed?

4. Draw a transformation schedule for a country that can trade one intermediate good for another, but which must have balanced trade separately in intermediates and final goods. If it is like country J in Figure 9.3, show how its transformation curve for final goods and its budget line shift if it can trade intermediates for final goods. Do the same for country N.

5. Explain why countries with relatively ample supplies of low-wage unskilled labor tend to produce goods at the "end" rather than the "beginning" of the product cycle.
6. With reference to the discussion of footloose factors in Section 9.4, suppose the fixed home labor costs for producing a unit of clothing and a unit of food are four hours and one hour, respectively, while comparable labor requirements in a foreign country are one hour apiece. Clothing production requires, as well, fixed units of some footloose productive input, A. Suppose the home country has an absolute advantage in its use of A: Only one unit of A is required to produce a unit of clothing, whereas two units of A are required abroad. Let the world price of food be $1. What are the pattern of production and the wage rate in each country if:
   a. The world price of clothing is $5.50 per unit and footloose factor A commands $2?
   b. The world price of clothing rises to $8 per unit and footloose factor A rises to $4?
   In case (b) suppose at home labor becomes more efficient in its production of food. Describe the impact on the production pattern at home and link the result to the phenomenon of the Dutch Disease.

SUGGESTIONS FOR FURTHER READING

Baumol, William J., Sue Ann Batey Blackman, and Edward N. Wolff. *Productivity and American Leadership: The Long View* (Cambridge, MA: M.I.T. Press, 1989). Natural resources and technological diffusion in the U.S. international economic position.

Bradshaw, Thornton F., et al., eds. *America's New Competitors: The Challenge of the Newly Industrializing Countries* (Cambridge, MA: Ballinger, 1988). Case studies and policy issues related to the NICs.

Frobel, F., J. Heinrichs, and O. Kreye. *The New International Division of Labour* (Cambridge, UK: Cambridge University Press, 1980). Part III reports extensive evidence on export processing activities.

Jones, R. W. "Comparative and Absolute Advantage," *Swiss Journal of Economics and Statistics*, 3 (1980): 235–260. A more detailed treatment of the material in Section 9.4.

Sanyal, K., and R. W. Jones. "The Theory of Trade in Middle Products," *American Economic Review*, 72 (1982): 16–31. Develops the view that intermediates and processed raw materials loom large in international trade.

Vanek, Jaroslav. "The Natural Resource Content of Foreign Trade, 1870–1955, and the Relative Abundance of Natural Resources in the United States," *Review of Economics and Statistics*, 41 (May 1959): 146–153. Traces the decline in relative abundance of natural resources in the United States.

Vernon, Raymond. "International Investment and International Trade in the Product Cycle," *Quarterly Journal of Economics*, 80 (May 1966): 190–207. Original statement of the product-cycle hypothesis.

———. "The Product Cycle Hypothesis in a New International Environment," *Oxford Bulletin of Economics and Statistics*, 41 (November 1979): 255–267. Autumnal thoughts on the product cycle.

10

INTERNATIONAL FACTOR MOVEMENTS AND MULTINATIONAL COMPANIES

Our focus so far has been on the international movement of goods and services. However, some of the most dramatic changes in the international economy have been caused by international movements of factors of production. In the nineteenth century the countries of Europe sent forth their workers and capital in great quantities to develop nearly empty regions. Today the countries of northern Europe supplement their work forces with migrants from southern Europe, and multinational companies carry on the international reallocation of capital. This chapter begins by examining how international factor movements are related to trade and economic welfare, and then explores the many policy issues relating to the multinational company.

10.1 FACTOR MOVEMENTS: THE EFFICIENCY OF WORLD PRODUCTION

Gains from trade occur because goods move from where their relative prices are low (in the absence of trade) to where they are high. Economic welfare can also be increased when factors of production move to places where they are better paid. For either factors or goods, when their prices equal their (marginal) values to society, the efficiency of the world economy is increased by a movement from a low-price location to a higher one.

Chapter 9 discussed the extra gains available to each trading nation if intermediate products and resources can be exchanged on world markets. Such gains are illustrated by outward shifts in the economy's production-possibilities curve when trade in such intermediates is balanced. For the world as a whole, efficiency is further served to the extent that primary factors, such as labor, can migrate from regions of relatively low returns to regions of higher returns. Production may contract in some countries and expand in others, but for the world as a whole such an international movement of factors serves to increase outputs. As will be discussed further in Chapter 12, such a conclusion presupposes that factor returns in various countries accurately reflect the productivity of factors. By contrast, if some countries use tariffs, subsidies, or taxes to attract foreign capital, such flows may be detrimental to world outputs and, indeed, may actually harm the countries into which the capital flows.

The Heckscher-Ohlin model, introduced in Chapter 7, illustrates how trade confined to final commodities may be sufficient to bring about the full equalization of factor prices without any international mobility of capital or labor. The severity of the assumptions, however, suggests the potential for further efficiency gains through factor mobility. For trade in commodities alone to bring about factor price equalization, countries must share the same technology and differ relatively little in the structure of their factor endowments, so that they also produce similar commodities. Certainly the most casual of observations reveals that these conditions may not be obtained in many cases.

10.2 FACTOR MOVEMENTS: THE EFFECT ON COMMODITY TRADE

One of the underlying themes of standard Heckscher-Ohlin theory is that international trade in commodities goes at least part way in substituting for international mobility of productive factors. Thus, world efficiency would be enhanced if capital, for example, could flow from capital-abundant to labor-abundant countries. Barring such a possibility, though, discrepancies in the returns to capital among countries are lessened by a trade pattern that allows relatively capital-abundant countries to export capital-intensive commodities. That is, the volume of international trade in commodities could be reduced if productive factors are freed to move to locations where their returns are higher. This view suggests that trade in commodities and international mobility of factors can be interchangeable.

Freeing primary factors to move internationally could cause trade in commodities to expand instead of contract. James Markusen analyzed this possibility by considering two countries differing in only one of the many ways that could encourage commodity trade.[1] Suppose, as in Heckscher-Ohlin theory, that two countries share the same technology but differ in relative factor endowments. If factors of production could move internationally, the basis for commodity trade would be eroded; trade and factor movements are interchangeable. Now suppose factor endowments are identical but trade is encouraged because the home country has a Ricardian technological superiority in producing the labor-intensive good. With trade, the home country is encouraged to increase its production of the labor-intensive good (so as to export it), which serves to drive up home wages compared to foreign wages. If, now, factors can move between countries, foreign labor is attracted to the home country, which serves to *expand* trade in commodities. The reason: Home exports of labor-intensive goods are encouraged by the inflow of labor.

The general results are clear. If the basis for the international exchange of final commodities resides in differences in factor endowments, allowing these factors to move directly between countries obviates the need for commodity trade. However, if

---

[1] See James Markusen, "Factor Movements and Commodity Trade as Complements," *Journal of International Economics*, 14 (May 1983): 341–356.

the basis for trade lies in other reasons (technological differences, as in Ricardo, increasing returns to scale, etc.), trade by itself will tend to raise the return to factors used intensively in each nation's export sector. Factor mobility that responds to such differentials adds a factor-endowment basis for expanded commodity trade.

Sometimes the international mobility of factors is a prerequisite for the development of commodity trade. Proponents of this view often point to the extraction and export of natural resources in many less-developed regions, extraction made possible by foreign investment undertaken by Europe and the United States.[2] On the other hand, deliberate protectionist policies may reduce trade significantly if they encourage the inflow of capital to avoid the tariff barriers. In such a case, factor mobility has enhanced the anti-trade nature of protection. Foreign investment may serve to expand production of a nation's exportables or, as above, to encourage production of import-competing products. Much of the large flow of American foreign investment to Europe during the 1960s was viewed as a response to the unified tariff walls of the newly created European Community, and capital flows similarly anticipated further internal unification 1992 (see Chapter 15).

10.3 MIGRATION AND INCOME DISTRIBUTION

Although factor movements can increase the efficiency of the world economy, they often are restricted by governments serving what they see as their national interests. Immigration of labor in particular is always under strict control. This section considers the effect of factor movements on income distribution and efficiency within the receiving country.

Gains from Migration

As Chapters 6 and 7 detailed, changing factor endowments alter the distribution of income in a way that depends on the nation's apparatus of production. The effect of an inflow of a factor from abroad is generally like that of a natural increase in its stock. Consider the mode, developed in Chapter 6, in which capital and land are specific factors used only in the clothing and food industries (respectively), but labor is mobile between industries. A wave of immigration drives down wages, as expected, but it raises the rewards to both land and capital. An inflow of capital depresses the returns to capital and raises wages; it also hurts the landlords because labor is pulled from food production into clothing and the marginal product of land falls. The capitalists and landlords would be expected to join in favoring free immigration but restricted capital inflows, and the workers to take the opposite position—but what of the national income as a whole? Is there any gain from immigration that could be divided up to make all the native factors better off?

We can gain some insight into this problem by considering a simple model in which all residents at home own the same bundle of two factors of production—labor and capital, for example. Suppose, also, that the country produces only one commodity and does not exchange goods with other countries. This situation is illustrated in

---

[2] See, for example, A. P. Schmitz and P. Helmberger, "Factor Mobility and International Trade: the Case of Complementarity," *American Economic Review*, 60 (September 1970): 761–767.

FIGURE 10.1   Immigration Benefits Home Residents

The community owns the labor and capital shown by bundle *A*. Preimmigration factor prices are given by the slope line *BB*. Immigration alters factor prices, allowing owners of bundle *A* to trade factor services to command output Q_3 at *D*, greater than initial Q_1.

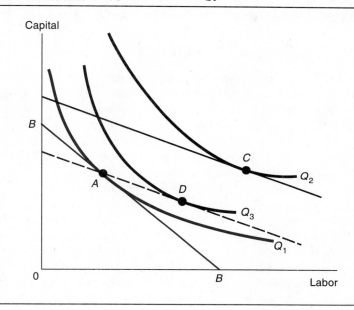

Figure 10.1. The original inhabitants possess the factor-endowment combination shown by point *A*, and the factor price ratio is given by the slope of line *BB* tangent to isoquant Q_1 at *A*. The community consumes what it produces, quantity Q_1. Suppose now that immigration is allowed, and that the new entrants bring with them, on average, less capital per person than the original group possesses. The new aggregate capital-labor bundle is a point such as *C*, with the enlarged community producing quantity Q_2 and the capital-poor immigration reflected in the lower wage/rental ratio shown by the slope of the Q_2 isoquant at *C*. The question raised concerns the fate of the original inhabitants. At the new factor prices the capital-labor bundle *A*, their endowment, is worth the same as bundle *D*. Yet *D* can produce quantity Q_3, which is greater than Q_1. In short, the original inhabitants can now consume more of the single commodity produced than they could before immigration.[3]

This argument is not new. It is a rehash of Chapter 2's account of the gains to be derived when a community can trade at prices different from those originally prevailing at home. The novel element is that there is only one commodity, and the new prices are factor prices. The original inhabitants, whose factor-endowment bundle is shown by point *A* in Figure 10.1, are viewed as trading *factor services* with an outside community at "terms of trade" for factors that would differ from those at home before

---

[3] The foregoing argument was suggested by Harry G. Johnson in "Some Economic Aspects of Brain Drain," *Pakistan Development Review*, 7 (August 1967): 379–411.

immigration. As long as immigration possess a different factor-endowment bundle than the original inhabitants, thus causing a change in the wage/rental ratio, the original community will gain. The major warning to be issued with this type of analysis is that it ignores possible effects of immigration on a country's terms of trade. Should the country attract primarily those skills and resources used intensively in its export sectors, local incomes could be hurt, as was explained in Chapter 4.

Migration of Unskilled Labor to Industrial Countries

The effects of immigration on the distribution of income have been an urgent policy question for most wealthy industrial countries. Every nation legally restricts the flow of immigrants, limiting the total inflow, regulating its national origin, and often favoring the immigration of skilled over unskilled labor. Nonetheless, the United States and the major European countries have all received large inflows of unskilled labor from lower-income countries, and these migrants have brought to the fore the issues of income distribution and national welfare just described.

In the 1960s the European countries faced what they perceived as shortages of unskilled labor. They devised programs for "guest workers" to come from lower-income European countries, presumably for temporary stays and without a change in their basic national allegiances. If the excess demand for unskilled labor should abate, it was thought, these guests could be hustled back to their homelands, in order to avert any unemployment problems in the host countries. The guests' stays proved a lot more permanent than had been anticipated, and in the latter 1970s they made up 10 to 20 percent of the work forces of some European nations. In the United States both legal and clandestine immigration (from Mexico, the Caribbean, and Central and South America) have been heavy. In 1980 about two million illegal immigrants resided in the United States (although some popular estimates were five times higher), and immigrants accounted for 38 percent of U.S. population growth in the 1980s.

Large flows of immigration always raise debates over the migrants' effects on national income and its distribution, not to mention the many questions of social welfare and hostility from directly affected groups of nationals. Researchers have explored the degree to which immigrants, mostly low-skill workers, have reduced the real wages or employment opportunities of closely competing low-skill natives. Some redistribution occurs, but fortunately it appears small. A doubling of immigrants in a typical U.S. industrial city would drive down native unskilled workers' wages by about 4 percent (and the immigrants' own wages by 3 percent). The labor-force participation of low-skilled natives has not fallen in areas with large influxes of immigrants, as it would if job opportunities for natives were foreclosed in the long run.[4]

Immigrants increase the U.S. supply of low-skill labor. Because industries that use low-skill labor intensively tend to be import-competing in the United States (see Section 7.3), we might expect them to enlarge the import-competing sector and possibly reduce the nation's overall participation in international trade. Indeed, in 1980 im-

[4] John M. Abowd and Richard B. Freeman, eds., *Immigration, Trade, and the Labor Market* (Chicago: University of Chicago Press, 1991), especially Chapters 6, 7, 10.

migrants made up 10.4 percent of the labor forces of import-competing industries but only 7.5 percent of the industries exporting most heavily. That pattern is consistent with immigration's having a negative effect on the real income of labor while increasing the incomes of other factors of production (including the human capital of skilled workers).[5]

10.4 INTERNATIONAL CAPITAL MOVEMENTS: SELECTED ISSUES

International capital movements are commonly divided into two classes, depending on whether the lender does or does not acquire decision-making control over the borrowing entity. Portfolio capital transfers occur when lending-country individuals or institutions purchase bonds or other liabilities issued by foreign countries or governments, or acquire foreign companies' equity shares in blocks too small to give the purchasers voting control over the companies. Direct investment, which does carry control over the borrowing entity, is mainly the domain of the multinational company, as is discussed in Section 10.5.

British Foreign Investment in the Nineteenth Century

Net portfolio capital transfers nowadays are quite small, with the major industrial countries rarely exporting capital totaling 1 percent of their gross national products annually. However, between 1870 and 1913 Great Britain placed 5.2 percent of its GNP in net foreign lending, France 2 to 3 percent, Germany somewhat less than 2 percent. Large flows of migration also occurred in those years. The experience still is instructive regarding the economic operation of large-scale international factor movements. The focus here will be on the British economy, which experienced the largest outflows.

It is expected that capital will flow abroad whenever it can earn a higher return than is possible at home. Indeed, during 1870–1913 British portfolio investments abroad did earn higher rates of return than did the portfolio of domestic securities held by British investors. The question is, "What long-run changes opened these gaps in returns to capital, and how did the capital transfers go about eliminating them?" The bulk of British portfolio investments went to the United States and to the overseas dominions, such as Australia and Canada. Ultimately, the capital flows served to complement the labor services of Europeans who emigrated to these areas in the development of the new countries' vast quantities of land and natural resources. This adjustment process can be seen as occupying three centuries—from the initial voyages of discovery and settlement to the beginning of the twentieth century.

In the period 1870–1913 the particular rhythms of this massive process of factor movement can be seen. British foreign investment moved in a somewhat cyclical fashion during this period. When capital was flowing abroad heavily, capital formation

---

[5] Peter Kuhn and Ian Wooton (in Abowd and Freeman, Chapter 10) argue, however, that the story may be more complicated. Skilled labor is used heavily in U.S. exporting industries, while the non-traded-goods sector (cement, electricity) relies heavily on physical capital, which is also the "middle factor" in the traded-goods industries. Increases in the stock of unskilled labor (through immigration or otherwise) could then increase the returns to physical capital while lowering those to both unskilled and skilled labor.

was depressed in Britain's home economy; when home investment revived, foreign investment fell off. These switches between home and foreign investment responded to shifts in rates of return in Britain and abroad, while these rates of return reflected shifts in Britain's international terms of trade for its manufactured exports relative to its imports of food and raw materials. When the country's terms of trade were poor, primary-product prices were high, and so was the profitability of expanding the capital stocks of the recently settled regions. British funds poured into railroad investments in the United States and Australia. Emigration to these areas also went in waves, but their timing was not closely related to the timing of British capital outflows. International capital flows depended not so much on the raw stocks of land and labor in the overseas regions as on the large-scale social capital investments being made there and the degree to which local savings could finance them.[6]

Another aspect of this large flow of capital exports is the "transfer process" that was explained in Section 4.4. Will a transfer of purchasing power disturb the equilibrium terms of trade between the lending and borrowing countries? It depends on how the borrower spends the proceeds and how the lender cuts back on expenditure that would otherwise be made. The changes in their spending decisions determine whether, without a change in the terms of trade, the balance of trade changes by the amount of the transfer. From the casual observation that people spend most of their incomes on locally produced goods, it is probable that the propensities are too low to adjust trade flows to the transfer without a deterioration of the lender's terms of trade. However, Britain was a major supplier of machinery and other manufactures to the borrowing countries as well as a major importer of raw materials from them. The borrowing countries' marginal propensities to import must have been high enough to change trade flows roughly by the amounts of the transfers, because history reveals no obvious evidence of terms-of-trade disturbances or their short-run monetary counterparts. Also, in a broader sense, the transfer of capital was surely smoothed by the simultaneous movement of labor from Britain. The exit of both factors from Britain reduced the pressure for changes in British wages relative to capital rents that otherwise might have arisen.

Models of international capital flows shed light on one historical controversy over these capital exports. J. A. Hobson, in his book *Imperialism* (1902), suggested that Britain's heavy capital outflow reflected "oversaving," which he thought occurred because income was being redistributed from the working classes (who saved little) to the capitalists (who saved large fractions of their incomes). If Hobson was right, these massive capital flows should have been "pushed" out of Britain by declining profits at home rather than "pulled" to the borrowers by high yields abroad. The declining profits would have reflected the fall in the marginal product that occurred as the high-saving capitalists sought to invest their funds at home. Edelstein found that rates of saving out of British national income did increase at times during the period, but he could not confirm that income redistribution was the cause. Also, "pull"

---

[6] Most of the analysis in this section is taken from these sources: A. K. Cairncross, *Home and Foreign Investment, 1870–1913: Studies in Capital Accumulation* (Cambridge, UK: Cambridge University Press, 1953), Chapters 7 and 8; Michael Edelstein, *Overseas Investment in the Age of High Imperialism: The United Kingdom, 1850–1914* (New York: Columbia University Press, 1982).

influences in the borrowing countries were obviously strong, and only at the end of the period was there much evidence that British capital was continuing to flow into Canada despite sinking returns in the borrowing country.[7]

LDC Borrowing in the 1970s

A major flow of international lending went to the less-developed countries (LDCs) in the 1970s and early 1980s. This flow passed chiefly to the larger and better-off LDCs, and its timing reflected the fact that their rates of economic growth in the past two decades (around 5 percent) comfortably exceeded the 3 to 4 percent growth managed by the industrial countries during those years. In a long-run perspective this transfer makes sense in terms of the Heckscher-Ohlin theory—moving capital to the countries with lower capital-labor ratios. However, the lenders' identity is actually a bit complicated. The LDCs did not simply sell bonds to industrial-country capitalists. Rather, they took out direct loans from international institutions (such as the World Bank) and especially from the large international banks. These banks are located in the industrial countries, but their depositors (who ultimately supply the capital) can be anywhere. In particular, a large amount of the privately supplied lending came ultimately from the oil-producing nations, which saved large proportions of their riches from oil sales (discussed in Section 13.2).

By the beginning of 1983, the twenty-one largest borrowers among the LDCs had run up total overseas debts of $514.5 billion, including short-term borrowings of $132.5 billion—as compared to their exports of $299 billion. Receiving these capital flows posed no transfer problem, because the LDCs typically use the bulk of their long-term borrowings to purchase capital goods from abroad, and short-term borrowings are associated with financing imports for consumption. As expected, these borrowings financed a bulge in capital formation. For the LDCs as a whole, gross domestic investment was more than 26 percent of gross national product in the late 1970s and early 1980s, while it was only 22 percent for the industrial countries.

So far, so good. However, in 1982 and 1983 many borrowers ran into trouble meeting their obligations to pay interest and repay principal on these loans. The troubles arose for several reasons. An increase of world oil prices in 1979 and a deep recession in the industrial countries in 1981–1982 dealt a double blow to the LDCs' terms of trade and trade balances, raising the cost of energy imports as demand for the LDCs' exports was falling. Real interest rates rose sharply worldwide and with them the LDCs' costs of borrowing. By 1983 about thirty LDCs and Eastern European borrowers were in arrears.

Many of these debts were incurred to fund projects that had seemed productive enough that their outputs would finance debt repayment. When circumstances foiled this expectation, an LDC government could in principle still reach into its taxpayers' pockets to meet the nation's repayment obligations. However, taxpayers can prove highly resistant, and many LDC governments lacked the power or the consensus

[7] Edelstein, op. cit., Part III.

needed to extract the purchasing power to repay.[8] When a domestic borrower defaults on a bank loan, the bank can often seize the debtor's assets. When the debtor is a sovereign nation, however, that option is lacking, and the main deterrent to defaulting is denial of access to future loans.

What followed during the 1980s was a diffuse process whereby the LDC debtors generally acknowledged their debts and sought to work out plans for repayment. The lending banks in turn wrote off some of the debts and converted some into equity claims on business assets in the developing countries (debt-for-equity swaps). Just as in previous episodes of default on international loans,[9] a process of forgive-and-forget ultimately takes over; by the early 1990s, both Latin American corporate and government borrowers with good prospects were again able to borrow abroad.

International Capital Flows in the 1980s

Although the LDCs were largely cut out as net recipients of international capital flows in the 1980s, the total volume of these flows increased perhaps threefold among the developed nations. The pattern of these flows differed greatly from that of the late nineteenth century, described earlier. Rather than being driven by differences in investment opportunities between lenders and borrowers, it mainly reflected differences in rates of saving. A major example was the large flows of lending from high-saving Japan to the low-saving United States; as a result the United States, once a major international creditor, became a large international debtor. Another key driver was efforts by holders of financial wealth to diversify their portfolios internationally, taking advantage of many innovative securities and falling transaction costs in international capital markets. In short, capital flows were dominated by considerations of managing existing wealth rather than creating new capital.[10]

10.5 MULTINATIONALS AND DIRECT FOREIGN INVESTMENT

Direct investment is a unique form of international capital flow because it affects both the nation's stock of productive factors and competitive conditions in its markets. Its uniqueness lies in two traits.

1. Direct investment represents a capital movement, but the capital involved is entrepreneurial or risk-bearing. It does not merely finance the construction of plant and equipment. In its entrepreneurial role, direct investment is usually linked to the transfer of managerial skills and knowledge from one country to another. The cor-

---

[8] There were also technical reasons why LDC governments had trouble extracting the real resources needed to make repayment. They might have restricted imports, squeezing domestic consumption and thereby effecting the net outflow of real resources needed for repayment. However, as we saw in Chapter 9, many imports are inputs into exports, so a general compression of imports pulls down exports as well. This response was estimated to be no less than 52 percent by Mohsin S. Khan and Malcolm D. Knight, "Import Compression and Export Performance in Developing Countries," *Review of Economics and Statistics*, 70 (May 1988): 315–321.

[9] For long-term perspectives, see Barry J. Eichengreen and Peter H. Lindert, eds., *The International Debt Crisis in Historical Perspective* (Cambridge, MA: M.I.T. Press, 1989).

[10] For a survey see Philip Turner, *Capital Flows in the 1980s: A Survey of Major Trends* (Basel: Bank for International Settlements, 1991).

poration establishing or expanding a subsidiary abroad is the typical agent of direct investment.

2. It is strongly *industry-specific*. Its economically significant traits arise not so much from the transfer of capital from country A to country B as from A's x industry to B's x industry. Specifically, much direct investment flows along two industrial channels. *Horizontal* investment occurs when a firm producing a product in the source (lending) country establishes a subsidiary to produce the same good in the host country. *Vertical* investment occurs when the firm establishes a subsidiary to perform the next stage forward, or the next stage backward, in the fabrication and sale of its product. Many small foreign subsidiaries only distribute and sell the parent company's products in the host country; these cases of "forward" vertical integration will be largely ignored. Much more important, in terms of the capital involved, are "backward" vertical integrations into the production of a raw material or input in the host country that then can be used by the parent company in the source country.

Because of these traits, the causes and effects of direct investment are best studied at the level of the individual market rather than that of the economy as an aggregate. However, the concepts of specific factors (Section 6.2) and of footloose production processes (Section 9.3) prove helpful.

Causes of Direct Investment

Why should a firm invest in production facilities abroad? It does not know the language, the laws, the customs, the local markets. The foreign government may not be its friend. There must be a general explanation as to why profit-maximizing firms, at least in certain industries, establish foreign subsidiaries in the face of these obstacles. The following explanation concentrates on horizontal investments.

This explanation begins with a factual observation: Foreign investment is seldom undertaken by a company before it becomes an established, substantial seller in its domestic market. At this stage it has acquired managerial know-how, patents, trademarks, and other such intangible assets. These assets allow it to earn at least normal profits on its invested capital. Having been acquired while the firm built a position in the domestic market, these assets are now available for use elsewhere, if a profitable opportunity can be found.[11] At this point, foreign markets are apt to fall under consideration.

Direct investment is sometimes an effective way to use these assets profitably abroad. Consider the company producing durable consumer goods. It has discovered how to devise and modify features of its products to attract a significant share of those demanding such goods. Its products have attained a reputation for satisfactory durability and service. Its trademarks, patents, innovative and marketing skills, and (to a degree) its reputation with customers can be transplanted to foreign markets when it establishes production facilities abroad through direct investment. Further-

---

[11] These forms of intangible capital consist of what economists call "public goods." When a technique or an idea is put to productive use in the United States, there is no less of it available for employment in Britain. The productive capacity of a machine obviously does not share this property. See Harry G. Johnson, "The Efficiency and Welfare Implications of the International Corporation," C. P. Kindleberger, ed., *The International Corporation* (Cambridge, MA: M.I.T. Press, 1970), Chapter 2.

more, owning local production facilities aids it greatly in penetrating foreign markets. Such facilities make it easier to design products for the special requirements of foreign markets and to modify the new product as information on consumer acceptance feeds back. Local servicing of such products may also lead to improved product performance.[12]

The firm described here clearly does not sell in purely competitive markets. Indeed, the marketing assets that make its foreign investment profitable describe *product differentiation* as a characteristic of markets. Section 2.3 noted that product differentiation can have distinctive effects on international trade. Rather than just exporting the differentiated product, or just importing it, a country may export some varieties while its consumers also buy some brands imported from abroad. Multinational companies, often based in such industries, similarly criss-cross the globe, spreading from various countries of origin to establish production facilities in each others' markets.

The industries that exhibit the most direct investment are, as expected, those whose products are the most differentiated. American firms producing automobiles, other consumer durables, rubber, and pharmaceuticals are very likely to have subsidiaries abroad, as are many firms supplying machinery and other important producer goods. These products are differentiated because each supplier offers a different mix of the product's primary attributes. What really turns these firms into foreign investors, however, are the close and enduring relationships they develop with their manufacturer-customers: When you depend heavily on a supplier, you prefer one nearby for the times when a "quick fix" is needed. On the other hand, there is less direct investment in some undifferentiated products with mature technologies, such as steel and paper; even successful firms may not accumulate intangible capital that is profitably exploited through direct investment. Also, some industries (such as aircraft) forgo direct investment because production scale economies confine their factory operations to one country or site.

The causes of foreign investment are quite different for subsidiaries supplying raw materials needed by their parents. The explanation of these investments at first seems obvious: How can a rubber company produce tires without crude rubber? The more interesting question, though, is why the raw material source is developed by a subsidiary of the company that will process it rather than by independent firms in the country where the raw material is found. The gain from this vertical direct investment seems to be the reduction of risk. Few companies in the world refine and fabricate copper. Important deposits of copper ore occur in only a few locations. If independent firms produced and refined the ore, both would be forced to commit funds to the construction of large fixed facilities without any guarantee regarding the bargain they could strike with the other party. What could the ore producer do if its smelter customer convincingly threatened to drop its business? What could the smelter do without an ore supply? "Vertical integration" in any industry reduces uncertainty.

---

[12] This account is closely related to the "product cycle" explored in Section 9.3. For such an interpretation, see Raymond Vernon, *Sovereignty at Bay: The Multinational Spread of U.S. Enterprises* (New York: Basic Books, 1971), Chapter 3.

Because the firms extracting raw materials must be located where the resources are and the firms processing and selling them where the markets are, foreign investment must be involved.[13]

Direct Investment and Other Forces in the International Economy

Because of its distinctive character, direct investment interacts with other forces in the international economy in ways that differentiate it sharply from other types of capital flow. These include the following.

Exports and Absolute Costs.   When the firm sees potential profits in markets abroad, exporting and direct investment often are alternative strategies for capturing them. They are not closely matched alternatives always, or in all respects. Exporting may prove clearly superior when the firm's foreign sales are not yet large enough to utilize an overseas plant of efficient scale. Also, the firm that has established a producing subsidiary may continue to ship substantial exports to the same market, using its subsidiary as a marketing agent. However, there will always be some companies close to the margin, with no clear preference for exporting or producing abroad.

This proposition implies an important contrast between direct investment and other capital movements: The flow of direct investment is sensitive to shifts in relative costs of production between countries. If some disturbance lowers the cost of making goods in the United States, for example, relative to other countries, this will suffice to tip some foreign enterprises toward investing in the United States (and discourage some U.S. companies from investing abroad). People need not expect this cost shift to be permanent for some effect to appear, although expected transience cuts the payout to responding. Such shifts in production costs involve changes in the terms of trade between factors of production located in different countries, manifested in changing money prices and production costs: A host country's inflation rate is lower than those of its trading partners, or the price of its currency (the exchange rate) falls. (These monetary adjustments are explored in Parts IV through VI.) The cheapening of the U.S. dollar relative to other currencies after 1973 was accompanied by a substantial net shift in foreign investment toward the United States. Foreign direct investment in the United States averaged only $0.9 billion in 1970–1972, $4.3 billion in 1974–1978. This experience was repeated after 1986, when the dollar's value plunged from a high level and foreign firms went on a spending spree, buying many U.S. companies.

Tariffs in Host Countries.   The choice between exporting and direct investment should reflect the producer's desire to serve a foreign market at the lowest cost. If the exchange rate potentially affects this choice, so should the level of tariffs surrounding the foreign market. Tariffs raise the cost of importing and tilt the decision toward direct investment. Surveys of foreign subsidiaries in host counties show that often they were

---

[13] Whether there are vertically integrated multinational companies or arm's-length markets for these internationally traded inputs seems to be highly dependent on market conditions. In several markets—crude petroleum, primary copper, iron ore—arm's-length markets have sprung up during the past quarter-century, and multinational companies have abandoned much of their vertical integration. When enough transactions proceed at arm's length to beget a smoothly functioning market in the intermediate goods, the remaining parties may find that multinational vertical integration no longer pays.

founded when the parent had been serving the market by exports that were slapped with an increased tariff. Many countries have used tariffs to lure direct investment in the past. Japanese auto manufacturers made large investments in the United States in response both to actual restrictions on vehicle imports from Japan and to the ever-present threat of such restrictions in the future.

Net Versus Gross Flows.   Capital is expected to flow from the country where the profit rate is low to where it is high. However, the industry-specific character of direct investment clouds this simple prediction. The corporation invests abroad because no domestic use for its funds offers a higher expected return, but the firm does not consider investment in *every* other home industry as an active alternative to investing abroad. International differences in profits within an industry are likely to be most influential. Thus, direct investment could be flowing from America to Britain in the automobile industry while moving from Britain to America in the petroleum industry. Indeed, such cross-hauls could even occur in the same industry when firms use direct investment to invade each others' markets.

Cross-hauls of foreign investment within the same industry have two distinct causes. They may be simply an extension of the intra-industry trade that is likely to occur when products are differentiated (see Section 8.3). That pattern is consistent with large numbers of sellers being present in the world market, as in the theoretical model of monopolistic competition. Cross-hauls also may result from oligopolistic rivalry among producers when only a few are present in the market. Then reciprocal market invasions can represent threats and counterthreats between rivals.[14]

Competition in Product Markets.   Multinational companies are regarded in some quarters as monopolists on whom public policy should keep a close eye. The kernel of truth behind this suspicion arises because some industries prone to foreign investment have relatively few companies competing in them. The lack of competition, however, arises mainly because the rivals are few in number, not because they are multinational. In fact, the formation of a new foreign subsidiary is likely to inject more competition into the subsidiary's local market—particularly if the multinational enters a "green field" with a new plant rather than buying up an established local company. The international cartels that operated in some worldwide oligopolistic industries before World War II depended on agreements under which members stayed out of each others' markets—that is, restricted their foreign investments.

Benefits from Direct Investment and Their Distribution

The significance of direct investment for economic welfare is a matter of controversy. On the one hand, its supporters laud it for transferring to the host countries not just capital but also technology and managerial skills. On the other, its critics charge it with exploiting the local market, impairing the nation's sovereignty, and frustrating its economic policies. It will therefore be necessary to define the benefits of foreign investment carefully and to explore their division between the source and host countries.

[14] See Asim Erdilek, ed., *Multinationals as Mutual Invaders: Intra-Industry Direct Foreign Investment* (New York: St. Martin's Press, 1985).

The primary gain (if any) from relocating productive resources is measured by the net increase in the value of output. This increase in turn should be reflected in the extra reward these resources receive in the new location. The extra profits an enterprise earns on its foreign investment, over the best domestic alternative, measure (on certain assumptions) the social benefit of the investment. The same applies to any rents accruing to its managerial talent or other assets utilized abroad. For intangible capital, such as patents, trademarks, and know-how, the gross rewards measure gain because use abroad does not preclude use at home. Who gets this gain? What other effects on welfare does foreign investment have? The following discussion examines the issues as seen in source countries (homes of multinational companies) and host countries (homes of their subsidiaries) in turn.

Policy Issues in Source Countries

Taxation of Corporate Incomes. An important factor determining how the benefits are divided between source and host is the way countries levy the taxes on corporate profits. The profits of American multinationals provide the basic gain from foreign investment for the United States. Yet the U.S. government is a major loser because standard tax practices both divert profits on the foreign investments of U.S. companies to foreign treasuries and induce the companies to shift their profits abroad (and thus into the foreign tax collector's hands). A common practice among countries is that the host country is the first to tax the subsidiary's profits, and the company's tax payments to the host country are then offset against its tax liability to the source country when those profits are repatriated. An example shows what is involved. Suppose that both source and host countries levy a corporate profits tax of 50 percent, and that a company earns a rate of profit (before tax) of 20 percent in the host country, whereas it could have earned only 16 percent had it invested the same funds at home. When the 20 percent is earned, the host country's tax authorities get 10 percent. The corporation keeps the remaining 10 percent; when it repatriates these profits, they become liable for taxation in the source country, but the credit for taxes paid to the host nation just offsets this. Had the direct investment not occurred, the corporation would have earned 8 percent after a tax payment of 8 percent to the source country. The real net return to the foreign investment of 4 percent $(20 - 16)$ exceeds the net gain to the corporation of 2 percent $(10 - 8)$. However, the host country gains more than the real net return (10 percent, compared to 4 percent), and the source country loses on the transaction; the corporation and the tax authorities together garner 16 percent from the domestic investment, but only 10 from the foreign. Thus, corporation profits taxation not only guarantees the host country a cut of the primary gains, but can even award it more than the extra real product, leaving the source country worse off. Economists have estimated that the United States was earning a negative social return on its foreign investment, because of this transfer; the gains to Canada (a major host country) from the same source were found to be as large as 2.5 percent of Canada's gross national product.[15]

---

[15] Herbert G. Grubel. "Taxation and Rates of Return from Some U.S. Asset Holdings Abroad, 1960–1969," *Journal of Political Economy*, 82 (May/June 1974): 469–487; Glenn P. Jenkins, "Taxes and Tariffs and the Evaluation of the Benefit from Foreign Investment," *Canadian Journal of Economics*, 12 (August 1979): 410–425.

U.S. tax law also creates an incentive for corporations to move profits onto their subsidiaries' books (e.g., by undercharging them for research or management services) whenever the host country's corporation tax rate is lower than that of the United States. This incentive arises because profits earned abroad are not subject to U.S. taxation until they are actually repatriated. A dollar of profit earned domestically cannot be reinvested before the tax collectors take their slice, but the whole of that same dollar earned abroad may be available for reinvestment.

Some economists have urged that the United States pursue its national interests by letting U.S. multinationals only deduct foreign taxes as a cost of doing business, as opposed to the prevailing and more generous practice of allowing them a credit on taxes paid to foreign governments. With a 50 percent tax rate, a credit of $1 for foreign taxes saves a company $1 of U.S. tax, while a deduction of $1 saves it only 50 cents. However, the tax-credit system used by the United States and some other industrial countries looks better from a world viewpoint than from that of any single country. That is, companies tend to make decisions concerning international plant locations in ways that maximize global welfare, whereas the tax-deduction rule maximizes the source country's welfare but not global welfare.[16]

Income Distribution.   If capital is invested abroad, less remains at home to work with labor in the source country. Unless relative factor prices are locked into place through their link to world product prices (see Chapter 7), wages are likely to fall just as the reward to capital rises. The process was described (for labor migration) in Section 10.3. In the early 1970s American labor became highly conscious of this possibility and pressed for legislation that would sharply restrict foreign investment in order "to protect American jobs."Although traditional economic theory says that labor was right, recent research in fact leans the other way. Foreign investment appears to an important degree complementary with U.S. exports; the subsidiary establishes distribution facilities and discovers markets abroad that actually encourage the parent's exports to that market and thereby increase its domestic output. Thus, it is not clear that American labor in fact loses. Some studies have estimated rather large losses for U.S. labor, but they neglect the link through product markets between American and foreign prices, which causes the estimated losses to be seriously biased upward.[17]

Policy Issues in Host Countries

Just as profits from foreign investment benefit source countries, the taxes collected on these profits are also an important benefit to the hosts. In addition, hosts gain from any activities of foreign subsidiaries that incidentally raise the productivity of their own factor stocks. The subsidiary may show its local suppliers how to achieve better quality control, or its method of distributing its output may improve the general

[16] For evidence that national tax rates affect the location of foreign investment, see Harry Grubert and John Mutti, "Taxes, Tariffs and Transfer Pricing in Multinational Corporate Decision Making," *Review of Economics and Statistics*, 73 (May 1991): 285–293.

[17] For a good discussion of these issues, see C. Fred Bergsten, Thomas Horst, and Theodore H. Moran, *American Multinationals and American Interests* (Washington: The Brookings Institution, 1978), Chapters 2–3.

productivity of the distribution sector. Some of the knowledge comprising the intangible capital of the multinational corporation may leak out to its local competitors as they seek to emulate its success (or resist its competitive pressure).[18] The size of these gains—indeed, whether they are substantial at all—will vary from subsidiary to subsidiary and from host country to host country. Subsidiaries of manufacturing firms operating in developed countries like Australia and Great Britain have been found to extend significant productivity benefits of this sort. At the other extreme, a capital-intensive subsidiary operating in a less-developed country and making few transactions with local enterprises may generate few secondary benefits.

Despite these benefits, hostility toward foreign investment is common in host countries. Even in the United States some members of Congress have expressed concern over the increasing number of foreign-owned enterprises! Some typical host-country issues will now be examined.

High Profits. Subsidiaries' profits are "too high." A firm can earn excess profits persistently for two quite different reasons, and the policies that these suggest for the host country also differ. One basis for excess profits is a noncompetitive market structure surrounding the multinational, which allows it some monopoly gains. In a market subject to elements of monopoly, the price that buyers pay is elevated above the marginal cost of supplying them, and a loss of economic welfare occurs. The government may be able to employ the tools of competition policy to remove the distortion and end the welfare loss. This potential welfare gain does not depend on whether the firm with monopoly power is foreign controlled or in domestic hands. The foreign-controlled monopolist, however, imposes an additional welfare cost on the nation. When a domestic monopolist elevates price above marginal cost and earns excess profits, those profits are a transfer from the real incomes of the product's buyers to those of the firm's owners; but both groups are home-country citizens, and so the redistribution itself does not reduce the national income. When a foreign monopolist elevates its price, however, the excess profit drains out of the national income stream and into the hands of foreigners. The host-country government can therefore increase its national welfare more by attacking a foreign monopolist than by attacking an otherwise identical domestic one. As will be seen in Section 13.3, it also can increase national welfare by helping a domestic firm increase its profits at the expense of a foreign-subsidiary rival, even if the monopolistic distortion (the excess of price over marginal cost) remains unchanged.

Natural-Resource Rents. The other way a firm can earn excess profits persistently is to enjoy some structural advantage that competing firms cannot replicate. The profit associated with such differential advantages is called a *rent*. Some foreign subsidiaries earn rents on the intangible assets (defined earlier) that their foreign parents first obtain in their home markets and then exploit abroad through the subsidiaries. Foreign subsidiaries engaged in extracting natural resources earn rents if the natural resources they control are of a higher quality than those owned and used by their competitors.

[18] For a survey of these effects see Magnus Blomström, "Host Country Benefits of Foreign Investment," *National Bureau of Economic Research*, Reprint No. 1703 (1991).

Resource rents have been a particular source of conflict between multinationals and host governments. When the host-country public sees a foreign enterprise carrying off the wealth from their soil, they applaud action by their government to intercept those rents. Indeed, the host government has every reason to tax these away, leaving the foreign subsidiary with only a normal profit. As long as it obtains a normal profit, the firm may shed tears over its lost rents, but it has no incentive to withdraw. The government obtains a pure transfer of wealth.

The actual sparring over resource rents between multinationals and host governments has shifted over time. In the 1950s and 1960s subsidiaries extracting natural resources were frequent targets of nationalization or expropriation, with the host government simply seizing control of their investments and handing over whatever amount of compensation it saw fit. Then the process took on a more subtle but no less invasive form—the "obsolescing bargain." Here the multinational commits a fixed investment to extract natural resources in a foreign land, on some understanding regarding the terms under which it will be taxed by the host government. Once the investment is in place, however, the host government starts raising the tax bill. The government need leave the company only enough revenue to cover its out-of-pocket costs in order to keep the operation going. The company may therefore suffer a large loss on its investment. Specifically, it not only loses any rents on the resources but also cannot recover the sunk cost of its investment.

The obsolescing bargain has a chilling effect on foreign investment in extractive projects. A company thinking about making such an investment recognizes that, once its capital outlay is sunk, the host country has every incentive to tax away its cash flow. The country may want the investment to take place, but has no way to pledge credibly that it will eschew punitive taxation. A partial solution has been new types of agreements whereby the host country pays for a project's sunk-cost components while the multinational company supplies management or other skills. If the host tries to encroach on the company's receipts, once such a deal is signed, the firm's managers and technicians can hop on a plane and depart. A giant mining establishment, on the other hand, is not so nimble.[19]

Research and Development.   Multinationals undertake most of their research in the source country and thus deny research and development activities to the host country. The multinationals usually centralize their basic research activities in their home country and undertake research in the host countries primarily to develop and adapt their products more efficiently to local conditions. Frequently, as in this instance, it is hard to grasp what alternative practices the complainers would prefer. Should the multinational corporation decentralize its research, perhaps losing some efficiency? It would still capture the profits from its discoveries (and incur the losses from its failures). More host-country nationals will get jobs in research, but it is not clear that they or the host nation will be richer in real income. People sometimes treat science and research as "consumption goods," as if the nation's benefit depended on the number of its citizens wearing white coats and shaking test tubes rather than upon its access to the fruits of research (wherever carried out). The ease with which research results travel across national boundaries suggests that this attitude is not rational.

[19] Bergsten, Horst, and Moran, op. cit., Chapter 5.

The most cogent reason for host countries to press multinationals for local research expenditures is the spillover benefits that may result—including training nationals and informing local firms, especially in developing countries.

Submission to Public Policy.   Because of its international connections the subsidiary enjoys alternatives not open to home-owned firms, and it can often take successive evasive action when the screws of public policy are applied. When confronted with new social legislation raising production costs (for example, by requiring the subsidiary to provide more benefits for its employees), the subsidiary may channel any expansion of capacity to another country. Its ease of lending and borrowing internationally may frustrate the use of direct macroeconomic controls for internal or external balance. Does this freedom warrant restricting its activities? Here again the question of the alternative arises. A policy that causes a subsidiary to move its activities elsewhere might simply put a home-owned firm in the same straits out of business. A government whose policies fight market forces should ask whether it is using the most effective possible policies. The answer may be no. Even if its policies must clash with the market, it is hardly clear, as a general proposition, that reducing firms' sensitivities to market forces improves economic welfare overall.

These complaints about the foreign firm have been arranged to move from the purely economic to the largely political. Evaluated broadly, they identify no systematic and severe economic costs of direct investment to the host country, although they certainly reveal offsets that must be chalked against the benefits conveyed. They do raise, however, the problem of national sovereignty, which pervades international economic policy. A nation would be most sovereign if it could mold its economic policy without heeding the economic or political reactions of the rest of the world. Yet perfect sovereignty is hardly conceivable without perfect isolation from the rest of the world. Therefore, gaining the benefit of specialization and exchange means tolerating economic and political links to the rest of the world that create both constraints and opportunities for policy-making, but in any case cannot be prudently ignored. Economists are prone to urge policies designed to get the best of both worlds— to secure the benefits of international exchange and to use the leverage for policy provided by international sensitivities rather than to fight it. But this is not a complete answer to the nationalist who would rather not deal with the rest of the world, even when this isolation results in some cost of real income to the nationalist.

10.6 SUMMARY

The efficiency of the world economy can generally be increased if factors of production are mobile among countries. Commodity trade can substitute for factor mobility but generally incompletely. However, inflows of a factor to a country generally redistribute incomes among factors already there, just as they raise real income overall. Immigration of labor reduces wages but raises the returns to capital. Inflows of a sector-specific factor depress the rewards to that factor and to other specific factors but raise the wages of the general factor, labor. The United States and other industrial countries have received large inflows of unskilled labor in the last two decades. These have raised controversies precisely because they depress the wages of low-skilled natives while raising national income overall. Fortunately that reduction seems quite small.

Funds moving internationally are direct investment when they obtain control over the receiving enterprise, portfolio investment when they do not. Portfolio investment moved in large flows from England and other European countries during 1870–1913. Bursts of foreign investment flowed to the overseas regions that supplied Britain's imports when import prices were high (Britain's terms of trade were poor). Capital stayed at home when Britain's terms of trade improved. There was no obvious transfer problem, because the overseas recipients naturally spent most of the proceeds on British capital goods. In the 1970s, the more successful of the developing nations received large inflows of portfolio investment to realize their strong development prospects. They ran into serious repayment problems because of unexpectedly high interest rates and a serious recession in the industrial countries (which cut export earnings). In the 1980s heavy capital flows among the industrial countries were related to differences in rates of saving and the diversification of wealth more than to differences in investment opportunities.

Direct investment typically involves the creation of a subsidiary abroad by a corporation. It is thus sector-specific, and usually occurs in certain market structures. Some companies invest abroad to obtain sources of raw materials or other inputs (backward vertical integration); others acquire subsidiaries that produce the same product line as their parent (horizontal integration). Horizontal investment is an alternative to exporting, and thus direct investment should be sensitive to the exchange rate. It is also influenced by the host country's tariffs. Like other factor flows, foreign investment tends to create a real benefit by moving resources from less to more productive uses. The profit earned by the multinational company constitutes much of this benefit for the source country, but established conventions on corporate income taxation may cause much of the gain to be captured by the host country. The host also benefits from foreign investment raising the productivity of its own factor stock. Host countries often criticize multinationals for their high profits or rents from natural resources, their centralization of research and development in the parent, and their access to alternative actions when squeezed by public policy.

CHAPTER PROBLEMS

1. Suppose that factor price equalization prevails in the world but a large migration takes place from country A to country B (because of some political disturbance, for example). Describe the adjustments that will occur if capital also is mobile internationally and what will happen if it is immobile.

2. In the early 1970s American trade unions campaigned vigorously (but without success) for restrictions on U.S. direct investment abroad, which they saw as costing them jobs. Were they perceiving their own interests correctly? What if the United States were embedded in a Heckscher-Ohlin world economy with factor-price equalization between countries?

3. It was suggested in the text that "oversaving" did not account for much of Britain's capital exports in the nineteenth century, because increases in capital outflows coincided with increases in rates of return to capital abroad rather than with declines at home. Using ordinary supply and demand curves, show why this conclusion follows.

4. Some observers have noted the occurrence of intra-industry flows of foreign direct investment, like the intra-industry trade discussed in Chapter 8. Given the nature of the multinational company, why might this happen?

5. What would be the effect on the amount of foreign direct investment of a decline in international transportation costs for merchandise? Of a decline in international costs of communication (satellite telephone linkages, personal travel, etc.)?

6. Developing countries sometimes encourage inflows of foreign direct investment by levying especially low tax rates on the net incomes of foreign subsidiaries. Evaluate the effect of this policy choice on the host country's income. Evaluate the suggestion that, instead, countries should lure the multinationals in with a package involving high tax rates on their profits but tariff protection high enough to make entry attractive.

SUGGESTIONS FOR FURTHER READING

Abowd, John M., and Richard B. Freeman, eds. *Immigration, Trade, and the Labor Market* (Chicago: University of Chicago Press, 1991). Studies of effects of U.S. immigration and its effects on natives' wages and employment opportunities.

Bergsten, C. Fred, Thomas Horst, and Theodore H. Moran. *American Multinationals and American Interests*. (Washington: The Brookings Institution, 1978). Treats many issues of behavior and public policy.

Blomstrom, Magnus. *Foreign Investment and Spillovers: A Study of Technology Transfers to Mexico* (London: Routledge, 1989). Survey of effects on one host country.

Caves, Richard E. *Multinational Enterprise and Economic Analysis* (Cambridge, UK: Cambridge University Press, 1982). Survey of concepts and evidence relating to multinationals.

Eichengreen, Barry, and Peter H. Lindert, eds. *The International Debt Crisis in Historical Perspective* (Cambridge, MA: M.I.T. Press, 1989). Compares episodes of default on international lending.

Graham, Edward M., and Paul R. Krugman. *Foreign Direct Investment in the United States* (Washington: Institute for International Economics, 1989). Survey of issues.

Sachs, Jeffrey D., ed. *Developing Country Debt and the World Economy* (Chicago: University of Chicago Press, 1989). Scholarly papers on this crisis and its resolution.

Thomas, Brinley. *Migration and Economic Growth* (Cambridge, UK: Cambridge University Press, 1972). Classic study of international migration.

Vernon, Raymond. *Sovereignty at Bay: The Multinational Spread of U.S. Enterprise* (New York and London: Basic Books, 1971). Survey of evidence on the behavior of U.S. subsidiaries abroad.

III

The Theory and Practice of Commercial Policy

11

TARIFFS AND THE
NATIONAL WELFARE

Free trade brings benefits to all nations. This theme forms the foundation for any basic discussion of international trade. However, for centuries most countries have felt compelled to interfere with the smooth flow of commodities by erecting tariff barriers or other obstacles to trade. Indeed, protectionist pressures in the United States seemed to reach new highs in the early 1990s. Part III of this book examines the nature of such impediments, asks how they may benefit special groups, and discusses attempts at cooperation in commercial policy both at the regional level (customs unions such as the European Community) and in larger groupings. The primary weapon of commercial policy used to be the tariff, whereas recent revivals of the protectionist spirit have sought other instruments whereby local interests can seek relief from foreign competition. It simplifies matters in the present chapter to focus on the use of tariffs and their effects on national and international welfare in the context of highly competitive national and world markets. Later (Chapter 13) we see how arguments for government intervention get altered if markets are imperfectly competitive.

11.1 THE TARIFF FOR A SMALL COUNTRY

A tariff is a tax on the importation of a commodity from abroad. If the country levying the tariff is small, the tariff has little effect on the world price of the commodity. Instead, the foreign commodity becomes more expensive at home behind the tariff wall both to producers of the commodity (who can be expected to support the tariff)

FIGURE 11.1   The Effect of a Tariff on Production

The initial free-trade prices are shown by line 1; production is at *A*, and national income, measured in units of food, is *OF*. A tariff on imports of food raises the domestic relative price of food, as is shown by line 2. Resources are shifted into food; production moves to point *B*. At world prices national income in food units has been reduced to *OD* (line 3 is parallel to line 1).

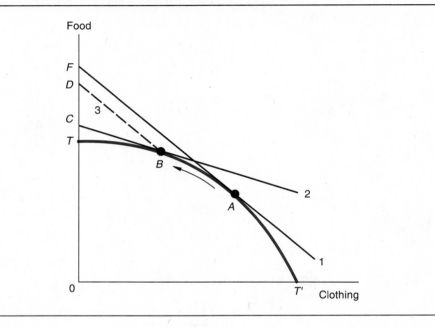

and to local consumers (who will likely oppose the duty). In general, a tariff attracts resources to the protected sector and shifts demand away from foreign goods. On both counts a tariff reduces a small country's imports.[1]

Tariffs and Production

Figures 11.1 and 11.2 are designed to highlight separately the impact of a tariff on production and on demand. Curve *TT'* in Figure 11.1 shows full-employment production possibilities for a small country initially producing food and clothing at point *A* and facing free-trade relative prices shown by the slope of line 1. Suppose the country imports food and proceeds to levy a tariff on food imports, thus raising the domestic relative price of food by the amount of the tariff. The posttariff *domestic* price ratio is shown by line 2, while the country's terms of trade are still given by the

---

[1] It will always be assumed that the tariff rate is quoted on an ad valorem basis; that is, the domestic price of imports, p_F, equals a multiple, $(1 + t)$, of the world price, p_F^*. The tariff rate is sometimes quoted as a percentage of the foreign price (e.g., $100t$ might be 28 percent). For a given tariff rate, t, the absolute wedge separating home and foreign prices would rise if the foreign price rises. A different kind of tariff is the *specific* tariff—a rate quoted in absolute dollars per physical unit (e.g., \$2.10 a ton). If t' denotes this amount, p_F would equal $(p_F^* + t')$. An inflation of world prices would in such a case leave the absolute tariff wedge unchanged (and diminish its relative significance).

FIGURE 11.2   The Effect of a Tariff on Demand

Production remains at *A* on the right-angled *TAT'* transformation schedule. A tariff raises the relative domestic price of food to line 2 (parallel to lines 3 and 4). Food consumption falls by the substitution effect (from *G* to *H*) plus an income effect (from *H* to *J*). Distance *EC* measures the tariff revenue in terms of food. The trade triangle shrinks from *GKA* to *JLA*.

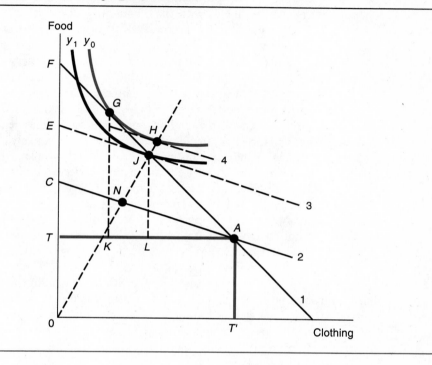

slope of line 1. The tariff attracts resources to food, driving up the opportunity cost in this sector until local costs reflect the new higher domestic food price, at *B*.

In terms of domestic prices, production point *B* maximizes the value of national production. Yet output evaluated at *world* prices has fallen: Line 3 is parallel to line 1, so that national income in food units at world prices is *reduced* from *OF* to *OD*. This is a signal that a small country in competitive world markets harms itself by levying a tariff on imports.

Tariffs and Demand

The analysis of the impact of tariffs on demand is complicated by the fact that a tariff not only drives up the relative price of food imports to consumers, it also raises revenue. The assumption typically made about the tariff revenue is that it is redistributed back to the public. This may take the form of reductions in other taxes (for example, income taxes) to balance the tariff revenue. In any case, it is assumed that the public's disposable income (and expenditure) consists now not only of produced income, but also of the tariff revenue.[2] This means, however, that import demand depends partly on how much tariff revenue is raised, and the amount of tariff revenue raised depends on the quantity of imports demanded.

Figure 11.2 illustrates the effect of a tariff on import demand when we abstract from production changes. The production-possibilities schedule is the right-angled box TAT', serving to keep production fixed at point A. The initial free-trade terms of trade are shown by line 1, with the community's best consumption point at G. Distance GK represents the free-trade level of food imports, matched by clothing exports of amount KA.

A tariff raises the relative price of food imports to consumers and also results in tariff revenues being collected and redistributed. The dotted line $ONJH$ in Figure 11.2 has been constructed to connect all possible consumption points consistent with the higher relative domestic price of food. (This locus is called an incomes-consumption line. For example, points N, J, and H are consumption bundles demanded at the new domestic prices and incomes shown by lines 2, 3, and 4, respectively.) Suppose posttariff prices are reflected in the slope of lines 2, 3, and 4 (all parallel). If consumers could stay on initial indifference curve y_0, the rise in food's price would evoke the substitution effect involved in moving from G to H. Income level y_0 cannot be maintained, however. The value of consumption at world prices must exactly match the value of production. Thus, point J is the consumption point chosen after the tariff is imposed because it is the only point on $ONJH$ that also lies on line 1 through production point A. All points on line 1 satisfy the requirement that quantities of clothing exported match demand for food as imports *at world prices*.

In terms of domestic prices, line 3 is the posttariff budget line. It is above a parallel line (2) through production point A. This reflects the fact that consumers' disposable income exceeds the value of production by the amount of the tariff revenue (EC in units of food). However, note that the tariff has harmed consumers—pushing them to consumption point J, which lies on a lower indifference curve than does G.

To summarize, the effect of a tariff on the demand for imports is tricky to analyze because tariff revenues form part of income, and income is one of the determinants of the demand for imports and thus tariff revenues. To cut through this simultaneity problem, Figure 11.2 shows that demand must satisfy two requirements in equilibrium: (1) the indifference curve must be tangent to a budget line reflecting *domestic* prices, and (2) the value of consumption must match the value of production at *world* prices. In Figure 11.2 this implies that the consumption bundle must lie both on ray $ONJH$ and on line AJF.

Tariffs and Imports

A nation's imports reflect both its demand for the importable commodity and its domestic production of that same commodity. Figure 11.1 shows how a tariff encourages a greater production of importables. Production was kept fixed in Figure 11.2 in order to highlight the effect of a tariff in cutting demand for importables.

---

[2] An alternative procedure has the government keeping the tariff proceeds and spending them according to its own taste patterns, which may differ from those of the private sector. Having the tariff proceeds redistributed makes it possible to consider a single set of preferences for the entire community.

These two strands are brought together in Figure 11.3. The free-trade equilibrium production and consumption points are represented by points A and G, respectively, with the slope of line 1 indicating the fixed relative world price of clothing to food. A tariff on food raises the relative domestic price of food and encourages greater local production. This effect is shown by the move from A to B, where line 2 shows posttariff domestic prices. Line 4 is parallel to line 1 and shows combinations of clothing and food that have the same value at world prices as the production point, B. The home country's consumption bundle after the tariff must lie somewhere along line 4; specifically, it must rest at J, where indifference curve y_1 has a slope equal to the *domestic* price ratio (line 3 is parallel to line 2). The home country's demand for imports has been reduced from GK to JL—a combination of greater production and lessened demand for food.

Tariffs and Welfare

In Figure 11.3 the tariff lowers real income from curve y_0 to curve y_1. At given world prices the tariff has lowered the aggregate value of production (compare OF with OD). Furthermore, point J is not even the best consumption point along line 4, because

---

FIGURE 11.3   The Effect of a Tariff on Imports

A tariff raises the domestic relative price of food (shown by lines 2 and 3) above the fixed world price (shown by lines 1 and 4). Domestic production of food rises from A to B. Domestic consumption of food falls from G to J. The trade triangle shrinks from GKA to JLB.

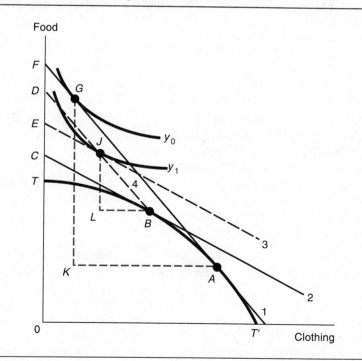

the tariff causes domestic prices (line 3) to be distorted away from world prices (shown by the slope of line 4).

This loss of real income may seem all the more noteworthy because with a tariff the home country receives tariff revenue, which, it is assumed, is passed on to consumers. Evaluated at the relative domestic price of food, the value of income earned in production after the tariff is distance OC in Figure 11.3. The tariff revenue is CE, and the budget line appropriate to domestic consumers is line 3, which lies *outside* the transformation curve (by the amount of the tariff revenue). However, the best point along line 3 (point J) is inferior to the best point (G) along the pretariff budget line 1, in which there was no tariff revenue.

Both domestic prices and world prices have a welfare significance that helps reveal why a tariff for a small country facing competitive foreign suppliers lowers national well-being. Domestic prices reflect the community's relative evaluation of commodities. (Marginal rates of substitution are equated to domestic price ratios.) World prices reflect costs of obtaining a commodity via trade. If a tariff is erected, the cost to the community of obtaining another unit of food imports (as measured by the required export of clothing at world prices) is lower than the value to the community of consuming another unit of food (as measured by the slope of indifference curves, or by the domestic price of food). This discrepancy between value and cost indicates that the purchase (at world prices) of another unit of food would yield more in satisfaction than would be sacrificed in cost. Yet the tariff has *reduced* imports instead and, thus, has lowered welfare. It has reduced imports by reducing demand *and* by increasing local production. (In Figure 11.3 food imports have been reduced from GK to JL.)

It has now been shown that a small country facing given world prices for its exportables and importables will, by levying a tariff, accomplish the following.

1. Encourage production of importables (though at the expense of production of exportables).

2. Create tariff revenue, which raises national income at domestic prices above the level of the value (at domestic prices) of all goods produced.

3. *Lower* welfare (compare y_1 to y_0 in Figure 11.3), despite the income derived from the tariff revenue. The tariff distorts domestic prices from the prices at which goods exchange on world markets. Such a distortion causes the value of goods produced, when evaluated at world prices, to fall from their free-trade value (compare line 4 with line 1 in Figure 11.3). Furthermore, the distortion encourages domestic residents to pick a consumption bundle that yields lower utility than could be obtained even granted the distorted production bias. (Point J is not the best point along budget line 4 in Figure 11.3.)

Such impact of a tariff on the level of a small trading community's imports also reveals the importance of the link between imports and exports. In Figure 11.3 the level of imports has been reduced from GK to JL. Exports have also been reduced, from KA to LB. Popular discussions of commercial policy often focus on the desirability of cutting back on foreign imports, perhaps because of the supposed benefit to employment in that sector of the economy. However, if exports are also cut back by such a move, the benefit via total employment or any other measure is clearly questionable. One of the real advantages of analyzing commercial policies in a manner that makes explicit the consequences for *all* sectors of the economy is avoiding the misleading conclusion that protection is beneficial just because it might favor the sector being protected—misleading because there are changes in other sectors that such an argument ignores.

Tariffs and Export Taxes

An export tax is an instrument of commercial policy that raises the foreign price of exportables above the domestic price. Although barred by constitutional provision in the United States, it is sometimes used by other nations. Indeed, in 1987 Canada levied a 15 percent export tax on shipments of softwood lumber to the United States as part of an arrangement whereby a threatened American import duty of 15 percent on softwood imports was recalled. The net effect: The Canadians pocketed the tax revenue.[3]

Although an import duty and a foreign export tax on the same item are comparable in their effect in creating a wedge between home and foreign prices, they differ in their distribution of the tax proceeds. If levied by the same country, however, an import duty and an export tax are identical in all regards (if levied on all importables or on all exportables). This is the famous Lerner symmetry theorem.[4] Because this discussion reveals that it is the *relative* price of exportables in terms of importables that matters, then clearly, as long as the country collects the tax revenue in either case, it does not matter whether the spread raises the foreign price of exportables above the domestic price or raises the domestic price of importables above the foreign. This symmetry helps point out that an import duty restricts a nation's exports just as much as would a direct tax on exports.

One notable consequence of this symmetry is that a nation imposing import duties as part of a stance of inward-looking protectionism can undo the protective effect indirectly—by granting matching export subsidies. This is a route pointing toward more open trade followed successfully by some of the NICs, such as South Korea and Taiwan. In addition, as will be discussed in Part IV, a uniform import tax plus an export subsidy replicates a devaluation of a country's currency.

11.2 THE IMPACT OF A TARIFF ON WORLD AND DOMESTIC PRICES

It has been shown that a tariff must reduce import demand and the supply of exports at the initially prevailing world prices. If the tariff-levying country is not small in relation to competitive world markets, its tariff will drive down the world relative price of imports or, equivalently, raise the relative world price of its exports. The tariff can improve a country's terms of trade.

This point can be illustrated by the net home import demand curve, M, and the foreign export supply curve, X^*, in Figure 11.4. The vertical axis measures the world

---

[3] Chapters 12 and 13 discuss in more detail the rationale behind the choice of protectionist instruments that, as in this case, divert tariff revenue to foreign hands.

[4] The reference is to Abba Lerner, "The Symmetry between Import and Export Taxes," *Economica*, N.S. 3 (August 1936): 306–313.

FIGURE 11.4   A Tariff Improves the Terms of Trade

The initial free-trade equilibrium is at Q, with the relative *world* price of food shown on the vertical axis at B. A tariff shifts the home import demand schedule down from M to M', and lowers the world relative price of food (to Q')

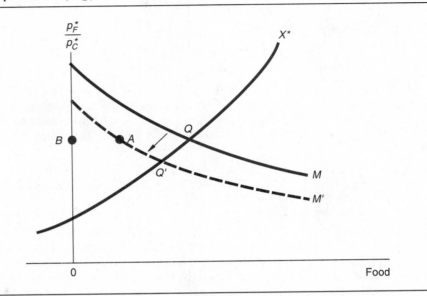

relative price of food (thus the asterisks). Section 11.1 showed that at any given terms of trade a tariff would cut back home demand for imports—from Q to A at the initial terms of trade in Figure 11.4. That is, the home demand curve for imports, M, shifts leftward to M'.

The home country is not "small" in Figure 11.4. This is revealed by the fact that the new world trade equilibrium at Q' shows that the home country's tariff has lowered the relative price of imported food on world markets. That is, a country can use a tariff to improve its terms of trade. It acts like a seller of a commodity that finds itself with some monopoly power. By controlling supply, the seller can exercise some influence over price. Just as a tariff reduces the home country's import demand at given world terms of trade, so does it reduce the quantity of exports supplied. Looked at in this way, a tariff is a means of forcing up the relative price of a country's exports on world markets. An improvement in the terms of trade means both a reduction in the world relative price of imports and an increase in the relative price of exports— they are the same thing. Remember that although the government of the tariff-levying country can act like a monopolist, it is still assumed that private firms are numerous enough to act competitively.

If a tariff depresses the *world* relative price of imports, the *domestic* relative price of imports cannot rise by the full extent of the tariff. This relationship points to a conflict in the motives lying behind the use of a tariff. Tariffs often aim to protect local import-competing industries, which wish to raise the domestic price of the commodities they produce. If the foreign supply curve is infinitely elastic, the domestic relative price of food rises by the full extent of the tariff. The foreign supply curve in Figure 11.4 does allow the tariff to depress the relative world price of food to some extent. If the foreign supply curve had been more inelastic, the world terms of trade would have improved by a greater amount.

There remains the curious possibility that a tariff might depress the relative world price of a country's import commodity to such an extent that the domestic price of imports falls as well.[5] The important feature of such a possibility is that the tariff fails to protect the import-competing sector of the economy. Instead, it drives resources toward the export sector. Yet this is just the case in which a tariff leads to a large gain in the world terms of trade.

The precise conditions required for a tariff to fail to protect are not a concern here. Needless to say, they require a low foreign elasticity of supply. Disturbances such as tariffs require large price adjustments when the response to price changes (which is what elasticities measure) is low.

11.3   TARIFFS AND DOMESTIC WELFARE

If a country can improve its terms of trade by commercial policy, why is it not always beneficial to keep levying higher and higher tariffs to obtain ever better terms of trade? The analysis of the small country case in Section 11.1 provided a warning that there is more to the argument than this; if a country cannot improve its terms of trade, a tariff will actually harm welfare. There are two conflicting forces regarding the impact of a tariff on domestic welfare.

Figure 11.5 shows how welfare is linked to the height of the tariff for a country able to improve its terms of trade by trade restriction. Assume there is some rate of duty, t_1, large enough to choke off all trade. If such a tariff were applied, all gains from trade would be wiped out. (Imposing tariff rates higher than t_1 would have no further effect on real incomes because dutiable imports have already been reduced to zero.) Free trade (a zero tariff) is superior to no trade (with a tariff equal to t_1 or higher), so the curve in Figure 11.5 is lower after t_1 than initially at A. Furthermore, the terms-of-trade improvement that would occur when a small tariff is first levied must improve welfare. Obviously, there must be some intermediate tariff rate, t_0, that is "optimal" in that it maximizes the level of domestic welfare.

The concern here is not to compute the value of the "optimal tariff."[6] Instead, it is to understand the nature of the conflict between the two effects of a tariff on welfare. A tariff improves the terms of trade by itself raising welfare. However, the terms-of-trade improvement has been deliberately engineered by having the tariff choke off local import demand, and any reduction in imports must serve to lower domestic welfare if the *cost* of obtaining these imports (as shown by *world* prices) is lower than

[5] The argument that a tariff may fail to raise the price of the protected commodity behind the tariff wall is found in Lloyd Metzler, "Tariffs, the Terms of Trade, and the Distribution of National Income," *Journal of Political Economy*, 57 (February 1949): 1–29; reprinted in Caves and Johnson, eds., *Readings in International Economics* (Homewood, IL: Richard D. Irwin, 1968), Chapter 2. The logic of the argument is explained in the supplement to this chapter. The appendix to this chapter constructs an offer-curve diagram to illustrate the possibility that a small tariff may fail to protect, but a sufficiently large tariff always benefits the import-competing sector.

[6] This is carried out in the supplement to Chapter 11 and illustrated by means of the offer-curve diagram in the appendix.

FIGURE 11.5   Domestic Welfare Depends on the Tariff Rate

Free trade leads to a level of real income indexed by OA. For a country with some influence on world prices, a tariff can improve its terms of trade and lead initially to a gain in real income. Rate t_0 is the optimum tariff. Higher rates of duty cost more in forgone opportunities to import than is gained by a lowering of import prices. Rate t_1 cuts off all imports and leads to a level of real income identical to that of the no-trade state, which is lower than the free-trade level, OA.

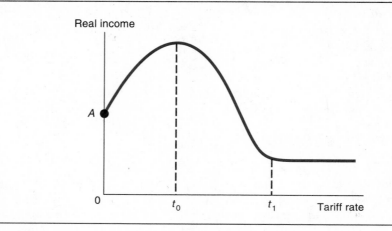

their *value* at home (as shown by *domestic* prices). A tariff is a wedge that raises domestic prices above world prices. Too high a tariff rate causes a greater loss through forgone opportunities to import than can be compensated for by the favorable price drop on remaining imports.

This discussion has assumed that the foreign country passively allows the home country to pursue whatever commercial practices it pleases while it retains a policy of free trade. This assumption overlooks the very real possibility that the foreign country will retaliate with its own tariff. Any foreign tariff worsens the terms of trade for the home country. If the foreign country does retaliate because of a tariff levied at home, it is no longer clear that the home country can benefit. Many outcomes of such a tariff war are possible. As will be related in Chapter 14, much of the tariff history of the major trading nations for the past forty years has been characterized by multilateral attempts to reduce tariff barriers, in full awareness of the dangers of escalation when a single country pursues an active commercial policy on its own.

11.4 TARIFFS AND WORLD WELFARE

Supporters of the free-trade doctrine point to the loss in *world* efficiency entailed by a tariff. Although the tariff-levying countries might gain, others stand to lose *more*. This argument focuses on the dead-weight loss introduced by the *distortion* that a tariff creates between prices in one country and another. To probe further, the argument will be presented in two stages: the effect of a tariff on world production, and the effect of a tariff on world consumption possibilities given the levels of production.

Tariffs and World Production

A tariff on food in the home country raises the relative price of food above its level in the foreign country. This higher price is reflected in a difference in the slopes of the two countries' transformation curves. Figure 11.6 superimposes the point showing production on the foreign transformation schedule (drawn upside down) on the point showing production at home. The production point is Q, for both countries, and the tariff wedge separating relative prices at home and abroad causes price line 1 at home to be flatter than price line 2 abroad. The point O^* shows posttariff *world* outputs of food and clothing relative to the axes through O. If the tariff were removed, resources in each country would be shifted into the commodity in which that country possesses a comparative advantage—clothing at home and food abroad. Points A and B represent possible free-trade production points. The slope of TT' at A equals the slope of $T^*T^{*\prime}$ at B, and if B were to be superimposed upon A, total world outputs would expand from O^* to C.

FIGURE 11.6   A Tariff and World Production

Point Q represents production at home and abroad. The foreign transformation schedule, $T^*T^{*\prime}$, is upside down so that total world production is shown by O^*. The home country's tariff on food imports leads to a higher relative price of food at home (shown by line 1) than abroad (shown by line 2). If the tariff is removed, both countries face the same price ratio (e.g., the common slope at A and B). If B is superimposed upon A, total world production expands from O^* to C.

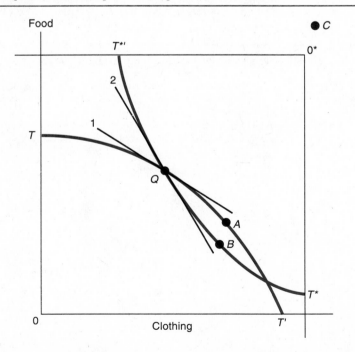

Tariffs and World Consumption Losses

One consequence of a tariff, therefore, is a reduction of world outputs below the free-trade level. From a world point of view, however, this is not the only consequence. Recall from Chapter 2 the discussion of the box diagram and the contract curve (Figure 2.8). For convenience the box is reproduced as Figure 11.7, which shows a *given* world total of food and clothing.

The imposition of the tariff on food in the home country causes domestic prices (as shown by the slope of line 1) to differ from foreign prices (given by the slope of line 2). Therefore, the tariff leads to a consumption allocation *off* the contract curve (such as point *A*). Compared with free-trade point *D* (the forces making *D* the free-trade point are not shown), the home country is better off with a tariff at *A* while the foreign country is hurt. In addition, world welfare has been reduced in that *A* is worse for *both* parties than some point on the contract curve, such as *B*.

11.5 SUMMARY

Tariff theory has both "positive" and "normative" aspects. The positive aspects are the effects of a tariff on prices, consumption, production, and trade. Proceeding first with a "small" country's tariff, it was shown that resources are shifted into the import-competing sector of the economy and demand is drawn away from the imported commodity. On both counts the country's demand for imports falls at the given world terms of trade. If a country is large enough for its actions to influence world prices, the contraction in import demand induced by the tariff will lower the country's relative price of imports and thus improve its terms of trade. There was a more ambiguous

---

FIGURE 11.7   The Tariff Pulls Consumption off the Contract Curve

---

Initial free-trade equilibrium is on the contract curve at D. The home country's tariff improves home welfare (to y_0) and reduces foreign welfare (to y_0^*) but pulls the consumption point off the contract curve (at A). A point such as B would improve *both* countries' welfare compared with tariff point A.

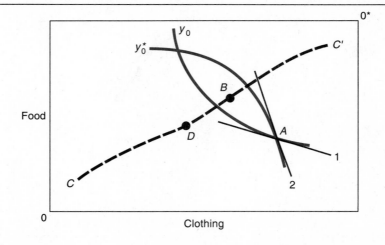

result concerning the relative domestic price of imports. Typically a tariff is "protective," because it raises the local price of the dutiable item, but if foreign response to price changes is sufficiently inelastic, the relative world price of imports could fall by more than the tariff itself. In that case a tariff on food would, paradoxically, lower the relative price of food behind the tariff wall.

The "normative" aspects of a tariff deal with its effect on welfare at home and abroad. The foreign country is hurt by the tariff—its terms of trade deteriorate. For the home tariff-levying country, however, there is more to consider than the possible improvement in the terms of trade. Once the domestic price of imports is higher than the world price, any further tariff increases may reduce imports of a commodity for which the cost of purchase abroad is less than the valuation at home (as measured by domestic prices). This loss in trade volume must be set against a terms-of-trade improvement in measuring the net benefits of a tariff. The extreme case of a tariff sufficiently high to choke off all trade shows that the optimal tariff must fall short of this. If the foreign country retaliates, the home country may end up with a lower level of real income than it obtained with free trade.

A tariff is an inferior way to redistribute income between countries. The reason? It introduces a distortion between domestic and world prices, and causes world outputs to settle at a suboptimal level while pushing consumption off the contract curve for any given levels of output. In this sense a tariff is a *second-best* instrument from a world point of view. Other means of redistributing income internationally (e.g., a direct gift from the foreign country to the home country) might allow both countries to emerge with a higher level of real income than a distortionary tariff provides. This "second-best" concept has wider applicability to other arguments for tariffs, as will be seen in Chapter 12.

CHAPTER PROBLEMS

1. A "small" country is one with no power to affect the world prices of commodities. Redraw Figures 11.4 and 11.5 for such a country.

2. The foreign supply curve of exports in Figure 11.4, X^*, has been drawn with a positive slope. This implies that foreign import demand for clothing is elastic. Suppose that for prices near the initial equilibrium point Q foreign import demand is inelastic. Draw the new X^* foreign supply curve of food exports. What is the effect of a tariff on imports of food? Would local food producers favor such a tariff?

3. In Figure 11.4 the tariff has shifted the demand curve for imports. Does the extent of the downward shift fall short of, equal, or exceed the amount of the tariff? (*Hint:* Ask what would happen to demand if world price were to fall by exactly the amount of the tariff— and decompose between substitution and income effects.)

4. Draw an initial free-trade equilibrium (for a small country facing given world prices) with a transformation schedule and indifference curves. Indicate in such a diagram the rate of the tariff that would completely wipe out trade. What happens to production and consumption if legislators are overzealous and the tariff rate is higher than this rate?

5. In the text it was assumed the government redistributes tariff proceeds back to the private sector. Instead, suppose the government spends the tariff revenues in a manner that differs from that of private citizens. Consider the two extreme forms of public spending: (a) the

tariff revenue is spent only on clothing, the commodity exported, or (b) the tariff revenue is allocated, instead, to purchases of food. Which scheme is more likely to be favored by producers who have clamored for protection? What might happen to the terms of trade in case (b)?

SUGGESTIONS FOR FURTHER READING

Jones, Ronald W. "Tariffs and Trade in General Equilibrium: Comment," *American Economic Review*, 59 (June 1969): 418–424. A brief analysis of basic tariff theory.

Metzler, Lloyd. "Tariffs, the Terms of Trade, and the Distribution of National Income," *Journal of Political Economy*, 57 (February 1949): 1–29. A more extensive account of tariff theory, concentrating on the effect of tariffs on domestic prices.

APPENDIX:
TARIFFS AND THE OFFER CURVE

The offer-curve construction described in the appendix to Chapter 3 is particularly useful in illustrating the impact of a tariff and the concept of the optimal tariff.

The Optimal Tariff

To pursue the geometry it is useful to introduce a simplifying assumption: The home country is completely specialized in producing its export commodity, clothing. The constant level of clothing output is shown in Figure 11.A.1 by distance $O_T O_C$. (O_T refers to the *trading* origin and O_C to the *consumption* origin.) The home offer curve, OR, intersects the foreign offer curve, OR^*, at point Q, establishing the slope of ray $O_T Q$ as the equilibrium terms of trade (the world relative price of clothing). That part of clothing production not exported is available for consumption at home, so that relative to the O_C origin any point in the diagram shows the home consumption bundle of food and clothing.

Two indifference curves have been drawn. The curve y_0 is tangent to ray $O_T D Q$; this is why point Q was selected at those prices. Clearly, other points on the foreign offer curve OR^* would represent more favorable trades for the home country. Point B lies on a higher indifference curve (not drawn). The curve tangent to the foreign offer curve, y_1, shows the maximal utility level possible for the home country.

How does the home country get to point A on curve y_1? By levying a tariff. As illustrated in the text, a tariff decreases the demand for imports and supply of exports at any given world terms of trade. That is, it shifts the home offer curve in toward the origin. The *optimal tariff* rate is that which leads to the home tariff–ridden offer curve $O_T R'$. Such a tariff has caused the relative *world* price of food, the commodity imported at home, to fall. This is shown by the greater slope of a ray from O_T through point A. The relative *domestic* price of food has slightly increased; the slope of indifference curve y_1 at its point of tangency with the foreign offer curve at A indicates

---

FIGURE 11.A.1   The Optimal Tariff

A tariff that shifts home offer curve OR to OR' is optimal. Home real income at point A is greater than at any other point on the foreign offer curve, OR^*

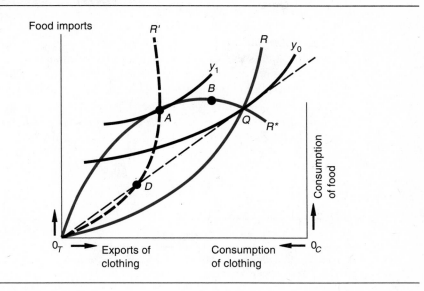

the domestic relative price of clothing. The wedge between the two prices shows the optimal tariff rate. (A formula for this rate is provided in the supplement.)

Imagine the country achieves the optimal tariff in small stages, gradually shifting its offer curve in until point A is reached. For equilibrium points between Q and B on the foreign offer curve, the home country clearly becomes better off, as each tariff increase results in greater home consumption of both commodities; this is the result of the foreign country's offer curve being inelastic in this range. Past point B increases in the tariff rate improve the home country's terms of trade, but at a sacrifice of a lower volume of trade. Finally, at point A, the loss from a further reduction in import volume (where the cost of imports—the world price—is lower than the value of imports—the domestic price) matches at the margin the gain from still better terms of trade.

The spirit of this analysis is that the home country has the power to set world prices, subject only to the constraint that at these prices foreigners buy and sell the amounts shown on their offer curve. This may not be borne out in practice; the foreign country might well retaliate with tariffs of its own. As will be seen in Chapter 14, tariff rates most often reflect a process of multilateral tariff negotiations.

The Protective Effect of a Tariff

As previously suggested, a tariff may fail to protect the home import-competing industry by improving the terms of trade so much that the relative domestic price of importables falls. The offer-curve diagram and yet another concept—*the income-consumption curve*—can usefully illustrate this possibility.

Figure 11.A.2 follows Figure 11.A.1 in illustrating the foreign offer curve, $O_T R^*$, with initial free-trade equilibrium at point Q along an inelastic section of the offer curve. The home indifference curve tangent to ray $O_T Q$ has been drawn. The income-consumption curve for the home country, IC, is the locus of points along home indifference curves for which slopes are the same as at Q (e.g., at point H). This IC curve cuts the foreign offer curve at point E.

As previously illustrated, a tariff levied on home imports of food shifts the home offer so that it cuts the foreign offer curve at a point such as G. A higher tariff would shift the home offer curve even more. The principal conclusion is that a home tariff leading to a new equilibrium anywhere in the stretch EQ along the foreign offer curve fails to protect the home food sector. The reason: At a point such as G the home indifference curve is steeper than at H (equal to the slope at Q). Therefore, the relative domestic price of food at G is less than the pretariff price at Q. This is called the *Metzler Paradox*. However, a tariff sufficiently high to place the new equilibrium point along the $O_T E$ stretch of the foreign offer curve must raise the home relative price of food.

FIGURE 11.A.2   The Tariff May Not Protect

IC is the income consumption curve for the home country, which cuts the foreign offer curve at E. A tariff that leads to an equilibrium in the EQ range of the foreign curve (e.g., at G) serves to lower the domestic relative price of importables, as is shown by the slope of the indifference curve at G. A tariff in range EQ fails to protect.

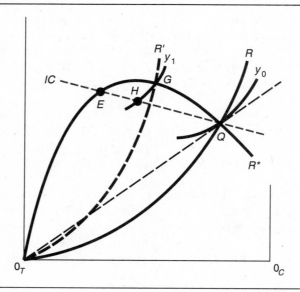

If the income-consumption curve is steeper than the foreign offer curve at Q, any tariff, no matter how small, must be protective. The condition for this, as is proved in the supplement to Chapter 11, is

$$\varepsilon^* > 1 - m$$

where ε^* is the elasticity of foreign demand for imports along $O_T ER^*$ at Q, and m is the home marginal propensity to import (food). Obviously, if foreign demand is elastic, this condition must be satisfied (as long as both commodities are "normal" at home, that is, the IC curve is negatively sloped).

12

THE POLITICAL ECONOMY OF PROTECTION

It would be naive to suppose that nations levy tariffs only after carefully weighing the pros and cons for the entire community. Instead, special sections or groups often find that their interests can be served by interfering with free trade despite a loss to others in the economy. Indeed, these groups often find that the potential gains from favorable commercial policies are worth a substantial investment of resources and lobbying efforts. They realize that the political process frequently rewards a minority with strong convictions in the face of relatively mild losses to each member of a majority. In addition, special circumstances may seem to warrant restrictive trade policies, although deeper analysis would reveal that other weapons in a nation's fiscal armor are more effective or impose lower social costs. Protection is frequently a "second-best" device in achieving social goals.

The bulk of this chapter is devoted to a discussion of this array of arguments for trade restriction. The chapter concludes with the recognition of what was stressed in Chapter 9—many items of commerce are not final consumer goods but raw materials and intermediate goods. Tariffs on intermediate goods require that a distinction be made between nominal tariffs on final consumer goods and the implied "effective" tariffs on their assembly within the nation's borders.

12.1 THE TARIFF AS A DEVICE FOR RAISING REVENUE

Long before the progressive income tax and other sophisticated instruments were devised to provide governments with necessary revenues, the government agent at the port of entry typically extracted a toll on the inflow of merchandise from abroad. Any tariff rate that is not so high as to be prohibitive is a source of revenue. Although modern industrial states rarely rely on customs duties to provide government income, less-developed regions often do.

The relationship between a tariff's impact on real income and on tariff revenue is expressed in Figure 12.1. A zero tariff yields no revenue. Tariff rate t_1 is assumed to be prohibitive, so higher rates of duty also yield no revenue. In the diagram it is

FIGURE 12.1   Tariff Revenue and Real Income

The curve showing tariff revenue reaches a peak at a higher tariff rate than does the curve showing real income.

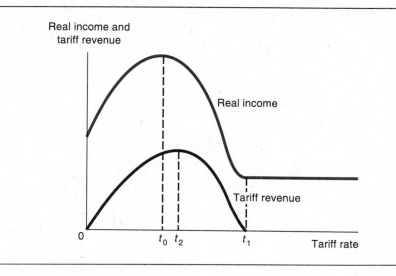

assumed that revenues rise continuously, reaching a peak for rate t_2, and, as imports dwindle, fall continuously to zero at rate t_1. The crucial point to notice is that the revenue-maximizing rate, t_2, exceeds the optimal tariff rate, t_0. An algebraic proof is provided in the supplement to Chapter 12. The geometric argument is provided in Figure 12.2.

Production in Figure 12.2 is assumed to be locked in at corner point A along the TAT' transformation curve. This simplifies the argument.[1] Consumption point B along indifference curve y_0 shows equilibrium with a tariff that has driven the domestic relative price of food imports to the height shown by lines 1 and 2.[2] Therefore distance CA measures the tariff revenue in food units. Suppose the existing tariff rate maximizes tariff revenue, such as at rate t_2 in Figure 12.1. Note what this implies: A slight increase in the tariff rate would leave tariff revenue (virtually) unaltered—at AC in Figure 12.2. If the relationship between real income and tariff revenue illustrated in Figure 12.1, whereby real income is falling at rate t_2, is to be confirmed, an increase in the tariff rate in Figure 12.2 must push consumers onto a lower indifference curve. This it does—the move from B on curve y_0 to D on curve y_1. Therefore, the tariff rate that maximizes revenue (t_2) must exceed the optimal tariff rate (t_0).

That these two critical rates are not equivalent underscores the point that pursuing commercial policy for revenue purposes is not optimal strategy. Thus, if at current

---

[1] The argument is strengthened if production responds along a smoothly bowed-out transformation schedule.

[2] The relative world price of clothing would be shown by the slope of a line connecting production point A with consumption point B.

FIGURE 12.2   The Maximum Revenue Tariff Exceeds the Optimal Tariff

---

Tariff revenue is shown by distance *CA*. Near a tariff that maximizes revenue, a small increase in the tariff rate will not change tariff revenue. Consumption point *D* is on a lower indifference curve than point *B* and corresponds to a higher tariff.

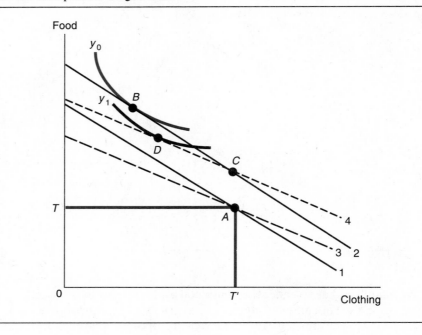

tariff levels an increase in the rate of duty would lower tariff revenues, the current levels are too high for optimal welfare.

It is well at this point to recall that for a small country that cannot influence the world prices of what it buys and sells, the optimal tariff rate is zero. A tariff to raise revenue must then be rationalized by other arguments, such as the ease of collection on international commerce as compared with local sales or income taxes.

12.2 TARIFFS, THE DISTRIBUTION OF INCOME, AND RENT-SEEKING ACTIVITIES

The American automobile industry is one among many that feels threatened by foreign competition. What attitude toward tariffs or other protective devices would be expected from an autoworker trained in tasks that have little application outside the auto industry, or from the owner of a specialized machine that cannot be used for any purpose other than making autos? Productive factors tied to one industry or occupation are very much affected by trade and commercial policies. Special interests and specific factors employed in import-competing industries will usually favor trade restrictions.

If protection favors inputs specific to import-competing production, a counter-argument for free trade can be mounted by factors tied to the nation's export industries.

The logic is there, but the argument is less obvious. It might not be recognized that dismantling barriers to imports encourages prices and production in the export sectors.

The impact of relative price changes on the incomes of specific factors of production was analyzed in Chapter 6. How does this compare with the impact on broad-based productive factors, such as relatively unskilled labor, that can move from one sector of the economy to another, earning roughly the same wage in each? The analysis in Chapter 6 suggested that these factors are much less apt to be affected significantly by the price changes brought about by a tariff than are the factors (skilled labor, specific capital equipment) tied more closely to particular industries.

This conclusion tends to modify the "pauper labor" argument, which asserts that laborers in high-wage countries are hurt by competition from low-wage labor abroad. This argument tends to ignore the fact that high wages reflect high productivity, made possible in part by ample supplies of cooperating productive factors (land, capital). Nonetheless, a germ of truth in the pauper labor argument is provided by the Heckscher-Ohlin model of production and trade, which was analyzed in Chapter 7. Suppose production in any sector requires only the services of two broad-based factors: capital and labor. Further, suppose that the high-wage country takes advantage of trading opportunities to import commodities that would be produced by labor-intensive techniques at home. A tariff that drives up the domestic price of these items serves to drive up the real wage as well. As was shown in the discussion in Chapter 7 of the Stolper-Samuelson result, a change in relative commodity prices gets transmitted into magnified changes in the returns to the two productive factors. One factor unambiguously gains from the tariff; the other factor loses. Such a strong result gets modified if there are more than two identifiable productive factors (as in the specific factors case). Nonetheless, if a particular factor (for example, labor) is intensively used in the production of import-competing goods, this factor may be expected to support a protectionist stance.[3]

Can a factor of production whose wage is hurt by a tariff find sufficient relief through receiving a cut of the tariff revenue? Once the possibility of income redistribution through fiscal devices is considered, it is only logical to ask how a tariff affects the community as a whole. This brings the discussion back to the optimal tariff argument discussed in Chapter 11. For a "small" country (unable to affect world prices) free trade was optimal. For a country with some influence on world prices, some finite degree of protection seems attractive, but only if the danger of foreign retaliation is ignored.

However attractive the possibility of income redistribution through taxes and subsidies may appear in principle, the political facts of life suggest that such redistribution often fails to counteract the impact of commercial policy. There is no doubt that for many groups protectionist legislation helps support "artificially" high levels of income, and that such groups are not apt to be fobbed off with arguments about the welfare of the community as a whole.

[3] Interesting early work concerning the question of whether employed factors tend to support protection for the industry in which they are employed (as would make sense for specific factors), regardless of whether the factor is capital or labor, is associated with papers by William Brock and Steve Magee. See, for example, their "The Economics of Special Interest Politics: The Case of a Tariff," *American Economic Review* 68 (May 1978): 246–250. A model describing how tariffs in a democratic system can reflect factor ownership patterns (whether of the Heckscher-Ohlin variety or the specific-factors type) is developed by Wolfgang Mayer, "Endogenous Tariff Formation," *American Economic Review*, 74 (December 1984): 970–985.

Rent-Seeking

Any restriction on production, exchange, or trade can alter the distribution of income, thus leading to resources being expended either to promote the imposition of these restrictions or to attempt to block their passage. A particularly clear example of restrictions on trade leading to income redistribution is the case of quotas imposed on imports. In a classic article, Anne Krueger described how competition to obtain the valuable import licenses that allow imports under a quota regime serves to waste resources.[4] The quotas create *rents*, and, as in any activity that promises profits, such a return attracts entrants.

The competition for rents created by the quotas takes many forms. Bribery of government officials is popular in some less-developed regions. This may take the indirect form of loading the payroll with relatives of government officials or passing out lucrative subcontracts to individuals with ties to important persons in the public sector. Expansion of plant capacity can be stimulated, even if it leads to excess capacity, if import licenses are directly related to that measure of potential production. To give some idea of the magnitude of the rents just from import licenses, Krueger cites rough figures of over 7 percent of national income for India (1964) and about 15 percent of GNP for Turkey (1968).

12.3 THE TARIFF AS A "SECOND-BEST" DEVICE

Commercial policy can affect the economy in a variety of ways—by changing prices, outputs, employment, and incomes. Tariffs (and import quotas or other forms of trade restriction) are not the only weapons available to governments for influencing the economy, however. Taxes or subsidies on sales, production, consumption, or incomes of particular groups can also be employed. In many respects these taxes (or subsidies) are substitutes for commercial policy, though not perfect substitutes. Is a subsidy to production better or worse than a tariff? It depends very much on the policy objective. The tariff can often be used to help implement some social objective, but it proves frequently to be "second-best" to some alternative policy instrument. The following three cases suffice to make the general point.

1. *Production Goals.* Suppose that the free-trade level of production of some commodity is thought to be too low. Perhaps labor receives special valuable training in the production of this item, or perhaps the community feels it should become more self-reliant on its own production in case foreign supplies are threatened in the future. (Witness the arguments about American dependence on foreign energy sources.) What is the optimal policy for encouraging greater domestic production?

The stage is set in Figure 12.3. The country is initially in a free-trade equilibrium at world prices reflected by the slope of line 1: Production is at *A*, consumption at *B*, and thus the country imports food. Now suppose the country wants to increase *production* of food, and compare two alternative policies available to accomplish this

[4] Anne O. Krueger, "The Political Economy of the Rent-Seeking Society," *American Economic Review* 44 (June 1974): 291–303. For a discussion of this phenomenon in a wider context, see James Buchanan, G. Tullock, and R. Tollison, eds., *Towards a General Theory of the Rent-Seeking Society* (College Station: Texas A & M University Press, 1980), or Jagdish Bhagwati, "Directly Unproductive, Profit-Seeking (DUP) Activities," *Journal of Political Economy* (October 1982): 988–1002.

FIGURE 12.3   Tariffs vs. Production Subsidies to Achieve a Production Goal

Free-trade production is at *A* and consumption at *B*. If *OJ* level of food production must be undertaken, a tariff that raises food's relative price at home to line 2 is sufficient. Consumption is then at *E*. A production subsidy could yield the same result for producers, but at a lower cost in welfare. Consumption is at *H*.

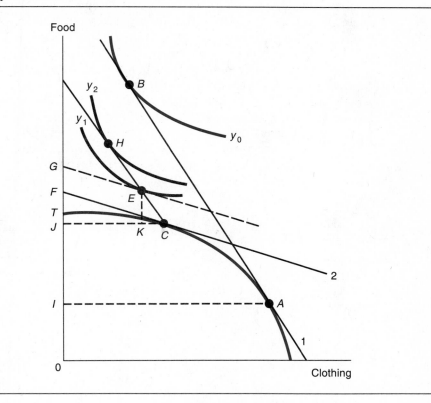

end—a *tariff* on imports of food or a *subsidy* to producers of food. Assume the desired production target is to raise food output from *OI* to *OJ*.

A tariff on food can be analyzed as in the preceding chapter. A duty high enough to move production to point *C* raises the domestic relative price of food to that shown by line 2. What is consumption behind this tariff wall? The consumption bundle must lie on an indifference curve whose slope reflects relative *domestic* prices, and it must have the same value as production point *C* at *world* prices. This is point *E*, and restricted imports are *EK*, matched at world prices by clothing exports *KC*.

The alternative strategy involves providing a subsidy to food producers sufficient once again to reach production point *C*. World food prices are reflected in line *HEC*, parallel to line 1, and food producers receive the higher (subsidized) price shown by line 2. But now home consumers are free to buy at world prices, and the best such point for them is *H* on curve y_2, which represents a higher level of satisfaction than does *E* on indifference curve y_1.

The moral of this comparison is clear. The objective is assumed to be a production goal. This can be achieved at a lower cost in terms of forgone real income if an instrument is used that focuses precisely on this goal. A production subsidy does exactly that, whereas a tariff (needlessly) distorts prices to consumers.[5]

2. *Consumption Goals.* Analogous remarks can be made about the desire that some governments express to restrict consumption of some items below the levels that the community would voluntarily choose in a free-trade situation. For example, the government may wish to restrict the private sector's consumption of automobiles or other items it deems to be unnecessary luxuries.

A tariff can accomplish the purpose, but so could a direct tax on consumption of the luxury item. These are different instruments, for a tax on consumption raises the price to consumers above the world level but leaves producers to face world competition at world prices. By contrast, a tariff raises the domestic price to producers as well as consumers and encourages a transfer of domestic resources away from exportables and toward production of the luxury item. If the government's desire is solely to restrict *consumption*, needless losses are involved by using a tariff, for the production shift away from exportables causes the value of income produced at world prices to fall below its free-trade level.

Arguments for tariffs are often aimed at altering the production or consumption pattern of a free-trade regime. Heeding the pleas of special consumer or producer interests involves a loss of welfare to the nation as a whole. Because the tariff affects both consumption and production, using it to alter either makes this loss larger than necessary. A more efficient instrument is a production tax or subsidy to change production or a consumption tax or subsidy to control consumption. In each case the instrument that works most directly on the objective should be used.[6]

3. *Domestic Distortions.* Market prices are not always perfect indicators of social costs and benefits. Occasionally elements of monopoly or of externalities in production or consumption distort market prices away from levels that represent social opportunity costs and values. For example, a commodity that enters a country's export lists may appear to have a low cost of production—and thus be exported—because pollution damage involved in the production process is not taken into account. (Firms may be dumping effluents into the country's streams and harbors at no cost to themselves but at considerable damage to the community.) In such cases it is possible to argue that levels of free trade are not optimal. Instead, those who would attempt to restrict exports (and imports) seem to find natural allies in ecologists and environmentalists. Once again, however, it can be shown that trade restrictions offer only a "second-best" solution to a problem that is better met directly by consumption or production taxes that attempt to remedy the distortion.

[5] This analysis can be found in W. M. Corden, "Tariffs, Subsidies, and the Terms of Trade," *Economica*, N.S. 24 (August 1957): 235–242.

[6] Other examples and a more detailed discussion of the material in this section can be found in H. G. Johnson, "Optimal Trade Intervention in the Presence of Domestic Distortions," in R. E. Baldwin et al., eds., *Trade, Growth, and the Balance of Payments* (Chicago: Rand McNally, 1965). See also J. N. Bhagwati, "The Generalized Theory of Distortions and Welfare," in J. N. Bhagwati et al., eds., *Trade, Balance of Payments, and Growth: Papers in International Economics in Honor of Charles P. Kindleberger* (Amsterdam: North-Holland, 1971), Chapter 4.

If social and private costs differ, there is not only the danger that export levels may be too high or too low; it is also possible that the *pattern of* trade itself is distorted. To return to the pollution example, suppose that private marginal production costs excluding pollution costs fall short of costs in the rest of the world by less than the costs of pollution abatement. Then forcing producers to bear these costs would entail that the industry shift from being net exporters to becoming importers.

The reason export taxes (or tariffs) are "second-best" devices in these examples is that it is either production or consumption levels that are distorted away from their socially optimal level, *not* trade levels. Commercial policy, which affects both domestic consumption and production, is usually inefficient as a device for controlling either separately.[7] Thus, even though the achieved levels of trade may not be socially desirable (e.g., in the pollution case), trade policies designed to correct the situation are wasteful because they involve unnecessary social costs.

An important type of "distortion" will be discussed at greater length in Chapter 13—that reflecting monopoly behavior or other forms of imperfect competition. Of particular interest is the case in which a domestic monopolist charges prices *to foreigners* that exceed marginal costs of production. Traditional public attitudes against using commercial (or other public) policy instruments to aid monopolistic firms have been challenged by recent arguments suggesting that government enter the fray on the side of our own contenders when they battle with foreign firms in world markets.

12.4 COMMERCIAL POLICY AND ECONOMIC DEVELOPMENT

No survey of the reasons why countries have used tariffs and other restrictive devices is complete without a brief look at the special complaint often voiced by less-developed countries. Nations at early stages of development frequently view free trade as a set of arrangements that deliberately or unintentionally impedes their own industrialization efforts, notwithstanding the many counterexamples of trade serving as an "engine of growth" for many nations settled and developed during the nineteenth century or of the recent experience of NICs in Southeast Asia tying high growth rates to export performance.

One complaint about life in a trading world is that any nation, especially a small, less-developed nation, to some extent loses control of its own destiny in being exposed to changes in world prices, demands, and supplies. This is an inevitable consequence of allowing production patterns to be based in large part not on local demands (over which the government presumably has some control) but on world tastes and the relative efficiency of local and foreign sources of supply. This introduces elements not only of "dependence" on foreigners, but also of uncertainty as to the future course of the terms of trade. Such uncertainty can play havoc with tightly budgeted central planning.

Leaving aside uncertainty and "dependence"—features of trade that even wealthy, advanced countries cannot avoid (as learned by the United States and Western Europe during the recurring energy crises)—less-developed countries often argue that trade

---

[7] As was remarked by Prof. Alan Deardorff of the University of Michigan, employing tariffs to attain a consumption goal or a production goal is like performing acupuncture with a fork.

adversely affects the local *structure* of the economy in ways that can partly be avoided by judicious use of tariffs, quotas, and other devices that restrict and control trade. As these arguments are surveyed, note the "second-best" flavor of the case for trade restriction as compared with alternative development strategies.

The Infant Industry Argument

The term "infant" refers to young or not yet established industrial activities that are prevented from developing because local prices are kept too low by foreign competition. If only the "infant" could be allowed to develop, so the argument goes, the nation could establish a comparative advantage in these industries or, at the least, compete successfully at home given the natural protective umbrella of international transport costs. This is a time-honored argument—used, for example, by the American iron industry in the nineteenth century—but what guarantee is there that the "infant" will grow up even with tariff protection?

To probe further, note that it is not sufficient to argue that a protected, larger scale of output could result in driving down costs. Could protection ultimately be removed? Is the local protected market of sufficient size to provide the scale required to lower costs to foreign levels? Even if these questions can be answered in the affirmative, protection may not be worthwhile for the community. Growing up takes time, and during this period consumers at home are paying more for goods than they would have done if resources had not been devoted to the protected sector. Any future gains must be discounted back to the present and set against these losses.

Suppose that even on such a calculation net gains may be realized from developing the industry. Why won't this be apparent to private entrepreneurs? Business firms often make investments, with returns spread out over future periods. That is, most investments involve a trade-off between present costs and future benefits, and if undertaken reflect an assessment that the present value of the benefits exceeds the costs. The argument for sheltering an industry during its growth is certainly weakened if prospective gains consist of economies of scale (average costs reduced with expansion of output) that are perceived by the firm.

The germ of truth in the infant-industry argument applies when the eventual gains from establishing the industry cannot all be recouped by those who have made the initial investments. Some form of externality must be present. To take an example, suppose workers gain by the skills learned during industrialization. These skills, deemed a gain to the community, can be transferred to other industries. That is, entrepreneurs in a particular sector may undergo costs of training the labor force that are subsequently lost to them if that labor moves to other occupations.[8] If so, it is maintained that protection should be given to offset these losses.

However, is tariff protection the best way of supporting these industries? In the case just cited, where labor is improving its skills by on-the-job training, a direct production subsidy would not involve the consumption distortion imposed by the tariff. An even better device would aim at subsidizing the use of labor if indeed the externality involves primarily their skills.

---

[8] Note, however, that it is possible to argue that if laborers are aware of the value of skills learned in an industry, competition will drive wages in that industry below wage rates prevailing elsewhere in the economy.

A variation on the infant industry argument has recently been put forth by Paul Krugman in the intra-industry framework for trade described in Chapter 8, in which a country produces a variety of differentiated products closely related in consumer tastes both to each other and to competing foreign brands.[9] A protective barrier placed against imports will shift demand onto locally produced products. Because production in this scenario is characterized by some degree of decreasing costs, a protected home market also implies an extra advantage in exporting these same products. The traditional infant industry argument envisioned sequential stages, with the home market being reserved for local producers; eventually costs are lowered, and then, it is hoped, the country might export once tariffs are removed. By contrast, the possibility of intra-industry trade with its mutual interpenetration of markets implies that even at early stages a country is both an importer and an exporter.

Growth, Protection, and Welfare

If a country devotes newly available resources to its traditional export sectors, won't this encourage a drop in export prices? As was discussed in Chapter 4, in any country in which growth is biased toward exportables, that country's terms of trade will tend to worsen. Tariff policy can be used to encourage the local production of import-competing commodities, thus forestalling such a price deterioration in the export sector.

This kind of argument loses its force if the country under discussion is too small to affect world prices of its export commodity. Suppose this is the case but nonetheless the developing country has imposed tariffs on imports to support an import-competing industry over and above its free-trade level. It was argued in Chapter 11 (see especially Figure 11.1) that such a diversion of resources entails real income losses. More can be said, however. As this country grows, the more it devotes its resources to the protected import-competing sector, the more its potential real income gains from growth are cut back. In extreme cases, growth at home could even result in a loss of welfare.

Figure 12.4 illustrates these possibilities. Line 2 indicates world prices. The country has protected its import-competing sector, food, and so line 1, showing domestic prices behind the tariff wall, is flatter than line 2. At these protected prices the community's optimal production point along transformation schedule TT' is at tangency point A and consumption is at A'.

Now suppose that world prices remain unchanged and the country's tariff structure is unaltered, but the value of produced income at domestic prices rises by 25 percent. That is, at domestic prices the country grows by 25 percent, but what industries have expanded? It makes a big difference, even for a small price-taking country. Points B, C, D, and E represent four possible alternative production points for which aggregate output at domestic prices would be 25 percent larger than at A. Point B is a point of balanced expansion relative to initial point A. For such a case, home consumption lies on a line through B with slope showing world prices (i.e., parallel to line 2), at

[9] See Paul Krugman, "Import Protection as Export Promotion: International Competition in the Presence of Oligopoly and Economies of Scale," in H. Kierzkowski, ed., *Monopolistic Competition and International Trade* (Oxford, UK, Oxford University Press, 1984), pp. 180–193.

FIGURE 12.4   Growth with Protection

With a tariff on food imports, line 1 showing domestic prices is flatter than line 2 showing world prices. A' is the initial consumption point corresponding to production along TT' at A. Growth to any of points B, C, D, and E shows a 25 percent increase in produced income at domestic prices. But corresponding consumption points B', C', D', E' are not equivalent.

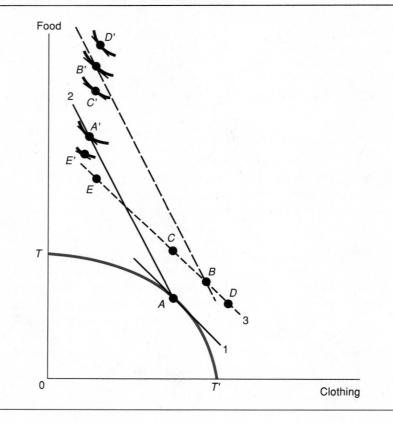

consumption point B'. Growth has increased real income. Now suppose instead that only the import-competing sector had been allowed to grow (point C lies directly above point A). The real income gains would have been cut back, an outcome underlined by comparing it to the alternative of letting only the export sector expand (point D lies to the right of A). Consumption point D' is preferable to B' (which is preferable to C').

The composition of output might have been altered even more radically by growth. Point E shows such a possible skewed growth point. Growth has been so biased in favor of the commodity (food) that is artificially high-priced at home that the seemingly higher-valued production point (compare E with A at domestic prices) represents an actual loss at world prices. This phenomenon could only occur if the import-competing sector is protected.[10] These comments reveal that in a growth context protection may impose costs that go beyond those described for a static economy.

Income Distribution and Domestic Saving

Most developing countries are concerned with raising levels of investment, in part by borrowing overseas but also by encouraging domestic saving. It has been seen that the distribution of income among productive factors can be radically affected by a policy of protection. Suppose that the factors differ in their propensities to save; owners of the factor used intensively in the import-competing sector save, for example, 10 percent of any extra incomes, while owners of the factor used intensively in exportables save only 5 percent. A trade restriction would then redistribute income toward the thriftier group and raise the average rate of saving. Many less-developed countries apparently believe that incomes earned by landowners from producing primary exports are not invested, or at least not invested in activities the government favors. If one makes that assumption, the most efficient policy is to tax landowner incomes directly. Export taxes, however, are often used as a second-best substitute.[11]

12.5   PROTECTION AND FOREIGN INVESTMENT

An argument sometimes raised in favor of protection is that it may encourage foreign investment in home markets. A tariff can affect the pattern of investment. If a country is initially importing a commodity, a protective tariff wall forces foreign firms either to cut prices, lose sales, or, alternatively, try to produce the commodity directly in the home market and thus avoid the tariff. Such "tariff-factories" are not rare, as evidenced, for example, in the number of automobile assembly plants located in Argentina, Brazil, South Africa, and other countries that do not possess a comparative advantage in automobile production.

Studies of the multinational corporation show that a tariff often causes it to invest in a country. Previously it has exported to the market in question, investing in advertising and customer good will but not in physical production facilities. When its exports to the market are struck with a tariff, direct investment becomes more attractive than the only alternative—writing off the firm's investment in good will and leaving the market entirely.

There is, however, something ironic about such a policy. Suppose a country is attempting to limit its dependence on foreign sources of supply by following a protectionist policy. It may also be anxious to diversify its productive structure by protecting its local industries from foreign competition. Keeping out foreign-made goods, however, may just encourage the foreigner to come in. In the years before the Free-Trade Pact Canada seemed bedeviled by a desire both to protect a whole panoply

---

[10] The possibility of welfare loss with growth, if an industry is protected, was pointed out by Harry G. Johnson, "The Possibility of Income Losses from Increased Efficiency or Factor Accumulation in the Presence of Tariffs," *Economic Journal*, 77 (March 1967): 151–154.

[11] As was explained in Chapter 11, export taxes and import taxes are symmetrical in their tendency to restrict the level of trade.

of secondary industries and to limit the incursion of American direct investment, which such a protected market seemed to attract.

Chapter 10 discussed various advantages and disadvantages to host countries of allowing foreign investment. Yet what can be said of using higher degrees of protection in order to attract more foreign investment? Chapter 11 argued that a country too small to improve its terms of trade by means of a tariff actually harms itself by protection. A tariff or other restriction on trade inserts a wedge between the cost of obtaining importables in world markets and the (higher) value of those importables to local consumers; cost is measured by world price, value by domestic price behind the tariff wall. Any action serving to cut back a nation's imports when an existing tariff wedge causes value to exceed cost must lower welfare at home. An increase in the tariff rate is one such action; such a rise causes a contraction in imports.

If foreign investment responds to changes in degrees of protection, the response is apt to exacerbate the damage such protection inflicts on the host country. An increase in levels of protection tends to attract investment into the protected sector and, by thus encouraging production, to cause imports to fall even further.[12] This phenomenon is not restricted to foreign investment in a nation's import-competing industries. Suppose foreigners have invested in the host country's export industries. An increase in tariffs on importables tends to favor that sector over exportables. For example, the squeeze may come through the tariff-inspired rise in wage rates that lowers returns to foreign investment in the export sector. A consequent *reduction* in foreign investment there cuts back on trade; importables (as well as exportables) are reduced and with them the nation's welfare, just as in the case of *increases* in foreign investment in the import-competing sector.

For a small country a policy of protection may lessen welfare by providing the wrong signal for local resource allocation. The international mobility of foreign productive factors may worsen the situation further as they also respond to the wrong signal.[13]

12.6 TARIFFS, EMPLOYMENT, AND THE BALANCE OF PAYMENTS: A PRELIMINARY VIEW

Two widely quoted arguments favoring tariff protection can only be mentioned here, as the flexible-prices, full-employment assumptions that have characterized the discussion so far need to be altered to do these arguments justice. This will be carried out in Part IV of this book.

The first argument states that tariffs (or other forms of protection) can save jobs, or create jobs, in those industries competing most directly with foreign goods. Even in our models this argument has validity: Protecting an industry does attract resources

[12] Here it is assumed the tariff does not wipe out imports. An alternative possibility is that any degree of protection attracts so much capital from abroad that the country becomes self-sufficient in production. In such a case foreign investment may actually increase welfare by circumventing the tariff. See R. A. Mundell, "International Trade and Factor Mobility," *American Economic Review*, 47 (June 1957): 321–335.

[13] The argument cited here is advanced in R. W. Jones, "Protection and the Harmful Effects of Endogenous Capital Flows," *Economics Letters*, 15 (1984): 325–330.

from other sectors. However, this does not necessarily mean that overall employment will rise. What is left out here is the question of employment in a nation's export industries. This problem becomes aggravated if foreign countries respond to the tariff by retaliating with barriers against home exports.

Although the argument for aggregate employment must be analyzed later (Part IV), a word should be mentioned about employment in each sector. Any change in world prices causes potential disturbances at home as the signal is given for some sectors to contract (and others to expand). Output changes, however, typically involve costs—relocation of labor from one industry to another and perhaps geographically as well. Frictions in readjustments could easily involve unemployment in some sectors, at least in the short run. It is understandable that an industry threatened by technical improvements or other forms of cost reductions abroad should plead for protection. Indeed, as Chapter 14 discusses, provisions involving such "peril points" are written into American law. Most readjustments are costly and take time. Tariff protection might postpone the adjustment, but once again it must be judged "second-best" relative to direct retraining and relocation assistance.

The second argument is that a tariff can improve the balance of payments. Here the assumptions that prices clear markets and a community spends exactly the value of its produced income stand in the way of a proper appraisal of the argument. A balance-of-trade surplus represents an excess of exports over imports, so it is tempting to argue that a tariff can create a surplus by restricting imports. However, a trade surplus also indicates that the nation is producing more than it is spending, and we must await the analysis of macroeconomic relationships in Part IV before asking how a tariff might create such an aggregate excess of output over spending.

12.7 EFFECTIVE PROTECTION

Actual production processes are rarely as simple as the theory presented here has assumed. In particular, commodities at various stages of fabrication are outputs of some productive activities and inputs into others. Flour to make bread, spun yarn to make clothing, sheet steel to make automobiles—these are only a few examples of interindustry flows in what economists call "intermediate commodities." Chapter 9 emphasized the large volume of international trade in these intermediate commodities; such a trade pattern has encouraged the development of a different concept in analyzing a country's commercial policy, that of the "effective rate of protection." It takes into account the fact that the "nominal" tariff applied to imports of a commodity does not by itself indicate the impact of protection for the domestic industry producing that commodity if that industry utilizes imported inputs that are subject to duty. The domestic industry "adds value" to the imported inputs, and the effect of protection on this "value added" is the key indicator of how protection affects resource allocation.

As an example, suppose the free-trade price of clothing on world markets is $1.00, and to produce a unit of clothing a country imports $.40 worth of spun yarn from abroad. The domestic industry then creates an additional $.60 worth of value added. Now suppose a 40 percent "nominal" tariff is levied on clothing imports, raising their domestic price to $1.40, and a 10 percent tariff is applied to imports of spun yarn, raising their cost to $.44 per unit of clothing behind the tariff wall. The domestic producer now receives as value added per unit of clothing $.96, the difference between $1.40 and the $.44 spent as outlay on imported cloth. This difference represents an increase of 60 percent over the original value added, $(1.40 - .44)/.60$. The tariff structure has yielded a 60 percent "effective rate" of protection to domestic clothing producers, whereas the "nominal" rate on clothing imports was only 40 percent. This example illustrates the kind of "escalation" that can be built into a nation's tariff structure if commodities at a lower level of fabrication or processing (steel, yarn) are charged lower duties than more finished items (automobiles, clothing).

The ingredients in the effective tariff rate emerge from this example. The rate attempts to measure the percentage by which value added can increase over the free-trade level as a consequence of a tariff structure. Let the fixed free-trade price of imports of the *final* good be denoted by p_j^*. With a tariff at rate t_j on these imports, the domestic price becomes $(1 + t_j)p_j^*$. Suppose the productive process uses an imported intermediate good, i, with a fixed world price, p_i^*. If a tariff at rate t_i is applied to imports of this intermediate good, its price behind the tariff wall is $(1 + t_i)p_i^*$. It is also necessary to know how much of the intermediate good is required per unit of final output. Let this be denoted by a_{ij}, and assume it is fixed. Then at free-trade world prices the value added per unit of final output is

$$v_j^* = p_j^* - a_{ij}p_i^*$$

Compare this with value added at domestic posttariff prices, v_j:

$$v_j = (1 + t_j)p_j^* - a_{ij}(1 + t_i)p_i^*$$

The effective rate of protection by definition is

$$\frac{v_j - v_j^*}{v_j^*} = \frac{t_j p_j^* - t_i a_{ij} p_i^*}{p_j^* - a_{ij} p_i^*}$$

Finally, divide both numerator and denominator by the world price of the final commodity, p_j^*, and let θ_{ij} denote the *share* of the intermediate commodity in a dollar's worth of final output at free-trade prices. That is, θ_{ij} is $a_{ij}p_i^*/p_j^*$. The effective rate of protection provided to the final commodity is thus:

$$\frac{t_j - \theta_{ij}t_i}{1 - \theta_{ij}}$$

In our numerical example, t_j was .40, t_i was .10, and θ_{ij} was .40. The effective tariff rate was 60 percent, although the nominal rate was only 40 percent.

In a study made for the World Bank, Bela Balassa computed the nominal and effective rates of duty for selected industry groups in seven developing countries. Some of the computations are rather startling. For example, in Chile in 1961 the nominal rate of duty on processed food was 82 percent.[14] This may sound high, but compare it with the calculated effective rate, 2,884 percent! Computations of effective rates have been used in bargaining sessions when tariff schedules are negotiated. It is useful

---

[14] These figures are from Balassa et al., *The Structure of Protection in Developing Countries* (Baltimore: Johns Hopkins University Press, 1971), p. 54.

for all parties to know which local productive activities receive especially favored rates of protection. The nominal rates are less helpful than effective rates in providing this information.[15]

12.8 SUMMARY

The basic theory of tariffs set out in Chapter 11 focused on the gain that a country may obtain if it has some monopoly power on world markets and can improve its terms of trade by levying a tariff. This gain provided the key valid argument for tariffs. This chapter surveyed a number of other arguments for protection. These ranged from redistributing income—by protecting certain industries and the factors used specifically or intensively by those industries or by controlling production or consumption levels in certain industries—to encouraging "infant" industries to develop, sheltered in early years from foreign competition.

In all the cases studied it was determined that tariffs or other forms of trade restrictions could help achieve any of these aims. In each case, however, a superior set of policies could also satisfy these objectives at a lower welfare cost. For example, if an industry seems to need a minimal home market, a tariff can be levied, though levying a tariff involves a consumption loss represented by the distortion between world and domestic prices. A production subsidy can achieve the same production goal and allow consumers to buy at world prices. The basic point is that tariffs interfere with *trade*, whereas the stipulated target or source of distortion often resides in production alone or consumption alone.

The final section introduced the concept of the effective rate of protection. This highlights the complexity in productive activity that exists in the real world. Domestic productive processes often rely on imported raw materials and intermediate products, and a tariff structure allocates resources more in line with the effective rates of protection on these processes than with the nominal rates on the end products.

Although few arguments have been made that clearly favor protection from a national point of view—and even fewer from an international point of view—voices clamoring for protection have become more strident in recent times. To the extent that special groups can be favorably affected by protection and that the political process may respond to their needs, it is not surprising that free trade is not a policy embraced by all. As well, recent work stressing the importance of international markets in which competition is less than perfect has challenged traditional free-trade tenets. This newer strand of argument is discussed in the next chapter.

CHAPTER PROBLEMS

1. Use the kind of diagrammatic argument represented by Figure 12.3 for the case of production subsidies to present the case that a nation wishing to restrict consumption of some item below the free-trade level would do better to levy a consumption tax instead of a tariff.

---

[15] We have already remarked that effective rates of protection are higher than nominal rates for processes in which nominal tariffs on outputs are higher than tariffs on intermediate good imports. Let e denote the effective rate. Then the formula can be rewritten as $(1 - \theta_{ij})e + \theta_{ij}t_i = t_j$. This states that the nominal rate is a weighted average of the effective rate and the tariff on inputs.

2. Suppose a capital-abundant country levies a tariff on its labor-intensive imports. (The country's productive structure is that of Chapter 7's Heckscher-Ohlin model.) Show why this must improve workers' real wage. What further changes in the country's real wage would be brought about if foreign countries counter with tariffs of their own on home exportables?

3. To expand upon Section 12.5's discussion of the relationship between protection and foreign investment, suppose the home country exports clothing, which is produced by labor and capital, and imports food, which is produced locally by labor and land. That is, assume the specific-factor production structure of Chapter 6. Let some of the capital used in the clothing sector be provided by foreign investment. If the home country protects its food industry with a tariff, trace through

   a. the effect on factor prices, production, consumption, and trade volumes if no more foreign capital enters or leaves the country.

   b. the further impact on factor prices, production, consumption, and trade if returns to capital in the clothing sector adjust to a given world rate of return via changes in the quantity of capital foreigners wish to place in the protectionist country.

   c. the effect on net home welfare in each case.

4. Show how a nation with higher tariffs on intermediates than on final goods may have negative effective rates of protection on some items. Consider the concept of effective rates of protection in a nation's exportable sectors.

SUGGESTIONS FOR FURTHER READING

Bhagwati, Jagdish. *Import Competition and Response* (Chicago: University of Chicago Press, 1982). A series of papers stressing difficulties of adjustment to competition from abroad.

————. *Protectionism.* (Cambridge, MA: M.I.T. Press, 1988). A popular discussion of free trade and arguments against it.

Black, John. "Arguments for Tariffs," *Oxford Economic Papers*, N.S. 11 (June 1959): 191–208. A discussion of various arguments for protection.

Brock, William, and S. Magee. "Tariff Formation in a Democracy," in J. Black and B. Hindley eds., *Current Issues in International Commercial Policy and Diplomacy* (London: Macmillan, 1980), pp. 1–9. Brief survey discussion of features of democratic governments that influence the formation of tariff policy.

Corden, W. M. "Tariffs, Subsidies, and the Terms of Trade," *Economica*, N.S. 24 (August 1957): 235–242. A lucid treatment of alternative protective devices.

Grubel, H. G. "Effective Protection: A Non-Specialist Guide to the Theory, Policy Implications, and Controversies," in H. G. Grubel and Harry G. Johnson, eds., *Effective Tariff Protection* (Geneva: General Agreement on Tariffs and Trade and Graduate Institute of International Studies, 1971). An introduction to the issues in effective protection.

Johnson, Harry G. "Optimal Trade Intervention in the Presence of Domestic Distortions," in R. E. Baldwin et al., *Trade, Growth and the Balance of Payments* (Chicago: Rand McNally, 1965). A general discussion of trade taxes and production and consumption subsidies, relying heavily on diagrammatic analysis.

Krueger, Anne. "The Political Economy of the Rent-Seeking Society," *American Economic Review*, 44 (June 1974): 291–303. The classic exposition of the loss in welfare as resources are devoted to obtaining import licenses.

————. "Asymmetries in Policy between Exportables and Import-Competing Goods," Chapter 10 in R. W. Jones and A. O. Krueger, eds., *The Political Economy of International*

Trade (Cambridge, UK: Blackwell, 1990), pp. 161–178. An interesting discussion of why import-competing industries receive governmental support more frequently than do export industries.

Krugman, Paul. "Import Protection as Export Promotion: International Competition in the Presence of Oligopoly and Economies of Scale," in H. Kierzkowski, ed., *Monopolistic Competition and International Trade* (Oxford, UK: Oxford University Press, 1984), pp. 180–193. A variation on the infant-industry argument when trade is of the monopolistic competition intra-industry type.

Stolper, Wolfgang, and Paul A. Samuelson. "Protection and Real Wages," *Review of Economic Studies*, 9 (November 1941): 58–73. The analysis of the effect of a tariff on wages and rents.

13

TRADE POLICY AND IMPERFECT COMPETITION

In this chapter the focus on trade policy shifts in two ways. We depart from the assumption that markets for goods, services, and factors of production are purely competitive and allow for elements of monopoly and oligopoly. The effects of these market structures are studied mainly in individual markets (partial equilibrium) rather than in the economy as a whole (general equilibrium, the setting of Chapters 11 and 12). Second, because many practical issues of trade policy, both old and new, turn on imperfect competition, we align the theory closely with its empirical applications.

13.1 MONOPOLY AND THE GAINS FROM TRADE

The most basic connection between imperfect competition and international trade lies in the ability of international competition to limit distortions caused by monopolies in a nation's product markets. This will be shown theoretically; then some evidence from real-world markets will be considered.

Monopoly and Import Competition

"The tariff is the mother of the trusts" was a charge heard often in the United States at the end of the nineteenth century. It meant that domestic producers who had worked out collusive agreements among themselves could not raise prices and exploit consumers without help from tariffs, which kept import competition away. Indeed, it can be shown theoretically that the gains from trade are amplified when foreign competition undercuts a monopoly's ability to raise its price above long-run marginal cost (the benchmark for an efficient, competitive price). This is illustrated in Figure 13.1, which shows not the monopoly's demand and cost curves but the effect of its behavior on resource allocation for the economy as a whole. If the economy were closed and both the clothing and food industries competitive, production and consumption would be at point C_1, and a tangent at that point would indicate the equilibrium price slope. It is assumed, however, that the food industry is monopolized.

FIGURE 13.1   Trade Breaks Up a Monopoly: Importables

Without trade, monopolized food production at F_M or F'_M is below the closed-economy competitive level. When trade is opened, food's price falls from P_M or P'_M to AC_2; the welfare gain is greater than that from y_1 to y_2.

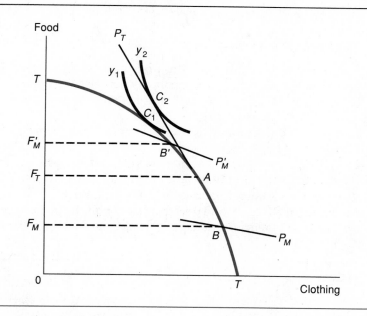

The monopoly maximizes its profits by producing less than the competitive output and charging a price higher than its marginal cost. Thus, in the two-good model of the economy, it restricts its output to some level such as F_M or F'_M, causing too many factors of production to be shifted into the clothing industry. The monopoly price distorts the economy's relative prices to some value indicated by an abbreviated price slope, such as P_M or P'_M. (The diagram does not show exactly how the monopoly's profit-maximizing quantity is determined, but price lines such as these will be tangent to community indifference curves.)

Suppose that the economy is now opened up to trade and the monopoly finds itself facing cheaper imports of food with a world market price shown by AC_2 (price slope P_T). Suppose further that the country is too small to influence world prices. The monopoly has now been turned into a pure competitor on the world market because it can only sell whatever output is profitable at the given world price. It chooses output F_T, the same output that a purely competitive food industry would select. It might contract its output (from F'_M) because of the cost disadvantage against foreign producers of food, or it might even expand output (from F_M), if its cost disadvantage is not too great, because it no longer pays to restrict output in order to raise price.

The economy gains more from trade in this case than if food production had been competitive. The economy's initial welfare was represented by a community indifference curve tangent to the price slope that intersects the production-possibilities curve at B or B'. This indifference curve (not shown) would lie below point C_1 and represent a lower level of welfare than community indifference curve y_1, which corresponds to a competitive economy without international trade. The overall welfare gain when trade is introduced can thus be decomposed into two parts: the movement from an indifference curve tangent to P_M (or P'_M) to C_1 due to eliminating monopoly, and the gain from C_1 to C_2 due to the advantages of international specialization.

Monopoly and Export Opportunities

It may be surprising that the gains from exposing a monopoly to international trade are essentially the same if the monopoly becomes the exporter; export opportunities change its behavior toward the home market in the same way as does the discipline of import competition. Figure 13.2 shows the effect of monopoly in the clothing industry. (The food industry is now assumed to be competitive.) In the absence of trade, output might be restricted to C_M or C'_M, corresponding to relative prices P_M or P'_M higher than would prevail in the competitive closed economy (at C_1). Exposing the monopoly to world price ratio AC_2 (price shown by the slope of line P_T) induces it to expand its output. Because it is assumed there is no restriction on imports of clothing at these same world prices, the monopoly can no longer exploit the downward-sloping domestic-demand curve. Instead it must sell on the foreign and domestic

---

FIGURE 13.2   Trade Breaks Up a Monopoly: Exportables

Without trade, monopolized clothing production at C_M or C'_M is below the closed-economy competitive level. When trade is opened at world prices P_T, the monopolist must trade as a pure competitor on the world market and produces C_T. Domestic price of clothing can either rise (from P'_M) or fall (from P_M).

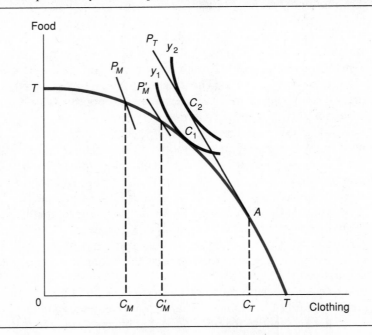

markets at the world price. Paradoxically, the actual domestic price of clothing could either rise or fall when the economy is opened to trade. The price might rise if the nation's comparative advantage is very great, so that high world price (relative to the monopoly's low costs) pulls up the domestic monopoly price (P'_M is flatter than P_T), but the force of international competition could also make it cut the price (P_M is steeper than P_T). Once more, the economy's total gain in welfare consists of the conventional gains from trade plus an extra gain that arises from elimination of the monopolistic distortion of production.

Monopoly and Exports in Practice: U.S. Steel in 1900

Time and again, trade has reduced the power of national monopolies. Still, its practical effect is both more limited and more complex than the preceding theory would suggest. Consider as an example the early years of the United States Steel Corporation, formed in 1898 by a consolidation of many previously independent companies. It controlled about two-thirds of U.S. production of the major steel products, and it also enjoyed tight control over the iron-ore deposits in Minnesota and Michigan, thereby gaining protection from the threat of entry in the following years by new domestic competitors. Just at the time of U.S. Steel's formation, the prices of pig iron (an intermediate product in steelmaking) and the major finished products nearly doubled. That increase itself was not the handiwork of the newly dominant firm, because it took place in British markets as well. However, outside the United States prices quickly retreated, while at home they were kept at this newly elevated level. Indeed, during the next decade the domestic pig-iron price stayed about 40 percent above the U.K. price plus the U.S. tariff. Transportation costs were apparently high enough that this differential led to substantial imports only in boom years, when the U.S. price became 70 to 80 percent higher than the U.K. price plus the U.S. tariff, setting off a burst of imports.

The United States had in fact become a significant exporter of iron and steel by this time, and U.S. Steel's elevated domestic price was a dire threat to its export sales. The problem had a simple solution: U.S. Steel charged its monopoly price on domestic sales while selling abroad for whatever price it could get. Prices of steel rails for export were sometimes only 75 percent of their domestic level. Transport costs and tariffs were high enough that it did not pay domestic rail buyers to bid these bargain goods away from favored foreign buyers. (This practice of selling cheaply abroad, known as dumping, will be considered in Section 13.4.) Thus, while international trade did limit U.S. Steel's monopoly power as theory suggests it would, the presence of high tariffs and transport costs and the feasibility of dumping left the company with access to generous monopoly profits in its early years.[1]

Economists studying trade and market competition in present-day industries often use statistical methods to compare the situations of different industries—those with substantial or little import competition and those with few sellers (perhaps approaching monopoly) or many sellers (close to pure competition). What they find repeatedly—not just in the United States, but for many countries and periods of time—is that

---

[1] This information is taken from Donald O. Parsons and Edward John Ray, "The United States Steel Consolidation: The Creation of Market Control," *Journal of Law and Economics*, 18 (April 1975): 181–219.

freedom from import competition is a necessary condition for such excess profits, as is a number of competitors small enough that they behave in a monopolistic fashion. A monopoly-elevated price pulls in more imports, which erode the monopoly's profits.[2]

Every industrial country maintains some type of antitrust or competition policy that seeks to avert monopoly-type distortions in domestic markets. It has been argued, quite properly, that applications of these policies should take international competition into account. The United States, for example, maintains "merger guidelines" to determine when rival firms that merge can be presumed to obtain market shares high enough to threaten monopoly. These guidelines now take account of import competition. While large countries whose domestic markets are only moderately affected by international competition tend to take competition policy seriously, most small ones with markets highly open to trade enforce it less vigorously.

13.2 CARTELS AND THE INTERESTS OF PRODUCING AND CONSUMING COUNTRIES

That international trade pays dividends by enforcing market competition and enlarging the gains from trade is a simple message—simple because each country's gains are independent of its neighbors' actions. Noncompetitive markets present a more complex issue, however, when monopoly overflows into international trade. The problem that arises is exactly that identified with the "optimal tariff" (Section 11.3). When a national monopolist earns profits on exports sold to foreigners, those profits both enrich the monopolist and enter into the exporting country's national income. When the monopolist snatches profits from domestic customers, these represent a transfer. (The deadweight loss that occurs when buyers cut back on purchases of monopolized goods is a real cost in either case.) Just as countries' interests clash when they attempt to monopolize their trade through tariffs, they may also clash over monopoly prices in international trade.

This section considers this issue in a traditional context—that of international cartels and the divergent interests of producing and consuming countries. Section 13.3 reviews some new thinking about national policies designed to capture monopoly gains or to fight off such raids.

The Organization of Petroleum Exporting Countries

This discussion can begin with the best known and most successful cartel in history, the Organization of Petroleum Exporting Countries (OPEC). For at least a dozen years starting in 1973, OPEC kept the price of crude oil far above what a competitive market would set. The excess profits are indirectly apparent in the OPEC members' cash build-ups that corresponded to their export surplus of $60 billion in 1974 and of almost twice that in 1980 after another price increase. These riches resulted from the OPEC members' agreement to charge a common high price for oil. Of course, that price reduced the world's consumption of oil, not only because any price increase

---

[2] Examples of these studies are Thomas A. Pugel, "Foreign Trade and U.S. Market Performance," *Journal of Industrial Economics*, 29 (December 1980): 119–129; and Dean A. DeRosa and Morris Goldstein, "Import Discipline in the U.S. Manufacturing Sector," *IMF Staff Papers*, 28 (September 1981): 600–634.

tends to cut the quantity demanded, but also because the disturbance reduced employment in the industrial economies, thus reducing their demand for all imports, oil included. For the cartel to hold together, its members had to accept a reduction in the quantities they produced and sold; the leading members made these cuts. However, in the 1981–1983 recession the cartel began to crumble after appropriating vast wealth for its members and inflicting further heavy indirect costs (unemployment, inflation) on the consuming countries. Three forces finally weakened OPEC's grip on the world's oil consumers. First, many oil users made the investments necessary to shift to the use of other fuels or to reduce their fuel usage overall. Second, other would-be producers went searching for oil, and many succeeded. In 1983 OPEC's share of Western production was one-third, down from two-thirds a mere five years earlier. Third, some members of the cartel themselves began to cheat on its agreed price, so that in early 1983 OPEC had to reduce its posted price from $34 to $29 a barrel to acknowledge that some of its members were making spot sales at prices much below list. The 20 percent decline in OPEC's real price between 1982 and 1983 meant a $40 billion loss of wealth to OPEC and a gain to the industrial countries equal to 0.4 percent of their combined GNP. The decline continued, bringing the price to $18 a barrel in 1987. That figure in real terms was still about twice the price that prevailed before the 1973 increase. In the early 1990s OPEC remained a passive force (but not one to ignore, in light of its increasing share of the world's known petroleum reserves).

OPEC serves as a classic example of a cartel that drains wealth to itself from customer countries and reduces the welfare of the world as a whole. Some economists have disputed that judgment, suggesting that OPEC's price is really a competitive one, because crude oil is an exhaustible resource, and new deposits get harder and harder to find. However, the evidence supports the simple monopoly interpretation. OPEC's price exceeds its marginal production cost by too much to make competitive status credible. Other defenders claim that OPEC should not count as a successful cartel in view of its declining price and market share. However, economic theory disagrees. If you are suddenly given a monopoly and wish to maximize the present value of the profits that it yields, your best strategy is probably to charge a price high enough that new competitors gradually enter your market; you eventually cease to dominate the market, but you extracted the maximum discounted value of profit that the monopoly will yield. Statistical evidence shows how OPEC held its price and reduced production as other producers expanded theirs.[3]

Commodity Agreements

The controversy over OPEC follows on a long history of attempts by countries or producer groups to manipulate their terms of trade. Primary-product cartels first became prominent after World War I. Most of them soon failed for reasons evident from the theoretical requisites of a successful cartel: It must face a price-inelastic demand (no actual or potential close substitutes). All important producers must join the arrangement. Members must be willing to cut back production, and an enforcement

---

[3] See James M. Griffin, "OPEC Behavior: A Test of Alternative Hypotheses," *American Economic Review*, 75 (December 1985): 954–963; M. A. Adelman, "Scarcity and World Oil Prices," *Review of Economics and Statistics*, 68 (August 1986): 387–397.

mechanism must be found that can curb their incentive to cheat once price has been elevated above their marginal costs. Last, buyers must be unable (or at least disinclined) to organize to ward off the exaction of monopoly rents. Most cartels soon collapsed for want of one or another of these conditions, even after producer governments became active participants in the 1930s.

The conditions for a successful cartel tend to make for unstable prices in a competitive market (low demand elasticity; also, producers' costs are substantially precommitted or sunk, so they keep producing when prices are low). Producer countries therefore often argue that associations of producers should be tolerated or even encouraged in order to stabilize prices. Indeed, there may be real economic gains from building up buffer stocks to raise prices in periods of excess supply and selling the stocks to mitigate price increases when demand exceeds production (see below). Producers of numerous commodities have sought to organize cartels (sometimes with consumer-country cooperation) in the name of price stabilization, although stabilization can be (especially for consumers) hard to distinguish from plain monopolistic price increases. With the competitive market-clearing price neither readily known nor agreed upon, observers may well disagree on whether price-raising efforts on a given day carry the market price toward or above that equilibrium price.

The operation of international commodity agreements since World War II reflects this ambiguity of objectives and also illustrates the ways in which the agreements can fail. Reflecting their unclear objectives, the agreements have employed a mixture of policy instruments—buffer stocks (usable mainly for price stabilization) and export quotas (needed to secure monopoly prices). Even those agreements that succeeded for periods of time collapsed through the failure of one or the other mechanism. An agreement of tin producers worked for a time because the producers were few and production was stable (unlike most agricultural crops). However, the buffer stock effectively ran out of resources and collapsed. The international coffee agreement, like others, failed because producers could not agree on reallocating quotas among themselves toward suppliers that were raising their efficiency (lowering marginal cost) or producing varieties in growing demand. After maintaining high and stable prices during 1980–1989, the agreement collapsed (and wholesale prices fell 40 percent) when Brazil left it; Brazil, a large but not high-quality producer, was unwilling to accept a reduced output quota and market share.[4]

Despite this woeful experience, in the 1970s the LDCs demanded through the United Nations Conference on Trade and Development (UNCTAD) an international program of commodity agreements as the keystone of a "New International Economic Order." It would involve agreements covering eighteen commodities, along with a Common Fund to finance the agreements and to assist LDC exporters in diversifying their economies. A much reduced version of the Common Fund was agreed to in principle in 1983, but ratification faltered.

Economic analysis offers several points to clarify the debate over the Common Fund proposal. It was originally intended to promote not just commodity-price

---

[4] See Christopher L. Gilbert, "International Commodity Agreements: Design and Performance," *World Development*, 15 (May 1987): 591–616; Takamasa Akiyama and Panayotis N. Varangis, "The Impact of the International Coffee Agreement on Producing Countries," *World Bank Economic Review*, 4 (May 1990): 157–173.

stabilization but also income transfers from consumers to producers through increased average prices. Unfortunately, transferring income to producers by having them restrict supply and raise their selling price is an inefficient procedure: It costs more real resources than if the buyer simply hands over an equivalent transfer of real income. Thus, any case for the monopoly element of the UNCTAD proposal must be political—that the industrial countries are more willing to give the LDCs foreign aid in the form of inflated commodity prices than as outright gifts, or that the recipients prefer the appearance of earning their keep rather than receiving handouts.

The stabilization aspects of commodity agreements are themselves somewhat complex, and economic analysis establishes that stabilizing a commodity price does not necessarily stabilize the incomes of the commodity's producers. That depends on whether the destabilizing disturbances come from the demand or the supply curve, as well as on the elasticities of these curves. Nonetheless, for producers and consumers together, there are real gains from running buffer-stock schemes to stabilize commodity prices. Even if their managers do not have perfect foresight in making their buying and selling plans, buffer stocks in many commodities could ideally produce welfare gains exceeding the costs of operating them (the costs of storing the commodities and the interest on capital tied up in them).[5] It is thus unfortunate that so much difficulty exists in untangling the monopoly and stabilization aspects of commodity agreements.

13.3 MONOPOLY AND POLICIES OF EXPORTING AND IMPORTING COUNTRIES

The world would be better off without monopolies, but most countries are happy to maximize their own incomes by using any monopoly power they may possess (or acquire through international cartels). This section considers some policies that nations can use to exploit their market power effectively—by exploiting foreign consumers or by snatching monopoly rents away from foreign exporters. The discussion will also examine the monopolistic practice of selling more cheaply abroad than at home (dumping) and importing countries' reactions to this practice.

Exploiting Monopoly Power over Exports

The interest of an exporting country in exploiting its monopoly power in trade is obvious enough. The optimal tariff lets it achieve that goal, as was demonstrated in Chapter 11 for a general-equilibrium model with purely competitive industries. The same problem is now considered in a broader context, where each industry or market is thought of as one of many making up the economy. If the U.S. passenger aircraft industry consisted of many small firms that failed to recognize their joint monopoly power, the government would maximize national welfare by imposing an export tax. The right tax rate, in this case, is one that "marks up" the export price over the industry's marginal cost by the same amount that a profit-maximizing monopolistic seller of aircraft would select.

---

[5] See David L. McNicol, *Commodity Agreements and Price Stabilization* (Lexington, MA: Lexington Books, 1978).

If the aircraft industry consisted instead of a single monopolistic seller (call it Boeing), the government would presumably find the private firm more than willing to set a price to maximize its profits from export and domestic sales alike. A welfare problem arises, however, because the excess of price over marginal cost to domestic buyers causes an undesired dead-weight loss to home consumers. The optimal policy is to compel the firm to sell domestically at a competitive price (that is, one equal to the monopolist's marginal cost). The only problem is to find a practical policy instrument that will effectively control the domestic price while allowing the producer to monopolize the overseas markets. In practice, governments have some means to regulate the degree of competition in an industry, but not much leverage for making it more competitive in its domestic than in its foreign sales. That shortcoming makes the government face a trade-off: The more monopoly it allows in the industry overall, the more monopoly profits are lifted from foreign pockets, but also the more surplus is lost by domestic buyers. The government can make a second-best choice—the right degree of monopoly has the property that a slight increase adds just enough income from exporting profits to offset the consequent, extra deadweight loss of domestic consumers' surplus. Other things being equal, the welfare-maximizing degree of monopoly corresponds to the proportion of its output that the domestic industry exports.

Manipulating the degree of monopoly in an exporting industry to attain this second-best outcome seems impractical and much more complicated than simply setting an optimal tariff (tax) on exports—and it is. Nonetheless, countries can be observed casting about for second-best ways to garner export profits without using export taxes. For the United States, at least, the explanation is easily found in the U.S. Constitution, Article I, Section 9, which prohibits taxes on exports. One substitute device, useful when the exporting industry comprise many competitive suppliers, is to allow them to form a cartel to manage their export sales, while forbidding them to collude in the domestic market. The United States permits such cooperative export agreements under the Webb-Pomerene Act, and other countries employ similar policies. Indeed, just as theory predicts, the more important an exporting activity is for a country, the more generously does the country allow collusion among its exporters (at the risk that this collusion will spill over onto the domestic market and cause deadweight losses to domestic consumers).[6]

National Welfare and International Oligopoly

In the years since World War II, the number of important trading countries in the world economy has grown continously. The European nations and Japan recovered from the war, then came increasingly close to matching the average per-capita income of the United States. More recently the emergence of the Newly Industrialized Countries has further enlarged the cast of significant trading nations. With more nations competing, situations in which individual countries, let alone single firms, possess substantial worldwide monopoly power over significant products have grown refreshingly less common. For that reason, OPEC has had no imitators (see Section 13.2), and in practice the exploitation of single-nation monopoly power is a minor issue.

---

[6] A. A. Auquier and R. E. Caves, "Monopolistic Export Industries, Trade Taxes, and Optimal Competition Policy," *Economic Journal*, 89 (September 1979): 559–581.

Nonetheless, some important industries are highly concentrated (that is, have few significant sellers) worldwide. Automobiles, semiconductors, large computers, large passenger aircraft, turbine generators, and aluminum are a few examples of world oligopolies (that is, industries with few sellers).

Economists have recently addressed the policy problem of how a country maximizes its welfare when it serves as the home base for only part of a world oligopoly. If it takes a leaf from OPEC's book, it simply works out an agreement with the other producing nations to run a joint monopoly at the expense of consuming nations. For reasons suggested in Section 13.2, this solution is seldom used. Rather, countries define the policy problem as a search for the best method of boosting the home producer's position relative to other members of the international oligopoly. Policy proposals all too often pass up economic terminology for sporting metaphors: "How can we strengthen our 'national champion' so that the firm can do battle more effectively with its international rivals?" Admittedly, driving the rivals out of business and enjoying a full-blooded monopoly has its economic attractions. Nonetheless, slaughtering one's oligopolistic rivals is usually infeasible, and if feasible it still may be unprofitable.[7]

Here some recent theories about national policy-making enter the picture. Suppose that a national firm faces just one competitor, located in a foreign country. That is, the market structure is an international duopoly, with both firms exporting to the rest of the world. Can the government do anything to help the national champion to a larger slice of the duopoly profit or to enlarge the world profit to be sliced? The scope available for national policy depends very much on how the two duopolists compete with one another. If they have formed an OPEC-style cartel to extract maximum joint profit from the world economy, there is probably little that the home government can do unless it can help the home firm bargain for a larger share of that profit.

The two duopolists might be less cooperative, however, and in that circumstance recent theoretical models become relevant. The theory of oligopolistic markets in general is indeterminate, meaning that the sellers may interact with one another in any of a number of ways; we can define some theoretical possibilities but cannot predict in general what output an oligopoly will produce, between the reference points of the outputs that purely competitive and purely monopolistic producers would select in the same circumstances. Despite this fundamental ignorance, a popular strategy for modeling oligopoly markets is to assume that the rival sellers do not cooperate in a joint monopoly; indeed, they do not cooperate at all, but instead act as if each expects no changes in its rivals' prices or outputs in response to its own moves in the market. Each duopolist knows that increasing its output will drive down the world price (because it is a big player on the world market), but it anticipates no response from its foreign rival. This assumption is implausible for a duopoly, but it makes more sense in oligopolies with enough firms that one rival holds no systematic expectation about competitors' responses. Also, the assumption is neither particularly

---

[7] Unprofitable, because to drive a rival from the market, the aggressor must charge low prices in the short run or otherwise run losses in order to inflict large (fatal?) losses on the victim. Even if the attack succeeds and monopoly profits then flow in abundance, they lie in the future, and their present value need not offset the profits forgone in the initial period of warfare. Those future profits themselves might induce new competitors to enter.

optimistic nor pessimistic: At best, when the home firm expands output, it might hope its rival would "move over," reducing output to keep the world price from falling; at worst, it might fear that the rival will come out swinging and expand its own output to maintain its market share, further depressing world price. Regardless, the assumption that a rival's output will not react to a competitor's output change is called the Cournot assumption, and it yields definite conclusions about what output the duopoly will produce and how much monopoly profit its members will earn. As expected, the output is greater than a cartel or joint monopoly would select, and the profit is less, because no collusion occurs.

Profits obtained by the home duopolist go into the national income. What can the government do to enlarge them? The appendix to this chapter shows that by subsidizing the home firm's output, it is possible to increase the profit it obtains (and thus national income) and to reduce the profit of the foreign rival (and its homeland's national income). The intuition behind the result is simple. If the duopolists' behavior follows the Cournot assumption, then an increase in the home firm's output (in response to the subsidy) causes its rival to contract output. World output still increases, and world profit falls, but the firm's enlarged market share gives it a sufficiently bigger share of the shrunken profit pie to make it—and the country—better off.

The Cournot model of duopoly (or oligopoly) is bothersome because most sellers seem to compete by quoting prices rather than setting outputs. The duopoly model can be reconstructed by assuming that each seller sets price on the assumption that its rival's price will remain unchanged—called the Bertrand assumption. The market equilibrium is similar to the Cournot equilibrium, if it is also assumed that the duopolists' products are differentiated from one another, and leads to a similar conclusion—that the market price will be set at a level lying above the pure-competition price and below the pure-monopoly price. (Without differentiation, the Bertrand assumption implies that duopolists will settle on the purely competitive price, which is implausible.)

If the world duopoly consists of Bertrand players, can the government once more maneuver the home champion into a superior postion? The answer is again affirmative, but—because the Bertrand assumption implies more aggressive behavior than Cournot's—the appropriate policy this time is to tax rather than subsidize the home company's exports. When the firm, hit with a tax, raises its price and supplies the smaller output that is demanded, its rival will respond by raising its price and probably lowering its output. Thus, the objective in each case is to induce less aggressive market behavior by the foreign firm.

At this point, the policy-maker asks the hard question: "How do I know whether the Cournot or the Bertrand assumption fits a given market, so I can tell whether to subsidize or to tax?" The answer, unfortunately, is that neither assumption can be confirmed by direct observation, and in fact neither approach comes very close to characterizing the behavior of any particular oligopoly. At this point, the policy advice stemming from these models of international duopoly tends to evaporate into nothing more than an engaging curiosity.[8]

_____

[8] Simple and judicious accounts of these and related models can be found in Paul R. Krugman, ed., *Strategic Trade Policy and the New International Economics* (Cambridge, MA: M.I.T. Press, 1986).

Fighting Off Monopoly Power over Imports

So far the discussion has concentrated on how a country might benefit from monopoly power over its exports. The importing country, however, faces the symmetrical problem of how to fight off such raids on its economic welfare by monopolists of the goods that it imports. While recent theoretical research supplies some new insights, it is necessary to recall the message of the optimum tariff for a single importing industry. If a country faces an upward-sloping supply curve for imports, it can benefit from purchasing them as a *monopsonist* (which is what a sole buyer is called). If a country faces a rising supply curve, each additional unit bought (per period of time) drives up the price and thus the cost of every other unit bought. The monopsonist cuts back the quantity bought to the point where the extra total cost due to the last unit is just equal to its marginal value to the user (normally the price that customers pay for a unit of the import).[9] The country could accomplish this cutback either by allowing some import agent to serve as the monopsony buyer or by setting a tariff rate that would achieve the same restriction of imports. The resulting gain is quite consistent with the imports being supplied competitively by their foreign producers. The essential condition is simply that when less is purchased, the asking price goes down.

However, what if the foreign supplier is a monopolist? When OPEC quadrupled the price of oil in 1973–1974, some people urged the United States to impose a tax on imported crude oil. They advanced, among other reasons, the likelihood that OPEC would react by backing off partially from its price increase. That prediction has some logic behind it, as can be seen in Figure 13.3, which shows the U.S. demand for imported petroleum as DD. It is assumed that OPEC can produce petroleum at a constant marginal cost of CC. That assumed constancy is important: In this model the buyer's gains do not depend on an upward-sloping cost or supply curve, as they do in the traditional monopsony model summarized in the preceding paragraph. The marginal-revenue curve corresponding to the U.S. import demand is MR. A profit-maximizing OPEC would set price P, and quantity Q would be imported. Now suppose that the government imposes an import duty of $\$X$ per barrel. U.S. consumers' willingness to pay for oil *net* of the newly imposed tax is described by demand curve $D_T D_T$, which is shifted downward uniformly by the amount $DD_T\ (=\$X)$. The profit-maximizing before-tax price charged by OPEC now falls to P_{NT}. U.S. consumers now pay a higher price gross of the tax of P_{GT} and accordingly purchase less than before (Q_T). While the consumers themselves are worse off than before the tax, the country as a whole is better off because the tax revenue, $(P_{GT} - P_{NT})Q_T$, is part of the national income and could be rebated to consumers or used to buy public goods.

This policy model shares one unhappy property with the model of international duopoly presented previously. Its policy prescription is sensitive to something of which little is known—in this case the exact shape of the demand curve. Figure 13.3 supplied a clear answer because it was assumed that the import demand curve is a straight line. If it had been assumed only that the curve slopes uniformly downward, however, local "wiggles" in the demand curve (and corresponding but enlarged wiggles in

[9] This decision is symmetrical with the action of a monopolistic seller, who equates its marginal cost to the net gain in total revenue (that is, marginal revenue) received when it pushes another unit onto the market and lowers the price.

FIGURE 13.3   Using Import Duty to Reduce Foreign Monopolist's Price

Import duty reduces demand for monopolized import from DD to $D_T D_T$. Monopoly reduces its price (net of tariff) from P to P_{NT}.

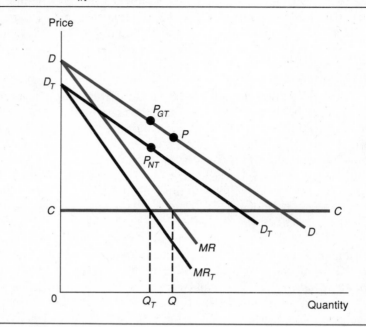

marginal revenue) could make a subsidy rather than a tax appropriate, depending on the exact point of equilibrium on the demand curve.[10] Once again, a seemingly confident policy prescription turns on empirical conditions that can be assessed only with difficulty, if at all.

The analysis of international duopoly previously set forth applies as well to the country that imports supplies that compete with the output of the domestic duopolist. The duopoly once more offers a "profit-shuffling" opportunity to the home government. Home consumers buy at a price that incorporates monopoly profits—some going to the domestic duopolist, some to the foreigner. If sales are shifted to the domestic seller, consumers still suffer the deadweight loss, but the profit slice remains in the national income rather than vanishing across the border.[11]

In conclusion, the analysis indicates that the importing country should probably consider restricting imports whose foreign suppliers possess monopoly power. Such

[10] See Homi Katrak, "Multi-National Monopolies and Commercial Policy," *Oxford Economic Papers*, 29 (July 1977): 283–291; James A. Brander and Barbara J. Spencer, "Trade Warfare: Tariffs and Cartels," *Journal of International Economics*, 16 (May 1984): 227–242; Ronald W. Jones, "Trade Taxes and Subsidies with Imperfect Competition," *Economics Letters*, 23 (1987): 375–379.

[11] An allegedly successful example of such a policy was studied by Richard Baldwin and Harry Flam, "Strategic Trade Policies in the Market for 30–40 Seat Commuter Aircraft," *Weltwirtschaftliches Archiv*, 125 (3) (1989): 484–500. Canada restricted imports from Brazil, shifting profits toward its domestic producer, while Brazilian export subsidies benefited world consumers.

restrictions provide a less than optimal solution to the problem, however, because they increase the deadweight loss to domestic consumers even when they shuffle some profits away from foreign monopolists (or oligopolists). Lost from sight among these strategies for exploiting and combatting monopoly power is the global interest of all participants in "competitive" prices (equal to long-run marginal costs). Such a global solution requires countries to agree that each will do its best to keep its domestic producers competitive, whether they sell at home or abroad. That might require the victims of successful monopolies to hand over bribes large enough to induce the tormentors to reduce price to the level of their marginal cost. That prescription sounds peculiar, yet its logic is straightforward. A monopolist benefits by a monopoly profit, while its customers' surplus is reduced by both the monopoly profit and a deadweight loss. If the customers trade the monopoly its erstwhile profit plus *part* of the deadweight loss for the privilege of buying at marginal cost, both parties are clearly better off. Unfortunately, not the least difficulty with this global-optimum solution is the way it conflicts with the fighting instincts of those imposed upon by monopolists.

Policy in Practice: Dumping

With these theoretical tools in hand, it is now time to inspect countries' actual policies to observe how practice corresponds to theory. It was suggested before that exporting countries at least occasionally pursue the gains from promoting and preserving their monopoly power. One could dip further into history, to the age of imperialism, when military actions could sometimes be read as keeping colonial markets open for the metropolitan country's exports. On the side of the importers, however, examples of effective actions against foreign monopolies are hard to find. Instead, what we encounter are anguished complaints that foreigners sell not too dearly but too cheaply—that they are "dumping" their goods abroad and damaging competing local producers. The first step here will be to consider why a profit-maximizing monopolist might indeed sell more cheaply abroad than at home (although not below "cost"). Then this practice will be evaluated from the viewpoints of the importing and exporting countries.

First of all, notice that a purely competitive firm would not sell identical goods in two different markets at different prices. Because the competitive firm perceives the market price to be unaffected by the quantity it sells, there is no reason to sell any output at less than the best price available. Therefore, dumping must be associated with departures from pure competition. Consider the domestic monopolist illustrated in Figure 13.4. Demand in the home market is given by D, marginal revenue by MR_d. If marginal cost is MC, the firm selling only in the home market maximizes profits by charging P_m, the sale price of the output for which $MC = MR_d$. The world price P_t is lower than P_m, but it still lies above MC over a substantial range of output, so the monopolist can profitably produce for export. Now suppose that different prices can be charged in the home and foreign markets, perhaps because a tariff protecting the home market keeps goods sold cheaply abroad from being reimported and undercutting the higher domestic price. A monopolist maximizes profits by setting a price that equates its marginal cost to the marginal revenue it can earn in each of its markets: If the marginal revenues were not equal, it would shift sales from the lower to the higher until the two are equalized. In Figure 13.4 the marginal revenue from

---

FIGURE 13.4 "Dumping" and Discrimination Between Domestic and Foreign Markets

Monopoly faces demand curve D at home and world price P_t. If it can charge different prices at home and abroad, it sets P_d and P_t, respectively, selling OB at home and BC abroad.

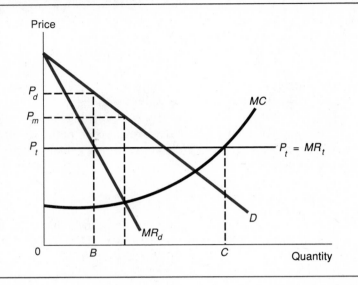

foreign sales is equal to the world price P_t, because that price is unaffected by the monopolist's level of exports. After it begins to export, the monopoly will sell in the domestic market at price P_d, which equates marginal revenue derived from the domestic market (MR_d) to that earned from foreign sales (MR_t). If total production is OC, marginal cost (MC) is equated to the common value of marginal revenue and profits are maximized. Exports are BC, domestic sales OB. Notice that this discrimination between the domestic and foreign markets has caused a higher price to be charged in the domestic market than if no trade were occurring (P_d exceeds P_m).

While the welfare effects of dumping on the *exporting* country are ambiguous, dumping's effects on the importer are clear. As long as the exporter finds that overseas markets are more competitive than the sheltered domestic market, the export price is set lower than the price to the exporter's home customers and lower than it would be in the absence of discrimination. The importing country therefore benefits from being offered a lower price. The welfare-maximizing importing country would encourage dumping. However, importing countries view the practice through very different spectacles. They tend to accept the self-serving perception of import-competing producers that dumping is "unfair" to them, or a predatory move designed to drive them out of business.

U.S. trade policy is fairly typical of industrial countries in assessing an antidumping tariff when there is evidence of injury to U.S. producers. Pursuant to the Antidumping Act of 1921, the dumping margin, used in turn to calculate the antidumping tariff, was computed as the difference between the import price and the imported goods' foreign market value. In 1974, however, the definition of dumping was changed. Dumping can now be found to exist if the price of imports is below the foreign cost of production (including a generous profit margin). When the foreign industry suffers excess capacity, the actual price for both domestic sales and exports sold to the United States might lie below this full cost,[12] and dumping can be inferred even when the overseas and U.S. prices of the imports are the same. Closely related to the antidumping laws are provisions for countervailing duties when exports to the United States are subsidized by the exporting country's government. Both dumping and subsidy cases are described as "less than fair value" cases.

In conclusion, importing countries do occasionally perceive that their welfare is being eroded by high prices set by foreign monopolists and seek to break that monopoly power or find ways to reduce the loss. However, the importers' most common public policy toward monopolistic foreign sellers is to compel them to charge their overseas customers just as stiff a price as the captive domestic market must pay. Once again, actual trade policy is hard to square with the maximization of national welfare.

13.4 INDUSTRIAL POLICY AND MARKET RIVALRY

International-trade policy has a lengthy history, and in no country has it long remained outside the realm of controversy. However, in the past decade it took a back seat in some quarters to "industrial policy," a new label that seeks to embrace trade policy and much more besides. It is considered here because the issues parading under the banner of industrial policy become economically interesting only in the context of markets that fall outside the orbit of pure competition.

What Is Industrial Policy?

While industrial policy defies neat definition, most observers associate it with any policy affecting the distribution of a country's economic activity among its various industries or sectors. Tariffs and other trade policies obviously fall under this heading—a tariff channels factors of production into import-competing industries and away from those producing exportables. So do many other policies, however. Subsidies or other encouragements promote the output of a favored sector or increase the stock of a factor of production that it uses, and short-run adjustment policies discourage the exit of resources from it or speed their influx; the opposite policies divert activity away from a sector. This definition casts a very broad net. For example, the corporation income tax becomes an instrument of industrial policy when it diverts activity from those sectors dominated by corporate organizations and toward those in which other forms prevail (partnerships, nonprofit organizations, etc.). The theory of international trade developed in Part I of this book shows why any policy that shifts the sectoral composition of activity will change the country's volume and composition of international trade. That is why the prescriptions offered under the label of industrial policy need to be examined.

The exact content of industrial policy (like trade policy) can be approached from two viewpoints—by asking what welfare economics prescribes, or by analyzing the

---

[12] For a theoretical analysis of this version of dumping, see Wilfred Ethier, "Dumping," *Journal of Political Economy*, 90 (June 1982): 487–506. In 1979 the European Community adopted a dumping code similar to that of the United States.

content of policies that governments actually select. Prescription and reality are rather different. What welfare economics prescribes for industrial policy was in fact covered in the treatment of second-best policies (Section 12.3). There it was seen that market forces tend to propel the nation's stock of factors of production into their best uses, under ideal conditions, and to assure that any given factor of production earns at least as much in the sector where it works as it could in any other. If product markets are competitive, then the marginal product of each factor is also the same in every industry. No reshuffling of factors among sectors—enlarging some, shrinking others— could enlarge real income. Industrial policy is called upon when these conditions fail. The natural tasks of industrial policy then become apparent: Fix any defects in factor markets that keep the wage or returns of a factor from being equalized among industries, and fix any defect in a product market that causes it to employ either too few factors (such as monopoly) or too many (restricted outward mobility). Section 12.3 showed that industrial policy and trade policy need to be distinguished carefully from one another. If a sector employs too few factors, one possible remedy is to restrict competing imports, thus raising the industry's profitability and pulling in more producing units. However, this was shown to be inefficient because it creates a needless distortion in consumption (when the product's price is raised by the trade restriction). The optimal policy is the direct one: Fix whatever causes the underallocation of resources to the sector.

Approaching industrial policy by reviewing the policies actually proposed or in force gives a very different picture. While industrial countries have many policies that affect the allocation of resources among sectors, most of these effects are incidental consequences of policies adopted for other purposes. That governments should aggressively pick and choose among industrial sectors is more a proposal than a policy in force.[13] Proponents often want to push sectoral allocations of resources in directions that have little to do with optimal allocation. It is said that the government should encourage high-technology sectors. It should favor sectors that pay high wages. It should push resources toward sectors that are growing rapidly. It should support those that add considerable value to the raw materials that they purchase. It is the economist's parlor game to demolish these proposals in their raw form. For example, a high-wage industry has no claim on additional labor if the high wages simply reflect the industry's need for skilled labor, which must be paid the same wherever it works; high wages call for policy intervention only if they result from a distortion such as a monopoly in the product or labor market, which keeps additional workers from entering the industry. Similarly, while some enterprises in high-technology sectors earn high profits, others fail; at the margin the factors recruited to the industry may anticipate no higher profits than they could earn elsewhere. That factors are pulled toward a high-technology or fast-growing sector by market forces does not mean (without additional evidence) that they are moving too slowly, so that the government should give a shove.[14] The prevailing weakness of these proposals for aggressive

---

[13] For a debate over trade policy in the guise of industrial policy see Robert Z. Lawrence and Charles L. Schultze, eds., *An American Trade Strategy: Options for the 1990s* (Washington: Brookings Institution, 1990).

[14] Adjustment policy and adjustment assistance when factors are pushed from sectors facing import competition will be discussed in Section 14.3.

industrial policy when subjected to economic scrutiny has led economists to dissent from most real-world proposals for industrial policy, even calling the proposals "sector fetishism."

That the goals of most industrial policy nostrums are not worth having is in some cases only part of the trouble. They can actually frustrate the very goals that they claim to pursue. Consider a high-technology intermediate good, such as integrated circuits. Because these serve as inputs into a whole range of modern producer and consumer electronics, the public is easily moved by a rousing call for the promotion of such an industry as a foundation for a phalanx of high-technology activities. When domestic producers of such an input gain tariff protection against foreign suppliers, the price of this input rises, and with it the costs of those allegedly desirable high-technology industries that incorporate the input. Rather than launching a whole sector, protecting an input can raise the costs of domestic users and cause them to cede the market to imported finished products. In 1991 the United States slapped a 62 percent tariff on screens for laptop computers imported from Japan, pursuant to a complaint under the antidumping law. This action might have cheered industrial-policy enthusiasts: A strong domestic laptop screen industry will surely encourage domestic production of laptop computers. Instead, the computer makers began moving their production overseas to escape the elevated cost.[15]

Industrial Policy and the Learning Curve: Integrated Circuits

Industrial policy should not necessarily be shunned, however, just because many fallacies about economic welfare parade under that banner. Some sectors with non-competitive structures indeed do present public policy with strategic problems involving both production and trade. The strategic element arises because countries may be able to capture or preserve a sector or activity that will provide a genuine surplus—an average reward to its share of the nation's factor stock that exceeds what it could earn in other uses. If this opportunity is spotted by several countries, each seeks a strategy to attract the activity and beat out the others.

Consider one trait that is popularly associated with high-technology industries—a "learning curve" such that unit costs of production decline with every additional *cumulative* unit produced. For example, every doubling of the number of a particular aircraft model produced might lower the variable cost of its production by 20 percent. This cost reduction occurs because workers and supervisors constantly learn more about the fine points of running a production process efficiently. Workers in assembly operations grow more skilled, learning to avoid wasted motions and to prevent defects. Managers of process technologies learn to wring more output by fine-tuning temperatures, pressures, and the like. These gains are not the same thing as economies of scale because they relate not to the rate of production per unit of time (a year, for example) but to the cumulative volume of output since production began.

The learning curve has important effects on the organization of a sector and its pricing behavior. First, the industry has room for relatively few producers. If the advantage of experience stays locked within the firm, then the first producer with X

---

[15] *Business Week*, December 2, 1991, pp. 38–39. Restricting imports of machine tools had different but equally adverse consequences (*New York Times*, October 7, 1991, pp. D1, D4).

units of output already behind it has a cost advantage over any latecomer. The later entrant may be unable to produce and sell enough output to move down its own learning curve and catch (or approach) the low costs attained by those who preceded it. Furthermore, a pioneering producer who correctly anticipates productivity gains stemming from experience factors them into its pricing decisions. The pioneer tends to set a low price at the outset, so that customers make large purchases, and the producer rapidly gains experience and lowers costs. This pricing strategy also disposes sectors with high rates of learning toward monopoly.

Now consider the implications for trade policy of a new industry subject to rapid proprietary learning. Suppose that one producer in the United States and one in Japan simultaneously start production of a new product subject to important learning effects. Suppose also that each not only serves its (large) home market but also exports to the other country.[16] Now suppose that the United States imposes an import duty on goods from the Japanese producer. Imports fall and with them the Japanese producer's output and the rate at which it learns to lower costs. Output of the U.S. producer rises, along with its rate of cost reduction. Those lower costs also lead to higher exports from the United States to Japan, and (as briefly noted in Section 12.4) import protection turns out to be a method of export promotion. As time passes, the U.S. producer's costs fall relative to those of the Japanese producer. Whatever pricing strategies the two firms employ, profits of the U.S. firm tend to rise, and the added profits taken on export sales are a net gain to the U.S. national income. Japan symmetrically is worse off than if the United States had not imposed its tariff.

Yet why should Japan passively endure this capture of advantage by the United States? While it may be assumed that the United States acts first, it is more plausible to suppose that each country understands the potential advantage of capturing the new industry, so that one's import restriction is promptly matched by the other. In that case, what happens to economic welfare? It is quite possible that both countries wind up worse off than if neither had imposed any protection. Each national industry comprises small producers serving just the domestic market; no producer learns very rapidly, and world welfare is less than if free trade had persisted. As is seen repeatedly in this chapter, neat schemes of policy toward noncompetitive industries exhibiting special conditions of production tend to be fragile, easily lowering rather than raising economic welfare if they are not applied under idealized conditions.

These points were illustrated by one study of a particular high-technology product, 16K random access memory (RAM) chips, which were produced by six major U.S. and three Japanese companies. While the U.S. market was open to imports, Japanese chip customers were palpably unwilling to buy from foreign sources, as if Japan maintained a prohibitive tariff. U.S. costs for that generation of integrated circuits were low enough that, without this barrier, Japanese producers could not have covered their costs, and U.S. firms would have dominated the market. So did the Japanese win? Probably not, according to Baldwin and Krugman. Without the Japanese import ban, the U.S. firms would have both enjoyed lower costs and been more numerous (and therefore competitive), and so would have driven down the price. The Japanese would have had no 16K RAM industry, but they would have been able to secure

---

[16] For reasons that will not be developed here, such intra-industry trade can occur in oligopolistic industries even if the product is entirely homogeneous.

chips at a lower resource cost. Thus, Japan's policy actually reduced the country's welfare unless (and this seems unlikely), by promoting the industry's development, producing 16K RAMs will have secured profits so great from subsequent product generations that this large welfare loss will be offset.[17]

The world would be best off if a new industry subject to learning advantages could be concentrated in whatever country is its most efficient location worldwide but then could be compelled to sell its output to all customers at a competitive price. Unfortunately, there is no international policy mechanism to attain this globally optimal solution. Countries can be expected to ply their industrial and trade policies in attempts either to capture a "hot" new industry or at least to sustain some domestic production for its competitive leverage against successful foreigners. As has already been seen, not everybody can win with these policies, and quite possibly nobody wins.

13.5 SUMMARY

International trade helps to make national markets competitive when the number of domestic producers is small, and this gain can occur whether the noncompetitive domestic producer faces import competition or has a comparative advantage and becomes an exporter. Either way, the gains from curbing monopoly are a dividend atop the usual gains from trade for a small country.

On the other hand, a country also can gain if its export activity enjoys monopoly status, either alone or in collusion with other producers. The OPEC cartel annexed enormous monopoly profits, although these were ultimately limited by the existence of substitute energy sources, competition from independent oil producers, and the incomplete cooperation of cartel members. International commodity agreements, even with the ostensible goal of stabilizing rather than raising prices, have nonetheless usually collapsed from attempts to hold the price above a market-clearing level in the short run.

A nation can extract available monopoly profits on its exports either by letting its national monopolist do the job or by setting an optimal tax on competitively produced exports. The former method has the disadvantage that the monopolist also imposes an undesirable deadweight loss on domestic consumers. When it shares monopoly power with a few other producers, its first objective is to collude with them for maximum joint profits (as with OPEC). If this proves infeasible, the government may be able to nudge the home producer into a more profitable position in the international oligopoly. Symmetrically, a country can increase its welfare when sellers of its imports enjoy some monopoly power. A tax on imports may cause the monopolist to reduce its price, or policies can be used to shunt business toward a competing domestic oligopolist (whose excess profits *are* part of the national income).

Dumping is a form of price discrimination between a competitive world market and a less competitive domestic market. One might expect importing countries to

---

[17] Richard Baldwin and Paul R. Krugman, "Market Access and International Competition: A Simulation Study of 16K Random Access Memories," in Robert C. Feenstra, ed., *Empirical Methods for International Trade* (Cambridge, MA: M.I.T. Press, 1988), pp. 171–197; and Paul Krugman, "Market Access and Competition in High Technology Industries: A Simulation Exercise," in Henryk Kierzkowski, ed., *Protection and Competition in International Trade* (Oxford: Basil Blackwell, 1987), Chapter 10.

welcome the practice, but instead it is generally restricted as being unfair to domestic producers.

"Industrial policy" refers to actions that a country may take to affect the mix of its industrial activities; thus defined, trade restrictions are instruments of industrial policy because they pull resources toward the import-competing sectors. Countries embrace industrial policy because they have collective preferences about the composition of these industrial sectors. While many of these preferences seem unrelated to the maximizing of national income, a salient example is efforts to develop an industry subject to learning-curve benefits by excluding imports and thereby denying learning to foreign producers. This updated type of infant-industry protection might increase a country's welfare, but the conditions are quite stringent.

CHAPTER PROBLEMS

1. The effect of import competition on a domestic monopolist was illustrated in Figure 13.1 in terms of general equilibrium. It can be illustrated equally well in terms of the standard graphical treatment of the monopolist in partial equilibrium. Draw this diagram, indicating the closed-economy monopolist's output and price determined by the intersection of its marginal-revenue and marginal-cost curves, and then show what happens when it is confronted by a fixed world price for its output.

2. Economists discussing the feasibility of international commodity stabilization agreements have pointed out that price stabilization is easier if the commodity can be stored at low cost. Why should that be so?

3. A country could exert its monopoly power over an export good either by organizing its competitive producers into a single monopoly seller or by imposing an export tax that corresponds to the monopoly's profit-maximizing markup of the export price over its marginal cost. Which policy yields the higher level of welfare, and why?

4. Suppose that a nation could tackle a monopoly over imported goods either by persuading the World Court to eliminate the monopoly or by banning imports of the monopoly's goods and giving the business instead to a domestic monopolist. Could the latter policy increase the nation's welfare? Why would it be inferior to the former?

5. A trademark gives a legal monopoly over the brand name or "good will" of a product, and controversies arise because trademarked goods are sometimes counterfeited and sold in international trade by firms other than the trademark's owner. Suppose that a Taiwanese counterfeit of a Swiss watch is imported to the United States and sold at a low price; it may or may not be equivalent to the Swiss product in physical quality. How is U.S. economic welfare affected by the practice? What difference would it make if the trademark's owner were American rather than Swiss?

6. Someone tells you that the United States needs an industrial policy to encourage fast-growing industries by subsidizing their exports and excluding competing imports. You know from your economics courses that private entrepreneurs tend to enter such industries only if they expect to earn positive profits. What market failures, if any, might then call for public policy to lend additional encouragement?

7. A foreign manufacturer of a differentiated good is considering whether or not to export it to the United States. The manufacturer has a monopoly at home, but in the U.S. market it faces close competition and would have to sell at a price lower than the one that maximizes profits in its home market. Nonetheless, such export sales would be profitable for it. However,

if it charges different prices at home and abroad, it is sure that its U.S. sales agency will be penalized heavily under U.S. antidumping laws. Explain why the manufacturer might choose, under those circumstances, not to export to the United States at all.

8. In 1988 the Ivory Coast, producer of one-third of the world's cocoa, was upset over the decline of the world price from $3.00 to $1.50 a kilogram over the preceding two years. That fall had resulted from heavy planting of cocoa trees in the late 1970s. The president of the Ivory Coast announced that his country would sell no cocoa at a price less than $2.00 a kilogram. Other cocoa-producing countries, however, were clearly willing to sell their available supplies at the world market price. Assume that cocoa supply is fixed (in the short run) and that marketwide demand elasticity is one (that is, world sales must be reduced by 1 percent in order to effect a 1 percent increase in price). What fraction of its crop must the Ivory Coast hold off the market in order to make $2.00 the equilibrium world price? What fraction must it withhold if the elasticity of demand is only one-half?

SUGGESTIONS FOR FURTHER READING

Bhagwati, Jagdish, and Hugh T. Patrick, eds. *Aggressive Unilateralism* (Ann Arbor: University of Michigan Press, 1992). Experience with retaliation and strategic trade policy.

Caves, Richard E. "International Cartels and Monopolies in International Trade," in Dornbusch, Rudiger and Jacob A. Frenkel, eds., *International Economic Policy: Theory and Evidence* (Baltimore: Johns Hopkins University Press, 1979), Chapter 2. Survey of theoretical models and evidence on this subject.

DeRosa, Dean A., and Morris Goldstein. "Import Discipline in the U.S. Manufacturing Sector," *IMF Staff Papers*, 28 (September 1981): 600–634. Statistical study of import competition with concentrated U.S. manufacturing industries.

Flamm, Kenneth. "Semiconductors," in Robert Z. Lawrence, ed., *Europe 1992: An American Perspective* (Washington: Brookings Institution, 1990), pp. 225–92. Analysis of nations' policies toward this sector.

Gilbert, Christopher L. "International Commodity Agreements: Design and Performance," *World Development*, 15 (May 1987): 591–616. Review of recent experience.

Griffin, James M., and David J. Teece. *OPEC Behavior and World Oil Prices* (London: Allen and Unwin, 1982). OPEC as a cartel.

Krugman, Paul R., ed. *Strategic Trade Policy and the New International Economics* (Cambridge, MA: M.I.T. Press, 1986). Summarizes recent theoretical research.

Lawrence, Robert Z., and Charles Schultze, eds. *An American Trade Strategy: Options for the 1990s* (Washington: Brookings Institution, 1990). Debate over strategic trade policy for the United States.

McNicol, David L. *Commodity Agreements and Price Stabilization* (Lexington, MA: Lexington Books, 1978). Good treatment of theoretical and welfare aspects.

APPENDIX:
INTERNATIONAL DUOPOLY AND NATIONAL STRATEGY

The following is a simple formal analysis of the model used by most researchers to identify a country's opportunity to gain from profit-shuffling. Suppose that the home firm (H) produces output Q, while its foreign rival (F) produces Q^*. They do not collude with each other; they make their market decisions independently. Specifically, each selects the quantity of output that it expects will maximize its profits on the assumption that the other's quantity is given and unaffected. Each has the same average unit costs, which are independent of its output (no scale economies or diseconomies).

Their behavior is illustrated in Figure 13.A.1, which shows the foreign firm's output on the horizontal axis, the domestic firm's on the vertical axis. The device used to derive the market equilibrium is a *reaction function*, constructed as follows. Consider H's choice of output, given whatever quantity F has decided to produce. If F were producing nothing, H would maximize profits by producing the output that maximizes monopoly profits from the world market. This is indicated by Q_M on the vertical axis. Now suppose instead that F had chosen to produce the competitive world output. The best response of H is to produce no output (point Q_C^*). When F selects any quantity that lies between nothing and the world competitive output, H's best responses will lie along the line between Q_M and Q_C^*. This is H's reaction function.

So far the discussion has not explained F's choice of output, only explored its consequences for H's output. Constructing F's reaction function is exactly symmetrical with constructing H's. If H were producing the world competitive output, Q_C, F would choose to produce nothing; if H were producing nothing, F would select Q_M^*. F's reaction function is the line connecting these two points. The industry equilibrium output for this duopoly is indicated by point K, where the two reaction functions intersect. This is called a Cournot equilibrium. It has the property that each duopolist is producing its most profitable output, consistent with the output choice made by

---

FIGURE 13.A.1   Possible Equilibria with Home and Foreign Duopolists

Duopolists might reach a Cournot equilibrium (K), or government may help the home duopolist to attain the more profitable Stackelberg equilibrium (S).

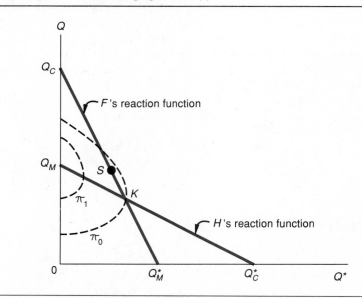

the rival. Each makes some profit because (it can be shown) the industry output is less than the world competititve output. It is also greater than the world monopoly output, so the duopolists together make less profit than would a world monopolist.

To understand the government's options for profit-shifting, we must consider the firms' profits more closely. H makes the maximum possible profit if production lies at Q_m, with H producing the world monopoly output and F producing nothing. Points farther to the right along H's reaction function yield lower and lower profits, going to zero at Q_C^*. Consider some profit level arbitrarily lower than the world monopoly profit. It could be attained at some point on H's reaction function, but also by other pairs of duopolists' outputs not lying on the reaction function. Those points would lie on a locus such as π_1, which can be shown to have the shape illustrated in the figure. π_1 is called an isoprofit locus, because every point on it yields the same profit. An important property is that, at its intersection with H's reaction function, it is tangent to a line perpendicular to the horizontal axis; indeed, that property defines the reaction function.

Now consider H's profit at the Cournot equilibrium, which lies on isoprofit locus π_0. Notice that a stretch of F's reaction function lies within π_0, meaning that if H selected a higher output than that corresponding to the Cournot equilibrium (but not too much higher), not only would F reduce its output, H's profits would increase. Should H now seize this new strategic opportunity, it maximizes profit by committing to select an output that corresponds to point S on F's reaction function. When H takes the initiative and picks its best point on F's reaction function, the result is known as a "leader-follower" or Stackelberg equilibrium. While H's profit is higher at S than at K, the opposite holds for F; the meek do not inherit the earth.

With this apparatus in hand, we return to the question of public policy toward international duopoly. H's profit is part of the national income, while F's is not. Therefore, some points lying above K on F's reaction function have the clear potential for increasing the home country's welfare. Profit is shifted from the foreign to the domestic duopolist, and home consumers also gain (because total output increases and price falls). The question is, what can the home government do to achieve this result? In the Cournot model, as was noted in the text, a subsidy may well have this effect. What determines whether equilibrium K or S materializes? Economic theory has no general answer to this because it depends on assumed perceptions of the market rivals. There has been much interest, however, in the possibility that government might make some binding commitment, such as a subsidy to H's research and development spending, that would effectively shift H's reaction function upward (increase the output it selects given any output of F) and make the Cournot equilibrium coincide with point S.[18]

[18] Barbara J. Spencer and James S. Brander, "International R&D Rivalry and Industrial Strategy," *Review of Economic Studies*, 50 (October 1983): 707–722.

14

TRADE CONTROLS IN PRACTICE

Without doubt, tariffs and other governmental restraints on trade have curbed international specialization and reduced world economic welfare. It is known, for example, that regions of the United States, trading freely with one another, are far more specialized in production than independent industrial nations of comparable size.[1] Explaining the persistence of widespread tariff protection poses a challenge for economists because it is seldom obvious that a nation's tariffs are advancing its own economic welfare, and they clearly reduce the welfare of the world as a whole. The preceding three chapters have dealt mainly with the reasons why a government maximizing the real incomes of its citizens would or (usually) would not restrict trade. Here we take a behavioral approach to the trade policies of the United States and other countries:

1. Why do they pervasively restrict international trade?
2. How effectively have they cooperated internationally to lower those restrictions or keep them from rising?

14.1 U.S. TARIFFS AND THEIR INCIDENCE

Makers of public policy in the United States were little impressed with the virtues of international trade until the last five decades. As Figure 14.1 shows, the American tariff through much of the nineteenth century averaged 40 percent or more on dutiable imports. It reached its high point in 1932 due to the Smoot-Hawley Act of 1930, then it began a substantial decline that was due in part to American participation in the multinational tariff reductions (see Section 14.2). The average duty paid on *total* imports declined even more than did customs revenue on dutiable imports, as duty-free imports (often raw materials) became more important. The decreased reliance on tariffs as a source of federal governmental revenue was striking. Customs revenues, now less than 1 percent of the federal government's budget receipts, were 89 percent

---

[1] Bela Balassa, "Effects of Commercial Policy on International Trade, the Location of Production and Factor Movements," in B. Ohlin, P. Hesselborn, and P. M. Wijkman, eds., *The International Allocation of Economic Activity* (London: Macmillan, 1977), Chapter 7, especially pp. 242–248.

FIGURE 14.1   **Long-Run Trend in U.S. Tariffs**

Average duty collected on dutiable imports was high until the 1930s, then fell sharply. Average duty on total imports has fallen more, because a larger proportion of imports has become duty-free.

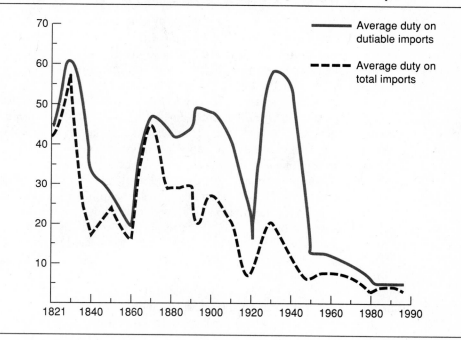

in 1821 (when they were the only tax easy to collect). Other industrial countries have shown similar patterns, and their average tariff rates in 1980 ranged from 0.8 percent (Italy) to 10.1 percent (Australia).

The history of tariff legislation is fascinating for its insights into the process of public decision-making. Early in the nineteenth century, America became a high-tariff country mainly for two reasons. One was acceptance of the infant-industry argument (see Section 12.4) that tariffs actually would raise real income by promoting economic development. The other reason was nationalism and a collective distaste for things British, notably imported British goods. Throughout the nineteenth century changes in the tariff reflected shifts in regional political strength—the manufacturing states in the northeast benefited from tariffs while the primary-product exporters of the South suffered. The Civil War swung the power balance decisively toward the manufacturers and enshrined a high tariff for the rest of the century.

Tariffs and Political Choice

Economists have recently taken a strong interest in how economic agents behave in the political sphere, as a basis for explaining the choice of economic policies. A number of models have been proposed and tested to explain the structure of present-day tariffs. One model addresses the democratic voting process. Its core could not be simpler: Each citizen gets one vote, so the economic policy chosen should be the policy that is expected to raise the welfare of a majority of the voters. On its face this model suggests a political preference for only those tariffs that maximize national welfare. The majority would certainly favor a policy that yields the greatest possible increase in national income (for example, by eliminating inefficient tariffs) and then divides up the gain so that all the voters (or a majority, in any case) are better off. The trouble with this interpretation is that losers actually are seldom compensated. Voters rationally size up a policy for its effect on their own real income if they keep the winnings or suffer the losses that come their way. A tariff proposal then wins if it redistributes income from a minority to a majority. For example, assume that the United States is a capital-rich country and that capital income is more concentrated among voters than is labor (wage) income. Then a majority will vote for tariffs in order to redistribute income from capital to labor.

Another model of tariff determination stresses interest groups. It assumes that groups lobby, support friendly candidates for office, and in other ways invest in securing political action favorable to the interest group. Sellers making up an industry are such a group. They rationally invest in securing tariff protection up to the point where the present value of the last benefits gained just equals the investment needed to secure them. Spending resources in order to gain access to a protected income stream is called *rent-seeking*.[2] One problem then is to explain which interest groups succeed in buying policies that advance their interests. This leads to the theory of collective action, which stresses the difficulty of organizing a group to secure benefits that are a collective gain to the group. It is difficult because group members can expect to enjoy the benefits even if they do not contribute to meeting the costs of securing them. The most effective groups are already organized for another purpose (professional and trade associations), or they consist of small numbers of beneficiaries (a concentrated industry with few sellers), so the problem of "free riders" is more easily solved. Members of geographically dispersed groups can readily catch the ears of many congressmen (bankers and steel fabricators). Consumers, on the other hand, have the dice loaded against them: They are numerous, and each has only a small monetary stake in a policy that affects them. The interest-group approach clearly can explain the persistence of many tariffs that do not contribute to national welfare.

Yet another approach notes that the government's job is to maintain certain collective goods, such as a sense that people are being treated fairly and not suffering unreasonably from economic misfortunes. This approach suggests that tariffs will protect low-income persons, such as unskilled labor. It also predicts that tariffs will be raised when an industry's competitive position is significantly undermined, causing unanticipated losses and unemployment.

---

[2] See Chapter 12. The term *rent* applies to any component of a supplier's income stream in excess of opportunity cost. It might arise because the government fends off competition (as here) or because the supplier enjoys a natural monopoly or gained possession of an especially productive asset (as in Chapter 10).

TABLE 14.1 Characteristics of Industries in Relation to Levels of Protection Given by U.S. Tariffs, Nominal and Effective, After Kennedy Round Reductions

Industry Characteristics and Tariff Measure	Industries Ranked by Level of Protection			
	Highest Quarter	Second Quarter	Third Quarter	Lowest Quarter
Labor-intensity (measured by payrolls as percentage of all factor payments)				
Nominal	46%	50%	53%	45%
Effective	47%	48%	52%	44%
Level of labor skill (measured by payroll per worker)				
Nominal	$6,000	$6,700	$7,200	$7,100
Effective	$6,000	$6,600	$7,500	$6,900
Size of manufacturing establishment (measured by value added per establishment in millions of dollars)				
Nominal	$1.8[a]	$1.4	$2.2	$3.6
Effective	$1.5[a]	$1.6	$3.2	$2.6

Source: Tariff rates—Robert E. Baldwin, *Nontariff Distortions of International Trade* (Washington: Brookings Institution, 1970), pp. 163–164; other data—United States Bureau of the Census, *1967 Census of Manufacturers: Summary and Subject Statistics* (Washington: Government Printing Office, 1971), Table 3.

[a] The "ordnance and accessories" sector was omitted from this class. The large establishments producing military wares hardly seem relevant to testing the effect of tariff protection.

Evidence on U.S. Tariff Structure

These models of political economy predict which industries will receive high tariff protection. Table 14.1 shows the results of a simple and casual test on the levels of protection that prevailed in the 1970s.[3] For each manufacturing industry, the average levels of both nominal and effective rates of protection were measured (including nontariff barriers, discussed in Section 14.3). Industries were ranked from the most protected to the least protected, and the ranked list was divided into quarters. Some traits of the industries included in each of the four quarters were then averaged.

Does the tariff protect labor intensive industries? The labor-intensity of an industry can be measured roughly by the share that payrolls constitute of payments to all the factors of production that it employs (the industry's value added). The top two lines of Table 14.1 show that the least protected industries are indeed the least labor-intensive. For the other three quarters, however, the hypothesis fails. The most heavily protected industries are not very labor-intensive. This does not strongly confirm the "majority voters" prediction that tariffs favor labor-intensive industries.

[3] These rates were reduced further in the Tokyo Round. Reductions have tended to be equiproportional, however, and the relative protection given to different goods has changed little since 1930. See Real P. Lavergne, *The Political Economy of U.S. Tariffs* (New York: Academic Press, 1983).

Does the tariff protect low-skilled labor? If the political process aims in part to redistribute income to the less fortunate, or to those who have suffered reductions in their incomes, high tariffs should protect industries that employ low-skill and low-wage labor. The next part of Table 14.1 shows that the low-wage industries do get the highest protection.

Does the tariff protect small (or big) business? The lobbying, or interest-group, model suggests that industries with small and widely dispersed production units can influence political decisions at low cost, thus securing high protection. On the other hand, the collective character of tariff benefits suggests that high protection goes to large, concentrated sellers. Thus, the theoretical predictions conflict. In any event, Table 14.1 suggests rather strongly that protection favors small plants.

That U.S. tariffs protect low-wage and small-scale industries emerges from other tests, more sophisticated versions of Table 14.1. The finding indicates that tariffs redistribute income toward the less fortunate, but it may also support the lobbying model: Industries with the greatest comparative disadvantage also have the most incentive to invest in higher tariffs.[4] Whatever the basis for their clout, industries that secure high tariffs also win heavy nontariff protection. So do geographically dispersed industries, consistent with the way congressional voting on tariff legislation reflects the interests of industries in congressmen's home districts.[5] The evidence does support the "political economy" approach to explaining levels of protection.

14.2 MULTILATERAL TARIFF REDUCTION

If it is possible to explain why some industries get heavy protection, what accounts for the *90 percent* drop in U.S. tariffs between the early 1930s and the present day? The answer to this question lies in the policy change that accounted for half of the decline—a program initiated by the United States whereby nations join in simultaneous reductions of their tariffs.

Origins of Trade Agreements Program

In the face of mountainous tariff rates imposed by the Smoot-Hawley Act of 1930, it was no wonder that the U.S. share of world trade dropped from 16 to 11 percent in the next five years. The world total also declined, as international trade shriveled in the face of the Great Depression of the 1930s. The combined effect on U.S. exports of the depression and of retaliatory increases in other countries' tariffs prompted a major shift in trade policy in 1934. Congress authorized the president to negotiate agreements with foreign trading partners to lower tariffs hampering American exports. In return, U.S. tariffs would be cut on selected goods exported by the partner. The president could offer to cut the rates of duty set by the Smoot-Hawley Act up to 50 percent. By 1940 the United States had entered into bilateral trade agreements with twenty partners, thereby establishing a ritual for these accords.

---

[4] Edward John Ray, "The Determinants of Tariffs and Nontariff Trade Restrictions in the United States," *Journal of Political Economy*, 89 (February 1981): 105–121.

[5] Ray, Table 4; Robert E. Baldwin, *Trade Policy in a Changing World Economy* (Chicago: University of Chicago Press, 1988), Chapter 3.

If the tariffs reduced by the agreement were not offsetting some specific failure of the market, their reductions should have increased world welfare. Did they also increase the welfare of each participating country? How were they consistent with the setting of tariffs through a process of political choice? One possible answer comes from the role of tariffs in extracting monopoly profits from international trade (see Section 11.3). If the tariff-cutting importer is large enough to influence its terms of trade, or if it merely *thinks* it gives benefits to foreigners by reducing its tariff, the reciprocal trade agreements make some sense. A tariff reduction now raises the world price of the imported good to the exporter's benefit. The size of this benefit depends on the initial volume of trade (as well as on the size of the tariff concession). This terms-of-trade gain to the exporter is a loss to the importer unless its tariff was higher than optimal. The importer might not gain from cutting a single tariff (even though the world does), but the importer's terms-of-trade loss on one product can be offset by its gain as an exporter when a reciprocal agreement is signed. In addition, these gains and losses are more likely to cancel if each party cuts tariffs on the same initial volume of trade.[6]

That all parties might gain through reciprocal tariff-cutting agreements is consistent with the political economy of tariffs. Suppose that a country has high tariffs in place, the result of the political processes described in Section 14.1. The government knows that national economic welfare has been impaired; it would like to reduce the tariffs and raise national welfare, but cannot get rid of tariffs one at a time. Therefore, it proposes a broad tariff-cutting agreement with its trading partners, which will benefit most of its export producers as well as consumers generally. Enough voters may perceive that they benefit significantly from the package that a majority coalition forms in favor of it. Both this process of forming coalitions in favor of freer trade and the monopoly-tariff story probably help explain the success of reciprocal trade agreements.

Multilateral Tariff Reductions and GATT

Whichever story is correct, the bilateral trade agreements program was running out of steam at the end of the 1930s. The United States and its trade-agreement partners tended to pick for liberalization goods for which each was the other's principal supplier. That choice is consistent with the dismantling of tariffs for monopoly, because the reduced tariffs applied to imports from all sources, not just from the partner. Suppose the United States and Brazil grant each other tariff concessions on coffee and computers, respectively. Each is a larger importer, and so their increased purchases raise the world prices of both goods. Both gain from lower trade barriers. The United States may also import coffee from Colombia, and Brazil may import some computers from Britain. The United States feels it has given away uncompensated benefits by paying a higher world price for Colombian coffee, Brazil by paying more for British

---

[6] Elements of monopoly and product differentiation in individual product markets probably contribute to causing the prices of a country's imports ex tariff to rise when a tariff is reduced. A study of U.S. tariff reductions in the 1950s found that nearly half of the price effects took the form of increased external prices, rather than reduced prices (including tariff) to domestic consumers. See M. E. Kreinin, "Effect of Tariff Changes on the Prices and Volume of Imports," *American Economic Review*, 51 (June 1961): 310–324.

computers. The United States and Brazil minimize these "spillover benefits" by cutting tariffs only on goods imported mainly from the partner country. Regrets over spillover benefits came to inhibit bilateral trade agreements and ultimately led to the development of multinational bargaining under the General Agreement on Tariffs and Trade (GATT). An important goal of the GATT was to preserve nondiscrimination in tariffs and to block retaliatory tariff increases.

The General Agreement is part of the machinery devised during World War II for restoring the international economy to health, and its most important function has been to provide a framework for multilateral tariff bargaining sessions.[7] The first five of these (1947–1958) consisted of simultaneous batteries of bilateral negotiations. Each party could match the spillover benefits flowing from its own concessions against the incidental benefits gained as a third party from other negotiations. A net loser on spillovers could demand additional compensation. Thus, each party could be sure of an equitable deal in both its bilateral negotiations and the incidence of spillover benefits. The GATT's bargaining procedure softened the inhibition that had threatened to strangle bilateral trade negotiations.

Even this multilateral procedure reached its limits as successive tariff reductions cut more and more sharply into the incomes of import-competing producers. A still more sweeping approach was needed to form a coalition that could offset the interest-group pressures favoring tariffs in the industrial countries. Therefore, the Kennedy Round of multilateral tariff bargaining, completed in 1967, departed even further from bilateral bargaining between principal suppliers. The chief industrial countries agreed on the target of an across-the-board 50 percent cut in all tariff rates. They would forgo balancing the reciprocal benefits stemming from this overall cut. Each country could propose to except some of its tariffs from the cut, presumably where unacceptable injury to domestic industries would result. Bargaining proceeded over the size of the exceptions lists, rather than over the 50 percent cut itself. The participants agreed to weighted-average tariff cuts of around 35 percent, making the Kennedy Round the most sweeping tariff reduction since the GATT went into effect.[8]

The Tokyo Round (1973–1979), continued the procedure of the Kennedy Round but also tackled the thorny problem of nontariff barriers to trade. In the tariff-cutting part of the agreement the industrial countries agreed to reduce their tariffs on average by another third over an eight-year period. Most of the major countries lowered individual tariffs by a formula that shaves more off those tariffs that were higher initially. The practice should cause *effective* rates of protection (see Section 12.7) to be lowered proportionally more than the average nominal rates. The Tokyo Round participants also agreed on a number of codes governing nontariff barriers (discussed in Section 14.3); not much has come of these, and in particular they did not succeed in propping up the dispute-settlement machinery of the GATT.

---

[7] The GATT also maintains a set of rules governing member nations' commercial policies and a forum in which international disputes over commercial policy can be mediated. The mediation function seemed to work well for a while, but in recent years the GATT has shown little ability to mitigate disputes over trade restrictions.

[8] Two studies of the Kennedy Round are Ernest H. Preeg, *Traders and Diplomats* (Washington: Brookings Institution, 1970); and John W. Evans, *The Kennedy Round in American Trade Policy: The Twilight of the GATT?* (Cambridge, MA: Harvard University Press, 1971).

FIGURE 14.2   Effects on Welfare and Government Revenue of Tariff on Individual Product

Domestic demand is DD', domestic supply is SS', world price is P_w. Imposing tariff $P_t P_w / P_w O$ leaves world price unchanged, raises domestic price to P_t, and causes a welfare loss (net) measured by triangular areas 2 and 4.

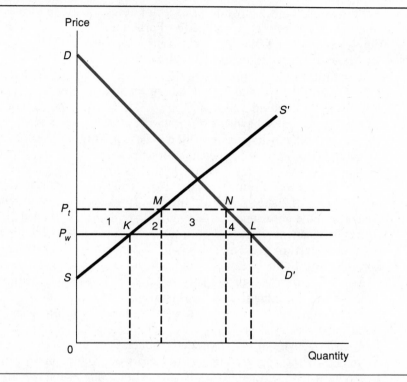

In 1992 another round of negotiations (the Uruguay Round), begun in 1986, remained under way. Emphasizing the difficult problem of liberalizing trade in agricultural commodities and limiting export subsidies for them, its prospects for success were poor.[9]

Gains from Trade Liberalization

Trade liberalization is always controversial. With the progressive reduction of tariffs by the industrial countries, some observers have begun to wonder whether the real welfare gains warrant the political effort involved. To discuss this and other problems

---

[9] Robert E. Baldwin and J. David Richardson, eds., *The Uruguay Round and Beyond: Problems and Prospects* (Cambridge, MA: National Bureau of Economic Research, 1991).

of quantifying the welfare effects of trade controls, the general-equilibrium analysis used in Chapters 11 and 12 can be translated into the familiar demand-and-supply version that economists use for measuring welfare effects in particular markets. Figure 14.2 illustrates the method.

The nation is a net importer of the product, and a small purchaser of it on the world market. Thus, the world price is not affected by its purchases, and it can take any desired quantity at price P_w. The horizontal line extending from P_w is thus the supply curve for imports. The demand curve for the product is DD'. The supply curve, SS', shows the domestic output at various prices.

If no tariff is in force, price P_w prevails in the domestic market. Domestic producers supply quantity P_wK, and import KL, of the total amount P_wL consumed. Suppose that a tariff is imposed at rate P_tP_w/P_wO. The world price cannot fall; therefore the domestic price (after payment of the tariff) must be elevated by the full amount of the duty to P_t (if any imports are still purchased). At this higher price, domestic supply is enlarged to P_tM, total consumption is reduced to P_tN, and imports shrink to MN.

Because the world price is fixed, the nation as a whole must lose by imposing the tariff. Figure 14.2 shows how the effect is spread among consumers, domestic producers, and the government. The total welfare that consumers derive from any given commodity can be measured by what they would pay rather than do without the good entirely. For reasons explained in introductory texts on economics, this is approximated by the area under the demand curve and above the market price line. In Figure 14.2 this "consumers' surplus" under free trade is measured by the triangular area beneath the demand curve and above P_wL; when the tariff is imposed, it shrinks to the area above P_tN and consumers lose an amount of welfare measured by the trapezoidal area P_wLNP_t.

A tariff likewise affects domestic producers' welfare. The area under the supply curve depicts the opportunity cost of factors of production (including normal profit to producers). Sometimes increases in output encounter rising marginal costs, and as in Figure 14.2 the supply curve acquires an upward slope. Then some factors employed in the industry earn more than the opportunity cost of their services and a "producers' surplus" results. This is measured by the area above the supply curve and below market price. Thus, when free trade prevails and the ruling price is P_w, domestic producers enjoy the surplus triangular area SKP_w. When the tariff is imposed, the surplus rises to SMP_t. Thus, domestic producers gain from the imposition of a tariff an amount measured by the area P_wKMP_t.

Before weighing these effects against one another, one more must be counted: the tariff revenue collected by the government. After the tariff is imposed, the government gathers P_wP_t on each unit of imports and MN is imported. The tariff yields revenue of $P_wP_t \cdot MN$, the area labeled 3 in the diagram. What significance does this have for welfare? It can be supposed either that the government hands the revenue back to the consumers or that it provides public services just as valuable to them (at the margin) as their private consumption. Either way, government revenue is dollar for dollar as good as surplus to the consumers.

Now the welfare effects of a tariff on domestic interest can be summarized. Consumers lose an amount equal to the sum of areas $1 + 2 + 3 + 4$. Producers' surplus increases by area 1. Government revenue grows by area 3. Thus, the net loss to the country from imposing the tariff is area $2 + 4$. Area 4 is often called the *deadweight loss* of consumers' surplus due to the imposition of a tax. Area 2 depicts the excess real cost of securing output $P_tM - P_wK$ from domestic sources rather than from imports.[10]

The gains expected from the Tokyo Round illustrate these concepts. Deardorff and Stern estimated the welfare gain for thirty-four countries from the reductions in tariffs (and some nontariff barriers). They calculated a gain of $4.8 billion annually, which is a modest 0.1 percent of the combined gross national product of these countries. Because of changes in their terms of trade, a few countries were expected to lose, although a few others would enjoy quite large gains.[11] This total gain seems small, so it should be placed in some perspective, as William Cline and associates did in reporting an earlier (and similar) estimate of Tokyo Round gains. They held that the experience of the European Community (see Chapter 15) warrants inflating this basic figure substantially to allow for greater scale economies and innovative gains that go with the static effects depicted in Figure 14.2. Furthermore, the scaled-up gain is an annual one, and it goes on applying to a larger volume of international trade each year. If trade grows at 5 percent a year after the Tokyo Round cuts are in place and future welfare gains are discounted at 10 percent annually, the present value of the total welfare gain rises to 100 times the figure given by Deardorff and Stern. From these gains should be subtracted the costs of reallocating resources to their better uses following tariff reduction, but Cline concluded that this offset is small.[12]

14.3 THE TREND TOWARD "MANAGED" TRADE

The undeniable success of multinational tariff reduction has occurred against a counterpoint of the replacement of tariffs by other forms of trade restrictions, along with some reimposition of tariffs that had been negotiated downward. While the GATT sought to install a stable regime of trade policy subject to simple and predictable rules, governments have chosen to intervene more and more closely in many important international markets, using nontariff controls and tariffs tailor-made to the perceived needs of protected domestic industries. One study[13] estimated that the proportion of countries' trade subject to nontariff barriers had risen as follows:

[10] An incidental virtue of Figure 14.2 is showing why efforts to bring about welfare-increasing changes in policy so often founder on the question of who gains and loses. Both the gains to consumers and the losses to domestic producers from eliminating the tariffs are likely to be large relative to the net benefit to the two groups taken together.

[11] Alan V. Deardorff and Robert M. Stern, "Economic Effects of the Tokyo Round," *Southern Economic Journal*, 49 (January 1983): 605–624.

[12] William R. Cline et al., *Trade Negotiations in the Tokyo Round: A Quantitative Assessment* (Washington: Brookings Institution, 1978), pp. 78–79 and Chapter 8. Dynamic gains from learning and the like were discussed in Section 13.3.

[13] Sam Laird and Alexander Yeats, "Trends in Nontariff Barriers of Developed Countries, 1966–1986," *Weltwirtschaftliches Archiv*, 126 (2) (1990): 299–326.

	1966 (%)	1986 (%)
United States	36	45 (12)
European Community	21	54 (19)
Japan	31	43 (14)
All developed countries	25	48 (16)

Although the increase shown here is evident on any reckoning, the levels may prompt an over-pessimistic interpretation, for nontariff barriers are defined to include both nontariff measures specifically intended to restrict trade and various domestic policies (technical or health and safety standards, border tax adjustments, etc.) that incidentally impose extra costs on foreign suppliers. If only the former restrictions are considered, the figures shown in parentheses for 1986 apply. These are still high, however, and they have increased greatly. The upward trend of these restrictions raises severe doubts as to whether recent successes in lowering tariff barriers reflect an actual reduction in protection. Instead, the principal feature of commercial policy in this period may be a substitution of diverse controls for explicit tariffs. This section reviews some theory of nontariff barriers to trade, then turns to important real-life forms of these barriers.

Theory of Quantitative Restrictions

A quantitative restriction (QR) has basically the same effect as a tariff, yet its incidental differences are important. The similarity is shown in Figure 14.3. The supply and demand curves for an imported product are shown by S and D; domestic supply is omitted. A quantitative restriction equal to OQ_0 per period of time is imposed. This is an effective restriction because it is smaller than the free-trade flow of imports (corresponding to point F). Imports are bought and sold on competitive markets. Thus, the prices that must prevail inside and outside the country's boundaries are known: P_t and P_w would clear the domestic and foreign markets, respectively, if OQ_0 imports are permitted. It is known that a tariff separates the domestic and foreign prices of an import and that in equilibrium a tariff rate must equal the proportion by which it elevates the internal above the external price. Thus, a quota that produces a price distortion of $P_t P_w / P_w O$ is equivalent in its *restrictive effect* to a tariff of that percentage; the equivalent tariff could be depicted by schedule S_t, which lies uniformly above S by that percentage and indicates the domestic price (including tariff) that must be paid for a quantity of imports.

Despite this proposition about equivalence, tariffs and quotas have important differences in practice. Some of these depend on what happens to the revenue representing the gap between the foreign and the domestic price. In Figure 14.3, a tariff of $P_t P_w / P_w O$ would generate for the government revenue measured by the rectangle $P_t DEP_w$. When imports are limited by quota, no tariff is ordinarily collected, yet the privilege of buying abroad at P_w and selling domestically at P_t is obviously valuable. The government might auction off licenses to import to the highest bidder. Competitive bidding by would-be importers would wipe out this potential profit and hand the government the same revenue as if it levied the tariff equivalent. On the other hand,

FIGURE 14.3   Comparison of Effects of Tariff and Quantitative Restriction

Demand and supply for imports are D and S, respectively. Imposing a quota OQ_0 drives domestic price up to P_t, external price down to P_w. The effect is thus equivalent to a tariff of $P_t P_w / P_w O$.

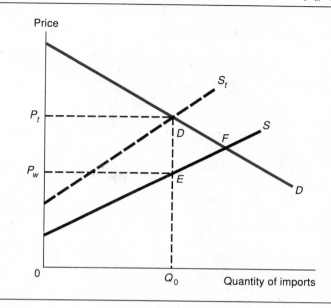

the government might give away import licenses to the domestic importers, in which case they capture the proceeds $P_t DEP_w$. If the government awards the licenses to foreign exporters, their country gains the scarcity rent. Note that the world welfare cost of the restriction, DEF, is the same in each case. The method of administering a quota only redistributes income.[14]

Another difference between tariffs and quotas arises if the domestic industry is a monopoly (rather than competitive, as was assumed in Figure 14.3). For example, a monopoly lobbying for protection would prefer a tariff to a quota that leads to the same equilibrium domestic price. The monopoly makes higher profits when the tariff is in force, due to the different ways in which the monopoly reacts to a tariff and a quota. The government, however, tends to prefer a quota because it obtains more public revenue by auctioning off the licenses to import the restricted quantity to the highest bidder than it does protecting the monopoly by a tariff.[15]

A special type of quantitative restriction now in widespread use is the so-called voluntary export restraint (VER), whereby the importing nation induces the exporting countries to curtail their shipments. In terms of Figure 14.3, this procedure simply hands over the proceeds ($P_t DEP_w$) to the exporters, who are expected to charge the

[14] At one time the Japanese government was financing its whole international commercial intelligence network (JETRO) from its cut of the profits of importers licensed to bring quota-restricted bananas into Japan.
[15] James H. Cassing and Arye L. Hillman, "Political Influence Motives and the Choice between Tariffs and Quotas," *Journal of International Economics*, 19 (November 1985): 279–290.

price that clears the market for the restricted volume of sales. A VER obviously maximizes the cost to the importing country's real income of restricting imports to Q_0. The following discussion will speculate on why the choice of VERs has been so popular among importing-country governments.

Management through VERs

The United States has made little use of quotas imposed unilaterally on imports of manufactured products, but it has used VERs extensively to regulate the quantities of goods that exporters ship to the United States. The VERs began with an informal agreement with Japan in 1957 to limit exports of cotton textiles in order to protect that U.S. industry. Curbing Japanese exports, however, merely created exporting opportunities for other overseas textile producers, and so the restraints were expanded to other exporters. Textile industries forbidden to export cotton textiles to the United States could expand production and exports of other types of textiles. Therefore, import competition increased in other textile lines and also in finished garments (because the U.S. garment industry lacked access to cheap textile inputs available to its foreign competitors). As a result, the negotiated restraints on textile exporters spread inexorably, leading eventually to the Multifiber Arrangement, an umbrella agreement covering bilateral quotas negotiated among a number of exporting and importing countries.

Initially, at least, most textile quotas negotiated by the United States held foreign suppliers not to fixed quantities, but rather to maximum rates of growth of their shipments or of their market shares. Such agreements were supposed to limit "disruption" of U.S. markets, and they are sometimes called *orderly marketing agreements*. Much of present-day governmental management of international trade aims to limit the rate of expansion of imports or the rate of contraction of the domestic industry, and not necessarily to guarantee the domestic industry's market share in perpetuity. Possible reasons for this are discussed below in connection with policies for adjustment assistance.

The restictiveness of VERs can be assessed by calculating export-tax equivalents of these quotas, like the import-tax equivalent of a quota administered by the importing country (Figure 14.3). Hamilton, however, could use an even more direct method by obtaining data from Hong Kong on the market values of quota allocations. That is, what competitive Hong Kong producers will pay for the privilege of exporting a given lot to a particular destination should equal the difference between their costs and the goods' sale value at the destination. He found tariff equivalents of 27 percent for the United States and 14 percent for the European Community; added to the conventional tariffs that continue to apply to these imports, the combined trade barriers are 56 percent for the United States, 33 percent for the Community.[16]

Why have U.S. policy-makers shown such a strong preference for VERs, with their high welfare cost? The answer probably lies in the bargaining power possessed by foreign exporters. When a large customer such as the United States raises its trade

---

[16] Carl Hamilton, "An Assessment of Voluntary Restraints on Hong Kong Exports to Europe and the USA," *Economica*, 53 (August 1986): 339–350.

barriers, it certainly inflicts short-run losses on foreign exporters and may permanently worsen their terms of trade. Exporting countries often have ways of retaliating, such as restricting imports from the United States. In addition, the United States may appear to be less protective if foreigners "voluntarily" restrain their exports than if U.S. quotas are imposed.

Management Through Special Protection

Important U.S. industries have obtained special protection through channels other than VERs, usually, but not always, following a bout of stiffened import competition. They have advanced their interests through the following legal or political channels:

1. Escape-clause relief (currently under Section 201 of the Trade Act of 1974) for industries that can blame their sufferings on GATT-round tariff reductions

2. Relief under various other statutory provisions, including national security, countervailing duties, antidumping rules, and special regulations covering agriculture[17]

3. Special protection (including VERs) obtained by going around these standard escape routes and appealing directly to the president and Congress

4. Preservation of longstanding high rates of statutory protection from reduction in the GATT rounds

Many, though not all, of these devices have been used for relatively short-run interventions to manage international trade on behalf of industries that have shown reduced profits or employment due (or allegedly due) to increased import competition. The one objective that most commonly leads to the management of trade is delaying or retarding a domestic industry's contraction. Industries that seek special protection usually flaunt scars that can be blamed on import competition, and policy-makers often rationalized special protection to assist an industry's adjustment to increased import competition. Therefore, it is necessary to observe how the patterns of special protection relate to adjustments by import-competing industries. Whether government should intervene in the adjustment process, in order to maximize welfare, is considered subsequently.

If special protection aims only to smooth the process of adjustment, it should be reasonably short-lived. The median industry that received escape-clause relief during 1950–1983 indeed had shelter for only four years, although industries protected under other provisions have enjoyed prolonged assistance. The textile and apparel sectors have been protected since 1957. However, protection has clearly not served to smooth the orderly exit of factors of production from this industry, in that one-third of all U.S. textile and apparel firms were less than six years old in 1982. Where protection has been long lived, its level or incidence has not necessarily been stable. In fact, there is a "catch-22" process in operation. When offering help to an industry reeling from import competition, the government admonishes the industry that the protection will last only while the industry takes appropriate steps to restore its profitability. However, the protection itself excludes competing imports and automatically improves the

---

[17] Antidumping and countervailing duties were considered in Section 13.3.

industry's profitability, even if no adjustment takes place. Then the government observes the recovered profits, proclaims that its assistance has succeeded, and removes or relaxes the protection. Yet the industry may have done little to reduce its capacity or increase its efficiency, or at least not enough to keep its profits from tumbling once protection is relaxed. Symptoms of ill-health return, and the cycle starts all over.[18]

How much adjustment actually takes place during these periods of special protection? Hufbauer and Rosen's study of thirty-one troubled industries that received special protection found that the median industry lost employment at a rate of 2.2 percent annually, while the market share held by imports continued to grow a bit (0.8 percent annually) despite the restrictions. Because any industry experiences a significant amount of natural turnover in its work force (retirement, job change), this rate of decline of employment means that in the typical case few workers actually lost their jobs. Therefore, the effect of special protection was really to slow the growth of competing imports, and thus the contraction of these industries, and to limit involuntary losses of jobs. Policy-makers awarding protection routinely urge the favored industry not to contract but to increase its efficiency and stand up to the cheaper imports. Such recoveries rarely happen, for the good reason that any available efficiency-raising investments would be undertaken by profit-seeking firms without the spur of import competition, and the arrival of an external competitive threat if anything reduces their expected payout. The only industries that successfully adjusted to imports either moved to lower-cost locations in the United States, thus costing the original workers their jobs anyway (bicycles), or were bailed out by demand shifts (motorcycles).

How costly has special protection been? Hufbauer and Rosen calculated that in 1984 special protection for thirty-one industries cost consumers $53 billion, and that society as a whole lost $8 billion (the deadweight loss in Figure 14.2). A more meaningful figure is the annual cost to consumers of each job preserved by special protection. The cost is usually more than the average worker's annual earnings—between $20,000 and $100,000 annually for most of Hufbauer and Rosen's industries, but in four cases exceeding $500,000. It is not obvious that the protected industries and their employees gained any benefits commensurate with the cost to the rest of the economy. It is even clearer that the amount of help given to imports-afflicted industries varied greatly from sector to sector, with the greatest protection going to large industries (steel, automobiles) and those otherwise able to seek political favors. Several observers have suggested that, because special protection can be considered politically inevitable, it should be provided through a single administrative forum (such as the International Trade Commission), thereby eliminating the special deals and political end-runs that have been common. Another question, considered in the following discussion, is whether adjustment could be offered more efficiently with policies other than the restriction of imports.[19]

[18] Vinod K. Aggarwal, Robert O. Keohane, and David B. Yoffie, "The Dynamics of Negotiated Protectionism," *American Political Science Review*, 81 (June 1986): 345–366. Legislation passed in 1988 moved toward requiring industries seeking relief from imports to show not only that they had been injured but also that they were capable of making "positive adjustment."

[19] See Gary Clyde Hufbauer and Howard F. Rosen, *Trade Policy for Troubled Industries* (Washington: Institute for International Economics, 1986); and Robert Z. Lawrence and Robert E. Litan, *Saving Free Trade: A Pragmatic Approach* (Washington: Brookings Institution, 1986).

How Special Protection Works: The Steel Industry

The major integrated steel producers of the United States have been important beneficiaries of protection since 1969, and the steel industry teaches several lessons concerning the political economy of protection. Import competition became significant in the 1960s, with imports' share rising to 17 percent of domestic steel consumption in 1968. The industry was losing its comparative advantage because the prime sources of ore and energy inputs, once abundant in interior North America, shifted overseas. Also, recent technical changes in steelmaking are not easily incorporated into old facilities, and new steel mills (mainly in Japan and the developing countries) are much lower-cost simply because they embody the latest technology from the ground up. Furthermore, the U.S. steel industry's prices had been high. Formerly it earned some monopoly profits. More important, substantial rents were captured by its unionized workforce: In 1982 a steelworker's compensation was double the average for production workers in U.S. manufacturing.

The first significant lesson from steel's experience concerns the form of the protection it has received. Steel is a large industry with considerable political clout. Repeatedly, steel has threatened to use the statutory machinery for special protection at times when a victory would prove embarrassing to U.S. diplomatic relations with major foreign steel-producing countries (Western Europe and Japan). The government responded with a series of special deals that would never have been available to a small industry. These included several rounds of voluntary export restraints, which recently helped to push imports' share of the U.S. market down from 26 percent (in 1984) to 19 percent.

The second lesson pertains to the adjustment process in an industry that is losing its comparative advantage. Outsiders typically urge such industries to hang tough and raise their productivity levels. However, investments to raise productivity can pay only if the industry has access to new technology that will not only lower the industry's costs, but lower them more than it lowers the costs of overseas competitors. The U.S. steelmakers had no such magic bullets. Therefore, the efficient choice was to run existing facilities until they could no longer cover their variable costs, then close them down. Two factors have impaired the efficient pursuit of this strategy of retreat. First, in the early 1970s optimism about future demand swept over the U.S. steel industry and led to a substantial amount of modernizing investment. The optimism was misplaced, and the investment did not pay out—affirming the proposition that a sector losing its comparative advantage cannot efficiently save itself by reinvesting. However, the closing down of production facilities has been complicated by obligations to make large severance payments to employees and incur other closing-down costs; the "salvage value" of a closed steel facility is actually negative and large.

The third lesson concerns the source of the major steel producers' difficulties. Public policy offers special protection against import competition, but usually not against the many adverse disturbances of domestic origin that can strike an industry. Therefore, an industry has an incentive to blame its troubles on imports even if they are a minor source, simply because public policy will respond. The U.S. integrated steel producers indeed lost markets to imports, but they lost nearly as much business to domestic "mini-mills," companies utilizing electric furnaces charged with steel scrap. The mini-mills operate efficiently at much smaller scales than traditional integrated facilities and attain much lower costs. They cannot make all steel products, but their product range continues to expand. The U.S. integrated producers could not hope to persuade the government to hobble the minis, so their rent-seeking (or rent-preserving) efforts were devoted instead to beating off the imports.[20]

Efficient Response to Import Competition: Adjustment Assistance

The evidence suggests that the United States has managed special protection by restricting imports in order to slow adjustment by import-competing industries. This policy has imposed large costs on consumers and a deadweight loss on society. Does it provide offsetting benefits by reducing the cost of reallocating America's productive resources? In order to focus on the normative issue, assume that, when the U.S. comparative advantage changes, the efficient policy in the long run is to let resources be reallocated to suit the new conditions in the world market. This assumption ignores the question of whether market forces pick the best speed and direction of their reallocation, or whether the government should intervene. The issue of efficient adjustment applies equally to the responses following any disturbance to the allocation of resources among sectors, and so it goes beyond international economics and cannot receive full treatment here. One conclusion from Section 12.3 can be adapted, however. Section 12.3 showed that it is inefficient to restrict trade when the underlying distortion lies elsewhere, such as in consumption or domestic production of the good in question. The proposition extends to the adjustment process. If factors are not reallocated at optimal rates when international (or other) disturbances displace them, the failings are presumably in the factor markets themselves, and remedies should be targeted there.[21]

Help for U.S. industries troubled by import competition has in fact come partly through adjustment assistance rather than protection. Since 1962 the United States has had a program whereby some firms and workers affected by import competition receive adjustment assistance as an alternative to elevated protection. The program was devised not so much to repair factor-market failures as to provide fair treatment to those injured by trade liberalization; in that sense it compensates the losers for going along with policies that raise the national income overall. The evidence on the performance of adjustment assistance is not very encouraging. Not many workers receiving it have actually been retrained, and many of them have experienced only temporary layoffs before returning to work in the same sector where they were employed before. Also, workers receiving adjustment assistance differed little from those getting general unemployment insurance, raising the equity question of why those who became unemployed through import changes should be treated differ-

---

[20] See Robert W. Crandall, "Steel Imports: Dumping or Competition?" *Regulation*, 4 (April 1982): 17–24; Donald F. Barnett and Robert W. Crandall, *Up from the Ashes: The Rise of the Steel Minimill in the United States* (Washington: Brookings Institution, 1986).

[21] People usually must incur some costs when they change jobs—retraining themselves and/or moving their homes. When an industry reduces its employment, it is generally efficient for wages to be reduced somewhat, in order to slow the rate at which jobs are lost and these job-change costs incurred. One example of a labor-market inefficiency would be downward-rigid wages that increase the losses of jobs and cause more job-change costs to be incurred.

ently.[22] Whatever the track record of adjustment assistance, the point remains that the way to correct any failings of adjustment processes in the factor markets is presumptively by repairing those markets and not by interfering with trade.

Export Subsidies: The Export-Import Bank

U.S. trade policy includes provision for countervailing duties against export subsidies. These subsidies are hard to square with the goal of maximizing the exporter's national income, as taxing exports for monopoly gain makes more sense. Paradoxically, the subsidies may raise world welfare when they offset a tariff that the importer levies on the same goods, just as the importer's levy improves world welfare if the export subsidy is taken as given. In any case, export subsidies abound despite GATT rules to the contrary. Some subsidies function like import duties to protect profits and employment in favored sectors. Others may pay homage to surviving mercantilistic beliefs that exports are good for the country and imports bad. Two types of export subsidy employed by the United States will be explored here. (Similar devices are used by many other countries.)

A popular way to subsidize exports is giving the purchaser a low-interest loan to finance the purchase. All the major industrial countries do this through agencies similar to the Export-Import Bank of the United States. Credits finance about 10 percent of exports for the United States but as much as 45 percent for Japan, France, and the United Kingdom. The subsidy can be measured by the difference between the interest rate actually charged to a favored purchaser and what the purchaser would pay for a commercial loan. The total value of the subsidies given by seven major industrial countries in 1980 was estimated to be between $1.5 and $3.5 billion.[23] These subsidies have two effects. They divert resources toward the export industries— those export industries favored by the subsidized loans—and they transfer income from the exporting to the importing country, except to the extent that the exporter can raise the price and capture the subsidy benefit going to the importer. About two-thirds of these subsidized loans are made by industrial countries to less-developed nations (over four-fifths, in the case of the Export-Import Bank), so the transfers pass from richer to poorer. Subsidized export credits are at the discretion of the credit-granting agency—often, it appears, to assist the country's exporters when they are competing keenly with exporters of other countries for large orders. These export subsidies seem to favor industries making big-ticket exports such as aircraft and machinery, and the industrial countries' export-subsidy agencies have sometimes become involved in price wars with one another in these markets.

The United States has at times offered extensive if disguised subsidies for the export of agricultural commodities. While U.S. subsidies of agricultural exports have been modest recently, the widespread management of agricultural trade by most countries

---

[22] J. David Richardson, "Trade Adjustment Assistance Under the United States Trade Act of 1974: An Analytical Examination and Worker Survey," in Jagdish N. Bhagwati, ed., *Import Competition and Response* (Chicago: University of Chicago Press, 1982), Chapter 12. The program was sharply curtailed by the Reagan administration.

[23] Heywood Fleisig and Catharine Hill, "The Benefits and Costs of Official Export Credit Programs," in Robert E. Baldwin and Anne O. Krueger, eds., *The Structure and Evolution of Recent U.S. Trade Policy* (Chicago: University of Chicago Press, 1984), Chapter 9.

is currently among the most serious issues of international economic policy. The problem arises because most countries maintain policies to increase the incomes of their farmers and these usually entail holding the prices of farm products above market-clearing levels. When the country is a net importer of the products in question, raising prices can be accomplished easily by restricting imports. When the country is a net exporter, however, any policy that raises prices will dry up the exports unless they are subsidized so that produce can be offered at a world price below what domestic consumers are forced to pay.

Because price-support policies increase farm production, an increasing excess of production over domestic demand clamors for export subsidies. Generous farm-price supports of the European Community countries, once net importers of major crops, have induced their farmers to produce exportable surpluses of many products, making the export subsidies a huge drain on the Community's budget. An international agreement to curb agricultural export subsidies was a major objective of the Uruguay Round, but one that seems doomed to frustration.

Managed Trade: The Prospects

This section will conclude by considering the prospects for managed trade. Will the management of international trade continue to proliferate, or will nations succeed in restoring the regime of progressive liberalization and stable rules fostered under the GATT? These questions pertain not just to the United States but to the major industrial countries in general.

The Tokyo Round recognized the increasing importance of nontariff barriers to trade, and members of the GATT agreed upon codes of behavior covering three significant nontariff barriers. (1) Government procurement rules invariably favor domestic suppliers, and countries are supposed to bring this degree of favoritism out into the open and give foreign suppliers a chance at orders. (2) Customs officials' methods of placing values on imports sometimes overstate their commercial value and thereby increase the effective rate of duty. The GATT code defines a series of preferred valuation methods, the ideal one being the actual transaction price. (3) Countries employ differing technical standards for electrical voltages, screw threads, and other such traits of manufactured commodities, and these standards can impede trade when they force the exporter to redesign a product to foreign specifications before it can be exported. These standards serve legitimate ends, but they are sometimes used opportunistically to give a country's suppliers an advantage over foreign competitors. The Tokyo Round code seeks to keep standards from creating unnecessary obstacles to trade and brings national standards codes into the GATT's purview as a basis for complaints. The Tokyo Round sought to address the more conspicuous devices for managing trade, such as export subsidies and countervailing duties to combat them, but the effects of these agreements seem to range from slight to nonexistent.

The Tokyo Round demonstrated that the adoption of harmonious general principles does little for the efficient flow of international trade if nations have no individual interest in heeding them. Worse yet, when countries manage their trade, they tend to fall into disputes with one another about the fairness of treatment that is involved. To see why, it will be helpful to turn to the longstanding issue of most-favored-nation (MFN) treatment in applying or removing trade restrictions. Tariff reductions under the GATT have, as a longstanding practice, been governed by unconditional MFN treatment. For example, when a country reduced a tariff in one of the GATT rounds conducted through bilateral bargaining, it lowered its tariff on goods imported not just from the principal supplier(s) with whom it negotiated but also from all other countries with which it had normal commercial relations. The importance of MFN treatment is its assurance that countries' tariffs are nondiscriminatory. Price discrim- ination, whether imposed by tariffs or otherwise, always involves some economic inefficiency.[24] Furthermore, it is an obvious source of international friction. However, each country always has parochial temptations to abandon MFN treatment for conditional reciprocity, a policy designed to make the most of every shred of bargaining power the country may possess. "I will cut my tariff on your exports only if you do some favor valuable to me," or "I will raise my tariff on your exports unless you do some favor for me."

This emphasis on bargaining power and perceived fairness reached a new height for the United States with the Omnibus Trade and Competitiveness Act of 1988, in which Congress sought to force the executive branch to "get tough" with exporting countries perceived to employ unfair trading practices. Unfairness could rest not just on violations of GATT or commitments under bilateral treaties but on any policy perceived by U.S. producers as competing unfairly: "export targeting," denial of work- ers' rights, or even the toleration of perceived anticompetitive practices among the foreign country's producers. Procedural changes made it more likely that complaints by American producers would lead to retaliatory actions by the U.S. government and less likely that they would be warded off out of concern for national economic welfare or foreign policy.[25]

Japan was the main target of congressional wrath, especially because of its large bilateral trade surplus with the United States. As we noted in Section 9.1, this surplus may well be a natural result of Japan's economic structure, which entails import surpluses from countries rich in natural resources that must be paid for by export surpluses with other countries. Economic equilibria are often perceived as unfair to somebody, which is why a criterion of fairness has such open-ended potential for supporting intervention in trade. Under the 1988 Act's mandate the administration indeed brought broad charges of unfair trade practices against Japan, India, and Brazil, but that particular authority expired in 1991.

The pursuit of strategic trade objectives under the 1988 Act sounds like the models of strategic industrial policy discussed in Section 13.4. They share the component of strategic action. However, they differ in that the objectives do not devolve from economic welfare but are politically defined, often by import-competing domestic producers whose sense of fairness, even when not openly self-serving,[26] may take no

---

[24] This is because the party paying the low price could, if it were feasible, strike a deal to resell to the party paying the high price so as to leave both better off. Other efficiency considerations besides this one may be relevant, however.

[25] For a convenient account see Earl L. Grinols, "Procedural Protection: The American Trade Bill and the New Interventionist Mode," *Weltwirtschaftliches Archiv*, 125 (3) (1989): 501–521. He points out that U.S. unfair-trade cases (under Section 301) had been increasing in the 1980s even before the 1988 Act.

[26] Producers often demand with seeming reasonableness a "level playing field" on which to compete with foreign rivals. Unfortunately, the theory of comparative advantage indicates that the playing field is intrinsically not level. Also, an apparently unfair practice (such as a high foreign tariff) may have its main (negative) effect on the welfare of foreign consumers, not that of U.S. producers.

heed of the welfare of consumers and other U.S. producers or even of the objective economic effects of the practice complained of. Many economists fear the rise of strategic trade policy not only because it is hard to implement efficiently even when well conceived (Chapter 13) but also because the political process stands all too ready to define strategic objectives at best independent of national economic welfare and at worst hostile to it. And it certainly flies against the spirit of GATT, which has sought the mutual reduction of trade barriers and the use of international rules and mediation to avoid or resolve direct clashes in national trade policies.

14.4 TRADE POLICY AND THE LESS-DEVELOPED COUNTRIES

The LDCs stayed largely aloof from the trade-liberalization movement, preferring to restrict trade severely in order to further their economic development. They tried to promote industry by using tariffs or other trade controls to raise the prices of imported manufactures. They hoped that factors of production could thereby be pulled into their import-competing manufacturing sectors out of subsistence agriculture, other low-productivity activities, or outright unemployment. Furthermore, LDCs have always relied much more heavily on tariff revenue to finance the government budget than the industrialized countries do, making LDCs' tariff rates on manufactures generally very high.[27] Quantitative restrictions and exchange control are commonly used as well as tariffs, and the local subsidiaries of multinational companies are required to act in various ways that may distort trade (as is explained later in this section).

In the 1970s the LDCs became disillusioned about the value of onerous trade restrictions. The import-substituting enterprise often turned out to be highly inefficient and to behave monopolistically in the domestic market. The infants receiving infant-industry protection were very slow to grow up. Furthermore, the opportunity costs of factors moved to import-competing manufactures could prove substantial. The trade balance could deteriorate sharply when sectors producing primary products for export were heavily taxed to provide capital for government projects. In addition, the import-competing industries turned out to be capital-intensive and ill-suited to the LDCs' labor-rich factor endowments, just as the Heckscher-Ohlin theorem suggests. The LDCs' interest therefore shifted visibly toward export-oriented industrialization and, by implication, lighter restrictions on trade.

LDC Exports and Tariff Preferences

This shift had its effect in rapid growth of exports of labor-intensive manufacturers from some LDCs in Asia and Latin America (see Chapter 9). A study by the Organization for Economic Cooperation and Development pointed out that a group of newly industrializing countries had expanded its share of world industrial exports from 2.5 percent in 1963 to more than 7 percent in 1977. The United States' percentage of manufactured imports bought from these countries rose from 5.9 percent in 1973

---

[27] See M. M. Kostecki and D. Seck, "Treasury Revenue and Foreign Trade Taxation," *Weltwirtschaftliches Archiv*, 118 (1982): 116–123. They found that import and export taxes were 28.4 percent of government revenue in 40 LDCs, 18.5 percent in 35 intermediate countries, and 4.2 percent in 18 developed countries.

to no less than 20.0 percent in 1977.[28] Furthermore, these imports shifted toward goods more intensive in skills and capital and more innovative than the LDCs' traditional manufactures. The nontraditional portion of the leading industrial countries' imports of manufactures from LDCs increased from 16 percent in 1970 to 30 percent in 1978.

This new openness to trade apparently had favorable effects on LDCs' rates of income growth. A statistical analysis of 30 developing countries showed that their growth rates of gross domestic product per capita (1970–1982) increased significantly with their openness to trade and their disuse of policy interventions such as export subsidies. Account was taken of other growth-affecting factors, such as rates of capital expenditure and the advantage that a country might have in catching up from a low initial level of income.[29]

It is clear why LDC exporters have been acutely conscious of the very high tariffs imposed on the kinds of goods they export by many industrial countries. It was seen in Section 14.1 that the U.S. tariff gives heavier protection to labor-intensive domestic industries, as do other industrial nations' tariffs. U.S. tariffs prevailing after the Tokyo Round were significantly biased against exports of the LDCs, even after controlling for product characteristics such as the labor intensity of their production processes.[30] Nontariff barriers raise the wall higher still. It might be expected that some developing countries gained from trade restrictions such as the Multifiber Arrangement (MFA) because of the rents they could collect on the exports that survived the restrictions. However, Trela and Whalley found that movement to free trade in textiles and apparel (no MFA, no tariffs) would raise real incomes for all developing countries except Hong Kong (a major beneficiary from rents due to MFA quotas).[31]

The LDCs urged successfully that they should be partially relieved of the burden of industrial countries' tariff barriers by a device that came to be known as the Generalized System of Preferences (GSP). Each industrial country would admit some quantity of imports from less-developed countries either free of tariffs or at a rate lower than what other exporters paid. This privilege would allow LDCs profitably to expand any exports that they could manufacture at a cost lying between the world price and the industrial country's tariff-ridden domestic price. To provide them this benefit the industrial countries would pay a price that can be identified in Figure 14.2. Suppose that tariff $P_t P_w / P_w O$ is in effect, so that the country purchases MN imports from industrial nations. A quota arrangement now allows LDCs to sell one-half of MN without paying the tariff. The total quantity of imports and their domestic price, P_t, will remain unchanged. The sole welfare effect on the industrial country giving the preference is its loss of tariff revenue equal to half of area 3. Despite this

[28] Organization for Economic Cooperation and Development, *The Impact of the Newly Industrializing Countries on Production and Trade in Manufactures: Report by the Secretary-General* (Paris, 1979). The OECD study includes Spain, Portugal, Greece, and Yugoslavia as newly industrializing countries, along with Brazil, Mexico, Hong Kong, Singapore, South Korea, and Taiwan.

[29] Sebastian Edwards, "Trade Orientation, Distortions and Growth in Developing Countries," Working Paper No. 3716, National Bureau of Economic Research, 1991.

[30] Peter Y. C. Chow and Mitchell Kellman, "Anti-LDC Bias in the U.S. Tariff Structure: A Test of Source versus Product Characteristics," *Review of Economics and Statistics*, 70 (November 1988): 648–653.

[31] Irene Trela and John Whalley, "Unraveling the Threads of the MFA," in Carl B. Hamilton, ed., *Textiles Trade and the Developing Countries: Eliminating the Multi-Fibre Arrangement in the 1990s* (Washington: World Bank, 1990), pp. 11–45.

cost, preferences have been granted to the LDCs by many industrial countries—including the United States, starting in 1976. The United States, like other countries, hedged its preferences with a number of restrictions. Domestic industries already facing heavy import competition were excluded, thus fencing off just the labor-intensive products that are the LDCs' most suitable exports. It is not surprising, therefore, most GSP imports come from the most advanced of the LDCs (although the GSP privileges of the strongest Asian exporters have now been revoked).

Imports to the United States that are duty-free under the GSP have been 11 to 12 percent of all imports from countries eligible for the GSP since the program began. In 1990, 130 countries remained eligible for GSP benefits. The benefits were highly concentrated in a few countries, with 64.5 percent of imports duty-free under GSP coming from just five sources: Mexico, Malaysia, Thailand, Brazil, and the Philippines. The program tends to favor nontraditional LDC exports and goods not subject to particularly high U.S. tariffs. Duty-free GSP imports have been kept away from the most protected U.S. industries, even though displaced non-LDC exporters should feel the main effects. It is estimated that in 1987 U.S. tariff revenue forgone was about $2 billion. There is no simple way to value the gains to the GSP beneficiaries. If the factors of production creating the GSP imports would otherwise have been idle or underutilized, the benefits could be as large as $15 billion. On the other hand, if the opportunity costs to the LDC exporters were nearly as high as the U.S. domestic price (P_t in Figure 14.2), then the benefits would be very small (less than the U.S. tariff revenue forgone). The GSP is cumbersome to administer. For the importing countries, it represents in essence a quota system; the quotas must be policed and allocated among the various authorized exporters. The exporting LDC's government must certify that the goods were in large part produced in that country and not merely transshipped. Thus, the net benefits of the GSP program cannot be large.[32]

Offshore Assembly Provisions

A feature of the U.S. tariff that has come to hold great importance for the LDCs is the provision for offshore assembly. The tariff collector usually insists that a good entering a country pay the standard tariff, even if the good was originally made in that country and then exported. The provisions for offshore assembly waive this practice to allow goods exported from the United States and subjected to further processing abroad to pay duty only on the value added abroad and not the whole value of the commodity imported. By 1978 the total value of goods imported under the offshore assembly provision had reached $9.3 billion, 9.9 percent of the total value of manufactured imports (19.1 percent in the case of manufactured imports from the LDCs). Of the $9.3 billion, $7.0 billion was value added abroad, $2.3 billion value from U.S. production.

Although the offshore assembly provision is not restricted to the LDCs, it has held special importance for them. It allows American firms to sort out the various processes required to make a finished product, sending partially finished goods overseas to have

[32] Tracy Murray, *Trade Preferences for Developing Countries* (New York: John Wiley, 1977); Edward John Ray, "The Impact of Special Interests on Preferential Tariff Concessions by the United States," *Review of Economics and Statistics*, 69 (May 1987): 187–193.

labor-intensive processes performed where they can be done more cheaply. Cut cloth is sewn into garments, wires are soldered onto electronic components. Of course, this maneuver works only if the goods are readily shipped and valuable relative to their weight; otherwise the two-way transportation costs swamp the savings from using lower-cost foreign labor. The LDCs benefiting most from these operations predictably have large supplies of low-skilled but efficient labor, not much other basis for establishing a comparative advantage in their exports, and a political and economic infrastructure conducive to carrying out these operations reliably.[33]

Trade and Performance Requirements for Foreign Investors

The LDCs maintain many indirect restrictions on trade via "performance requirements" for multinational companies establishing subsidiaries in their territories. A would-be entrant must negotiate with the government, which likely requires that the company buy inputs from national suppliers ("content requirements"), supply its technology to national citizens, maintain at least some minimum level of employment or activity, and/or export some minimum volume of products. The fact that these allocative choices are imposed on the multinational entrant as requirements indicates that it would not voluntarily undertake them in the course of maximizing its own profits. If the foreign investor were entering a competitive local market where it could at best earn normal profits, it would turn down a deal that forced it into such costly policies. However, if the entrant has the prospect of some monopoly power (perhaps because it gains protection from competing imports), it may be willing to accept such a deal. That is, the host government makes it the "all or nothing offer" of some protected monopoly profits in exchange for extra local content, exports, and the like.

If the host-country economy consisted of efficiently functioning competitive markets, a policy of performance requirements would be inefficient. The protected monopoly would cost its citizens a deadweight loss. The local-content purchases from domestic suppliers would come at the expense of supplies more efficiently obtained by import. The required exports would exceed the quantity that the market would efficiently choose. In the conditions of a developing economy afflicted with various market distortions, however, it is impossible to be so dogmatic about the inefficiency of such a policy, especially the exporting requirement.

In any case, 29 percent of the overseas affiliates of U.S. multinational companies operating in LDCs are subject to performance requirements. So are 6 percent of affiliates operating in industrial countries such as Canada and Australia, where an economic justification of the practice is unlikely to hold. U.S. policy has opposed performance requirements for multinationals, and the United States has tried to get the practice onto the GATT agenda for the Uruguay Round.[34]

---

[33] Michael Sharpston, "International Sub-Contracting," *Oxford Economic Papers*, 27 (March 1975): 94–135; J. Peter Jarrett, "Offshore Assembly and Production and the Internalization of International Trade Within the Multinational Corporation" (Ph.D. dissertation, Harvard University, 1979), Chapters 7, 8.

[34] Harvey E. Bale, Jr., "Trade Policy Aspects of International Direct Investment Policies," in Robert E. Baldwin, ed., *Recent Issues and Initiatives in U.S. Trade Policy* (Cambridge, MA: National Bureau of Economic Research, 1984), pp. 67–100.

14.5 SUMMARY

Although U.S. tariffs have fallen greatly in the last fifty years, many industries still receive significant protection. Because economists find it hard to explain U.S. tariffs (or those of other countries) on the criterion of maximizing national welfare, they have turned to economic models of political behavior to explain how those tariffs arose. Several independent models have been developed: (1) Governments are elected by majorities and thus will favor tariffs that redistribute income from a minority to the majority. (2) Producer interest groups invest in lobbying for tariff protection if the present value of the expected extra profits and wages exceeds the lobbying cost. (3) Governments aim to provide what their citizens perceive as fair treatment, and fairness calls for tariffs (or other measures) to help those who are badly off or have suffered unexpected losses. These models do help to explain why rates of protection differ among sectors.

In the 1930s the United States sought an escape from high levels of tariff protection worldwide by negotiating reciprocal reductions with other countries. Eventually, concern with incidental terms-of-trade gains given to third parties impeded bilateral deals of this type. After World War II, international tariff cutting was put on a multinational basis in successive rounds of bargaining under the General Agreement on Tariffs and Trade. These international tariff-cutting agreements account for at least half of the large reduction of U.S. tariffs over the last fifty years.

Running counter to the trend toward lower tariffs has been the increased tendency for countries to "manage" international trade in pursuit of objectives related to particular problem sectors of their domestic economies. Management often involves the use of quotas or voluntary export restraints, which generally impose on the importing nation higher welfare costs than do tariffs with equal incidence. The principal use of special protection is to delay adjustment in troubled industries that face increasing competition from imports. If such delays have a welfare justification, it must be due to the imperfection of short-run adjustment processes in the factor markets. Such imperfections would better be tackled directly, although adjustment assistance to labor has not worked very well. Export subsidies seek to expand or preserve exports. Export assistance is important for major capital goods (subsidized through cheap credit to customers) and agricultural commodities (an adjunct to domestic price-support programs). The Tokyo Round of negotiations sought to reduce nontariff as well as tariff barriers, but it is not clear that such international efforts, can halt the trend toward managed trade.

LDCs have been uninterested in cutting their tariffs under GATT negotiations. However, in the 1970s they swung heavily from promoting import-replacing industrialization with high tariffs to promote the production of labor-intensive manufactures for export. The Generalized System of Preferences seeks (probably with small effect) to give their exports limited tariff-free access to industrial countries' markets. Their export-oriented industrialization has been helped by the rapid growth of offshore assembly operations, in which labor-intensive stages of fabrication are undertaken in LDCs, with the inputs imported from industrial countries and the output shipped back to them.

CHAPTER PROBLEMS

1. You are asked to estimate the welfare cost of a tariff imposed in a market like that depicted in Figure 14.2. You are told that imports were $100 million before the tariff and $50 million (valued at world prices) after it was imposed; the tariff rate is 20 percent. Can you estimate the approximate loss in national welfare due to the tariff?

2. Suppose that the trade restriction described in the preceding problem were due not to a tariff, but to a voluntary export restraint. Then what would the welfare loss be?

3. Exporting countries sometimes administer export restraints by creating transferable rights to export to the restricted market, which domestic manufacturers can trade among themselves. Suppose you learn that Hong Kong shirtmakers pay $20 for the privilege of exporting a dozen shirts to the United States, and that the shirts have a world market value of $60. What conclusions can you draw about the tariff equivalent of the export restraint?

4. Some evidence on the incidence of U.S. tariffs suggests that large industries gain higher levels of protection than do small ones. In terms of the economic models of political behavior advanced to explain tariffs, why might that be?

5. You are a domestic manufacturer persuading the government to protect your industry. You can secure either a 20 percent tariff or a fixed quota that is equivalent to it. You expect the market to grow in real terms. Will that fact affect whether you choose the tariff and the quota?

6. Governments in some European countries are believed to make substantial use of industrial subsidies to avert the contraction of some industrial sectors. What difference does it make for national welfare whether the subsidy applies to domestic sales, export sales, or both? Governments do not find it easy to raise tax revenues to finance such subsidies. Does that fact help explain why such governments would rather subsidize an industry's export sales than its sales in the domestic market?

7. In 1986 the United States and Japan reached an agreement setting minimum prices on Japanese semiconductor chips sold by Japanese manufacturers not just directly to the United States but also to all other export markets. At the time, producers in both countries had considerable excess capacity because demand was unexpectedly low. Explain why chip prices in Japan plummeted and why third-country chip buyers started to obtain their supplies from intermediaries and brokers in Japan.

8. Producer groups sometimes urge that "fair trade" requires that Japan's tariff on goods that they export be no higher than the tariff protecting their home (U.S.) market. What should be the consequences of this policy for the home industry's quantity and profits if (a) markets are purely competitive and both countries are small, (b) markets are competitive but both are large, and (c) markets are not purely competitive (oligopoly, product differentiation)?

SUGGESTIONS FOR FURTHER READING

Baldwin, Robert E. *The Political Economy of U.S. Import Policy* (Cambridge, MA: M.I.T. Press, 1985). Detailed study of political mechanism of import restriction.

———, and Anne O. Krueger, eds. *The Structure and Evolution of Recent U.S. Trade Policy* (Chicago: University of Chicago Press, 1984). Contains useful analytical papers on many features of U.S. policy.

Bayard, Thomas O., and Kimberly A. Elliott. *An Evaluation of Aggressive Trade Policies* (Washington: Institute for International Economics, 1992). Pro and con arguments and experience since the early 1980s.

Cline, William R., ed. *Trade Policy in the 1980s* (Washington: Institute for International Economics, 1983). Another volume of useful papers on various facets of U.S. policy.

————— *The Future of World Trade in Textiles and Apparel* (Washington: Institute for International Economics, 1990). The Multi-Fiber Arrangement and its prospects.

Grinols, Earl L. "Procedural Protection: The American Trade Bill and the New Interventionism," *Weltwirtschaftliches Archiv*, 125 (3) (1989): 501–521. How the Omnibus Trade and Competitiveness Act pursues fair trade.

Hufbauer, Gary C., et al. *Trade Protection in the United States: 31 Case Studies* (Washington: Institute for International Economics, 1986). Protection and its consequences for individual industries.

—————, and Kimberly A. Elliott. *The Costs of U.S. Trade Barriers*. (Washington: Institute for International Economics, 1992). Quantitative estimates of effects on employees, consumers, and so forth.

Lawrence, Robert Z., and Robert E. Litan. *Saving Free Trade: A Pragmatic Approach* (Washington: Brookings Institution, 1986). On minimizing the cost of managed trade.

Ratner, Sidney. *The Tariff in American History* (New York: D. Van Nostrand, 1972). A useful short history.

Yarbrough, Beth V., and Robert M. Yarbrough. *Cooperation and Governance in International Trade* (Princeton, NJ: Princeton University Press, 1992). Analytical treatment of approaches to trade liberalization.

15

PREFERENTIAL TRADING ARRANGEMENTS

Chapter 14 reviewed the mutual efforts of countries to remove impediments to trade. Campaigns for trade liberalization are not confined, however, to freeing trade around the world. Some groups of nations try to ease trade restrictions among themselves while leaving them intact against the outside world. This chapter will deal with such efforts at partial liberalization.

Preferential trading arrangements now follow one after another. In 1957 six nations of Continental Europe formed the European Economic Community, prompting seven others to organize the European Free Trade Area. These two groups are now engaged in a process of consolidation, with the European Community (EC), as it is now called, including twelve full members. In 1989 Canada and the United States began to implement a far-reaching free-trade agreement, and in 1992 the United States and Mexico were negotiating a similar arrangement. The LDCs, especially in Latin America and Africa, have gathered into similar if less far-reaching unions. Such preferences are not a recent discovery: Great Britain and her Commonwealth associates in 1931 agreed to levy lower tariff rates on goods imported from each other—Commonwealth Preference tariffs.

The economic effects of these arrangements, usually undertaken for both political and economic reasons, raise a number of important questions. Do the participants gain economically? If so, what factors control the size of the gain? Do the outsiders lose? If so, can the world as a whole become worse off? The theory of regional trading arrangements will be explored in the first two sections of this chapter, then some of its predictions will be tested against the experience of the EC. This chapter will also take up another distinctive regional group—the socialist block of countries, whose trading arrangements are in transition as their economies grope toward market systems.

15.1 FUNDAMENTAL EFFECTS OF TRADE PREFERENCES

A set of countries forms a preferential trading arrangement when they place lower restrictions on trade with each other than they do on trade with the outside world. The members need not be neighbors, but because they often are, these will be called "regional arrangements." Likewise, the preferences need not extend to all products traded, but common practice will be followed in assuming that they generally do. Even assuming that preferences are given on all goods, it is possible to imagine several different arrangements. The following terms for describing them have come into fairly standard usage:

1. *Free-Trade Area.* Members eliminate tariffs among themselves but keep their original tariffs against the outside world. The Canada-United States free-trade agreement provides an example.

2. *Customs Union.* Members not only eliminate all tariffs among themselves but also form a common tariff against the outside world.

3. *Common Market.* Members proceed beyond the requirements of a customs union to eliminate restrictions on movements of factors of production among the member countries. The European Community, often called "the Common Market," largely fits this definition.

4. *Economic Union.* Members proceed beyond the requirements of a common market to unify their fiscal, monetary, and socioeconomic policies. Belgium and Luxembourg formed an economic union in 1921, and the EC plans ultimately to go most of the distance to an economic union.

These preferential arrangements are analytically interesting—and complex—because they both distort and liberalize trade. Trade is freed because some flows face lower restrictions than before. However, trade is also distorted because goods coming into a member country pay different tariffs depending on their origin—the external tariff if from outside the group, a preferential or zero rate if from a partner. The distortion amounts to price discrimination, that is, charging or (in this case) paying different prices for identical goods at a given market location. Because of this two-faced character of preferential arrangements, they can either improve or worsen the economic welfare of their members or of the world as a whole. This section will analyze the effects of preferences in the simplest possible way, to show how they can either improve or worsen the allocation of resources. Section 15.2 will push a short distance into the general-equilibrium analysis of preferential arrangements.

Trade Creation and Trade Diversion

Jacob Viner first showed that preferences could either improve or worsen allocation, in that they could lead either to *trade creation* or to *trade diversion*.[1] Suppose that *A* and *B* form a customs union, leaving *C* (the rest of the world) outside. Previously, *A* produced part of its requirements of good *x* at home, inefficiently, behind its tariff wall. Partner *B* is the most efficient producer of *x* and the sole world exporter. When

---

[1] Jacob Viner, *The Customs Union Issue* (New York: Carnegie Endowment for International Peace, 1950), Chapter 4.

A abolishes tariffs against *B* (and all the necessary market adjustments have taken place), *A*'s inefficient *x* industry is partly competed down, as *A*'s imports from *B* expand. Trade has been *created*. The gains are the same as if *A* had eliminated its *x* tariff completely.

Because trade creation works just like the removal of a tariff against all foreign suppliers, the analysis of it is a replay of Figure 14.2. In Figure 15.1 *A*'s demand and domestic supply curves for *x* are respectively shown as *D* and *S*. Suppose that *x* is produced in *B* under conditions of perfectly elastic supply, so that an unlimited quantity is available at price *OP*. *A*'s external tariff is set at the rate *PT/OP*. Before the customs union was formed, the supply function for imports after payment of tariff was *TT'*; thus *A* produced amount *OM* of its consumption (*ON*) of *x*, importing *MN* from *B*. Elimination of the tariff against *B* now makes *PP'* the relevant import supply schedule and causes consumption to expand to *ON'*, imports to expand to *M'N'*, and domestic production to shrink to *OM'*. The four numbered areas in the diagram measure the welfare gain. *A*'s consumers of *x* enjoy a gain in surplus measured by the whole area 1 + 2 + 3 + 4, but not all of this is net gain to the country. Area 1 formerly was profit to *A*'s protected producers of *x*, so this gain to consumers is offset by the loss to producers. Likewise, area 3 formerly represented tariff revenue collected by *A*'s government that is now lost when the preference is given to *B*. If the government was spending its revenues on useful things, such as parks and schools, there is no presumption that any net social benefit derives from (in effect) giving the revenue measured by area 3 to the consumers of *x*; therefore, it is assigned no net welfare significance. Two triangles remain, both measuring net gains to *A*. Area 2 formerly

---

FIGURE 15.1   Welfare Effects of Trade Creation

PP' is the partner-country supply curve. Tariff removal cuts domestic price from *OT* to *OP*, expands imports to *M'N'*, and raises welfare by areas 2 + 4.

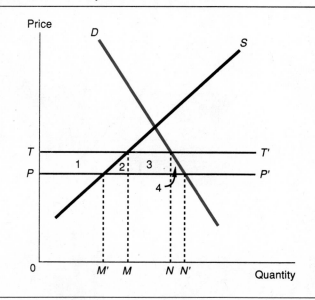

represented part of the real cost of securing OM of domestic production; it is assumed that those resources are now put to other uses, so the extra surplus measured by 2 is a net benefit. Likewise, area 4 represents a pure gain in consumers' surplus not subject to any offset. The net benefit is areas 2 + 4.

Trade diversion can occur for another good y if A's consumption of y was formerly supplied by outsider C and if C is the world's most efficient producer.

Suppose that B can also produce y—not as efficiently as C, but efficiently enough to undercut C in A's market when C pays A's tariff but B does not. In Figure 15.2 A's demand for y appears as DD. Suppose that C's supply of y is perfectly elastic at a domestic cost (and price) of P_C; likewise, B can supply y at the higher constant cost (and price) of P_B. Before the customs union is formed, A imposes an ad valorem tariff on imports of y equal to $P_C T_C / O P_C$ or $P_B T_B / O P_B$—they are the same. A would buy from the least costly source after paying the tariff and thus would import OM_C at price OT_C. Forming the customs union allows B's exports of y to enter duty-free, and A's consumption expands to OM_B. Areas in the diagram are labeled to illustrate the significant effects on welfare. Once again, lowering a tariff (even preferentially) allows a gain to A's consumers of y (areas 3 + 4). The meanings of these areas match their counterparts in Figure 15.1: Area 3 shows tariff revenue formerly collected on imports from C, its loss offsetting the congruent gain in consumer's surplus; and area 4 depicts the remaining pure gain in consumer's surplus that is not subject to any offset. A loss occurs, however, in the form of area 5. Areas 3 + 5 measure the total tariff revenue formerly collected on imports OM_C. This revenue now is lost to A's government, and

---

FIGURE 15.2   Welfare Effects of Trade Diversion

P_B indicates pretariff supply price in partner country, P_C pretariff supply price in rest of the world. Tariff preference lowers internal price from T_C to P_B. Welfare loss occurs if area 5 exceeds area 4.

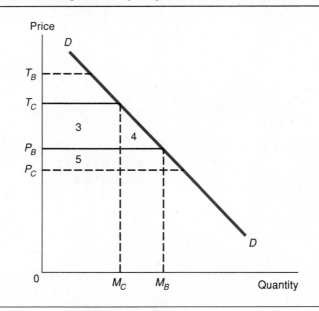

the part denoted by 5 instead paid by A's consumers to the higher-cost producers of y in B. It is pure social loss.[2] A *net* welfare loss from trade diversion occurs if area 5 is larger than area 4. It need not be, of course: The loss from switching to a less efficient source of supply could be more than offset by the gain from reducing a distortion of consumers' spending. If a supply curve for domestic producers had been incorporated in Figure 15.2, another gain would have resulted, because protected output falls when the domestic price declines from OT_C to OP_B (an area of gain like 2 in Figure 15.1). Also, notice that welfare increases in the trade-creation case even if the former tariff sheltered no protected production. (The welfare gain is just area 4.)

Net Gains or Losses?

What can be said about the net influence of these forces? If A and B consume and trade many commodities, is it possible to establish any presumption that a union leads to net gains? An accurate evaluation depends on the facts of each case. Nonetheless, some rough tests can suggest whether trade creation (which must raise welfare) is likely to prevail over trade diversion (which may or may not). For trade creation to predominate, the economies of A and B should be *actually competitive* (before the union) but *potentially complementary* (after it comes into effect). Trade-creation gains are greater with protected production to be reduced, since protective tariffs have made the two economies' output pattern look similar before they join in a customs union. Thus, they should appear actually competitive. However, each member must also be the most efficient producer of goods protected and inefficiently produced by its partner—this condition guarantees trade creation rather than trade diversion.

Other simple tests for a union's welfare significance can also be used. Higher initial tariffs mean greater potential benefit. Higher initial tariffs enlarge area 4 in Figures 15.1 and 15.2. If a common external tariff is formed (as in a customs union), the chances of benefit are enlarged if the new common tariff is lower than the previous individual ones—making trade diversion less likely, reducing the distance $P_C T_C$ (in Figure 15.2), and thus lowering the possibility that P_B will fall within it. A larger preferential arrangement is more likely to be beneficial. This condition is obvious if we imagine enlarging a hypothetical customs union until it includes nearly all the world's economic activity. With little production taking place outside, the union is almost sure to include the most efficient producer; trade diversion is therefore curtailed.

Another factor affecting the balance of welfare effects works in a different way. When countries form a customs union, they must decide on a common external tariff. Of the many possible methods, they usually choose to average the members' previous national tariff rates. Because of the averaging process, there is less variation of the resulting rates among the different classes of imported commodities than existed in the previous national schedules. That reduced dispersion is itself a source of welfare gain, because the relative prices of commodities inside the tariff wall are then less distorted from those in the world at large. If each of two products is subject to a 10

---

[2] No welfare gain for country B is involved because the resources drawn into the production of y presumably were engaged in other activities where their value productivity was just as high.

percent tariff, both domestic prices are raised 10 percent, and the relative price is the same as in the outside world.[3] Thus, the more tariff schedules are homogenized, the greater the welfare gain.

15.2 DISTRIBUTION OF GAINS AND LOSSES FROM PREFERENCES

One more building block is needed for this analysis of the effects of tariff preferences. The technique for measuring the welfare effects of trade creation and diversion set forth in Figures 15.1 and 15.2 assumes that the country's terms of trade remain unchanged. That assumption is built into the perfectly elastic supply for imports. If the partner's terms of trade with the outside world change, or if one member's terms of trade with its partner change, redistributions of real income take place. The total effect of preferences on any one country's welfare is the sum of effects due to trade creation or diversion and any redistribution stemming from changed terms of trade.

You might suppose that a country would pick its partners for a preferential arrangement so that it would get a terms-of-trade gain or so that the members would select each other in order to extract a gain from the rest of the world. Countries seem to pick their partners primarily on political grounds, not from economic motives or calculations. Still, whether intended or not, a preferential arrangement is likely to change its members' terms of trade with the outside world and with each other. The possible results are diverse, but consideration of preferential arrangements in the context of general equilibrium reveals some likely outcomes.

Start with a question that has a simple answer. Suppose that A and B decide to form a preferential arrangement, excluding C (the outside world). What tariff structure will maximize their joint gain from the venture? In the absence of any special market distortions, A and B should clearly adopt free trade with each other and levy the optimum tariff against the outside world (that is, the tariff that maximizes their joint monopoly gain). Even if each member's tariff was optimal before, from its own viewpoint, each gains from the expansion of previously restricted trade with the other. If their individual tariffs were not optimal, a further gain accrues from switching to the optimal tariff. Notice that their joint monopoly power in trade could well be greater than that of either separately. If they are sole exporters of a product and each previously calculated its optimal tariff taking the other's as given, further monopoly gains should accrue to them from setting their external tariff jointly. Should A and B form a free-trade area without changing their former external tariffs, the elimination of internal tariffs is still apt to improve their terms of trade with the outside world. The only requirement is the occurrence of some trade diversion. The switch of trade away from C, as A and B adopt preferences and increase their mutual trade, has the same effect on C as if A's and B's demand curves for imports from C were shifted inward. (Conversely, the preferential arrangement gains from trade creation with no corresponding loss for the outside world.)[4]

---

[3] Both theory and evidence on this point were developed by Pan A. Yotopoulos and Jeffrey B. Nugent, *Economics of Development: Empirical Investigations* (New York: Harper & Row, 1976), pp. 352–355.

[4] This terms-of-trade improvement was analyzed and estimated for the EC by Howard C. Petith, "European Integration and the Terms of Trade," *Economic Journal*, 87 (June 1977): 262–272. He suggested that Germany's terms of trade may have improved as much as 7 percent, France's as much as 9 percent.

15.3 PREFERENTIAL ARRANGEMENTS IN PRACTICE

Customs unions and free-trade areas have been popular in the last several decades among both industrial and less-developed countries. The European Community (EC) was formed in 1957 by France, West Germany, Italy, the Netherlands, and Belgium-Luxembourg. Other Western European nations acceded over time, and as of 1992 only Norway and Switzerland had chosen to remain outside. The initial members moved to eliminate tariffs among themselves by staged reductions completed in 1968, and 1992 was the target year for removing many remaining types of nontariff restrictions. The EC members also adopted a Common External Tariff, its rates set (with some exceptions) by averaging the rates for individual products that previously appeared in the member nations' tariff schedules.[5] Canada and the United States negotiated a free-trade arrangement in 1987.

Interest in such arrangements has also run high among the LDCs, although political difficulties have led to much frustration. For example, eight South American nations plus Mexico agreed to form a Latin American Free-Trade Area, and five Central American countries agreed to create a Central American Common Market. In 1991 Argentina, Brazil, Paraguay, and Uruguay entered into the Southern Common Market (Mercosur). Each union is propelled by political and economic objectives, with the latter including the real-income gains described in Section 15.2, and others, such as economic growth and economies of scale in production for small countries.

This section will review some empirical evidence on the effects of preferential arrangements, in order to illustrate and give perspective to the theoretical concepts presented in Sections 15.1 and 15.2.

Trade Creation and Diversion in the European Community

We saw in Section 15.1 that the welfare effects of a preferential arrangement are related to trade creation and diversion. Consider the effect of the EC on international trade in manufactures. It would be insufficient to simply look at the sizes of trade flows—external and internal—before and after the EC was formed. They changed in response to forces other than tariff rates, such as the growth of national incomes, to take the most obvious. One reasonable way to estimate trade creation and diversion, however, is to look at changes in the sources of supply of manufactures to the EC countries, as Mordechai Kreinin did.[6]

The reduction of internal tariffs resulted in trade creation that was reflected in a reduced share of each EC country's consumption of manufactures supplied by its domestic producers. Trade diversion was detected in the increased share of EC countries' imports coming from exporters in EC partner countries. Even without the EC, these shares would have changed because of movements in prices and incomes differing between the EC and the rest of the world. Kreinin experimented with various adjustments to control for these movements; finding none clearly superior to the others, he suggested taking an average of their results. He concluded that, as of 1969 and

---

[5] For a description of the EC, see D. Swann, *The Economics of the Common Market*, 4th ed. (Harmondsworth, UK: Penguin Books, 1978).

[6] Mordechai E. Kreinin, *Trade Relations of the EEC: An Empirical Investigation* (New York: Praeger, 1974), Chapter 3.

1970, the EC had caused trade diversion of $1.1 billion, but trade creation in the amount of $8.4 billion. Estimates by other investigators using somewhat different methods all yield the same general conclusion: Trade creation exceeded trade diversion by a generous margin. Furthermore, trade creation took just the course predicted by the theory of comparative advantage. If a country had the Community's lowest price for a certain line of goods before internal tariffs were removed (i.e., 1958), then it tended to gain a large share of Community exports to other EC countries by 1966, when internal tariffs were 80 percent eliminated.[7]

To the static welfare analysis of customs unions set forth here, and that of trade liberalization in Chapter 14, many students respond: "Is that all there is in it?" Are there no dynamic gains from greater scale economies, more vigorous competition, new incentives to invest and innovate? The economist's answer is: "If you believe that markets are competitive and always pretty much in equilibrium, yes, that's all there is." If that assumption fails to hold, however, the gains from tariff reduction, whether preferential or general, may be greatly enlarged. Consider these alternative assumptions.

1. Most producers (outside the primary sector) make goods that are specialized and differentiated, so each faces a downward-sloping demand curve for its own output.

2. Elements of oligopoly may be present (especially in pre-EC Europe), so that producers' efforts to maintain and share out their collusive profits discourage them from making major plant expansions or otherwise getting an innovative jump on their rivals.

3. Business investment is subject to considerable uncertainty, so indications of an expanding market may increase the rate of capital spending that businesses desire to undertake.

Either of the first two assumptions suffices to predict that trade liberalization (preferential or general) will induce producers to make a dash for larger-scale and more efficient plants. Under the first assumption, each individual producer foresees the possibility of enlarged export markets that will absorb a substantially increased quantity of output. Under the second assumption, collusion gets harder to sustain when tariff barriers fall and foreign producers not in the cartel offer their wares at more competitive prices; erstwhile loyalists of the cartel abandon that ship and try instead to make their activities as efficient as possible within a larger and more competitive market. Finally, the third assumption implies that these productivity-raising microeconomic adjustments not only increase the productivity of investment but increase the rate of capital formation as well.

There is evidence that these dynamic gains occur and are important. Producers in the original EC countries rationalized their product lines, concentrating on what they could make most efficiently, and plant sizes ran to more efficient scales. Increased rates of domestic saving and investment were observed. Indeed, one study found that nearly all customs unions have brought significant dynamic gains in faster rates of capital formation and productivity growth following their formation.[8]

[7] H. Glejser, "Empirical Evidence on Comparative Cost Theory from the European Common Market Experience," *European Economic Review*, 3 (November 1972): 247–258.

[8] Josef C. Brada and Jose A. Mendez, "An Estimate of the Dynamic Effects of Economic Integration," *Review of Economics and Statistics*, 70 (February 1988): 163–168.

Despite these gains, the EC has its less-than-rosy side. A keystone of the Community is a scheme to provide massive protection to European agriculture. This protection has imposed large costs of trade diversion, especially on Great Britain, which before joining had a relatively efficient policy toward agriculture. High food prices in the EC have fostered excess supplies of crops that could be disposed of only through massive export subsidies, which now squander the bulk of the Community's budget. These have exacerbated the EC's relations with the United States, a competing agricultural exporter on a large scale, and they were central to the difficult negotiation of the Uruguay Round under the General Agreement on Tariffs and Trade (see Section 14.2).

"Europe in 1992"

Although the EC nations long ago removed tariffs on trade among themselves, in 1988 they attracted considerable attention by agreeing to remove many nontariff restrictions—all internal economic barriers and customs posts—by 1992. In 1985 the European Commission compiled a list of 300 remaining national nontariff restrictions on intra-EC trade. These represented a generous assortment of the types of nontariff barriers described in Chapter 14. Some of them were no doubt erected as substitutes for the tariffs removed under the original (1957) agreement forming the Community. These barriers include inconsistent product-safety standards (children's toys, oxygen tanks), national differences in professional licensing requirements (for professions such as accounting), and restrictions on the entry of firms into certain sectors, such as financial services. Not the least of these barriers is so-called administrative protection—the sheer cost of documenting imported goods at the customs post: Intra-EC highway trucks had to file up to 75 forms in order to comply with border-crossing regulations.

If the EC countries keep their promises, removal of these nontariff barriers will add substantially to the EC countries' incomes. The mere administrative costs of customs frontiers to shippers and governments are estimated to be 1.8 percent of the value of goods traded. The removal of these, of the diverse national standards mentioned earlier, and of various inefficient government-procurement policies are expected to add 2.5 percent to gross domestic product in the EC. Observers fear, though, that some offsetting costs may arise from elevated restrictions on the EC's trade with the rest of the world. Competitive pressures due to the removal of internal nontariff barriers could easily be relieved by higher barriers against outside competitors.[9]

Free-Trade Agreements in North America

In 1987 the United States and Canada negotiated a free-trade arrangement. Starting in 1989, the arrangement calls for removal during the following decade of all tariffs and quotas between the two countries on most categories of goods and services. The Canadians expressed concern that the United States government would take away— via ad hoc trade restrictions—what it gave in the agreement, and so provision was

[9] Michael Emerson et al., *The Economics of Europe in 1992*, Oxford: Oxford University Press, 1988. Also see papers by Richard N. Cooper and Merton J. Peck in *Brookings Papers on Economic Activity*, 1989:2.

made for international dispute-settlement panels to replace U.S. courts in final appeals of administrative decisions. While the agreement left various forms of special protection in place, it did eliminate others in each country. U.S. trade with Canada already constitutes 21 percent of total U.S. trade, and the Canada-U.S. bilateral trade flow is by far the world's largest. The geographical proximity of the two countries and the substantial levels of protection previously in force (especially Canada's) mean that this free-trade agreement could have very important effects.

The Canadian economy is roughly one-tenth the size of the United States'. That difference implies that Canada will get proportionally larger benefits, for two reasons. First, the established trade restrictions have caused different sets of relative prices to prevail within the two countries. Free trade will bring these prices together, but with most of the change coming in Canada's prices. As the smaller country, Canada gets the advantage of trading at an "alien" set of prices.[10] Second, when a small country protects its domestic market (and its exports are limited by foreign tariffs), it not only forgoes the usual gains from trade but also suffers because production units in some industries cannot grow enough to exhaust the available scale economies serving only the domestic market. Thus, the combined effect of the Canadian and U.S. tariffs has been an estimated cost to Canada of about 6 to 10 percent of its potential welfare.[11] Over the long run, the free-trade arrangement ought to retrieve that loss. Thus, Canada will experience a very large reallocation of its resources, relative to the United States, but it will also get proportionally much larger benefits in the form of productivity increases due to greater economies of scale.

During 1992 the United States and Mexico sought to negotiate a similar free-trade agreement. This arrangement would link an industrial with a developing nation. Because each country heavily protects its domestic producers of goods supplied by the other, the scope for trade creation is large. However, there is also much room for trade diversion; in Mexico, for example, sophisticated U.S. industrial machinery is likely to be a better substitute for machinery from Japan or Germany than it is for machinery produced in Mexico. The static welfare economics of the arrangement therefore are not obviously favorable (dynamic gains for Mexico might be large, however, even if trade diversion is predominant).

Like the United States, Mexico is a large country, and so free trade should involve substantial adjustments in each country. With its low-skill but fairly literate labor force, Mexico's comparative advantage evidently lies in labor-intensive activities and that of the United States in activities intensive in physical and human capital. The arrangement could thus redistribute income in both countries, away from labor in the United States, toward it in Mexico. The ease with which American multinational firms, already prevalent and successful in Mexico (see Section 9.3), could expand their operations speaks for the potential extent of trade creation but also underlines the possible redistribution of factor incomes.[12]

The possible U.S.-Mexico arrangement has raised concerns that Canada's gains from trade creation in the Canada-U.S. free-trade deal might be eroded in trade

---

[10] This point was made in Section 10.3 in the context of welfare effects of immigration.

[11] Richard G. Harris, "Applied General Equilibrium Analysis of Small Open Economies with Scale Economies and Imperfect Competition," *American Economic Review,* 74 (December 1984): 1018–1032.

[12] Peter Morici, *Trade Talks with Mexico: A Time for Realism* (Washington: National Planning Association, 1991).

diversion following a U.S.-Mexico deal. Partly for this reason a trilateral Canada-U.S.-Mexico free-trade area has been proposed. More generally, if the U.S. should pursue free-trade deals with other nations in the Americas, each might find itself impelled to join in order to avert losing from trade diversion stemming from free-trade agreements that other labor-rich nations had already reached with the United States.[13]

Preferential Arrangements Among Developing Nations

Preferential arrangements have been popular among the LDCs, especially while import-substituting industralization behind high tariff walls remained a popular development policy. The small sizes of most LDCs' national markets meant that for many manufactured goods production facilities designed for the LDC's home market would suffer serious diseconomies of small scale.

A customs union might avoid this problem. Rather than starting one small inefficient plant each in Colombia, Ecuador, and Paraguay to manufacture (or assemble) farm tractors, why not form a free-trade area and agree to put the tractor plant in one country, a maker of radios in a second, a tire factory in the third? Each country would benefit its industrial sector, yet the disadvantages of small scale would be mitigated if each plant served all three markets. Furthermore, the expansion of trade among them should be balanced. This goal has been an important motive for both the Latin American Free-Trade Area and the Central American Common Market (where national markets are hopelessly small). A study found that the nations of the Latin American Free-Trade Area, by locating plants of six important manufacturing industries at the cost-efficient sites, could save around 10 percent in production costs over a situation in which every member (or nearly every member) started its own protected production. Further gains would accrue in consumers' benefits (like area 4 in Figure 15.1). Another study found potential gains from integration between Ghana and the Ivory Coast amounting to 33 and 22 percent, respectively, of their gross outputs. The bulk of the gains would arise not from conventional trade creation but from scale economies and the offsetting of divergencies between private and social cost.[14] The actual performance record of customs unions in developing countries is quite mixed.

Finally, note that the Generalized System of Preferences, described in Section 14.4, can be analyzed as a limited customs union, with the industrial-country donors giving limited duty-free access to LDC imports. GSP will be trade-diverting insofar as LDC imports replace imports from other countries, trade-creating insofar as LDC imports force the contraction of the donors' import-competing industries. The many restrictions that hedge the GSP tend to assure the predominance of trade diversion.

[13] Ronald J. Wonnacott, *The Economics of Overlapping Free Trade Areas and the Mexican Challenge* (Washington: National Planning Association, 1991).

[14] Martin Carnoy, "A Welfare Analysis of Latin American Economic Union: Six Industry Studies," *Journal of Political Economy*, 78 (July/August 1970): 626–654; Scott R. Pearson and William D. Ingram, "Economies of Scale, Domestic Divergences, and Potential Gains from Economic Integration in Ghana and the Ivory Coast," *Journal of Political Economy*, 88 (October 1980): 994–1008. See *Business Week*, May 4, 1992, pp. 50–51, for examples from Mercosur.

15.4 TRADE PROBLEMS OF THE EASTERN
EUROPEAN COUNTRIES

The centrally planned economies of Eastern Europe were long studied as a regional trading group. They chose to do much of their trading with each other. Furthermore, because of both ideology and the operating methods of their planned economies, they effectively discriminated against trade with the rest of the world. Their principal trading association, the Council for Mutual Economic Assistance (CMEA), has been called a trade-destroying customs union: Economic planners pursued the goal of self-sufficiency for each nation, closing off efficient trade with outside nations and generating what often appeared to be inefficient trade among CMEA members.[15] To everyone's surprise, the political regimes that kept central planning in place vanished almost overnight, leaving their stranded economic systems to find their own paths of transition toward Western-style market economies.

The pace and direction of this transformation, indeed its very occurrence, are quite unsure at this time. To help understand the process and its implications for international trade, we provide a brief account of the now-crumbling systems of central planning and the trade patterns that they created. Then we can consider what developments in international trade may attend the transformation.

The Legacy of Central Planning

The managers of the centrally planned economies excluded private business enterprises from most sectors and made no use of prices for allocating resources among activities and uses. State-owned production units were told what and how much to produce on the basis of a central plan. That plan selected a mix of final outputs—consumption goods, investment goods, military equipment, etc.—and then devolved detailed instructions causing the state enterprises to deliver all the various inputs required to satisfy the planned final output. The enterprises bargained not with the "customers" who received their outputs but with the central planners over what and how much they should produce. Prices functioned only at the retail level to ration out consumption goods to households.

International trade was generally regarded by the CMEA countries not as an opportunity to benefit from specialization but as a way to fill otherwise intractable excesses of plan requirements over domestic supplies. Exports were merely the trading stock for securing imports—a contrast to the mercantilistic habits of Western governments that tend to treat exports as desirable and imports as a necessary evil. This aversion to international trade was not wildly unrealistic for the vast and diversified Soviet Union, but it made no sense for the small countries of Eastern Europe when they copied the Soviet planning practices. It is no surprise that the foreign-trade turnover of the CMEA countries was estimated to be no more than one-third of that expected of Western market economies comparable in size and income levels.[16]

---

[15] Franklyn D. Holzman, "Comecon: A 'Trade-Destroying' Customs Union?" *Journal of Comparative Economics*, 9 (1985): 410–423.

[16] See Frederic L. Pryor, *The Communist Foreign Trade System* (Cambridge, MA: M.I.T. Press, 1963), Chapter 1.

FIGURE 15.3   Effect of CMEA Pricing Practices on Potential Gains from Trade

Production takes place at P. With world prices P_w, the socialist economy would gain from producing consumer goods for export and trading to point C. Internal prices P_c, set to favor producer goods, cannot guide trade because they imply an inefficient specialization in producer goods.

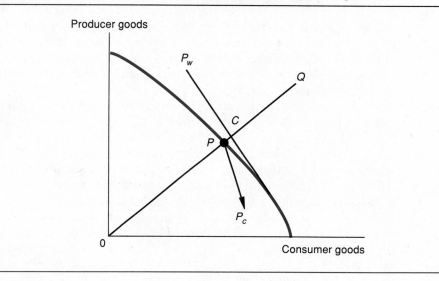

The centrally planned economies may not have used prices when they selected goods to be produced, consumed, and traded. Nonetheless, their decisions implicitly made some goods cheap by producing large quantities, whereas others were expensive because little was available. In particular, producer goods were favored over consumer goods and expanding plant capacity was favored over raising the productivity of capacity in place. An arbitrary choice of that sort can have an adverse effect on the welfare of a country taking part in international trade. Consider Figure 15.3, which shows a transformation function for producer and consumer goods. Suppose that the planners allocate output between these two classes in the proportion given by line OQ, making no systematic use of international trade (except to meet temporary shortages or dispose of temporary surpluses). The relative prices in Western markets are indicated by price slope P_w. It suggests that, by taking full advantage of international trade, the CMEA country could export consumer goods, obtaining for final use the producer and consumer goods indicated by point C, superior to bundle P actually produced and used. On the other hand, the implicit prices used by the CMEA countries, P_c, render producer goods cheaper. If Western traders were allowed to make offers at these internal prices, the CMEA country would export producer goods, and wind up at an inferior point somewhere along PP_c.[17]

---

[17] The real cost of these allocative distortions to the USSR was not small. A study of the misallocations of resources among eight major sectors of the Soviet economy found that its cost is 10 percent of the economy's attainable output, and rising. See Padma Desai and Ricardo Martin, "Efficiency Loss from Resource Misallocation in Soviet Industry," *Quarterly Journal of Economics*, 98 (August 1983): 441–456.

The CMEA countries' actual trade with the West has been strangled by many factors. With no prices at which Western buyers could "shop," East-West trade has been confined to barter conducted by the foreign-trade organizations of the CMEA countries. The exportables that these agencies could offer (other than raw materials) were arbitrary artifacts of the planning process. Manufactured exportables have suffered from not meeting design and quality standards expected by Western buyers. Indeed, an important failure of the central-planning system has been that producers respond to quota incentives and not to the direct wants of buyers. At a time when Western producers increasingly develop close and sustained contacts with their customers, as a way to assure the quality and suitability of products, CMEA production units are accustomed to meeting only quantity targets.

Trade among the CMEA countries themselves has also been both constricted and distorted. Like East-West trade it was not based on any systematic plan to produce exportables as a way to obtain importables for consumption. Only during the 1970s did the CMEA countries make any progress in coordinating their sectoral plans among countries so that these could be coordinated in a multilateral trading pattern. Before that, the coordination of trade and production was confined to narrow intra-product specialization within industries. Exchanges among the CMEA countries were based partly on Western prices but primarily were bargained out by the parties. Apparently the Soviet Union has been a loser in this bargaining. Hewett's calculations suggest that the USSR could have shifted the factors of production it used producing exports shipped to other CMEA members into producing goods to replace what it imported from them and would have wound up with more goods overall.[18]

Future of Eastern European Trade

What will happen to the trade of the former CMEA members, if indeed their economies are reorganized on a market basis? A considerable expansion of their international trade will surely accompany a successful transformation. Statistical studies indicate that the present foreign trade of these countries is low even relative to their present-day real incomes, and a market transformation should expand trade by raising overall income and production capacity as well as rationalizing the use of production capacity now available. Because the former CMEA countries account for about 13 percent of world income, their reorganization presents a significant new trading opportunity for the rest of the world. Of course it also raises the fears of some policy-makers that some of their domestic producers will suffer from the expansion of competing exports from the East. That concern arises particularly in the European Community, which for geographic reasons alone is likely to experience the predominant share of growth in East-West trade.[19]

How do we project the likely pattern of trade for the former CMEA members? Scholars have relied on various rough techniques suggested by international-trade theory. They have based forecasts on the apparent factor endowments of the CMEA

[18] Edward A. Hewett, *Foreign Trade Prices in the Council of Mutual Economic Assistance* (New York: Cambridge University Press, 1974).

[19] See Susan M. Collins and Dani Rodrik, *Eastern Europe and the Soviet Union in the World Economy* (Washington: Institute for International Economics, 1991).

countries.[20] They have employed the principle of "revealed comparative advantage," which holds simply that a country's comparative advantage lies in those goods for which its exports make up the largest proportions of world exports. The evidence tends to agree that the former USSR's comparative advantage probably lies in exporting raw materials and energy sources, the other CMEA members in these, agricultural products, and simple basic and miscellaneous manufactures: products intensive in natural resources and labor, not in physical or human capital.

This judgment on the factor-endowment basis for the transformation of East-West trade is consistent with most organizational assessments of the problem of transforming the centrally planned economies. Managers in these countries lack experience in supplying goods that in quality and design meet the direct wishes of customers (as mentioned above). They also lack experience with large-scale market-oriented enterprises (and the financial and services markets that support them). These lacks are consistent with the trade pattern just predicted. They also help to explain why the transformation from central planning to a market price system will be so difficult. Resource allocation by central planning and by a price mechanism are fundamentally different systems, and there is no such thing as a gradual transition from one to the other.[21] Yet the working of the price system itself depends on the effectiveness with which market-oriented business organizations can operate. Possibly the expansion of East-West trade will help this process. Western market prices provide a rough set of opportunity indicators to help guide the allocation of resources in the former CMEA countries. Furthermore, at the level of institutions, contact through trade with Western enterprises (and possibly Western foreign investment in these countries) may aid the development of market-oriented business enterprises.

15.5 SUMMARY

Preferential arrangements among groups of countries—trading clubs, free-trade areas, customs unions, etc.—are now a popular way to cut tariffs. They can either raise or lower economic welfare, in that they both free trade (among their members) and distort trade (with the outside world). Beneficial trade creation results when protected production is competed down and trade expanded between members. The effects are like those of the nondiscriminatory removal of tariffs. Trade diversion occurs when a preference causes a country to switch its purchases from a more efficient to a less efficient supplier. That switch itself imposes a welfare cost, but that cost could be offset by a gain for consumers. A trade union is most likely to benefit the world when a lot of protected production is competed down, when very high tariffs are lowered, and when the union comprises a large proportion of the trading world.

A preferential arrangement is likely to shift the terms of trade of each party. The members would maximize their joint welfare by freeing trade among themselves and

[20] Some time ago the Soviet Union's trade was shown to follow a seemingly rational pattern in terms of the Heckscher-Ohlin theorem. The USSR's exports to industrial countries were more labor-intensive than its imports from those countries, while the reverse was true of the USSR's trade with developing countries. See Steven Rosefielde, *Soviet Foreign Trade in Heckscher-Ohlin Perspective* (Lexington, MA: Lexington Books, 1973).

[21] Richard E. Ericson, "The Classical Soviet-Type Economy: Nature of the System and Implications for Reform," *Journal of Economic Perspectives*, 5 (Fall 1991): 11–27. The issue contains other useful articles on the transition in Eastern Europe.

levying the optimal tariff against outsiders. A member who gives a preference to its partner loses (and the partner gains) if the member's terms of trade with the outside world fail to improve; if they improve, however, the member and the partner may both benefit. Speaking broadly, preferences seem likely to improve their members' terms of trade and welfare and to impose a cost on the outside world.

The European Community seems to have created a good deal of trade and diverted little. The modest diversion may be due to the way the common external tariff was formed by averaging members' previous tariffs. The EC has probably enjoyed dynamic gains much larger than its static effects. Dynamic gains are predicted if it is supposed that many markets are imperfectly competitive. The removal of nontariff barriers in 1992 is expected to bring large gains in reduced transaction costs. A U.S.-Canada free-trade arrangement will give large gains to Canada as the small partner because the removal of U.S. tariffs will grant Canada access to a new set of relative prices as well as to scale economies that will increase its productive efficiency. Both extensive creation and diversion of trade could result from a proposed U.S.-Mexico free-trade area. While bringing gains to both partners, it could also redistribute income within each country. Customs unions among the LDCs can aid in achieving efficient production scales in developing industries.

The centrally planned economies of the former Council of Mutual Economic Assistance extinguished trade with the West without effectively pursuing competitive advantage among themselves. Their central plans eschewed the use of prices in allocating resources among sectors, denying the role of opportunity cost and providing little incentive for product quality or productivity. As these planning systems collapse, world-trade prices may help to guide the reallocation of resources in these countries.

CHAPTER PROBLEMS

1. Why is it that, as a customs union encompasses a larger proportion of the trading world, its formation becomes more likely to promote net welfare gains for the world at large?

2. A form of economic integration used occasionally is the elimination of trade barriers among countries in the goods produced by a particular sector; an example is a free-trade arrangement in automobiles and parts between the United States and Canada. If the parties keep their tariffs on all other goods, why might freeing trade in one sector cause the wrong country to specialize and export?

3. Suppose that a customs union causes a substantial expansion in its members' real incomes and output through the attainment of scale economies. How does this gain affect the chances that the rest of the world will lose from worsened terms of trade with the customs union?

4. Countries that recently joined the European Community (Spain, Portugal, and Greece) have factor endowments that are much more labor-rich and capital-poor than those of the other EC members. Does this fact suggest any presumption about the amounts of trade creation and diversion associated with their accession?

5. One type of preferential trading arrangement is a one-shot barter deal, as when McDonnell Douglas sells a jet aircraft to Poland in exchange for canned ham (more, one trusts, than is needed for the company cafeteria). How could this transaction differ from the alternative in which each party simply sells its wares for cash on the open market? Why might they make the barter deal?

6. The trading practices used among members of the CMEA block tended to require that trade be balanced between each pair of members (A's exports to B equal B's exports to A). Exactly how can bilateral balancing keep a country from obtaining the maximum gains from trade?

7. Provide a diagrammatic explanation as to why the removal of U.S. tariffs in the U.S.-Canada free-trade arrangement would increase Canadian welfare.

SUGGESTIONS FOR FURTHER READING

Collins, Susan M., and Dani Rodrik. *Eastern Europe and the Soviet Union in the World Economy* (Washington: Institute for International Economics, 1991). Analyzes the process of transformation to market economies.

Fieleke, Norman S. "One Trade World, or Many: The Issue of Regional Trading Blocks," *New England Economic Review*, May/June 1992, pp. 3–20. Review of development of regional trading arrangements.

Hufbauer, Gary Clyde, ed. *Europe 1992: An American Perspective* (Washington: Brookings Institution, 1990). Covers evolving policy in the EC and its implications for the United States.

Jacquemin, Alexis, and Andre Sapir, eds. *The European Internal Market: Trade and Competition* (Oxford: Oxford University Press, 1989). Analytical papers on economic integration.

Morici, Peter, ed. *Making Free Trade Work: The Canada-U.S. Agreement* (New York: Council on Foreign Relations, 1990). Problems in operation of this free-trade area.

————. *Trade Talks with Mexico: A Time for Realism.* (Washington: National Planning Association, 1991). Issues raised by a U.S.-Mexico agreement.

Sachs, Jeffrey. *Capitalism in Europe after Communism* (Cambridge, MA: M.I.T. Press, 1992). Prospects for conversion of the centrally planned economies.

Schott, Jeffrey J. *More Free Trade Areas?* (Washington: Institute for International Economics, 1989). Relation between free-trade areas and the General Agreement on Tariffs and Trade.

IV

Money, Income, and the Balance of Payments

16

THE BALANCE OF PAYMENTS
ACCOUNTS

Parts I through III of this book concentrated on the behavior of "real variables" in the international economy, on the quantities of goods produced, consumed, and traded. Prices were crucial in securing equilibrium, but only as the relative prices of goods (the terms of trade) or of factors of production. The focus now turns to the "monetary side" of international economics.[1] This requires an examination of the behavior of monetary magnitudes—the quantity of money itself and various prices that are measured in currency units. These include overall price levels, wage rates, and the foreign exchange rate, which is the price at which currencies exchange for one another.

The subject of international monetary economics has grown rapidly in interest and importance over the last twenty years. Much has happened over this period in the world economy. In 1973 the major industrialized countries moved from a system under which exchange rates were fixed by governments—a system that had held sway since World War II—to a new, unfamiliar system in which exchange rates are determined in the marketplace. We now have twenty years of experience with this system from which to draw lessons.

Meanwhile, both goods markets and financial markets have become more highly integrated, forcing even previously insular American macroeconomists to recognize the importance of the foreign sector; oil price changes (upward in the 1970s, downward in the 1980s) have induced economists to build back into their view of the macroeconomy some of the real factors that had been left behind; and large new macroeconomic policy disturbances and unprecedented trade imbalances in some countries have tested the limits of the modern financial system. At the same time, thinking on the subject has been stimulated by new developments in the macroeconomic theory of closed economies: The intellectual revolutions that in a few short years saw monetarism adopted as a standard description of long-run equilibrium (if not of short-run reality), "rational expectations" adopted as standard methodology, and "real business cycle" theory adopted as a representation of supply shocks.

---

[1] The field is also known as "the macroeconomics of open economies." The term "international finance" is also applicable, particularly to the material covered in Parts V and VI.

Variables

This half of the book will introduce eight or ten factors, or variables, that received little or no attention in the first half of the book. The variables include the exchange rate, output and employment (emphasizing the cyclical components of each), the interest rate, stocks of money and reserves, the aggregate price level, the relative price of non-traded goods, international flows of portfolio capital, and expectations. Understanding how the macroeconomic system works can be quite difficult if one tries to consider all ten variables simultaneously. These variables will be introduced one at a time, so that each can be assimilated—understood in terms of its interaction with the other variables in the macroeconomic system—before the next is introduced. Thus, we need not discard what we have used at each stage as we move on to the next stage and the next variable. Rather, we can consider what came before to be the right answer when the variable in question is held constant; when the variable is allowed to change, we will examine the corresponding change in the results.

Before proceeding, however, we briefly enumerate the different variables. Chapter 17 will introduce the exchange rate, and will show how it helps determine a country's balance of trade. The effect of the exchange rate on the trade balance will first be examined in the most controlled environment, in which price levels, income levels, and all other variables are held constant. Then Chapter 18 will allow for cyclical fluctuations in income. Unlike changes in output considered previously, these fluctuations will represent changes *relative* to potential output, changes associated with unemployment of labor and unutilized capacity. They are the consequence of wages and prices that are rigid, or at least "*sticky*"—that resist moving to equilibrate the labor and goods markets. This represents a sharp departure from the first half of the book, in which all prices were assumed to be flexible enough that they adjusted to ensure that supply always equalled demand. Some of the results, such as the existence of unemployment and excess capacity, are familiar from standard macroeconomics textbooks. However, much will be new and different in the open economy. For example, when prices are not free to adjust, the exchange rate can sometimes be used to restore equilibrium.

In the last part of Chapter 18 the money supply and the interest rate together will make their appearance. At this point we will address how five variables—trade balance, exchange rate, level of income, money supply, and interest rate—all interrelate. Here, and throughout the last half of the book, a key question concerns the effects of monetary and fiscal policy on the open economy. In Chapter 19 two more factors are added. The first half of the chapter introduces the stock of international reserves (for example, gold) that is held by the central bank. The second half of the chapter examines, for the first time, the overall price level. Chapter 20 distinguishes between traded and non-traded goods, providing a particularly useful model for LDCs and other countries that are small in world trade.

The core of Part V, the international flow of capital, is the most powerful factor in the modern world macroeconomy. In Chapter 23 wages also play a significant role. To simplify: Parts I through III concentrated on the international flow of goods, with the trade balance generally constrained to zero; Part IV introduces the international flow of money, allowing nonzero payments balances; and Part V introduces the international flow of portfolio capital (assets such as stocks and bonds). Because an asset is a claim to future consumption, international trade in assets is what allows countries to spend more than they earn in some periods, then make up for it by spending less than they earn in other periods. Part VI examines the determination of exchange rates in international asset markets, where expectations arise as a key variable.

We will see that two particular aspects of the structure of the world economy as it has evolved over the 1970s and 1980s—the great ease of international capital movements and the system of market-determined exchange rates—have completely altered how policy changes and other macroeconomic disturbances operate. These aspects of the modern economy have important implications for the resolution of international payments imbalances and other policy problems that the world faces in the 1990s.

Before we begin exploring the operation of the international macroeconomy, it is necessary to go through the mechanics of balance of payments accounting in the present chapter. This tool would be necessary even if the subject were as tedious as matters of accounting sometimes appear. Balance of payments accounts, however, have attained a new fascination in recent years. Some measures of the balance of payments are closely watched by the press and policy-makers.

Considerable insight into present international payments imbalances can be gained simply from the accounting identities, even before the discussion turns to the more interesting questions of economic causality. An "accounting identity" is an equation that must hold precisely, as a matter of definition or arithmetic, as opposed to "behavioral equations," which represent theories of economic behavior that are not expected to hold precisely.

16.1 BREAKDOWN OF THE ACCOUNTS

A nation's balance of payments accounts is the statistical record of all economic transactions taking place between its residents and the rest of the world. These are most conveniently broken up into three accounts, as shown in Table 16.1. First, the *current account* (*CA*) is the record of trade in goods and services and other current transactions, as opposed to trade in *assets*, which are obligations regarding the future. Trade in assets appears in the capital accounts. If the asset is traded among private citizens of the countries, then it appears on the *private capital account* (*KA*). If the buyer or seller of the asset is a central bank—i.e., the monetary authority of either the domestic or foreign government—then the transaction appears on the *official reserve transactions* account (ORT).

Each of these three accounts is in turn divided into sub-accounts. Within the current account the first sub-account is merchandise trade, consisting of exports and imports of goods, which includes all movable goods either sold, bought, or otherwise transferred (perhaps given away) between domestic and foreign owners.

The second sub-account within the current account is services (also known in the United Kingdom as "invisibles," as opposed to "visibles," which refers to merchandise). Some of the important international service transactions are as follows.

1. Transportation services include freight and insurance charges for the international movement of goods and also the expenditures on international travel of tourists and other passengers.

TABLE 16.1   Schematic Representation of the Balance of Payments

Accounts and Sub-Accounts	*Cumulative Balances*

Current Account
  Merchandise . . . . merchandise balance
  Services
    ● tourism
    ● transportation
    ● professional and other services . . . . "resource transfer"
  Investment income . . . . balance on goods, services, and income
  Unilateral transfers
    ● government grants
    ● private remittances . . . . current account balance

Private Capital Account
  Direct investment
  Portfolio investments (securities
    and banking flows)
    ● long-term . . . . basic balance
    ● short-term . . . . overall balance of payments

Official Reserve Transactions
  Changes in foreign central banks'
    holding of domestic assets
  Changes in domestic central banks'
    holding of foreign assets
    ● gold
    ● IMF credits and SDRs
    ● foreign exchange reserves

Each balance at the right is the sum of the previous balance and the additional items listed before the dotted line.

2. Tourist services include all expenditures by a country's citizens in foreign countries (on food, lodging, local transportation, etc.).

3. Business and professional services make up a diverse class of international transactions. International trade in the services of engineering firms, management consulting firms, and so forth is a rapidly growing component of trade. Royalties and license fees, paid for the use of a work or invention when the copyright or patent is held by the citizen of another country, are also counted as payments for a service.

A third sub-account within the current account is investment income. Interest payments or dividends appear here because they are considered payments for the services of capital that is "working" abroad. The profits earned by a factory owned by a foreign resident, for example, are payments for the services of the capital embodied in that factory (somewhat as royalties and license fees can be considered payments for the services of "intellectual capital"). It is important to distinguish these payments for the *services* of capital, which appear in the current account, from the original investment itself, which appears in the capital account.

Unilateral transfers are a fourth sub-account. This sub-account consists of government grants (foreign aid) and private remittances (from emigrant workers to their families, from pensions to retired people living abroad, etc.). Transfers appear in the current account rather than the capital account because they do not create any obligation for repayment in the future, as a loan does.

Within the capital account,[2] the key distinction is between direct investment and portfolio capital. Portfolio investment in turn can be divided into long-term and short-term.

1. *Foreign direct investment* occurs when the residents of one country acquire control over a business enterprise in another country. The acquisition may involve buying enough stock in an existing enterprise to become a controlling shareholder (defined for this purpose as 10 percent ownership), taking over the enterprise outright, or building a new factory or enterprise from scratch (including, as well, the purchase of real estate). When an investor buys only a small fraction of the shares of a foreign company, however, it is an example of long-term portfolio investment.

2. *Long-term portfolio investment* involves international transactions in financial assets with an original term to maturity greater than one year. Such investment consists of purchases of securities (stocks, also called "shares" or equities, and bonds) and long-term bank loans. Often the distinction between long-term and short-term capital flows is arbitrary, as when an investor buys a 10-year government bond, intending to resell it in a short time, or a bond that has already been held for $9\frac{1}{2}$ years and is about to mature.

3. *Short-term capital flows* involve assets with original terms to maturity of less than one year. Examples are treasury bills, commercial paper, and certificates of deposit (short-term claims on the government, corporations, and banks, respectively). Also included as short-term capital flows are any international shifts in the ownership of liquid funds, such as an interest-earning deposit, or even a check or cash which does not pay interest. For example, British pound notes, or deposits in a British bank, are assets giving a claim on future British goods and services, just as surely as British treasury bills. The distinction between short-term and long-term is still reported in Japan, Germany, and other countries, but not in the U.S. accounts, mainly because it is difficult to disentangle the two types of portfolio investment in the data.

Finally, the ORT account consists of central bank transactions in international reserve assets: gold, foreign exchange reserves, credits issued by the International Monetary Fund (IMF), and Special Drawing Rights.[3] Central banks hold these reserve assets to back up the liabilities they issue (domestic currency and the other assets that add up to the monetary base), much as commercial banks hold reserves to back up the liabilities that they issue (checking account deposits and the other assets that add up to the total money supply).

---

[2] "Capital account" will generally be used to refer to the private capital account, as distinct from the transactions of central banks. (It does include, however, any international transactions undertaken by government agencies other than the central bank—for example, credit to U.S. armed forces stationed abroad.)

[3] Special Drawing Rights, sometimes described as "paper gold," are an asset created by the IMF. Their value is defined in terms of five currencies: the dollar, yen, mark, pound, and French franc.

16.2 HOW INDIVIDUAL TRANSACTIONS ARE RECORDED

The key rule for recording transactions is as follows: Whatever enters the country, such as imports, is recorded as a debit; whatever leaves the country, such as exports, is recorded as a credit. The examples that first come to mind concern trade in merchandise (goods). An import of an automobile appears as a debit in the merchandise account because something is entering the country; the export of jet engines appears as a credit because something is leaving the country. (Of course, the country that exports the automobile earns a credit on its merchandise account; and the country that imports the jet engines receives a debit.)

There are many other examples for exports and imports of various services, and for each of the other sub-accounts as well. When an American importer arranges transportation with a Greek shipping company, or American tourists cross the Atlantic on a foreign airline, the import of the service is recorded as a debit in the U.S. transportation service account. When foreign firms hire American ships to carry goods, or when foreign tourists come to the United States, the export of the service is recorded as a credit. The spending of American tourists in Europe is recorded as a debit, again on the service account, and the spending of Japanese tourists in the United States as a credit. When business firms ship statistical data abroad to Korea, Ireland, and elsewhere to be transcribed on tapes (for electronic data processing back in the United States), a service import of the United States again appears. When a foreign student comes to an American university to study or a foreign medical patient comes to an American hospital for surgery, it appears as a U.S. service export.

The convention is that gifts and other transfers are recorded under unilateral transfers. Even though a transfer to another country does not create any obligation for future monetary repayment as does a loan, a device for remembering that it appears as a credit might be to think of the transfer as the export of a political or moral "IOU." In the first half of 1991, the United States received large payments from Japan and other allies to finance operation Desert Storm. These credits did not appear on the trade account because they were not *literally* exports of "military services" but appeared instead as transfers. Emigrants' remittances are an important source of credits for Mexico and countries around the Mediterranean; the corresponding debits are incurred in the United States and Northern European countries (also Persian Gulf states) that host the immigrant workers.

The acquisition of an asset in a foreign country counts as a debit on the capital account, because the asset, or at least the claim to the asset, is entering the home country. As a device for remembering that an investment abroad counts as a debit, think of it as the "import" of an asset. (The equivalent term—"capital outflow"—may be less helpful here, in that it may not sound like an import, even though it is one.) When General Electric builds a factory in Europe, an outflow of direct investment, a debit, equal to the value of the equity that GE acquires in the factory, is recorded in the U.S. balance of payments. In this sense the purchase of machine tools bolted down to a factory floor in Scotland is similar to the purchase of Scottish machine tools imported into the United States, but in the former case the debit appears on the capital account and in the latter case it appears on the merchandise trade account. An American purchase of the bonds of a Canadian provincial government is recorded as a portfolio capital outflow, a debit on the long-term portfolio capital account. The

American acquisition of a short-term asset in another country—whether it is a treasury bill, corporate IOU, certificate of deposit, check, or currency—counts as a debit on the short-term portfolio capital account. This point should be emphasized because it will be important for understanding the accounting to follow: Remember that the reason this acquisition counts as a debit is that an American has increased individual holdings of a foreign asset, even if the asset is only foreign currency.

Ever since 1982, the U.S. capital account has shown many more credits than debits. Foreign citizens have been acquiring assets of every sort in the United States: currency, treasury bills, bank loans, bonds, stocks, and direct investment. The term "credit" makes it sound like a good thing for the receiving country. In one sense this is true: It can be viewed as a vote of confidence when foreigners decide to invest in the United States. The "downside," of course, is that U.S. citizens will have to service the debt (i.e., pay interest, and eventually repay the principal) in the future; or, in the cases of sales of stocks and inward direct investment, dividends and profits will have to be repatriated abroad in the future.

If American citizens resell to a foreign resident a bond originally issued by a foreign government, or any other foreign asset that they acquired in the past, that too counts as a credit. There is no economic difference between an increase in your obligations to a foreigner or a decrease in a foreigner's obligations to you. Both are described as a decrease in the net foreign investment position of the United States, which is simply one more way of saying "capital inflow" or "credit on the capital account." Similarly, if an American buys back a U.S. treasury bill from a foreign resident who acquired it in the past, it counts as a debit in the U.S. capital account in the same way as when the asset the American purchases from the foreign resident is one that was originally issued by some foreign government or other institution.[4]

The final place where credits and debits can appear is the Official Reserve Transactions account. When the domestic central bank buys foreign currency or gold its purchase counts as a debit, just as when a private investor does so, but it appears on the ORT account rather than the private capital account. As a device for remembering that it counts as a debit, the purchase can be thought of as an import of gold or foreign currency by the central bank. In this sense it is like the import of gold jewelry or shares in a foreign gold mine, except that in the jewelry case the debit appears in the merchandise trade account and in the gold mine case in the capital account. Only when the central bank makes the purchase does it appear on the ORT account. Another example arises if the country in question is one whose currency is used by other central banks as a reserve asset (as are the dollar, the yen, the mark, and several other currencies[5]); when a foreign central bank buys some of the domestic currency, its purchase counts as a credit, just as when a private foreigner does it.

[4] As a matter of fact, increases in U.S.-held assets issued abroad and decreases in foreign-held assets in the United States are reported separately in the detailed balance of payments accounts published every quarter by the Department of Commerce, and even in the simplified version of them shown in Table 16.2. Economic discussions of the balance of payments usually focus only on the net capital flows, however. (Don't be confused by the cryptic headings in Table 16.2, "U.S. Assets Abroad" and "Foreign Assets in the U.S." They refer, respectively, to assets held by U.S. citizens issued in foreign countries, and assets held by foreign citizens issued in the United States.)

[5] Only *convertible* foreign currencies are held as foreign exchange reserves. Central banks do not hold Albanian leks as reserves because neither the government nor private banks will freely convert them into gold, dollars, or other international reserve assets.

16.3 DOUBLE-ENTRY BOOKKEEPING

A critical point is that every complete economic transaction is recorded twice, once as a debit and once as a credit, as a matter of accounting. The reason is that in every complete transaction there is something leaving the country in exchange for something entering the country; if there were not, then one party or the other would be giving up something for nothing.[6] One case where this is easy to see is barter. If Argentina exports wheat to Russia, for example, in exchange for tractors, then both the credit for the wheat export and the debit for the tractors import appear on the merchandise trade account. Similarly, if Russia accepted the claim to some Argentine farmland in payment for the tractors, the Argentine balance of payments statistics would show a debit on the trade account and a corresponding credit under foreign direct investment.

Usually, however, transactions are paid for in an immediate sense through the banking system.[7] Argentina pays for the tractors by writing a check on a bank; the credit that corresponds to the debit on the trade account appears on the short-term capital account. Recall that any time a foreign resident acquires an asset or a claim on the domestic country, even if it is a bank deposit rather than a more tangible investment, it counts as a credit on the capital account. It is quite likely that the Russian tractor manufacturer will quickly cash in its check, a claim on an Argentine bank, to buy something more directly useful to it than Argentine pesos (perhaps that Argentine wheat), but this would count as an entirely separate transaction and would appear in the accounts as a new credit-debit pair.

Other than paying for transactions by cash or check, the only common method is trade-credit: The tractor manufacturer extends the Argentine importer the credit to buy the tractors (that is, the importer does not have to pay until a date, for example, six months in the future) or else a bank extends the credit to the importer. Then, however, the credit item again appears in the short-term capital account: A foreign resident has acquired a short-term claim against an Argentine resident. In this sense paying for an import on short-term credit looks just like paying cash; both appear as credits in the same line of the balance of payments.

As a final set of examples, consider how the purchase of an asset is paid for. If a Japanese company buys an office building in Los Angeles and pays by check, the U.S. balance of payments registers a credit under direct investment (a foreign company has increased its holdings of U.S. real estate) and a debit under banking flows (an American company has increased its holdings of short-term claims on foreigners— it has the Japanese check). If an American firm buys a Canadian bond and pays by

---

[6] The unique case where one party does in fact give up something for nothing is the unilateral transfer, discussed previously. When the United States donates grain to an African country, for example, a debit is assigned to the trade account of the African country (or to its capital account if the donation consists of money) because something is entering the country, and a credit is assigned to the United States because something is leaving the country. As was already noted, the unilateral transfers account is where accountants, by convention, also assign a credit to the recipient country and a debit to the donor country.

[7] There is a rapidly growing type of international transaction called "countertrade," in which the exporter of goods to a country promises to bring a corresponding import of goods from that country. However, most countertrade transactions are still paid for through the banking system; relatively little of it is outright barter for goods, as this is awkward. (Countertrade is discussed by Norman Fieleke in *The World Economy Under Stress*, [Cambridge, MA: Ballinger Books, 1988], pp. 47–52.) The practice is particularly popular among Eastern European countries.

check, the U.S. balance of payments shows a debit on portfolio capital (the firm has increased its holdings of foreign securities) and a credit under banking flows (a foreign firm has increased its holdings of short-term claims on Americans). If an American buys a three-month Certificate of Deposit in the United Kingdom and pays by check, both the credit and the debit appear under banking flows (two short-term assets have been exchanged). In some cases it is difficult to say which side of the transaction is paying for the other. There is nothing wrong with this; the seller of the good or asset is acquiring something (usually money) just as surely as the buyer is.

It may be clearer now why it makes accounting sense to enter a payment abroad as a capital account credit at the same time that a debit is entered for the other half of the transaction (e.g., on the trade account in the case of an import of merchandise). Take the case of an American company paying for an import in dollars (either cash or a check on its banking account). If the foreign company were to hold on to the dollars rather than cashing them in for its own currency, that is, if there were no second transaction undoing the capital flow, this would have to mean that the foreign company had made a deliberate decision to increase its holdings of dollars. This *should* count as a capital account credit; it constitutes foreign investment in U.S. assets, just as if the foreign company had increased its holdings of U.S. stocks or bonds. Again, normally the foreign company would be expected to cash in the dollars for something more useful, but doing so would count as a separate transaction. If the foreign company sells the dollars to the central bank, the second transaction consists of a debit on the U.S. short-term capital account (a foreign private company has now reduced its holdings of short-term U.S. assets) and a credit on the ORT account (the Federal Reserve has exported some foreign currency reserves).

It has been assumed so far that the U.S. importer can make payment in dollars. The story is similar, however, if it pays in foreign currency. Assume first that the U.S. importer has on hand a stock of foreign currency just for such purposes. Initially the current account debit is paid for by a short-term capital account credit: A U.S. company has reduced its holdings of foreign assets, which represents a capital inflow just as if it had sold off a security. (Recall that when the U.S. company decreases its credit position vis-à-vis foreign companies, it is as if foreign companies had increased their credit position vis-à-vis U.S. companies.) However, if the importer obtained the foreign currency by drawing down some transactions balances that were kept on hand for the purpose, subsequently it will probably want to replenish its stock of foreign currency by buying some in the foreign exchange market. If the importer does not have a stock of foreign currency to begin with, then again it has to go into the foreign exchange market to obtain some. Either way, the importer needs foreign currency, and there will be a second transaction in which it is obtained. If the importer obtains the foreign currency from its Central Bank, the second transaction consists of a debit on the short-term capital account and a credit on the ORT account, exactly as in the first example.

On the other hand, if the importer allows its stock of foreign currency to remain lower at the end of the period than it was at the beginning (or goes into debt in foreign currency), then it must have decided deliberately to decrease its (net) holdings of foreign assets. The net credit then remains on the capital account—as when foreign companies increase their claims on domestic companies—rather than being transferred to the ORT account.

16.4 THE BALANCES

Every year, the country adds up the debits and credits arising from the international transactions that have taken place. For most purposes in economics, the only concern is *net* flows, or total credits minus total debits. Within any given line of the balance of payments, there will be many credits and debits that cancel each other out. For example, short-term banking flows are typically very high in gross terms, as banks buy and sell short-term positions in foreign currency and send checks back and forth for collection, while the net flow is much smaller.

The country then adds together the net flows, or subtotals, from various lines in the accounts to determine various balances, such as the trade balance. If credits outweigh debits, then the balance in question is positive. A positive balance is commonly referred to as "favorable." If debits outweigh credits, the balance is negative, or "unfavorable."

Note the gravitational pull of the semantics. The export side owns all the positive words—and has done so ever since the eighteenth-century mercantilists made a national virtue of selling abroad more than one bought in order to "store up treasure." Although economists from Adam Smith on have proclaimed that economic welfare ultimately depends on the goods available for the nation's use and not on the money earned from exporting, they have never conquered this linguistic remnant of mercantilism. When the term "unfavorable" is used in reference to a negative trade balance, remember that it may be perfectly appropriate for a country to run a trade deficit, depending on the circumstances. An example is Korea, which ran large trade deficits in the 1970s. This practice was perfectly appropriate, as the country was growing rapidly and needed to import, for example, capital goods in order to invest in plant and equipment. Korea was necessarily borrowing from abroad to finance its current account deficit. Because it spent the funds well, it now has the level of capital stock, particularly export capacity, necessary to generate export earnings with which to repay that debt.

Because every debit has an offsetting credit somewhere, $CA + KA + \text{ORT} \equiv 0$. (Three bars are used in the equality sign to indicate that this is an accounting identity.) The three-account sum is not a very interesting statistic! Two interesting statistics are (1) the current account balance and (2) the sum of the current and capital accounts, which is what is generally meant by the overall balance of payments (*BP*): $BP \equiv CA + KA$. These statistics reveal whether the country is spending beyond its means, and whether there is a net supply of or demand for its currency. A country that is running a current account deficit—for example, the United States since 1982— is borrowing from abroad to do so, running down its net foreign asset position. A country that is running a current account surplus—for example, Japan—is accumulating claims on foreigners, building up a positive net foreign asset position.[8] If the foreign assets are acquired by the private residents of the domestic country, then

---

[8] This may be the appropriate place to introduce the distinction between *stocks* and *flows*. Flows have a "per unit time" dimension, while stocks are absolute and dimensionless. Examples of stocks are the level of reserves held by a central bank and the level of assets held by private investors, whether money, bonds, equities, or physical capital. Examples of flows are the balance of payments, the current account, income, spending, and saving. A flow is the rate of change of a stock.

the capital account deficit offsets the current account surplus and the overall balance of payments is zero. In this case, $KA = -CA$, so ORT $= 0$.

On the other hand, if a country is running a current account surplus and its private residents are *not* acquiring foreign assets, then it must be the central bank that is acquiring foreign assets: In this case, $KA = 0$, so ORT $= -CA$. Such a country is running a surplus, not just on its current account, but also on its overall *BP*. *BP* is sometimes called the "official settlements balance" or "official reserve transactions balance." (Note, however, that it is the *negative* of the sum of the items on ORT account: ORT $\equiv -BP$.) The overall balance of payments is the net supply of foreign currency (or the net demand for domestic currency, which is the same thing), after the private sector has made all its desired current account and capital account transactions. If it is a positive number, the ORT is negative, which means that the central bank is adding to its foreign exchange reserves (or is supplying the domestic currency that private agents in the foreign exchange market want, which is the same thing). If *BP* is a negative number, then ORT is positive, which means that the central bank is selling foreign exchange reserves (or is buying the domestic currency that private agents in the market want to sell).[9]

The monthly U.S. merchandise trade balance numbers that appear in newspapers receive more attention than any other measure of the balance of payments. They become available more quickly than other components of the balance of payments because they are reported directly to the Commerce Department by the Customs Service. The merchandise trade numbers are important precisely because they are available monthly and because they do receive so much attention. However, they are not in truth a very good measure. First, they are not intended to measure net exports of services, only net exports of goods. Second, they are subject to large short-term fluctuations (due in part to lags before imports arrive in port to be counted) and sometimes have to be substantially revised at a later date. This means that any one month's merchandise trade balance is not a very good indicator of future trends.

There is no reason, conceptually, to focus on exports and imports of goods while ignoring services. Thus, a better measure than the merchandise trade balance is the *balance on goods, services, and income*, although (like the current account) it is only reported quarterly. The balance on goods, services, and income is the point of juncture between the international payments statistics and national-income accounts. Gross domestic product, the chief measure of a nation's economic output in one year, consists of goods and services produced at home for consumption, investment, government

---

[9] A story illustrates how important it can be to know the differences among the definitions of the various balances. In 1984, with the U.S. trade balance deteriorating at an alarming rate, some congressmen held hearings to see whether they might be able to invoke a provision in a trade bill that had been passed ten years earlier allowing the imposition of a 10 percent tariff surcharge in the event of a large deficit in the U.S. balance of payments. Along with the many other reasons the congressmen were given as to why such a tariff surcharge would be a bad idea was the simple point that the earlier law in any case did not apply: The law's language did not refer to a *trade* or *current account* deficit, but rather to a deficit in the overall balance of payments, which the United States was not in fact running in 1984. (At the time the bill had originally been written, amid the wreckage of the Bretton Woods system, the U.S. government had been most concerned with the overall excess demand for foreign currency and the threat to U.S. gold reserves, not just with the trade balance.) The congressmen were forced to look elsewhere for ways to block imports.

use, and export. The statisticians measure these flows of goods, however, not as they are *produced* but as they are *purchased*. Some of these purchases (whether by house-holds, firms, governments, or foreign residents) consist of imports—goods that are produced abroad. Therefore, after all purchases are added up, the statisticians must then subtract out imports in order to arrive at the desired measure of domestic production. The import total is ordinarily shown as a subtraction from exports. Thus,

$$\text{GDP} \equiv C + I + G + (X - M)$$

The term in parentheses is, under U.S. income definitions, the balance of goods and services. In the national-income accounts it is called "net exports of goods and services." Conceptually, it is the most deserving of the name "trade balance," even though the newspapers usually call the monthly merchandise trade numbers by that name.[10]

There used to be a presumption of causality running from items reported higher in the accounts shown in Table 16.1 to items reported lower. Trade, for example, logically came first. Suppose a line is drawn under the entries for trade in goods and services. Then, if the balance is in deficit, it could be financed by transfers, by borrowing (KA), or by reserve loss (ORT). All items "above the line" are considered *autonomous*, as causing items "below the line," which are financing or *accommodating*. There has been much debate as to where to draw the line. Obvious places are the CA balance, with KA and ORT as accommodating, or BP, with ORT alone as accommodating. However, there are other places to draw the line, as shown along the right in Table 16.1.[11]

Another place to draw the line is above interest payments but below net exports of merchandise and services. This "trade balance in merchandise and services" is particularly useful when we examine the situation of a country, as with many in Latin America, that must run a trade surplus in order to service a large foreign debt accumulated in the past. If the country runs an overall deficit on this measure, then its creditors are lending it new money in excess of that required to pay the interest on the existing debt. Such was the case for many Latin American countries until 1982. However, if the country runs a surplus in merchandise and services, then its creditors are lending it less new money than required to pay the interest. This was the case for most Latin American countries after August 1982, when the banks became worried about the countries' credit-worthiness and so cut back sharply on lending. The trade balance in merchandise and services is often called the "resource transfer," which indicates how much money is flowing from the debtor country to the creditor country to service the debt.[12]

[10] Even when services are included, the trade balance numbers also differ from "net exports" in the national income and product accounts in a number of other minor technical ways. For example, the goods and services number in the balance of payments statistics include as services interest payments to foreign holders of U.S. government bonds, while the national income and product accounts classify these interest payments as transfers rather than services.

[11] Charles P. Kindleberger, "Measuring Equilibrium in the Balance of Payments," *Journal of Political Economy*, 77(6) (1969): 873–891. (Reprinted in his *International Money*, [London: George Allen & Unwin, 1981].)

[12] The distinction among (1) the balance on goods and noninterest services, (2) the balance on all goods and services, and (3) the current account balance is roughly similar to the distinction between (1) gross domestic product (which includes only income from domestic production), (2) gross national product, which includes also profits from abroad ("net factor income"), and (3) total national income, which includes also income from transfers. The United States began to emphasize GDP over GNP in 1991.

We have already explained the current account balance, the measure of the balance of payments that adds to trade in goods trade in all services, as well as transfers. Recall that the current account is important because it represents the net acquisition of foreign assets (whether by private citizens of the home country or by the central bank). Also discussed was the overall balance of payments (also called the ''official settlements balance''), which adds to the current account all private capital account transactions and is important because it represents the net acquisition of foreign reserve assets by the central bank. Some economists have argued that the line should be drawn between these two, that ''exports'' of claims to factories, along with other forms of foreign direct investment and sales of long-term assets, should count above the line—as do exports of goods. Thus, the *basic balance* adds these long-term capital inflows to the current account. The accounting shows that this balance must be financed, or accommodated, either by short-term private capital flows or by official reserve transactions. The basic balance is no longer reported for the United States. Indeed, it cannot even be computed because the statistics collected no longer distinguish between long-term and short-term portfolio investment. The balance is still reported for Japan and other countries.

Originally, the reason for "drawing the line"—whether at the merchandise trade balance, goods and noninterest services, goods and services, current account, basic balance, or overall balance of payments—was so that transactions below the line could be thought of as financing or accommodating (being caused by) transactions above the line. This reasoning is now somewhat out-of-date.

A more modern view of causality in the balance of payments accounts has evolved from the transition to floating exchange rates on the part of most major industrialized countries in 1973.[13] The definition of (pure) floating is ORT = 0: The central bank does not buy or sell foreign exchange, so there are no official reserve transactions to record. Obviously, in this case BP is not an interesting statistic, as it is now always equal to zero.

Currently, central banks at times *do* participate in foreign exchange markets to try to influence the exchange rate.[14] This is ''managed floating,'' rather than pure floating. Yet there is no clear sense in which central bank sales or purchases of international reserves necessarily accommodate (i.e., are caused by) private trade and capital flows, rather than the other way around. For example, in the late 1960s, under fixed exchange rates, it made some sense to say that large U.S. balance of payments deficits caused foreign central banks to buy up unwanted dollars. In the case of the deficits run by the United States in 1977 and 1978, however, and the much larger deficits in 1986 and 1987, it was at least as correct to say that the voluntary decision by foreign central banks to buy dollars allowed, or even "caused," the U.S. deficits. Similarly, when in the 1970s the Saudi Arabian Monetary Authority and other institutions in the Organization of Petroleum Exporting Countries (OPEC) held much

---

[13] Robert Stern, "The Presentation of the U.S. Balance of Payments: A Symposium," *Essays in International Finance* No. 123, Princeton University, August 1977.

[14] During the first Reagan Administration (1981–1984), the United States followed a policy of not intervening in the foreign exchange market at all, that is, a policy of pure floating. In 1985 the United States joined its largest trading partners (the other members of the "G7" or Group of 7) in intervening in the market from time to time.

of their new-found riches in the form of short-term claims on the United States, this was a commercial investment decision, not an accommodating transaction.

This point is even more applicable when assets are sold to foreign private residents rather than to foreign central banks. A surplus on the private capital account is what allows, or even "causes," a country to run a deficit on the current account, as much so as the deficit on the current account gives rise to the surplus on the capital account. The most prominent example is the large current account deficit that the United States began to run after 1982. To say that the decision by private foreigners to increase their holdings of U.S. assets caused the U.S. current account deficits is as correct as saying that the decision by Americans to import more goods and services caused the current account deficits, which then had to be financed by borrowing from abroad. The important point is that no clear presumption exists as to the direction of causality. In general, the various accounts are in reality determined simultaneously. For this reason, the distinction between autonomous and accommodating transactions is no longer observed.

In fact, even the net figures for the capital account and the overall balance of payments are no longer explicitly reported for the United States, as can be seen from the actual balance of payments statistics reproduced in Table 16.2. To find the net capital account balance, the entries for U.S. private assets abroad must be added to entries for foreign private assets in the United States. For example, we can compute that in 1983 the U.S. capital account turned sharply from deficit into surplus, as foreigners began to acquire U.S. assets in record amounts. Then we add the capital account number to the balance on current account (a large deficit since 1983) to find the overall balance of payments. At first the private capital inflow was sufficient to finance the U.S. current account deficit. In 1986–1990, however, the private capital inflow fell far short of the current account deficit, and foreign central banks made up the difference, as evidenced in Table 16.2 under "foreign official assets." In other words, the United States began to run a deficit, not just on its current account, but also on its overall balance of payments.[15]

Making these calculations can be instructive even though we have abandoned the presumption that the U.S. balance of payments deficit was necessarily *causing* central banks to buy up unwanted dollars, rather than the other way around.

16.5 STATISTICAL ERRORS IN THE PAYMENTS ACCOUNTS

When government statisticians assemble the record of a nation's international transactions, they do not observe directly the two sides of every transaction. Errors creep in for two reasons: Some transactions are valued incorrectly, so that the quantity recorded for one side of the transaction fails to equal that for its compensation, or one side of a transaction is omitted entirely. While the statistician measures each

---

[15] Notice, however, that the U.S. current account was in surplus briefly in early 1991, as Desert Storm transfers from allies were enough to offset the trade deficits.

TABLE 16.2 U.S. Balance of Payments Statistics in Summary Form

[Millions of Dollars. Credits (+), Debits (−)]

Period	Merchandise[1,2]			Services			Investment Income[4]			Balance on Goods, Services, and Income	Unilateral Transfers, net[3]	Balance on Current Account
	Exports	Imports	Net Balance	Net Military Transactions[3]	Net Travel and Transportation Receipts	Other Services, net[4]	Receipts on U.S. Assets Abroad	Payments on Foreign Assets in U.S.	Net			
1980	224,269	−249,749	−25,480	−2,577	−997	7,794	72,506	−42,119	30,387	9,126	−7,593	1,533
1981	237,085	−265,063	−27,978	−844	144	12,552	84,975	−53,626	31,349	15,223	−8,331	6,892
1982	211,198	−247,642	−36,444	112	−992	12,981	85,346	−57,097	28,250	3,907	−9,775	−5,868
1983	201,820	−268,900	−67,080	−163	−4,227	13,859	81,972	−54,549	27,423	−30,188	−9,956	−40,143
1984	219,900	−332,422	−112,522	−2,147	−9,153	14,042	92,935	−69,542	23,394	−86,385	−12,621	−99,006
1985	215,935	−338,083	−122,148	−4,096	−10,788	14,008	82,282	−66,115	16,166	−106,859	−15,473	−122,332
1986	223,367	−368,425	−145,058	−4,907	−8,939	18,551	80,982	−70,013	10,969	−129,384	−16,009	−145,393
1987	250,266	−409,766	−159,500	−3,662	−8,006	18,012	90,536	−82,908	7,629	−145,527	−14,674	−160,201
1988	320,337	−447,323	−126,986	−5,743	−3,844	19,925	110,669	−105,317	5,353	−111,294	−14,943	−126,236
1989	361,451	−477,368	−115,917	−6,204	−2,621	25,998	128,651	−125,963	2,688	−90,814	−15,491	−106,305
1990	388,705	−497,558	−108,853	−7,220	−4,140	29,456	130,091	−118,146	11,945	−69,794	−22,329	−92,123
1991r	415,962	−489,398	−73,436	−5,524	17,118	33,307	125,315	−108,886	16,429	−11,710	8,028	−3,682

[1] Excludes military.

[2] Adjusted from Census data for differences in timing and coverage.

[3] Includes transfers of goods and services under U.S. military grant programs.

[4] Fees and royalties from U.S. direct investments abroad or from foreign investments in the United States are excluded from investment income and included in other services, net.

r Revised.

Source: Department of Commerce, Bureau of Economic Analysis.

319

TABLE 16.2 (continued)

[Millions of Dollars]

Period	U.S. Assets Abroad, Net [Increase/Capital Outflow (−)]				Foreign Assets in the U.S., Net [Increase/Capital Inflow (+)]			Allocations of Special Drawing Rights (SDRs)	Statistical Discrepancy Sum of the Items with Sign Reversed	U.S. Official Reserve Assets, Net[1] (Unadjusted, End of Period)
	Total	U.S. Official Reserve Assets[1]	Other U.S. Government Assets	U.S. Private Assets	Total	Foreign Official Assets	Other Foreign Assets			
1980	−86,118	−8,155	−5,162	−72,802	58,112	15,497	42,615	1,152	25,736	26,756
1981	−110,951	−5,175	−5,097	−100,679	83,032	4,960	78,072	1,093	19,934	30,074
1982	−124,490	−4,965	−6,131	−113,394	93,746	3,593	90,154		36,612	33,958
1983	−56,100	−1,196	−5,006	−49,898	84,869	5,845	79,023		11,374	33,747
1984	−31,070	−3,131	−5,489	−22,451	102,621	3,140	99,481		27,456	34,934
1985	−27,721	−3,858	−2,821	−21,043	130,012	−1,083	131,096		20,041	43,186
1986	−92,030	312	−2,022	−90,321	221,599	35,588	186,011		15,824	48,511
1987	−62,937	9,149	1,006	−73,091	229,828	45,343	184,485		−6,690	45,798
1988	−86,057	−3,912	2,966	−85,111	221,534	39,657	181,877		−9,240	47,802
1989	−128,610	−25,293	1,320	−104,637	216,549	8,624	207,925		18,366	74,609
1990	−57,706	−2,158	2,976	−58,524	86,303	32,425	53,879		63,526	83,316
1991r	−62,220	5,763	3,397	−71,379	66,980	18,407	48,573		−1,078	77,719

[1] Consists of gold, special drawing rights (SDRs), convertible currencies, and the U.S. reserve position in the IMF.

r Revised

Sources: Department of Commerce (Bureau of Economic Analysis) and Department of the Treasury; *Economic Indicators*, Council of Economic Advisors, Washington, D.C.

class of transaction as accurately as possible, because of these and other errors the sums of credit and debit items do not come out equal. Therefore, the statistician simply inscribes an item, "Statistical discrepancy," or "errors and omissions," equal to this difference. These measurement errors are no small problem. The error in the U.S. statistics began to run wild in the 1980s indicating an unmeasured net inflow of money, as can be seen in Table 16.2. This inflow was due in part to unrest in some foreign countries that impelled funds to seek a safe haven in the United States. The acquisition of such claims by foreigners often is clandestine and goes unrecorded.

Another major discrepancy appears when the net current-account positions of all countries are added together. Because every export is some country's import, these accounts would sum to zero if all countries got their measurements right. The discrepancy ran over $100 billion in 1990. It appears as though the world were running a deficit with other planets.[16] The measurement error arises in part because exports of services are often missed or undervalued. Developing countries are generally supposed to run current account deficits, borrowing from wealthier countries to finance their growth. Thus the Earth's deficit confirms the widespread impression that other civilizations are more advanced than our own!

16.6 SUMMARY

The study of international monetary economics begins with the balance of payments accounts. The current account adds up all credits and debits arising from trade in goods and services and from transfers, the private capital account covers the purchase and sale of assets, and the official reserve transactions account consists of changes in international reserve holdings by the central bank.

We now turn from rules of accounting to models of economic behavior. Throughout most of the book the sub-accounts will usually be ignored, and the focus will be on the $CA/KA/$ORT level of aggregation. For example, the discussion will often abstract from transfers to speak interchangeably of the trade balance (TB) and current account (CA).

CHAPTER PROBLEMS

1. In this question you must play balance of payments accountant.

   The Rules
   • On the current account, exports are credits; imports are debits.

---

[16] For example, many countries record payments to ships that fly "flags of convenience" as debits under transportation services in their accounts, with no corresponding credits recorded by Panama or Liberia (the countries where such ships are often registered) or any other country. There are also examples of discrepancies in the other direction. When the United States donates excess dairy products to a poor African country, the value of the produce shipped may be recorded by the United States at the artificially high price it uses in its domestic agricultural support program, while the recipient country may record the value of the goods received at the much lower price of the world market.

- On the capital account, capital inflows are credits (like exports of stocks, bonds, etc.); capital outflows are debits (like imports of stocks, bonds, etc.).
- On the official reserve transactions account, reserve losses are credits (like exports of gold, foreign currencies, etc.); reserve gains are debits (imports of gold, foreign currencies, etc.).
- Every autonomous debit (e.g., a merchandise import) must have an accommodating credit (e.g., an inflow of short-term capital to pay for the import), and vice versa.

For each of the following transactions indicate (a) on which account the debit occurs, and (b) on which account the credit occurs. Your choices are merchandise, services, income transfers, direct investment, long-term capital, short-term capital, and official reserve transactions. Also, in each case indicate (c) the effect on the current account balance ($+$, 0, or $-$) and (d) the effect on the overall balance of payments ($+$, 0, or $-$). Answer only for the transaction specified; do not assume that the recipients of payments from abroad necessarily exchange foreign currency with the central bank as you would if capital flows were assumed zero. (The United States is the domestic country.)

1. U.S. imports BMWs from Germany, pays by check in marks.
2. U.S. exports grain to Japan, is paid by check in dollars.
3. U.S. imports coffee from Brazil, agrees to pay in dollars three months later.
4. U.S. tourists spend francs in Paris.
5. Mexico buys locomotives from U.S. firm, which agrees to let the Mexicans pay in dollars eighteen months later.
6. German firms and banks, because they are accumulating more dollars than they want or than U.S. banks will accept, turn them in to the Federal Reserve Board, which agrees to give them marks.
7. U.S. investor buys a Canadian 2-year treasury bond, pays by check.
8. U.S. firm builds a factory in Mexico, pays for land, local labor, and so on, in pesos.
9. U.S. government sends foreign aid to Pakistan, which Pakistanis hold in the form of dollars.
10. China buys nuclear reactors from the U.S. government, pays in gold. (No central bank is involved.)
11. Portuguese immigrant sends money back to his family in Lisbon in the form of a ten-year U.S. savings bond.
12. U.S. firm receives profits in the form of pesos from the factory it previously built in Mexico.
13. Dutch holding company buys a controlling interest in an American firm, pays in dollars.
14. U.S. ship is leased to carry beef from Australia to U.K. Payment is in dollars.
15. Federal Reserve Board sells gold to support the value of the dollar.

2. We hear of financial transfers to "launder" illegally acquired funds. For example, a South American smuggler might deposit income from illegal exports in a Miami bank, and arrange for the bank to relend it to the smuggler to invest in a legitimate activity.

   a. How would this transaction appear in the U.S. balance of payments accounts if it were recorded correctly? How would it appear in the accounts of the South American country?

   b. What error will it create in the accounts if the exporter's claim on the Miami bank is not recorded in the exporter's home country, but the other transactions are recorded? (This could be the case if the commodity exported is legal, but the exporter leaves the dollar proceeds in the Miami bank to evade taxes.) What will this do to the worldwide current account discrepancy?

c. What error will be created in the two countries' accounts if the exporter's claim on the bank is not recorded in either country (but the export is reported in both)? (To minimize the chances of getting caught, the exporter simply fails to inform the Miami bank that he or she is not a U.S. citizen.) What would this error do to the worldwide current account discrepancy?

SUGGESTIONS FOR FURTHER READING

Kester, Anne, and Robert Baldwin. *Behind the Numbers: U.S. Trade in the World Economy* (Washington, D.C.: National Research Council, National Academy Press, 1991). How should the U.S. address growing measurement errors in the balance of payments statistics?

17

THE FOREIGN EXCHANGE MARKET AND TRADE ELASTICITIES

The foreign exchange market is where domestic money (for example, dollars) is traded for foreign money (for example, pounds sterling). The exchange rate is usually defined as the price of foreign currency in terms of domestic, though it could as easily have been the reverse,[1] and this convention will be followed here. Note that a *depreciation*, a decrease in the value of the domestic currency, is an *increase* in the exchange rate, because it is an increase in the price of foreign currency. Some find it counterintuitive that a decrease in the value of the currency is called an increase in the exchange rate. Yet just as economists often talk about an increase in the prices of commodities (inflation) rather than the equivalent depreciation of money's purchasing power over commodities, so it is often intuitive to talk about an increase in the price of foreign currency rather than the equivalent decrease in the value of the domestic currency. In any case, this is the standard way of defining the exchange rate.

It is simplifying to speak of "*the* exchange rate" facing a country. In reality, each country has many exchange rates, one for every other currency in the world. The United States, for example, has the dollar/mark rate, the dollar/yen rate, the dollar/pound rate, and so on. Although these exchange rates tend to be highly correlated, the measure of the movements in the home country's currency depends on which exchange rate is used. To get a good idea of the value of the currency overall, it is necessary to use an exchange rate index, known as the *effective exchange rate*, which computes a weighted average of the exchange rates against the other individual countries. Typically the weights used are the countries' shares in trade.

[1] In the United Kingdom, for example, the practice is to speak in terms of the dollar/pound rate, an exception to the general rule because the pound is the domestic currency.

17.1 THE FLOW OF SUPPLY AND DEMAND FOR FOREIGN EXCHANGE

We can think of the supply and demand for foreign exchange or foreign currency as functions of the currency's price—the exchange rate—just as with any commodity. Unless otherwise specified, supply and demand refer to private sources (i.e., transactions on the current account and private capital account, not official reserve transactions by the central bank). In Figure 17.1 the supply curve and demand curve are (for the moment) simply assumed to slope the conventional ways: upward and downward, respectively.

The behavior of the exchange rate varies considerably depending on which *regime* is in effect: floating exchange rates or fixed exchange rates. Under pure floating, the exchange rate is whatever it must be to equilibrate supply and demand in the private market. Consider an increase in the demand for foreign exchange, an outward shift of the curve in Figure 17.1(a) from D to D'. Such an outward shift in the demand for foreign currency could result, for example, from an increase in demand for imports (as will soon be seen) or from an increase in investors' demand for foreign assets (as Part V will show). Under floating, the increased demand for foreign currency causes an increase in its price, the exchange rate, just as an increase in demand for a commodity causes an increase in the price of the commodity.

With a completely fixed or "pegged" exchange rate, on the other hand, the central bank stands ready to buy or sell foreign currency whenever private supply and demand

---

FIGURE 17.1 Increase in Demand for Foreign Currency

When the demand for foreign currency shifts out from D to D', the result depends on the exchange rate regime. Panel (a) illustrates a floating exchange rate: An increase in the price of foreign currency is necessary to equilibrate the private market. Panel (b) illustrates a fixed exchange rate: The central bank intervenes by supplying the excess amount demanded out of its foreign exchange reserves.

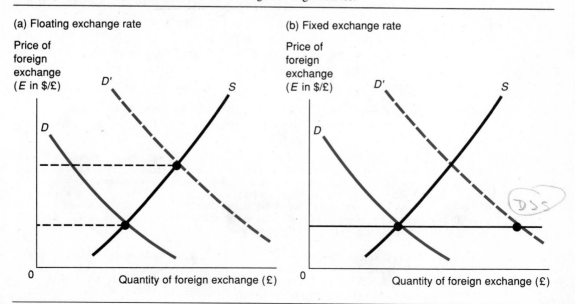

(a) Floating exchange rate

(b) Fixed exchange rate

are not equal at the fixed rate. The official exchange rate would only by coincidence be the rate that precisely equates private supply and demand. Under this regime, an increase in demand, illustrated in Figure 17.1(b), would result in an excess demand for foreign currency that must be met by central bank sales of foreign currency. From the discussion of the balance of payments accounts, it is clear that the country runs a balance of payments deficit. The central bank keeps the domestic currency from depreciating by buying up the excess supply. Obviously, the central bank can continue this only as long as it has foreign exchange reserves. (The other country's central bank also could use its own currency to buy up the unwanted domestic currency, if it were willing to do so.) There are policy changes (which will be examined later) that the domestic government can make to reduce the deficit instead of financing it, but such policies generally take time to have an effect. If the deficit continues, eventually the central bank will run out of foreign exchange reserves and be forced to withdraw support from the domestic currency.[2] The central bank must then either (1) set a new, higher exchange rate at which it will stand ready to sell foreign exchange from then on, or (2) cease foreign exchange operations and allow the market to determine the rate. The first option constitutes a *devaluation* of the currency, the second the floating of the currency.[3]

Deriving Supply and Demand for Foreign Exchange from Exports and Imports

What determines the supply and demand for foreign exchange? Three assumptions together will provide a preliminary answer to this question.

Assumption 1.   Assume (until Part V) that *there are no net capital flows* ($KA = 0$). Thus, the private supply and demand for foreign exchange are determined entirely by the trade account. Most of the results in this part of the book would be unaffected if it were assumed that capital flows were constant or exogenous, without necessarily being zero. In the 1950s, capital flows indeed consisted largely of government loans (for example, the Marshall Plan) and foreign direct investments that were not very responsive to short-term factors such as the interest rate.

Furthermore, assume now that two goods are traded: an importable good and an exportable good. Thus, the first assumption is that the balance of payments is simply sales of the export minus spending on the import.

Assumption 2.   Assume (through the remainder of this chapter) that *domestic residents look only at prices expressed in domestic currency*. Thus, in the case of domestic

---

[2] If the central bank's level of reserves is beginning to run low enough, speculators will see what is coming (a devaluation), and will seek to trade in domestic currency in exchange for foreign currency, in order to protect themselves from the former's expected loss in value. The central bank may very quickly lose very large amounts of its foreign exchange reserves in such an episode, which is known as a *speculative attack*. The effort to defend the fixed exchange rate usually proves to be futile, and the authorities are forced to abandon the rate earlier than they would in the absence of the speculative attack, or else face the loss of all their reserves. This was the proximate cause, for example, of the end of the Bretton Woods system.

[3] The appendix to the present chapter shows how stability in the foreign exchange market depends on the slopes of the supply and demand curves in Figure 17.1(a). This analysis holds whether or not the curves are derived from exports and imports, as in the next subsection. Chapter 21 will discuss the mechanics of how foreign exchange is actually bought and sold under the floating rate system, most of it by banks.

consumers, the demand for imports depends only on the price of the import expressed in domestic currency. In the case of domestic firms, the supply of exports depends only on the price of the export expressed in domestic currency. Similarly, assume that *foreign residents look only at prices expressed in foreign currency* when choosing the supply of imports to the home country (in the case of foreign firms) or the demand for the home country's exports (in the case of foreign consumers). Changes in demand due to changes in income are ignored. This assumption, representing the defining characteristic of the "elasticity approach" to devaluation, will be relaxed in Chapter 18.

Assumption 3. Finally, assume for now that firms set a price and then meet any forthcoming demand. In other words, assume that *supply is infinitely elastic.* This assumption can be regarded as a "Keynesian" special case that is a realistic description of the short run. In light of Assumption 2, the price at which domestic firms supply exportables infinitely elastically must be set in domestic currency—call it *P*—and the price at which foreign firms supply the home country importables must be set in foreign currency—call it *P**. Assumption 3, as well, will later be relaxed.

By Assumption 3, output levels are determined by demand. The demand for imports, M_D, is a decreasing function of the imports price expressed in domestic currency, which is the fixed price in foreign currency times the exchange rate.

$$M = M_D(E\overline{P}^*)$$

If a Range Rover costs £20,000 and the exchange rate is \$2.00/£, then the price to an American is (\$2.00/£)(£20,000) = \$40,000. Americans will buy fewer Range Rovers when the dollar price goes up, without distinguishing whether it is the exchange rate or the pound price that has changed. Figure 17.2 graphs prices in terms of foreign currency, to facilitate calculation of export revenue and import spending. Thus, the import demand curve is drawn for a given exchange rate, *E*. A change in *E* would shift the entire M_D curve. The demand for exports, X_D, is a decreasing function of their price expressed in foreign currency, which is the fixed price in domestic currency divided by the exchange rate.

$$X = X_D(\overline{P}/E)$$

If a Ford costs \$20,000 and the exchange rate is \$2.00/£, then the price to a Britisher is \$20,000/(2.00/£) = £10,000. Britishers will buy fewer Fords when the pound price goes up, regardless of whether it is the dollar price that rose or the exchange rate that fell.

A devaluation, an increase in *E*, lowers the price of exports to foreigners. This is a movement down the curve in Figure 17.2(b), increasing the quantity of exports demanded, X_D in Figure 17.2(b). The devaluation also raises the price of imports to domestic residents, reducing their demand, M_D. This is represented in Figure 17.2(a) as a proportionate downward shift of the entire import demand curve, because the curve was drawn contingent on the exchange rate.[4]

---

[4] If the vertical axes had been expressed in domestic currency instead of foreign currency, the devaluation would have been a *movement* (up) *along* the import demand curve and an (upward) *shift of* the export demand curve, instead of the other way around. (The effect on the quantities would have been the same as in Figure 17.2.) The general rule is that a devaluation is a *movement along* the curve that describes the behavior of the people (domestic or foreign residents) whose currency is on the vertical axis; it *shifts* the curve that describes the behavior of the people whose currency is not on the axis.

FIGURE 17.2   Effect of a Devaluation on Trade

Panel (a) shows how a devaluation lowers the quantity of imports. Panel (b) shows how the devaluation raises the quantity of exports. The effects on import *spending* and export *revenue*, respectively, are shown by the areas of the shaded rectangles.

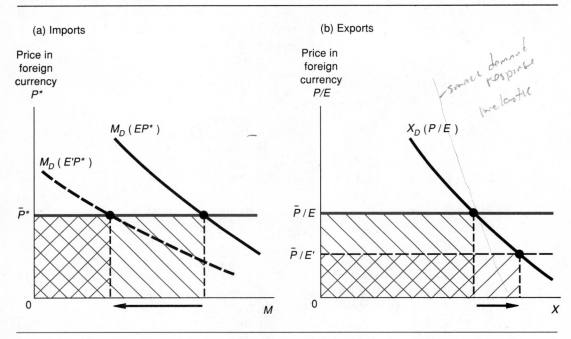

Now consider the market for foreign exchange. Assumption 1 means that the demand for foreign exchange is identical to import spending: In the absence of borrowing, foreign exchange must be obtained on the market to pay for imports. Import spending is quantity times the foreign-currency price. (Even if the imports can be paid for in domestic currency, the foreign exporter is assumed not to hold on to it, which would be a net capital flow, but rather to cash the domestic currency in on the foreign exchange market, again adding to the demand for foreign exchange.) The supply of foreign exchange is identical to export revenue: All foreign exchange earned through exports is cashed in on the foreign exchange market. Export revenue is export quantity times foreign-currency price. (Again, even if exports earn domestic currency, the foreigner must obtain the currency on the foreign exchange market, thus adding to the supply of the foreign country's currency.) So the demand for foreign currency prior to the devaluation is P^*M, the shaded rectangular area in Figure 17.2(a), and the supply is $(P/E)X$, the area in Figure 17.2(b). The net supply of foreign exchange is

$$(\overline{P}/E)X - \overline{P}^*M$$

which is also the trade balance measured in foreign currency, TB^*.

The appendix to this chapter considers the question of stability in the foreign exchange market: "Does an increase in the exchange rate reduce the net demand for foreign exchange?'' This question is identical to the question, ''Does a devaluation improve the trade balance?'' The two questions are the same because no capital flows have been assumed. Domestic consumers cannot borrow abroad to get the foreign exchange they need for imports, so the trade balance is the same as the net supply of foreign exchange. We will now derive the condition under which the answer to the two questions is ''yes.''

The Marshall-Lerner Condition

The effect of a devaluation on the trade balance can be decomposed into three factors. (1) A devaluation reduces the real quantity of imports (the number of Range Rovers imported, in the example) and, because their nominal price is fixed in foreign currency, unambiguously reduces the amount of foreign exchange spent on imports. The rectangular area in Figure 17.2(a) unambiguously shrinks. This factor helps the trade balance. (2) The devaluation also increases the real quantity of exports. This factor also helps the trade balance. (3) However, any given quantity of exports earns less foreign exchange than before, because their nominal price is set in domestic currency. This factor *hurts* the trade balance.

The net effect on foreign-currency export revenue is ambiguous. The size of the rectangular area in Figure 17.21(b) may either increase or decrease, depending on the elasticity of export demand. If the demand response (factor 2) is small enough, export revenue may actually fall. This will be the case if the elasticity of export demand is less than 1. The case just described, in which an increase in the price of foreign exchange reduces the total foreign currency earned from exports, is the case of a backward-bending supply curve for foreign exchange, as in Figures 17.A.1(b) and 17.A.1(c) in the appendix. Export revenue could fall, and yet be outweighed by a reduction in imports, so that the total trade balance would still improve. However, if the demand response on the import side (factor 1) is also small enough, the trade balance will actually worsen: The net supply of foreign exchange will fall. (This is the case when the foreign exchange market is unstable, the third case illustrated in Figure 17.A.1(c) in the appendix.)

At this point a fourth assumption is added to those required by the elasticities approach.

Assumption 4.   Assume that *the economy is initially in a position of balanced trade* ($TB = 0$). Given this, the necessary and sufficient condition for the devaluation to improve the trade balance, or for the foreign exchange market to be stable, is the Marshall-Lerner condition. The supplement to Chapter 4 includes a derivation of the Marshall-Lerner condition. Here, with price levels fixed in each country, the exchange rate plays the role of the price of foreign goods in terms of domestic. The condition is

$$\epsilon_X + \epsilon_M > 1$$

where ϵ_X and ϵ_M are the elasticities of demand for exports and imports, respectively. For example, if exports have an elasticity of exactly 1, a devaluation leaves export revenue unchanged in foreign currency (the second and third factors just described cancel out); then, if import demand has any elasticity, the devaluation reduces imports, thereby improving the trade balance. Alternatively, if imports are more-than-unit elastic and exports have any elasticity, or if both elasticities are greater than one-half, then the third factor previously described will be outweighed by the first two and the trade balance again will improve.[5]

We have discussed the supply and demand for foreign exchange, but we could as easily have discussed the demand and supply of *domestic* exchange. Assuming again that the starting point is a position of balanced trade, the Marshall-Lerner condition applies unchanged to the question of the trade balance expressed in domestic currency.[6]

The model can be generalized in two directions. First, Assumption 4 can be relaxed. In particular, note that in practice a country seldom devalues unless it starts from a position of deficit, rather than balanced trade: $TB < 0$, or $EP^*M > PX$. Now, it makes a difference whether the trade balance is measured in terms of domestic currency or foreign currency. If trade is measured in terms of domestic currency, the necessary condition for a devaluation to improve the trade balance is more stringent: The elasticities must be higher than those given by the Marshall-Lerner condition.[7] The economic reason is that, given the relatively large initial value for imports M, the valuation effect on import spending is more negative. For example, the export elasticity could be as high as 1, and yet if the import elasticity—even though positive—is not high enough, the trade balance could worsen. A 10 percent devaluation may raise exports 10 percent, yet this accomplishes little if exports initially were a small number; meanwhile, the already-large import bill increases by almost 10 percent.

Another generalization involves relaxing Assumption 3—that firms exhibit infinitely elastic supply. Figure 17.3 illustrates this general case. Prices are no longer exogenously fixed. True, a devaluation still shifts the import demand curve and the export supply curve (which was a horizontal line in Figure 17.2) down. In addition, it remains true that import spending falls, and the effect on export revenue is ambiguous, since any given quantity of exports translates into a smaller value when expressed in foreign currency. Thus, the basic conclusions are similar, but the relevant condition necessary for the trade balance to improve includes supply as well as demand elasticities.[8]

According to "general equilibrium theory," consumer demand should be a function not of nominal prices, but of *relative prices and real income*. The elasticities approach is frequently criticized for the partial equilibrium nature of Assumption 1. ("Partial equilibrium" means that some important variables are held constant.) For example, an increase in demand for a country's exports should raise its real income, thus raising its demand for imports, but in the elasticities model there are no such effects. Chapter

---

[5] The proof of the Marshall-Lerner condition in the present context (i.e., where the exchange rate takes the role of the relative price) is given in the supplement to this chapter.

[6] The proof of the Marshall-Lerner condition in terms of domestic currency is left to the student, in Problem 5 at the end of the chapter.

[7] You are asked to show this in Problem 5b at the end of the chapter.

[8] See Problem 6 at the end of the chapter.

FIGURE 17.3   Effect of a Devaluation with Less Than Infinitely Elastic Supply

The devaluation can lower prices when expressed in foreign currency. Panel (a) shows the effect on imports, and (b) on exports.

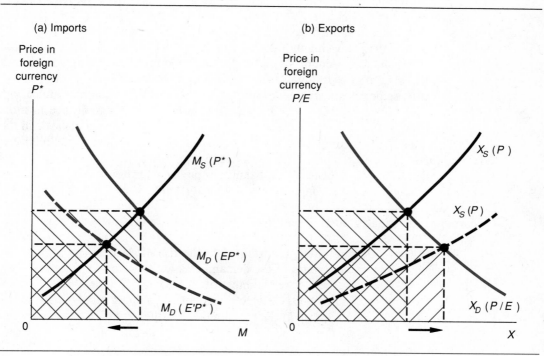

18 begins to remedy this deficiency by introducing income as a variable in the import demand function.[9]

17.2 EMPIRICAL EFFECTS OF DEVALUATION ON THE TRADE BALANCE

Clearly, much depends on the magnitude of the import and export elasticities. Are they large enough in practice for a devaluation to improve the trade balance? It is now time to turn to the empirical evidence.

[9] Restrictive conditions under which the elasticities approach is theoretically correct after all are adduced by Rudiger Dornbusch, "Exchange Rates and Fiscal Policy in a Popular Model of International Trade," *American Economic Review*, (December 1975). These conditions include the requirement that exports and imports are a sufficiently small proportion of income relative to non-traded goods. In general, however, a devaluation has further effects beyond those covered in this chapter, via the relative price of non-traded goods, as will be seen in Chapter 21. The partial equilibrium nature of the elasticities approach was also shown by Ronald Jones, "Stability Conditions in International Trade: A General Equilibrium Analysis," *International Economic Review* 2(2) (May 1961): 199–209.

Elasticity Pessimism

In the 1940s a view known as elasticity pessimism arose, suggesting that actual trade elasticities were too low to satisfy the Marshall-Lerner condition. Several factors contributed to this view. First, floating exchange rates in the 1930s were unstable, in that they were highly variable. The Appendix to this chapter shows that the Marshall-Lerner condition is also the necessary condition for a stable foreign exchange market under floating rates. Thus, highly variable exchange rates seemed to imply low trade elasticities. Second, many countries on fixed exchange rates found their trade balance in fact worsening after a devaluation, rather than improving.

Both of these points are still made with respect to the current floating-rate period. The second point acquired new force when oil assumed such significance in most countries' imports after 1973. Because the demand for oil is relatively inelastic in the short run, many small countries discovered that a devaluation against the dollar just raised their oil import bill proportionately, when expressed in domestic currency, thus worsening their trade balance. When balance of payments problems drive a country to borrow money from the International Monetary Fund, banks and other lenders, the Fund usually asks—among other policy changes—that the country devalue its currency; the country often argues that its elasticities are too low for a devaluation to help.

A third factor that originally contributed to the rise of elasticity pessimism was that early econometric estimates of the demand elasticities were low, frequently less than one-half. However, there were a number of problems with these estimates. They ignored the possible simultaneous existence of an upward-sloping supply relationship, problems of aggregation, errors in the measurement of the variables, and the crucial role of *time*.[10] Some studies measure only relatively short-run elasticities, but there is abundant evidence that the factor of time is important. Elasticities are higher in the long run, which makes the Marshall-Lerner condition more likely to hold.

The J-Curve

Some studies that allow for lags of import demand in response to changes in relative prices have found that only about 50 percent of the full quantity adjustment takes place in the first three years, and 90 percent in the first five years.[11] For example, although the dollar began its long steady appreciation in 1980, U.S. exports did not fall absolutely until 1982. The trade deficit set a record in that year, which approximately doubled in 1983 and doubled again in 1984. The magnitude of these deficits is attributed primarily to the continued appreciation of the dollar. The dollar peaked in March 1985 and then depreciated over the subsequent two years, but because of these lags, the effect on the quantities of exports and imports did not begin to show

---

[10] Faulty measurement of prices is particularly common in foreign trade. For example, importers in some countries "underinvoice," that is, understate the price of their imports, so as to minimize the import duty they must pay. Also, where laws require exporters to turn over all their foreign exchange earnings to the government, exporters might understate their prices and so retain some of the scarce foreign exchange for themselves. Such demand errors in the price data make it more difficult to discern a relationship.

[11] Helen Junz and Rudolph Rhomberg, "Price Competitiveness in Export Trade Among Industrial Countries," *American Economic Review*, (May 1973).

up until the end of 1986, and the effect on the dollar trade balance did not begin to show up until the end of 1987.

In the case of the 1981–1985 appreciation and 1985–1986 depreciation of the dollar, contrary to what we have assumed, dollar prices of imports did not respond immediately or fully to the exchange rate—because many importers, rather than passing exchange rate changes immediately through to import prices, at first absorbed in their profit margins much of the difference between foreign-currency prices and domestic-currency prices. The delayed pass-through to import prices added an extra lag at the beginning, before the elasticities could even begin to come into play. The case of the United States is unusual in that only a small portion of an exchange rate change tends to be passed through to import prices.

There are a number of reasons why demand elasticities rise over time, and so why the quantities demanded are slow to respond even after the change in the exchange rate is passed through to import prices. First, there is a lag due to imperfect dissemination of information, during which importers recognize that relative prices have changed.

Second, there is a lag in deciding to place a new import order. In the case of firms' imports of inputs, it may take months or years before inventories are depleted or machinery is worn out, and replacements are needed. Also, a firm may be tied to a particular supplier, through implicit or explicit contracts. In the case of consumers' imports, changing habits takes time. For example, when the price of energy jumped upward in 1973, the continued strong demand caused many observers to assert that the energy demand was essentially inelastic. With the passage of time, however, the energy demand fell considerably. The adjustment process required not only overcoming the momentum of old patterns of consumption but also changing where people live and what kind of cars they drive.

Third, after a new import order has been placed, there may be production and delivery lags before it is filled. Much of internationally traded merchandise is still transported by ship, requiring weeks or months in transit. Payment is typically not made before delivery, even though the contract may have been signed months earlier.

The fourth reason why trade quantities respond more fully with the passage of time, and the reason that can potentially draw out the process the longest, is that producers sometimes relocate their factories in the country where costs are lower because of an exchange rate advantage, regardless of whether it is the home country of the producer or the country where the goods are sold. For example, when the dollar appreciated so greatly in 1981–1984, some U.S. firms, such as Caterpillar Tractor, that had previously been producing in the United States and exporting with great success, found that they were losing out to competition from countries with lower cost. (Japan's Komatsu was Caterpillar's biggest competitor.) To compete more effectively, Caterpillar moved some operations to other countries with lower-valued currencies, such as Scotland. Thus, sales in the world market that were previously counted under U.S. exports came to be counted under Scotland's exports.

Similarly, when the dollar underwent a large depreciation in 1985–1986, the big cost disadvantage to producing in the United States disappeared and companies began to move their operations back home. Foreign-based corporations—for example, Japanese auto companies—also increased their operations in the United States, as the cheaper dollar reduced relative costs. Thus, sales in the United States that were previously counted as U.S. imports ceased to be counted. In fact, some production that was moved to the United States began to be exported.

Obviously, the response of export and import quantities after an exchange rate change is greater in the long run than in the short run, as companies are able to relocate their plant and equipment. The transition costs are large. For this reason, a company is unlikely to relocate until the change in the exchange rate has endured enough to convince the company that the fluctuation is not transitory. Such an endurance test may take as long as five or ten years. Indeed, even after the exchange rate has returned to old levels, a company that decided to move operations abroad when the dollar was high might never move back, after having incurred the costs of moving. The word *hysteresis* is used to describe such not-easily-reversed reactions.

The tendency of the elasticities to rise over time results in the commonly observed phenomenon of the J-curve. The trade balance following a devaluation is observed first to worsen, then to improve, in the "J"-like pattern of Figure 17.4. (The figure assumes an initial trade balance of zero.) At the moment of the devaluation, quantities have had no time to adjust, and the Marshall-Lerner condition fails. In fact, if quantities do not respond at all initially, then only the negative valuation effect remains: The trade balance worsens by the initial level of exports times the percentage decrease in their foreign currency value caused by the devaluation.[12] However, as time passes, export demand begins to pick up and import demand begins to fall. A point is reached

---

[12] If it takes time before the exchange rate change is passed through to domestic prices of imports, as described in reference to the United States in the 1980s, the initial worsening in the trade balance is spread over a longer period; the down-sweep of the J would then be more round than shown in the figure. This is the major reason why even the *real* U.S. trade balance, that is, the physical quantities of exports and imports, did not begin to improve until the end of 1986, 1 1/2 years after the dollar depreciation began.

FIGURE 17.4   The J-Curve

In the aftermath of a devaluation, the trade balance (1) initially worsens, due to the perverse valuation effect, (2) gradually improves over time as the elasticities rise, and (3) surpasses its starting point when the Marshall-Lerner condition is satisfied.

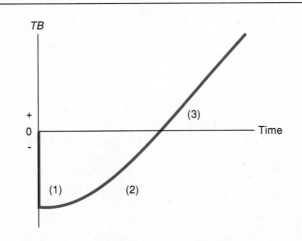

where the curve crosses the zero axis, which means that the elasticities are high enough to sum to one and the trade balance is back at zero. After that point, the Marshall-Lerner condition holds and the trade balance moves into surplus. The surplus must run for a while if the reserves accumulated are to outweigh the reserves lost during the initial period of deficit.

All this assumes that exporters in the home country continue to supply whatever quantity is demanded at the same fixed price. This may get increasingly harder, especially if they are operating close to full capacity. The exporters in the devaluing country will be tempted to raise their prices in response to the increasing demand. Alternatively, their workers may demand higher wages in response to the greater cost of imported consumer goods, and the firms will be "forced" to pass through the higher labor costs in the form of higher prices. However, we will stay with the fixed-price assumption until Chapter 19.

17.3 SUMMARY

The exchange rate is defined as the price of foreign exchange in terms of domestic currency. Under a floating-exchange-rate system, the central bank does not intervene in the foreign exchange market, and the exchange rate is determined by supply and demand in the market: An increase in the demand for foreign exchange causes an increase in the price of foreign exchange (a depreciation of the domestic currency). Under a fixed-exchange-rate system, an increase in demand for foreign exchange means that the central bank has to supply the difference—the net demand for foreign exchange, which is the balance of payments deficit—out of its foreign exchange reserves.

In this chapter the first and simplest model of what determines the balance of payments was adopted. Part IV does not include capital flows. This chapter looked only at the effect of the exchange rate on the trade balance, holding constant the level of income, interest rate, price level, and other macroeconomic variables that will be introduced in subsequent chapters. A devaluation of the currency (or, under floating exchange rates, a depreciation) increases the quantity of exports demanded by foreign residents and decreases the quantity of imports, working to improve the trade balance. A third effect works to worsen the trade balance, however: the higher cost in domestic currency of any given quantity of imports that have prices set in foreign currency. Only if the sum of the import and export elasticities is high enough, as in the Marshall-Lerner condition, will the quantity effects dominate and the trade balance improve after the devaluation.

Empirically, the elasticities do appear to be high enough for a devaluation to improve the trade balance, but only after enough time has passed. In the short run, the trade balance often worsens, which gives rise to the "J-curve" pattern of response.

CHAPTER PROBLEMS

1. The newspaper reports that the dollar/mark exchange rate has risen.
   a. Does this news mean that the value of the dollar has risen or fallen? The value of the mark?
   b. Does this mean that the dollar/yen rate is more likely to have gone up than down?

   c. Does this mean that the mark/yen rate is more likely to have gone up than down? (*Hint:* If neither the dollar/yen rate nor the mark/yen rate has changed, what does that imply for the dollar/mark rate?)

2. Assume that the United States is currently exporting 10 million calculators at a price of $10 apiece and importing .002 million BMWs at a price of 100,000 DM apiece, and that the current exchange rate is 50 cents per mark. Calculate in a table the effect of a 10 percent devaluation of the dollar on each of twelve variables under each of four sets of assumptions about the elasticities (assuming infinitely elastic supply and no income effects). You may round off.

	Before the Devaluation		After the 10% Devaluation			
	(a)		(b)	(c)	(d)	(e)
		Export Elasticity:	0	$\frac{1}{2}$	1	4
		Import Elasticity:	0	0	$\frac{1}{2}$	1
(1) Export quantity	10m					
(2) Import quantity	.002m					
Expressed in $ { (3) Export price	$10					
(4) Import price						
(5) Export earnings						
(6) Import spending						
(7) Trade balance						
Expressed in DM { (8) Export price						
(9) Import price	100,000 DM					
(10) Export earnings						
(11) Import spending						
(12) Trade balance						

3. a. In the example from Problem 2, comment on the trade balances in (b) and (c) versus those in (d) and (e).
   b. In which case is spending on imports in dollars very close to what it was before the devaluation? Why?
   c. In which case are earnings from exports in marks very close to what they were before the devaluation? Why?
   d. Starting from a position of importing .003 million BMWs, with everything else remaining the same, what would be the initial trade balance in dollars? For given elasticities, for example, (d), would the devaluation cause the trade balance to improve (i.e., the trade deficit decrease) by more than, less than, or the same amount as in Problem 2? (A numerical answer is not necessary, but is fine if you can't do it intuitively.)

4. The trade balance expressed in domestic currency, with prices normalized to 1, is $TB = X(E) - EM(E)$.
   a. Illustrate the effect of a devaluation graphically, that is, repeat Figure 17.2, but with domestic-currency prices on the vertical axis.
   b. If the import elasticity is greater than 1 and the export elasticity is greater than 0, then the Marshall-Lerner condition holds. Is this condition sufficient to imply that TB, the

trade balance expressed in domestic currency, improves? (You may assume the starting point is $TB = 0$.) Explain why, in terms of export revenue and import spending.

Extra Credit

5. a. If you know calculus, prove that the Marshall-Lerner condition is still the correct condition necessary and sufficient for a devaluation to improve TB, the trade balance expressed in domestic currency, starting from $TB = 0$.
   b. Starting from $TB < 0$, is the Marshall-Lerner condition too strong or too weak for a devaluation to improve the trade balance?
   c. Assume we start from a deficit and the elasticities sum approximately to one. From (b) we know that dTB/dE and dTB^*/dE are of opposite sign. At the same time we know that a devaluation that brings the country back from deficit to zero trade balance must do so in either currency, because $TB^* = 0$ implies $(E)(TB^*) = 0$. How do you reconcile this apparent contradiction?
6. It is possible (if old-fashioned) to stay within the "partial equilibrium" elasticities approach and yet relax the assumption that supply is infinitely elastic. The Bickerdicke-Robinson-Metzler condition for a devaluation to improve the trade balance is

$$\frac{\epsilon_M \epsilon_X (1 + \sigma_M + \sigma_X) - \sigma_M \sigma_X (1 - \epsilon_M - \epsilon_X)}{(\sigma_M + \epsilon_M)(\sigma_X + \epsilon_X)} > 0$$

where σ_M and σ_X are the supply elasticities of imports and exports, respectively.
   a. Prove that in the limit, as σ_M and σ_X go to infinity, the formula reduces to the Marshall-Lerner condition.
   b. Does the presence of the supply elasticity terms make the condition more or less stringent than the Marshall-Lerner condition?

SUGGESTIONS FOR FURTHER READING

Bergsten, C. Fred, ed. *International Adjustment and Financing, The Lessons of 1985–1991* (Washington: Institute for International Economics, 1991). Did the dollar depreciation reduce international trade imbalances as promised?

Bryant, Ralph, Gerald Holtham, and Peter Hooper, eds. *External Deficits and the Dollar: The Pit and the Pendulum* (Washington: Brookings Institution, 1988). Analyzes the causes of the U.S. trade deficits of the 1980s.

Feldstein, Martin, "Correcting the U.S. Trade Deficit," *Foreign Affairs* (Spring 1987). The former Chairman of the Council of Economic Advisors explains his widely cited view that the dollar must depreciate further to eliminate the trade deficit.

Hooper, Peter, and Catherine Mann, *The Emergence and Persistence of the U.S. External Imbalance: 1980–87*, Studies in International Finance, (Princeton: International Finance Section, 1989). Authoritative analysis of the causes of the U.S. trade deficit in the 1980s.

Leamer, Edward, and Robert Stern, *Quantitative International Economics* (Boston: Allyn and Bacon, 1970). Chapter 2 explains the econometric methodology of estimating trade elasticities.

McCulloch, Rachel, "Trade Deficits, Industrial Competitiveness, and the Japanese," *California Management Review*, 27(2): 140–156. Reprinted in Robert Baldwin and J. David Richardson, eds., *International Trade and Finance*, 3rd ed. (Boston: Little Brown, 1986). Are U.S. trade deficits due to declining American "competitiveness," to unfair Japanese trade policies, or to macroeconomic factors?

APPENDIX:
STABILITY OF THE FOREIGN EXCHANGE MARKET

The focus now turns from the comparative statics of the foreign exchange market, considered in Section 17.1, to the question of stability under a floating exchange rate. The theoretical question of whether a market equilibrium is stable (as in Chapter 4) is not the same as the question of whether the market price moves around a lot. The theoretical question is the following: If an equilibrium price is displaced slightly, will it tend to return to its original value?

Think of foreign exchange traders as individuals who buy and sell foreign exchange with each other on the floor of centralized exchanges in New York and elsewhere or, in the case of the trading divisions of banks, on a network of telephones and computer terminals. Assume that whenever foreign exchange traders find that demand exceeds supply, they raise the exchange rate; whenever supply exceeds demand, they lower it. Consider the following three cases.

1. Assume that the demand curve slopes down and the supply curve slopes up, as in Figure 17.A.1a. If the curves are derived from import spending and export earnings, respectively, this first case is the one where the elasticity of demand for exports is greater than one. In response to an increase in demand, from D to D', the traders raise the exchange rate. This raises export revenue, reduces the excess demand for foreign exchange, and causes a move toward the new equilibrium. The market is stable.

2. Next, assume that the demand curve slopes down and the supply curve slopes down also, but more steeply, as in Figure 17.A.1b. Again, in response to an increase in demand, the traders raise the exchange rate, causing a move toward equilibrium. Again the market is stable. This is the case where the elasticity of demand for exports is less than one (so the increase in the exchange rate *lowers* export revenue) but the sum of the two elasticities is nevertheless high enough to satisfy the Marshall-Lerner condition.

3. Finally, assume that both curves slope down, but the supply curve is less steep, as in Figure 17.A.1c. This is the case where the Marshall-Lerner condition fails. This time, when the traders respond to the increase in demand by raising the exchange rate, they cause a move *away* from the new equilibrium. At the higher exchange rate, excess demand is even greater, so the traders raise the exchange rate again, and the situation is farther still from equilibrium. The market is unstable. These examples show that the required condition for stability is that the supply curve slopes upward or, if sloping downward, is steeper than the demand curve.

As a practical matter, a floating exchange rate usually will not shoot off to infinity. One possibility is that there are two stable equilibria surrounding an unstable one, much as is shown in Figure 4.A.1. Even if the market is stable in the technical sense, however, it may be "unstable" in the sense that the market-clearing price is highly variable. Very small changes in demand may produce large jumps in the exchange rate. High variability in the exchange rate may create uncertainty and imply high costs for importers and exporters. These are often cited as an argument against floating exchange rates. This chapter showed that if the demands for exports and imports are relatively inelastic, then the curves representing the supply and demand for foreign exchange will be relatively steep. Resulting exchange rates may be highly variable if the exchange rate is called upon to clear the trade balance.[13]

---

[13] It has been argued that the trade elasticities facing the United States may have become lower in the 1980s than they were previously. The reason is that exchange rates move around more than they used to, so that firms now regard a given movement in the exchange rate as less likely to be permanent and thus pay less attention to it (much as insects become more resistant to some insecticides, the more they are used). Paul Krugman, *Exchange Rate Instability* (Cambridge, MA: M.I.T. Press, 1988). With lower trade elasticities, it is then hypothesized that larger swings in exchange rates will be required to eliminate. given trade imbalances than used to be necessary.

FIGURE 17.A.1 Stability in the Foreign Exchange Market

The market is stable if the increase in the price of foreign exchange that results from an increase in demand for foreign exchange works to eliminate the excess demand. In cases (a) and (b) the market is stable, but in (c) it is not.

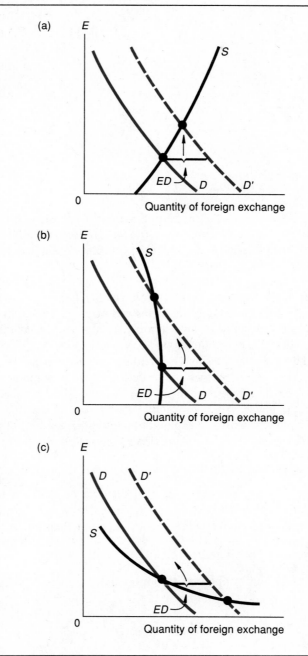

18

NATIONAL INCOME AND THE TRADE BALANCE

This chapter will examine the interaction of income and the trade balance. We use the simple Keynesian multiplier model familiar from introductory macroeconomic textbooks but open up the model to international trade. This will turn out to make quite a difference.

Here "Keynesian" means simply that prices are assumed to be fixed (in terms of the currency of the producing country, as in Chapter 17) and that changes in demand are therefore reflected in output instead of price. This assumption is realistic for the short run, especially in an economy with unemployed labor and excess capacity. Empirical observation shows that prices are not perfectly flexible (to come in Chapter 19). In addition to the short-run realism, a second reason for continuing to make this assumption here concerns the structure of the remainder of the book. Chapter 17 focused on the effect of changes in the exchange rate. This chapter adds the effect of changes in income. Only in Chapter 19 will we be ready for changes in the price level, followed by international capital flows and other factors. The introduction of all these variables at once would be quite confusing, so they will be introduced one at a time.

18.1 THE SMALL-COUNTRY KEYNESIAN MODEL

This section recognizes that import demand depends on more than just a relative price term, as in Chapter 17 (which is just the exchange rate, E, given the maintained assumption that suppliers fix prices in terms of their own currencies). It also depends on income, Y.

$$M = M_d(E, Y) \tag{18.1}$$

The marginal propensity to import out of income[1] is represented by m.

$$M = \overline{M} + mY \tag{18.2}$$

---

[1] From this point on imports will be defined in domestic units, not foreign units. In other words, if the economy is the United States, M (like Y and the other variables) is expressed in dollars. Because the price level is assumed to be fixed, this is the same as expressing everything in units of U.S. output: number of automobiles, bushels of wheat, and so on.

This linear import function is analogous to the standard Keynesian consumption function

$$C = \overline{C} + cY \tag{18.3}$$

where c is the marginal propensity to consume. The essence of the Keynesian consumption function is that households' consumption increases, but less than proportionately, in response to an increase in households' disposable income.

Equation 18.2 does not show the exchange rate explicitly because the first step will be to consider the case of a fixed exchange rate. Although most major industrialized countries have highly variable exchange rates, there are several reasons for beginning with the case of a fixed exchange rate. First, it will provide a greater understanding of the 1950s and 1960s, when almost all countries had pegged exchange rates. Second, it will aid in understanding the many small or less-developed countries that, today, still have pegged exchange rates. Most Western European countries sought to stabilize their exchange rates vis-à-vis each other in the 1980s, under the European Monetary System, and are currently undertaking steps to tie their currencies even more tightly together. Third, it will make it easier to evaluate the frequently heard proposals to restore stability in exchange rates—ambitious schemes for a complete return to fixed rates (supported by proponents of a gold standard), as well as more moderate proposals for target zones.[2] Finally, with the exchange rate held fixed, it is easier to understand how the economy operates—before proceeding to what happens when the exchange rate can change.[3]

The demand for exports (foreigners' imports) should be a function (analogous to Equation 18.1) of relative prices and *their* income, Y^*.

$$X = X_d(E, Y^*) \tag{18.4}$$

Most countries are small enough that, although developments in the rest of the world have important implications for the domestic economy, any impact of the domestic economy on the rest of the world can be safely ignored. Thus, this section begins with the "Keynesian small-country assumption" that foreign income is exogenous. (This is as opposed to the very different *classical* small-country assumption, which is that relative prices are exogenous. That assumption is ruled out when export prices are set in domestic currency.) Now we have the simplified export demand function,

$$X = X_d(E)$$

or, staying with a fixed exchange rate for the moment,

$$X = \overline{X} \tag{18.5}$$

In other words, exports are given exogenously. Thus, from Equations 18.2 and 18.5, the trade balance is given by

$$TB = X - M = \overline{X} - (\overline{M} + mY) \tag{18.6}$$

---

[2] Studies of proposals to stabilize exchange rates include Ronald McKinnon, "Monetary and Exchange Rate Policies for International Financial Stability," *Journal of Economic Perspectives* (Winter 1988): 83–103; and John Williamson, *The Exchange Rate System*, Institute for International Economics (June, 1985).

[3] Each of these motivations—particularly the goals of understanding the early postwar period and LDCs—applies also to the assumption of no capital movements, which will be maintained through Chapter 20.

The definition of equilibrium in the Keynesian model is that output supplied, Y, is equal to output demanded. In the closed economy, demand comes from three sources: consumption by households (C), investment by firms (I),[4] and spending on various goods and services by the government (G). In the simple Keynesian version with which this chapter begins, investment, like government expenditure, is taken to be exogenous (which is shown by a bar over the letter) even though consumption is endogenous. The open economy factors a fourth source of net demand for domestic goods—that coming from foreign residents—into the total demand for domestic goods. Net foreign demand for domestic goods is, of course, the trade balance, or net exports ($TB = X - M$). So the equilibrium condition is as follows:

$$Y = C + I + G + X - M$$
$$= \overline{C} + cY + \overline{I} + \overline{G} + \overline{X} - (\overline{M} + mY)$$

Solving for the equilibrium level of income,

$$Y = \frac{\overline{A} + \overline{X} - \overline{M}}{s + m} \tag{18.7}$$

where for notational simplicity we have defined the exogenous component of aggregate demand as $\overline{A} \equiv \overline{C} + \overline{I} + \overline{G}$, and the marginal propensity to save as $s \equiv 1 - c$. (That part of each additional dollar of income that is not consumed must be saved.

The multiplier for government spending, or for other autonomous components of spending, is as follows:

$$\frac{\Delta Y}{\Delta A} = \frac{1}{s + m} \tag{18.8}$$

In practice, s and m are fractions totaling less than 1. Thus, the multiplier is greater than 1: An autonomous increase in spending of a given amount raises income by a greater amount. The explanation is that those who produce the goods and services to which the spending goes see an increase in their income and so raise their spending, which in turn raises the incomes of other producers, who raise their spending, and so forth. The infinite series has a finite sum for the same reason as in a closed economy: At each round of spending some "leaks out" of the system through saving, so each round is smaller than the previous round. Notice that in the special case of a closed economy, where $m = 0$, the multiplier reduces to the familiar $(1/s)$ or $1/(1 - c)$. In general, however, the open-economy multiplier is less than $(1/s)$, because there are two leakages from the spending stream: through imports as well as through saving.

To look at the Keynesian model graphically, it will be easier to work in terms of saving, equal to disposable income minus consumption, than in terms of consumption itself. To do so, it first must be recognized that, besides decomposing GNP into the sectors to which the output is sold ($C + I + G + X - M$), an alternative is to

[4] Investment includes not only additions to plant, equipment, and inventories by firms, but also residential construction by households.

decompose income from the viewpoint of those who earn it: consumption (C), saving (S), and taxes (T).[5]

$$C + S + T = \text{GNP}$$
$$= C + I + G + X - M$$

Subtract C from both sides and rearrange.

$$S + (T - G) - I = X - M$$

Think of the government budget surplus ($T - G$) as government saving or, inasmuch as the number is often negative, think of the government budget deficit ($G - T$) as government "dissaving." Define total national saving as $NS = S + (T - G)$. Then the equation is

$$NS - I = TB \qquad (18.9)$$

Equation 18.9 is described as follows: National saving exceeds investment by an amount equal to the trade balance, which is the rate of accumulation of claims on the rest of the world. Intuitively all national saving, NS (whatever is left over after financing the government), goes into building up either the stock of capital or the stock of foreign claims. For example, in the 1980s, a very low rate of U.S. national saving, consisting especially of high federal budget deficits, translated into very high deficits in the trade balance and current account balance. Ever since 1917, the United States had been accumulating claims on the rest of the world, but a few years of enormous deficits in the 1980s wiped out that accumulated investment position. The official statistics show that the country passed from net creditor status to net debtor status in early 1985. Italy, which has also had very large government budget deficits, by contrast has a high rate of private saving to offset them. As a result, Italy's overall NS is higher than the United States' (as a share of GNP) and its trade deficit is much closer to zero.

Another way of viewing Equation 18.9 is in terms of the funds available to finance domestic investment, I. Investment must be financed either by the nation's domestically generated savings, NS, or by funds made available for the use of the home country by the rest of the world, that is, foreign lending to finance the domestic trade deficit. In Italy most investment is financed domestically, while in the United States more investment is in effect financed abroad.

The "saving gap" ($NS - I$) is an increasing function of Y, with slope s, as in Figure 18.1: Higher income means higher saving.[6] The other line in the figure represents the trade balance ($X - M$), a decreasing function of Y, with slope $-m$: Higher income means higher imports. Equation 18.9 states that equilibrium occurs where the two lines cross. Figure 18.1 shows the initial intersection as occurring when savings equal

[5] If we wish to include government transfers such as unemployment compensation and social security in the model, then T should be defined as taxes *net* of these transfers.

[6] If it is recognized that tax revenues (T) depend positively on income, then the slope of NS is higher than s (by the amount of the marginal tax rate). For simplicity in what follows, taxes (T) will be treated as if they were exogenous. The marginal tax rate is introduced, however, in Chapter Problem 4.

FIGURE 18.1   Fiscal Expansion in the Keynesian Model

The Saving-Investment line slopes up because higher income, Y, means higher national savings, NS. An increase in government spending of G shifts the line down. Point D is the new intersection with the $X - M$ line.

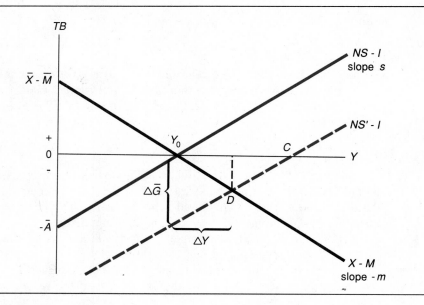

investment and exports equal imports, but the choice of this location is arbitrary; equilibrium could occur as easily above or below the zero axis.

Let us consider as our first experiment a fiscal expansion $\Delta \overline{G}$. It shifts the $NS - I$ line down by that amount, because $NS = S + (T - G)$. It raises equilibrium income to point D, the intersection on the new line $NS' - I$ in Figure 18.1. Notice again that the change in income is less than in the closed-economy case: A closed-economy equilibrium would occur where the $NS' - I$ line crosses the zero axis at point C, which lies further to the right than D.

The multiplier formulas could also be derived geometrically. In the closed economy [Figure 18.2(a)], $\Delta G = s\Delta Y$ because s is the slope of the hypotenuse of the triangle. In the open economy [Figure 18.2(b)], $\Delta G = s\Delta Y + m\Delta Y = (s + m)\Delta Y$ because s is the slope of the hypotenuse of the lower triangle and m the slope of the hypotenuse of the upper triangle. Again, $\Delta Y/\Delta G$, the multiplier effect on income, is smaller in the open economy than in the closed economy because there is leakage through imports in addition to the leakage through savings.

The convenient aspect of this graph is that it depicts not only income, Y, measured on the horizontal axis, but also the trade balance, $TB = X - M$, measured on the vertical axis. In Figure 18.1, the fiscal expansion pushes the trade balance into deficit because the higher income draws in more imports. Algebraically,

$$\Delta TB = -\Delta M = -m\Delta Y$$

FIGURE 18.2   Closed-Economy and Open-Economy Fiscal Multipliers

The fiscal multiplier is the ratio of the change in income, Y, to the change in government spending, G. It is smaller for an open economy (b) than for a closed economy (a) because spending leaks out through higher imports rather than only through higher saving.

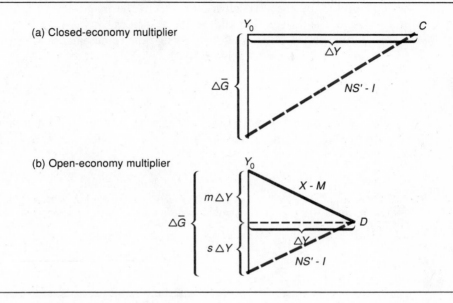

(a) Closed-economy multiplier

(b) Open-economy multiplier

Now use the multiplier, from Equation 18.8, to substitute for ΔY.

$$\Delta TB = -\frac{m}{s + m} \Delta \overline{G} \qquad (18.10)$$

Equation 18.10 shows that the effect of a fiscal expansion on the trade balance is clearly negative.

  An illustration of this relationship occurred in 1976–1978, when the United States followed expansionary policies that stimulated recovery from the 1974–1975 recession. As a consequence, the expansion moved the country from a position of trade balance surplus to one of deficit. In 1980, as the United States contracted sharply, imports fell and the balance on goods and services went back into surplus. In 1983, a strong fiscal expansion consisting of tax cuts and increased military spending again propelled the economy into a strong expansion. Partly as a consequence, imports soon soared and the trade balance registered the record deficits mentioned previously. In the U.S. recession of 1990–1991, the trade balance again improved.

  Another example of this relationship was the situation in France in 1981. When the Socialists came to power under François Mitterand in 1981, they initiated an expansion that led to higher imports and a balance of payments problem.

  Now consider the effect of a devaluation. Assume that the Marshall-Lerner condition is satisfied. This analysis could apply equally well to other exogenous sources of improvement in the trade balance, such as the imposition of a tariff, a shift in tastes away from foreign goods, or an exogenous increase in foreign income. Algebraically, these changes are represented as an increase in $\overline{X} - \overline{M}$. Graphically, they are represented as an upward shift in the $X - M$ line by the distance $\Delta\overline{X}$ in Figure 18.3.[7] If changes in income could somehow be ignored (as in Chapter 17), the trade balance would improve by the vertical distance $\Delta\overline{X}$. (The magnitude $\Delta\overline{X}$ depends on the magnitude of the devaluation and of the elasticities.)

In addition to the obvious effect of raising the trade balance, however, the devaluation stimulates income. Algebraically,

$$\Delta Y = \frac{1}{s + m} \Delta\overline{X}$$

The higher income means higher imports, according to the marginal propensity to import, and so the improvement in the trade balance is less than if income were held fixed.

[7] The exogenous increase in net exports is represented by $\Delta\overline{X}$ for simplicity, even though it could be a fall in imports as well as a rise in exports. One might want to think of the special case where the import elasticity is 1.0, so total import spending is unaffected by changes in the exchange rate, and the entire improvement in the dollar trade balance comes from export earnings X.

FIGURE 18.3   Devaluation in the Keynesian Model

The devaluation shifts up the $X - M$ line (assuming the Marshall-Lerner condition is met). Income, Y, rises. The trade balance also rises, but less than it would if income were held constant.

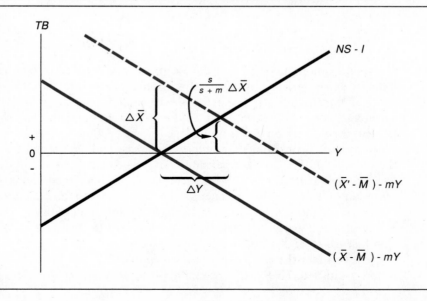

$$\Delta TB = \Delta \overline{X} - m\Delta Y$$

$$= \Delta \overline{X} - m\,\frac{1}{s+m}\,\Delta \overline{X} \qquad (18.11)$$

$$= \frac{s}{s+m}\,\Delta \overline{X}$$

The key point is that $\dfrac{s}{s+m} < 1$; the trade balance improves by less than the full exogenous increase in net exports because of the higher imports that are drawn in by higher income. Yet the effect is still positive: Imports do not go up as much as exports.

The Transfer Problem

The Keynesian model can be applied to an old problem in international macroeconomics. As was discussed in Chapter 4, the transfer problem originated with war reparations payments, such as those from Germany to France after World War I, yet it can be applied whenever there is a transfer of income from one country to another. More recent examples abound. The OPEC price increase at the end of 1973 could be modeled as an exogenous transfer from the oil-importing countries to OPEC. The 1982 LDC debt crisis could be modeled as an exogenous transfer from the debtor countries to the creditor countries (the increase in debt-service requirements).

The important issue is the extent to which the recipient country will spend the transfer on imports and the transferor will cut back on its imports. Recall that the current account is defined as the balance of trade on goods and services *plus* transfers. Let us consider a small country that has just received a transfer. If it spends the entire transfer on imports and its trade balance worsens by precisely this amount, then the overall current account is unchanged at the existing exchange rate. In this case, the transfer is considered "fully effected," meaning that the *financial* transfer leads to the intended matching transfer of *real goods*. If the recipient spends most of the money on its *own* goods, its overall current account will improve at the old exchange rate—the negative effect on the trade balance will be smaller than the transfer. In this case the transfer is "undereffected."

We saw in the model of Chapter 4 that a transfer may or may not be undereffected. In the Keynesian model, however, the transfer is *necessarily* undereffected.[8] The change in the trade balance is less than the transfer. Why?

Recall the identity that output less consumption is given by

$$Y - C = I + G + X - M$$

All output that is not consumed is either saved or goes to the transfer:[9]

$$S + T = I + G + X - M$$

---

[8] The first to show this was not Keynes, but Lloyd Metzler, "The Transfer Problem Reconsidered," *Journal of Political Economy*, (June 1942): 397–414.

[9] Here it is assumed for simplicity of notation that the money for the transfer is raised by taxation of the public, T. In the recipient country, the proceeds are distributed to the public as a tax cut.

Given that G and I are exogenous, it follows that the trade balance $X - M$ would decrease by exactly the transfer ΔT if S were unchanged. In a Keynesian model, however, the increase in disposable income causes a rise in saving. Therefore the trade balance falls by less than the transfer.

The point can be demonstrated graphically in Figure 18.4 by putting disposable income, Y_d, on the horizontal axis in place of total income, Y (because both saving and imports depend on Y_d, not Y, once the distinction is acknowledged). The current account, CA, depends on disposable income with the same slope as the trade balance ($-m$, the marginal propensity to import). If there is no transfer, then the trade balance coincides with the current account. Consider, however, the case of a country that has to undergo a negative transfer, say a post-1982 debtor that is required to make large debt-service payments. An outward transfer ΔT shifts the CA line down. Saving-investment equilibrium is given where the new CA line intersects $NS - I$, at point R. At this lower level of disposable income, imports have fallen and the trade balance is in surplus at point S. Yet the trade balance, TB, is not as large as the outward transfer, ΔT. The overall current account, $CA - TB - \Delta T$, necessarily goes into deficit at point R. So long as the $NS - I$ curve is not flat—that is, so long as the marginal propensity to save is greater than zero—the transfer is undereffected.

FIGURE 18.4   Transfer Worsens the Total Current Account

A transfer to a foreign country improves the domestic trade balance, $X - M$, because imports fall when domestic disposable income falls and exports rise when foreign disposable income rises. Nevertheless, in the Keynesian model the overall current account, $X - M - T$, falls.

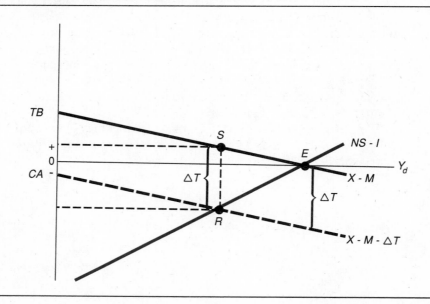

18.2 THE TWO-COUNTRY KEYNESIAN MODEL

So far we have assumed exports to be exogenous with respect to domestic income. This section relaxes that assumption, taking into account how exports depend on developments in the rest of the world. In the examination of a large country, developments in the rest of the world, in turn, depend on developments in the home country. The country and the rest of the world are interdependent.[10]

Repercussion Effects

If income, Y^*, increases in the foreign country, foreigners import more from the home country.

$$X = \overline{X} + m^*Y^*$$

The foreign marginal propensity to import is represented by m^*. In Equation 18.7, $\overline{X}$ is replaced by the new expression for exports, resulting in the new formula for equilibrium income.

$$Y = \frac{\overline{A} + \overline{X} - \overline{M} + m^*Y^*}{s + m} \tag{18.12}$$

Obviously, domestic income depends positively on foreign income. Figure 18.5 graphs this relationship. The slope $\Delta Y/\Delta Y^*$ is $m^*/(s + m)$, which is less than 1 unless the foreign country is very much more open to imports than the home country.

---

[10] The seminal work on the Keynesian two-country model was done by a Nobel Prize winner: James Meade, *The Theory of International Economic Policy*, Vol. I: The Balance of Payments (London, Oxford University Press, 1952), Chapters 4 and 5.

FIGURE 18.5   Transmission from Foreign Income to Domestic Income

When foreign income, Y^*, rises, imports into the foreign country rise, that is, exports from the domestic country rise; as a result, domestic income, Y, also rises.

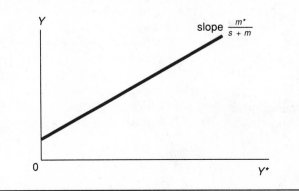

The relationship explains how expansion in one country is transmitted to its trading partners through the trade balance. For example, in 1977–1978 the United States pressured Germany and Japan to expand their economies. The plan, known as the "locomotive theory," was to help pull the rest of the world out of recession. In 1983–1984, the United States was the locomotive pulling the world out of recession. In 1985–1987, the United States was once again pressuring Germany and Japan to help out by expanding. In each episode, the smaller, more open, and less-developed countries were anxious for the big three industrialized countries to expand, because the economies of the smaller countries depend particularly on foreign income. Of course, contraction is transmitted across countries, as well. The prime example is the Great Depression of the 1930s, when declining income in one country resulted in declining imports, and thus declining income, among its trading partners.

Now we are ready to drop the assumption that foreign income is exogenous. The rationale has been that the domestic economy is too small to affect foreign income. However, when a country as large as the United States (or Germany or Japan) expands, and consequently imports more from its trading partners, those imports are a large enough component of world demand to raise income significantly, and thus expenditure, among the trading partners. Then a large enough fraction of the foreign expenditure is spent on domestic goods that foreigners' imports from the home country in turn rise significantly. In other words, part of the spending that leaks out, flows back. The result is that income increases in the home country, the one that began the expansion, by more than one would expect based on its spending alone (the model in Section 18.1). The feedback through the trading partner can be called a repercussion effect. To model the repercussion effect, we now consider two countries that are each large enough to affect the other's income.

To make foreign income endogenous, the foreign country is modeled analogously to the home country, recognizing that its exports are the home country's imports, a function $\overline{M} + mY$ of the home country's income; similarly, its imports are the home country's exports, a function $\overline{X} + m^*Y^*$ of the foreign country's income. Then the solution for equilibrium foreign income is

$$Y^* = \frac{\overline{A}^* + \overline{M} + mY - \overline{X}}{s^* + m^*} \qquad (18.13)$$

where $\overline{A}^*$ represents the autonomous components of foreign expenditure and s^* the foreign marginal propensity to save. This is simply the other country's version of Equation 18.12. The graph of foreign income as a function of domestic income is analogous to Figure 18.5. It must be turned on its side in Figure 18.6 to show it on the same axes as Figure 18.5. Equilibrium income for each country is indicated graphically at the intersection of the two lines, point B.

Equilibrium income for each country is indicated algebraically by solving the two equations simultaneously.[11] The multiplier for a domestic expansion turns out to be

[11] You are asked to do this in Problem 6a at the end of the chapter.

$$\frac{\Delta Y}{\Delta A} = \frac{1}{s + m - \dfrac{m^*m}{s^* + m^*}}$$ (18.14)

The important point is that it exceeds the small-country multiplier $1/(s + m)$ derived in Section 18.1. In terms of Figure 18.6, the expansion results in a move to the new *intersection at D'*, whereas the intersection would be at point D if foreign income Y^* were kept constant. Why? Some of the expenditure stream that "leaks out" as imports now returns as exports. For every dollar increase in domestic income, imports go up by m; because the other country's exports go up by m, its income goes up by $m/(s^* + m^*)$, and so it imports move from the home country. This effect is represented by the term $(m^*m)/(s^* + m^*)$ in Equation 18.14. Because it reduces the denominator, it increases the multiplier. The small-country multiplier is the special case where a negligibly small proportion of foreign expenditure falls on domestic goods ($m^* = 0$), so this term can be ignored. On the other hand, the multiplier is necessarily *less* than the closed-economy multiplier, $1/s$ (as long as m and $s^* > 0$). It is impossible that *all* the expenditure that leaks out through the trade balance will come back, as long as any foreign income is saved.

FIGURE 18.6   Simultaneous Solution for Both Countries' Incomes

A relationship runs from domestic income, Y, to foreign income, Y^*. A domestic expansion shifts the domestic line up so that the new intersection occurs at D'. The increase in Y is greater than in the small-country model—which ignored the repercussion effect of higher income abroad (point D).

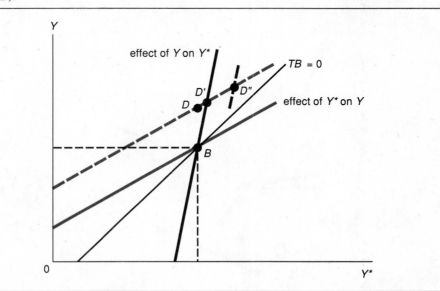

We can continue to use the $X - M = NS - I$ graph of Figure 18.1. Because

$$\Delta TB = m^*\Delta Y^* - m\Delta Y \tag{18.15}$$

we can substitute

$$\Delta Y^* = \frac{m}{s^* + m^*}\Delta Y$$

from Equation 18.13 and so find the new slope of the $X - M$ line:

$$\Delta TB = \left(m^*\frac{m}{s^* + m^*} - m\right)\Delta Y$$

$$\frac{\Delta TB}{\Delta Y} = -\frac{ms^*}{s^* + m^*} \tag{18.16}$$

Notice that the slope is close to $-m$, the slope of the TB line in the small-country case, if m^* is small. In general, however, the slope is less in absolute value than $-m$, as evidenced in Figure 18.7. It is possible to see from the intersection with the $NS' - I$ line at point D' the proposition already shown algebraically: An expansion (rightward shift of $NS - I$) has a greater effect on domestic income in the two-country model than in the small-country model because there is less leakage through the trade deficit.

FIGURE 18.7   Repercussion Effect Increases the Multiplier

The effect of a fiscal expansion is greater in the two-country model (point D') than in the small-country model (point D), because some of the spending that leaks out of the country through imports leaks back in through exports.

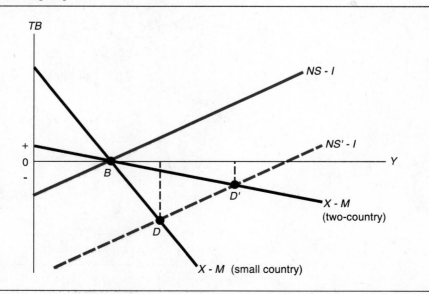

Empirical Evidence on Growth and Import Elasticities

Figure 18.8 shows the U.S. balances, on merchandise trade, goods and services, and current account (as shares of GDP) for the last 40 years. In the 1970s the trade balance went into deficit for the first time since World War II, but the current account balance still averaged zero. The trade deficit re-emerged in much greater magnitude in 1983. By 1987, on a goods and services basis it had reached more than ten times the record deficits of the late 1970s. On a merchandise basis it reached the unheard-of level of $160 billion. (Counting imports on a c.i.f. basis, the newspapers reported a 1987 trade deficit of $170 billion.) These very large trade deficits generated tremendous concern throughout the U.S. economy. They represented lost output and employment in those sectors or firms that in the past had relied on overseas customers for a rising share of their sales, as well as in those sectors or firms that faced tough competition from rapidly rising imports. Furthermore, the equally enormous current account deficits meant that the country was going rapidly into debt to foreign investors. Congressmen and editorial writers railed against the deficits, many adopting protectionist views for the first time. Why did these deficits occur?

Part of the answer is that in 1983–1984, the United States was expanding more rapidly than its trading partners were. As is seen from Equation 18.15, if the home country expands faster than the foreign country, the home country suffers a worsening in its trade balance—assuming the two countries have the same marginal propensity

FIGURE 18.8   Current Account Balance, Balance on Goods, Services, and Income, and Merchandise Balance Expressed as a Percentage of GDP (1946–1991)

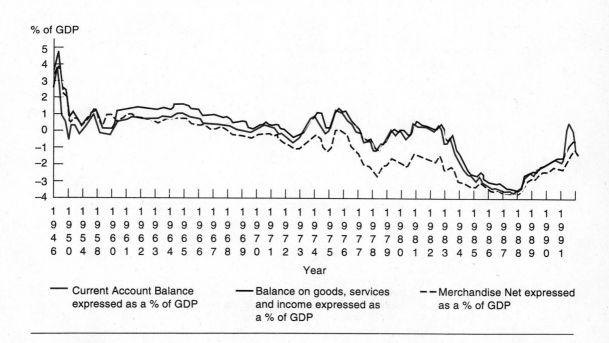

to import. The point is also illustrated in Figure 18.6. The line that gives U.S. income, Y (as a function of foreign income, Y^*), shifts out faster than the line that gives foreign income (as a function of U.S. income). In terms of Equations 18.12 and 18.13, $\overline{A}$ increases faster than $\overline{A}^*$. The intersection moves up faster than it moves to the right. As at point D'', it lies above the trade balance equilibrium schedule (the slope of which is m^*/m, as we can see by setting $\Delta TB = 0$ in Equation 18.15). The United States goes into deficit because its imports go up faster than those of its trading partners.

What happens if both countries expand together, if income growth is equal? If the two countries have the same elasticities of import demand with respect to income, then there is no effect on the trade balance. The elasticity of demand with respect to income is the marginal propensity to import ($m = \Delta M/\Delta Y$) divided by the ratio of imports to income: $(\Delta M/\Delta Y)/(M/Y)$. The usual way to think of it is the *percentage* change in imports that results from a given *percentage* change in income: $(\Delta M/M)/(\Delta Y/Y)$. There is some evidence that imports are more elastic with respect to income in the United States than they are in many of its trading partners.[12] The same may be true of some European countries. The LDCs (and perhaps Japan) are the countries with lower income elasticities. One possible explanation is that U.S. private-sector demand for imports is in truth no more income-elastic than LDC demand, but that LDCs have relatively constant trade barriers, while the United States tends to erect protectionist barriers to LDC products (e.g., steel, textiles, copper, sugar, etc.) during recessions and to remove them during booms, so U.S. import volumes vary considerably as the level of U.S. income varies.

One implication that follows for LDCs and any other countries exporting goods that face highly income-elastic demand is that their incomes tend to be highly procyclical: When the world is in recession, demand for their goods tends to fall more than demand for goods produced by other countries, and so their incomes fall more than proportionately. The high variability in income is particularly severe for LDCs that produce a single commodity, such as copper or oil, that serves as an intermediate input in other countries' production processes with little scope for substitution.

A second implication would also follow if these elasticities were assumed to apply to long-run, as well as short-run, changes in income: There will be a long-run secular trend in the trade balance in favor of these countries, and against the United States and the other producers of manufactured goods facing demand that is less income-elastic. Indeed, this could be part of the explanation for the long-term trend toward deficit in the U.S. trade balance reported in Figure 18.8.

On the other hand, it has been suggested that the long-term income elasticities are in reality not as high as the short-term elasticities, when care is taken to separate long-term growth in income from exogenous trends such as increased supply capacity in the Newly Industrialized Countries (NICs). Some have discerned a secular trend in trade adverse to the raw materials produced by LDCs.[13] The NICs, such as Hong

---

[12] Some empirical evidence on how the income elasticities of import demand vary across countries is presented by Hendrik Houthakker and Stephen Magee, "Income and Price Elasticities in World Trade," *Review of Economics and Statistics* 51(2) (May 1969), pp. 111–124.

[13] Some studies, however, show only a slight negative trend in the prices of primary commodities relative to those of manufactured goods for the twentieth century, or none at all. John Cuddington and Carlos Urzúa, "Trends and Cycles in the Net Barter Terms of Trade: A New Approach," *Economic Journal*, 99, June 1989, pp. 426–442.

Kong, Singapore, South Korea, and Taiwan,[14] have achieved strong trade positions through policies of growth led by exports, not of traditional raw materials, but of manufactured goods (beginning with labor-intensive manufactures such as textiles and electronics). The pattern that fits them best may be the product cycle.[15] For any given technology, a secular trend exists against the United States and in favor of those countries able to adopt the technology to produce the same goods at lower cost. Yet the United States and other technological leaders have always innovated, staying one step ahead—at least until recently.

Estimates show that the average U.S. growth rate over the entire period 1980–1987, only slightly higher than trading partners' growth rates, accounts for a relatively small part of the $150 billion deterioration in the U.S. trade balance over this period. The big 1981–1985 appreciation of the dollar had the greatest effect, as is seen in Chapter 17. However, an adverse trend relative to the NICs and other LDCs is also important, especially if we consider the effects of the international debt problem that surfaced in 1982: The United States lost $20 billion in net exports to Latin America from 1981 to 1983.

18.3 TRANSMISSION OF DISTURBANCES

Section 18.2 showed how income in one country depends on income in the rest of the world through the trade balance. The effect varies considerably, depending on what is assumed about the exchange rate. This section compares the two exchange rate regimes, fixed and floating, with respect to the international transmission of economic disturbances.

Transmission Under Fixed Exchange Rates

The starting point here will be the regime of fixed exchange rates. For simplicity, return to the small-country model. In other words, ignore any repercussion effects via changes in foreign income. As Equation 18.8 showed, an internal disturbance such as a fall in investment demand, $\Delta \bar{I}$, changes domestic income by

$$\frac{\Delta Y}{\Delta \bar{I}} = \frac{1}{s + m}$$

in the small-country model. Recall that the multiplier is smaller than the closed-economy multiplier because some of the change in aggregate demand leaks out, or is transmitted to the rest of the world. An external disturbance such as a fall in export demand, $\Delta \bar{X}$, changes income by the same amount.

$$\frac{\Delta Y}{\Delta \bar{X}} = \frac{1}{s + m}$$

In this case some of the *foreign* change in aggregate demand is transmitted through the trade balance to the *home* country.

---

[14] These four entities are now sometimes called Newly Industrialized Economies, or NIEs, instead of NICs, in deference to the People's Republic of China, which is set to retake responsibility for the British colony of Hong Kong in 1997 and which has never recognized the independence of Taiwan.

[15] See the discussion of the product cycle in Chapter 9.

The two-country model would serve as well here. The domestic spending multiplier would be a little higher, as in Equation 18.14, because some import leakage returns in the form of exports. The same applies to the export multiplier. The important point is that, in general, under fixed rates disturbances are transmitted positively from the country of origin to the trading partners, via the trade balance.

Transmission Under Floating Exchange Rates

Now assume that the central bank does not participate in the foreign exchange market. Thus, the exchange rate adjusts automatically to ensure $BP = 0$. Continue to assume no capital flows (or transfers), so $TB = 0$ as well. In the case of an internal disturbance, a fall in investment demand, $\Delta \bar{I}$, would cause a fall in income and a consequent trade surplus under a fixed exchange rate. The $S - I - G$ line shifts up, as is seen in Figure 18.8(a). However, under floating exchange rates a surplus is impossible because the central bank is no longer in the business of buying or selling foreign exchange. In response to what would otherwise be an excess supply of foreign currency, the price of foreign currency automatically falls, that is, the domestic currency automatically appreciates. The effect of an appreciation of the currency is that imports are stimulated and exports discouraged, and the $X - M$ line shifts down (assuming the Marshall-Lerner condition is satisfied). The shift will be whatever is required to restore the trade balance to equilibrium. The required change in the exchange rate could be computed if the trade elasticities were known.

Whatever the exchange rate change, the ultimate effect is such that the trade balance remains at zero: $\Delta TB = 0$. From Equation 18.6,

$$\Delta TB = \Delta \overline{X} - m\Delta Y$$

So floating exchange rates imply that

$$\Delta \overline{X} = m\Delta Y$$

the downward shift in the component of net exports attributable to the appreciation must be sufficient to offset the decrease in imports attributable to lower income. To compute the change in income, note that

$$\Delta Y = \frac{\Delta \bar{I} + \Delta \overline{X}}{s + m}$$

$$= \frac{\Delta \bar{I} + m\Delta Y}{s + m}$$

$$\Delta Y = \frac{\Delta \bar{I}}{s}$$

Compare this to the multiplier under fixed rates shown on the preceding page. The internal disturbance has a greater effect under floating rates than under fixed rates. The disturbance induces an exchange rate change that reinforces the effect on aggregate demand. In fact, the disturbance has the full closed-economy multiplier effect. The reason is that when the exchange rate fluctuates to keep the trade balance at zero, it reproduces the effect of a closed economy. All disturbances are "bottled up" inside the country rather than being partially transmitted abroad. The point can also be shown graphically. The $X - M$ line becomes irrelevant. Equilibrium income is determined wherever the $NS - I$ line crosses the zero axis because the floating exchange rate automatically ensures that the $X - M$ line crosses there as well. Because the $NS - I$ line has slope s, a disturbance that shifts it up by $\Delta \bar{I}$ reduces income by $\Delta \bar{I}/s$.

In the case of an external disturbance, a downward shift of the $X - M$ line, as in Figure 18.9(b), would cause a fall in income and a trade deficit under fixed rates. The incipient trade deficit causes the currency to depreciate automatically, however, shifting the $X - M$ line back up until balanced trade is restored. At this point the effect on income is eliminated as well. The floating exchange rate insulates the economy against foreign disturbances. Again, by adjusting to keep the trade balance at zero, it reproduces a closed economy.

To sum up, floating rates (in the absence of capital flows) restrict the effects of disturbances to the country of origin. This result suggests one possible basis on which a country could choose between fixed and floating exchange rates. If the goal is to minimize the variability of domestic output, then the absence of international transmission is desirable to the extent that disturbances originate abroad, because the home country is insulated from them. However, the absence of transmission is undesirable to the extent that disturbances originate domestically; the floating rate

FIGURE 18.9 Insulation Under Floating Exchange Rates

Panel (a) shows how domestic disturbances are "bottled up" inside the country. A fall in investment, I, has a greater effect on income under a floating rate than under a fixed rate, because the currency appreciates and discourages net exports. Panel (b) shows how the country is "insulated" from foreign disturbances. A fall in foreign demand causes the domestic currency to depreciate, which stimulates net exports.

(a) Internal disturbance under floating rates

(b) External disturbance under floating rates

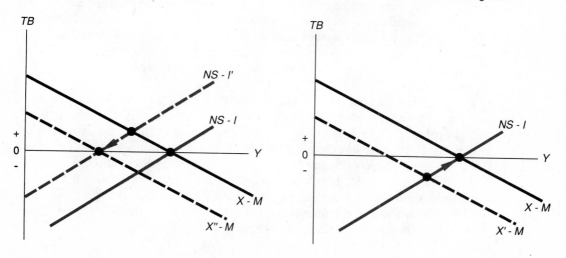

prevents these disturbances from being "passed off" to the rest of the world. On the other hand, if the goal is to allow each country to pursue its own independent policies, then the absence of transmission constitutes an argument for floating exchange rates. In the late 1960s, when the world was still on fixed rates and excessive expansion in the United States was transmitted to the European countries as unwanted inflation, floating rates were suggested as the ideal solution. They would allow each country to pursue its preferred policies independently.

The conclusion that floating rates prevent transmission extends to the two-country model. As long as the trade balance is always zero, income must be determined by domestic demand. Chapter 22, however, will show that this conclusion does not extend to models with capital mobility, because the trade balance need not equal zero. Furthermore, although foreign disturbances have no effect on domestic output and employment in the model of this chapter, they do affect domestic real income. The currency depreciation illustrated in Figure 18.9(b) turns the terms of trade against the home country: The price of imports rises in domestic terms, causing a fall in the real purchasing power of a given quantity of domestic output. Domestic residents will feel poorer even though national output is unchanged. Such changes in the terms of trade can have further implications for the level of spending and other variables; they are considered in the chapter appendix.

18.4 EXPENDITURE-SWITCHING AND EXPENDITURE-REDUCING POLICIES

Sections 18.1 through 18.3 explained the use of the Keynesian model in determining income and the trade balance. This section uses the model to show the most effective ways for government policy-makers to combine the tools at their disposal to achieve their policy goals.

Expenditure-switching policies and expenditure-reducing policies are alternative ways to reduce a trade deficit. Measures to reduce overall expenditure, such as reductions in government expenditure or increases in taxes, work to reduce a trade deficit because some of the eliminated expenditure would have fallen on imports. Conversely, measures to increase expenditure increase the trade deficit, as was evidenced earlier in this chapter (for example, in Figure 18.1 and Equation 18.10). There exist expenditure-reducing policies other than fiscal contraction, including monetary contraction. Monetary policy will be covered following a discussion of expenditure-switching policies.

Expenditure-switching policies are those that, for any given level of expenditure, work to improve the trade balance by switching expenditure away from foreign goods and toward domestic goods. In the case of domestic expenditure, the result is a fall in imports. In the case of expenditure by foreigners, the result is a rise in exports to them. The expenditure-switching policy focused on so far is devaluation, as in Figure 18.3 and Equation 18.11. Expenditure-reducing and expenditure-switching policies are equally valid ways of eliminating a trade deficit. The most important difference between the two is that the former accomplishes this by reducing income and employment, while the latter does so by—or at least with the effect of—raising income and employment.

Types of Expenditure-Switching Policies

There are many possible expenditure-switching policies. One is price deflation, which makes domestic goods more attractive to residents of both countries. In practice, price deflation can usually only be achieved by expenditure reduction (though wage-price controls are an alternate possibility). The period of low income and high un-employment that must be endured before wages and prices begin to come down is usually long and painful. We continue to assume in the Keynesian model that because of the existence of minimum wage laws, unions, contracts, implicit contracts, money illusion—for whatever reasons—wage and price deflation is so difficult in the short run as to be ruled out.

A devaluation might be described as a Keynesian expenditure-switching policy (i.e., one that takes rigid prices as given). Direct trade controls are also Keynesian expenditure-switching policies.

A common form of direct trade control is a tariff, which raises the price of imports, thus discouraging domestic residents from buying them. Export subsidies, which lower the price of exports, so encouraging foreign residents to buy them, are also sometimes used. A uniform 10 percent import tariff combined with a uniform 10 percent export subsidy would have the same effect on the relative prices facing each country as a 10 percent devaluation. The devaluation analysis would apply, in large measure un-changed.

In practice, tariffs and subsidies are enacted more often to help specific industries that are in trouble (or that have sufficient political clout) than to further macro-economic purposes. Pure trade theory provides some persuasive microeconomic ar-guments against them, as is explained in Part III of the text. Nevertheless, these measures are sometimes imposed for macroeconomic reasons. In the 1930s, the United States adopted the Smoot-Hawley tariff in an effort to switch expenditure toward domestic goods generally. Policies of this type, which are designed to switch spending to domestic products at the expense of other countries, are called "beggar-thy-neighbor"[16] The consequences in that case were disastrous, as was seen earlier in this text. Trading partners responded by putting up tariffs of their own to protect their trade balances, and the result was a global collapse in trade. Following World War II, the GATT was set up to negotiate reductions in tariffs. One example of lifting trade restrictions for macroeconomic purposes was European countries in the 1950s, who liberalized in steps when they developed trade surpluses.

Partly as a consequence of the GATT's success, protection has shifted emphasis away from tariffs and toward other direct controls on trade, that is, toward non-tariff barriers. One non-tariff barrier is the quantitative restriction or quota. The United States, for example, has restrictions placed on the quantity of sugar it will import and has persuaded Japan to place so-called "voluntary" quotas on exports of autos and other goods to the United States. These are called voluntary export restraints (VERs). The Japanese, for their part, have long had quotas on agricultural imports. Europe also employs quotas, joining the United States in having quotas on imports of textiles from many countries.

---

[16] "Beggar" is used as a verb here, meaning "to impoverish."

The economic analysis of an import quota is similar to the analysis of a tariff, in that a quota raises the domestic price. The two would be practically equivalent if the government auctioned off the licenses to import, so that the revenue accrued to the domestic government instead of to the importers fortunate enough to get the licenses. In practice, governments rarely auction off quotas. In the case of a tariff, that the revenue goes to the domestic government is an obvious advantage, from the national viewpoint, relative to a voluntary export restraint, where the "revenue" goes to the foreign country. If the alternative is a domestically imposed quota, then the revenue generally accrues to domestic residents, as with a tariff. From a macroeconomic viewpoint, however, there is still an important difference between a tariff, under which the revenue accrues to the domestic government, and a quota, under which the revenue accrues to the domestic private sector. An increase in tariffs, like any tax increase, reduces the private sector's disposable income and constitutes a contractionary fiscal policy (assuming the government does not spend the revenue right away). Thus, it has an expenditure-reducing side in addition to the expenditure-switching side and may have a bigger effect on the trade balance than would a domestically imposed quota.

Another non-tariff barrier used sometimes when a government has a pressing trade balance crisis is advanced deposits on imports. An importer must place on deposit with the government a certain amount of money for a certain length of time, such as six months, without interest. The effect is the same as a tariff equal in amount to the interest on the deposit lost by the importer. If the deposit were refunded only after six months, with the deposit equal to the value of imports and the importer's cost of borrowing 10 percent per annum, the deposit requirement would be equivalent to a 5 percent surcharge on imports. Like a tarriff, this barrier withdraws money from circulation, and thus it has an expenditure-reducing effect in addition to the expenditure-switching effect.

The topic here is barriers to trade; barriers to capital flows will be discussed later. Nevertheless, one device for discouraging the outflow of money bears mentioning: the two-tier exchange rate.

Suppose that Belgium is experiencing a substantial inflow of capital and upward pressure on the price of its currency. Because it wants to avoid worsening its trade balance, as would follow if it revalues the Belgian franc, the central bank maintains its present fixed exchange rate for current-account transactions, but requires parties making capital-account transactions to use the competitive foreign-exchange market. There the exchange rate is left free to find its own level. Those clamoring for Belgian francs to buy Belgian assets, that is, to export capital to Belgium, find the supply limited to the flow of currency made available by Belgians desiring to export capital to their countries. Capital exports and imports would be equated by the market-determined exchange rate for capital transactions, and no *net* international capital transfers could take place. This device could similarly be used to avert a devaluation when a country is experiencing capital outflows. The two-tier foreign-exchange market is difficult to administer because it requires elaborate controls. If the price of Belgian francs is higher in the competitive market for capital-account transactions, those exporting capital to Belgium have an incentive to gain access to its currency at the cheaper rate for current-account transactions. In addition, Belgian importers who must buy foreign exchange at the (for them) less favorable current-account rate have an incentive to sell Belgian francs to buyers in the capital-account market. Controls must keep these parties apart, if the system is to work.

Capital controls can impair economic efficiency because they keep capital from moving to where it earns a higher return. If the difference in returns faced by the lender is also a difference in real social productivity, the control imposes a welfare cost. One cannot be dogmatic, though, about the welfare costs of capital controls, because governments use the interest rate—the return to capital—extensively as a policy variable. When the central bank is influencing the price of credit, the connection between the market price and social productivity of capital is no longer certain.

Another barrier that has been used by LDCs is multiple exchange rates. The government charges a higher price for foreign exchange when it is used to purchase luxury consumer goods than when it is used to purchase, for example, capital goods or—considered most essential of all—spare parts and fuel. Other non-tariff barriers, which are seldom even claimed to be temporary macroeconomic measures, are official preferences in government purchasing, and administrative and technical barriers.

The Swan Diagram

Assume that the government authorities have two policy goals. First, they want to attain external balance: a trade deficit equal to zero. Second, they want to attain internal balance: output equal to full employment or potential output. (The situation in which demand exceeds potential output, $\overline{Y}$, can be considered undesirable because it leads to inflation.) There is a general principal that attaining two different policy goals requires two independent policy tools. In this case the two policy tools are expenditure-switching and expenditure-reducing policies, or, for concreteness, devaluation and government expenditure.[17] Each policy will be considered in isolation before we consider the use of both at once.

As was already seen, government fiscal expansion raises output but worsens the trade balance. If the government were restricted to the use of fiscal policy, this would represent a dilemma. The government could adopt a contractionary fiscal policy to achieve external balance ($TB = 0$) at the expense of unemployment ($Y < \overline{Y}$), at point X in Figure 18.10(a), or could adopt an expansionary fiscal policy to attain internal balance at the expense of a trade deficit ($TB < 0$), at point N. The government cannot, however, attain external and internal balance simultaneously, except by coincidence. Such simultaneous balance demands another policy tool.

A devaluation also raises output, but improves the trade balance. This presents another dilemma—whether to choose a low exchange rate, that is, revalue to achieve internal balance ($Y = \overline{Y}$) at the expense of a trade deficit ($TB < 0$) at point N in Figure 18.10(b), or to choose a high exchange rate, that is, devalue, to achieve external

---

[17] The general principle originated with Jan Tinbergen. The application to the open economy was developed by James Meade. The application of the principle to an economy with international capital mobility, which will be studied in Chapter 22, was developed by Robert Mundell.

balance ($TB = 0$) at the expense of excess demand ($Y > \overline{Y}$) at point B. Obviously, to attain balance in both sectors, both policies must be used together. The case depicted in Figure 18.10 requires an intermediate exchange rate policy together with an intermediate fiscal policy.

Heavy use has been made of Figure 18.10, the diagram of income and the trade balance, with one schedule that holds for a given level of government expenditure and another that holds for a given level of the exchange rate. Now the situation will be inverted, shifting to a diagram of government expenditure and the exchange rate, with one schedule that holds for a given level of income and another that holds for a given level of the trade balance. Same model, new graph.

Assume that, by coincidence, the starting point is a position of both external and internal balance, point A in Figure 18.11(a). To begin, consider external balance. If the government increases its expenditure, it also must devalue in order to maintain external balance, as at point B. Otherwise, it will go into deficit. For trade balance equilibrium to hold, G and E must vary together: Higher expenditure must be accompanied by a higher exchange rate. This means that the combinations of G and E that imply external balance in Figure 18.11(b) are represented by an upward-sloping line: the BB schedule.

FIGURE 18.10   Dilemma: External Balance or Internal Balance?

Panel (a) shows how the government, using just fiscal policy, can attain either a zero trade balance at point X or full employment at N but not both. Panel (b) shows how the government, using just exchange rate policy, again can attain either one goal at B or the other at N but not both.

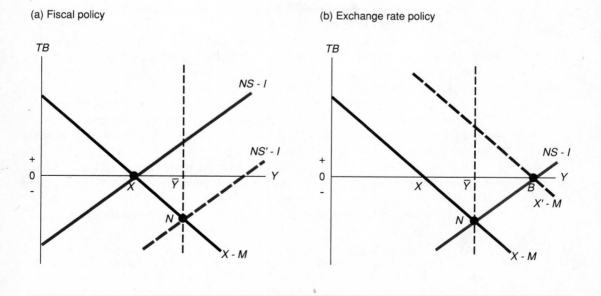

FIGURE 18.11 Policy Combinations That Give External Balance

After a fiscal expansion, there must also be a devaluation if the trade balance is to be restored to its original level. In panel (a), the axes represent the policy goals. In panel (b), the axes represent the policy instruments.

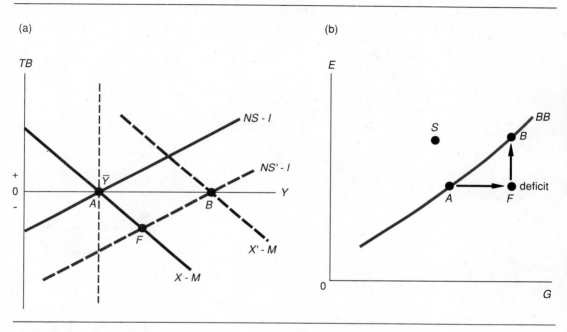

It is quite possible that the economy is at a point off the line *BB*. At any point *F*, below and to the right of *BB*, *E* is too low, or *G* too high, for external balance. This is a point of trade deficit. Total expenditure is too high, or too large a fraction of expenditure falls on foreign goods. It is necessary to reduce expenditure (cut *G*) or switch expenditure toward domestic goods (raise *E*) to return to balanced trade. Similarly, at any point *S*, above and to the left of *BB*, *E* is too high, or *G* too low, for external balance. This is a point of trade surplus. *G* would have to be increased, or *E* reduced, to return to balanced trade. Only under a floating-exchange-rate regime will the economy necessarily be on the *BB* line. In that case, the exchange rate adjusts automatically, so as to maintain an external balance. Under fixed rates it is possible to be anywhere on the graph.

Now consider internal balance. Return in Figure 18.12(a) to point *A* and the exercise of an increase in government expenditure. Now observe, however, that the government will have to *revalue* if it wants to maintain internal balance, as at point *C*. Otherwise, the economy will suffer from excess demand. To stay at the same level of demand, output, and employment, *G* and *E* must vary inversely: Higher expenditure must be accompanied by a lower exchange rate. This result yields the *YY* schedule in Figure 18.12(b). The combinations of *G* and *E* that imply internal balance are represented by a downward-sloping line.

FIGURE 18.12 Policy Combinations That Give Internal Balance

After a fiscal expansion, there must also be a *revaluation* of the currency, if the level of output is to be restored to its original level. In panel (a), the axes represent the policy goals. In panel (b), the axes represent the policy instruments.

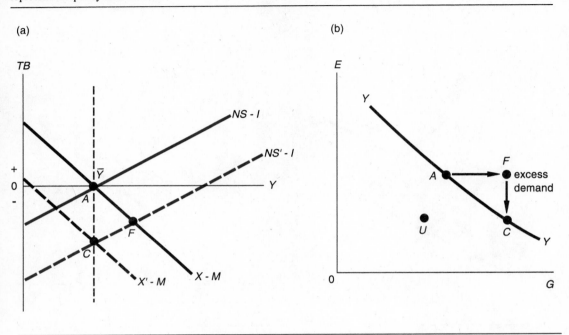

Again, it is perfectly possible that the economy is off the line YY. At any point F above and to the right of YY the exchange rate E is too high, or too large a fraction of expenditure falls on domestic goods. It is necessary to reduce expenditure (cut G) or switch expenditure toward foreign goods (reduce E) if the country is to return to potential output. Similarly, at any point U below and to the left of YY, E is too low, or G is too low, for internal balance. This is a point of excess supply, or unemployment. G or E would have to be increased to return to full employment. In general, there is no reason necessarily to be on the YY line.

Figure 18.13 shows the BB and YY schedules together, in a graph known as the Swan Diagram.[18] There are four zones. Zone I indicates a trade deficit and excess demand, Zone II a deficit and unemployment, Zone III a trade surplus and unemployment, and Zone IV a surplus and excess demand. There is only one point of full equilibrium, A. Again, both tools are needed to attain it. For example, many countries

---

[18] The Swan Diagram was invented by Trevor Swan, "Longer-run Problems of the Balance of Payments," 1955; reprinted by the AEA, op. cit pp. 455–464. It was further developed in W. Max Corden, "The Geometric Representation of Policies to Attain Internal and External Balance," *Review of Economic Studies* 28, (1960), pp. 1–22.

FIGURE 18.13 The Swan Diagram of Internal and External Balance

The BB schedule shows the combinations of government spending, G, and the exchange rate, E, that give the desired trade balance. The YY schedule shows the combinations that give the desired level of output. Only by deliberately using both independent policy instruments could the government attain both policy goals, at point A.

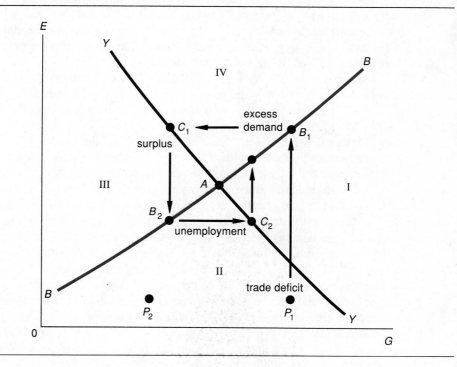

find themselves at a point like P_1: deficit and unemployment. They could raise G to reach full employment at the expense of a greater deficit or cut back G to attain balanced trade at the expense of greater unemployment. The correct strategy is to cut G and devalue, attaining internal and external balance simultaneously. Of course, policy-making is not always this easy in practice. For example, the symptoms at point P_2 are the same, deficit and unemployment, and yet the correct strategy here is to devalue and *raise* G. In practice, this might only be discovered by experimentation: devaluing and then waiting to see what happens before deciding whether to change expenditure.

The Assignment Problem

Imagine a decentralized government in which the central bank determines the exchange rate and the treasury determines fiscal policy, and the two bodies do not coordinate policy effectively. Which agency, the central bank that sets E or the treasury that sets G, should be responsible for external balance and which for internal balance? This question is known as the "assignment problem."

Consider the consequences of assigning external balance to the central bank and internal balance to the treasury. Call this assignment Rule 1. Whenever the trade balance is in deficit, the bank raises E; whenever it is in surplus, the bank lowers E. Whenever output falls short of full employment, the treasury raises G; whenever it exceeds full employment, the treasury lowers G. The analysis will be pursued here in discrete time. Assume that the two agencies take turns. For example, the budget is drawn up and enacted only at yearly intervals, and the exchange rate is changed only in periodic devaluations or revaluations.

Start from point P_1 in Figure 18.13. Let the central bank go first. Because of the trade deficit, Rule 1 tells the bank to devalue until balanced trade is reached, at B_1. Now the stimulus to net exports has moved the economy into the region of excess demand. When it is time to set the annual budget, Rule 1 tells the treasury to contract until internal balance is attained, at C_1. However, the reduction in expenditure has created a trade balance surplus. The rule tells the central bank to revalue until balanced trade is restored, at B_2. Now, however, unemployment means that the treasury will expand until reaching full employment again, at C_2. Once again, a trade deficit tells the central bank to devalue, and the counterclockwise cycle repeats.

As the graph is drawn, the line spirals in on the equilibrium point, A, at which the goal of simultaneous balance in both sectors is achieved. The reason for spiraling in rather than spiraling out is that the YY schedule is drawn steeper (in absolute value) than the BB schedule. This claim can be demonstrated by making the slopes more extreme. Try this yourself: Draw the external balance schedule to be much steeper than the internal balance schedule. When Rule 1 tells the treasury to contract because of excess demand at point B_1, the trade surplus that opens up is larger than the initial imbalance. When the central bank revalues, the country moves farther away from internal balance than it was previously. This system is unstable, moving farther and farther from full equilibrium.

Now try Rule 2. External balance is assigned to the treasury. Whenever the trade balance is in deficit, the treasury cuts G; whenever it is in surplus, the treasury raises G. Internal balance is assigned to the central bank. Whenever output falls short of full employment, the central bank raises E; whenever it exceeds full employment, the bank lowers E. Starting from a point such as P_1, a reduction in G leads to unemployment, an increase in E, and so forth. The path now progresses around the graph clockwise, not counterclockwise as under Rule 1. If the YY schedule is the steeper one, as in Figure 18.13, there is a spiral *out*. Rule 2 does not work. Yet if the BB schedule is steeper, there is a spiral in to equilibrium. Rule 2 works.

Thus, the selection of the assignment rule should be based on the relative slopes of the schedules. Which case is more likely, a YY schedule that is steeper than the BB schedule, or one that is flatter? Problem 8 at the end of the chapter involves computing the relative slopes of the two lines. It turns out that the YY line is steeper only if the economy is not very open to imports. In that case Rule 1 should be used; Fiscal policy should be used for internal balance. Otherwise—i.e., for an economy that is highly open—fiscal policy should be assigned to external balance. Intuitively, if the marginal propensity to import is high, then expenditure-reducing policies are an effective way of improving the trade balance because a high proportion of the eliminated expenditure goes to foreign goods. Mundell's principle of "effective market classification" states that policy tools should be assigned responsibility for those policy variables on which they have a relatively greater effect.

In practice, while it may take time for policy-makers to enact major policy changes, they should monitor economic conditions continuously and try to update their policies accordingly. If they are unable to do so, policy activism may exacerbate macroeconomic fluctuations rather than dampen them.

Monetary Factors

The discussion of policies to change the level of expenditure has so far focused on fiscal policy. However, it is easy enough to put monetary policy into the Keynesian model. The mechanism of transmission from the money supply to income is the interest rate. Assume that expenditure, in particular investment—which has been treated previously as exogenous—is now a decreasing function of the interest rate, since the interest rate is the cost of borrowing to firms. If it falls, firms are more likely to undertake investment projects. Households may raise their expenditure as well and so reduce savings. Residential construction and purchases of consumer durables (automobiles, household appliances, and so forth) are often particularly sensitive to interest rates. Figure 18.14 shows how a decrease in the interest rate shifts the $NS - I$ line down. Equilibrium occurs at a higher level of income, $Y_2 > Y_1$. Thus, an inverse relationship between the interest rate and income is traced out, describing equilibrium in the goods market. This relationship is none other than the IS curve, from the familiar closed-economy IS-LM analysis of intermediate macroeconomics courses.

What would make the interest rate fall to begin with? The obvious answer is monetary policy. The central bank could simply set the interest rate directly. In the 1980s, however, it became more common—and more realistic—to treat the central bank as setting the money supply. The interest rate then adjusts to equilibrate the money supply with money demand.

Individuals balance their portfolios between money and other assets, such as stocks and bonds. Their demand for money is a decreasing function of the rate of return on alternative assets, represented by the interest rate. Yet even though money pays no interest, people must hold some with which to undertake transactions. The demand for real money balances is thus an increasing function of real income. If income were to go up, and nothing else changed, the demand for money would go up. For a given real money supply, to maintain equilibrium in the financial markets (demand equals supply) something else must change: The interest rate must rise to make bonds more attractive and money less attractive. Only then will money demand be equal to the existing money supply. Thus, the lower part of Figure 18.15 traces a positive relationship between the interest rate and income, describing equilibrium in the financial market. For a given real money supply, the two variables must move together, precisely because they have offsetting effects on money demand. This relationship is the familiar LM curve. The intersection of the two curves gives the equilibrium level of income and interest rate.

Notice that there is a unique critical level of income that implies a zero trade balance, Y_1, in the upper panel of Figure 18.15. Anywhere to the right of Y_1 is a point of trade deficit because imports are too high. Anywhere to the left of Y_1 is a point of

FIGURE 18.14   Effect of a Fall in the Interest Rate, i

If monetary policy lowers the interest rate from i_1 to i_2, then it stimulates investment from I_1 to I_2. The Saving-Investment line shifts out, raising the level of income from Y_1 to Y_2. This inverse relationship between i and Y is the IS curve.

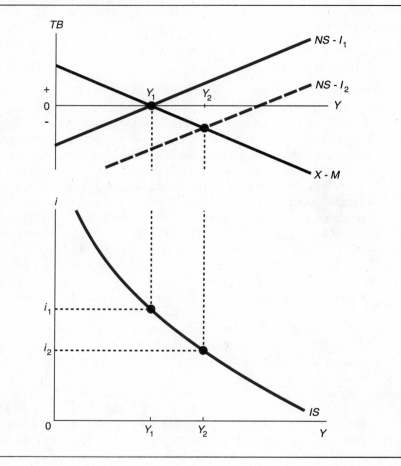

surplus because imports are too low. An expenditure-switching policy that shifts the $X - M$ line will change the critical level of income.

The following analysis will begin from a point where the equilibrium level of income given by the $IS = LM$ intersection also implies a zero trade balance, point E in Figure 18.15. We will consider in turn the effects of three policy changes: a monetary expansion, a fiscal expansion, and a devaluation.

The monetary expansion shifts the LM curve to the right. For the higher money supply to be willingly held, either the interest rate must fall or income must rise. In fact, both happen; the interest rate falls and stimulates investment and thus income. The new equilibrium occurs at point M. Because this is to the right of the $TB = 0$ point, clearly the higher level of expenditure stimulated by the expansion has pushed the country into trade balance deficit.

FIGURE 18.15   Monetary Expansion

The upward-sloping *LM* curve gives equilibrium in the money market. An increase in the money supply shifts the *LM* curve out, driving down the interest rate, *i*, at point *M*, and as a result increasing income, *Y*. The trade balance worsens.

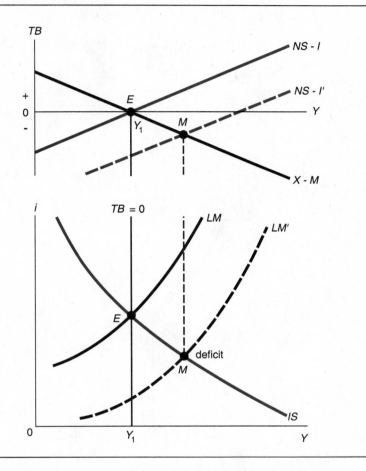

Figure 18.16 depicts an increase in government expenditure, ΔG. The fiscal expansion shifts the *IS* curve to the right: Any given interest rate and consequent level of investment, which previously implied a particular level of income, now imply a higher level of income. In fact, the distance that the fiscal expansion shifts the *IS* curve to the right can be precisely stated. The simple Keynesian multiplier analysis of Section 18.1 showed that, for a given interest rate, income increases by

$$\Delta Y = \frac{1}{s + m} \Delta \overline{G}$$ (Equation 18.8). Previously, that formula was the complete answer

to the question of how much income increases, because the interest rate was assumed constant. Now it only answers the question of how much the curve shifts, because the interest rate is no longer necessarily constant. The increases in expenditure and

FIGURE 18.16   Fiscal Expansion with Crowding-Out of Investment

An increase in government spending shifts the *IS* curve to the right by the amount of the simple Keynesian multiplier. However, the actual increase in income is somewhat less than this, at point *F*, because an increase in the demand for money drives up the interest rate and "crowds out" investment.

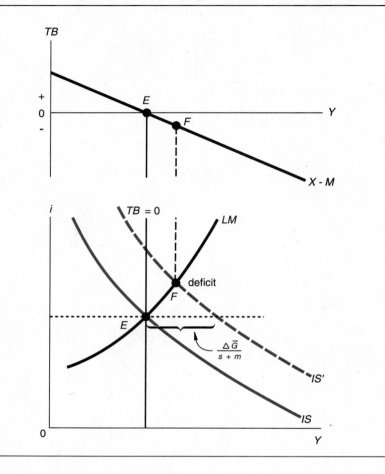

income raise money demand, forcing the interest rate up, which in turn discourages private investment. The new equilibrium occurs at point *F*. Income is still higher than at point *E*, but some of the effect of the fiscal expansion has been offset by the crowding out of investment. The overall effect on income is somewhat *less* than the full open-economy multiplier effect, $\Delta Y = \dfrac{1}{s + m} \Delta \overline{G}$.[19]

---

[19] The $NS - I$ schedule has not been explicitly drawn in the upper half of Figure 18.16. It initially runs through point *E*; then the fiscal expansion shifts it to the right, by $\Delta G/(s + m)$, and the increase in i immediately shifts it part of the way back to the left. It ends up intersecting the $X - M$ line at point *F*.

Notice that the economy is again in trade deficit at point F because of higher imports. In this model, monetary and fiscal expansions operate in the same way. Both raise expenditure, thus raising income and worsening the trade balance. They differ only in their implications for the composition of the given level of output, a monetary expansion favoring private investment and a fiscal expansion favoring government spending (or, in the case of a tax cut, favoring consumer spending).

We now turn from the two kinds of policies affecting the level of expenditure to an expenditure-switching policy, devaluation. Figure 18.3 showed that, assuming the Marshall-Lerner condition holds, a devaluation shifts the $X - M$ line up by some positive amount, called $\Delta \overline{X}$. For any given level of investment, equilibrium occurs at a higher level of income. Thus, for any given interest rate, the equilibrium point in the lower panel of Figure 18.17 shifts to the right. From Section 18.1, it is even possible to state by how much it shifts to the right: For a given interest rate, $\Delta Y = \dfrac{1}{s + m} \Delta \overline{X}$. The actual overall effect on Y is less, as can be seen at the new $IS - LM$ intersection, point D.[20] Like the increase in demand from the government sector, the increase in demand from the foreign sector raises output, but the effect is partly offset by the investment that is crowded out by higher interest rates.

Despite the move to the right, point D brings a trade surplus, not a trade deficit. As shown in the upper panel in Figure 18.17, the critical level of income that implies a zero trade balance has shifted to the right. Furthermore, the $TB = 0$ line has shifted to the right by *more* than the IS curve. How do we know this? Imagine for a moment a perfectly flat LM curve (the famous "liquidity trap"), such that the devaluation causes a move to point L. Section 18.1 showed that the trade balance would improve, by $\Delta TB = \Delta \overline{X} - m\Delta Y = \Delta \overline{X} - m \dfrac{1}{s + m} \Delta \overline{X} = \dfrac{s}{s + m} \Delta \overline{X} > 0$. *The marginal propensity to import times the increase in income is only a partial offset to the improvement in the trade balance.* When the LM curve has some slope, the change in the trade balance is still $\Delta TB = \Delta \overline{X} - m\Delta Y$, but now crowding out means that ΔY is smaller than the simple multiplier formula indicates. The marginal propensity to import has even less of an offsetting effect on the trade balance. If there is surplus at L, there is even greater surplus at D. This proves that the vertical $TB = 0$ line shifts right by more than income increases, leaving D to the left of the new line.[21] Intuitively, income would not have increased in the first place if devaluation did not, on net, stimulate the trade balance.

Most of this closely resembles material covered in an intermediate closed-economy macroeconomics course. Opening the economy up to foreign trade has added little to the analysis; it has merely appended the trade balance as a function of income. Nor has anything of significance been added to the open-economy analysis presented

---

[20] In terms of the upper panel, the $NS - I$ schedule has shifted to the left (again because of the increase in i), so that it intersects $X' - M$ at D.

[21] The $TB = 0$ schedule shifts to the right by $\Delta \overline{X}/m$. (Only if $m\Delta Y = \Delta \overline{X}$ is TB unchanged.) However, as can be seen in the figure, the IS curve shifts to the right by a smaller amount: $\Delta \overline{X}/(s + m)$.

FIGURE 18.17   Devaluation with Crowding-Out

A devaluation shifts the *IS* curve to the right by the amount of the simple Keynesian multiplier (at point *L*). However, the actual increase in income is somewhat less than this, because investment is crowded out at *D*. The trade balance improves.

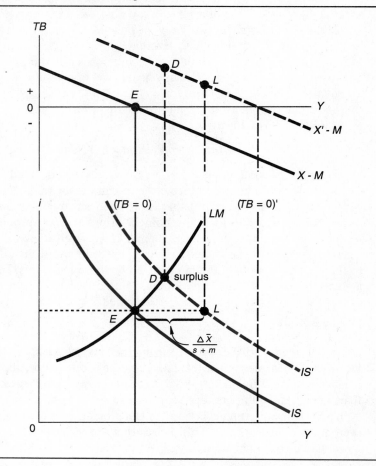

in Sections 18.1 through 18.3. This section has only shown how the effectiveness of fiscal expansion or devaluation in stimulating demand is reduced by crowding-out and how monetary expansion is an alternate policy for stimulating expenditure. Chapter 19 will return to the *IS-LM* graphs to analyze the effects of reserve flows, and Chapter 22 will explore the effects of international capital mobility. Chapter 22 will also present greater synergy between the financial markets and the foreign sector. The existence of a balance of payments surplus or deficit will ultimately have much wider implications for the entire economic system in those chapters.

The Absorption Approach

In the 1950s, the phrase "absorption approach" originated as an alternative to the elasticities approach studied in Chapter 17.[22] The idea is simple. Begin with the definition of the trade balance as the domestic country's earnings from exports minus its expenditure on imports. Add the country's expenditure on domestic goods and subtract its earnings from domestic sales, which are the same quantity. The trade balance is given by *total* earnings, income Y, minus total expenditure, or absorption A.

$$TB = Y - A$$

A country running a deficit is earning less than its expenditure; intake is exceeded by absorption. As $A \equiv C + I + G$, the equation is simply the national income identity— the starting point for the Keynesian model. Indeed, the model usually associated with the absorption approach is the Keynesian one developed in this chapter, with a role given to the monetary effects mentioned in Section 18.3.

According to Harry Johnson, the new insight gained from the "absorption" terminology was that a country that is in deficit, and so spending more than it is earning, is decumulating international reserves. Over time, this change in the stock of reserves has implications for the money supply and thus for expenditure itself. These lead to the monetary approach to the balance of payments, the subject of Chapter 19.

18.5 SUMMARY

This chapter added a second factor, in addition to the exchange rate, in the determination of the trade balance: national income, or GNP. When income increases, the demand for imports increases, which works to decrease the trade balance. The trade balance is in turn a component of income, so the determination of both variables must be considered simultaneously.

Because we have maintained the assumption that the prices of domestic goods are fixed (in terms of domestic currency), the resulting model is "Keynesian": Changes in demand are reflected in output, not in prices. Two types of exogenous policy changes were studied: expenditure-switching policies such as devaluation, and expenditure-reducing (or -increasing) policies such as government spending. This chapter also examined the effects of changes in such policy instruments on the two policy targets: internal balance (GNP at the "full-employment" level, for example) and external balance (the trade balance at zero, for example). A general principle was demonstrated: If a country is to attain both policy targets, the government must use two independent policy instruments, such as fiscal policy and the exchange rate.

The most important conclusions were evident even in the simplest form of the

---

[22] The term "absorption approach" was coined by Sidney Alexander, "The Effects of Devaluation on a Trade Balance," *IMF Staff Papers*, (April 1952), 359–373. A confusing debate followed. The confusion was attributed in part to the terminological question of whether a "neutral" monetary policy meant keeping the interest rate constant, as in Meade, or the money supply constant, as in more modern parlance (a constant *LM* curve, in terms of Section 18.4): S. C. Tsiang, "The Role of Money in Trade-Balance Stability: Synthesis of the Elasticities and Absorption Approaches," *American Economic Review*, (December 1969), pp. 389–412.

Keynesian model, in which (in addition to holding the price level constant) the level of foreign income is held constant, which is realistic given the assumption that the domestic country is too small to affect foreign income, and the domestic interest rate is held constant as well, which is accurate given the assumption that the central bank follows an accommodating monetary policy. The first conclusions concern changes in government spending: (1) Such changes have a multiplier effect on national income because at each round of spending some proportion of the income earned is passed on in a new round of spending, but (2) the effect on income is smaller than in closed-economy textbooks, because at each round of spending some leaks out of the country in the form of higher import spending and a higher trade deficit. Feedback effects via foreign income, which only need be taken into account if the home country is large, work to increase the effect of an expansion on domestic income. On the other hand, crowding-out effects via the domestic interest rate, which must be taken into account if the central bank keeps the money supply constant, decrease the effect of a fiscal expansion on domestic income.

The next conclusions concern devaluations: (3) If the Marshall-Lerner condition is met, a devaluation will raise the trade surplus, as in Chapter 17,[23] and will in turn improve income because of the multiplier, but (4) because the higher income means higher imports, the increase in the trade surplus will be less than it was when income effects were omitted.

Several other important questions can also be explored with the simple Keynesian model. (5) When a country makes an exogenous transfer to its trading partner (reparations, foreign aid, or interest payments), it will generally experience an improvement of its trade balance that is smaller than the amount of the transfer, so its total current account will deteriorate (at a given exchange rate). (6) Under a regime of fixed exchange rates, disturbances are transmitted from one country to another, while a regime of floating rates helps to insulate countries from each other's disturbances because the exchange rate adjusts automatically to equilibrate the balance of payment.[24]

The chapter concluded by introducing money into the model for the first time, thus leading to the subject of Chapter 19.

CHAPTER PROBLEMS

1. In the Keynesian multiplier process, at each round of spending some proportion of the income is passed on by its recipients as a new round of spending. The number of rounds is infinite. Does this mean that the total effect on income is infinite? Why not?

2. Would you expect the multiplier to be highest in Australia, Belgium, or Singapore?

3. Assume there is an increase in a country's government budget deficit.
   a. What must happen to private saving, investment, or the trade balance, according to the national saving identity? In the Keynesian model (leaving out any interest rate

[23] The appendix explores a qualification to this conclusion that arises if saving depends on the terms of trade (the "Laursen-Metzler-Harberger" effect).

[24] This chapter continues to assume the absence of international capital flows, so the overall balance of payments is the same as the trade balance. Part V of the book will introduce capital flows; one consequence will be that floating exchange rates do not provide complete insulation.

effects on investment), which of these alternatives, or what combination of them, results from a tax cut? What is the answer if investment is allowed to depend on the interest rate?

b. If there is a recession because of an exogenous fall in $\overline{C}$, what is the effect on the budget deficit? Are the effects on private saving and the trade balance the same as in 3a?

c. If there is a recession because of an exogenous fall in exports, what are the effects on the budget deficit, saving, and the trade balance?

4. Output is given by

$$Y = C + I + G + TB$$

where consumption (C), disposable income (Y_d), investment (I), government expenditure (G), and the trade balance (TB) are given as follows:

$$C = \overline{C} + (1 - s)Y_d$$
$$Y_d = Y - tY$$
$$I = \overline{I}$$
$$G = \overline{G}$$
$$TB = \overline{X} - (\overline{M} + mY_d).$$

This model differs from Section 18.1 by the introduction of t, the marginal tax rate.

a. (i) Solve for the equilibrium level of income Y_0 as a function of exogenous variables.

(ii) What is the open-economy fiscal multiplier $\Delta Y_0/\Delta\overline{G}$? Is it larger or smaller than the multiplier in a closed economy $1/s$? What is the intuitive explanation?

(iii) Is the multiplier larger or smaller than the open-economy multiplier in Section 18.1? What is the intuitive explanation?

(iv) What is the effect on the trade balance $(\Delta TB/\Delta\overline{G})$?

b. Assume that export demand increases exogenously by $\Delta\overline{X}$—for example, because of a devaluation that raises exports by $\Delta\overline{X} = \epsilon\Delta E$ (think of ϵ as the export elasticity times $\overline{X}/E$), and has no direct effect on imports in domestic currency (import elasticity is 1.0).

(i) What is the effect on income $(\Delta Y/\Delta\overline{X})$?

(ii) What is the effect on the trade balance $(\Delta TB/\Delta\overline{X})$? How does this answer compare with the elasticities approach and why?

(iii) Assume (just for this question) that floating exchange rates are in effect so that E always increases by the amount necessary to guarantee $TB = 0$. What is the floating-rate fiscal multiplier $\Delta Y_0/\Delta G$? How does it compare with the fixed-rate and closed-economy multipliers in Problem a(ii)? What is the effect of a fiscal expansion on the exchange rate $(\Delta E/\Delta\overline{G})$?

5. This question concerns the relative virtues of the regimes of fixed and floating exchange rates in automatically stabilizing real growth in the economy. Assume that the goal is to minimize Variance (ΔY), in the presence of domestic disturbances $\Delta\overline{A}$ and foreign disturbances ΔX (which are assumed to be independent of each other). The variance is a measure of variability that has the following three properties in general.

$$\text{Variance } (au) = a^2 \text{ Variance } (u)$$
$$\text{Variance } (b + v) = \text{Variance } (v)$$
$$\text{Variance } (u + v) = \text{Variance } (u) + \text{Variance } (v)$$

where a and b are parameters or exogenous variables and u and v are independent disturbances. Assume the simple Keynesian model of Section 18.1.

a. (i) How does Variance (ΔY) depend on Variance $(\Delta\overline{A})$ and Variance $(\Delta\overline{X})$ under fixed exchange rates?

(ii) Under floating exchange rates?

   b. (i) Which regime would be preferable if the variance of foreign disturbances is much larger than the variance of domestic disturbances?

     (ii) If the two kinds of disturbances are similar in magnitude, and the country is very open (m is large)? Which is a better candidate for a fixed exchange rate, Australia or Luxembourg?

6. This question concerns the two-country model.
   a. Solve Equations 18.12 and 18.13 simultaneously, to determine Y.
   b. Use Equations 18.16 and 18.14 to solve for the effect of a spending rise on the trade balance:

$$\frac{\Delta TB}{\Delta \bar{A}} = \frac{\Delta TB}{Y}\frac{\Delta Y}{\Delta \bar{A}}$$

   c. Compare your answers to b with the analogous expression in the small-country model. In which case is the fall in the trade balance greater and why?

7. In Section 18.1 we applied the transfer problem to a small country, but the problem is more often applied to two countries of approximately equal size (such as France and Germany).
   a. The transfer, ΔT, can be viewed as an exogenous decrease in the income of the transferring country and an exogenous increase in the income of the recipient country. The answer to 6b gives the effect of the first factor on the trade balance, and the analogous equation for the foreign country gives the effect of the second factor. Show that

$$\frac{\Delta TB}{\Delta T} = \frac{ms^* + m^*s}{s^*s + ms^* + m^*s}$$

   b. Is the ratio necessarily less than 1? What if the marginal propensities to save are zero? How would the special case when the domestic country is so small that the foreign country spends almost nothing on its goods look?
   c. Show the effect on the current account $\Delta CA = \Delta TB - \Delta T$. Does the current account of the transferor improve or worsen?

8. Returning to the small-country model of Section 18.1, compute the ratio of the slope of the internal balance line (YY) to the slope of the external balance line (BB):

$$\frac{(\Delta E/\Delta \bar{G})|_{Y=\bar{Y}}}{(\Delta E/\Delta \bar{G})|_{TB=0}}$$

(*Hint:* The numerator refers to the change in E that is required to offset a given change in G, in such a way as to leave Y at the original level of $\bar{Y}$, and is given by

$$-\frac{\Delta Y}{\Delta \bar{G}}\bigg/\frac{\Delta Y}{\Delta E}$$

This applies analogously to the denominator.)
How is this ratio relevant to the assignment problem?

Extra Credit

9. In this question the interest rate is allowed to vary. (Think of it as having been held constant by monetary policy in the preceding problems.)
   In the preceding model, replace the exogenous specification for investment (I) with an equation in which it depends inversely on the interest rate (i):

$$I = \bar{I} - bi$$

and add an equation for the demand for money. (We now use M to stand for money.)

$$M/P = KY - hi$$

a. Derive the *IS* curve, giving Y as an inverse function of i. [For notational simplicity, use α to denote the answer to 4a(ii).]

b. Combine your answer to 4a with the *LM* curve (the money demand equation with real money demand M/P equal to the exogenous real money supply $\overline{M}/P$) to solve for Y as a function of exogenous variables. Solve for i as well.

c. What is the fiscal multiplier $\Delta Y/\Delta G$ now? How does it compare with the answer to 4a(ii) (call it α), and why? What happens if h is very high (i.e., money demand is very sensitive to i)?

d. What is the monetary multiplier $\Delta Y/\Delta(\overline{M}/P)$? What happens if h is very high?

SUGGESTIONS FOR FURTHER READING

Corden, W. Max, "The Geometric Representation of Policies to Attain Internal and External Balance," *Review of Economics Studies* 28, (1960) 1–22; Reprinted in Richard Cooper, ed., *International Finance* (Baltimore: Penguin Books, 1969). Further development of the "Swan Diagram."

Goldstein, Morris, and Mohsin Khan, "Income and Price Effects in Foreign Trade," in Ronald Jones and Peter Kenen, eds., *Handbook of International Economics*, Vol. II, (Amsterdam: Elsevier, 1985), Chapter 20, pp. 1041–1105. Comprehensive reporting of econometric estimates of the elasticities of demand for imports and exports, including the distinction between short- and long-run elasticities of demand with respect to income.

Johnson, Harry, "Toward a General Theory of the Balance of Payments," (1958). Reprinted in Richard Cooper, ed., *International Finance* (Baltimore: Penguin Books, 1969); and in Jacob Frenkel and Harry Johnson, eds., *The Monetary Approach to the Balance of Payments* (Toronto: University of Toronto Press, 1976). The first half interprets the "absorption approach" as pointing the way to the monetary approach to the balance of payments by emphasizing reserve flows. The second half develops the distinction between expenditure-switching policies and expenditure-reducing policies.

Krugman, Paul, *Adjustment in the World Economy*, Occasional Paper No. 24 (New York: Group of Thirty, 1987). Argues, using the logic of the transfer problem, that the U.S. trade deficit should not be eliminated by U.S. fiscal contraction alone (even together with foreign fiscal expansion). Depreciation of the dollar is also needed.

Sachs, Jeffrey, "The Current Account and Macroeconomic Adjustment in the 1970s," *Brookings Papers on Economic Activity* 1, 1981, pp. 201–268. A clear exposition of the current account as the outcome of the two-period saving decision (as in the appendix to Chapter 22), with special reference to the oil shocks of the 1970s and countries' responses.

APPENDIX:
THE LAURSEN-METZLER-HARBERGER EFFECT

When a devaluation worsens the terms of trade, there may be real consequences beyond the simple fact that purchasing power has fallen. This observation leads to the Laursen-Metzler-Harberger effect.

Expenditure and the Terms of Trade

Up to now, we have assumed that the marginal propensities to save and consume are specified in domestic terms. (In Equation 18.3 C and Y were both defined in domestic units.) This has meant that a change in the terms of trade between domestic output and foreign output has had no effect on the $NS - I$ schedule when the horizontal axis measures income in domestic terms, as in Figure 18.3. An increase in the exchange rate has affected only the $X - M$ line, shifting it up if the Marshall-Lerner condition is satisfied. One implication has been that the Marshall-Lerner condition is the necessary and sufficient condition for a devaluation to improve the trade balance. The change in income, and therefore imports, reduces the effect on the trade balance but does not reverse it.

However, there is little justification in theory for measuring income in domestic terms when determining saving. When the exchange rate rises, the terms of trade worsen. (The terms of trade are defined as the price of exports divided by the price of imports.) Any level of income given in domestic terms translates into less when measured in terms of foreign goods, or in terms of the appropriate consumption-weighted basket of domestic and foreign goods. If consumption, saving, and imports were proportional to income, it would not matter what numeraire we used for measurement. In the Keynesian model, however, a fall in income is hypothesized to induce consumers to reduce their consumption *less than proportionately*. In other words, the elasticity of consumption with respect to income is less than 1:

$$\frac{\Delta C/\Delta Y}{C/Y} = \frac{c}{(\overline{C} + cY)/Y} < 1$$

It is argued that a fall in real income, even if it results from a worsening in the terms of trade rather than from a fall in domestically measured income, should be reflected in a similar less-than-proportionate fall in real spending. If measurements are made in domestic terms, this is reflected as an increase in spending, or a decrease in saving, for any given level of income domestically measured. In other words, an increase in the exchange rate, in addition to shifting the $X - M$ schedule up, shifts the $NS - I$ schedule down, as in Figure 18.A.1. Consumers reduce their saving to maintain living standards in the face of the worsened terms of trade. This terms-of-trade factor is called the Laursen-Metzler-Harberger effect.

The Condition for a Devaluation to Improve the Trade Balance

There are two implications of the Laursen-Metzler-Harberger effect. The first is that the fall in saving, or increase in expenditure, has a negative effect on the trade balance. Thus, the trade balance could go into deficit (depending on the elasticities) even if the Marshall-Lerner condition is satisfied. That is the way Figure 18.A.1 is drawn. If we recall that the trade balance is equal to saving minus investment, it is intuitively clear why the Laursen-Metzler-Harberger effect would work to reduce the trade balance when it works to reduce saving.

Evidently the necessary condition for a devaluation to improve the trade balance is more stringent than

$$\epsilon_X + \epsilon_M > 1$$

In the two-country context the necessary condition is

$$\epsilon_X + \epsilon_M > 1 + m + m^*$$

FIGURE 18.A.1   Increase in the Exchange Rate with the Laursen-Metzler-Harberger Effect

As usual, the devaluation shifts the $X - M$ line up. If the saving rate depends not just on income measured in domestic terms (Y), but also on the terms of trade, then the $NS - I$ line shifts down, as households seek to protect their standard of living.

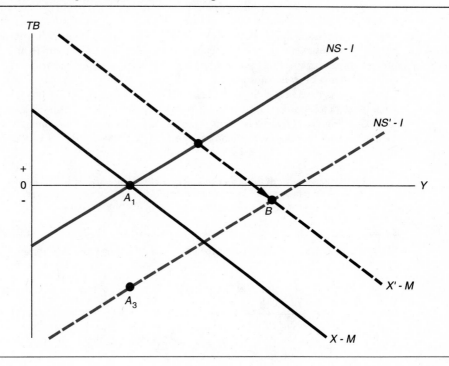

This condition will not be derived.[25] Note, however, that in addition to the price effects of the devaluation, the stimulus to domestic real income from increased exports will raise imports to an extent that depends on the domestic marginal propensity to import, and the fall in foreign real income from the fall in foreign exports will lower their imports to an extent depending on the foreign marginal propensity to import. Thus, the effect of the devaluation depends on the magnitudes of the elasticities compared to the marginal propensities to import. This much was also true earlier, when expenditure was based on income measured in terms of the country's own goods. In that case, however, aggregate incomes did not begin to change until the elasticities were high enough that the trade balance was going to improve, no matter what the income effects; the propensities to import could only dampen the improvement. Now, with the Laursen-Metzler-Harberger effect, because the change in the exchange rate necessarily starts changing *real* incomes even before the Marshall-Lerner condition is satisfied, the propensities to import must be overcome before there can be improvement in the trade balance.

[25] The condition for a devaluation to improve the trade balance was originally derived by Arnold Harberger, "Currency Depreciation, Income and the Balance of Trade," *Journal of Political Economy*, (February 1950): 1147–1160; reprinted in R. Caves and H. Johnson, eds., *Readings in International Economics* (Homewood, IL: Irwin, 1968), pp. 341–358.

Implications for Transmission Under Floating Rates

The second implication of the Laursen-Metzler-Harberger effect has to do with the question, considered in Section 18.3, of the international transmission of disturbances.[26] This is illustrated in Figure 18.A.2, with the economy initially at point A. It is no longer true that a floating exchange rate completely insulates domestic output and employment from foreign disturbances. As before, a fall in exports due, for example, to a foreign contraction, leads to a depreciation to prevent the trade deficit that would otherwise emerge at point B in Figure 18.A.2. In the standard Keynesian model, the depreciation would increase exports and reduce imports, causing a return (instantaneously) to point A. With the Laursen-Metzler-Harberger effect, however, the worsened terms of trade cause saving to fall. Thus, the $NS - I$ line shifts down and a further depreciation is necessary if the trade balance is to avoid going into deficit. Equilibrium occurs when the depreciation is sufficient to restore the trade balance to zero despite the fall in saving, point C in Figure 18.A.2. This point occurs at a higher level of income than A, even though the chain of events began with a contraction of foreign income. The disturbance is transmitted in reverse.

[26] The transmission of disturbances that occurs despite floating exchange rates was the motivation behind the original paper, Svend Laursen and Lloyd Metzler, "Flexible Exchange Rates and the Theory of Employment," *Review of Economics and Statistics*, 32 (November 1950): 281–299.

FIGURE 18.A.2   External Disturbance Under a Floating Exchange Rate

---

In the presence of the Laursen-Metzler-Harberger effect, a fall in foreign demand can actually *raise* domestic output. The reason is that the domestic currency depreciates, which causes saving to shift down.

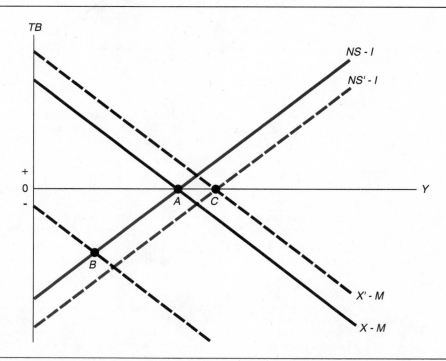

The empirical importance of the Laursen-Metzler-Harberger effect has been questioned, partly because the result that disturbances are transmitted in reverse is counterintuitive. Yet one possible instance of this phenomenon occurred in 1977–1978. When the United States expanded its economy, beginning in 1975, the resulting record U.S. trade deficits caused a large sustained depreciation in the dollar. From the earlier model the exchange rate change would be expected to insulate Europe from the effect of the U.S. expansion. We might even have expected the Europeans to be happy at this improvement in their terms of trade, especially because the reduction in their import prices helped in the fight against inflation that was uppermost in their minds. Nevertheless, loud complaints about the falling value of the dollar were heard from across the Atlantic, and the changed exchange rate did slow down the recovery in Europe by reducing the demand for their goods. While there are other possible ways of explaining these facts, some economists argued that this was an example of the Laursen-Metzler-Harberger effect. The improved terms of trade led to an increase in saving in Europe and stagnant output.

Temporary Versus Permanent Shifts in the Terms of Trade

The Keynesian consumption function, on which the Laursen-Metzler-Harberger effect is based, cannot be applied to long-run permanent changes in real income. When there is an adverse shift in the terms of trade, or any other reduction in real income, consumers can only reduce saving (or borrow) to maintain expenditure levels *if* conditions are expected to improve in the future, allowing the consumers to make up the lost savings (or pay back the loan). It has long been recognized that the marginal propensity to consume out of a permanent change in real income is higher than the marginal propensity to consume out of a temporary change in income. The latter will be close to zero in the limit of a very short-lived change in real income, which has no effect on a rational individual's expectation of lifetime wealth or permanent income, and thus no effect on consumption plans.[27]

It is reasonable to think of standard Keynesian propensities to consume and save as applying in the intermediate case, in which a change in real income is observed but is not known to be necessarily either temporary or permanent. Thus, the Laursen-Metzler-Harberger effect applies in this general, intermediate case. It should be modified, however, if there is additional information on the permanence of the change.[28]

One illustration was the sharp increase in the price of oil in 1973. For an oil-importing country, this was an adverse shift in the terms of trade analogous to a devaluation. One might have expected all oil-importing countries to incur large trade deficits due to the increase in their oil import bills. Yet the industrialized country that ran the largest deficit was Norway, which had North Sea oil reserves that it could develop in the future. The Norwegians knew that their real income loss was temporary and that they would be wealthier in the long run. Accordingly, they reduced saving relative to investment, borrowing from the rest of the world

---

[27] These ideas regarding the consumption function began with Milton Friedman's Permanent Income Hypothesis and Franco Modigliani's Life Cycle Hypothesis. The appendix to Chapter 22 shows that a country of optimizing consumers will borrow from abroad if it can expect income to be higher in the future than today.

[28] The theory is updated to include explicit intertemporal utility maximization by consumers in Maurice Obstfeld, "Aggregate Spending and the Terms of Trade: Is There a Laursen-Metzler Effect?" *Quarterly Journal of Economics* 96 (May 1982); and Lars Svensson and Assaf Razin, "The Terms of Trade and the Current Account: The Harberger-Laursen-Metzler Effect," *Journal of Political Economy* 97 (1) (February 1983): pp. 97–125. The first paper makes strong enough assumptions to rule out the Laursen-Metzler-Harberger effect; the second paper is more general.

to finance the development of their oil reserves. Norway's current account balance declined by 7 percent of GNP from the period 1965–1973 to the period 1974–1979. Other oil importers, who had little prospect that their loss in real income would be temporary, had no choice but to adjust. The United States and Germany each had no change in their current account positions between the two periods. In other words, they increased exports of other goods to pay for the higher oil import bill.

19

MONEY SUPPLIES, PRICE LEVELS, AND THE BALANCE OF PAYMENTS

Chapter 17 considered the impact of changes in the exchange rate alone on the balance of payments; in effect, income was held constant. In Chapter 18, we allowed income to vary. Similarly, the interest rate was held constant in the first part of Chapter 18, then it too was allowed to vary in the last part of the chapter. Chapter 19 will continue this pattern, of letting additional macroeconomic variables vary, by introducing the price level, which was assumed constant in the preceding chapters.

The determination of the price level, a monetary variable, was relatively neglected until its importance was pointed out by economists of the monetarist school of thought. This chapter considers not only changes in the price level but also changes in a second monetary variable: the central bank's holdings of international reserves. These two variables are fundamental to the monetary approach to the balance of payments. The monetary approach was originally developed in the 1960s, in large part at the University of Chicago but also at the International Monetary Fund. Its central point was that the balance of payments is a monetary phenomenon. The monetary approach to the balance of payments was and is often used by the IMF staff when they must figure out why a country is running a balance of payments deficit and what should be done about it.

19.1 THE NONSTERILIZATION ASSUMPTION

The monetary approach to the balance of payments is sometimes presented as an object of controversy, a model in conflict with the previously discussed elasticity and Keynesian approaches. The controversy is more apparent than real. This chapter will show that no necessary connection exists between the *monetary* approach to the balance of payments and *monetarism*. The debate between monetarists and Keynesians *is* a proper object of controversy, but is not directly at stake here. The beginning of this chapter will apply the monetary approach within the context of the Keynesian model of Chapter 18, and the second half will show how the price level is determined.

The Definition of Sterilization Operations

What *is* at stake here is "sterilization." It is important to understand the difference between what happens when the central bank practices sterilization of international reserve flows and what happens when it does not. This distinction is relevant for understanding the difference between how major industrialized countries, especially the United States, conduct monetary policy today and how it was conducted under the classical gold standard of the nineteenth century (and is to an extent still conducted today in many small open economies).

To begin, consider the definition of a country's *monetary base* (sometimes called "high-powered money," to distinguish it from broader definitions of money such as M1). The monetary base consists of currency plus other liabilities issued by the central bank, for example, credit extended by the central bank to commercial banks. A checking account that an individual holds at his or her commercial bank is included in M1, but not in the monetary base.

When a country runs a balance of payments deficit, its central bank is necessarily buying the country's own currency and selling international reserves.[1] If the bank takes no other action, then the monetary base is decreasing. One way of thinking of this is that there is less domestic currency in the hands of the public.

Another way of thinking of the effect on the money supply is to recognize an alternate, equivalent definition of the monetary base in terms of the assets held by the central bank: international reserves (claims against the rest of the world) plus domestic credit (the central bank's holdings of claims against its own government).

$$MB \equiv Res + DC$$

where MB is the monetary base, Res is reserves, and DC is domestic credit. This definition of the monetary base is identical to the first definition because the assets on the bank's balance sheet must —by the rules of accounting[2]—add up to the same sum as the liabilities. (As was noted earlier, with accounting identities the equality sign is drawn with three lines.) As detailed in Chapter 16's discussion of the balance of payments accounts, a country's overall balance of payments is the same thing as the current period's change in the central bank's international reserves.[3]

$$BP \equiv \Delta Res$$

If reserves fall (because the balance of payments deficit, ΔRes, is negative), and domestic credit, DC, is unchanged, then the monetary base, MB, falls by the same amount.

---

[1] The effect on the level of reserves is the same whether the balance of payments deficit is a deficit on current account trade or on the private capital account. That is why the name is the "monetary approach to the balance of payments," rather than "the monetary approach to the balance of trade." Nevertheless, this chapter will continue to omit capital flows and so will refer to the determination of the trade balance. Chapter 22 will show how the monetary approach to the balance of payments changes in the presence of international capital movements.

[2] The balance sheet of a bank, or any other institution, is where it keeps track of all its assets and liabilities. One item appearing on the asset side is "net worth," which is defined as the value of all the *other* assets minus the sum of the liabilities. This is why the sum of the assets on the balance sheet is the same as the sum of the liabilities.

[3] Assume here that the country's currency is not held by other countries' central banks, so their actions are not relevant.

The central bank *sterilizes* the reserve outflow if it prevents it from reducing the domestic money supply. The most standard way of doing this is to create money by expanding domestic credit, at the same rate as the reserve outflow is contracting the money supply, so that there is no net effect. If $\Delta DC = -\Delta Res$, then $\Delta MB = 0$. In the United States, when the Federal Reserve wishes to expand domestic credit, it does so through open market operations in which it buys U.S. Treasury securities on the private market. In this way, any changes in the Federal Reserve's holdings of reserves are sterilized immediately.

When a country runs a balance of payments *surplus*, its central bank is necessarily selling its own currency in the foreign exchange market, thus adding to its stock of international reserves. Again, the central bank sterilizes the reserve inflow if it prevents the increase in reserves from increasing the domestic money supply. The most obvious way of doing this is to extinguish money by contracting domestic credit so that no net effect on the total monetary base results. In the United States, the Federal Reserve sells U.S. Treasury securities on the private market.

Most countries do not have as highly developed bond markets as does the United States, and open market operations are less feasible. For these countries, expanding domestic credit may be done by buying securities directly from the treasury, and so monetizing the budget dificit, or else by extending credit to domestic commercial banks or other enterprises, especially any that may be owned by the government. In some LDCs, the central bank lends money directly to such enterprises as public utilities, industrial development banks, and agricultural cooperatives.

Contracting domestic credit means cutting back on loans to the government, state-owned enterprises, or the banking system. However, it is usually difficult to control the budget deficit of the government or state-owned enterprises, even in the long run, let alone on short notice. In LDCs and other countries where the central bank is obligated to finance these deficits, domestic credit is not a viable tool for sterilization (that is, for offsetting reserve flows) on a short-run basis. An alternative possibility is to allow the high-powered money supply or monetary base—the liabilities of the central bank—to change, but to offset the effect on monetary aggregates such as M1. M1 represents the liabilities of the entire consolidated banking system, including not only claims on the central bank (such as currency) but also claims on commercial banks (such as checking accounts). Even on a relatively short-term basis, the central bank can regulate the amount of credit banks extend to the public—for example, by varying the reserve requirements to which banks are subject.

In many countries where the central bank has little short-run control over domestic credit, reserve flows simply are not sterilized. In the nineteenth century this was mostly true of countries that participated in the gold standard. If money is directly backed with gold, then balance of payments deficits are necessarily financed by gold sales that reduce the domestic money supply: They cannot be sterilized via offsetting changes in the liabilities of either the central bank or the private banking system.[4] If reserve flows are not sterilized, then a balance of payments deficit or surplus implies that the money supply is, over time, decreasing or increasing. (If $\Delta DC = 0$, then $\Delta MB = \Delta Res$.)

---

[4] Appendix B to this chapter explains the gold standard at somewhat greater length. The system did not, in fact, function precisely in the idealized way generally assumed.

This is bound to have effects on expenditure and the entire system and is the essence of the monetary approach.[5]

Hume's Price Specie-Flow Mechanism

The monetary approach to the balance of payments can be traced back to eighteenth-century philosopher and economist David Hume. Hume attacked the mercantilists, who believed that a country's power depended on amassing gold and silver ("specie"), and who restricted trade so to maximize the inflow of specie through the balance of payments. Hume, like Adam Smith and other writers of the Enlightenment, believed in maximizing the welfare of free, atomistic, rational individuals, not the power of an autocratic state. He believed further that the welfare of the individuals residing in a country depended on the economy's productive capabilities, not on the country's stock of gold or money. Money goes where it is demanded, which is where goods are being produced and sold. Assume that a country acquires a new stock of gold but is not especially productive. (Hume mentioned the example of tribute brought to Spain from the New World.) Then the country will spend the gold on the goods of countries that are productive. (Hume had in mind the England of the Industrial Revolution.) The gold flows out through the balance of payments and will continue to do so until the country's gold stock returns to what it was originally.

Hume attributed this process to the *price specie-flow* mechanism. If a country, previously in equilibrium, experiences an increase in its gold supply, then in the short run its price level will be driven up. However, the higher price level will discourage export demand and stimulate import demand, worsening the trade balance. The corresponding outflow of specie will continue until it, and thus the price level, returns to its original level and the trade balance returns to zero. The automatically equilibrating process is described by Hume in terms that evoke the tendency of physical systems toward equilibrium.

> *All water, wherever it communicates, remains at a level. Ask naturalists the reason; they tell you that, were it to be raised in any one place, the superior gravity of that part not being balanced must depress it, till it meet a counterpoise; and that the same cause, which redresses the inequality when it happens, must for ever prevent it, without some violent external operation.*
>
> *Can one imagine, that it had ever been possible, by any laws, or even by any art or industry, to have kept all the money in Spain, which the galleons have brought from the Indies? Or that all commodities could be sold in France for a tenth of the price which they would yield on the other side of the Pyrenees, without finding their way thither, and draining from that immense treasure? What other reason indeed is there why all nations, at present, gain their trade*

---

[5] The monetary approach to the balance of payments is less applicable to the United States or other major industrialized countries under the current system than it is to many smaller countries, to which it is often applied by the International Monetary Fund. An early contribution by a Fund figure is J. J. Polak, "Monetary Analysis of Income Formation and Payments Problems," *Staff Papers*, 6 (November 1957): 1–50. A more recent statement by Fund staff is Mohsin Khan and Malcolm Knight, "Stabilization Programs in Developing Countries: A Formal Framework," *Staff Papers*, 28 (1981): 1–53.

with Spain and Portugal; but because it is impossible to heap up money, more than any fluid, beyond its proper level?

—David Hume: *On the Balance of Trade*

Mundell's Income Specie-Flow Mechanism

[handwritten: ? Monetary Approach - no sterilization IMF approval in small countries]

Harry Johnson and Robert Mundell revived Hume's view in the 1960s, under the name, "the monetary approach to the balance of payments." They were more specific about price determination than Hume had been. First we consider Mundell's income flow mechanism, under which prices were assumed fixed for Keynesian reasons. This is simply the Keynesian model of Chapter 18 plus an analysis of the effects over time under the assumption of nonsterilization of reserve flows. One way to think of the Keynesian model is with a perfectly flat Aggregate Supply curve, so that outward shifts of demand are reflected entirely in output and not at all in price. As already mentioned, the assumption of a constant price level will be relaxed later in the chapter. At that point we will consider the opposite extreme—a perfectly vertical Aggregate Supply curve—in which increases in demand are reflected entirely in prices and not at all in output. Chapter 23 will examine more closely where the Aggregate Supply curve comes from and how its slope might be determined at some intermediate position between flat and vertical.

We begin with the effects of a monetary expansion. Given the Keynesian assumption of fixed prices, the monetary expansion does not alter the price level. Instead, the expansion shifts out the *LM* curve and raises expenditure and income, thus raising imports and worsening the trade balance, as was detailed at the end of Chapter 18. Figure 19.1 is a reproduction of Figure 18.14. The monetary expansion moves the economy from point *E* to point *M*. The deficit at point *M* means that reserves are declining over time.

If the central bank sterilizes the reserve outflow, the money supply remains at the new higher level. The effect would be to keep income high and the trade balance in deficit. The central bank could keep the economy at point *M* indefinitely, or at least until it exhausts its international reserves. However, assume now that the central bank is either unable or unwilling to sterilize the reserve outflow. Over time, the reserve outflow reduces the money supply. The *LM* curve shifts back. The effect is that expenditure and income fall, and the trade balance improves. The process continues as long as the trade balance is in deficit, which is until the economy returns to *E*. Once the trade balance is back at zero, no reason exists for reserves or any other variables to be changing. Notice that in the long-run equilibrium income has not changed from what it was before the monetary expansion. Thus we have our first result under the monetary approach to the balance of payments: a monetary expansion, though it raises income and worsens the trade balance in the short run, has no effect *[handwritten: Conclus]* on either in the long run. Conversely, a monetary contraction reduces income and improves the trade balance in the short run, but has no effect in the long run. Only continuing growth in the money supply (in excess of growth in money demand) could cause a continuing deficit.

When the IMF observes a country with a persistent and excessive balance of payments deficit, it often concludes that the central bank is increasing the supply of money faster than the country's demand for money is increasing. The IMF advises

FIGURE 19.1   Effects of a Monetary Expansion Over Time

In the short run, an increase in the money supply raises output and worsens the trade balance. If the loss of reserves is not sterilized, however, then the money supply falls over time and output returns to its original level at E.

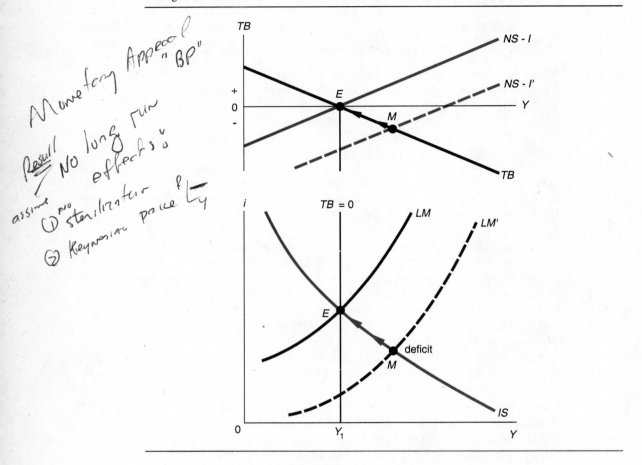

[handwritten margin notes: Monetary Approach "BP" / Result: No long run effects? / assume ① no sterilization ② Keynesian price Ly]

the country to cut back the money growth rate. The country may have no choice but to take the advice, especially if the balance of payments problem is severe enough that the country must borrow from abroad and if the IMF's approval is a prerequisite for such borrowing. Even if the country does not want to borrow directly from the IMF, most banks and governments will not lend unless the troubled borrower country is in good standing with the IMF.[6]

---

[6] Countries are often reluctant to take the IMF's advice. This does not mean that the advice is bad. Typically, the advantages of monetary stabilization are counterbalanced by politically powerful interest groups that stand to lose from Fund programs. For example, if central bank credit to steel mills or farms is cut back, the workers, managers, and owners of those steel mills and farms will be upset. It is often the case that, even though one might prefer the country not to have to make such sacrifices, there is little alternative to adjusting because the country will otherwise run out of reserves before long.

Now consider the effects of a fiscal expansion—for example, an increase in government spending. Figure 19.2 is a reproduction of Figure 18.15. The fiscal expansion shifts out the *IS* curve. This raises income. The higher income at point *F* causes a trade deficit. The deficit means that reserves are declining over time.

As before, the central bank could sterilize the reserve outflow to keep the money supply constant and remain at *F*. Under the assumption of nonsterilization, however, the money supply falls over time. The *LM* curve shifts back, income falls, and the trade balance improves. Eventually, income and the trade balance return to where they were before expansion at *B*. There is one difference between the new equilibrium at *B* and the old equilibrium at *E*. The interest rate is higher, meaning that a reallocation of output between sectors has taken place: The government sector has expanded at the expense of private investment. We have our second result under the monetary

FIGURE 19.2   Effects of a Fiscal Expansion Over Time

In the short run, an increase in government spending raises output and worsens the trade balance. If the loss of reserves is not sterilized, then the money supply falls over time and output returns to its original level at *B*.

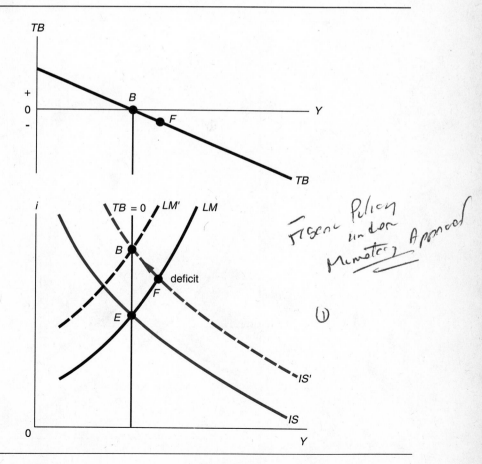

approach: A fiscal expansion, though raising income and worsening the trade balance in the short run, has no effect on either in the long run.

Finally, consider the effects of a devaluation. Figure 19.3 is a reproduction of Figure 18.16. The devaluation shifts out the *IS* curve. At point *D* income has increased. The devaluation shifts the vertical $TB = 0$ line farther out than the *IS* curve, so the trade balance improves at point *D*. As a consequence of the trade surplus, reserves are increasing over time. The central bank could sterilize the reserve inflow to keep the money supply constant and remain at point *D*, but under the assumption of non-sterilization the money supply rises over time and the *LM* curve shifts out. Income rises and the trade balance worsens. Eventually, the trade balance returns to zero, at point *C*. In this case, however, income ends up at a permanently higher level. The *TB* line in the upper panel of Figure 19.3 shows the magnitude of the long-run increase in income. The line's slope is $-m$, so $\Delta Y_{LR} = \dfrac{1}{m}\Delta \overline{X}$.

FIGURE 19.3   Effect of a Devaluation Over Time

In the short run, a devaluation improves the trade balance and raises output. If the inflow of reserves is not sterilized, then the money supply rises over time, and output rises further to *C*.

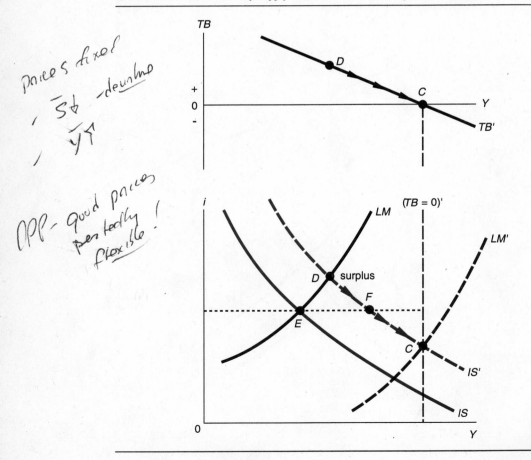

Intuitively, we can see that money keeps flowing in through the trade surplus until income has risen enough for increased imports ΔM to cancel out the initial stimulus of the devaluation of $\Delta \overline{X}$. This returns the trade balance to where it was before the expansion.[7]

It is interesting to compare the effect of the devaluation (at point C in Figure 19.3), $\Delta Y_{LR} = \dfrac{1}{m} \Delta \overline{X}$, to what it would be in the simpler Keynesian multiplier model (at

point F), that is, in the absence of crowding-out: $\left[\dfrac{1}{s+m} \right] \Delta \overline{X}$. The former is larger.

Under the monetary approach to the balance of payments, the long-run effect is not only greater than the short-run effect but is even greater than the short-run effect without crowding-out. The conclusion that a devaluation is an effective means of raising income even in the long run is a very "unmonetarist" conclusion; it stems from the Keynesian assumption that prices are fixed. This assumption is not very realistic for the long run and will be relaxed in the following section.

19.2 THE PURCHASING POWER PARITY ASSUMPTION — "monetarist" assumpt

The previous section defined the monetary approach to the balance of payments by the assumption of nonsterilization, but there is a second proposition often associated with proponents of the monetary approach. It is called Purchasing Power Parity (PPP), and requires the assumption that goods prices are perfectly flexible. Thus, the time has come to consider the determination of the price level.

Unlike the nonsterilization assumption, which is simply appropriate or inappropriate depending on what the central bank does, the assumption of price flexibility is a bigger issue, one that generates ideological controversy. The issue is similar to the Keynesian-monetarist debate in closed-economy macroeconomics. Many writers continue to confuse the monetary approach (nonsterilization) with monetarism (perfectly flexible prices). However, the difference is clear in a passage written by two of the central figures in the area:

> *The monetary approach to the balance of payments . . . can be readily applied to conditions of price and wage rigidity and consequent response of quantities–employment, output, consumption–rather than money wages.*[8]

Indeed the application to price and wage rigidity constitutes Mundell's income mechanism, developed in the preceding section.

Marina Whitman has suggested that the open-economy proponents of perfect price flexibility be referred to as "global monetarists" to distinguish them from the adherents of the more general monetary approach.[9] The global monetarists adopt the non-

[7] The way Figure 19.3 is drawn, the long-run interest rate is lower, and therefore I is higher, after the devaluation than before. We know that this must be right. Otherwise, with $X - M$ unchanged, $Y = C + I + G + X - M$ could not be higher after the devaluation.

[8] Jacob Frenkel and Harry Johnson, "The Monetary Approach to the Balance of Payments: Essential Concepts and Historical Origins," in Jacob Frenkel and Harry Johnson, eds., *The Monetary Approach to the Balance of Payments* (Toronto: University of Toronto Press, 1976), p. 25.

[9] Marina Whitman, "Global Monetarism and the Monetary Approach to the Balance of Payments," *Brookings Papers on Economic Activity*, 3 (1975): 491–536. The exposition corresponds to the two-country monetarist model of this chapter's Appendix B.

[handwritten margin note: —PPP— no short run deviation!]

sterilization assumption, but they have a slight quarrel with Hume's price specie-flow mechanism. Hume said that a monetary expansion will raise prices and worsen the trade balance, which will lead to an outflow that in the long run returns the prices to their original level, whereas the global monetarists ask how prices can be higher in one country than another even in the short run. Why would consumers buy any goods at all from the country with the higher prices? Would it not suffer an instantaneous trade deficit of unlimited size?

[handwritten note: ① — Composition different ② — Various production ③ — Monopoly power]

PPP: Definitions

[handwritten margin note: A Condition]

Purchasing Power Parity, or PPP, is simply the name for the following equation:

$$P = EP^*$$

[handwritten: $\$ = \left(\frac{\$}{DM}\right) DM$]

where E is the exchange rate and P and P^* are the domestic and foreign price levels respectively. It could also be written,

$$E = P/P^*$$

[handwritten: $\ln E = \ln A + (\ln P - \ln P_0) - (\ln P^* - \ln P)$]

We are not ready to draw any conclusions about causality, about whether changes in E cause changes in P or the other way around. PPP is just a condition, not in itself a complete theory of determination of the price level or the exchange rate.

The equation has a long history. Many economists consider it discredited. Certainly it is inconsistent with the Keynesian model, in which price levels are not free to adjust whenever the exchange rate changes. However, others consider it a necessary and logical consequence of economic rationality. The right answer depends on how one defines P and P^*.[10]

Arbitrage and the Law of One Price

If P and P^* are defined to be the price, in domestic and foreign currency respectively, of the identical good, then the formula is indeed a logical consequence of economic rationality and competitive markets. Under this interpretation, the equation is called the "Law of One Price." It is practically a definition of what it means to be a single good. The Law of One Price should hold because of international *arbitrage*.

When the price of the good in one country begins to rise above the price in another country (expressed in a common currency), it will become profitable for middlemen to buy the good in the low-price country, sell it in the high-price country, and pocket the difference. Such activity is what is meant by arbitrage.

For example, in 1984–1985, when the dollar had appreciated to roughly double its 1980 value against the mark, luxury German automobiles were selling for lower prices in Germany than in the United States. A "gray market" developed rapidly, in which people bought BMWs, Mercedes, and Porsches in Germany and shipped them to the United States, either to use themselves or to resell. Another example of arbitrage arose in 1988–1992, when the dollar had depreciated and it was the yen that

---

[10] Surveys of PPP are offered by Rudiger Dornbusch, "Purchasing Power Parity," in J. Eatwell, M. Milgate and P. Newman, eds., *The New Palgrave*, Vol. 3, New York: Macmillan, 1987, pp. 1075–1085; and Lawrence Officer, "The Purchasing-Power-Parity Theory of Exchange Rates: A Review Article," *International Money Fund Staff Papers* 23, (1976): 1–60.

was at its highest level in forty years. Then the arbitrage went in the other direction: Japanese visitors to California would load up on consumer goods that were cheaper than the same goods back home.

Arbitrage will tend to drive the price up in the low-price country, by adding to demand there, and down in the high-price country, by adding to supply. The process should continue until the price is equalized in the two countries. Hence, the Law of One Price.

An interesting question is why the arbitrage in 1984–1985 was not powerful enough to force retailers of German autos in the United States to lower their prices to match the lower dollar prices of the autos sold in Germany. Evidently the costs involved in buying an auto in Germany and shipping it to the United States are large enough that most American customers preferred to continue buying from authorized dealers despite the higher price. Part of the explanation is that a BMW bought in Germany is not precisely the same commodity as a BMW bought from an authorized U.S. dealer. Even leaving aside the shipping costs, some changes must be made in pollution control equipment to satisfy U.S. regulations. Furthermore, when consumers buy automobiles from an authorized dealer, one thing they get is a warranty, the ability to have mechanical problems fixed at no cost. Needless to say, this is difficult to do if the dealer is in Stuttgart.

Do note that this phenomenon of the importer ''pricing to market''—setting prices with an eye more on prices of competing products in the customers' market than on the price of the import good in its country of origin—is predominantly a phenomenon of the U.S. market. In other countries, exchange rate changes tend to be more fully and immediately passed through to the prices of imports. A possible reason is that Americans are less accustomed to foreign currencies than are residents of most other countries.

Because the Law of One Price is so basic, we have been implicitly assuming all along that it holds. In the preceding two chapters even though we assumed that the price of BMWs produced in Germany was set rigidly in terms of marks (refer to the discussion of Assumption 3 in Section 17.2), we took as given that the price of BMWs in the United States was simply the mark price times the dollar/mark exchange rate. In other words, we assumed that arbitrage enforced the Law of One Price for BMWs, and we will continue to do so, notwithstanding the anomaly just noted.

This is not as strong as the assumption that the price of *American-made* automobiles is equal to the mark price of German automobiles times the exchange rate. Chryslers and BMWs are, after all, different products. Arbitrage between the two does not operate, given the reasonable assumption that consumers view American and German automobiles as sufficiently different products. This fact allows U.S. manufacturers to set their prices in dollars with some degree of rigidity (at least in the short run), at the same time allowing German manufacturers to set theirs in marks.

Reasons for Failure of PPP

The term "purchasing power" connotes a basket of goods rather than a single good. If identical goods entered the domestic and foreign consumption baskets with identical weights, and the Law of One Price held for each good, then PPP would necessarily hold.

We will use P and P^* to refer to actual price indices in use, such as the Consumer Price Index (CPI) or Producer Price Index (PPI). Such indices inevitably refer to different baskets of goods, which immediately allows the possibility that the equation $P = EP^*$ will fail to hold. Note that aggregate price indices are expressed relative to a base year (e.g., 1980 = 100) rather than in absolute dollar or pound terms. Thus the concept here is known as "relative PPP," rather than "absolute PPP":[11] Relative to the base year, the domestic price goes up by the same percentage as the foreign price level plus the percentage change in the exchange rate. If a bushel of wheat or a ton of steel is now, and in the past has always been, more expensive in France than China, this will not show up in the calculations of relative PPP. In other words, the equation $P = EP^*$ holds only up to a multiplicative constant. For convenience, the multiplicative constant usually is not shown explicitly. Another way of stating the proposition that relative PPP holds is to say that the *real exchange rate*, defined as EP^*/P, is constant over time.

There are four reasons why Purchasing Power Parity can fail to hold. Each is associated with its own typical pattern of movement in the real exchange rate.

1. *Tariffs and transportation costs* create a band in which prices can fluctuate before arbitrage becomes profitable.[12] Only if the price in one country exceeds the price in the other by more than the size of any tariffs, other trade barriers, and shipping costs, will arbitrage start to operate. We might rescue the Law of One Price by claiming that a bushel of wheat delivered in New York City at 12:00 noon on a particular day is a different good than a bushel of wheat delivered in London, or delivered on a different day. (Contracts for spot or forward delivery of agricultural and mineral commodities do in fact specify time and place, and the price can vary accordingly, especially if there are substantial tariffs or transportation costs. In any case, PPP is defined to apply to price indices that aggregate together, not only wheat, but all goods, so these geographical factors clearly allow deviations from PPP. Figure 19.4(a) represents these deviations as fluctuations of the real exchange rate within a band.

2. *Permanent shifts in the terms of trade* between traded goods occur, such as the upward shift that occurred between oil and manufactured goods in 1973–1974 or the reverse shift that occurred in 1986. Oil and manufactured goods can have very different weights in the price indices of the two countries, particularly if we consider producer price indices rather than CPIs. An oil-producing country, for example, will experience a "real appreciation" of its currency when the relative price of oil goes up, whether in the form of a nominal appreciation of the currency or in the form of an increase in the producer price index, P. If the oil price goes up by 50 percent and oil has a weight that is 20 percentage points higher in an oil-exporting country than in another country, then the effect on the real exchange rate will be 10 percent. To take another example, automobiles could have the same weight in two countries' price indices, but

---

[11] It is difficult to get the data necessary for computing absolute PPP; we cannot use standard statistics on price indices that governments publish, as we can when computing relative PPP. It means sending a team of researchers to different countries to sample the prices of a standardized set of goods, as has been done in a long-term research project by Irving Kravis and Robert Lipsey; "Toward an Explanation of National Price Levels," *Princeton Studies in International Finance*, No. 52, 1983.

[12] A classic reference is Paul Samuelson, "Theoretical Notes on Trade Problems," *Review of Economics and Statistics*, (May 1964): 145–154.

FIGURE 19.4   Patterns of Deviation from Purchasing Power Parity

(a) Tariffs and transportation costs create a band within which the real exchange rate can fluctuate.
(b) Permanent shifts in the terms of trade move the real exchange rate unpredictably. (c) A long-term trend
in the relative price of non-traded goods (e.g., upward, in a rapidly growing country) will cause a trend in
the real exchange rate. (d) The real exchange rate works its way back to equilibrium after a devaluation, as
goods prices adjust, but the process can be slow.

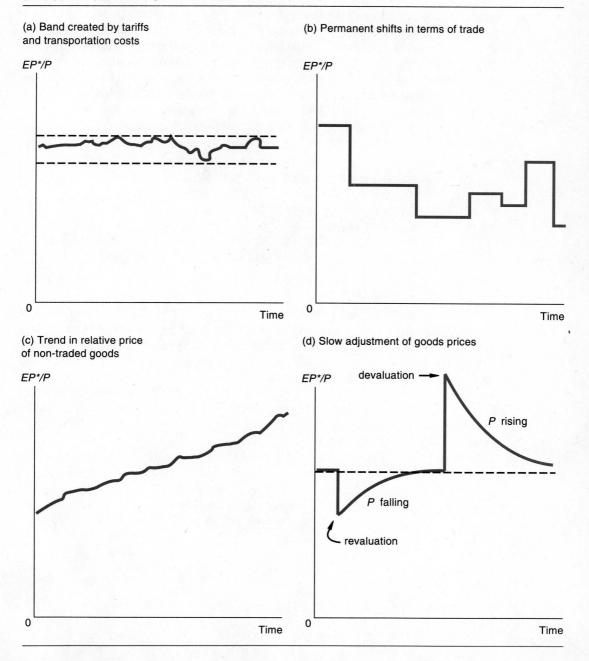

if one produces smaller, more fuel-efficient cars, then it is likely to experience a real appreciation in the event of an oil price increase that causes demand to shift toward its products.

In the case of tariffs and transportation costs, when the real exchange rate nears the top of the band it cannot go much farther. However, in the case of permanent shifts in the terms of trade, no natural limit exists on how far the real exchange rate can drift in one direction or the other. In the absence of any particular theory predicting changes in the terms of trade, the real exchange rate can move up from its current position as easily as down. Accordingly, in Figure 19.4(b), the shifts in the terms of trade are shown as "permanent." When a change in the real exchange rate is observed, there is no way to know whether it will in the future continue to move further in the same direction or will reverse itself. When changes in the level of a variable such as the real exchange rate are not predictable, we say that the variable follows a "random walk," like a drunken reveler walking down an empty street. But this should just be a statement of our ignorance of what the real exchange rate will do; it does not take the place of an economic theory.

3. Even if the traded goods baskets are identical in both countries, if the indices include prices of *non-traded goods and services*, which cannot be arbitraged internationally, PPP may fail. If the prices of non-traded goods in each country happen to move proportionately to the prices of traded goods, then PPP will still hold. If there are shifts in the relative prices of traded goods and non-traded goods, PPP will fail. (Models with non-traded goods are discussed at greater length in Chapter 20.)

Consider the real exchange rate defined in terms of consumer price indices.

$$E_{real} = E[CPI^*/CPI] \tag{19.1}$$

In each country, a weighted average of non-traded goods and traded goods constitutes the CPI. The real exchange rate will change if the *relative* price of non-traded goods (i.e., the price of non-traded goods in terms of traded goods) changes in either the foreign country or the domestic country.[13] For example, the Swiss franc has often appeared overvalued relative to Swiss housing and other non-traded goods and services. An even clearer example is Japan; the long-term trend in the yen over the past four decades shows a strong real appreciation, with housing leading the way in the Japanese price index (along with golf-club memberships, a non-traded good particularly important in Japan!).

Bela Balassa and others have identified a pattern based on differential economic growth.[14] Growth of a country's income is associated with increased productivity in traded goods, which then fall in price relative to non-traded goods. In other words, the relative price of non-traded goods in terms of traded goods rises. Growth also may cause a rise in the relative price of non-traded goods and services if they are superior

---

[13] Refer to Problem 2c at the end of the chapter.

[14] Bela Balassa, "The Purchasing Power Parity Doctrine: A Reappraisal," *Journal of Political Economy*, 72 (1964): 584–596. This is the sort of "real trade theory" explanation for changes in the real exchange rate that we would like to have to explain the shifts in the terms of trade discussed above, as opposed to the agnostic ("ignorance is bliss") position that is content with describing the real exchange rate as following a random walk.

goods in consumers' demand functions.[15] Either way, since the prices of traded goods are tied to world prices, a rise in the relative price of non-traded goods can only mean an increase in the price of non-traded goods relative to world prices. Therefore, the CPI, which includes non-traded goods, rises relative to world prices. The domestic currency will appear to be overvalued by PPP calculations. The real exchange rate, E (CPI*/CPI), will appear too low (i.e., either E will appear too low or CPI too high).

In short, countries with strong growth rates tend also to have upward trends in their relative prices and therefore in the real foreign exchange value of their currencies, as is shown in Figure 19.4(c). In other words, such countries often show trends of real appreciation in their currencies.[16]

4. In Chapter 17, lags due to *imperfect information, contracts, inertia in consumer habits,* and so forth, rendered elasticities lower in the short run than in the long run. This implies that two goods that are highly substitutable in the long run may be very imperfect substitutes in the short run. This low degree of substitutability allows prices to be "sticky" and allows large deviations from PPP in the short run without inducing large-scale international arbitrage. For example, following a devaluation or revaluation, firms do not readjust their prices fully, but absorb the (finite) increase or decrease in demand by varying the quantity sold. If the goods are close substitutes in the long run, then prices will adjust to PPP eventually; if they did not adjust, demand levels might rise or fall without limit. Figure 19.4(d) illustrates the process. If a sudden increase in the nominal exchange rate occurs, with prices fixed in the short run it translates fully into an increase in the real exchange rate. This real depreciation stimulates the demand for domestic goods, putting upward pressure on prices. As prices gradually rise, the real exchange rate comes back down toward its long-run equilibrium. However, it is always possible that before equilibrium is reached, another sudden exchange rate change will occur.

The precise nature of the microeconomics of sticky prices is not well understood, but the empirical evidence is clear, as we will see in the following section. Of these four ways in which PPP can fail, the last is the one with the most macroeconomic content. From now on, any reference to the possibility of short-run failure of PPP will be a reference to the macroeconomic, sticky-price interpretation. While permanent changes in the real exchange rate due to productivity differences and other real factors do occur (e.g., the real appreciation of the yen against the dollar over the last forty years), they tend to be slow long-term trends. When we talk about failures of PPP, we will be referring to short-run deviations from those trends.

[15] "Superior" goods are goods that experience a relative increase in demand when real income increases. Jeffrey Bergstrand, "Structural Determinants of Real Exchange Rates and National Price Levels: Some Empirical Evidence," *American Economic Review*, 81 (1) (March 1991) pp. 325–334.

[16] David Hsieh, "The Determination of the Real Exchange Rate: The Productivity Approach," *Journal of International Economics*, 12 (1982): 355–362, finds evidence in time series data for Germany and Japan more supportive of the Balassa hypothesis than does Officer (op. cit.). These studies look at relative PPP. Cross-country evidence on absolute PPP is summarized by Irving Kravis and Robert Lipsey, "National Price Levels and the Prices of Tradables and Nontradables," *American Economic Review*, 78, (2) (May 1988): 474–478; it too shows that the price of non-traded goods relative to traded goods increases with the level of the country's per capita income.

Any empirical study of PPP shows very large deviations, at least in the short run. Relative to the Bretton Woods period of fixed exchange rates, most countries' real exchange rates have been especially variable in the years since 1973, including Great Britain and the United States. This is reflected in Figure 19.5, which graphs the real pound-sterling/dollar rate. A useful measure of variability is the standard deviation.[17] The standard deviation of the real pound/dollar rate was 16 percent over the period 1973–1987.[18] In general, it takes a band of two standard deviations either way to encompass 95 percent of the fluctuations in a variable (assuming a normal distribution). These numbers imply that departures from PPP as large as 32 percent occur (2 times 16 percent = 32 percent). These are large swings to be occurring regularly in the relative prices of countries' goods.

[17] If you are familiar with the statistical concept of the *variance*, the standard deviation is simply the square root of it.

[18] Jeffrey Frankel, "Zen and the Art of Modern Macroeconomics," in William Haraf and Thomas Willett, eds., *Monetary Policy for a Volatile Global Economy*, Washington: The AEI press, 1990, pp. 117–123.

FIGURE 19.5   119 Years of Purchasing Power Parity Between the Dollar and Pound

---

Changes in the real exchange rate are not purely random. Rather, it tends to regress slowly toward its long-run equilibrium (until a new disturbance comes along). In the case of the United States and United Kingdom, the long-run equilibrium appears to have been constant.

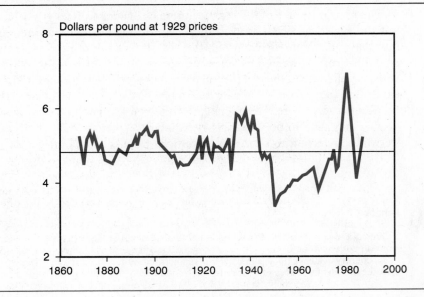

In comparison, the standard deviation of the real pound/dollar rate was only 9 percent over the fixed-rate period 1945–1972.[19] The 1973 increase in the variability of the real exchange rate against the United States was particularly great for Germany; this is clear in Figure 19.6, which shows monthly changes in the real mark/dollar rate.[20] The pre-1973 vs. post-1973 comparisons suggest strongly that fluctuations in the nominal exchange rate may be a cause of fluctuations in the real exchange rate.

Another explanation is that the greater variability in real exchange rates after 1973 was due to the greater magnitude of worldwide real "disturbances" such as oil shocks, and would have happened even under a regime of fixed exchange rates (in which case the variability would have shown up in the price levels). This alternative view holds that changes in the nominal exchange rate do not *cause* changes in the real exchange rate, but that both occur in response to exogenous real disturbances such as productivity changes.[21] One problem with this view is that no one has identified these real shocks. It would seem that if there were a change in productivity or consumer tastes which applied to hundreds of different industries in a country, such that all of them experience an increase in price when the currency appreciates (relative to their counterparts in foreign countries), then we should be able to identify what that change is. A few cases, in fact, do suggest explanations. The rapid fall in the value of the yen and the mark against the dollar when the price of oil quadrupled at the end of 1973 surely resulted because those two countries' economies were more dependent on imported oil than was the United States'. It is hard to see what changes in worker productivity or consumer tastes could possibly explain the 50-plus percent real appreciation of the dollar between 1980 and 1985, however, or its reversal over the following three years.

One way to check if the comparison of the fixed-rate and floating-rate periods might be contaminated by larger supply shocks after 1973 than before is to look at Canada, the one country to have a floating exchange rate in the 1950s. The real exchange rate in Canada was highly variable at the time, while those in fixed-rate countries were much less so. Another piece of evidence is offered by the case of Ireland. From 1957 to 1970 the Irish currency was pegged to the pound, and thereby to the dollar and mark as well, until the currencies began to float against each other. From 1973 to 1978 the Irish currency was again pegged to the pound, which meant it floated

---

[19] Some of the variation in the real exchange rate during this period was due to differences in inflation rates between the two countries, but much of the variation was accounted for by a few discrete devaluations of the pound. The exchange rate was not literally "fixed" permanently; it was "fixed, but adjustable." For some statistics on other countries, see Hans Genberg, "Purchasing Power Parity Under Fixed and Flexible Exchange Rates," *Journal of International Economics*, 8 (May 1978): 247–786; or Rudiger Dornbusch and Alberto Giovannini, "Money in the Open Economy," in Frank Hahn and Benjamin Friedman, eds., *Handbook of Monetary Economics*, Amsterdam: North-Holland, 1988.

[20] Monthly variability in the U.S.-German rate tripled after 1973. The source is Dornbusch and Giovannini. We have concentrated here on the U.K. case rather than the German one, or others, because the time series extends unbroken much farther back in history.

[21] Such theories have been constructed, for example, by Alan Stockman: "The Equilibrium Approach to Exchange Rates," *Economic Review*, Federal Reserve Bank of Richmond, (March–April 1987): 12–31. Other relevant work includes Elhanan Helpman, "An Exploration in the Theory of Exchange Rate Regimes," *Journal of Political Economy*, 89 (October 1981): 865–890; and Torsten Persson and Lars Svensson, "Exchange Rate Variability and Asset Trade," *Journal of Monetary Economics*, 23 May 1989): 485–509.

FIGURE 19.6   Changes in the Real Mark/Dollar Exchange Rate

Short-run exchange rate volatility has been very high since exchange rates began to float in 1973. It appears that the higher volatility of nominal exchange rates translates into higher volatility of real exchange rates.

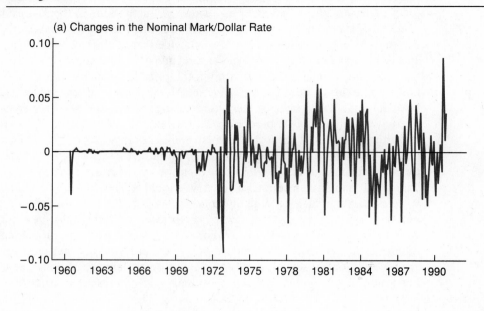

(a) Changes in the Nominal Mark/Dollar Rate

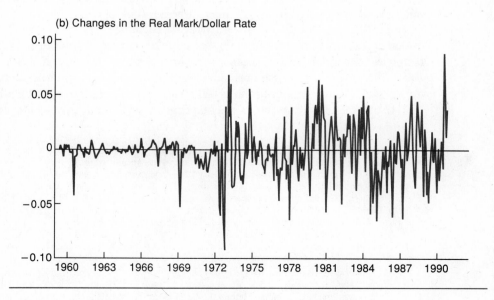

(b) Changes in the Real Mark/Dollar Rate

against the dollar and mark. Then from 1979 onward Ireland was in the European Monetary System, and the currency, the punt, was thereby tied to the mark, which meant it floated against the dollar and pound (until the latter joined as well in 1990). In each of the three periods, the choice of *nominal* exchange rate regime for the punt corresponds very well with the observed degree of *real* exchange rate variability vis-à-vis each of the three trading partners. Stickiness of prices explains the pattern. Otherwise it would be quite a coincidence that real variability vis-à-vis the mark, say, should fall and vis-à-vis the pound should rise at precisely the same moment that the nominal variabilities, respectively, fall and rise as well.[22] A third way of evaluating whether real exchange rate variability is related to the exchange rate regime is to consider earlier historical experience. History demonstrates that the variability of real exchange rates was larger under floating-rate regimes than under fixed-rate regimes, not just during the period after World War II, but before the war as well.[23]

These findings would be difficult to explain with perfectly flexible goods prices.[24] It seems more likely that prices are sticky and that nominal exchange rate variability is indeed a primary source of real exchange rate variability. Estimates on the yearly U.S.-U.K. data indicate that fluctuations in the nominal exchange rate are 92 percent reflected as fluctuations in the real exchange rate.[25]

There have been some studies of PPP, or the Law of One Price, for disaggregated categories of goods matched across countries, which are the smallest, most narrowly defined, SITC categories (Standardized International Trade Classification). These studies find large deviations even on these disaggregated data. They need not be interpreted as a failure of economic rationality or the Law of One Price. One partial explanation is that most foreign trade takes place under 30- to 90-day contracts, so prices cannot be reajusted for 30 to 90 days after a disturbance. More fundamentally, manufactured goods of different firms are actually different goods, as was noted earlier.[26]

Even goods that are marketed in the same location and differ in little more than brand name—for example, a Japanese television set and the identical item manufactured by the identical firm but under an American label—violate the Law of One Price. Different manufacturers vary with respect to reputation or warranty offered, and different retailers vary with respect to their sales and maintenance service. Long-term customer relationships are thought to be particularly important in Japan and give rise to what are sometimes called *implicit* contracts: A Japanese corporation will hesitate before raising prices when there is excess demand, in the anticipation that this will build loyalty among customers, who will continue to buy from it in other periods of excess supply.

---

[22] Michael Mussa, *Exchange Rates in Theory and in Reality*, Essays in International Finance No. 179, (December 1990), Princeton University.

[23] Barry Eichengreen, "Real Exchange Rate Behavior Under Alternative Monetary Regimes: Interwar Evidence," *European Economic Review* 32 (June 1988): 363–371.

[24] An ingenious, if convoluted, explanation of this sort has been constructed by Alan Stockman, "Real Exchange Rate Variability under Pegged and Floating Exchange Rate Systems: An Equilibrium Theory," in K. Brunner and A. Meltzer, eds., *Carnegie-Rochester Conference Series on Public Policy*, 1988: 259–294.

[25] From 1869 to 1987. Frankel, op. cit.

[26] Peter Isard, "How Far Can We Push the Law of One Price?" *American Economic Review*, 67 (December 1977): 942–948.

This point recalls a distinction made by Arthur Okun and others between homogeneous "auction goods"—for which the Law of One Price holds instantaneously and worldwide, and heterogeneous ''customer goods''—for which the Law of One Price fails, at least in the short run. Auction goods are usually basic commodities such as agricultural and mineral products, while customer goods are usually heterogeneous manufactured goods that bear brand names. However, the rapidly evolving semiconductor industry provides an example of each kind of good: So-called "commodity chips" tend to be all the same regardless of the producer and are sold in perfectly competitive markets resembling those for agricultural or mineral commodities, while "specialty chips" are designed to fulfill more specific functions and tend to fit more the description of "customer goods."

If PPP holds in the long run but not in the short run, the obvious empirical questions become: How long is the short run? How quickly do deviations from PPP disappear? The speed with which the real exchange rate adjusts back toward its long-run equilibrium has been estimated at about 3 percent a month for the floating-rate period: The best guess in a given month as to what will be the gap between the real exchange rate and its long-run equilibrium is 97 percent of what it was in the preceding month. After two months, 94 percent of the gap will remain ($.97^2 = .94$), and so forth. After one year 69 percent of the gap will remain ($.97^{12} = .69$). In other words, the speed of adjustment has been estimated at 31 percent per year. This speed of adjustment is not implausibly slow, but it is sufficiently slow as to be difficult to detect statistically in the data, given that large new disturbances come along frequently. This is especially true if only a few years of data are available. We must look at a long time period, such as the 119 years of data in Figure 19.5, for clear manifestation of the tendency of the real exchange rate to return to equilibrium.[27]

19.3 THE MONETARIST MODEL OF THE BALANCE OF PAYMENTS

This section adopts the monetarist assumption that prices are perfectly flexible, so that PPP holds.

$$P = EP^* \tag{19.2}$$

Why is PPP assumed here, when the empirical evidence reviewed above does not support it? There are several reasons. First, just as assuming fixed prices allowed us to focus on the determination of output in the preceding chapter, assuming flexible prices and full employment is a simplification that allows us to focus on the determination of the price level. (We will relax the assumption of full employment in Chapter 23 to study the complete case where increases in demand go partly into output and partly into prices.) Second, some economic analysts write as if PPP does hold. It helps to understand their viewpoint. Third, the flexible-price full-employment assumption is fairly realistic for thinking about the *long run*, just as the rigid-price assumption is fairly realistic for thinking about most countries in the short run.

[27] Hyperinflation is one context in which PPP in a sense works well empirically (because the long run in effect ''telescopes'' into the short run). This is explained in Appendix A to the chapter. Hyperinflations are also discussed briefly in Chapter 24, which looks at the question of how monetary factors determine the exchange rate.

Finally, PPP is fairly realistic, even in the relatively short run, for thinking about very small, very open economies. Hong Kong and Singapore are good examples. Why is PPP a good assumption for some countries but not for others?

The Aggregation of Traded Goods for Small Countries

For most countries, even relatively large ones, prices of import goods can be taken as given exogenously in the short run, fixed in terms of foreign currency—as was assumed in the preceding two chapters—because a typical country constitutes a small fraction of the world demand for any given product and so has very little "monopsony power." The situation is more varied when it comes to the country's export goods. Many countries have some monopoly power in their export goods. Even if the country is only one of many that produces, for example, automobiles, foreign consumers will not treat its autos as perfect substitutes for other countries' autos. This makes it possible for producers to set a price for the product in domestic currency without fearing an instantaneous large loss of demand due to adverse changes in the exchange rate or in the prices charged by foreign competitors. This was the sort of country we considered in Chapters 17 and 18. But we now consider a different kind of country.

Many countries are so small in world markets that they have very little monopoly power in their export goods and can take prices of export goods as exogenous, fixed in terms of foreign currency. In the case of agricultural and mineral commodities, the output of different countries often can be considered perfect substitutes. Sugar or tin, for example, is basically the same regardless of where it is produced. In addition, if the country doesn't happen to produce a large proportion of the world output of the agricultural or mineral product, then it is safe to assume it accepts the world price. In other words, if it tried to charge more than the going price, it would quickly find itself without customers. In the case of manufactured goods, some labor-intensive products such as textiles are sufficiently similar among a wide range of countries that their prices too can be taken as essentially given on world markets. Then the analysis returns to the definition of a "small country" used in the first half of the book: a country that is too small in international markets to affect world prices.

As these examples show, less developed countries are more likely to take export prices as given than are larger industrialized countries. (Note, however, that the assumption that the country can sell any quantity it wants on the world market at the going price can go wrong for another reason: Major customers may apply country-by-country quotas to purchases of the commodity. Industrialized countries maintain such quotas against both sugar and textiles.)

If a country is so small that it takes not only its import prices as given but its export prices as well, then it is possible to aggregate the two kinds of goods together at their (given) relative price. The composite commodity thereby created is referred to as "traded goods." Under the assumption that the small open country can buy or sell all of the traded goods it wishes to, the trade balance becomes the quantity of traded goods it chooses to produce minus the quantity it chooses to buy. With this analysis, the question of how a given change in the trade balance breaks down into the change in imports and the change in exports is left unanswered. However, it is usually the overall trade balance in which we are interested anyway.

In reality, the relative prices of some of the goods within this composite commodity, the traded good, will sometimes change. When this happens, it will not be useful to talk in terms of traded goods in the aggregate. Worldwide changes in the relative price of oil, as occurred in 1973 and 1979 (upward) and 1986 (downward), are an important example. But for purposes of studying changes that do not affect relative prices, such as changes that originate in domestic macroeconomic policy, this aggregation will be useful. The next chapter will continue to aggregate all traded goods, as well.

The Determination of the Balance of Payments in the Monetarist Model

This chapter considers only fixed exchange rates. This is probably just as well, because most very small, very open economies (such as Hong Kong) do in fact seek to maintain a fixed exchange rate. The monetary approach under floating rates will be taken up in Chapter 24. The goal here is to analyze the effect of monetary policy and devaluation on the two target variables, income and the trade balance. Furthermore, this section considers the small-country version of the monetarist model, which means that the world price level is taken as exogenous.[28] Since both the exchange rate and the foreign price level are determined by Equation 19.2 the domestic price level is also determined. This method of determining the domestic price level is very different from the Keynesian way in which it was exogenously set. The difference will become obvious when we later consider devaluation. PPP states that the devaluation is instantly reflected as a proportionate increase in the domestic price level, whereas in the Keynesian model the domestic price level did not change.

Desired money balances are proportional to nominal income.[29]

$$M^d = KPY \qquad (19.3)$$

Individuals adapt actual money balances to desired money balances through saving (in excess of investment), represented by H. This part of the book ignores assets other than money, such as bonds. (They will enter in Part V.) For this reason, saving can only take the form of additions to holdings of money balances. H is thus equal to $\dot{M}$, defined as the change in the money stock; $\dot{M}$ tells us how much the money supply is going up per year. H is assumed proportional to the current gap between the desired money stock and the actual money stock, M,

$$H = \dot{M} = \delta(M^d - M)$$

where δ is the speed with which money balances are adjusted. Now we use Equation 19.3 for long-run desired money balances.

$$H = \delta(KPY - M) \qquad (19.4)$$

---

[28] Appendix B to this chapter relaxes the small-country assumption to look at the two-country version of the monetary approach to the balance of payments, which is relevant when the country is large enough to affect the world price level. (As long as world prices are perfectly flexible and PPP holds, it continues to be a "monetarist" model, as opposed to the Keynesian model previously examined.)

[29] M here represents the money stock, not imports as in previous chapters. Desired money balances M^d refers to a long-run notion of money demand; it differs somewhat from the short-run notion of money demand in $IS = LM$, where the interest rate adjusts so that money demand is always equal to money supply, even in the short run. (The two notions of money demand can be made to coincide in the long run if the interest rate tends to a constant.)

Under the key nonsterilization assumption of the monetary approach, the rate of change of the money supply, $\dot{M}$, is the same as the rate of accumulation of reserves, the balance of payments surplus, BP (holding constant domestic credit). The equation becomes

$$BP = \dot{M} = \delta KPY - \delta M \qquad (19.5)$$

Equation 19.5 looks unlike any balance of payments expression seen before. An increase in the money supply M has a negative effect on the surplus, as in the last chapter. While the Keynesian model was quite specific about the channel through which the increase in the money supply increases spending (it lowers the interest rate and thus stimulates investment), the monetarist explanation is more general. A monetary expansion worsens the balance of payments because individuals, when faced with an excess supply of money, increase spending to adjust their excessive money holdings back down to the level of their money demand. (These two explanations can be made entirely consistent if investment depends linearly on the interest rate.[30])

Another difference between the two models is that the monetary approach says the outflow occurs through the overall balance of payments, without differentiating between the current account or capital account, whereas the Keynesian approach specifies that it occurs through the trade balance. However, since we have not yet introduced capital flows into the Keynesian model, it is difficult to tell the difference.

Still, these differences are not especially important. The crucial difference, remember, between the monetarist and Keynesian models is price flexibility.

The assumption of perfect wage and price flexibility in the global monetarist model implies completely inelastic aggregate supply. Because income is always at the full-employment level, $Y = \overline{Y}$, the balance of payments in Equation 19.5 varies only with the price level, P, and the money supply, M. Figure 19.7 graphs the relationship between the balance of payments and the price level for a given M, with the balance of payments measured on the horizontal axis, and refers to it as the "H schedule."[31] As the equation says, the horizontal intercept is $-\delta M$ and the slope is the inverse of $\delta K \overline{Y}$. Again, the reason the schedule slopes upward is that a higher price level means a higher demand for money, which causes residents to cut back on spending so they can earn the desired money balances through a balance of payments surplus.

The exogenous foreign price level, $\overline{P}^*$, and the given fixed exchange rate, E, together determine the domestic price level, $P = E\overline{P}^*$, by Equation 19.2. This price level, P, is represented in Figure 19.7 by a horizontal line. Point B in the figure is the starting point, a position of balance of payments equilibrium. Two policy changes will be considered: monetary policy and devaluation.

The Effect of a Monetary Expansion in the Monetarist Model

A monetary expansion shifts the H schedule to the left. The size of the leftward shift is determined by the size of the change in the horizontal intercept ($\delta \Delta M$) The economy moves to point M. Any given P implies a certain level of money demand.

---

[30] The reduced form of the linear *IS-LM* system (i.e., with the interest rate substituted out) is the same as the monetarist formulation. This is Chapter Problem 5b.

[31] Earlier monetarist writings referred to the accumulation of money through saving as "hoarding," thus the symbol H, but the term did not catch on.

FIGURE 19.7   Monetary Expansion in the Monetarist Small-Country Model

An increase in the money supply shifts the "H schedule" left. With the price level, P, tied down by PPP, this leads to an excess supply of money and a balance of payments deficit ($BP < 0$ at M). Over time, money flows out of the country and balance is restored ($BP = 0$ at B).

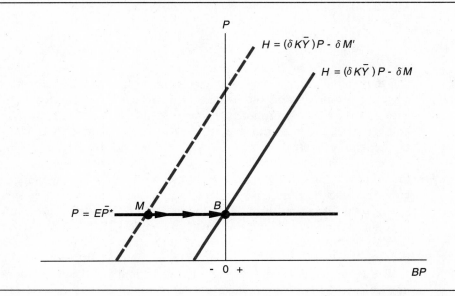

At the level implied by the exogenously given $P = E\bar{P}^*$, an excess supply of money is evident because money supply is greater than money demand. (*Any* point to the left of the vertical axis is a point of excess money supply.) People will increase spending or decrease saving. In fact *dis*saving, a balance of payments deficit, can be read off the horizontal axis at point M. Recall again the essence of the monetary approach, the identification of the balance of payments deficit with the rate of decumulation of the money supply.

The H schedule shifts whenever the money supply changes. As time passes and money flows out through the balance of payments deficit, the H schedule shifts to the right. The intersection with the price level line gradually moves rightward from M. As the excess supply of money is worked off, the deficit falls, as can be read off the horizontal axis. This process continues until (in the long run) the economy returns to point B, where money supply again equals money demand and there is no further need for dissaving: The balance of payments has returned to zero. Only then, when the reserve stock is no longer changing, has it reached long-run equilibrium.

Conversely, a monetary contraction initially shifts the H schedule to the right, improving the balance of payments. However, the payments surplus itself leads to an increasing money supply, which over time shifts the H schedule back to the left until, again, in the long run it returns to balance of payments equilibrium.

In the case of either expansion or contraction, there is no long-run effect on the level of the money supply, but there may be an effect on its composition. Expansion or contraction of domestic credit is permanent. It is the foreign component of the monetary base—international reserves—which changes to offset the change in domestic credit.

The Effect of a Devaluation in the Monetarist Model

Now consider the effect of a devaluation. An increase in the exchange rate from E to E' means that the exogenous world price level, $\overline{P}^*$, now translates into a higher domestic price level, $E'\overline{P}^*$, represented by a higher domestic horizontal price line in Figure 19.8. The higher value of P implies a higher level of domestic money demand. With an unchanged level of money supply, there is an excess demand for money at point D. (Any point to the right of the vertical axis is a point of excess money demand.) People reduce their spending or increase their saving. A balance of payments surplus results. That devaluation leads to a surplus is a common observation, but in this case the cause is not a change in relative prices stimulating exports. There can be no change in relative prices in this model. Rather, the higher price level raises the demand for nominal money balances.

The balance of payments surplus at D means that the money supply is increasing. Over time, the H schedule shifts to the left, as the excess demand for money is alleviated by the increasing supply. In the long run it moves to point C, where money supply again equals money demand and the balance of payments is back at zero. The new

---

FIGURE 19.8 Devaluation in the Monetarist Small-Country Model

---

An increase in the exchange rate from E to E' raises the price level, P, proportionately, leading to an excess demand for money and a balance of payments surplus ($BP > 0$ at D). Over time, money flows into the country and balance is restored ($BP = 0$ at C).

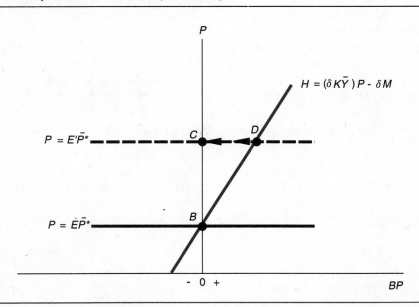

equilibrium after the devaluation features not only a higher price level but a higher money supply as well, both nominal variables having increased in the same proportion as the exchange rate.

Let us now consider an exogenous increase in the world price level, $\overline{P}^*$, as might result, for example, from an expansion in the world money supply. It acts just like the devaluation pictured in Figure 19.8 so far as the small country is concerned. It is instantly transmitted as a proportionately higher domestic price level, $P = E\overline{P}^*$. The excess demand for money shows up as a temporary balance of payments surplus. Notice again that the favorable effect of the foreign price increase on the balance of payments does not take place through *relative* prices, as in the elasticities or Keynesian approaches, but rather through the effect of the price *level* on money demand.

Finally, consider an exogenous increase in domestic money demand. Such an increase in money demand might result, for example, from an exogenous increase in domestic output, $\overline{Y}$. Since this chapter assumes full employment, the increase in output must come from the supply side: an increase in the capital stock, labor force, or productivity. In any case, the increase in money demand causes people to cut back spending so that they can acquire the desired money balances. It acts like the decrease in money supply previously considered, in that it creates an excess demand for money and shifts the hoarding schedule to the right. (More precisely, if the increase in M^d comes from an increase in Y, then it rotates the H schedule in the clockwise direction; refer to the slope in Equation 19.4. The point remains: A higher H now corresponds to a given P.) The cutback in spending thus leads to a balance of payments surplus. Over time money flows in through the payments surplus, until equilibrium returns with a higher money supply and a zero balance of payments, as always.

Notice the sharp contrast to the Keynesian model, in which an increase in income caused an immediate trade deficit, rather than a surplus. The Keynesian model should be thought of as correct for income growth induced by increases in spending (because it is a model in which the economy can be below full employment). The present result—growth causing a payments *surplus* due to higher money demand—is appropriate for exogenous supply-induced growth. A prime motivation for the development of the monetary approach in the 1960s was the observed fact that the fastest-growing countries, such as Japan, Germany, and other European countries, ran balance of payments surpluses while the United States ran a deficit. That the monetary approach could explain this situation accounted in part for its growing popularity.[32]

Extensions of the Monetary Approach

The monetary approach to the balance of payments has given rise to a number of theoretical offshoots. The following chapter will introduce non-traded goods into the model. Chapter 24 will consider the monetary approach to floating exchange rates.

As noted, the conclusions regarding effects on the balance of payments could apply either to the current account or capital account, but capital flows will not be explicitly

---

[32] The argument was made by Robert Mundell, "Growth and the Balance of Payments," Chapter 9 in his *International Economics* (New York: Macmillan, 1968). For good examples from the current era (in which Japan and Germany have floating rather than fixed exchange rates), recall the cases of Taiwan and the other newly industrialized economies of East Asia which have tended to experience rapid supply-side growth with surpluses in their balances of payments.

introduced until Chapter 22. There the basic conclusion of the monetary approach will be seen to be unchanged. Under a fixed exchange rate, any increase in the money supply will flow out through a balance of payments deficit, leaving no long-run effect. A devaluation will cause an inflow of money through a payments surplus, so that in the long run the money supply will have increased by the same proportion as the exchange rate and price level.

There is another model, called the portfolio-balance approach, that grew out of the monetary approach and is formally analogous to it.[33] In the portfolio-balance model of fixed exchange rates the demand, not only for money, but for all assets (including, in particular, bonds) is assumed to depend on income. Under a fixed exchange rate, an equiproportionate increase in money *and bonds* will flow out through a *current account* deficit, leaving no long-run effect (as opposed to the monetary approach, where it is specifically an increase in money that flows out through a balance of payments deficit).[34] Similarly, a devaluation will cause an inflow of money *and bonds* through a current account surplus, so that in the long run holdings of both assets will have increased in the same proportion as the exchange rate and the price level. Chapter 25 will consider assets other than money, and a portfolio-balance model will be presented in the context of floating exchange rates.

19.4 SUMMARY

This chapter introduced two new concepts into our study of economies that operate under fixed exchange rates. The first concept was the flow of international reserves into or out of a country through the balance of payments, which changes its monetary base endogenously over time if the central bank either cannot or does not choose to sterilize (offset or neutralize) these reserve flows. Such changes in the monetary base then have further implications over time for the economy. The second concept was Purchasing Power Parity (PPP). Both of these concepts are associated with the monetary approach to the balance of payments.

We studied the effects of two policy experiments: a change in the money supply and a devaluation. An increase in the money supply creates an excess supply of money, which leads to a higher level of private expenditure and a balance of payments deficit in the short run, the same as at the end of the preceding chapter. The difference is that under the nonsterilization assumption, the balance of payments deficit implies that the level of the money stock falls gradually over time, which in turn undoes the increase in expenditure and the balance of payments deficit. A devaluation leads to a balance-of-payments surplus in the short run, again as in previous chapters. The level of the money stock rises gradually over time, which in turn undoes the balance-of-payments surplus. Whatever the policy experiment, in the long run the balance of payments must be zero under the monetary approach, so that the stock of reserves is no longer changing.

---

[33] Two early statements of the portfolio balance approach under fixed exchange rates were William Branson, *Financial Capital flows in the U.S. Balance of Payments* (Amsterdam: North-Holland, 1968); and Lance Girton and Dale Henderson, "Financial Capital Movements and Central Bank Behavior in the Two-Country Short-Run Portfolio-Balance Model," *Journal of Monetary Economics*, (1976): 33–61.

[34] Figure 19.7, exactly as it is drawn, could be used to describe securities flowing out of the country through a current account deficit, instead of just money.

These results apply regardless of what is assumed about the second concept associated with the monetary approach to the balance of payments: Purchasing Power Parity (PPP). PPP states that the domestic price level is given by the exchange rate times the foreign price level. There are a number of reasons why this relationship can fail in theory, why the *real* exchange rate is not constant. The most important in practice, at least in the short run, is that prices are "sticky," meaning that prices require time to adjust after a change in the nominal exchange rate. Thus, the fixed-price assumption (which we made in Chapters 17 and 18 and will return to in Chapter 22) is realistic for the short run. Nevertheless, in the last part of the present chapter we explored the implications of the assumption of price flexibility and PPP. One motivation is to think about the long run. Another motivation is to think about very small, open economies.

In the flexible-price version of the monetary approach, which we call monetarist, a devaluation translates directly into a proportionate increase in the domestic price level, so no change occurs in the real exchange rate. Nonetheless, there is an effect on the balance of payments, through what is called the real-balance effect. The increase in the price level reduces the real money balances held by the public. In response to the resulting excess demand for money, people cut back on expenditure, which in turn leads to the improvement in the balance of payments. The next chapter will include some additional effects that devaluations have for small, open countries, particularly less-developed countries.

CHAPTER PROBLEMS

1. What effect does a revaluation of the currency upward have on income and the trade balance, in the short run and in the long run? Answer diagrammatically for each of the two monetary models.
   a. The monetary model with fixed goods prices (Section 19.1).
   b. The monetarist model with Purchasing Power Parity (Section 19.3).
2. The real exchange rate is defined to be E (CPI*/CPI).
   a. If PPP holds, what is the rate of change of the CPI when the foreign inflation rate is 3 percent per year and:
      (i) the nominal exchange rate is fixed?
      (ii) the domestic currency is depreciating at 7 percent per year?
      (iii) the domestic currency is appreciating at 3 percent per year?
   b. Assume that PPP holds, the foreign price level is fixed, the parameter K measures the sensitivity of desired money balances to nominal income, and the parameter δ measures the sensitivity of the balance of payments to the excess demand for money, as in Equation 19.5. In each of the following cases, what is the (short-run) effect on the balance of payments? Assume that nominal GNP is initially C 100 (C stands for the local currency).
      (i) The central bank decreases domestic credit by C 1.
      (ii) Domestic output grows by 1 percent.
      (iii) The country devalues its currency by 1 percent.
   c. Let CPI $= P_n^a P_t^{(1-a)}$, where P_n is the price of non-traded goods, P_t the price of traded goods, and a the weight given to the former in the consumption basket. Define CPI* analogously. Express the real exchange rate as a function of the relative price P_n/P_t in each country. (Assume the Law of One Price for traded goods.)

    d. If the domestic and foreign CPIs each give weight two-thirds to non-traded goods and one-third to traded goods, what is the rate of change of the real exchange rate if
       (i) the relative price of non-traded goods is rising at 3 percent per year in the domestic country (and is constant in the foreign country)?
      (ii) the relative price of non-traded goods is rising at 3 percent per year in both countries?
     (iii) the relative price of non-traded goods is constant, but within traded goods there is an increase in EP_t^*/P_t—a shift in the terms of trade, running against the home country—at 3 percent per year?

3. a. Assume that the gold standard is in effect and that huge new deposits of gold are discovered in California. What happens to the U.S. price level and trade balance and the world price level?
   b. In *The Wizard of Oz*, Dorothy thinks that powerful men in the Emerald City have the answers to her problems, only to discover at the end of her journey that their power is based on sham and illusion and that she, the girl from Kansas, knew the answer all along. What city do you think this is? (See appendix B, footnote 41.)

Extra Credit

Problems 4 and 5 deal with the monetary approach to the balance of payments. The rate of change of the money supply is given by the balance of payments.

$$\dot{M} = TB$$

Problem 4 maintains the fixed-price assumption of the Keynesian model of Chapter 18. Problem 5 goes to the opposite "monetarist" extreme, fixed output.

4. Assume the model of Problem 9 in the problem set for Chapter 18.
   a. Continuing Problem 9b, what is the initial short-run effect of a fiscal expansion on the balance of payments: $\Delta TB_{SR}/\Delta G$? What happens over time? What is the effect on income in the long run, defined as the time when the money supply is no longer changing ($\dot{M} = 0$): ΔY_{LR}?
   b. Continuing Problem 9d from Chapter 18, what is the initial effect of a monetary expansion on the balance of payments: $\Delta TB_{SR}/\Delta(\overline{M/P})$? What is the effect on income in the long run: ΔY_{LR}?

5. Think of the balance of payments, now equal to the desired rate of accumulation of money balances, as a function of the gap between the actual current money supply, M, and desired (long-run) money, M^d, where the latter is proportional to nominal GNP:

$$M = -\delta(M - M^d)$$

$$M^d = \frac{1}{v}PY$$

   a. Using BP to represent the balance of payments, equal to the nominal trade balance in the assumed absence of capital flows, express it as a function of M and PY. What is the effect of ΔM on ΔBP, and why?
   b. Is the effect of a monetary expansion on the trade balance in the Keynesian model of Problem 4b consistent with its effect in the monetarist model of 5a? (Note that the Keynesian model used TB to denote the real trade balance; the nominal trade balance is given by P times it. It made no difference when P was exogenous and normalized to 1.)

c. For the first time, the assumption of a fixed price level is relaxed and replaced by the assumption of purchasing power parity:

$$P = E\overline{P}^*$$

where the "monetarist small-country" assumption (that the world price level P^* is exogenous) is adopted, along with the assumption that income is exogenous because flexible prices guarantee full employment ($Y = \overline{Y}$).

Returning to the monetarist notation of Problem 5a, what is the effect of a devaluation, ΔE, on the balance of payments in the short run? In the long run?

SUGGESTIONS FOR FURTHER READING

Dornbusch, Rudiger. "Purchasing Power Parity," in J. Eatwell, M. Milgate and P. Newman, eds., *The New Palgrave*, vol. 3, (New York: Macmillan, 1987). A good survey.

———. "Stabilization Policy in LDCs: What Lessons Have We Learned?" *World Development*, (September 1982). Reprinted in his *Dollars, Debts and Deficits* (Cambridge, MA: M.I.T. Press, 1986). In the late 1970s, Argentina, Brazil, and Chile each sought to keep their currencies at a high level, under the "monetarist" theory that PPP would bring inflation down costlessly. What went wrong?

Eichengreen, Barry. *The Gold Standard in Theory and History* (New York: Methuen, 1985). Important papers, including Barro, Cooper, Hume, and Triffin, on how the gold standard operated, and whether it did or did not correspond to the idealized version represented by the monetary approach to the balance of payments.

Frenkel, Jacob, and Harry Johnson, eds., *The Monetary Approach to the Balance of Payments* (Toronto: University of Toronto Press, 1976). Includes, among other relevant papers, two important, easily readable accounts of the overall monetary approach: "The Monetary Approach to Balance of Payments Theory," by Johnson, and "The Monetary Approach to the Balance of Payments: Essential Concepts and Historical Origins," by both editors.

Katseli, Louka. "The Re-emergence of the Purchasing Power Parity Doctrine in the 1970's," *Special Papers in International Economics*, No. 13, (Princeton: Princeton University Press, 1979). Documents the increased popularity of PPP that came with the rise of monetarism.

Mundell, Robert. *International Economics*. (New York: Macmillan, 1968). Includes "Barter Theory and the Mechanism of Adjustment" (Chapter 8), a classic reference on the monetary approach; "Growth and the Balance of Payments" (Chapter 9), which makes the argument that real growth leads to a surplus, not a deficit as in the Keynesian model; and "The International Disequilibrium System" (Chapter 15), which develops the model of the income flow mechanism (though this paper, like much of the book, allows for capital mobility, and thus is most relevant for our Chapter 22).

Wanniski, Jude. "The Mundell-Laffer Hypothesis—A New View of the World Economy," *The Public Interest*, 39 (Spring 1975): 31–52; reprinted in Robert Baldwin and J. David Richardson, eds., *International Trade and Finance*, 2nd ed. (Boston: Little, Brown and Co., 1981), pp. 374–388. The author, a former editorial-writer for the *Wall Street Journal*, offers a heartfelt proclamation of the view that changes in the exchange rate have no effect on relative prices and therefore no effect on the trade balance (which he calls the Mundell-Laffer hypothesis).

Whitman, Marina. "Global Monetarism and the Monetary Approach to the Balance of Payments," *Brookings Papers on Economic Activity*, 3 (1975): 491–536. Introduced the distinction between the "monetary approach" and "global monetarism"; the exposition corresponds to the two-country monetarist model of this chapter's Appendix B.

APPENDIX A:
PURCHASING POWER PARITY IN A HYPERINFLATION

As was mentioned earlier in a footnote, hyperinflation is one context in which PPP in a sense works well empirically. Jacob Frenkel found that an OLS regression testing the relationship between the exchange rate E and the relative price level P^*/P in the Germany hyperinflation of 1920–1923 produces a coefficient close to one, whereas similar regressions for the more recent floating-rate period produce much smaller coefficients.[35]

There is another sense in which PPP works poorly during a hyperinflation. Paul Krugman finds that the standard deviation of the real exchange rate was 21 percent in Germany's hyperinflation—the real exchange rate was even more variable then than it has been since 1973.[36] The explanation for these seemingly conflicting findings is that PPP holds fairly well in the long run, but there are large short-run errors that can push both the exchange rate and the price level away from PPP endogenously. In a hyperinflation, the long run arrives quickly.[37] Figure 19.5 demonstrates the tendency for the real exchange rate to return to its average value in the long run.

APPENDIX B:
THE GOLD STANDARD

The monetarist model is useful for thinking about the gold standard, the subject of this Appendix. The two-country version of the model, which is developed in the Supplement to Chapter 19, is particularly useful for thinking about international flows of money between Britain and the United States under the nineteenth-century gold standard—roughly the period 1880–1914.

The Idealized Gold Standard

There are many senses in which the world "lost its innocence" in World War I. The era before 1914 often is recalled with fond, and sometimes overly idealized, nostalgia as an era of unprecedented economic growth and stability under the gold standard. The definition of a gold standard is that central banks fix the value of their currencies in terms of gold. This means that they set a price of gold in terms of domestic currency and then stand ready to buy or sell gold to whatever extent is necessary to maintain that price. They must, of course, hold reserves of gold to meet any fluctuations in demand.[38]

---

[35] "Purchasing Power Parity: Doctrinal Perspective and Evidence from the 1920's," *Journal of International Economics*, 8 (2) (May 1978): 169–191; and "The Collapse of PPP During the 1970s," *European Economic Review*, 16 (May 1981): 145–165.

[36] As compared to standard deviations for the first four years of floating exchange rates (July 1973–December 1976) of 8 percent for Germany and 6 percent for Great Britain, each measured relative to the United States. "Purchasing Power Parity and Exchange Rates: Another Look at the Evidence," *Journal of International Economics*, 8 (3) (1978): 397–407.

[37] When there is a sufficient trend in the nominal variables, due either to a long enough time sample or to hyperinflationary conditions, even large errors appear small, and the coefficient of one emerges in a regression. However, when the trend in the nominal variables is less, the errors appear large, and bias the coefficient toward zero. This is a standard "errors in variables" problem in econometrics. N. Davutyan and J. Pippenger, "Purchasing Power Parity Did Not Collapse During the 1970s," *American Economic Review*, 75 (5) (December 1985): 1151–1158.

[38] Relevant papers are collected in Barry Eichengreen, ed., *The Gold Standard in Theory and History* (New York: Methuen, 1985).

A gold standard is a special case of a system of fixed exchange rates. It is easy to show this: If the Federal Reserve has fixed the price of gold in terms of its currency (i.e., in dollars/ounce) and the Bank of England has fixed the price of gold in terms of its currency (in pounds/ounce), then they have in effect fixed their exchange rate (the ratio of the two, in dollars/pound).

The nineteenth-century gold standard, when visualized in its idealized form as a system of smooth and automatic adjustment to any disequilibrium, has two distinguishing characteristics. They correspond to the two defining assumptions of the monetary approach to the balance of payments laid out in the chapter.

First is the assumption that wages and goods prices are perfectly flexible and so adjust quickly to maintain equilibrium in the labor and goods markets. Earlier in the chapter, this cornerstone of the global monetarist view was discussed at length. Here it is worth noting that the assumption of flexible prices and wages was less unrealistic in the pre-1914 period than it is in the modern era of differentiated brand products, labor unions, and myriad forms of government intervention in the marketplace (such as minimum-wage laws).

The second aspect of the monetary approach to the balance of payments, the emphasis on international reserve flows, takes on an especially simplified form in the case of the idealized gold standard. The idealization leaves out reserves held in the form of foreign currency and thus treats gold as the only form of international reserve.[39] Furthermore, it leaves out domestic credit (purchases of domestic bonds by the central bank) and thus treats gold as the only component of the monetary base. Finally, it leaves out credit created by the commercial banking system, so that gold is treated as the only component of the money supply. This need not mean that gold literally circulates among the public; it is enough if the banking system always holds exactly the right amount of gold to back up one-for-one the domestic currency that it issues. (This is called "100 percent reserve backing," as opposed to the modern system of "fractional-reserve backing," under which the monetary base is only a fraction of the money supply in the hands of the public.) It follows that under this idealized version of the gold standard, the central bank could not sterilize international reserve flows even if it wanted to. The money supply necessarily varies one-for-one with the country's holdings of gold, evaluated at the set price. This appendix will use freely the word "gold" interchangeably with "reserves," or "money."

In truth, domestic credit creation and fractional reserve backing began long before 1914. Central banks did not in fact always allow reserve outflows to translate fully into monetary contraction as they were supposed to under the "rules of the game." It is probably true, however, that in the nineteenth century central banks made much less of a practice of sterilizing reserve flows so as to set the money supply where they wanted it than they do today. It was only after World War I that central banks began to acquire responsibility for deliberate setting of monetary policy to respond to problems such as unemployment. (One possible interpretation is that the motivation for them to do so stems from the greater degree of rigidity of wages and prices in the modern era mentioned earlier.[40])

The Ups and Downs of the Gold Standard

When the world's money was tied to gold, the world price level was determined by the world supply of gold, relative to world real income, precisely as in Equation 19.S.4 in the Supplement. This relationship is the key both to arguments in favor of a gold standard and to arguments

[39] This ignores the fact that under the gold standard, central banks held much of their reserves in the form of pounds sterling because they knew that the pound was convertible into gold.

[40] See Robert Triffin, "Myths and Realities of the So-called Gold Standard;" and Donald McCloskey and J. Richard Zecher, "How the Gold Standard Worked, 1880–1913," both reprinted in Eichengreen, op. cit.

against it. The "pro" argument is that it prevents central banks from creating money at an excessive rate and generating sustained inflation. Excessive money creation and inflation in the 1970s inspired some Americans to propose a return to the gold standard, or some related form of "commodity standard."

There are several "con" arguments. Tying the money supply to gold prevents central banks from responding to cyclical downturns with more expansionary monetary policy. (This is not considered a disadvantage by the gold-standard proponents; they would prefer that the government not have such discretionary power, because they do not trust that it has the good faith and competence to use the power well.)

Furthermore, tying the money supply to gold also prevents the steady long-term growth in the world supply of money and reserves necessary to satisfy the transactions demand that comes with growing output and trade. If there is no increase in the supply of available gold, then money will get tighter and tighter, creating a drag on world growth. The absence of major discoveries of gold between 1873 and 1896 helps explain why price levels fell dramatically over this period (53 percent in the United States and 45 percent in the United Kingdom).[41] On the other hand, the gold rushes in California in 1849 and in South Africa and Alaska in the late 1890s were each followed by upswings in the price level of similar magnitude. Clearly, the system did not in fact guarantee price stability. Opponents of the gold standard ask why one would want to make the world economy hostage to chance gold discoveries and the other arbitrary vicissitudes of supply and demand in the world gold market. They also question the efficiency of a system that requires the use of resources to dig gold out of the ground laboriously, only to bury it back in the ground at Fort Knox.[42]

After World War I, it was considered very important to Britain to restore convertibility of the pound into gold. However, a misplaced faith in the usefulness of Purchasing Power Parity as a guide to the proper exchange rate led the British to peg the pound at too high a value (that is, to set too low a price for gold in terms of pounds). The result was a balance of payments deficit and severe contraction that ended in collapse of the system, rather than in smooth adjustment to the disequilibrium.[43]

Officially, gold was also the reserve asset of the Bretton Woods system founded in 1944. World growth would have soon run into the constraint of a basically fixed supply of gold, were it not for the fact that the dollar immediately became the *de facto* reserve asset. Central banks held much of their reserves in the form of dollars because the dollar was convertible into gold (in the same way that central banks had earlier held much of their reserves in the form of pounds). This is why the Bretton Woods system was sometimes called a Gold-Exchange

---

[41] The deflation of these years inflicted economic hardship, in particular, on American farmers, who had debts that were set in dollar terms but who produced commodities and owned land whose prices were falling in dollar terms. This was the era of Snidley Whiplash threatening to foreclose on poor Nell's farm and of the rise of populism in the American Midwest. The populists wanted the United States to abandon the gold standard so as to expand the money supply and get prices up. William Jennings Bryan, their candidate for President in 1896, warned that the farmers would not be "crucified on a cross of gold." Incidentally, the book *The Wizard of Oz* was really an allegory about populism. Oz stands for "ounces" (gold). Dorothy is the "innocent" from Kansas, the Scarecrow represents the Farmer, the Tinman is the downtrodden urban worker (with whom the populists might have hoped to make a political alliance), and the Lion is William Jennings Bryan. Their enemies are the Wicked Witch of the East, representing the East Coast bankers (who were suspected of conspiring to keep money tight) and the Wicked Witch of the West, representing drought (only water can kill her).

[42] Perhaps the best introduction to the topic is provided by Richard Cooper, "The Gold Standard: Historical Facts and Future Prospects," *Brookings Papers on Economic Activity*, 1 (1985): 1–45. It includes the latter day controversy over proposals to return to the gold standard in order to restore price stability, and the statistics on the price level swings that in fact characterized the 19th century.

[43] Much has been written on this period. See Barry Eichengreen, *Elusive Stability: Essays in the History of International Finance, 1919–1939* (Cambridge, UK: Cambridge University Press, 1989), Chapter 10: "The Gold-Exchange Standard and the Great Depression."

Standard. Before long, however, the system came under increasing strain. The reason was that beginning in 1958, the United States ran balance of payments deficits. Foreign central banks' holdings of dollars rose relative to the gold in Fort Knox, and foreigners (particularly Charles DeGaulle, the gold-conscious leader of France) began to doubt the ability of the U.S. government to redeem its dollar liabilities in gold. This was the beginning of the long, drawn-out breakdown of the Bretton Woods system.

The monetarist model can be used to illustrate the emergence of U.S. balance of payments deficits in 1958. Let the countries in the two-country model of the Chapter Supplement be the United States and Europe. In the 1950s the European economies grew more rapidly than the United States as they recovered from the devastation of the 1940s. Their rapidly growing levels of income led to rapidly growing demand for money. To acquire international reserves, they had to run balance of payments surpluses against the United States. The model was used in the 1960s to show the sense in which emergence of U.S. deficits was a natural consequence of the system that had been set up in 1944.

The world monetary system was faced with the "Triffin Dilemma."[44] If the United States was allowed to continue running balance of payments deficits, eventually there would be a crisis of confidence, as foreigners all tried to cash in their dollars for gold before it was too late, and thereby exhausted the U.S. gold reserves. On the other hand, if steps were taken to end the U.S. deficit, then the rest of the world would be deprived of sufficient liquidity in the form of a steadily growing stock of reserves.

Economists and policy-makers debated the problem throughout the 1960s. There were two sorts of proposals to increase the world supply of reserves, both of them radical departures from the system agreed upon at Bretton Woods. The first was to increase the price of gold— that is, to devalue the dollar in terms of gold—thereby raising the nominal value of the world supply of reserves. The second was to create an artificial reserve asset, a sort of "paper gold."

Eventually, both changes were made, though it had not been planned that way. The artificial asset was the Special Drawing Right which the members of the International Monetary Fund agreed to create in 1968. By the time the batch of SDRs was phased into use (1970–1972), other events had intervened. In August 1971, in response to the worsening U.S. balance of payments,[45] President Nixon unilaterally suspended convertibility of the dollar into gold, not just for private residents, but for foreign central banks as well. When the leading countries met at the Smithsonian Institution in December 1971 to agree on a new set of exchange rates, the realignments included a 10 percent devaluation of the dollar against gold. This attempt to shore up the system of fixed exchange rates did not last long, and in March 1973 the system was abandoned completely. The market price of gold increased twentyfold (in dollars) over the remainder of the decade.

[44] Robert Triffin, *Gold and the Dollar Crisis* (New Haven: Yale University Press, 1960).

[45] 1971 was the first year since World War II that the United States ran a deficit, not just on the private capital account, but on the trade account as well. The U.S. trade surplus had been diminishing steadily since 1964. The cause was overly expansionary macroeconomic policies, as the Johnson Administration—followed by the Nixon Administration—increased military spending on the war in Vietnam and domestic spending at the same time.

20

LDCs and Other Small Open Economies with Non-Traded Goods

Imagine the dilemma faced by the finance minister of a small LDC that needs to improve its trade balance. Advisors strongly urge that some combination of devaluation and contractionary demand policies be adopted; they base their reasoning on standard macroeconomic models such as the ones developed in the preceding chapters.[1] The finance minister has little faith in these models, believing that they were designed to fit the experience of relatively large industrialized countries, not small LDCs. On the other hand, the finance minister also does not believe the simple small-country monetarist model developed in Chapter 19.[2] This chapter departs temporarily from the central focus of the text to consider the implications of a few of the characteristics of typical LDCs.

If a country were so open to international trade and so small in world goods markets that Purchasing Power Parity held, then by definition a devaluation could not change relative prices. Hong Kong and Singapore have been cited as relatively close approximations of such a country.

[1] Such recommendations are often highly unpopular politically, especially when they are perceived to be imposed by the International Monetary Fund (IMF). Richard Cooper, "Currency Devaluation in Developing Countries," *Essays in International Finance* No. 86 (June 1971), reported that most finance ministers lose their jobs in the year following a devaluation. A deficit country often has little choice whether to take the IMF's advice, however, as IMF lending rests on the principle of *conditionality* (the program is conditional on country compliance with an agreed-upon package of policy changes), and other banks and governments will not lend to a country that does not have the IMF "seal of approval." For a summary of the political consequences of IMF-type austerity programs, see Henry Bienen and Mark Gersovitz, "Economic Stabilization, Conditionality, and Political Stability," *International Organization*, 39(4) (Autumn 1985). Urban riots regularly follow food-subsidy cutbacks enacted as parts of austerity programs in North Africa, for example, and even contributed to the overthrow of President Nimeiri of Sudan in 1985. Similar riots in Venezuela, which President Perez blamed in part on the IMF, caused roughly 300 deaths in early 1989.

[2] Blind adherence to PPP and an overly simplified version of the monetarist model (among other things) got the countries of the "Southern Cone" of Latin America (Argentina, Chile, and Uruguay) into trouble in the late 1970s. Vittorio Corbo and Jaime de Melo, "Liberalization with Stabilization in the Southern Cone of Latin America," *World Development*, Special Issue, 13(8) (August 1985): 893–916.

417

In Chapter 19 a devaluation could affect the trade balance only through the real money balance effect. Even countries that are small in terms of world trade often have large internal markets, however. China and Australia, for example, are probably too small in world markets to affect their terms of trade, though they are certainly not called ''small'' countries in ordinary speech. This chapter will continue to consider countries that are sufficiently small and open that they take the prices of all traded goods (exports and imports) as determined outside the country and fixed in terms of foreign currency. However, the existence of goods that are not internationally traded will also be recognized. The discussion will reveal that, as a consequence, such countries experience relative price effects when they devalue, along with the real money balance effect already explored.

20.1 NON-TRADED GOODS

We first introduced non-traded goods in Section 5.7. Chapter 19 explained that the existence of non-traded goods is one reason why PPP fails to hold in practice.

The primary examples of non-traded "goods" are not goods at all, but services. Some services, such as insurance, shipping, and tourism, are internationally traded, and these have been growing in importance in recent years. Nevertheless, most services are too localized to be traded internationally, for example, personal services like those offered by barbershops and dry cleaners. Some larger sectors, such as housing, utilities, and local transportation, also fit in this category.

Many commodities are also non-traded, specifically those where the cost of transporting them internationally is prohibitively high. Highly perishable food is a good example. More commodities will qualify as non-traded in a country far removed from the rest of the world geographically, like Australia, than in one centrally located, like Germany. Prohibitively high trade barriers can also render goods non-traded. Particularly in LDCs, transportation costs and trade barriers often insulate much of the economy from the rigors of international competitition. In Latin America, for example, high import tariffs and quantitative restrictions on imports of manufactured goods (and barriers to Latin American exports in the industrialized countries) historically have put into the non-traded category some industries that might otherwise be in the category of traded goods. A final case is that in which cultural tastes are such that foreigners are not interested in consuming the good in question.

We now develop the appropriate model for thinking about a small open economy with non-traded goods.[3] We recall that if the country is too small to affect its terms of trade, then we can aggregate together tradable goods, for the reasons explained in Section 19.3. We begin by drawing the production-possibility curve, or transformation schedule, showing the different quantities of non-traded goods versus traded goods that the economy can produce if its labor and other resources are fully employed. Figure 20.1 shows this curve, with traded goods measured on the horizontal axis. The curve has the usual bowed-out shape, meaning that there are diminishing returns as

---

[3] A country's "openness" could be defined as the ratio of its production of traded goods to its total GNP. Thus, this chapter focuses on countries that, though small as in the monetarist model of Chapter 19, are not *100 percent* open. Because Chapters 17 and 18 and the remainder of the book do not include non-traded goods, this chapter is in a sense a digression.

FIGURE 20.1   Output and Consumption of Traded and Non-Traded Goods

Production occurs where the transformation curve is tangent to a relative price line. Consumption occurs where the budget line is tangent to an indifference curve. As drawn, the two points coincide, so output of traded goods, TG, equals consumption of traded goods and the same is true for non-traded goods, NTG.

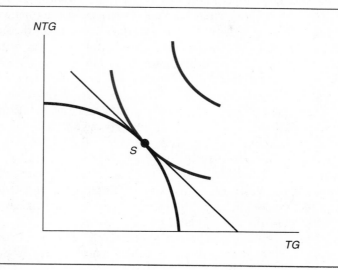

more and more labor is shifted out of non-traded goods into traded goods. Chapter 5 considered the special case of Ricardian production, in which this production-possibility curve was flat. In that case the relative price of traded goods in terms of non-traded goods is determined entirely by the relative labor costs of producing the two goods, which is a constant (the slope of the line). In general, however, the relative price will vary and with it the quantities of the two kinds of goods that are profitable to produce (as in Section 6.7).

Assume that the relative prices are given by the slope of the straight line in Figure 20.1. P_N will denote the relative price of non-traded goods. $P_N = P_n/P_t$, where P_n and P_t represent the (nominal) prices of non-traded goods and traded goods, respectively. P_N gives the number of units of traded goods required to buy one unit of non-traded goods. When P_N is low, non-traded goods are relatively cheap and the budget line in Figure 20.1 is steep: A resident can buy a larger quantity of non-traded goods for any given quantity of traded goods.

In the most general case, any combination of outputs is "fair game," including points that lie inside the production-possibility curve (points at which the supplies of labor and other resources are not being fully utilized, so that output of both goods is less than it could be). In this chapter, however, the discussion will be restricted to the assumption that labor and other resources are fully employed, as in Chapter 19. In this case, the quantities of output of the two goods, X_N and X_T, are given by the point S, where the line is tangent to the curve. The output quantities are the outcome of supply decisions that firms make when faced with the prevailing prices. Keep in mind that output of traded goods includes not only specific products that the home country might currently be exporting but also specific products that might be *imported* if the demand from domestic consumers exceeds domestic output.

The trade balance is given by the quantity of traded goods produced minus the quantity of traded goods consumed. If some of the output produced remains after domestic households have bought what they want, it is exported and the country runs a trade surplus. There is no question as to whether there will be sufficient demand for the goods outside the home country, because under the small-country assumption the rest of the world will take all goods that the country has to offer at the going world price. If, on the other hand, domestic consumption of traded goods exceeds domestic output, then the difference is imported and the country runs a trade deficit. This way of thinking of the trade balance—as the difference between the output and the consumption of traded goods—is the same as in the small-country monetarist model of Chapter 19, the only difference being that there *all* goods were traded goods. It is very different, however, from the way we thought of the trade balance in Chapters 17 and 18—as foreigners' demand for the export goods of the home country minus domestic residents' demand for the imports. In the present model, with all traded goods aggregated together, it is impossible to say what determines the level of exports and the level of imports. Fortunately, though, it is not necessary to know either level to determine the trade balance.

What determines the pattern of consumption? Assume, as in Figure 5.6 in Chapter 5, that we can draw community indifference curves. Along any given indifference curve, consumers are equally happy with the different possible combinations of non-traded and traded goods consumed, C_N and C_T. The slope of the indifference curve is called the *marginal rate of substitution* between the two; it tells the amount of consumption of non-traded goods the consumer is willing to give up to get one more unit of traded goods. Indifference curves farther from the origin are better, of course, because more consumption is better than less. The curves are convex because of the diminishing marginal rate of substitution.

To attain the highest level of welfare available to them, consumers will determine their quantities purchased, C_N and C_T, at the point on an indifference curve where the given price line is tangent, that is, where the marginal rate of substitution is set equal to the relative prices of the two kinds of goods. It is possible that this will be the same point, S, in which case the quantity of traded goods consumed will equal the quantity of traded goods produced. If this happens, the trade balance is zero. If we were to rule out gaps between expenditure and income, thereby ruling out trade deficits or surpluses, as in most of the first half of the text, we would necessarily be at S. Indeed, under this restriction, the relative price line would have to be determined endogenously by the unique point where the production possibility frontier was tangent to an indifference curve.

Now we allow for countries to "spend beyond their means." We assume expenditure is at some level, A [measured in terms of traded goods: $A \equiv C_T + P_N(C_N)$], which is greater than the level of income, Y [also expressed in terms of traded goods: $Y \equiv X_T + P_N(X_N)$]. For example, there may have been a tax cut or an increase in expenditure on the part of the government. A and Y are measured along the horizontal axis in Figure 20.2. The budget line is the one that passes through A, with consumers

FIGURE 20.2   Increase in Expenditure, Followed by Decrease in Relative Price of Non-Traded Goods

Assume expenditure exogenously increases to A, beyond income, Y. If relative prices are unchanged, consumption is at F, implying excess demand for NTG and excess demand for TG. If the relative price of traded goods is increased, it raises output of TG at X and may also lower consumption of TG at B.

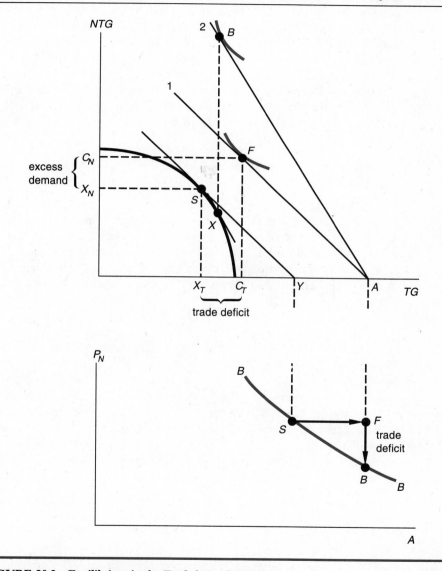

FIGURE 20.3   Equilibrium in the Traded Goods Market

In the aftermath of an increase in expenditure, A, if the relative price of non-traded goods, P_N, is decreased far enough, it will eliminate the excess demand for TG, which is the trade deficit. Thus, equilibrium in the TG market gives the downward-sloping BB schedule.

assumed to face the same relative prices as producers. (There are no taxes or subsidies on the goods.) C_N and C_T are located where the budget line is tangent to an indifference curve, at point F. This is where consumers attain the highest level of welfare, given their budget constraint. In Figure 20.2, consumption of both goods exceeds output. In the case of traded goods, the difference $(C_T - X_T)$, which can be measured horizontally on the graph, is simply the trade deficit. Consumers are satisfying their excess demand for traded goods abroad. In the case of non-traded goods, the difference $(C_N - X_N)$, which can be measured vertically, is the excess demand for non-traded goods. According to the definition of "non-traded," this excess demand cannot be satisfied abroad, but can be thought of as being satisfied out of inventories held by firms (temporarily, until they run out).

Other conditions could exist in these markets as well: trade surplus if F occurs anywhere to the left of S, and excess supply of non-traded goods if F occurs anywhere below S. The next thing to consider is what determines these points of consumption and output.[4]

20.2 EXPENDITURE AND THE RELATIVE PRICE OF NON-TRADED GOODS

This section will examine the effects of exogenous changes in the level of relative prices P_N and the expenditure A. Subsequent sections will show how exogenous changes in exchange-rate policy and monetary policy bring about changes in relative prices and expenditure. For the moment, take P_N and A as given.

The effect in the traded goods market will be examined first. Starting from a position of zero trade balance, S in Figure 20.2, an increase in expenditure with no change in relative prices will move the country into trade deficit because a certain share of the new expenditure falls on traded goods. Remember that importable and exportable goods are aggregated together. It does not matter here whether the additional purchases are imports or goods that would otherwise have been exported; in either case the result is a worsening of the trade balance. When the new spending comes from the private sector—for example, in response to a tax cut—the deterioration in the trade balance is the marginal propensity to spend on traded goods times the increase in expenditure. When it is government expenditure that has increased, the import content could be either higher (as it usually is in the case of military weapons, construction equipment, or other capital goods) or lower (as in education or health services). For simplicity, assume that the government's marginal propensity to spend on traded goods is in general the same as that of the private sector.

Maintaining Equilibrium in the Traded Goods Market

Let us now ask what would have to happen, after an increase in expenditure such as that illustrated in Figure 20.2, to restore trade balance, without stating that this will necessarily happen in fact. To restore trade balance, the relative price of traded goods

---

[4] Figure 20.1 is known as the Saltzer diagram because it originated with W. E. G. Salter, "Internal Balance and External Balance: The Role of Price and Expenditure Effects," *Economic Record* (August 1959): 226–238. Salter, like a number of the other authors who developed the model that features both traded and non-traded goods, was Australian. Australia fits the model relatively well because the two categories of goods are fairly clearly drawn. (The model goes by various names: Australian, non-traded goods, dependent economy, and small open economy. A version known as the Scandinavian model is illustrated in Problem 6 at the end of the chapter.)

would have to rise to eliminate an excess demand for traded goods. This could happen if the country decides to devalue, that is, to increase the price of foreign currency. The price of traded goods will rise by the same percentage as the price of foreign currency. If the price of non-traded goods remains the same, or at least fails to rise as much as the price of traded goods, then the relative price of traded goods will have risen.[5] In other words, the relative price of non-traded goods, P_N, will have fallen.[6]

It certainly sounds plausible that an increase in the relative price of traded goods will help eliminate an excess demand for traded goods, just as an increase in the relative price of chocolate will help eliminate an excess demand for chocolate. But we have to see how this would work. In Figure 20.2 the change means that the relative price line has become steeper (line 2 instead of line 1): Each unit of traded goods is now worth more units of non-traded goods. The effect on production of traded goods will clearly be favorable. As resources shift out of non-tradables into tradables, we move down along the production-possibility frontier from S.

What incentive induces resources to shift from one sector to the other? Within the tradable industry, the higher price at which firms can sell their products means that at S the real wage in terms of traded goods (W/P_T) is now below the marginal product of labor. These firms thus find it profitable to hire more workers. They will continue to hire workers until they reach the point at which the marginal product of labor is down to the level of the new real wage. In a full-employment model with flexible wages, the increased demand for labor from the tradables sector will quickly bid up the nominal wage—not just in that sector, but throughout the economy, assuming that workers are basically the same in both sectors. Firms in the non-traded sector now find that the real wage in terms of *their* product has risen. They now find it less profitable to produce on the same scale as previously, so they release labor and contract in size. Under the full-employment assumption, the workers who lose their jobs in the non-traded sector are the same ones hired in the expanded traded sector. We continue to move down the curve until we reach X, the new point of tangency with the relative price line. By reading off the horizontal axis, we can see that the quantity of tradable goods has risen.[6]

The effect of the increase in the relative price of tradables on consumption is not quite as clear as the effect on production. There is an unambiguously positive substitution effect: The steeper relative price line means a move upward along any given indifference curve to lower levels of consumption of traded goods. However, there is also an income effect that may go the other way. It depends on what is assumed about the level of expenditure. The experiment that we are examining is an exogenous

[5] If the price of non-traded goods is fixed in terms of domestic currency because firms supply these goods with infinite elasticity—the same assumption that we made for domestically produced goods in Chapters 17 and 18—then a devaluation is the *only* way that the country can increase the relative price of traded goods. In this case, with normal prices fixed, we could speak interchangeably of the nominal exchange rate and the relative price of traded goods.

[6] Incidentally, the relative price of traded goods in terms of non-traded goods in small open economies (particularly in Latin America) is sometimes called the real exchange rate. [See, for example, Arnold Harberger, "Economic Adjustment and the Real Exchange Rate," in Sebastian Edwards and Liaquat Ahamed, eds., *Adjustment and Exchange Rates in Developing Countries* (Chicago: University of Chicago Press, 1986).] Since others use the term "real exchange rate" to denote the price of imports in terms of exports—a variable that here is assumed constant—we will avoid this alternative use of the term.

increase in expenditure and the associated change in relative prices that would be necessary if balanced trade is to be restored. In this experiment, when the relative price of traded goods rises, the expenditure line remains tied down at its new bottom endpoint (expenditure remains fixed at the new level, A, in terms of traded goods).[7] The expenditure line swivels to its new steeper slope, the same slope as the new price line facing producers. The new consumption point will be located at a point such as B, where the steeper expenditure line is tangent to a new indifference curve. This point could be located either to the right or left of the old point, F: The consumption of traded goods could either rise or fall.

The trade balance is the difference between the production and consumption of traded goods. Thus, even if consumption fails to fall because of the income effect, the trade balance would still probably improve because of the unambiguously positive effect on production. Assume that the production effect and the substitution effect in consumption are large enough to outweigh the negative income effect in consumption, and so the net effect on the trade balance is positive. The new trade balance is the distance, measured horizontally, between X and B. If the increase in the relative price of traded goods is large enough, then it will eliminate completely the trade deficit that opened up when expenditure was increased. This is the case shown in Figure 20.2: B is directly over X.

Now consider, on a graph of its own, the relationship between expenditure, A, and the relative price of non-traded goods, P_N, necessary to maintain trade balance equilibrium. Figure 20.3 shows expenditure on the horizontal axis and the relative price of non-traded goods on the vertical axis. Again, S denotes the initial point of both external balance (a zero trade balance) and internal balance (no excess supply or demand for non-traded goods). Increased expenditure causes a horizontal move to the right (by precisely the same distance as the movement of the expenditure point along the horizontal axis in Figure 20.2). Point F lies in a region of trade deficit, because expenditure on traded goods has increased, and a sufficiently large increase in the relative price of traded goods would be needed to restore balanced trade. This is the same as a sufficiently large decrease in the relative price of non-traded goods, represented by a movement vertically downward from point F to point B in Figure 20.3. For each level of A, there is a corresponding level of P_N that is necessary to maintain balanced trade. We can trace out a whole series of points representing combinations of A and P_N, which is downward-sloping, as shown in the graph. We label this curve BB, for balance of trade.

[7] Because we are considering changes in relative prices, how we draw the graph depends in part on whether we define expenditure in terms of traded goods or in terms of non-traded goods. In other words, the precise question we are asking is slightly different depending on whether we hold expenditure constant in terms of one type of good or the other, so naturally the precise answer is slightly different. The decision is arbitrary as to which question we should examine, but because the subject of this chapter is small open economies, we have decided to use internationally traded goods as the "standard of value." That is why we defined expenditure A in terms of traded goods. (When a visiting team of economists analyzes the macroeconomic situation in a Latin American country, they sometimes convert the components of output from units of local currency into dollars. This is roughly the equivalent of expressing these magnitudes in terms of internationally traded goods.)

Maintaining Market Equilibrium for Non-Traded Goods

There is no reason why an increase in expenditure will necessarily be accompanied by a decrease in the relative price of non-traded goods to maintain equilibrium in the market for traded goods. This requires something like a deliberate decision by the government to devalue. Notice in Figure 20.2 that, although the excess demand for traded goods has been eliminated by the change in relative prices, there is now a large excess demand for *non-traded* goods: Point B lies far above point X. Policy-makers may be just as concerned about equilibrium in the market for non-traded goods and the related problem of unemployment as they are about trade balance equilibrium. We now consider what would have to happen to maintain equilibrium in the market for non-traded goods instead of traded goods.

We return to the initial increase in expenditure that moves the economy to point F in Figure 19.2. Some of the increased expenditure falls on non-traded goods. Thus, point F is a point of excess demand for non-traded goods. The excess demand can be measured vertically as the gap between consumption and output, on either Figure 20.2 or the equivalent, Figure 20.4. In terms of Figure 20.3, or the equivalent, Figure 20.5, the increase in expenditure causes the move rightward from S to F into a region of excess demand.

Eliminating this excess demand for non-traded goods would require that the relative price of non-traded goods rise. Again there are effects on both production and consumption. The higher price of non-traded goods makes their production more prof-

---

FIGURE 20.4   Increase in Expenditure, Followed by Increase in Relative Price of Non-Traded Goods

---

Again, an exogenous increase in expenditure, A, beyond Y, moves consumption to F while leaving output at S, if relative prices are unchanged. If the relative price of traded goods is decreased, it raises output of NTG at X and lowers consumption of NTG at G.

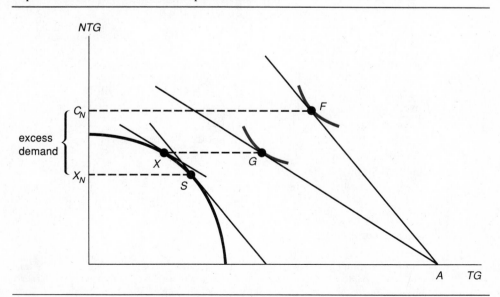

FIGURE 20.5   Equilibrium in the Non-Traded Goods Market

In the aftermath of the increase in expenditure, A, if the relative price of non-traded goods, P_N, is increased far enough, it will eliminate the excess demand for non-traded goods. Thus, equilibrium in the NTG market gives the upward-sloping NN schedule.

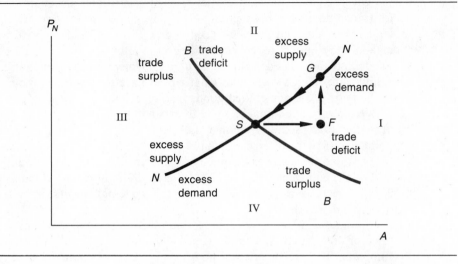

itable. Resources shift out of the other sector into non-traded goods, causing a move up along the production-possibility frontier from S, as shown in Figure 20.4, until reaching a point of tangency, X, with the new, less-steep relative price line. Thus, X_N rises. The higher relative price of non-traded goods also means that consumers substitute away from them into the cheaper traded goods. The income effect, like the substitution effect, reduces consumption of non-traded goods, as is seen when the relative price line is rotated downward to the new tangency. The income effect is not ambiguous, as it was when considering the demand for traded goods. C_N unambiguously falls.[8]

If the increase in the relative price of non-traded goods is sufficiently large, then the upward movement of output and the downward movement of consumption will be sufficiently large that the point X and the point G will be at the same horizontal level: The excess demand for non-traded goods that opened up when expenditure increased will have been eliminated. In terms of Figure 20.5, a sufficiently large increase in the relative price of non-traded goods, P_N, returns the country to equilibrium in the domestic market at point G. There is an entire set of combinations of A and P_N, such as S and G, that give equilibrium in non-traded goods. These points constitute the upward-sloping internal balance schedule, NN. To recap the reason for the NN schedule's upward slope, an increase in expenditure A must be accompanied by a sufficiently large increase in P_N if the potential excess demand for non-traded goods is to be eliminated.

---

[8] If expenditure had been set in terms of non-traded goods rather than in terms of traded goods, then a change in relative prices would have an ambiguous effect on the demand for nontraded goods and an unambiguous effect on the demand for traded goods. This is the method used in the dependent economy model in Rudiger Dornbusch, *Open Economy Macroeconomics*, 2nd ed., New York: Basic Books, 1989.

The external balance schedule, *BB*, and the internal balance schedule, *NN*, together divide the policy instrument space into four quadrants, or four "zones of economic unhappiness." (I) Any point such as *F* has a trade deficit and an excess demand for non-traded goods, as we have seen. Proceeding counterclockwise through the other three regions, we have (II) trade deficit with excess supply, (III) trade surplus with excess supply, and (IV) trade surplus with excess demand for goods. In general, the government would need to set both policy variables, *A* and P_N, to hit both targets. Only at point *S* are both the traded and non-traded goods markets in balance simultaneously. (The graph is conceptually the same as the Swan Diagram derived in Chapter 18, although the curves are flipped vertically because that chapter showed increases in the exchange rate as movements up the vertical axis, rather than down.[9])

To take an example from recent history, many Latin American countries in the period 1974–1982 were at points like *F*, as the result of high levels of government spending: They experienced excess demand for non-traded goods together with large trade deficits, which they financed by borrowing from foreign banks.[10] Many also had overvalued currencies, and thus were at points like *G*, even farther from external balance than *F*. After 1982, the typical Latin American country was obliged to cut the level of government expenditure and devalue its currency to generate more foreign exchange earnings, thereby helping to pay the interest bill on the debts that it had incurred. It moved into the left-hand region of the diagram, with a trade surplus and excess supply of non-traded goods. Turkey and Korea are two debtors that made their adjustments earlier, in 1980, and were in far better shape than the Latin American countries thereafter.[11] Table 20.1 shows the dramatic increase in trade balances that developing countries in Latin America and other parts of the world were obliged to make after 1982 in response to decreased availability of loans to finance their current account deficits.

20.3 THE MONETARY APPROACH WITH NON-TRADED GOODS

Even if the government does not undertake any deliberate policy change in response to a trade deficit or in response to excess demand for non-traded goods at a point like *F*, there are two automatic mechanisms of adjustment that may be set in motion. First, in response to the excess demand for non-traded goods, producers of these

[9] More substantively, the Keynesian model focused on the price of exports in terms of imports, whereas this chapter uses the price of traded goods in terms of non-traded goods. It might be noted that Swan originally developed his diagram in the context of the nontraded goods model, not in the context of the Keynesian model. Trevor Swan, "Economic Control in a Dependent Economy," *Economic Record* (November 1956): 239–256.

[10] The other major source of financing for government deficits in the Latin American countries was printing money. A point like *G* in Figure 20.5 is shown to correspond to a high rate of money growth and inflation under the "old paradigm," in Rudiger Dornbusch, "Stabilization Policy in LDCs: What Lessons Have We Learned? *World Development* (September 1982); reprinted in his *Dollars, Debts and Deficits* (Cambridge, MA: M.I.T. Press, 1986). It would follow that a prerequisite to eliminating inflation is eliminating the budget deficit (while simultaneously undergoing a real devaluation, if seeking to avoid excess supply of domestic goods). In the late 1970s, Argentina, Brazil, and Chile each attempted to peg their currencies at high levels, under the "new" theory (the monetarist model of Chapter 19) that PPP would bring inflation down costlessly. It did not work.

[11] See the papers by Merih Celasun and Dani Rodrik, and Susan Collins and Won-Am Park, respectively, in Jeff Sachs, ed., *Developing Country Debt and the World Economy* (Chicago: University of Chicago Press, 1989).

TABLE 20.1   Trade and Current Account Balances of Developing Countries

(in billions of U.S. dollars)	1981	1982	1983	1984	1985	1986	1987	1988	1989	1990	1991
Merchandise trade balances											
All developing countries	39	8	39	68	54	22	60	38	40	38	−2
Africa	−4	−6	2	7	12	3	7	1	3	9	4
Asia	−22	−21	−17	−4	−12	2	18	7	0	−4	−13
Europe	−20	−13	9	10	4	8	10	6	−8	−29	−22
Middle East	89	41	16	17	17	−7	7	2	16	34	12
Latin America	−4	6	29	38	33	16	19	23	29	29	17
Current account balances											
All developing countries	−48	−86	−43	−13	−18	−34	13	−11	−19	−25	−104
Africa	−22	−22	−12	−8	−1	−11	−5	−11	−8	−3	−9
Asia	−19	−17	−13	−3	−13	5	22	10	1	−2	−12
Europe	−14	−8	9	13	4	9	11	8	−6	−24	−22
Middle East	50	3	−17	−13	−5	−20	−6	−9	1	10	−43
Latin America	−43	−42	−9	−1	−2	−17	−9	−10	−7	−7	−18

Source: World Economic Outlook (October 1988 and 1991), International Monetary Fund, Table A36 (Figures for 1991 are estimates.)

goods would be expected to raise their prices. If the market for non-traded goods operates with sufficient flexibility, the prices of non-traded goods, and therefore P_N, will rise sufficiently quickly to restore equilibrium at *G*.

In practice, this is likely to be a more gradual process. The adjustment process can be especially slow if the country finds itself in a position of excess supply, as at point *H* in Figure 20.6, because then a fall in the price of non-traded goods is required. There may be a prolonged recessionary period, with unemployed labor if wages adjust slowly. In such circumstances, a case can be made for speeding up the process by a change in government policy. One possibility is to devalue the currency, thus accomplishing the required reduction in the relative price of non-traded goods, immediately jumping downward in Figure 20.6 to equilibrium on the *NN* schedule. Another possibility is to increase expenditure, moving rightward in Figure 20.6. Unfortunately, a policy change bringing the country closer to internal balance may move it farther from external balance.

Reserve Flows

A second possible automatic mechanism of adjustment, which operates in response to external imbalances, is the flow of international reserves that we studied in Chapter 19 under the "monetary approach to the balance of payments." As we saw there, the money supply is one of the policy variables that determines the level of expenditure in the country. When the country is running a balance of payments deficit, at a point like *F* in Figure 20.5, its level of reserves is decreasing over time. If the reserve loss translates into a reduction in the total money supply, then it will exert a contractionary effect on expenditure. A declining level of expenditure means a gradual movement leftward over time and a diminishing balance of payments deficit. The movement

FIGURE 20.6   Adjustment with Excess Supply of Non-Traded Goods

At a point to the left of *BB* such as *H*, excess supply of non-traded goods puts downward pressure on the price of *NTG*. Even when the *NN* schedule is reached, however, there is still a trade surplus. If the reserve inflow is not sterilized, expenditure, *A*, increases over time.

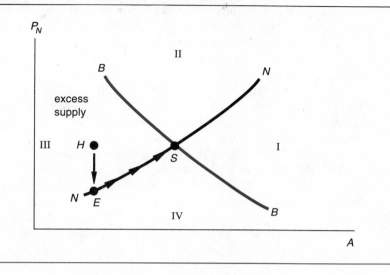

stops at a point on the external balance line, *BB*, because the rate of change of reserves is zero when the balance of payments is zero. On the other hand, if the government offsets the effect of the reserve loss on the money supply by expanding domestic credit (i.e., sterilizes), then there will be no leftward movement. However, the country cannot continue to intervene in the foreign exchange market forever. As the central bank's level of reserves approaches zero, the government will eventually be forced to react, either by reducing expenditure or—if it is too late for that—by devaluing the currency.

Similarly, when the country is running a balance of payments surplus, at a point like *H* in Figure 20.6, its level of reserves is increasing over time. If the upward effect on the money supply is not offset, then expenditure will be increasing. There is movement rightward in the graph, with the balance of payments surplus gradually decreasing over time, until equilibrium is reached somewhere on the *BB* schedule. Again, the government can forestall this process by reducing domestic credit (sterilizing), which it may choose to do if it is politically or emotionally attached to its trade surplus. Indeed, unlike the situation facing a deficit country, there is nothing to force a surplus country to adjust. For example, in the 1980s Taiwan ran enormous surpluses, and allowed its reserves to pile up to levels that in absolute terms (let alone proportionate to GNP) rival the very largest and wealthiest countries in the world.

Reserve inflows can create serious problems, however. One cause of potentially undesirable reserve inflows is the Dutch Disease, discussed in Section 6.7: a natural resource boom, as experienced by the Netherlands in the 1960s (a producer of natural gas) and a variety of other countries in the 1970s (producers of oil, coffee, and various other mineral and agricultural products).[12] Another possible source of large reserve inflows is a successful monetary stabilization program, as some of the countries in the Southern Cone of Latin America (Chile, Argentina, and Uruguay) undertook in the 1970s. Whatever the cause of the reserve inflows, the difficulty arises when real appreciation of the currency causes a loss of competitiveness for exports of manufactured goods (or for any other tradable-goods industry, excluding, of course, an industry experiencing an export boom that is the original source of the reserve inflow).

How does a reserve inflow lead to real appreciation of the currency? There are two possible ways. If the monetary authorities keep the exchange rate fixed, then the monetary approach to the balance of payments indicates that the reserve inflow will cause the money supply to swell, which may in turn lead to increases in wages and the prices of non-traded goods; in this case the real appreciation takes the form of inflation. On the other hand, the monetary authorities may respond to the reserve inflow by allowing the currency to appreciate in *nominal* terms, bringing about the real appreciation directly. Taiwan, for example, eventually responded to its growing reserves and began to let its currency appreciate against the U.S. dollar in 1986–1987. To take another example, the value of Colombia's currency tends to move with the international price of its leading export, coffee.[13] However, a country experiencing a commodity boom can avoid a real appreciation of its currency by careful policy-making. An example is Indonesia after 1978, when it saw the value of its oil exports soar.[14] Another is Cameroon, which experienced both a coffee-and-cocoa boom in 1976–1977 and an oil boom in 1978–1980.[15]

Even when events like the Dutch Disease create difficulties for manufactured exports, this does not mean that the country as a whole is worse off. A country would be foolish to turn down a windfall gain on its commodity exports. After all, no country would welcome a *fall* in the value of an exportable resource. Examples of sudden falls in the price of a basic export commodity leading to real depreciation and (often) sharp recession include Chile in 1974–1975 (copper), Bolivia in 1985 (tin), and Mexico in 1986 (oil).[16]

---

[12] On the Dutch Disease in general, see W. Max Corden, "Booming Sector and Dutch Disease Economics: A Survey," *Oxford Economic Papers*, 36 (1984): 359–380. On the monetary aspects, see J. Peter Neary and Sweder van Wijnbergen, "Can an Oil Discovery Lead to a Recession? A Comment on Eastwood and Venables," *Economic Journal*, 94 (1984): 390–395.

[13] When world coffee prices rise, Colombia experiences reserve inflows that can cause non-coffee sectors to lose competitiveness. See Sebastian Edwards, "Coffee, Money, and Inflation in Colombia," *World Development*, 12 (1984): 1107–1117. Sebastian Edwards, "A Commodity Export Boom and the Real Exchange Rate: The Money-Inflation Link," in J. P. Neary and S. Van Wijnbergen, eds., *Natural Resources and the Macroeconomy* (Cambridge, MA: M.I.T. Press, 1986), 229–248.

[14] Wing Thye Woo and Anwar Nasution, "The Conduct of Economic Policies in Indonesia and Its Impact on External Debt," in Jeff Sachs, ed., *Developing Country Debt and the World Economy*, (Chicago: University of Chicago Press, 1989). Unlike most Latin American and African countries, economist "technocrats" and rural producers of export goods have had sufficient influence over policy-making in Indonesia to prevent overvaluation of the currency.

[15] The dependent-economy model of this chapter is used to illustrate how three West African countries have responded to changes in prices of their export commodities, see Shantayanan Devarajan and Jaime de Melo, "Adjustment with a Fixed Exchange Rate: Cameroon, Cote d'Ivoire, and Senegal," *World Bank Economic Review*, 1(3) (May 1987): 447–488.

[16] See the papers by Juan Antonio Morales and Jeffrey Sachs and by Edward Buffie, respectively, in Sachs, op cit.

The Effects of an Increase in the Money Supply in the Non-Traded Goods Model

We now formally examine, within the context of the non-traded goods model, the implications of the two assumptions associated with the monetary approach to the balance of payments: Goods prices are perfectly flexible, and reserve flows are not sterilized.[17] The first assumption means that the automatic mechanism of adjustment in the home (non-traded goods) market described earlier not only exists but functions instantly. Whenever the economy finds itself at a point of excess demand for non-traded goods, prices rise rapidly to clear the market, causing a jump vertically upward to the NN line. Whenever the economy finds itself at a point of excess supply of non-traded goods, prices fall rapidly to clear the market, causing a jump vertically downward to the NN line. In short, we assume that the economy is always on the NN line (which has the benefit of simplifying the analysis). The second assumption means that the other automatic mechanism of adjustment described earlier, via the balance of payments, is in effect as well. It will not operate instantly, however. As long as large-scale rapidly responding capital flows continue to be ruled out, the rate of reserve flow is restricted to the same finite scale as the trade balance.

Consider first the effects of an increase in the money supply. Figure 20.5 showed how an increase in expenditure A—whatever its causes—resulted in a move from point S to point F, featuring excess demand for non-traded goods and a trade deficit. A monetary expansion is precisely the sort of policy change that would cause such an increase in expenditure. Now that we are incorporating automatic adjustments in the market for non-traded goods, however, we recognize that point F represents an equilibrium that cannot last for long. Producers respond to the excess demand for non-traded goods by raising the nominal price. This is equivalent to raising the relative price, P_N, because the nominal price of traded goods is tied down (by the exogenous foreign-currency price of traded goods and the fixed exchange rate). We move vertically upward from point F in Figure 20.5 until we reach point G on the NN line, where the excess demand has been eliminated. We assume that this adjustment takes place very rapidly, so that following the increase in the money supply we virtually jump from point S to point G.

At point G, the country is still running a trade deficit. In fact, the increase in the relative price of non-traded goods has moved the country even farther from trade balance equilibrium than it would be at point F (because the price change discourages the output of traded goods and encourages the consumption of traded goods). The balance of payments deficit means that reserves will be steadily flowing out of the country. Under the assumption that the reserve outflow is not sterilized, the money supply is declining over time. As the money supply declines, the level of expenditure, A, declines, so there is a move leftward in Figure 20.5. At the same time, however, P_N must decline, so as to eliminate any incipient excess supply of non-traded goods that would otherwise result from the declining expenditure and keep the country on the NN schedule. In other words, the movement is down-and-to-the-left, until eventually we return to balance of payments equilibrium at point S. Only when the rate

[17] The model that follows was developed by Rudiger Dornbusch, "Devaluation, Money and Non-traded Goods," *American Economic Review* (December 1973): 875–880.

of change of reserves, equal to the balance of payments, is zero will there be long-run equilibrium. In the long run the monetary expansion has changed absolutely nothing except the composition of the central bank's balance sheet: The original expansion in domestic credit has been offset by an equal decrease in the central bank's holdings of international reserves.

The Effects of a Devaluation

The primary motivation for introducing the monetary approach to the balance of payments in the presence of non-traded goods is to use it to study the effects of a devaluation. A devaluation should improve the balance of payments through two independent routes. First is the contractionary effect on expenditure introduced in Chapter 18 (the "real balance effect"). Second is the effect of the decrease in the relative price of non-traded goods, which was introduced in this chapter (the effect of an increase in the "real exchange rate," in the alternative use of the term as the relative price of traded goods).

Consider an increase in the exchange rate. Under the assumption that the country takes the world price of traded goods as given, this causes a proportionate increase in the price of traded goods, P_t, expressed in domestic currency. The first effect of the devaluation occurs even if for some reason there is no change in the relative price of non-traded goods, that is, even if the prices of all goods rise by the same percentage. For example, assume that n stands for nuts instead of non-traded. What would happen if P_n, the price of nuts, along with P_t, the price of tin, rose by the same percentage as the devaluation? In Figure 20.6 this constraint would prevent any movement off a horizontal line through S. The economy moves from S to H. An increase in the price of traded goods reduces the real money supply. The reduction in real money supply (or, equivalently, the increase in nominal money demand) results in an excess demand for money. At H, households and firms cut back their spending to restore their level of real money balances.

In terms of Figure 20.1, the reduction in expenditure means that the budget line shifts inward, with an unchanged slope if relative prices remain unchanged, so that the consumption point, the point of tangency with an indifference curve, occurs inside the production-possibility frontier. Both consumption of traded goods, C_T, and consumption of non-traded goods, C_N, fall. Some of the decrease in spending takes the form of an "excess supply," or surplus, of traded goods. This is the first favorable effect of the devaluation on the trade surplus. The rest of the decrease in spending, however, takes the form of an excess supply of non-traded goods. Inventories of nuts are piling up (because demand is lower than producers of nuts anticipated). Only if nuts really were a traded good, so that the excess supply could be unloaded on the world market at the going price, would the relative price of nuts and tin be unchanged (*both* P_n and P_t having gone up in proportion to the devaluation). Nuts are a non-traded good, however. To equilibrate the market for non-traded goods, their relative price, P_N, will have to fall. This means that the budget line in Figure 20.1 will become steeper.

Since we have already derived the NN schedule, it is easier to see the effects in Figure 20.6. The fall in the relative price of non-traded goods moves the economy from point H to point E on the NN schedule. (Under the current assumption that the market for non-traded goods always clears, the first of the two distinguishing assumptions of the monetary approach, this movement takes place instantaneously.) That is, if nuts are non-traded, then their price does not rise by the same proportion as tin and other traded goods.[18] The decline in the relative price of non-traded goods yields the second favorable effect of a devaluation on the trade balance: As we saw earlier in the chapter, for any given level of expenditure, a lower relative price of non-traded goods means that more traded goods are produced and fewer consumed. The trade surplus is larger at point E, where both effects are operating, than at point H, where only the real balance effect was allowed to operate.[19]

The second aspect of the monetary approach now appears: the non-sterilization of reserve flows. At point E the country is running a trade surplus. If the money flowing into the country through the trade account is not offset elsewhere, then it will increase expenditure, which reduces the trade surplus. We move up along the NN schedule: As expenditure rises, the price of non-traded goods must continuously rise to eliminate what would otherwise be an excess demand for non-traded goods. Money continues to flow into the country and expenditure continues to rise, until in the long run the country is back at S and the trade surplus has been completely eliminated, as always in the monetary approach.

This process illustrates some principles that recur throughout the study of devaluation. First, to have an effect on the trade balance, some variable must be "sticky" in the short run, in other words, it must be restricted from jumping discontinuously. A nominal devaluation reflected as equal increases in all nominal magnitudes would have no real effects. In Chapters 17 and 18, the sticky variable was the price of export goods; thus the devaluation changed the relative price of export and import goods. In the monetary approach to the balance of payments, the sticky variable is the stock of foreign reserves. Because the devaluation changes the real money supply, it has an effect on the trade balance in the short run even in the absence of slow adjustment in the goods or labor markets.[20]

Second, the sticky variable adjusts over time. When the sticky variable is the stock of international reserves, it adjusts via the balance of payments. (Analogously, when the sticky price variable is the price level, it adjusts via excess demand.) In the long run, when all adjustments are complete, all nominal magnitudes have increased by the same percentage as the devaluation, which is to say that no real magnitudes have changed.

---

[18] The nominal price of non-traded goods, P_n, probably stays about the same in the short run, or rises a little (less than the nominal price of traded goods). It is even conceivable that P_n falls. It depends on the elasticities of demand and supply of non-traded goods. All that is certain is that the *relative* price of non-traded goods, P_n/P_t, falls.

[19] To see the increase in the trade surplus graphically, think of successive waves of downward-sloping "iso-trade-surplus" lines emanating from the BB schedule in Figure 20.6, each one corresponding to a different level of the trade balance. Point E lies on an iso-trade-surplus line that is farther from BB than is H, so the trade surplus is larger, as it must be as a result of the fall in P_N.

[20] Both the real balance effect and the relative-price-of-non-traded-goods effect constitute counterexamples to an extreme claim that is known in some circles (notably the *Wall Street Journal* editorial page) as the Mundell-Laffer hypothesis. The claim is that in a small open economy a devaluation cannot improve the trade balance because all prices go up by the same proportion as the exchange rate. Jude Wanniski, "The Mundell-Laffer Hypothesis—A New View of the World Economy," *The Public Interest*, 39 (Spring 1975): 31–52; reprinted in Robert Baldwin and J. Davidson Richardson, eds., *International Trade and Finance* (Boston: Little, Brown and Co., 2nd. ed. 1981), pp. 374–388.

This last point does not mean that there can never be lasting changes in the real exchange rate. Real disturbances can and do affect the real exchange rate. An example is the debt burden acquired by Latin American countries and other LDCs, and the sudden 1982 fall in banks' willingness to continue lending to them. As we saw, servicing the debt meant, among other things, real devaluations of these nations' currencies to generate trade surpluses. These real devaluations were not purely transitory; the equilibrium itself will entail a lower real value of the currency for as long as it is necessary to service the debt. In terms of Figure 20.5, the relevant *BB* schedule for a typical debtor country shifted downward in 1982. In the absence of a deliberate policy change, a long slow deflation (falling prices of non-traded goods) might have eventually brought the country to the new long-run equilibrium. However, a devaluation of the currency speeds up the process.[21]

20.4 POTENTIAL CONTRACTIONARY EFFECTS OF DEVALUATION IN LDCs

In the Keynesian model in Chapter 18, a devaluation had a clear expansionary effect on output and employment. As long as the Marshall-Lerner condition was satisfied, net foreign demand for domestic products, that is, the trade balance, increased, working to raise output and employment. However, countries forced to devalue, usually because they are running out of foreign exchange reserves and sometimes as part of a program administered by the International Monetary Fund, often express the view that devaluation has a contractionary effect on output and employment rather than an expansionary one.[22] There are a number of channels through which such effects could possibly occur. Although some are also very relevant for large industrialized countries, many are peculiar to small countries and LDCs. We will consider ten possible contractionary effects that can arise in various contexts, the first seven operating through the demand for domestic goods and the last three operating through supply. Many of these concern structural characteristics of typical LDCs that are of interest in their own right.

Negative Effects on Aggregate Demand

The first problem arose in Chapter 17: If the country begins with a high initial volume of imports—and countries generally devalue only when they have a trade deficit to begin with—then because the devaluation raises the cost of imports in domestic terms, the trade balance may worsen in domestic terms, even if the demand elasticities are high enough to satisfy the simple Marshall-Lerner condition. If domestic demand does not rise at the same time, then the total effect on the demand for domestic goods will be contractionary. Of course, sufficiently large elasticities will solve this problem. LDCs often argue, however, that their elasticities are low. This is particularly true of their elasticity of demand for those imports that they cannot produce domestically,

---

[21] One might say that deviations of the real exchange rate from long-run equilibrium are purely transitory but that in 1982 the equilibrium value of the currency fell.

[22] There are other drawbacks to devaluation, particularly the exacerbation of inflation, regardless of the effect on output.

such as oil, luxury consumer goods, or capital goods. It can be argued that the world demand for the exports of even a small country may fall far short of the infinite elasticity that has been assumed in the preceding three sections of this chapter. Textiles produced in Mexico are, after all, not perfect substitutes for textiles produced in Thailand.

As was pointed out earlier, many of the products exported by LDCs face import barriers from the industrialized world (not to mention from other LDCs). If the devaluing country is constrained from increasing its exports, and its import bill increases with the devaluation, then domestic output will suffer from a loss in demand.

The second contractionary effect of devaluation is the real balance effect, first developed as part of the monetary approach in Chapter 19, then extended in Section 20.3. A devaluation raises the price of traded goods proportionately, thereby raising the general price level and reducing the real money supply to the extent that traded goods are important in the output basket. The lower real money supply then reduces expenditure. In the flexible-price model that we have been using recently, total output and employment, by assumption, do not fall. The contractionary effect on domestic spending is offset one-for-one by the stimulus to net exports, so the total is unchanged. However, if we allow for slowly adjusting prices of non-traded goods, the contractionary effect on domestic expenditure can translate into an excess supply of goods. Total output and employment in the economy may fall if the demand for non-traded goods falls by more than the net foreign demand for traded goods rises. To take a recent example, a feature of Poland's "cold turkey" reform program of January 1990 was a devaluation of almost 50 percent. The real balance effect, though helping to produce a trade surplus, also helped to produce a sharp fall in output and employment.[23]

The third effect of a devaluation, attributed to Carlos Diaz-Alejandro, enters when we introduce distinctions between different classes of consumers.[24] When wages, W, are sticky, a devaluation reduces real wages by increasing prices. Indeed, the only way it stimulates the production of tradable goods is by reducing W/P_t, the real wage in terms of traded goods. It is easy to see why workers might object to a devaluation. However, if workers' share of national income falls, then firm owners' share of national income rises. Thus, it is more difficult to see why there should be a contractionary effect on total demand, as is often claimed, rather than simply a negative effect on evenness of the distribution of income.

Diaz-Alejandro's argument is that different sectors have different marginal propensities to consume. Owners of firms might have a lower propensity to consume than workers. The specific example he had in mind was Argentina, where the most important tradable goods are wheat and cattle, which are raised by large landowners. A devaluation raises the prices of these commodities and causes a redistribution of income away from urban workers (who consume wheat and meat, and import other goods that are also now more expensive), and toward the landowners. If the landowners have a lower propensity to consume than the urban workers do, the net effect on

[23] John Williamson, *The Economic Opening of Eastern Europe* (Washington: Institute for International Economics, 1991).

[24] Carlos Diaz-Alejandro, "A Note on the Impact of Devaluation and the Redistribution Effect," *Journal of Political Economy* (December 1963): 577–580.

aggregate demand will be negative. Such distributional effects of a devaluation are likely to be more important for LDCs than for industrialized countries.[25]

The fourth potential contractionary effect of a devaluation concerns debt rather than money. Small countries that find they must devalue often have already accumulated sizable debts to the rest of the world, in the form of bonds that they have sold to foreign residents or loans that they have taken from foreign banks. Such debts are almost always denominated in dollars or other foreign currencies; foreign investors would be reluctant to hold assets denominated in local currency precisely because they fear that the country will devalue the local currency and thereby reduce the value of those assets to foreigners.[26] Residents of the home country lose if their debt is denominated in a foreign currency, such as the dollar, and the country is forced to devalue. Because it now costs more units of local currency to buy one dollar, servicing the debt—that is, making the interest payments and paying off the principal in installments—is more expensive in terms of the local currency. Households and firms may respond to the deterioration in their net wealth position (the increase in the valuation of their liabilities) and in their cash flow (the increase in their debt service requirements) by cutting back expenditure.[27] After the international debt crisis surfaced in August 1982, Brazil, to take one example among many, was forced to devalue. The resulting increase in the cost of the large outstanding dollar debts bankrupted some businesses and contributed to a recession in Brazil.

A fifth potential effect of a devaluation concerns the speculative buying of goods. Speculative buying of goods may be the only way that people can protect the real value of their wealth against high expected inflation rates, particularly in countries where a full range of bonds and stocks are not available because financial markets

[25] In LDCs (excluding a few like China) differences in income, and especially in wealth, are often much greater than in industrialized countries. An increase in firms' profits is likely to be distributed less widely through the population. (It is useful to recall that in the United States workers' pension funds constitute the largest category of the holders of corporate equity.) Furthermore, those living closer to the margin of subsistence are likely to have little savings and even less scope for borrowing, so their marginal propensity to consume is likely to be very close to one. This is why redistributional effects are likely to be larger in LDCs.

[26] The problem created for the incentives facing the local country is known as a "moral hazard" problem. The only country in the world that sells bonds to foreigners denominated in its own currency, on a large scale, is the United States. Until recently, foreign investors were fairly confident that the United States would not "inflate away" the real value of its debt by printing a lot of money and/or devaluing the dollar. But many of these investors saw the value of their holdings of dollar bonds fall in half in terms of their own currencies over the period 1985–1987, and may be increasingly reluctant to buy more in the 1990s.

[27] The net wealth of the citizens of a country in the aggregate is a determinant of private spending (along with such variables as their income). There is an interesting question as to what sort of bonds should be counted as part of net wealth. We usually do not count citizens' holdings of corporate debt because the corporations are owned by other citizens, so in the total the assets and liabilities cancel out, much as with an "IOU" between two individuals. (This is called "piercing the corporate veil.") Some economists argue analogously that citizens' holdings of bonds issued by their government should not be counted as net wealth. The argument is that an increase in the national debt means that the government will have to raise taxes at some point in the future, and far-sighted citizens will weigh those implicit future tax liabilities negatively when figuring their net wealth, so they fully cancel out the positive effect of the bonds held. This doctrine is called "Ricardian equivalence," but most people, including Ricardo and a majority even of modern economists, find it implausible that individuals in fact calculate that far into the future. The subject is addressed in an appendix to Chapter 22. In any case it is clear that holdings of foreign bonds (or indebtedness to foreigners) count positively (or negatively) in net national wealth, as do holdings of factories and other physical capital.

are not fully developed. If people think that a devaluation and consequent price increases are coming in the future, they may buy consumer durables and other such goods in anticipation. In Chile in the mid-1970s, for example, many residents believed that the government would be unable to maintain the peso at its high value; in anticipation of future devaluation, they bought consumer appliances and other durable goods in large numbers.[28] Although such purchases can have an expansionary effect at the time of the purchases (if some of the goods are produced at home), the devaluation itself may remove this speculative motive for spending and result in a contraction.[29]

A sixth potential contractionary effect occurs if import quotas are removed at the same time as the devaluation. This often happens with the devaluation intended to substitute for import controls as a policy addressing trade balance difficulties. Often the adoption of a more realistically valued currency in place of existing trade distortions is required as part of an agreement with the International Monetary Fund or its sister institution the World Bank. The removal of import controls can in the short run result in a large inflow of imports, which compete with domestic products, reducing domestic output.[30] Of course, it is not strictly correct to attribute such effects to the devaluation itself rather than to the distinct change in trade policy.

A similar point holds with contractionary monetary and fiscal policies, which are often adopted as part of a package at the same time as a devaluation. Though the policy changes are distinct and have distinct effects, it can be difficult to disentangle them empirically. The tendency for such policy changes to occur at the same time may account for some claims that devaluations are observed to have negative effects on output.[31]

The seventh contractionary effect that has been identified arises when there are important tariffs on tradable goods that are ad valorem tariffs, that is, are levied as a percentage of the money spent on the import. (Tariffs expressed in domestic currency per unit of the traded good are less common.) A devaluation will raise the price of the traded good proportionately and therefore the amount of tariff revenue that must be paid to the government. As with any tax increase, this will have a negative effect on the private sector's disposable income and therefore on its expenditure. This effect

[28] Rudiger Dornbusch, "External Debt, Budget Deficits, and Disequilibrium Exchange Rates." in Gordon Smith and John Cuddington, eds., *International Debt and the Developing Countries*,World Bank, 1985. Reprinted as "Overborrowing: Three Case Studies," (with other relevant essays) in R. Dornbusch, *Dollars, Debts and Deficits*, (Cambridge, MA: M.I.T. Press, 1986).

[29] Contrary effects are also possible (for example if the devaluation causes speculators to suspect that further devaluations are likely in the future rather than the reverse).

[30] Many countries have a history of proclaiming trade liberalization programs and then reversing them subsequently. Anne Krueger, *Foreign Trade Regimes and Economic Development: Liberalization Attempts and Consequences* (Cambridge, MA: Ballinger Press for National Bureau of Economic Research, 1978). The rush to buy imports after the government enacts a liberalization will be particularly large if buyers suspect that trade barriers may go back up in the future. Guillermo Calvo, "Incredible Reforms," in G. Calvo, R. Findlay, J. de Macedo, and P. Kouri, eds., *Debt, Stabilization and Development*, New York: Basil Blackwell, 1989.

[31] Richard Cooper, "Currency Devaluation in Developing Countries," *Essays in International Finance* No. 86 (Princeton: Princeton University Press, 1971), offers a classic and highly readable account of devaluation in LDCs which presents the six contractionary effects discussed so far.

is likely to be far more important in LDCs than in industrialized countries because only the former tend to rely on tariffs for a significant fraction of government revenue (income taxes being more difficult to enforce in such countries).[32]

Negative Effects on Aggregate Supply

The three remaining effects of devaluation arise in relation to aggregate supply rather than aggregate demand; they work to raise the price level for any given quantity of output supplied or, equivalently, to reduce the quantity of output supplied for any given price level. Thus, they can be more troublesome than the seven contractionary effects by way of demand, which can in theory be offset by expansionary monetary or fiscal policy.

Effect number eight, one of the most important for industrialized countries and LDCs alike, relates to the prices of raw materials and other imported inputs. (These are the "intermediate goods" of Chapter 9.) In Mexico in 1982–1983, for example, foreign exchange became very scarce, mostly because of successive devaluations of the peso in response to the international debt crisis. As a result, many companies were forced to cut output severely—even of products for which there was adequate demand—for lack of necessary industrial materials, mechanical parts, and other inputs that had previously been imported.[33]

For oil-importing countries, the most important imported input is, of course, oil. Energy is a factor of production like labor and capital. Most countries can take the price of oil and other fossil fuels as determined completely on world markets. Thus, a devaluation translates directly into a proportionate increase in the price that firms have to pay for fuel expressed in domestic currency. The increase in marginal cost relative to the price of the good the firm is producing will induce it to reduce output. The outcome can be analogous to the recession suffered by most countries in 1974 following the quadrupling of the world price of oil. The negative effect on a country's aggregate supply is the same, whether the reason for an increase in the price paid for imported oil is a worldwide price increase or an increase in the individual country's exchange rate.[34]

A parallel supply effect, again as important for many industrialized countries as for LDCs, concerns wages. When workers see increases in the prices of tradable goods that they consume, they may ask for increases in their nominal wages to make up for the loss in purchasing power. In some countries, particularly those with a past history of high rates of inflation, wage contracts may be indexed, that is, they may be written so that increases in the Consumer Price Index that occur during the period of the contract are automatically reflected in the wage rate. Thus, a devaluation will in part be passed through to higher wages. The increase in labor costs means that

[32] Paul Krugman and Lance Taylor, "Contractionary Effects of Devaluation," *Journal of International Economics*, 8(3) (August 1978): 445–456, introduce the effect via tariff revenue, and provide a description of some of the earlier contractionary effects as well.

[33] Intermediate inputs and capital goods account for over 90 percent of Mexico's total imports. On the contractionary effects of Mexico's "import compression," see Edward Buffie, "Mexico 1958–1986: From Stabilizing Development to Debt Crisis," in Jeffrey Sachs, ed. *Developing Country Debt and the World Economy* (Chicago: University of Chicago Press, 1989).

[34] Such "supply shocks" are analyzed in Chapter 23.

firms again face higher marginal costs relative to the product price and may respond by reducing supply.[35]

Examples are not hard to find. When Chile devalued its currency in 1981 to speed up the adjustment of the relative price of non-traded goods, it found that its existing wage-indexation arrangements were an obstacle to adjustment.[36] Israel and Brazil are two countries that carried indexation of wages (and indeed of most prices and other nominal magnitudes) the furthest in the 1970s and early 1980s. As the inflation rate accelerated, the Brazilians began to adjust wages automatically for inflation with greater frequency.[37] Also note that in some LDCs, the process whereby urban workers fight for increases in nominal wages to make up for the loss of purchasing power through higher prices of the tradable goods that they consume often involves strikes and other forms of social conflict that are very costly to the entire country in terms of lost output, not to mention the noneconomic costs. (Argentina is one of the best examples. A desire to divert public attention from economic problems of this type is considered to be one of the reasons why the Argentine military government invaded the Malvinas/Falkland Islands.)

The final potentially contractionary effect on the supply side comes through the cost of "working capital." Capital (in the sense of physical plant and equipment) is usually assumed to be the factor of production that is fixed in the short run, so that variable costs consist only of labor and intermediate inputs, such as oil. However, it is sometimes argued, particularly in countries with less-developed securities markets, that another variable factor of production is working capital—short-term funds to carry inventory, meet payroll, and so on. Given such a financial structure, if a devaluation reduces the real volume of credit available and forces up the interest rate, firms may face an adverse supply shock analogous to an increase in wages or oil prices. The mechanism that drives up interest rates is similar to that previously described under the real balance effect, but the contractionary effect here is believed to come on the supply side rather than the demand side.[38]

Thus, there are many possible routes through which a devaluation might have contractionary effects on output. For any given country, however, only some of the

[35] Wage indexation in industrialized countries is another topic covered in Chapter 23.

[36] It has been argued that this is one reason why Chilean unemployment rose sharply thereafter. Vittorio Corbo, "Reforms and Macroeconomic Adjustments in Chile during 1974–1984," in *World Development*, Special Issue on Liberalization with Stabilization in the Southern Cone of Latin America, 13(8) (August 1985): 893–916. He uses precisely the model developed earlier in this chapter to argue that an increase in spending (due in part to a swelling of the money supply in 1980) and an overvalued currency moved Chile in 1981 to a point of balance of payments deterioration like *G* in our Figure 20.4. He further argues that the government at first relied on the monetary approach to the balance of payments to restore equilibrium but failed to realize that an immediate fall in the relative price of non-traded goods was necessary to reverse the deterioration in the trade balance.

[37] Israel reduced its degree of wage indexation in 1985, as part of a comprehensive program to reduce the inflation rate. Brazil, under pressure from the IMF, decreased its degree of wage indexation in 1984. Although the motivation of such attempts to eliminate indexation is to reduce *both* the price inflation rate and the wage inflation rate, wages in practice tend to lag behind prices in the transition. (In 1986 the Brazilian government attempted a disinflation program on its own, known as the Cruzado Plan, but its success was much shorter lived than that of the Israeli program.)

[38] Sweder van Wijnbergen, "Exchange Rate Management and Stabilization Policies in Developing Countries," in S. Edwards and L. Ahamed, eds., *Economic Adjustment and Exchange Rates in Developing Countries* (Chicago: University of Chicago Press, 1986).

effects will be important. Furthermore, some effects could lead to increased output. Most important, remember the original and primary reason for believing that a devaluation will have an expansionary effect: It stimulates exports and discourages imports. What is the net effect of all these factors likely to be on output? Sebastian Edwards has studied the effect of devaluation on output for twelve developing countries during the period 1965–1980. He found that devaluations generate a small contractionary effect in the first year, but the effect is completely reversed in the second year and becomes expansionary. In the long run, there is no effect, presumably because price levels and other nominal magnitudes adjust, so the nominal devaluation ceases to be a real devaluation.[39]

20.5 SUMMARY

Most LDCs (and industrialized countries as well) have a substantial internal market where prices do not adjust instantly in response to a devaluation, so that the monetarist model of Chapter 19 is not applicable. However, a majority of such countries are too small in world markets to be able to set the price of their exports, so the Keynesian model is also not relevant. This chapter examined the effects of exchange rate and monetary policies in such small, open countries with non-traded goods.

The trade balance can be thought of as the country's excess supply of internationally traded goods. We focused on two key variables: the level of expenditure and the relative price of non-traded goods (in terms of traded goods). One possibility is that these variables adjust automatically to ensure equilibrium in the two markets. Whenever there is a trade deficit, reserves flow out of the country; under the monetary approach to the balance of payments, the level of expenditure falls until trade balance equilibrium is restored. Whenever there is excess supply of non-traded goods, the price of non-traded goods falls until equilibrium in this market is restored as well.

In practice, these automatic mechanisms of adjustment are likely to work slowly at best. Thus, there is an argument for the government to use its available policy tools to speed up the process. The government can adjust the level of expenditure by changing the money supply. The government can adjust the level of the relative price of non-traded goods by changing the exchange rate and thus changing the price of traded goods.

We saw that a devaluation works to improve the trade balance in a small country through two effects. In addition to the real-balance effect of Chapter 19 (whereby the higher price level creates an excess demand for money and leads to a reduction in spending), there is a second effect. When the price of traded goods goes up in proportion to the devaluation, the relative price of non-traded goods goes down; in response, resources shift out of the production of non-traded goods into production of traded goods. Thus, the trade balance improves by more than it would have if the price of

---

[39] Sebastian Edwards, "Are Devaluations Contractionary?" *Review of Economics and Statistics*, 68(3) (August 1986): 501–508. Some support for positive effects of devaluation on real growth was found by Michael Connolly, "Exchange Rates, Real Economic Activity, and the Balance of Payments: Evidence from the 1960s," E. Classen and P. Salin, eds., *Recent Issues in the Theory of Flexible Exchange Rates* (Amsterdam: North-Holland, 1983). A recent study of sixty devaluations between 1953 and 1983 finds no evidence of contractionary effects: Steven Kamin, "Devaluation, External Balance, and Macroeconomic Performance: A Look at the Numbers," *Princeton Studies in International Finance*, No. 62 (August 1988).

non-traded goods had gone up by the same proportion as the price of traded goods. In the long run, however, all nominal magnitudes are likely to go up in proportion to the devaluation, leaving no permanent effect on the trade balance.

The chapter concluded by mentioning a variety of special factors that characterize some LDCs and that might lead to a devaluation reducing total output and employment rather than raising it. Some of the factors concern demand: If a devaluation makes people poorer, they will spend less. Some concern supply: If a devaluation raises the prices of inputs, firms will cut back production. The empirical evidence seems to suggest, however, that in most devaluations, once sufficient time has passed for consumers to respond to the higher prices of imports and producers to respond to the higher prices of exports, the net effect on GNP is positive.

CHAPTER PROBLEMS

1. The country of Lampong used to import grain but now produces enough to feed itself; during the last few years imports have been essentially zero (as have exports). Does this mean that grain is a non-traded good?

2. You are the governor of the central bank in the country of Salesia, which is running a large balance of payments surplus as the result of recent discoveries of valuable natural resources. You are worried that the inflow of reserves through the balance of payments surplus is causing excessive growth in the money supply. Indeed, you have already exceeded the year's money supply target that you and the International Monetary Fund team agreed on at the time of their last visit. On the other hand, you don't want to allow the currency to appreciate, causing your exporters in the manufacturing sector to lose competitiveness. What should you do?

3. You have just been called in to advise the government of Gondar. The country has been running a large trade deficit for years and is in trouble with its international creditors. Other economic statistics, however, are unreliable. There seem to be more than the usual number of people wandering the capital looking for odd jobs. Also, prices of hotel rooms, pedi-cabs on the street, and the local delicacy in the countryside have all fallen since your last visit. In what quadrant of Figure 20.5 would you tentatively place the country's economy?

4. You are the Finance Minister of Rajistan. The country has started running a balance of payments deficit as the result of a bad harvest in the countryside, but the rest of the economy appears to be booming. Your foreign advisors suggest that you devalue your currency to eliminate the payments deficit. Do you agree with this course of action? If you are worried about inflationary pressures, how should you respond?

5. You are Minister of Trade in Santa Maria, which is undergoing an acute balance of payments crisis. In desperation you are considering cutting off imports of cotton, which is the country's largest import because it is used by the large textile industry. Is this a good idea?

6. You are advising the Prime Minister of Phoenesia. Traded goods constitute half of workers' consumption basket. The other half consists of non-traded goods. The price of non-traded goods, P_n, is a simple proportionate markup to wages, W. Industry and the labor unions have agreed on a contract stipulating that two-thirds of any increases in the CPI will be passed through to wages.
   a. For every 1 percent nominal devaluation, what is the effect on the price of non-traded goods?
   b. Assume that firms in the traded goods sector show an elasticity of supply (with respect to P_t/W) of 1.0. If the government wants to increase output of traded goods by 10 percent, how large an increase in P_t/W is required?

c. Putting together your answers to a and b, how large must the nominal devaluation be to bring about the desired increase in output of traded goods? How large is the resulting increase in the wage, W? In the CPI?[40]

SUGGESTIONS FOR FURTHER READING

Begg, David. "Economic Reform in Czechoslovakia: Should We Believe in Santa Klaus?" *Economic Policy* No. 13, 1991. A discussion of extensive macroeconomic and micro-economic reforms instituted in 1991 by the pro-market Czech finance minister.

Corden, W. Max. *Inflation, Exchange Rates and the World Economy* (Chicago: University of Chicago Press, 1977). Includes a verbal exposition of the dependent economy model.

————. "Macroeconomic Policy and Growth: Some Lessons of Recent Experience," *Annual Conference on Development Economics*, The World Bank, 1990. Lessons from seventeen developing countries.

Dornbusch, Rudiger. "Devaluation, Money and Non-traded Goods," *American Economic Review* (December 1973): 871–880. The classic model of the monetary approach to devaluation in small open economies. Non-traded goods are introduced in the second half of the paper.

————. "Our LDC Debts," in Martin Feldstein, ed., *The United States in the World Economy*, (Chicago: University of Chicago Press, 1988). An introduction to the issues involved in the LDC debt crisis that surfaced in August 1982.

————. "Policies to Move from Stabilization to Growth," *Annual Conference on Development Economics*, The World Bank, 1990. How can growth be restored to the debtor countries?

Edwards, Sebastian. "The International Monetary Fund and the Developing Countries: A Critical Evaluation," *Carnegie-Rochester Conference Series on Public Policy* 31 (1989): 7–68. Discusses the model used by IMF staff to generate advice to borrowing countries (essentially the monetary approach to the balance of payments), and the evidence whether IMF programs help countries.

Lipton, David, and Jeffrey Sachs. "Creating a Market Economy in Eastern Europe: The Case of Poland," *Brookings Papers on Economic Activity* 1, 1990: 75–142. Two key advisers to Eastern European governments describe the "shock therapy" adopted in Poland in 1990, featuring devaluation of the zloty and restoration of convertibility, price liberalization, and control of domestic credit creation.

Sachs, Jeffrey. "External Debt and Macroeconomic Performance in Latin America and East Asia," *Brookings Papers on Economic Activity*, 2, 1985. Why did one group of debtor countries fare so much worse than another in response to the same deterioration in the international environment in the early 1980s?

————, ed. *Developing Country Debt and the World Economy*. (Chicago: University of Chicago Press, 1989). Papers on aspects of the debt crisis by Dornbusch, Edwards, Eichengreen, Fischer, Haggard and Kaufman, Lindert and Morton, Krugman, Sachs, and others, as well as country studies for Argentina, Bolivia, Brazil, Indonesia, Korea, Mexico, the Philippines, and Turkey.

---

[40] A simple version of the dependent model along the lines of the calculations laid out in Problem 6 is sometimes known as the "Scandinavian model." Non-traded goods are called the "sheltered" sector (sheltered from the international competition), and traded goods the exposed or competitive sector.

————. "New Approaches to the Latin American Debt Crisis," *Essays in International Finance*, No. 194 (Princeton: Princeton University Press, July 1989). The argument for debt forgiveness, a major departure from the strategy adopted by the creditor countries after 1982 to manage the LDC debt crisis. (The "Brady Plan" of 1989 moved a step in this direction.)

Williamson, John, ed. *Latin American Adjustment: How Much Has Happened?* (Washington: Institute for International Economics, April 1990). Reviews recent progress among Latin debtors.

V

International Financial Markets and Their Macroeconomic Implications

21

THE INTERNATIONALIZATION OF FINANCIAL MARKETS

Part IV introduced the international movement of money but left out the factor that by the 1980s had become the most important aspect of the world monetary system: the international movement of capital. In the 1950s, it was possible to ignore international capital flows without seriously endangering the accuracy of the analysis. The world financial system, which had facilitated large volumes of international capital movement in the nineteenth century,[1] had become badly fragmented in the course of two world wars and the Great Depression. Even in the countries where financial markets were the most developed, such as the United States, the United Kingdom, and Switzerland, governments in the 1950s and 1960s maintained controls preventing the free international flow of capital.

Innovative bankers and others began to find ways around these controls. The Euromarkets developed, outside the reach of national governments. Then, in the 1970s, many of the larger countries removed their capital controls. Meanwhile, transaction costs were gradually falling because of technological progress in telecommunications and computers. In the 1980s, the process of internationalization of financial markets continued as a result of further liberalization by governments and further innovation by the private markets. Chapter 21 will trace the process whereby the world's financial markets have become highly integrated over the last twenty years. Then the primary focus in the remainder of the text will be the implications of this financial integration for the operation of the world economy.

The increasing degree of international capital mobility is crucial for macroeconomics in many ways. With large volumes of short-term capital poised to shift back and forth among countries every time investors' preferences change, financial markets are highly volatile and prices of stocks, bonds, and foreign exchange highly variable. Interest rates in each country are increasingly determined by financial conditions abroad rather than by domestic policy alone. Income and employment, in turn, are increasingly affected by economic developments abroad.

[1] Chapter 10 discusses portfolio capital in the nineteenth century.

The structure of the world's financial markets over the last twenty years has been profoundly affected by a number of trends. From the viewpoint of individual countries' financial markets, the trend has been "internationalization" or "globalization": National markets are increasingly influenced by foreign investors, foreign assets, foreign financial intermediaries, and developments in foreign economies.

Integration, the breakdown of the barriers separating nations' financial markets, began with the development of the Euromarkets. The trend continued with "liberalization" and "deregulation" on the part of national governments (the removal of controls, regulations, and taxes) and "innovation" on the part of the private sector (the development of new financial instruments and new ways of issuing and trading them). Innovation in the 1980s includes "securitization": Where previously a borrower would have relied on bank loans, securities such as stocks and bonds are now increasingly sold directly to investors, often without the participation of banks ("disintermediation"). We will examine the Euromarkets in Section 21.1, liberalization in Section 21.3, and innovation in Section 21.4.

After World War II, the steps taken to restore and encourage international trade in goods did not apply to international trade in financial assets. While the Articles of Agreement of the International Monetary Fund, worked out in 1944 at Bretton Woods, New Hampshire, incorporated a presumption of the desirability of free trade, there was no analogous presumption that free capital movements were necessarily desirable.[2] No mechanism analogous to the GATT was set up to negotiate reductions in barriers to capital movements. Most countries retained controls on such movements. Indeed, in the 1960s, the United States adopted increasingly more stringent controls in an effort to prevent capital from flowing out of the country; U.S. policy-makers were concerned that they would run out of international reserves, thereby jeopardizing the viability of the Bretton Woods exchange rate system. For example, there was an "interest equalization tax," designed to reduce the rate of return on foreign assets relative to domestic U.S. assets, thus making the foreign assets less attractive to investors. There was also a voluntary foreign credit restraint program that placed ceilings on banks' foreign lending. The controls were not entirely effective, in part because of the development of the Euromarkets.

21.1 THE EUROMARKETS

The Euromarkets began in the 1960s with deposits denominated in U.S. dollars but placed in banks located in London and elsewhere outside the United States. The banks, many of which are European branches of major American banks, accept these deposits and use them to make short-term loans to borrowers of any nationality. This market is like any other for bank deposits and bank loans, except that the transaction is not denominated in the currency of the country where it takes place. Indeed, the

---

[2] One can make a good theoretical case that the free movement of capital maximizes welfare, just as the free movement of trade in goods does. International trade in assets allows countries to reallocate consumption from high-income periods to low-income periods. (This point is developed in the appendix to Chapter 22.) It also allows countries to share risk internationally, thereby reducing the amount of risk that each must bear. Some policy-makers, however, including the architects of the Bretton Woods system, have always questioned whether capital markets left to themselves would function as efficiently as the theoretical ideal.

fundamental purpose of this market is to sever the location of the bank from the nationality of the currency in which it deals.

At the inception of the Eurodollar market, some of the most important depositors were central banks of the Soviet Bloc countries, which held dollar balances in order to conduct trade with the West, but were loath to place them on Wall Street, the bastion of capitalism. They may have been worried that in the event of a crisis U.S. authorities could freeze any deposits held in the United States.

In the 1960s, the markets thrived primarily because they offered a way to avoid capital controls and other U.S. financial regulations (such as Regulation Q, which placed a ceiling on the interest rate that a bank could pay to attract deposits). Banks are required to hold a certain ratio of reserves (which do not pay interest to the bank) against deposits in the United States, while there is no reserve requirement for deposits in the Euromarket. Even today, this remains the chief advantage of the latter, from the bank's viewpoint. As recently as 1982, banks had a sufficient preference for deposits in the Euromarket that they were willing to pay 1.0 percent per annum more in interest on these deposits. U.S. banks became heavy borrowers in the Euromarket whenever credit conditions were tightened by the Federal Reserve System. From early on, depositors in the Eurodollar markets included U.S. corporations, which earned a higher return on their liquid balances there than at home. Depositors also include many non-Americans who transact large volumes of business in dollars and so prefer to hold funds in dollars.

It is important to recognize the circumstances under which a Eurodollar transaction involves an international capital movement. We need take account only of transactions between depositors and ultimate borrowers, intermediated by the banks. When a Eurodollar changes hands between citizens of different nationalities, the borrower's country experiences a short-term capital inflow from the depositor's country. When their nationalities are the same, no international flow occurs. The fact that the currency denominating the transaction may be foreign to one or both parties is not significant.

The size of the Euromarkets increased rapidly after 1973.[3] In the aftermath of the oil price increase of that year, the OPEC countries had far larger dollar earnings than they could usefully spend, and they invested these "petrodollars" in Euromarket bank deposits. The banks in turn "recycled" these dollars by lending them to LDCs and other oil-importing countries that needed to finance current account deficits.

The Euromarkets have expanded in several dimensions in addition to size. First, in the 1960s they began to deal not just in U.S. dollars, but in pounds, yen, marks, and all other major currencies. The dollar proportion has declined over time. Second, the geographical location has spread, first from London to European capitals such as Zurich, then to Caribbean islands such as the Bahamas and the Cayman Islands, and more recently to rapidly growing Asian financial centers such as Hong Kong, Singapore, and Bahrain. As a result of this geographical extension, the Euromarkets are effectively open twenty-four hours a day. Third, the instruments that the system

---

[3] Although one of the original motivations for the Eurodollar market—escaping U.S. international capital controls—was removed after 1973, escaping the U.S. domestic banking regulations remained a relevant motivation. Indeed, it has been argued that escaping domestic regulation was the only motivation all along: Gunter Dufey and Ian Giddy, "The International Money Market: Perspective and Prognosis," 1978; reprinted in R. Baldwin and J. D. Richardson, eds., *International Trade and Finance*, 3rd ed. (Boston: Little Brown, 1986).

uses to relend deposits to borrowers on a longer-term basis have evolved over time. In the 1970s the money reached LDCs and other borrowers by means of the syndicated bank loan—a large number of banks lending together under the same terms. In the latter part of the decade, innovation was evident in the shift from loans at fixed interest rates at long terms to loans indexed to short-term dollar interest rates, usually the London Interbank Offered Rate (LIBOR) or the U.S. treasury bill rate. The goal was to protect against the risk of changes in inflation and interest rates. The process of innovation accelerated with the growth of Eurobonds and other new instruments, as Section 21.4 will discuss.

Throughout the history of the Euromarkets, and international financial trading in general, there has been a steady trend of reduced costs due to improved communications and transaction technology. The real cost of sending a telegraphic message from New York to London in 1985 was only 8 or 9 percent of what it was in 1900. The real cost of a three-minute off-peak telephone call between Washington and Frankfurt was only 5 percent of what it was in 1950.[4] The *Financial Times* of London is now available in New York on the day it is published. Recently, new computer technology has merged with telecommunications advances to further the revolution in international finance. Regardless of home base, an investor can now analyze the day's developments in Washington, monitor reactions in the financial markets in Tokyo, take a position in a foreign currency in London, and make payment through a bank in New York, all with little effort and little time lag. As a result of the reduction in communications and transaction costs, together with the other processes of liberalization and innovation to be discussed in Sections 21.3 and 21.4, the boundaries between the Euromarkets and many countries' domestic financial markets began to break down in the 1980s. Today, the Euromarket exists wherever transaction costs are the lowest.[5]

21.2 THE FOREIGN EXCHANGE MARKET

The size of the world foreign exchange market has increased dramatically. This "market" is really a loose network of banks and other financial institutions, linked by telephone and computer, that buy and sell currencies. Because there are so many participants, and the "products" being traded are so homogeneous (i.e., a deutschemark deposit is the same, wherever you buy it), this market fits exactly the classical economists' model of perfect competition.

The precise size of the foreign exchange market is unknown. In April 1989, the Federal Reserve Bank of New York surveyed known foreign exchange dealers. Banks reported foreign exchange transactions of $111 billion per day, up 121 percent from 1986. This figure includes, along with regular spot transactions (63 percent), trading

---

[4] Richard Cooper, "The United States as an Open Economy," in R. Hafer, ed., *How Open Is the U.S. Economy?* (Lexington, MA: D.C. Heath, 1986), p. 10.

[5] Eurobanks have usually offered smaller spreads between deposit and loan interest rates than do U.S. banks, consequently pulling considerable business away from them. See Gunter Dufey and Ian Giddy, *The International Money Market* (Englewood Cliffs, NJ: Prentice-Hall, 1978), Chapters 1 and 2. Beginning in December 1981, U.S. banks were allowed to participate in an arrangement resembling a domestic Euromarket, by establishing International Banking Facilities (IBFs), which are simply a separate set of deposit accounts without reserve requirements. See Alec Chrystal, "International Banking Facilities," *Federal Reserve Bank of St. Louis Review* (April 1984): 5–11. Japan also now allows IBFs.

in forward contracts and some other contracts. A "spot" purchase of foreign exchange is the purchase of a contract for immediate delivery of the currency (actually within two days). The other contracts are explained in Section 21.4. Other financial institutions reported another $18 billion in transactions, for a total of $129 billion per day in the United States.

In the same month, the Bank of England surveyed banks and brokers in London, who reported a total of $187 billion per day, while the Bank of Japan surveyed the Tokyo market, obtaining a total of $115 billion per day.[6] Thus, the three largest financial centers add up to over $430 billion per day. Other financial centers in Europe (Zurich, Frankfurt, Paris, and Milan) and in the Pacific (Singapore, Hong Kong, Australia, and New Zealand) were not surveyed at that time. The total volume worldwide, however, is well over $500 billion per day, especially allowing for the continued growth since 1989.

This number does not include the many countries where there is no organized private foreign market, often because the government in these countries owns the banking system and prohibits private trading. In these countries, the government buys and sells foreign exchange instead (though informal trading may go on in an illegal "black market" or officially-tolerated "parallel market," at an exchange rate usually very different from the official rate).

Bid-Ask Spreads and Arbitrage in the Spot Market

One reason for the large volume of foreign exchange transactions is their low cost. The cost of the transaction usually appears in the form of a "spread between the bid and ask," that is, a gap between the price at which the bank is willing to buy a given currency and the price at which it is willing to sell it. The size of the spread is determined by the type of customer. A tourist who buys foreign exchange at a bank will typically pay a large cost, approximately 1 percent. A firm that conducts a great deal of international business will receive a much better rate from its bank. When banks or brokers deal with each other, the spread is yet another order of magnitude smaller. The quoted spread on the Reuters screen averages around .05 percent, and in practice banks and brokers may negotiate still smaller spreads.

These transaction costs are lower than those in the past[7] because of the technological factors mentioned previously and the economies of scale involved in large transactions and "thick," or highly liquid, markets.[8] However, the bid-ask spread still widens at times, especially for less-important currencies that are thinly traded. A

---

[6] The Tokyo foreign exchange market has been growing very rapidly since 1984, when the Japanese Ministry of Finance began to remove some restrictive regulations.

[7] The average bid-ask spread in DM in New York was twice as large in 1973, at 0.11 percent, according to Kenneth Froot, "Multinational Corporations, Exchange Rates, and Direct Investment," in William Branson, Jacob Frenkel, and Morris Goldstein, eds., *International Policy Coordination and Exchange Rate Fluctuations* (Chicago: University of Chicago Press, 1989).

[8] Notice the multiple directions of causality. While higher transaction volume is partly a result of low bid-ask spreads, low bid-ask spreads are partly a function of high transaction volume (the economies of scale). Some evidence on the determination of the bid-ask spread is given by Paul Boothe, "Exchange Rate Risk and the Bid-Ask Spread: A Seven Country Comparison," *Economic Inquiry*, 26 (July 1988): 485–492; Debra Glassman, "Exchange Rate Risk and Volatility: Evidence from the Bid-Ask Spread," *Journal of Finance* (December 1987): 479–490.

major determinant of the bid-ask spread is the volatility of the spot rate itself. Every time a bank buys foreign currency from a customer, it runs the risk that before it can resell the currency, there will be a large movement in the exchange rate and the currency will lose value. Clearly, this risk is higher when exchange rate volatility is higher, one reason why the bid-ask spread is larger at some times that at others.

Exchange rates in different financial centers are kept nearly identical by foreign exchange arbitrage. As we saw in Chapter 19 *arbitrage* is a general term that means buying something where it is cheap and selling it where it is expensive, thus working to reduce the differential by driving the first price up, the second price down, or both. In this case, the "commodity" being bought and sold is currency. If the dollar price of Swiss francs in New York falls below the dollar price of Swiss francs in London by more than the small transaction cost, it pays to buy in New York and sell in London. The arbitrage will bid up the price of Swiss francs in New York, and bid down the price in London, until the difference disappears.

Arbitrage also keeps exchange rates among three or more currencies consistent with each other. Suppose you buy $1000 worth of sterling in New York, sell it in London for German deutschemarks (DM), then sell the DM for dollars in Frankfurt. If you wind up with either more or less than $1000, the exchange rates were not consistent. If you made a profit, you (and other arbitragers) will repeat the transaction until the market rates are forced to be consistent. If you lost in the transaction, you went around the circuit the wrong way; the opposite series of purchases and sales would have yielded an arbitrage profit. This process is called *triangular arbitrage*. Subject to the limits of transaction costs, it maintains consistency among the bilateral "cross rates," connecting all the world's internationally traded currencies. In other words, the $/£ exchange rate times the DM/$ rate equals the DM/£ rate (as you can tell by crossing out currencies in the numerators and denominators).

Interbank Trading of Foreign Exchange

The large volume of foreign exchange transactions seems puzzling. The 1989 survey showed that the amount of foreign exchange traded in the major markets was in excess of $430 billion per day. Of this almost all consisted of trading the U.S. dollar for another currency. ("Cross-currency" transactions, foreign exchange transactions not involving the dollar, were only 4 percent of the total in New York.)

By contrast, U.S. imports plus exports totaled $839 billion for the entire *year*. Adding in the gross purchases and sales of assets and gross investment income payments, the total comes to an average of $4 billion per calendar day. Why is the volume of dollar transactions in the foreign exchange market approximately 100 times larger than this?

Section 21.3 provides a bit of the explanation, relevant to the dollar in particular, and Section 21.4 provides the rest of the explanation. Briefly, the answer is that most of the foreign exchange transactions involve trading among banks rather than providing services for importers, exporters, and other customers: 82.0 percent of the foreign exchange trading reported by U.S. banks was with other banks. Only 4.9 percent of their trading was with nonfinancial customers.

When a bank buys, for example, French francs from a customer who has just earned them from exporting to France, the bank will not choose to hold the francs unless (1) it has good reason to expect that another customer will want to buy them before long or (2) it expects that the foreign exchange value of the francs is about to go up.[9] Otherwise, it will quickly try to unload the francs to some other bank. That bank may itself try to unload them on another bank, and so on, until the francs find someone who wants them, either to spend on imports from France or to hold as an investment.

Vehicle Currencies

In any center of foreign exchange trading, most business is carried on in only a few foreign currencies. This does not necessarily imply that the market is imperfect or that it discriminates against the smaller trading countries. Rather, it demonstrates the convenience to all parties of picking one or two leading currencies—known as *vehicle currencies*—and using them as focal points for trading. For that reason, a high proportion of transactions in the foreign exchange market is explained by exchanges of U.S. dollars for another currency. In an overseas financial center such as Paris, foreign exchange transactions in U.S. dollars are much more prominent than French commercial transactions with the United States would suggest. Particularly for currencies traded in small volumes, it proves more efficient to convert, for example, Greek drachmas into dollars and then into Portuguese escudos than it is to find a transaction partner for a direct drachma-escudo exchange.

Vehicle currencies are used not only to facilitate foreign exchange transactions but also, to some degree, for invoicing trade in goods (and services). As a reason for this, Ronald McKinnon cites the risks facing exporters of various types of goods. McKinnon draws a contrast between homogeneous goods and materials (particularly agricultural and mineral commodities), which are sold on competitive world markets, and the differentiated finished goods, whose manufacturers control their own prices even if they face substantial competition. This is essentially the same distinction made earlier between "auction goods" and "customer goods." Chapter 19 emphasized that competitive, homogeneous, auction goods tend to obey the Law of One Price. Here the point is that producers of such goods face less risk if they invoice in the most important currency, the dollar, even when it is not their own currency, because the exchange rate and the local price of the commodity are likely to be highly correlated. In the event that a producer's currency suddenly depreciates against the dollar, the price of the commodity in terms of the producer's currency is likely to go up by a similar amount due to the Law of One Price. The producer would be in trouble if she had invoiced in her own currency but will find herself still operating at the going world price if she invoiced in dollars. By contrast, the sellers of differentiated finished goods incur most costs in their home currency and control the home-currency price of exports, so they minimize risks to the profit margin by quoting in home currency.[10]

The widespread use of a currency in one area will contribute to its widespread adoption in another area. For example, if all foreign exchange transactions must pass

---

[9] Under the existing "multiple dealer" system, banks must provide quotes on both sides of the markets, both bid and ask, and then must accept a trade offered at the quoted price.

[10] Ronald Mckinnon, *Money in International Exchange: The Convertible Currency System*, New York: Oxford University Press, 1979, Chapter 4.

through dollars, then the convenience of settling transactions is an extra incentive to use the dollar for invoicing of trade. Arguments similar to those made regarding the currency choice for invoicing trade can also be made regarding the choice of vehicle currencies to denominate assets. Another area in which vehicle currencies are in evidence, in addition to foreign currency trading, invoicing of merchandise trade, and denomination of assets, is the form in which central banks choose to hold their foreign exchange reserves.

Before World War I, the pound sterling was the clear world choice for vehicle currency. Subsequently, the dollar came to be used more widely, as the United States gained economic power and political prestige relative to Great Britain. Since World War II, the dollar has been the clear choice for vehicle currency. Table 21.1 shows the roles of major currencies in three of the areas mentioned: foreign exchange trading, asset denomination, and reserve holdings. The dollar's share is much greater than the United States' share in world output, trade, or assets. For several decades the mark was in second place and the yen in third. The yen has been gaining, however. In the 1980s it passed the mark in importance in the international financial markets by some measures. The question of fourth place depends very much on the criterion used. The pound still does rather well in foreign exchange trading and external bank loans, the Swiss franc in international bond issues, the French franc and SDR in the number of small countries that peg their currency to them, and the ECU in international reserve holdings (among European central banks).

Some observers, watching the relative decline of the United States and the relative rise of Japan by such measures of economic power as productivity growth, income, and wealth, are suggesting that the use of the yen in transactions may eventually supplant the use of the dollar. Not long ago, the government of Japan resisted the idea that its currency should become increasingly used internationally. Since 1984, however, the Japanese government has begun to look more favorably on the increased use of the yen, partly in response to U.S. pressure.[11]

Despite the rise in the yen share of transactions evident in Table 21.1, the yen, like the mark, is still a long way from replacing the dollar. Everyone—banks, importers, exporters, borrowers, lenders, and central banks—tends to use the currencies that other market participants are using. The choice of currency is based not only on the relative importance of the respective countries in the world economy but also on the relative use of the various currencies in the recent past. The dollar will undoubtedly remain the world's principal vehicle currency for many years to come.[12]

The world monetary system features two "composite" currencies, the SDR (Special Drawing Right), created by the IMF, and the ECU (European Currency Unit), created by the European Community (EC). Both assets are assured a certain level of usage in reserve transactions among central banks. The SDR, whose value is determined as a weighted basket of the dollar, yen, mark, pound, and French franc, is also used by some small countries with widely diversified trade as a unit on which to peg their own currencies. However, it has not caught on widely as a currency for denominating

---

[11] The major disadvantage to a country of having its currency used as an international currency is that the demand for the currency may be subject to larger fluctuations than before. The major advantage is that the country earns *seignorage* on the other countries' holdings of its currency: The other countries have to give up real goods and services in order to add to their currency balances.

[12] Paul Krugman, "The International Role of the Dollar: Theory and Prospect," in J. Bilson and R. Marston, eds., *Exchange Rate Theory and Practice* (Chicago: University of Chicago Press, 1984).

TABLE 21.1 The Importance of Major Currencies (Shares in International Use)

	Official Use of Currencies		Currency of Denomination in Private Transactions				
	Pegging of Minor Currencies[1]	Foreign Exchange Reserves Held by Central Banks[2]	Foreign Exchange Trading in World Markets[3]	External Bank Loans[4]	External Bond Issues[5]	Euro-currency Deposits[6]	Invoic-ing Trade[7]
U.S. dollar	.51	.50	.45	.65	.38	.53	.38
Japanese yen	.00	.09	.14	.02	.13	.05	.13
Deutsche-mark	.02	.19	.13	.06	.07	.16	.21
Pound sterling	.00	.03	.07	.13	.09	.04	.10
Swiss franc	.00	.02	.10	.00	.09	.06	NA
French franc	.28	.02	.02	NA	.04	.02	.11
Canadian dollar	.00	.00	.01	NA	.03	NA	NA
Italian lira	.00	.00	NA	NA	NA	NA	.08
Dutch guilder	.00	.01	NA	NA	.01	NA	NA
Australian dollar	.02	.00	NA	NA	.02	NA	NA
ECU	.00	.12	.00	.08	.08	.05	NA
Other	.06	.03	.07	.06	.06	.09	NA

[1] *Source: International Financial Statistics*, IMF. Data pertain to mid-1991. EMS countries are not counted as pegging to the ECU.

[2] *Source:* IMF *Annual Report*, 1991. Data are for 1990.

[3] All data pertain to April 1989. All figures have been divided by 2 so that total adds to 100% rather than 200%. Figures for the major currencies pertain to trading in 21 financial centers. (*Source:* George Tavlas and Yuzuru Ozeki, *The Internationalization of Currencies: An Appraisal of the Yen*, Washington, D. C., International Monetary Fund, [1991] Table 23.) Figures for the Swiss franc, French franc, and Canadian dollar (which exclude cross-currency trading) pertain to trading in New York, London, and Tokyo which constitutes 60% of total world trading. (*Sources:* Federal Reserve Bank of New York, Bank of England, and Bank of Japan press releases, September 13, 1989).

[4] *Source:* Table 23 in Tavlas and Ozeki, *op.cit.* Data pertain to 1990.

[5] Ibid. Data pertain to 1990. (Includes international issues, foreign issues, and special placements.)

[6] Ibid. Data pertain to 1990. ("Other" includes foreign currency position of U.S. banks for which no currency breakdown is available.)

[7] Calculation based on Stanley Black, "Transactions Costs and Vehicle Currencies," *Journal of International Money and Finance* 10 (4) (December 1989): 512–526, Table 2. Data pertain to 1987. The original data pertain only to trade undertaken by the six largest industrialized countries plus OPEC, and to their six currencies.

trade or finance in private markets. The ECU is having more success as a product of European integration. Aside from the fact that European governments use the ECU to settle transactions among themselves, a substantial number of bond issues are now denominated in ECUs, as can be seen in Table 21.1. If the European countries achieve total monetary integration, as they are attempting, the ECU could replace the individual national currencies in the twenty-first century.

Is Most Foreign Exchange Trading "Speculation"?

The dollar's status as a vehicle currency explains why dollar foreign exchange trading is such a high proportion of the total. However, it does not explain why total foreign exchange trading among banks is so large, relative to the foreign exchange sales and purchases required by customers for exports, imports, borrowing, and lending.[13]

A major economic activity for banks is trading with other banks. Many banks and other financial institutions report profits from their foreign exchange business each year. This trading is extremely short-term: Most traders are under instructions to close out their open positions, that is, to unwind any sales or purchases of foreign currency, by the end of the day.[14] Longer-term positions are apparently considered too risky by banks.

It is clear that most purchases and sales of foreign exchange by spot traders (those trades not accounted for by the needs of customers) are made as a gamble that the exchange rate will change in the trader's favor by the end of the day. Thus, these transactions meet the definition of "short-term speculation." (Chapter 24 and 25 will analyze speculation—the holding of assets in expectation of increases in their value.) What is not clear is whether the spot traders in the banks are able to outguess the general public, as many of them claim they can, so that their total profits exceed the transaction costs they charge their customers. The alternative possibility is that, while on any given transaction somebody must gain and somebody lose, the aggregate profits banks report from foreign exchange trading are nothing more than the normal payment they earn in return for providing foreign exchange services for customers.[15]

The remainder of this chapter discusses the successive waves of liberalization and innovation that over the last twenty years have increasingly broken down the barriers between the various financial markets around the world—not only the markets for money, but also the markets for stocks, bonds, and loans.

21.3 LIBERALIZATION

After the system of fixed exchange rates was abandoned in March 1973, the United States and several other major countries no longer needed the capital controls that had been put in place in the 1960s and the early 1970s and so reduced or removed them.

Liberalization by Countries Controlling Inflows

In Germany and some of its neighbors, such as the Netherlands, the controls in place in the early 1970s were primarily designed to discourage the acquisition of assets in these countries by foreign residents, to discourage the inflow of capital rather than

[13] The special role of the dollar could at most explain why trade or capital flows between non-dollar countries result in foreign exchange transactions of twice the magnitude. When a Frenchman buys something from a Spaniard, for example, double the transactions are incurred: First francs have to be exchanged for dollars, and then dollars for pesetas.

[14] A decline since the 1970s in the size of open positions that risk-averse banks are willing to carry overnight is reported by Patricia Revey, "Evolution and Growth of the United States Foreign Exchange Market," *Federal Reserve Bank of New York Quarterly Review* , 6 (Autumm 1981): 32–44.

[15] The view among banks that their spot trading operations make profits *above and beyond* the bid-ask spread is reported by Charles Goodhart, "The Foreign Exchange Market: A Random Walk with a Dragging Anchor," *Economica* 55 (November 1988): 437–460.

the outflow. The German government essentially prohibited the payment of interest to nonresidents on large bank deposits, taxed any new credits by nonresidents to German banks, and prohibited nonresidents from buying German bonds. A primary motive behind such controls was to limit the flow of capital from the United States to Germany, which was putting unwanted upward pressure on the mark at the same time as it put downward pressure on the dollar. Another, related, motive behind the barriers to capital inflow was concern over possible loss of control over the money supply: If a large volume of reserves flowed in through the balance of payments, the countries' central banks might not be able to sterilize the effects on the money supply, and inflation might result. Both motives were more or less eliminated after March 1973, insofar as countries were no longer supposed to be concerned about preventing their exchange rates from fluctuating. Most of these controls were removed in 1974.

One way to determine the extent to which a country's capital controls are effective is to look at the differential between the domestic interest rate and interest rates outside the country. If a higher rate of return is being paid on assets inside the country than outside, this is a good indication that controls are preventing foreign residents from bringing in their capital; otherwise it would be difficult to explain why foreign residents would settle for a lower rate of return in their own countries.[16] On the other hand, if the domestic rate of return always moves closely with foreign rates of return, this indicates that financial markets are open and that arbitrage is keeping the rates in line with each other—by means of borrowing where interest rates are low and lending where they are high.

For such a test, it is important that the two interest rates be expressed in terms of the same currency. The dollar interest rate in the United States is not directly comparable with the mark interest rate in Germany, for example. A differential that appeared in such interest rates would not truly be a difference in expected returns if it simply compensated investors for the likelihood that the dollar will depreciate against the mark during the period in question. Fortunately, the Euromarket allows observations of interest rates on currencies (like the mark) outside the home country.

Dooley and Isard report that during the period 1970–1974 the mark interest rate in Frankfurt exceeded the Euromark interest rate. In early 1973 the interest differential was as high as 10 percent per annum.[17] We can view this differential as a measure of the magnitude of the barrier discouraging capital from flowing into Germany. The differential fell sharply thereafter, tangible evidence of the government liberalization.

One country that maintained stringent controls on capital inflows in the period 1975–1979 is Japan. Foreign residents were prohibited from holding assets in Japan. The motive, again, was concern over monetary independence. Japan, like Germany and Switzerland, had a reputation for maintaining a strong currency, and potential demand for yen assets by international investors was growing. Sudden large capital inflows would give the Bank of Japan an unpleasant choice. It could respond by allowing the yen to appreciate, or it could buy up the surplus dollars—in which case

[16] An exception to this rule of thumb, particularly relevant for long-term interest rates, arises if the country has a history of political instability, large budget and international deficits, or defaults on debt. In such cases, a higher rate of return on domestic assets than on foreign assets is probably a premium to compensate investors for risk.

[17] Michael Dooley and Peter Isard, "Capital Controls, Political Risk and Deviations from Interest-Rate Parity," *Journal of Political Economy*, 88 (2) (April 1980): 370–384.

the increase in its reserve holdings would, it was feared, have inflationary implications for the money supply. During this period, the Japanese were particularly worried that either a nominal appreciation of the yen or an increase in prices would erode their competitive price position on international export markets.

In 1979, the yen reversed its long-term trend and began a period of depreciation against the dollar, a movement magnified in the early 1980s by shifts in U.S. macroeconomic policy, as will be shown later. By this time, the Japanese were more confident of their exporters' ability to compete on world markets, and the government did not consider a sharp depreciation of the yen desirable. There was also political pressure from foreigners seeking to buy Japanese assets. For such reasons, the Ministry of Finance in 1979 removed the prohibition against foreign investment.

The effect of the liberalization is visible in the differential between yen interest rates in Tokyo and overseas, shown in Figure 21.1. From January 1975 to April 1979, the differential between the three-month interest rate in Tokyo (a freely determined rate called *Gensaki*) and the Euroyen interest rate in London averaged 1.8 percent, showing the efficacy of the controls on capital inflow. During the period May 1979 to November 1983, the differential fell sharply, to negative 0.3 percent. The fact that the differential was actually negative during this period is evidence that the controls that remained were working to discourage outflow rather than inflow. This suggests that the U.S. plan of November 1983 for Japan to remove its remaining controls should have been expected to accelerate the capital outflow and yen depreciation. This, in fact, turned out to be the result of the May 1984 "Yen/Dollar Agreement" between the U.S. Treasury and the Japanese Ministry of Finance. Since then the differential has been essentially zero, showing evidence of continued liberalization.[18]

Liberalization by Countries Controlling Outflows

More countries use capital controls to discourage outflows than to discourage inflows. These are usually countries that are concerned about a balance of payments deficit or a depreciating currency.

The United Kingdom maintained controls on capital outflows until 1979. Even though the largest Euromarket was physically located in London (in the old financial district known as "the City"), effective legal restrictions required that British banks keep their "offshore" accounts separate from their domestic accounts. Again, the effectiveness of these restrictions is shown by the interest differential. In 1978, the three-month Europound interest rate averaged 1.4 percent per annum higher than the U.K. interbank interest rate. The controls were preventing British residents from getting at the higher-paying assets that were so close at hand. However, as is illustrated in Figure 21.2, the differential fell to 0.3 percent per annum in 1979, and to zero soon thereafter.[19]

[18] Jeffrey Frankel, *The Yen/Dollar Agreement: Liberalizing Japanese Capital Markets* (Washington: Institute for International Economics, 1984).

[19] That a U.S.-U.K. interest differential remained in the 1970s can be seen in some papers by Jacob Frenkel and Richard Levich: "Transaction Costs and Interest Arbitrage: Tranquil versus Turbulent Periods," *Journal of Political Economy*, 85 (6) (1977): 1209–1226; and "Covered Interest Arbitrage in the 1970s" *Economic Letters*, 8 (3) (1981): 267–274. That the differential dropped sharply in 1979 can be seen in Michael Artis and Mark Taylor, "Abolishing Exchange Control: The UK Experience," in A. Courakis and M. Taylor, eds., *Policy Issues for Interdependent Economies*, (London: Macmillan Press, 1990).

FIGURE 21.1   Financial Liberalization in Japan

In the 1970s, capital controls prevented foreign residents from acquiring assets in Japan, which paid a higher return than equivalent yen assets offshore. In 1979, these controls were removed, and arbitrage caused the interest differential to fall.

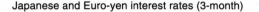

Japanese and Euro-yen interest rates (3-month)

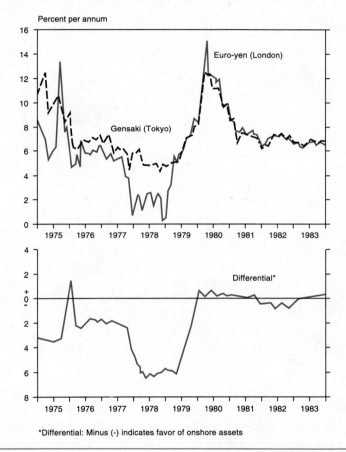

*Differential: Minus (-) indicates favor of onshore assets

J. Frankel, *The Yen/Dollar Agreement* (Washington: Institute for International Economics, December 1984).

Thus, by the end of the 1980s, the list of countries with essentially open capital markets included, in addition to the United States, a majority of the Group of Ten largest industrialized countries (G-10): Canada, Germany, Switzerland, the Netherlands, the United Kingdom, and Japan. The magnitudes of the interest differentials for these six countries vis-a-vis the Euromarket have averaged 0.2 percent since 1982. The list also includes two NICs: Hong Kong and Singapore. The magnitudes of their interest differentials vis-à-vis the Euromarket have also averaged 0.2 percent in recent years.[20]

[20] The statistics refer to covered interest differentials, described in Section 21.4.

FIGURE 21.2   Financial Liberalization in the United Kingdom

In the 1970s, capital controls prevented British residents from acquiring assets offshore, which paid a higher return than equivalent assets in London. In 1979, these controls were removed, and arbitrage caused the interest differential to fall.

U.K. and Euro-dollar interest rates (3-month)

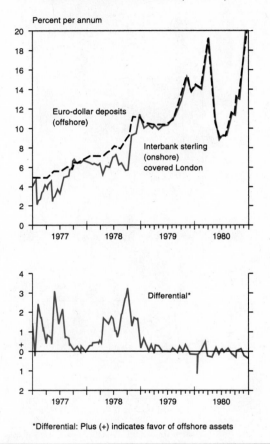

*Differential: Plus (+) indicates favor of offshore assets

The two largest countries maintaining effective capital controls into the 1980s were France and Italy. Among the G-10 countries, Belgium also maintained controls, though they were of a different sort—separate exchange rates for trade and financial transactions. Both France and Italy are members of the European Monetary System (EMS) and were periodically threatened with capital outflows. Consequently, they had difficulty keeping their commitments to maintain their exchange rates within the bands of plus or minus 2.25 percent (6 percent in the case of Italy until 1990) against stronger member currencies such as the German mark. At such times, France and Italy had the option of raising domestic interest rates to keep capital inside the country. However, they too wanted to maintain some measure of independence in their monetary policies, which would not be possible if their interest rates were completely tied to foreign interest rates. This was their motive for maintaining controls on capital outflow. Indeed, France had to tighten its controls when the Socialist François Mitterrand was elected president in 1981 and many residents rushed to get their money out of the country.

The differential between the three-month Eurofranc interest rate in London and the most comparable domestic interest rate in Paris was larger and more variable in the 1980s than that for the other major industrialized countries discussed. Most of the time it was only 1 to 2 percent per annum. Evidently, all along there were outflows in moderate quantity. (For example, there is the technique applicable in many countries with capital controls, of *leads and lags* in trade credit. Exporters request early payment from their foreign customers in foreign exchange, and importers try to delay payment of foreign exchange to their foreign suppliers. If an importer or exporter succeeds in shifting the timing of the payment from what it would normally be by, for example, six months, this is equivalent to a six-month capital outflow.)

At times, however, the interest differential on Eurofrancs would shoot up sharply. These episodes occurred when investors suspected that the franc was about to be devalued within the EMS. If the capital markets had been free, then franc interest rates would have risen in Paris and London equally, to compensate holders of franc assets for the anticipated loss in value. Instead, a shortage of investors willing to hold Eurofrancs caused the interest rate to be bid up offshore, while most Frenchmen—because they could not get their money out of the country fast enough—were stuck with the lower domestic rate. These episodes ended as soon as the question of devaluation was resolved, usually when the suspected EMS realignment actually took place and investors decided it was safe to hold French assets again for another year. This same pattern was evident in Italy.[21]

Liberalization became quite a popular trend in the 1980s. After 1986, France and Italy dismantled their capital controls to meet a 1990 deadline for liberalization set by the EC Twelve. Of the four EC countries that required a later deadline, Spain and Portugal began liberalizing in the late 1980s, but Greece and Ireland lagged behind. Sweden and Austria appear to have open financial markets. Elsewhere in the world, Australia began the process of financial liberalization in the early 1980s[22] and New Zealand followed suit. In 1987, Taiwan removed some controls on capital outflows that had become unnecessary.

Most other countries still retain serious barriers to international capital movements. Several South American countries, such as Chile, attempted international capital market liberalization in the 1970s. The experiments were largely unsuccessful, because of a wave of borrowing from abroad that turned out to be excessive.[23] Most of the

[21] Francesco Giavazzi and Marco Pagano, "Capital Controls and the European Monetary System," *Capital Controls and Foreign Exchange Legislation*, Occasional Paper, Milano: Euromobiliare, 1985; and Charles Wyplosz, "Capital Flows Liberalization and the EMS: A French Perspective," *European Economy*, European Economic Community (June 1988).

[22] Victor Argy, "International Financial Liberalisation—The Australian and Japanese Experiences Compared," *Bank of Japan Monetary and Economic Studies* 5 (1987): 105–168.

[23] Carlos Diaz-Alejandro, "Goodbye Financial Repression; Hello Financial Crash," *Journal of Development Economics*, 19 (September/October 1985).

various plans for economic reform in the former Soviet Union and Eastern Europe in the 1990s postpone to last the complete removal of restrictions on international capital flows. Nevertheless, financial liberalization around the world does seem to be the continuing trend.

Changes in Tax Laws

Tax reform can have important effects on international capital flows. Countries' income tax rates may have less of an effect on international investors' decisions concerning where to put their money than one would think, however. The mere fact that the citizens of one country are taxed at a higher rate than those of another does not necessarily create an incentive for capital flows, assuming that either group of citizens is taxed at the same rate on its foreign interest earnings as on its domestic earnings. However, high corporate taxes, as opposed to personal income taxes, will reduce the return to corporate equity for any investor. As part of a tax reform, the government of Japan decided to reduce its corporate income tax in 1989 and 1990 so that large differences vis-à-vis the United States and other countries would not encourage Japanese companies to shift operations offshore. Furthermore, investors sometimes evade taxes by keeping their money in tax havens, in the Caribbean or elsewhere. Thus, the existence of taxes does give rise to substantial capital flows.

The United States has become something of a haven for investors seeking to avoid taxation or the possibility of future controls or even confiscation in their own countries, especially in Latin America. Comparisons in the 1980s of the current account deficits of countries such as Argentina, Mexico, and Venezuela with the debt incurred by those countries to foreign banks suggested that there had been a large increase in unrecorded overseas claims by citizens of those countries, the well-known problem of *capital flight*. Many Latin Americans with wealth seek to hide it in Miami real estate.

Until recently, the major industrialized countries sought to ensure that all interest income they generated was taxed somewhere. Investors receiving interest payments could pay the taxes to their own government, provided that government has a bilateral tax treaty with the government of the country where the interest was paid; otherwise the taxes would be withheld directly by the latter country. This withholding tax was abolished by the United States in July 1984. France and Germany soon reduced or eliminated their own withholding taxes in order to "remain competitive" in the eyes of international investors.

The abandonment by the U.S. and other governments of the attempt to ensure that all interest income is taxed could be positively or negatively viewed. On the one hand, some distortions have been eliminated. For example, the abolishment of the withholding tax means that U.S. corporations have stopped setting up dummy subsidiaries in the Netherlands Antilles to do their international borrowing for them at untaxed rates. On the other hand, this trend has facilitated tax evasion around the world. The trend is not just toward reducing distortions between countries; it actually creates incentives for residents of each country to hold assets in another country, incentives that would not exist in a no-tax world.

Turnover taxes are an altogether different tax, one that affects the amount and location of trading in financial assets rather than the international flow of capital.[24] Stock market participants in Germany, Switzerland, and Japan have to pay a tax on every transaction. Authorities in these countries are under some pressure to remove these turnover taxes, so that Frankfurt, Zurich, and Tokyo do not lose business to other financial centers.[25]

In any case, with respect to taxes, the apparent trend is toward increased international capital mobility.

Liberalization of Domestic Financial Markets

When governments consider liberalizing controls on international capital movements, they often simultaneously consider other types of economic liberalization: that related to domestic capital markets and, perhaps, that related to distortions affecting trade in goods and services.

Domestic financial market liberalization involves the removal of ceilings on interest rates. Regulation Q in the United States, for example, has been phased out. The Japanese have also been phasing out their interest rate ceilings: Until recently the interest rates paid to small savers in Japan—through the enormous Postal Savings System, for example—were artificially kept quite low.

Domestic financial liberalization also involves the removal of other restrictions on the permissible activities of banks. Examples of restrictions in the United States are the prohibition against interstate banking and the Glass-Steagall Act, which since the 1930s has prohibited commercial banks from dealing in securities as do investment banks. Unlike in the United States, separation of banks by region and by function is minimal in Canada, Switzerland, and Germany, and will henceforth be absent throughout the EC under the 1992 process of integration.

Such differences in banking regulation in different countries raise interesting questions regarding the desirable goal in international trade negotiations: "national treatment," meaning that the other country's regulators treat your banks the same way they treat their own, or "reciprocity," meaning that the other country's regulators treat your banks the same way you treat theirs. U.S. banks benefited more from the national-treatment provision in the 1988 U.S.-Canada Free Trade Agreement, for example, than they would have from reciprocity. Under reciprocity, the United States would have had to allow Canadian banks to practice throughout the fifty states and to deal in securities, as banks are allowed to do in Canada. Under national treatment,

---

[24] Some observers are skeptical of the benefits of "perfect" international financial markets, and have proposed reducing the volume of speculative trading by taxing foreign exchange transactions, with the aim of dampening volatility in the market. James Tobin, "A Proposal for International Monetary Reform," *Eastern Economic Journal*, 4 (3–4)(1978): 153–159; and Rudiger Dornbusch, "Flexible Exchange Rates and Excess Capital Mobility," *Brookings Papers on Economic Activity*, 1 (1986), 209–226. A majority of economists believe that speculation is stabilizing, so that the proposal would result in more volatility rather than less.

[25] A majority of trading in Germany government bonds takes place in London and Luxemburg in order to avoid the turnover tax in Frankfurt. With the abolition of fixed commissions for brokers in the "Big Bang" of 1986, London became the most efficient financial center in Europe in which to trade securities. But one reason why the United Kingdom feels compelled to participate in European financial integration is that London may otherwise lose business to Frankfurt, Paris, or Milan.

Canadian banks operating in the United States are subject to the prohibition against interstate banking and to the Glass-Steagall Act as long as U.S. banks are.

In the United States, some political support for phasing out the Glass-Steagall Act stems from U.S. banks' sudden drop from the international "league tables" of the largest ten banks in the 1980s. However, Japan, the home of most of the banks that pushed the U.S. banks out of the Top Ten, also has rules separating their banks by the functions they perform, one of a number of ways in which the Japanese economic system set up after World War II emulated the American system. The current size of Japanese banks has more to do with the enormous pool of savings available in Japan (and perhaps the lack of alternative investment outlets available to Japanese citizens) and the strength of the yen in recent years than with differences in regulation.

In countries at an earlier stage of financial development, there may be little resembling a private banking system to deregulate. The government may have to begin by selling off banks that it had previously owned (this process is known as privatization) and by abolishing existing prohibitions on private banking. One school of thought states that "repression" of the financial sector in many LDCs retards economic development by keeping the real rate of return low, thus discouraging people from saving, and by interfering with the efficient allocation of whatever saving is available among possible uses.[26]

Liberalization of Trade in Goods and Services and Direct Investment

Trade liberalization is the removal of tariffs, subsidies, quotas, and other barriers to trade in goods. Its theoretical motivation stems from the argument in the first half of the text (particularly Chapters 2 and 11), regarding the welfare gains from free trade. Firms' losses due to competition with imports are generally outweighed by the gains on the part of consumers, firms that export, and firms that use imported inputs. For the liberalization arguments to succeed politically usually requires the promise of reciprocal reductions in import barriers by trading partners, as in successive rounds of GATT negotiations.

The United States formally proposed that trade in services be included in trade liberalization, along with trade in goods, in 1986 (at the meetings held in Uruguay, setting off the latest seven-year round of GATT negotiations). The United States is primarily concerned with insurance, banking, and other financial and information services (which it would export—not construction, household work, or other labor services, which it would import!). It had already sought, through bilateral pressure, to induce countries as diverse as Brazil, Japan, and Korea to allow U.S. banks, securities houses, and other financial institutions to operate in their domestic markets. Japan has recently given U.S. securities firms seats on the Tokyo Stock Exchange. Japan and other major countries have begun to allow securities companies of other nationalities to "lead-manage" international bond issues denominated in their own currency. In the 1988 U.S.-Canada Free Trade Agreement, both sides agreed that, as they proceed to liberalize their own financial markets, they will extend any resulting

---

[26] Ronald McKinnon, *Money and Capital in Economic Development*, Washington: The Brookings Institution, 1973; Edward S. Shaw, *Financial Deepening in Economic Development* (New York: Oxford University Press, 1973).

benefits to the financial institutions of the other country under the national treatment principle. If, like the liberalization of capital controls, this trend becomes more widespread, it will probably further facilitate borrowing and lending between countries.

The issue of direct investment in plant and equipment is related to the issue of trade in goods and services in several ways.[27] A government's decision to allow a multinational corporation to put a factory in its country can lead to imports of machinery and other intermediate products in the short run and to exports or import-competing production in the long run. Japanese auto companies establish plants in the United States to avoid U.S. import quotas and in Europe to avoid European quotes. Many countries place performance requirements on any foreign direct investment, such as "domestic-content" legislation that prohibits such plants from importing a high proportion of the final product's value added—for example, in the form of auto parts that are only assembled in the host country. A Canadian law in the 1970s required that each foreign direct investment project be individually approved.[28] Such issues are also important in ongoing steps of integration in the EC. In addition, these issues are becoming increasingly important in the United States, as Americans begin to show the political sensitivity to inward foreign direct investment that has in the past been more common in other countries. A provision in the 1988 Omnibus Trade Bill empowers the president to investigate and block foreign direct investment for reasons of national security.[29] In truth, direct investment (1) is a smaller component of the capital inflow into the United States than is portfolio investment, and (2) is less likely to be destabilizing for the American economy than is portfolio investment, which can be cut off at any time.

The Optimal Order of Liberalization

An important practical question that arises for policy-makers undertaking a program of liberalization along multiple fronts is the optimal order of liberalization. Should international capital liberalization proceed more rapidly or more slowly than domestic capital liberalization? Than trade liberalization? In theory, the optimum (first best) is to remove all distortions immediately, but this strategy is seldom practical. The wrong order of liberalization can misallocate resources and give an unsatisfactory "third-best" outcome. What order is "second best"?

These questions were considered in the late 1970s when several countries in the Southern Cone of Latin America—Chile, Argentina, and Uruguay—embarked on general liberalization plans. More recently, the optimal order of liberalization has again become an urgent question in the context of plans for economic reform in Eastern Europe.[30] The consensus seems to be that international capital liberalization

[27] Refer back to Chapter 10 for a more complete discussion of foreign direct investment.

[28] Under the 1988 agreement with the United States, Canada now screens only the largest investments, and performance requirements are precluded. (Jeffrey Schott and Murray Smith, *The Canada-U.S. Free Trade Agreement: The Global Impact*, Institute for International Economics, 1988. Canadian book publishing and film distribution are still specially protected; Canadians live in fear of being swamped by American popular culture.)

[29] All these restrictions are examples of so-called TRIMs (trade-related investment measures). The Uruguay Round included efforts to reduce TRIMs, for the first time in GATT negotiations.

[30] Ronald McKinnon *The Order of Economic Liberalization: Financial Control in the Transition to a Market Economy* (Baltimore: Johns Hopkins University Press, 1991).

should come last. The argument is that if international controls are removed prematurely, massive capital flows might occur in response to distorted incentives. For example, trade liberalization in Chile resulted in a large trade deficit financed by a large increase in borrowing, leaving the country with a clearly excessive debt in the 1980s.[31] There is also an argument that the removal of capital controls should be postponed until after the reduction of a large existing government budget deficit, to prevent overborrowing while the government deficit is still stimulating demand, and until after the completion of any planned monetary stabilization program, again to prevent foreigners from rushing to buy domestic assets.

To take another type of example, Japan in the 1980s pursued international financial liberalization more rapidly than domestic financial liberalization: It removed its controls on international capital flows before it allowed interest rates paid to Japanese investors to rise. This may have accelerated the outflow of capital in search of the higher interest rates available in the United States, thereby increasing the Japanese current account surplus and exacerbating trade friction with trading partners. However, there was a reason why the Japanese Ministry of Finance chose to pursue international liberalization in advance of domestic liberalization. In an environment where banks, brokers, and the rest of the financial sector have grown highly protected, regulated, and dependent on longstanding customer relationships, they may lack experience at competing in terms of the fees they charge for their services or at adapting to new ways of doing business. Like any vested interest group, they may be able to oppose liberalization politically. In such an environment, if international liberalization comes first, the" demonstration effect" of seeing foreign financial companies operating in their markets may teach them new ways of doing business. In any case, the political opposition will soon become irrelevant, as banks are forced to offer competitively high interest rates to their depositors and brokers are forced to charge competitively low fees to their clients to avoid losing business to the foreign newcomers.

The subject of increasingly competitive financial services markets leads to the next topic: innovation by the private financial sector.

21.4 INNOVATION

Innovation in domestic financial markets reduces the cost differential between the rate of return paid to the investor and the cost of capital paid by the ultimate borrower. Innovation in international financial markets works similarly and therefore, like liberalization, increases the degree of capital mobility across national borders. The original key innovation was the development of the Euromarkets, out of reach of regulation by national authorities. However, the innovation process continued after 1973, and indeed accelerated in the 1980s. Financial centers in London, New York, Chicago, Tokyo, Singapore, and elsewhere are awhirl with new ''products'' and new ways of buying and selling them.

---

[31] To be fair, the Chileans did in fact seek to keep liberalization of the international capital barriers for last. Other factors, such as the plummeting of the world price of a key export, copper, and the increase in world interest rates, were the proximate causes in the 1980s of the debt crises in Chile, as in other countries that had borrowed too heavily in the 1970s. See Sebastian Edwards (1984), "Stabilization with Liberalization: An Evaluation of Ten Years of Chile's Experience with Free-Market Policies, 1973–1983," *Economic Development and Cultural Change* (December 1985): 223–254.

Innovation can be driven by exogenous technological developments, such as those in telecommunications and computers already mentioned. Often, however, innovation is an endogenous response to some new problem in the financial environment, such as uncertainty. After exchange rates began to float in 1973, exchange rate uncertainty increased. Interest rate uncertainty also increased, at first due to the higher and more variable inflation rates of the 1970s, and thereafter due to other shifts in macroeconomic policies. Another result of macroeconomic shifts in the 1980s was heightened exchange rate variability. Variable exchange rates and interest rates create risk for international investors. In response, a variety of new ways to protect against risk in exchange rates and interest rates were developed.

The Forward Exchange Market

The most standard technique for dealing with exchange rate risk is by means of the *forward exchange market*. This market rate enables transactors, after they commit themselves to a transaction but before they get paid, to protect themselves against a change in the exchange rate. Japanese exporters invoicing exports to the United States in dollars run the risk that the value of the dollar in terms of the yen will fall before the date comes when they are paid and can convert the dollars into their own currency (which may be three months later). The Swedish portfolio manager who acquires a sterling treasury bill in the United Kingdom runs the risk that the value of the pound in terms of the Swedish krona will fall by the time the treasury bill matures in three months. In each case, if the prospective recipients (Japanese and Swedish) of the foreign currency do not wish to bear this risk, they can protect themselves against it by *hedging*, or "selling the currency forward." This involves entering into a contract with a bank, under which they agree to sell the foreign currency for their own currency, with the exchange to take place in 90 days but with the price set at the time the contract is agreed upon. The price received is the current going forward exchange rate, as opposed to the uncertain spot exchange rate that will prevail in 90 days.

There are other market participants besides exporters and investors for whom hedging on the forward exchange market is often beneficial. The Italian importing a German product invoiced in marks runs the risk that the lira price of the mark will go up by the time payment is required. Similarly, the Australian borrowing in U.S. dollars runs the risk that by the time the debt needs to be repaid, the cost of doing so in Australian currency will have gone up. In each case, the party obliged to pay foreign currency in the future (the Italian or Australian) can avoid the risk of changes in the exchange rate by hedging, which in this case means *buying* the currency forward. Thus, the future cost of the obligations in terms of domestic currency is locked in today. The ability to hedge risk on the forward exchange market has meant that the high degree of volatility exhibited by exchange rates since 1973 has not been as costly as it otherwise would have been to firms engaged in international business.

The forward exchange market has developed since the advent of floating exchange rates, as Milton Friedman predicted it would,[32] in that more currencies are traded more widely around the world. New York banks report that as of 1989, about 33

---

[32] Milton Friedman, "The Case for Flexible Exchange Rates," in *Essays in Positive Economics* (Chicago: University of Chicago Press, 1953).

percent of their foreign exchange business consists of forward transactions.[33] While most trading is in the pound, mark, yen, and Swiss franc (all against the dollar), many other currencies are traded as well. In addition to the popular 90-day maturity, contracts are also traded at 30 days, 60 days, and one year.

There are other participants in the forward exchange market besides those importers, exporters, investors, and borrowers seeking to hedge against currency risk. A second group is made up of "speculators," that is, anyone who takes an "exposed" (open or risky) position in the foreign exchange market in expectation of gains when the exchange rate changes. Speculators expecting the currency in question to appreciate to a value higher than the going forward rate will buy a forward contract in that currency. A profit will result if the currency does appreciate as expected, but a loss will result if it does not. If the speculator expects the currency to depreciate to a value lower than the going forward rate, then she can sell a forward contract in that currency. Now profits result only if the currency depreciates in the expected way. Speculators are thus the ones who accept the risk that the hedgers shun.[34]

Covered Interest Arbitrage

The third set of participants in the forward exchange market are called *covered interest arbitragers*. Covered interest arbitrage is a powerful force in forward exchange market equilibrium under modern conditions, that is, in well-developed financial markets without barriers to international transactions. Indeed, covered interest arbitrage is sufficiently powerful that it can be considered the sole determinant of the forward exchange rate, provided the spot rate and the interest rate are taken as given.[35] We will now see how it works.

Consider an asset-holder facing the choice between putting money into a one-year certificate of deposit (CD) denominated in dollars at a U.S. bank, or a one-year CD denominated in pounds at a U.K. bank. If there is a difference between the interest rates on the two assets of 1 percent per annum in favor of the U.K. asset, it might appear that the U.K. asset is the better investment. However, there is the risk that the pound/dollar exchange rate will change during the course of the year. To eliminate this risk, the investor must use the forward exchange market.

Assume that the investor has $1 million to invest. By putting it into the U.S. CD, at the end of the year the investor will get back $\$(1 + i_{US})$ million, where i_{US} is the U.S. interest rate. The alternative is:

1. to take the $1 million and buy pounds on the spot exchange market, getting $(1/S)$ million pounds, where S is the spot exchange rate in dollars per pound;[36]

---

[33] Counting not only forward transactions but also foreign exchange swap contracts, which constitute the simultaneous execution of a spot and forward transaction (in opposite directions).

[34] The minimum contracts in the forward market are too large for individuals. If you feel the urge to speculate, you should—after considering the large risks involved!—investigate the closely related futures market or the options market, both discussed later in this chapter.

[35] For a country that still has barriers to international capital movements, it takes all three groups—hedgers, speculators, and covered interest arbitragers—to determine together the equilibrium value for the forward exchange rate (again taking the spot rate and interest rates as given). This is the model of the forward exchange market originally developed by S. C. Tsiang, "The Theory of Forward Exchange and the Effects of Government Intervention in the Forward Market," *Staff Papers*, International Monetary Fund (April 1959).

[36] Previous chapters have designated the exchange rate as E, but now the spot exchange rate, S, must be distinguished from the forward exchange rate, F.

2. then to take the $(1/S)$ million pounds and put them into a British CD, which in one year's time will pay off $(1/S)(1 + i_{UK})$ million pounds, where i_{UK} is the U.K. interest rate; and finally

3. to sell the $(1/S)(1 + i_{UK})$ million pounds on the current forward exchange market, where it will fetch $F(1/S)(1 + i_{UK})$ million dollars, F being the current forward exchange rate in dollars per pound. Because the forward rate is known at the time the initial investment is made, the complete investment strategy is riskless in terms of dollars. The investor has "covered" the holdings of foreign securities, just as a homeowner is "covered" when buying fire insurance.

Which should the investor buy, the U.S. asset, or the U.K. asset covered (hedged) on the forward exchange market? In both cases, the investor would be putting $1 million in today, and getting back a certain amount of dollars in one year. Assuming that the two investments are the same with respect to taxes, risk of default, and so on, the investor should clearly buy whichever one pays the higher return. If $(1 + i_{US}) < (F/S)(1 + i_{UK})$, then the investor should buy the U.K. asset and cover it. When many investors do this, they will add to the supply of pounds on the forward market, thus driving down the forward price of pounds F and reducing the inequality. (If the investors also drive up the spot price of pounds S by their purchases of pounds in the spot market, or drive down the British interest rate, i_{UK}, by their purchases of pound CDs, this too will tend to reduce the inequality.) This is covered interest arbitrage at work.

To engage in covered interest arbitrage, it is not necessary to be a wealth-holder with a stock of dollars to allocate. If the U.K. interest rate exceeds the U.S. interest rate on a covered basis, as in the preceding inequality, it is possible to make a profit even without initial capital. Begin by borrowing the $1 million at the relatively low U.S. interest rate, i_{US}, and then proceed as before: Exchange the dollars for pounds on the spot market, invest the proceeds in a U.K. CD, and, finally, sell the pounds forward. The dollars received in one year as a result of the forward transaction will be enough to settle the dollar debt incurred at the beginning, with some left over as a profit; this is what the inequality tells us. Anyone engaging in this form of arbitrage will be adding downward pressure on the forward rate.[37]

If transaction costs are low, such arbitrage will continue until the inequality is eliminated. The result is a condition called *covered interest parity*.

$$(1 + i_{US}) = (F/S)(1 + i_{UK}) \tag{21.1}$$

If the inequality goes the opposite way, with the right-hand side of the expression being less than the left-hand side, then arbitrage will run in the opposite direction. Investors will convert pounds (which they may have borrowed at the relatively low interest rate i_{UK}) into dollars (at the relatively favorable spot exchange rate S), invest them in a U.S. CD (at the relatively high interest rate i_{US}), and sell the dollar proceeds

---

[37] Even though anyone could engage in this sort of arbitrage if the inequality held (i.e., it is not the sort of thing where "it takes money to make money"), one has to incur four transaction costs to do so: borrowing, spot, investing, and forward. In practice those who already have money and are investing it all the time anyway (or hedgers who are already engaging in forward transactions anyway) have an advantage in covered interest arbitrage because they have fewer additional transaction costs to incur. Alan Deardorff, "One-Way Arbitrage and Its Implications for the Foreign Exchange Market," *Journal of Political Economy* 87 (April 1979): 351–364.

forward for pounds (at the relatively favorable rate of $1/F$), thereby locking in a riskless profit. Such arbitrage, again, will tend to push the rates and prices back into line with Equation 21.1, putting upward pressure on E, until covered interest parity is restored.

Let us define the forward discount: $fd \equiv (F - S)/S$. If F is greater than S, the foreign currency is more expensive—or the domestic currency is less expensive—on the forward market than on the spot market. The forward discount on the domestic currency is the percentage rate at which "the forward market thinks the currency will depreciate." If the current spot rate is \$2 per pound, and the one-year forward rate is \$2.02 per pound, then the forward discount on the dollar is 1 percent.[38] Thus, in Equation 21.1, F/S can be thought of as "1 plus the forward discount."

$$(1 + i_{US}) = (1 + fd)(1 + i_{UK})$$

Multiplying out,

$$(1 + i_{US}) = (1 + fd + i_{UK} + fd\, i_{UK})$$

The forward discount and the interest rate are both normally fractions, relatively small number such as 0.04 and 0.08 (or even smaller numbers such as 0.01 and 0.02 if the calculations are done on a 90-day basis rather than per annum). Thus, the last term, the product of these two terms, is likely to be very small—for example, 0.0032 (or 0.0002 on a 90-day basis)—and can be omitted, with the approximation remaining accurate.[39] Canceling out the two "1s" that appear as well, the equation becomes an alternate statement of covered interest parity, which may be more intuitive than Equation 21.1.

$$i_{US} = fd + i_{UK} \tag{21.2}$$

This equation implies that when the U.S. interest rate is higher than the U.K. interest rate, U.S. assets are not necessarily a better investment. If there are no barriers to capital mobility, then the dollar will be selling at a discount in the forward exchange market, at a rate fd that precisely cancels out the interest differential.[40]

During the 1980s, for example, dollar interest rates were higher than mark, yen, and Swiss franc interest rates by three or four percentage points per annum. As a result, the dollar sold at a forward discount of the same magnitude. The dollar has often sold at a forward premium against the pound, French franc, and lira, reflecting British, French, and Italian interest rates that are higher than U.S. interest rates.

---

[38] If the forward rate F is less than the spot rate S, then there is a forward *premium* on the dollar. (Check that you understand the arithmetic of covered interest parity, including for the case where the maturity is for less than one year, by doing problem 3 at the end of the chapter.)

[39] The approximation is fairly safe when dealing with stable industrialized countries, where the inflation rates, interest rates, and forward discounts are usually in single digits. But when dealing with Latin American countries or others where these rates can go to 100 percent per annum or higher, one must be very careful how these rates are expressed; one cannot go back and forth instantly between equations like Equation 21.1 and Equation 21.2.

[40] There is another way of getting to the approximation of covered interest parity, Equation 21.2, if you know enough about logarithms to apply them to Equation 21.1

$$\log (1 + i_{US}) = \log F - \log S + \log (1 + i_{UK})$$

Since the log of $1 + i_{US}$ is approximately equal to i_{US}, and the same for i_{UK}, this equation is simply Equation 21.2 with the forward discount expressed in logarithmic terms.

The theory of covered interest parity is clear. Does it hold precisely in practice? This depends on where interest rates are observed. If the dollar interest rate, the mark interest rate, and the dollar-DM forward discount are all observed in the same location, such as the London Euromarket, then covered interest parity holds extremely well—to within the very small margins of interbank transaction costs. Indeed, banks in the Euromarket determine the forward rate they offer their customers by calculating it from the spot and Euromarket interest rates using the covered interest parity equation. It is more interesting, however, to see whether the condition holds across national boundaries—for example, with the dollar interest rate observed in New York and the mark interest rate observed in Frankfurt. Section 21.3 pointed out that, even for some of the G-7 industrialized countries, nonzero differentials in interest rates remained in the 1970s (the U.K. and Japan as recently as 1979, and France and Italy as recently as 1986), and they remain today for other countries, especially LDCs. The reason is capital controls, tax differences, and the other barriers to the movement of capital across national boundaries that have been discussed.

The covered interest differential, the deviation from Equation 21.1 (which Figure 21.2 illustrated for the case of the U.K. liberalization of 1979), is essentially the same as the Eurocurrency onshore interest differential (which Figure 21.1 illustrated for the case of the Japanese liberalization).[41] Statistics on covered interest differentials for the 1980s confirm that only eight industrialized countries (plus Hong Kong and Singapore) began the decade with relatively open financial markets, but ten more countries liberalized significantly during the 1980s. Those that made the most rapid progress were Portugal, Spain, France, New Zealand, Denmark, Australia, and Italy.[42]

The countries with covered interest differentials throughout this period that were not large or variable are the same as those found to have essentially open capital markets in Section 21.2.[43]

Other Ways of Managing Risk in Exchange Rates and Interest Rates

In addition to the market in forward exchange, there is also an active market in foreign exchange *futures*. Like a forward contract, a futures contract is a commitment to buy foreign exchange in the future. One difference is that a deposit must be put down to buy a futures contract. Then, each day, if the market rate moves the wrong way, the investor may receive a "margin call" requiring payment for any losses, whereas a forward contract does not have to be settled until maturity. Another difference is

---

[41] This is because covered interest parity holds so perfectly *within* the Euromarket. Consider the yen example illustrated in Figure 21.1. Within the Euromarket we have $i_E^¥ = i_E^\$ - fd$, where $i_E^¥$ is the Euroyen interest rate, $i_E^\$$ is the Eurodollar interest rate, and fd is the forward discount on the dollar (the rate at which "the forward market thinks" that the dollar will depreciate against the yen). The interesting question is whether there is a covered interest differential across national boundaries. The covered interest differential is $i_T^¥ - (i_E^\$ - fd)$, where $i_T^¥$ refers to the Tokyo rate. Given covered interest parity in the Euromarket this is the same differential as the one discussed earlier: $i_T^¥ - i_E^¥$.

[42] Jeffrey Frankel, "Measuring International Capital Mobility: A Review," *American Economic Review* 82 (2) (May 1992).

[43] Important references on covered interest parity include Robert Aliber, "The Interest Rate Parity Theorem: A Reinterpretation," *Journal of Political Economy* 81 (1973): 1451–1459; and those by Frenkel and Levich referenced in footnote 19.

that futures contracts mature on specific dates: the third Wednesday of **March, June, September, and December**. Forward contracts, by contrast, are tailored to the customer seeking foreign currency, for example, 90 days into the future, regardless of the current date. Another difference is that futures contracts are traded on centralized exchanges like the Chicago Mercantile Exchange, whereas forward contracts are arranged through the banking system. A large investor or importer that wants to lock in the rate on foreign currency needed in the future may be more likely to use the forward market. A small speculator buying or selling foreign exchange on a short-term basis in anticipation of exchange rate changes is more likely to use the futures market.[44]

Foreign currency and interest rate options were introduced in the United States in 1982, and grew rapidly in popularity. When buying an option on pound sterling, an investor acquires the right, but not the obligation, to buy pound sterling in the future at a price agreed upon at the time the option is purchased. The buyer has the right to buy the pounds at what is called the *strike price*; it will not be in the buyer's interest to exercise that right until such time as the market price of pounds rises above the strike price. The option gives the investor protection against possible future increases in the spot price of pounds (the exchange rate), protection that could be useful if the investor is planning on buying British goods or securities in the future and will need to pay in pounds. Alternatively, an individual may buy an option because of a desire to speculate in pounds, betting on an increase in the pound's value. Finally, an option is a way for a trader to take a position on the volatility of a currency. The higher the volatility of the currency is, the more valuable the option is, because the higher the probability is that the exchange rate will reach the strike price in the time allotted.[45]

Whether the motive for buying the option is hedging or speculation, a similar goal could be accomplished by buying pounds in the forward market. In a forward contract, however, the agent would be committed to complete the transaction whether the spot rate goes up or down. Of course, in buying the option the individual must give up some return for the advantage of not having to buy the pounds if the price goes down in the future.[46] Options are often used for speculation, and it is sometimes charged that they add to the volatility of the underlying spot price on the day that they mature. However, they are also an effective way for the individual international investor to manage risk arising from exchange rate or interest rate volatility.[47]

---

[44] For more on futures, see Norman Fieleke, "The Rise of the Foreign Currency Futures Markets," *New England Economic Review* (March/April 1985): 38–47. Reprinted in R. Baldwin and J. D. Richardson eds., *International Trade and Finance*, 3rd ed. (Boston: Little Brown, 1986).

[45] The famous Black-Scholes formula, relating the options price to volatility, was extended to foreign exchange by Marc Garman and Steven Kohlhagen, "Foreign Currency Option Values," *Journal of International Money and Finance* 2 (1983): 231–238.

[46] The right to *buy* pounds in the future is a "call" option. The other sort of option, the right to *sell* pounds, is a "put"; here the investor is speculating that the value of the pound might fall in the future.

[47] Two accessible references on options are Ian Giddy, "The Foreign Exchange Option as a Hedging Tool," in J. Stern and D. Chew, eds. *New Developments in International Finance* (Cambridge, MA: Basil Blackwell, 1988); and Brian Gendreau, "New Markets in Foreign Currency Options," *Business Review*, Federal Reserve Bank of Philadelphia, (July/August 1984): 3–12, reprinted in Robert Baldwin and J. David Richardson, eds., *International Trade and Finance* 3rd ed., (Boston: Little Brown, 1986).

Forward exchange contracts (along with futures and options) are widely available only for horizons up to one year at the longest. An investor considering the purchase of a long-term bond in a foreign currency, or a borrower considering issuing a long-term bond abroad in a foreign currency, will be exposed to exchange rate risk that cannot be readily hedged on the forward exchange market. An important innovation that began in the early 1980s is the *currency swap*. The technique has become extremely popular, though the transactions involved sound somewhat complicated.

To take an example, assume that the Coca-Cola Corporation is sufficiently well known in Switzerland that it can borrow at a slightly lower cost there than it can at home (where investors already have all the Coca-Cola bonds they want), provided the debt is denominated in Swiss francs, the currency Swiss investors prefer to hold. Coca-Cola, however, may wish to avoid the uncertainty of not knowing what the exchange rate will be in the future, and thus not knowing the cost of debt service in terms of dollars. At the same time, the Nestlé Corporation, a Swiss company, may wish to know its debt service ahead of time in terms of Swiss francs. Coca-Cola, or its bank, goes to Nestlé and proposes that each corporation issue bonds denominated in the other's currency and that they then swap the obligations to service each other's debt, Nestlé paying interest in Swiss francs to the investors who bought the Coca-Cola bond, and Coca-Cola paying interest in dollars to the investors who bought the Nestlé bond.[48] This technique has allowed hundreds of corporations to go beyond their own countries' capital markets and borrow internationally when it otherwise might not have been convenient for them to do so.

Even more popular than the currency swap is the interest rate swap, one of several techniques for managing risk associated with uncertain future interest rates. When interest rates first became more variable in the 1970s, investors became wary of holding longer-term bonds that paid fixed interest rates because the value of these bonds fell every time interest rates went up. In the 1980s, borrowers became more aware of interest rate risk, as decreases in nominal interest rates caused them to seek refinancing at lower rates. Thus, borrowers began to offer investors debt at floating interest rates: The interest rate would be tied to that on, for example, U.S. treasury bills. Borrowers also began offering shorter-term debt and rolling it over when it matured, which is equivalent to floating rate debt in terms of interest rate risk. Floating rate notes first became popular in the Euromarkets in 1983.

To understand how interest rate swaps work, consider this example. Assume that Coca-Cola is a sufficiently well-known borrower that it can borrow relatively cheaply at fixed interest rates, but that it does not wish to be exposed to the risk of future decreases in interest rates. In other words, if interest rates fall, it wants to be free to take advantage of the new lower cost of borrowing, rather than being committed to a fixed interest rate. If there is another corporation that does not mind the commitment of a fixed interest rate, Coca-Cola may issue a fixed-rate bond and the other corporation a floating-rate bond, with the two borrowers swapping interest obligations. Each borrower then has the interest rate risk situation that it desires.

---

[48] In practice, the corporations do not necessarily have to deal with each other directly. Rather, the bank may swap a dollar obligation for the corporation's foreign currency debt, and it is then up to the bank to match up with another corporate borrower (and to guarantee the other side of the transaction against default).

Securitization

In the 1960s and 1970s bankers led the assault on international financial barriers, particularly in the Euromarkets. In the 1980s, however, new waves of exotic financial weaponry succeeded the now-mundane bank loan.

International banking was dealt a major blow by the LDC debt crisis, which first surfaced in August 1982 when Mexico informed its creditor banks that it was unable to service its debts on the original schedule. The crisis rapidly spread to other debtor countries, and banks became much less willing to put new money into LDCs. Bank lending to developing countries fell from $51 billion in 1982 to $8 billion in 1985 and then turned negative. In the second half of the 1980s, repayment of previous loans exceeded new loans.

At the same time, public concerns regarding the stability of the banking system arose, fueled by reports of problems at financial institutions (though bad loans to the domestic farm, energy, and real estate sectors were in fact more a source of banks' difficulties than bad loans to other countries). The Federal Reserve and other regulatory agencies put pressure on banks to raise the ratio of their capital to their outstanding loans. One consequence of these developments was that banks sought to earn more of their fees through "off balance sheet" activities, like swaps, which do not involve recording a loan on their books.[49] Another consequence was that borrowers and lenders began to rely less on banks for intermediating between them, and more on the selling of bonds and other securities. In 1984, foreign purchases of U.S. securities surpassed bank liabilities as the largest component of capital flows to the United States (on either a gross or net basis), and the trend continued in subsequent years. This is the process of international disintermediation, or *securitization*.[50]

We have already covered a number of the innovations, such as swaps, that facilitate issuing international bonds. Another such innovation is the *note issuance facility*, in which a corporation arranges repeated offerings (over five to seven years) of short-term debt, underwritten by its banks, where previously it might have simply borrowed from the bank itself. "Underwritten" means that the bank is committed to buy any notes the borrower is unable to sell directly to outside investors. By 1986, however, note issuance facilities were overtaken by yet another innovation: *Eurocommercial paper*, which allows borrowers to dispense altogether with the underwriting service provided by the banks. Further innovation undoubtedly will follow.

The new methods of selling bonds have helped them to become increasingly important relative to bank loans.[51]

Total international bond issues (which include both bonds sold in the Euromarkets and other bonds sold abroad) grew exponentially in the mid-1980s. The capital account

---

[49] In the Basle Agreement of 1987, Central Banks of the Group of 10 set common "harmonized" rules (taking effect in 1993) for the minimal capital requirements that they impose on their countries' banks and also set some reserve requirements to cover off-balance-sheet items.

[50] Disintermediation describes the phenomenon of borrowers (e.g., firms) and lenders (e.g., individual investors) starting to do business directly, rather than via financial intermediaries (i.e., banks). This normally means the borrower selling securities (i.e, stocks and bonds) to the lender. (The term "securitization" is sometimes reserved for the transformation of a given bank loan into a security, e.g., debt-equity swaps. Here it used more broadly to denote any increased share of securities in international capital markets, at the expense of bank lending.)

[51] Ralph Bryant, *International Financial Intermediation* (Washington: Brookings Institution, 1987), p. 56.

of the U.S. balance of payments shows that sales of bonds to foreigners roughly doubled every two years in the first half of the 1980s. In 1985, foreigners bought $72 billion of U.S. securities, nine times the level of 1980. Japanese residents constituted a remarkable share of the foreign purchases of Treasury securities in 1985: 85 percent according to U.S. statistics.

The overwhelming majority of international bond issues are by industrialized countries. Nevertheless, in light of disenchantment with bank loans as a vehicle for LDC borrowing in the 1980s, there was a trend toward securitization in this area as well. Banks began to resell some of their LDC loans on a secondary market to reduce their exposure to problem countries. Once resold on a secondary market, a loan essentially becomes a security like a bond. The banks can only resell the loans at a discount, that is, at a price less than the full "face value" of the asset. Table 21.2 lists the discounts from the secondary market for fifteen of the most important problem debtors. These market prices fluctuate weekly with prospects for the country in question and for the debt problem as a whole.

Initially, only smaller banks, which may have hoped to eliminate altogether their lending to LDCs, participated; the larger banks were more concerned about jeopardizing the value of the rest of the large loans that they held. In recent years, however, the larger banks have participated more in the secondary market, as part of a general movement to acknowledge formally the reduced value of their loans to LDCs.

Some economists argue that the existence of the large *debt overhang* constitutes a disincentive to the debtor countries that discourages them from investing in projects that would generate earnings of foreign exchange, due to fears that the payoff would just go to the foreign creditors. They further argue that outright *forgiveness* or writing-down of the debt would encourage investment and growth, resulting in a larger economic "pie" for all parties to share. Paul Krugman has provided theoretical support for this argument by pointing out that, if the disincentive effect is sufficiently large, a reduction in the quantity of debt outstanding might increase the probability that

TABLE 21.2 Secondary Market Prices of Selected LDC Debt

Country	8/18/86	7/13/87	4/4/88	4/13/89	1/18/90	9/91	5/22/92
Argentina	66.5	47.0	28.0	16.8	12.6	79.2	48.8
Bolivia	6.0	10.0	11.0	11.5	11.5	NA	11.3
Brazil	74.0	57.0	49.5	37.5	27.9	54.2	39.5
Chile	66.0	68.0	58.0	58.9	64.7	88.7	89.8
Colombia	84.0	81.0	65.0	NA	60.2	78.0	78.0
Ecuador	65.0	45.0	31.5	NA	15.0	NA	27.3
Ivory Coast	75.0	60.0	30.0	NA	7.0	6.0	8.2
Mexico	57.0	54.0	51.0	42.9	38.4	59.5	64.6
Morocco	70.0	65.5	50.0	NA	38.0	52.8	47.6
Nigeria	50.0	28.0	28.5	20.5	30.0	41.7	40.5
Peru	20.0	11.0	6.0	3.5	6.0	14.5	16.1
Philippines	66.0	68.0	51.0	47.0	48.2	71.6	52.8
Uruguay	63.0	70.0	59.5	NA	50.7	NA	55.7
Venezuela	74.0	69.0	54.2	38.0	35.6	67.5	61.9
Yugoslavia	79.0	73.0	46.5	NA	54.5	33.5	NA

Note: Full face value (zero discount) would be 100.0.
Source: Salomon Brothers and J.P. Morgan.

the remaining debt would be repaid—and thus raise the market price—so much that the total value of the debt (price times quantity) to the banks might rise rather than fall.[52] Initially, the official U.S. government strategy for dealing with the international debt problem called for (in addition to policy adjustment by the debtor countries) increased lending, by both private banks and official creditors, to help the countries overcome what was supposed to be a temporary *liquidity problem*. The Brady Plan, put forth by the U.S. Treasury in 1989, constituted something of a reversal of this position, a step in the direction of debt reduction. There have even been proposals for a new agency to facilitate debt reduction.[53] Most of the banks remain unconvinced, however.

LDC bonds have been tried before as an alternative to bank loans for lending to LDCs. In the nineteenth century and in the period between the wars capital flowed from industrialized countries to colonies and developing countries via this route. Defaults occurred periodically, however, culminating in the widespread defaults of the 1930s.[54] Capital also reached the LDCs through foreign direct investment. However, when LDCs gained their political independence, most did not want foreigners owning controlling shares of their natural resources, land, or plant and equipment.[55] Even when an LDC government does proclaim its willingness to accept foreign direct investment, investors may be concerned that a future government will nationalize it. Thus, there is considerable interest in devising some new mode of capital flow to LDCs, other than bonds, direct investment, or bank lending.

The obvious candidate is equity investment. Unlike bonds or bank loans, the cost of such an obligation does not stay fixed in dollar terms when the ability of the country to earn export revenue falls because of a world recession or a collapse in commodity prices. (Another idea is the possibility of tying the repayment terms on bonds or loans to export prices or export revenues, which would make them more like equity: The cost of the obligation automatically falls when the ability to pay falls, thus reducing the risk to the borrower.) Unlike direct investment, the foreigner does not have a controlling interest in investment projects.

Most Third World countries do not have well-developed equity markets. Two new trends have developed, however. The first is *debt-equity swaps* (not to be confused, with any of the other swaps that have been discussed). These allow debt-troubled countries and their creditor banks to reduce the debt on the banks' books. It requires a third party eager to acquire a stake in an investment project in the LDC, provided there is a sufficient discount. The third party may be a resident of the country itself;

---

[52] Krugman, "Financing versus Forgiving a Debt Overhang: Some Analytical Notes," *Journal of Development Economics*, 1989. The author coins the phrase "Debt-Relief Laffer Curve" to describe the hump-shaped relationship between the quantity of debt and its total market value, but "Debt-Relief Krugman Curve" would be more appropriate.

[53] Peter Kenen, "Organizing Debt Relief: The Need for a New Institution." A contrary view is offered by Jeremy Bulow and Kenneth Rogoff, ''Cleaning Up Third World Debt Without Getting Taken to the Cleaners.'' They appear in *Journal of Economic Perspectives* 4 (Winter 1990): 7–18 and 31–42, with related papers.

[54] The parallels between the 1980s debt crisis and the experience of the 1930s are striking. Barry Eichengreen and Richard Portes, "Debt and Default in the 1930s: Causes and Consequences," *European Economic Review* 30, 599–640. Albert Fishlow, "Lessons from the Past: Capital Markets During the 19th Century and the Interwar Period,'' in Miles Kahler, ed., *The Politics of International Debt* (Ithaca, NY: Cornell University Press, 1986) pp. 37–94. See Section 10.4 for more on the history of LDC debt.

[55] Chapter 10 discussed such resistance to foreign direct investment.

in this case the goal is to reverse capital flight, the savings that local residents have sent out of the country to less risky havens abroad. In any case, the bank, if anxious enough to unload the debt, will be willing to do so at a discount. If the discount is large enough, the country will be willing to swap an equity claim in return for the cancellation of the bank debt. The technique has been successful (on a relatively small scale) in Chile and a few other countries.

Second, and more relevant for LDCs that do not already have severe debt problems (such as many of the rapidly growing East Asian countries), are *equity funds.* Foreign residents may think they do not have adequate information on specific companies in, for example, Korea to make individual selections. Korea, for its part, may only allow foreigners to participate in certain segments of the economy. So the Korean government arranges with foreign investors a mutual fund (the Korea Fund is one), in which they can invest on a portfolio basis. Although total equity investment in LDCs is still small, it may become important in the future if the host countries adopt policies to encourage it, or at least do not discourage it.[56]

Equity markets are, of course, far more developed in the United States and other industrialized countries. The United States and the United Kingdom have historically had the largest stock markets, but the Japanese market has grown rapidly in recent years, rivalling the U.S. market. *International* equity trading has been surprisingly low until recently. In 1986–1987, foreigners eagerly participated in a surging U.S. stock market. One reason for this trend (and for securitization in general) is that a large share of savings are now invested by managers of pension funds and mutual funds rather than by individuals. These managers are better able to acquire the information needed to invest in foreign securities than are most individual investors. While it will take time for investors everywhere to hold similar widely diversified portfolios, movement is clearly in that direction. The strengthening links among countries' stock markets are reflected in the increasing tendency for market indexes to rise or fall together. The stock market crash of October 1987, for example, was transmitted within hours from the United States to markets in Asia and Europe.

20.5 SUMMARY

This chapter showed how the rise of the Euromarkets, governments' removal of capital controls, the development of new financial instruments, and other forms of liberalization and innovation have all worked to reduce barriers to the international flow of capital. This increase in the degree of international capital mobility makes an enormous difference, not just for those who live in these markets, but for the entire macroeconomy as well, as the following chapters will show.

CHAPTER PROBLEMS

1. When Israel's annual inflation rate exceeded 100 percent in the early 1980s, Israelis took to quoting domestic transaction prices in U.S. dollars and converting them to Israeli currency at the exchange rate of the moment. Does this behavior illustrate the convenience of using

---

[56] Besides Korea, mutual funds have recently been floated on Wall Street for Taiwan, Thailand, and India, among others.

vehicle currencies, the undesirability of holding a fast-depreciating currency, or the transaction costs of adjusting price quotations for rapid inflation?

2. You have acquired an option to buy Swiss francs at a "strike price" of $.70 per Swiss franc. (At the time you bought the contract, the spot exchange rate was only $.50 per Swiss franc.) In each of the following three cases, answer whether you would choose to exercise the option: either "definitely yes," "definitely no," or "maybe yes, maybe no in order to wait to see if the spot exchange value of the Swiss franc goes higher."

   a. The current spot exchange rate is $.60 per Swiss franc.

   b. The current spot exchange rate is $.80 per Swiss franc, and the contract is about to expire.

   c. The current spot exchange rate is $.80 per Swiss franc, and the contract still has two months to run.

   d. Would the option be more or less valuable if the Swiss franc is thought to be highly volatile this year?

3. Suppose you are a U.S. exporter expecting to receive a payment of DM 100 in 12 months. The one-year interest rate on DM deposits is 5 percent per annum. The one-year interest rate on dollar deposits is 8 percent per annum. The present spot exchange rate is $.50 for DM.

   a. What is the one-year forward exchange rate?

   b. Assuming you ultimately need dollars, you have two ways to cover yourself from the exchange rate risk. Describe them and show their equivalence computationally.

   c. Now suppose your claim on DM 100 is due in six months. The interest rate on six-month DM deposits is 4 percent per annum. The interest rate on six-month dollar deposits is 8 percent per annum. What is the six-month forward exchange rate?

   d. What do a and c imply about "the market's expectations" regarding the future path of the exchange rate?

   e. The Swiss franc (SF) is worth 1 DM today and obeys the six-month and one-year relationships to the dollar given in a and c Suppose, however, that today investors know with certainty that in one year 1 SF = $.53 in the spot market. Suppose that the U.S. interest rate remains the same. (America is a big country.) What will investors do? What level will they drive the one-year forward exchange rate to? What will that imply for the interest rate on one-year deposits in SF?

4. Refer to Table 21.2, which gives secondary market prices for the debt of fifteen countries. What was the general trend in the value of these loans for most of these debtors in the 1980s? The early 1990s? Which three countries do bankers believe are most likely to default on their debts? Of these three, which one declared a partial suspension of debt-service payments in 1985–1987, and which one adopted a stabilization program that succeeded in restoring price stability over this same period?

SUGGESTIONS FOR FURTHER READING

Bank for International Settlements, *International Banking and Financial Market Developments*, Basel (May 1991). A detailed explanation of new financial instruments.

Chrystal, K. Alec. "A Guide to Foreign Exchange Markets," *Federal Reserve Bank of St. Louis Review* (March 1984): 5–18. Reprinted in James Wilcox, ed., *Current Readings on Money, Banking and Financial Markets*, (Boston: Little Brown, 1987). An introduction to how the markets work, including such concepts as foreign exchange options and covered interest arbitrage.

Dornbusch, Rudiger. "Our LDC Debts," in Martin Feldstein, ed., *The United States in the World Economy*. (Chicago: University of Chicago Press, 1987). A good introduction to the international debt crisis that erupted in 1982 and subsequently lingered longer than many had expected.

Edwards, Sebastian. "The Order of Liberalization of the External Sector in Developing Countries," *Essays in International Finance* No. 156 (Princeton: Princeton University Press, 1984). An analysis of whether international trade should be liberalized before or after capital markets, and related issues.

Frankel, Jeffrey. "Quantifying International Capital Mobility in the 1980s," in D. Berheim and J. Shoven, eds., *National Saving and Economic Performance* (Chicago: University of Chicago Press, 1991), pp. 227–260.

Goodfriend, Marvin. "Eurodollars," *Instruments of the Money Market*, Federal Reserve Bank of Richmond (1986): 53–64. Reprinted in James Wilcox, ed., *Current Readings on Money, Banking and Financial Markets* (Boston: Little Brown, 1987). Clear explanation of the Euromoney markets, and their relationship to the U.S. banking system.

Grilli, Vittorio. "Europe 1992: Issues and Prospects for the Financial Markets, "*Economic Policy* (October 1989). Will European monetary integration make transactions easier? Which city will become the dominant financial center?

Kindleberger, Charles P. *International Capital Movements* (Cambridge, U.K.: Cambridge University Press, 1988).

Levich, Richard. "Financial Innovations in International Financial Markets," in Martin Feldstein, ed., *The United States in the World Economy* (Chicago: University of Chicago Press, 1988). Discusses innovation, securitization, liberalization, globalization, and increased competition among financial institutions.

McKinnon, Ronald. *Money in International Exchange: The Convertible Currency System* (New York: Oxford University Press, 1979). Good chapters on participants in the forward exchange market.

FISCAL AND MONETARY POLICY WITH INTERNATIONAL CAPITAL MOBILITY

Mundell Flemming
① - country
small country

This chapter adds international capital flows to the basic model, continuing the process of adding new factors one by one to the analysis of the balance of payments. Chapter 17 examined the effects of changes in the exchange rate, holding everything else constant. Chapter 18 allowed first the level of income and then the interest rate to change; then Chapter 19 introduced international money flows and the price level.

In Chapter 21 we saw in detail that the degree of international capital mobility has been increasing steadily over the past twenty years. This chapter and those to follow will demonstrate that international capital mobility has important implications for the operation of macroeconomic policy. For example, the most dramatic shift of the 1980s in the economic interaction of the industrialized countries, the emergence of enormous trade deficits in the United States, was not primarily caused by changes in trade policy or competitiveness. Rather, it had its origin in the international flow of capital to the United States. This flow of capital, in turn, was caused primarily by fiscal and monetary policies enacted in Washington, D.C.

International capital flows in reality depend on many factors. Perhaps the most important are the rates of return that various countries are offering on their assets. This chapter will simplify and assume that the rates of return on all assets offered by a given country (other than money) move together sufficiently closely within the country that they can be represented by a single nominal interest rate, i. In other words, we aggregate together bonds, stocks, and other nonmonetary assets. It is further assumed here that the differential between the domestic and foreign interest rate is the only determinant of the net capital inflow or outflow. Chapter 24 will add other determinants of the behavior of the international portfolio investor besides interest rates, in particular investors' awareness that future changes in exchange rates will affect the returns they earn.

When investors in a low-interest-rate country buy assets in a high-interest-rate country, they exploit the principle of comparative advantage, just as consumers do when buying goods from a foreign country that can produce them at lower cost. Chapters 2 and 3 introduced the concept of "autarky": the hypothetical situation that would prevail if a country were closed off from international trade in goods (for example, because of prohibitively high tariff barriers), so that agents could consume only those goods produced domestically. It was shown that, once the country opens up to international trade, the pattern of trade is dictated by the prices that would hold in autarky: If one good would sell for a lower price in the foreign country than in the domestic country (whether because demand for it is lower or supply higher), then domestic residents will import that good as soon as they have the opportunity.

A similar concept can be applied to international trade in bonds. Autarky now would prevail if a country were closed off from international trade in bonds, that is, from borrowing or lending abroad (for example, because of prohibitively high capital controls). In autarky the interest rate in each country would be determined so as to equilibrate the supply and demand for bonds versus money. The last part of Chapter 18 introduced monetary policy and the interest rate, i, into the model, but did not allow for international capital flows. In Figure 18.15, for example, a high interest rate was required for equilibrium in the home country. There had been an increase in government demand for funds that reduced total national saving, thus driving up the interest rate and crowding out private investment. (Do not be concerned if your recollection of the graph is hazy; it will be covered again momentarily.)

Imagine now that in autarky a lower interest rate prevails in the foreign country. Then, once the countries open up to international capital flows (removing capital controls, for example, as Japan did at the start of 1980s), the pattern of trade in bonds is dictated by the rates of return that would hold in autarky. If the home country has the higher interest rate, then domestic residents will borrow from abroad, where the cost of funds is lower. Equivalently, foreign residents will lend to the home country, where the rate of return is higher. Either way, the point is that capital flows from the low-interest-rate country to the high-interest-rate country.[1]

We represent the net (private) capital account balance by KA. Thus,

$$KA = \overline{KA} + k(i - i^*) \tag{22.1}$$

To the extent that the domestic interest rate, i, rises above the foreign rate, i^*, foreign investors will find domestic assets more attractive than their own and will seek to acquire them, while domestic residents will be less eager to buy foreign assets and may even borrow abroad at the lower foreign interest rate. Whether foreigners invest in the home country or domestic residents borrow abroad, the transaction counts as a capital inflow and the domestic capital account shows a surplus: KA is positive. Conversely, if the domestic interest rate falls below the foreign rate, domestic residents will buy foreign assets and foreign residents will borrow in the home country; there is a capital outflow and KA is negative.

Why, if one country is offering a higher interest rate than another, would investors be willing to hold *any* assets of the low-rate country? This is a question well worth

---

[1] To carry the analogy with the two-good trade model one step further, the "good" that the foreign country obtains is the ability to consume more in the future, in exchange for consumption today. This point is spelled out in the appendix to this chapter.

asking, and there will be an answer to it that holds even under conditions of perfect integration of financial markets (that is, the possibility of future changes in the exchange rate, to be introduced in Chapter 24). For the moment, assume that there are still some transaction costs, capital controls, or other impediments to the movement of capital across national borders that prevent investors from completely arbitraging away interest differentials.[2]

This chapter inserts the capital flow equation, Equation 22.1, into the model used to determine national income, Y, in Chapter 18. The chapter also returns to the ("Keynesian") assumption made there that the speed of adjustment of goods prices is so slow that it can be ignored in the short run, so that changes in demand are entirely reflected as changes in output. (As before, much of the analysis developed here would also apply in a world of flexible prices, with changes in the price level substituting for changes in output when there are changes in aggregate demand.) Because Chapter 18 assumed a capital account constrained to zero, the model did not look radically different from the *IS-LM* model of closed-economy textbooks. Now, however, international capital flows will change the model radically, particularly regarding the effects of monetary and fiscal policy.

In the first half of the chapter we consider a regime of fixed exchange rates. Then we consider a floating exchange rate regime. At every stage, the discussion explores not just what difference it makes to have *some* degree of capital mobility ($k > 0$) but also the different implications of high versus low capital mobility. Section 22.3 will consider the limiting case of perfect capital mobility ($k = $ infinity). This logical progression—from no capital mobility to low, high, and finally perfect capital mobility—mirrors the historical evolution of the international financial system, as the processes of innovation and liberalization have gradually diminished the barriers between countries.

22.1 THE MODEL UNDER FIXED EXCHANGE RATES

We set down equations for the *IS* and *LM* relationships from Chapter 18:

$$IS: \qquad Y = [\overline{A} - b(i) + \overline{X} - \overline{M}]/(s + m) \qquad (22.2)$$

$$LM: \quad M/P = L(i, Y) \qquad (22.3)$$

The curves appear in the figures used throughout this chapter.

To review, the *LM* curve is the relationship between income, Y, and the interest rate, i, that gives equilibrium in the money market, where equilibrium is defined as real money supply (M/P) equal to real money demand. A given curve represents a given real money supply. The curve slopes upward because i and Y have opposite effects on money demand. An increase in Y raises the demand for money because people undertake more transactions. If there is no accommodating increase in the money supply, then the interest rate will be driven up, thus reducing the demand for money back to its original level. If the central bank adopts an expansionary monetary

[2] Again, to point out the analogy with trade in goods, the existence of transportation costs, tariffs, or other impediments to the movement of goods across national boundaries would prevent the prices for the identical goods from being equalized between the two countries.

policy, under the assumption that the short-run price level is fixed, the increase in the nominal money supply is also an increase in the real money supply; it shifts the *LM* curve to the right so that a higher level of *Y* can be sustained for any given interest rate.

The *IS* curve is the relationship between output, *Y*, and the interest rate, *i*, that gives equilibrium in the goods market, where equilibrium is defined as a point where the amount of goods produced equals the amounts of goods demanded. The curve slopes downward because *i* has a second role (in addition to the return paid to households on nonmonetary assets) as the cost to firms of borrowing funds to finance investment in plant and equipment or the cost to households of borrowing to finance an automobile or other consumer durable. An increase in *i* reduces such expenditures and in turn (through the multiplier effect) leads to a lower level of output throughout the economy. Just as the *LM* curve is drawn contingent on a given level of the money supply, so is the *IS* curve drawn contingent on a given level of government expenditure, *G*. *G* is subsumed in the intercept term for the equation, along with the exogenous components of consumer spending and business investment. An increase in any of these exogenous components of spending ($\Delta \overline{A}$) shifts the *IS* curve to the right by an amount equal to the simple Keynesian multiplier ($\Delta Y = [1/(s + m)]\Delta \overline{A}$). Similarly, a reduction in the tax rate would leave households with more disposable income and would exogenously increase consumption. The multiplier, $1/(s + m)$, is smaller than it would be $(1/s)$ if the economy were closed to international trade, because some of the spending leaks out into imports from abroad. The effect on income in complete *IS-LM* equilibrium is smaller still, because the higher transaction demand for money drives up the interest rate and discourages investment.

The *IS* curve shifts to the right not only when there is an exogenous increase in demand for domestic goods coming from domestic residents (*A*), but also when there is an exogenous increase in demand for domestic goods coming from foreign residents, that is, when there is an increase in net exports (*TB*). This would be the case, for example, if there is a shift in foreign tastes toward domestic products or if quotas are imposed on imports. The same occurs if there is a devaluation (assuming the Marshall-Lerner condition is satisfied). It will often be necessary to take into account this source of shifts in the *IS* curve.

The *BP* Relationship

In Chapter 18 a third line, labeled $TB = 0$, was drawn. At that stage in the analysis, the balance of payments consisted solely of the trade balance because there was no capital account. That can be considered the approximate situation of the world economy in the 1950s, when capital flows were not free to respond to rates of return. (This is not to say that the capital account was literally zero. There was an exogenous component, $\overline{KA}$. An example of such exogenous capital flows is lending to Europe under the Marshall Plan after World War II.) The interest rate had no effect on the balance of payments, so the line representing the balance of payments was vertical: A unique level of income *Y* was consistent with balance of payments equilibrium. Any point to the right was a point of deficit, because higher income means higher imports, and any point to the left a point of surplus, because lower income means lower imports. The position of this line, however, like the position of the *IS* curve, shifts to the right when there is a change in the exchange rate. Some points that previously represented a trade deficit now represent a trade surplus.

In this chapter the third line, which we will now call the *BP* line, still represents equilibrium in the overall balance of payments, but this no longer means the trade balance alone. It includes both the trade balance, *TB*, which depends negatively on income and positively on the exchange rate as before, and the capital account, *KA*, which depends positively on the interest differential $(i - i^*)$ as in Equation 22.1:

$$BP = TB + KA = 0 \qquad\qquad (22.4)$$
$$= \overline{X} - \overline{M} - mY + \overline{KA} + k(i - i^*) = 0$$

The third line represents combinations of income and the interest rate that would give an overall balance of payments equal to zero. To help graph it on the same diagram as the *IS* and *LM* curves, we can solve the equation to show the level of the interest differential that corresponds to any given level of income, *Y*:

$$i - i^* = -(1/k)(\overline{X} - \overline{M} + \overline{KA}) + (m/k)Y \qquad\qquad (22.5)$$

This chapter will assume that the home country is relatively small in world financial markets, so that it can take the rest of the world's interest rate as given $(i^* = \overline{i}^*)$. Figure 22.1 graphs the relationship shown in Equation 22.5. Notice that an increase in income must be associated with an increase in the interest differential to maintain a zero overall balance of payments. This is because imports increase with income, and the interest rate must be raised to attract the capital inflow to finance the trade deficit. Notice also that the slope of the line depends inversely on the degree of international capital mobility, *k*. The larger is *k*, the flatter is the $BP = 0$ line: The

---

FIGURE 22.1   Balance of Payments Equilibrium Schedule

The *BP* schedule appears on the same axes as *IS-LM*. An increase in income, *Y*, raises imports and causes a trade deficit; it thus requires an increase in the interest rate, *i*, to attract a capital inflow, if the overall balance of payments is to remain at zero.

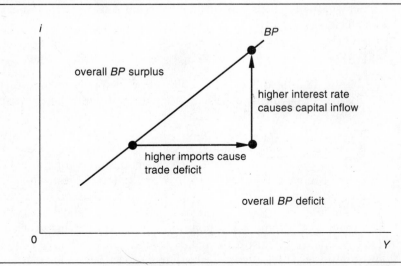

smaller is the increase in the interest rate necessary to attract a given required capital inflow. If k is small, the $BP = 0$ line is steep: It would take a large increase in the interest rate to attract the required capital inflow. The previous case of no capital mobility ($k = 0$) is the case where the line is vertical: No finite increase in the interest rate would be enough to attract the capital. The slope also depends positively on the marginal propensity to import, m.[3]

Notice also that an increase in the exchange rate, or anything else that exogenously increases the trade balance, still shifts the BP curve to the right: For any given interest rate, the condition that the balance of payments is zero would now permit a higher level of income. (The BP curve shifts to the right by precisely the same distance as it did in the absence of capital mobility: $(1/m)\Delta\overline{X}$.)

The economy is always at the intersection of the IS and LM curves, under the assumption that there is always equilibrium in the goods and asset markets. The demand for goods equals the output of goods supplied, and the demand for money equals the supply of money. There is not necessarily any reason to be also on the BP curve. The balance of payments will be nonzero, and the economy will be off the BP curve, if the central bank is buying or selling foreign exchange reserves. The following discussion will assume that the starting point just happens to be a point where the balance of payments equals zero, so that all three curves intersect simultaneously.

The model will now be used to examine the effects, first, of a fiscal expansion, and, second, of a monetary expansion.

Fiscal Policy and the Degree of Capital Mobility

Consider the case of an increase in government expenditure, beginning as in the case of zero capital mobility, shown again in Figure 22.2(a) for convenience. The IS curve shifts to the right to IS', with the new intersection at point G. Income, Y, increases, and the higher transaction demand for money drives up the interest rate. There are now different implications for the balance of payments, however. In the case of no capital mobility shown in Figure 22.2(a), the only effect on the balance of payments came via imports and the trade deficit. The balance of payments went into deficit, with the central bank buying up the unwanted domestic currency (under the regime of fixed exchange rates, the one considered in this section). But now, when we include the capital account, the higher interest rate attracts a capital inflow into the country, which works to improve the overall balance of payments. On the other hand, the higher level of income still draws in imports and worsens the trade balance, which works to worsen the balance of payments. Which effect dominates? It depends on the degree of capital mobility. If capital flows are not very sensitive to interest rates, then the improvement in the capital account will be small and the trade deficit will dominate. However, if capital flows *are* highly responsive to the interest rate, then the capital inflow will dominate and the overall balance of payments will improve.

Figure 22.2(b) shows the upward-sloping BP curve as relatively steep—steeper than the LM curve. This is the case of "low" capital mobility. It is the case where the

[3] Most countries have gradually become more open to international trade in the postwar period, so that m has gradually been increasing. However, the degree of capital mobility, k, has been increasing more rapidly in most industrialized countries, so the slope m/k has been gradually diminishing.

FIGURE 22.2   Fiscal Expansion Under Fixed Exchange Rates

(a) Regardless of the degree of capital mobility, a fiscal expansion shifts the *IS* curve out, raising *Y* and *i* at *G* and worsening the *TB*. If capital mobility is low (b), then the capital inflow, *KA*, is smaller than the trade deficit and the overall *BP* is negative. If it is high (c), then *KA* is larger than the trade deficit and *BP* is positive.

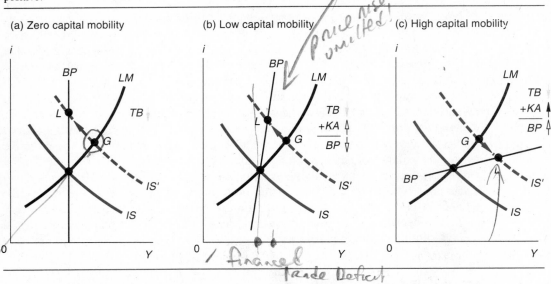

[handwritten annotations: "price rise omitted", "with Sterling con stay here!", "financed", "Trade Deficit"]

new *IS-LM* intersection at point *G* occurs to the right of, or below, the *BP* curve. Any point to the right of or below the *BP* curve is a point of deficit: Either the level of income, and therefore imports, is too high for balance of payments equilibrium, or the level of the interest rate, and therefore the capital inflow, is too low. Thus, the fiscal expansion in Figure 22.2(b) gives a balance of payments deficit, as in the case of zero capital mobility, with the central bank using its foreign exchange reserves to buy up the unwanted domestic currency on the foreign exchange market. Yet there is a difference: The deficit is not as large as in Figure 22.2(a), because the capital inflow does partially offset the trade deficit. This is the *only* difference. *Y* and *i* are the same as in the earlier case.

In Figure 22.2(c) the *BP* curve is relatively flat—flatter than the *LM* curve. This is the case of "high" capital mobility. The fiscal expansion again produces the same increases in *Y* and *i*. Now, however, the new intersection of the *IS* and *LM* curves occurs at a point, *G*, to the left of, or above, the *BP* curve. The increase in *i* attracts a capital inflow more than sufficient to finance the higher imports resulting from the increase in *Y*. Thus, the overall balance of payments is in surplus. Under fixed exchange rates, the central bank is accumulating foreign exchange reserves, not losing them, as with a lower degree of capital mobility.

Which case, (a), (b), or (c), is most realistic in practice? Clearly, all countries have at least some degree of capital mobility. The degree of capital mobility for the United States and Canada has been high enough to put them in category (c) ever since capital controls were removed in 1974. Still, many other countries have lagged behind in liberalizing their financial markets, as was seen in Chapter 21. The United Kingdom was still in category (b) at least as recently as 1978, and Japan perhaps as recently as 1984. None of these countries is on fixed exchange rates, so the complete analysis relevant to them will have to await Section 22.2, which deals with floating rates.

Nevertheless, the continental European countries do maintain relatively fixed exchange rates against each other as part of the European Monetary System (EMS), so the analysis of this section can be applied to them. Consider the example of France, which undertook an expansion when the Socialists were elected in 1981. At the time, capital controls placed the country in category (b). The balance of payments went into deficit, so the French franc was in excess supply (vis-à-vis the German mark) and President Mitterrand was forced to reverse the expansion. In other words, France had difficulty attracting the foreign capital to finance fiscal expansion.

Since then, liberalization has moved France from category (b) to category (c), where most Western European countries are now. Deficits are easily financed. In Spain, for example, an increase in interest rates in 1989–1990, brought about by an increase in spending, attracted such a large capital inflow that it put strong upward pressure on the peseta, even vis-à-vis the traditionally strong mark.

Completely fixed exchange rates are most common in small LDCs. However, small countries usually have a high marginal propensity to import, so a fiscal expansion leads to a large trade deficit (especially if the government spends the money on military equipment or large investment projects that are very import-intensive). Most LDCs naturally have less-developed financial markets. As a result, interest rates may not be free to rise in response to a fiscal expansion, or, even if interest rates do rise above the level in the rest of the world, the degree of capital mobility is likely to be low enough that the overall balance of payments worsens rather than improves. In other words, they are in case (b).

This analysis has assumed that the central bank holds the money supply constant. The effect of the fiscal expansion on income would be greater if the central bank at the same time were to follow an expansionary monetary policy so as to prevent interest rates from rising (an "accommodating" monetary policy). The Federal Reserve generally followed such a policy in the 1960s when expansionary fiscal policies were adopted: the 1964 tax cut proposed by President Kennedy and the subsequent increases in spending by President Johnson. (It was not until later that the Fed allowed interest rates to rise sharply.) Accommodating monetary policies have also been common in other countries. We will now consider the effects of an increase in the money supply in itself.

Monetary Policy and the Degree of Capital Mobility

Figures 22.3(a), (b), and (c) again illustrate the cases of zero, low, and high capital mobility, respectively. From the initial equilibrium, a monetary expansion shifts the *LM* curve to the right. In each of the three cases, the effects of the increase in the money supply on the interest rate and income are precisely the same. The interest rate, i, falls, stimulating spending, thus raising income, Y, at the new intersection, point M. In each case, higher income means higher imports and a trade deficit. However, the presence of international capital mobility has implications for the balance of payments. This time there is a capital outflow, resulting from the fact that i has fallen below the foreign rate, i^*. Because the capital account moves in the same

FIGURE 22.3   Monetary Expansion Under Fixed Exchange Rates

(a) Regardless of the degree of capital mobility, a monetary expansion shifts the *LM* curve out, lowering *i* and raising *Y* at *M*, and worsening the *TB*. (b) With low capital mobility, an outflow through the *KA* supplements the trade deficit, so the overall *BP* deficit and speed of reserve outflow are greater. (c) With high capital mobility, the speed of reserve outflow is greater still.

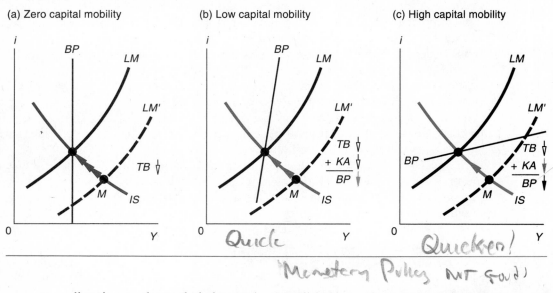

(a) Zero capital mobility   (b) Low capital mobility   (c) High capital mobility

direction as the trade balance, the overall balance of payments is in deficit in each of the three cases. Because the lower interest rate causes larger capital outflows the higher the degree of capital mobility, the overall balance of payments must deteriorate by more in case (b) than in case (a), and by more in case (c) than in case (b).

If a country is running a balance of payments deficit, as in Figures 22.3(a), (b), and (c) [or Figures 22.2(a) and (b)], it is losing foreign exchange reserves continuously over time. Because it only has a certain level of reserves, it cannot continue to do this indefinitely or it will run out. Eventually, it must adjust. One way it could adjust deliberately is by reversing the monetary (or fiscal) expansion. Yet there is also the possibility of automatic adjustment of the money supply through the balance of payments deficit if the central bank does not sterilize reserve outflows. Nonsterilized reserve flows will be considered momentarily.

A final way to adjust is to let the exchange rate change. A deliberate devaluation would stimulate net exports and shift the *BP* curve to the right. The automatic version of this mechanism of adjustment is to *allow* the currency to depreciate on the foreign exchange market, when the central bank follows a rule of not intervening, as we will see in our discussion of floating exchange rates. So far in this chapter, capital mobility has affected only the balance of payments, not income. However, under either of these two possible (automatic) mechanisms of adjustment—reserve flows or exchange rate changes—the changes in the balance of payments already derived will in turn have implications for the level of income.

When Money Flows Are Not Sterilized

If the central bank does choose to sterilize reserve flows, the economy can remain at point M in Figure 22.3, or at point G in Figure 22.2, as long as the stock of reserves holds out. Now, however, the analysis adopts the assumption of the monetary approach to the balance of payments: Changes in the level of reserves are not sterilized and are thus allowed to be reflected one-for-one as changes in the level of the total money supply. The preceding analysis still explains what happens to income and the interest rate in the short run, but now it is necessary to trace the implications of the money flow over time.

We begin by picking up the experiment where the central bank undertakes a deliberate increase in the money supply. The combination of a lower interest rate and higher level of income at point M is only a short-run equilibrium. Even without any capital mobility, as in Figure 22.3(a), the trade deficit at point M in itself implies that reserves are flowing out of the country over time. If the central bank does not choose to sterilize this loss in reserves, then the money supply is decreasing, which means that the LM curve is shifting back to the left over time. The sequence of intersections back along the IS curve is shown by the arrows in Figure 22.3(a). They bring to mind the principle illustrated in Figure 19.1, when the monetary approach to the balance of payments was first encountered. As the money supply falls, the interest rate rises, discouraging business investment and other interest-sensitive components of spending. This process continues as long as the balance of payments is still in deficit. In the long run, the economy is back where it started. The entire increase in the money supply has flowed out through the balance of payments, leaving no permanent effect on income.

The story is similar when we add some degree of capital mobility, as in Figure 22.3(b). Because the lower interest rate induces a deficit on the capital account as well, the overall balance of payments at point M is in greater deficit than it was in the absence of capital mobility. As in the case without capital mobility, if the central bank opts not to sterilize the reserve outflow, then the economy follows the sequence of arrows until in the long run it is back where it started, with no effects. Is this case then identical to the case illustrated in Figure 22.3(a)? The two graphs look quite similar, but there is a difference. Because the balance of payments deficit is greater in the case of capital mobility illustrated in Figure 22.3(b), the rate at which the money supply decreases over time is greater, and therefore the economy returns to its starting point more rapidly.

The case of high capital mobility, illustrated in Figure 22.3(c), proceeds in the same way. The balance of payments deficit at point M means that the addition to the money supply is flowing out of the country over time. In the long run, the economy is again back where it started. What difference does the higher degree of capital mobility make? Because the capital outflow is greater for the same differential in interest rates, the rate of reserve loss is even greater in Figure 22.3(c) than in Figure 22.3(b), and so the return to the long-run equilibrium will be that much faster.

We now turn from the experiment where the government undertakes a deliberate monetary expansion to the experiment where it undertakes a deliberate fiscal expansion, such as an increase in government expenditure. Figure 22.2 showed an outward shift in the *IS* curve and an increase in income. Recall that the higher level of income resulted in a trade deficit, just as in the monetary expansion.

When a fiscal expansion results in a balance of payments deficit, the money supply will gradually decrease over time if the central bank does not sterilize the reserve outflow. The declining money supply will shift the *LM* curve leftward and the interest rate will rise. We now move up the new *IS* curve (*IS'*) in a sequence of *IS-LM* intersections, with interest-sensitive expenditures declining. As expenditure declines, the trade balance improves. This process continues until the economy has returned to a zero balance of payments. Only then are we in long-run equilibrium, because only then is the money supply no longer changing. The arrows in Figure 22.2(a) show this process for the case of zero capital mobility and remind us of the lesson learned from Figure 19.2: In the long run (point *L*), the fiscal expansion is completely offset by the outflow of money and there is no effect on the level of output. In the case of low capital mobility illustrated in Figure 22.2(b), the balance of payments deficit that exists at point *G* again means that reserves will be flowing out over time and that under the nonsterilization assumption the money supply and level of income will be declining over time. In this case, however, the long-run equilibrium at point *L* features a level of income that, while below the short-run level at point *G*, is still somewhat higher than before the fiscal expansion. Despite the fact that income is higher at *L*, the overall balance of payments is zero: The higher interest rate attracts a capital inflow sufficient to finance the higher imports that result from the higher level of income.

We have already seen that in the case of high capital mobility, illustrated in Figure 22.2(c), the short-run equilibrium at point *G* is a point of balance of payments surplus, rather than deficit. The capital inflow is more than enough to offset the trade deficit. This represents a qualitative departure from the other five cases illustrated. It means that the stock of international reserves is increasing over time, not decreasing. If the central bank opts not to sterilize, but rather allows the total money supply to increase over time, then the *LM* curve will again shift, but to the *right* this time. From point *G*, the economy moves to the right along the *IS'* curve, with the higher money supply driving down the interest rate and stimulating spending. The long-run equilibrium occurs at *L*, where the capital inflow is no more than needed to finance the trade deficit. Unlike the case with low capital mobility, the level of income in the long run is not just higher than it was before the fiscal expansion, it is also higher than in the short run.

It is appropriate here to note a pitfall that may be encountered when analyzing international money flows. A capital inflow such as results from the increase in interest rates shown in Figure 22.2 is sometimes referred to as an "inflow of money." This is permissible terminology, because foreign residents will usually be paying for the stocks and bonds they buy, in the first instance, with money. However, it is important to realize that, at the same time that money is flowing "in" through the capital account, it may be flowing "out" through the trade account. It takes money to buy goods, just as it takes money to buy securities. Money is only truly flowing in, on net, if the total balance of payments is in surplus, both the trade account and the capital account, as in the short-run equilibrium at point *G* in Figure 22.2(c). Even then, the total money supply does not increase unless the central bank lets it, by refraining from sterilizing the inflow. It is probably safest to avoid altogether using the term "inflow of money" to describe an inflow of capital. Then there will be no danger of confusing it with a change in the money supply. There are many other more suitable synonyms for capital inflow to choose from (borrowing from abroad, foreign financing, foreign investment in the domestic country, decrease in the net international investment position, foreign purchases of domestic assets, etc.).

As we have seen repeatedly, under the monetary approach to the balance of payments, the overall balance is zero in the long run. At point L in Figure 22.2, however, there must be a continuing capital inflow, because the domestic interest rate remains above the world interest rate. "Money" is flowing in through the capital account at precisely the same rate it is flowing out through the current account. Another implication is that, in the long run, all three curves intersect (at the same point L), not just the IS and LM curves.

Other Automatic Mechanisms of Adjustment

Within the context of the monetary approach to the balance of payments, the findings of Figure 22.2(b) and (c) are unfamiliar. As a general rule, it is expected that in the long run, when the economy has had enough time to adjust to a change in macroeconomic policy, there are no real effects left. Yet it has just been shown that under conditions of capital mobility, a fiscal expansion has a permanent effect on real output. Even in the case of zero capital mobility in Figure 22.2(a), though there is no long-run effect on output at point L, there is a long-run real effect on investment and other interest-sensitive components of spending. The loss of output in these sectors must be equal to the gain in output in the government sector—a case of 100 percent crowding out—for aggregate GNP to be unchanged. It is clear why some effect on output remains even in the long run in this model: The only automatic mechanism of adjustment is the flow of money through the balance of payments, which is shut off at point L. However, there are other automatic mechanisms of adjustment that have been omitted here.

One is the adjustment of the price level over time in response to an excess demand for goods and labor. Inflationary pressure may exist at points like G in Figure 22.2 or M in Figure 22.3, assuming that the starting point before the fiscal or monetary expansion was the point at which the economy was at potential output and full employment. Chapter 19 showed that an increase in the price level reduces the real money supply, which works to discourage expenditure and return the economy to its long-run equilibrium. Chapter 23 will add the gradual adjustment of goods prices to the model of this chapter.

Another possible automatic mechanism of adjustment omitted here is changes in the stock of bonds. This point is particularly relevant in Figures 22.2(b) and 22.2(c). At point L, the government is still running a budget deficit, and—as a consequence— the country is still running a current account deficit, even though the capital inflow is large enough to finance these deficits. When the government runs a budget deficit, the supply of government bonds in the hands of the public increases over time, assuming that the deficit is not monetized (i.e., assuming that the bonds are not bought by the central bank—which they are not, under the assumption that the central bank is holding the money supply constant). Analogously, when the country runs a current account deficit, the supply of foreign bonds in the hands of the public decreases over time. In other words, the public borrows, or runs down the asset position vis-à-vis foreigners that it has accumulated in the past, in order to pay for its trade deficit.

Note that when the government borrows from domestic residents, who in turn borrow from foreign residents, it is as if the government were borrowing directly from foreign residents. In the case of the government deficits of many Latin American countries in the 1970s, much of the borrowing was in fact directly from foreign banks. In the case of the record federal government deficits of the United States in the 1980s, many of the treasury securities were sold directly to foreign residents, but the majority were sold to American residents. American residents in turn borrowed from abroad via, for example, U.S. corporate bonds issued in the Euromarket.

The stock of bonds (i.e., the accumulated *level* of bonds issued, as opposed to the *flow*, i.e., the deficits), either domestic or foreign, has no role to play in the model developed here. However, there are possible effects left out of the model. For example, holdings of bonds, along with money and other assets, are a component of the *wealth* or *net worth* of households and thus have an effect on the level of spending. If spending declines at point L in Figure 22.2(c) because households are running down their holdings of foreign bonds at the rate of the current account deficit, then the IS curve will shift back to the left, just as it does when there is any exogenous fall in domestic spending. The process may continue until the current account is back to zero and the stock of bonds back to where it started, by analogy with the monetary approach to the balance of payments, in which the adjustment process continues until the overall balance of payments is back to zero and the money supply back to where it started. This added posssible mechanism of adjustment will not be pursued here. The discussion, rather, is based on the model in which changes in the stock of bonds have no effect, so that it does not matter whether it is changing over time or not.

Monetary and Fiscal Policies for Internal and External Balance

The last section of Chapter 18 introduced a fundamental principle of policy-making: To attain the two independent policy targets of internal balance (output equal to a desired level, such as that consistent with the natural rate of unemployment and low inflation) and external balance (the trade balance at a desired level, such as zero), at least two independent policy instruments are required. In Chapter 18, the two policy instruments were government spending and the exchange rate. So far in this chapter we have been keeping the exchange rate fixed, ruling out one of the instruments. (Section 22.2 will return to the case of flexible exchange rates.) On the other hand, a new policy instrument, the money supply, has been added since the issue was last considered. Monetary and fiscal policy are each thought of as domestic policy instruments. Will the two, used together, nevertheless allow the two targets, external and internal balance, to be attained simultaneously? The answer will turn out to be "yes," but only because the model now allows for international capital movements.[4]

[4] Much of the analysis of this section is based on R. A. Mundell, "The Appropriate Use of Monetary and Fiscal Policy under Fixed Exchange Rates," *IMF Staff Papers*, 9 (March 1962): 70–77. Mundell (a native Canadian) had particularly in mind the example of policy-making in Canada. Capital mobility became crucial for Canada, because of the high degree of integration with the United States, earlier than for many other countries.

To study the problem from the viewpoint of the government policy-maker, the same model will be viewed with a different graph. In Figures 22.2 and 22.3, changes in fiscal or monetary policy showed up as shifts of the *IS* or *LM* curves. Figure 22.4, however, shows the two policy instruments directly on the axes. Here the level of government expenditure, *G*, appears on the horizontal axis. The interest rate, *i*, the instrument of monetary policy, appears on the vertical axis.

For major industrialized countries, it is somewhat old-fashioned to think of the interest rate as the instrument of monetary policy; late in the 1970s most of their central banks began thinking of the money supply as the instrument of monetary policy. However, in the absence of exogenous shifts in money demand, it makes no difference which we choose: When the central bank sets a money supply, it implicitly determines the interest rate as well. The money supply might just as well be on the vertical axis. Here we use the interest rate for the policy instrument so that the implications for international capital flows can readily be seen.[5] Furthermore, many smaller countries and LDCs, who tend to be on fixed exchange rates, continue to think of the interest rates as their primary instrument of monetary policy because interest rates are administered directly by the goverment rather than being determined in the marketplace. Even in the case of the United States and other large industrialized countries, innovations in banking, such as payment of interest on checking accounts,

[5] Also because this is the way Robert Mundell did it originally.

FIGURE 22.4   External Balance under Fixed Rates

An increase in government spending, *G*, causes a trade deficit. If overall balance of payments equilibrium is to be maintained, the interest rate, *i*, must be raised to attract a capital inflow. Thus, the *BB* schedule slopes up.

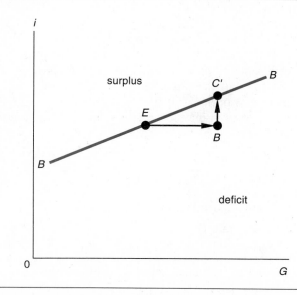

have blurred the distinction between money and other assets. Consequently, the money supply is no longer considered the unambiguously superior measure of monetary policy that it was at the end of the 1970s. Thus, focusing on the interest rate has once again become respectable.

We will use Figure 22.4 to derive the combinations of the two policy instruments consistent with the targets. Assume that internal balance and external balance both hold at the starting point, E. Consider an increase in government expenditure, G, a rightward movement from point E. Figure 22.2 showed that such a fiscal expansion affects both policy targets. It raises income and, as a result, raises imports and worsens the trade balance. (The discussion here is concerned only with the short-run equilibrium at point G in Figure 22.2; endogenous effects of reserve flows on the money supply are not under consideration for the moment because the focus is deliberate changes in monetary and fiscal policy.)

Consider first external balance. At point B, the increase in government spending has moved the trade balance into deficit. To eliminate the balance of payments deficit resulting from the trade deficit, the government must generate a surplus on the capital account. It can do this by following a contractionary monetary policy. The higher interest rate for any given level of income will attract a capital inflow into the country. (This policy mix, a fiscal expansion with monetary policy kept sufficiently tight to allow interest rates to rise, describes well the United States expansion in the years 1981–1984. The predicted result emerged: a large trade deficit, financed by large-scale borrowing from abroad attracted by high interest rates.)

If the interest rate rises far enough, the surplus on the capital account will be sufficient to offset the deficit on the current account and the overall balance of payments will be restored to zero. In terms of Figure 22.4, if the increase in G (a rightward movement) is accompanied by a sufficiently large increase in i (an upward movement), then overall external balance will be maintained at point C'. Thus, the set of combinations of G and i that give external balance constitutes an upward-sloping relationship, which is labeled the BB curve. There is no reason necessarily to be on the BB curve, because there is no reason why the balance of payments must necessarily be zero. Indeed, the advantage of the graph is that it shows where the economy is *relative* to the policy goals. Any point below and to the right of the BB schedule is a point of balance of payments deficit because policy is expansionary. One way of thinking of it is that the capital account balance is low because the interest rate is low; the other way of thinking of it is that the current account balance is low because income is high. Any point above and to the left of the schedule is a point of balance of payments surplus, because policy is tight. The capital account balance is high because the interest rate is high, or the current account balance is high because income is low.

Now consider internal balance. When the government increases G, income goes up; thus, the rightward movement from point E to point B in Figure 22.5 causes a move into the zone of excess demand, where the level of income exceeds the full-employment level and creates inflationary pressure. If the government is to restore internal balance, it must undertake a monetary contraction, raising the interest rate to dampen demand. If the interest rate is increased by enough, it will restore income back to the full-employment level. In terms of the graph, if the increase in G is accompanied by a sufficiently large increase in i, to a point like C, then internal balance is maintained. Thus, the set of combinations of G and i providing internal balance constitute another upward-sloping relationship, which is labeled the YY curve. Again, there is not necessarily any reason to be on the YY curve, because in the absence of instantaneous flexibility in wages and prices there is no reason why output should necessarily be at the full-employment level. Any point below or to the right of the YY schedule is a point of excess demand. Any point above and to the left is a point of excess supply.

What determines the relative slope of these two upward-sloping curves? It might seem, reasoning from the BP curve in the earlier graphs, that the answer to this question depends on the degree of capital mobility. It is true that the higher the degree of capital mobility, the flatter the slope of the BB curve, because if k is higher, then it takes a smaller increase in i to attract the necessary capital inflow to finance any given trade deficit. However, it turns out that even if the degree of capital mobility is relatively low, so that the BB curve is relatively steep, it cannot be any steeper than the YY curve. To see this, consider the movement from point E to point C, a simultaneous fiscal expansion and monetary contraction calculated to leave income unchanged at the full-employment level. Is point C a point of balance of payments surplus or deficit? There is no reason for the trade balance to have changed, as income is unchanged, but because the interest rate is higher, there is a capital inflow that puts the balance of payments in surplus. Only points above and to the left of the BB schedule are points of surplus. Therefore, C must be above the BB schedule, which implies that the YY schedule is steeper.

This logic applies whatever the degree of capital mobility k, so long as it is greater than zero. In the event that k is zero, the balance of payments is no higher at C than at C' or E. In this case the BB curve has the same slope as the YY curve. This is a return to the situation of no capital mobility, as in Chapter 18, in which case monetary and fiscal policy are not *independent* policy instruments. Monetary policy has no extra effect on the balance of payments beyond the same effect that fiscal policy has via income and imports. In general, C lies above C' because the interest rate has an effect on the capital account above and beyond its effect on the trade balance.

Combinations of Monetary and Fiscal Policy

Figure 22.5 is divided into four zones. In zone I there is a payments deficit and excess supply (unemployment), in zone II a deficit and excess demand (inflation), in zone III a payments surplus and excess demand, and in zone IV a surplus and excess supply. There is only one point of full equilibrium, E. Both policy tools are needed to attain it.

Conclusions about the proper direction of change in the policy instruments can be drawn from Figure 22.5. Point A lies in zone II, and a deficit and inflationary pressure call for both a contraction of public spending and a rise in the rate of interest. The same problems at point B, however, would be solved by a contraction of fiscal policy alone; monetary policy is already tight enough to secure overall balance once the appropriate change in fiscal policy is made. At point C', external balance and inflationary pressure coexist. Fiscal policy must be tightened, but monetary policy eased somewhat, to keep the contraction from throwing the balance of payments into surplus as inflationary pressures abate. At point D, however, a monetary contraction

---

FIGURE 22.5   External and Internal Balance

The *YY* schedule shows internal balance (*Y* at full employment). It also slopes up, because an increase in *G* would cause excess demand for goods at *B* (which is inflationary), requiring that the monetary authority raise *i* to eliminate the excess demand at *C*. However, the *BB* schedule is not as steep as the *YY* schedule when an increase in *i* has the added effect of attracting a capital inflow.

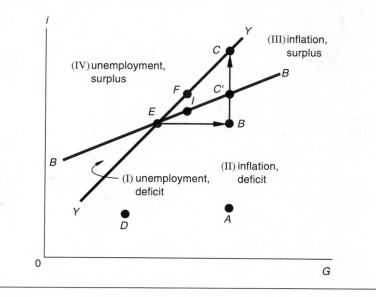

must be associated with fiscal expansion to secure a relatively large improvement in the balance of payments while removing only a relatively small amount of inflationary pressure. In zone II, and in zone IV as well, the proper direction of change for both instruments depends on the relative sizes of the internal and external disequilibria.

On the other hand, in zone I it is possible to tell unambiguously the right direction of change for both instruments. In zone I unemployment and payments deficit are always fought by expansionary fiscal policy coupled with a tightening of monetary policy. The rising interest rate combats the restoration of full employment but does less harm there than the good it does in eliminating the payments deficit, and the interest rate at any point in zone I is lower than it must be if balance is secured at point *E*. The corresponding statements apply to zone III.

Were monetary and fiscal policy used as independent instruments during the era of fixed exchange rates in the way that this analysis suggests is possible? In the late 1950s and early 1960s, the United States suffered from unemployment combined with an external deficit (zone I). Some economists urged on the basis of these theoretical considerations that fiscal policy should be eased and monetary policy tightened. Indeed, taxes were cut by the Kennedy Administration to pull the country out of recession, and for some time an attempt was made to allow short-term interest rates to rise in order to attract capital from abroad. Yet for the most part, U.S. fiscal and monetary policy moved in the same direction—either relaxed together or tightened together—in the 1950s, 1960s, and 1970s. The first time fiscal and monetary policy went strongly in opposite directions was the 1980s, as will be seen subsequently.

We have seen that capital flows, if responsive to monetary policy, allow countries to secure overall balance without changing their exchange rates. The more mobile is capital, the smaller is the required interest rate change when monetary policy is used to secure overall balance. At the limit, when capital is perfectly mobile, the interest rate is fixed at the world level, i^*, and the BB schedule becomes a horizontal line. Monetary policy can affect external balance without changing interest rates measurably. At the same time, changes in the money supply do not influence internal balance at all. This case, in which monetary policy becomes ineffective because capital is perfectly mobile, is examined in Section 22.3.

Difficulties of Policy-Making

The model and diagrams discussed so far make it sound as if policy-making should be perfectly easy. The government simply ascertains where the economy lies relative to internal and external balance, calculates how much it needs to move the monetary and fiscal policy levers to restore equilibrium, and proceeds. Is it possible that policy-making is this easy in practice?

There are four problems that make policy-making much more difficult than this. First, there are considerable *lags* between the time a policy instrument is changed and the time the economy responds. Chapter 17 considered a major lag, between an exchange rate change and its effect on the trade balance: the J-curve. There are also important lags between the time that monetary or fiscal policy is changed and the time that households and firms fully adjust their plans for consumer spending and business investment.

If lags were the only problem, it would not be so difficult to select the appropriate policies. The policy-makers would simply need to plan ahead so that their policy changes would have the desired effects at the right time. However, the process is complicated enormously by the existence of *uncertainty*. There are three kinds of uncertainty: (1) uncertainty about the current position of the economy relative to the "full employment" level of output and the desired trade balance; (2) uncertainty about future disturbances or "shocks" (such as sudden shifts in the demand for money or in private spending); and (3) uncertainty about the correct model (such as the correct value of the marginal propensities to save and import, the slope of the LM curve, and other parameters). Any of these three forms of uncertainty can lead to policy errors.

In the 1970s, for example, policy-makers saw the United States and the world as being at levels of income substantially below full employment, and therefore decided to use both fiscal and monetary policy to expand. (The expansion began with a tax cut by the Ford Administration in 1975 and was continued by the Carter Administration in 1977–1979.) Inflation reached double-digits by the end of the decade, and—in retrospect—the expansion is generally considered to have been excessive. One way of interpreting the error is that there were unanticipated shifts in some key economic relationships. There was a sizable downward shift in the demand for money—an outward shift in the LM curve—which meant that the planned rate of money growth translated into a higher demand for goods than had been anticipated. In 1979 there was also a new increase in oil prices associated with the fall of the Shah of Iran. (Chapter 23 will examine the effects of such supply shocks.)

The third problem for policy-making is the elusive factor of public *expectations*, particularly as they relate to inflation. If moving into a zone of excess demand caused the inflation rate in the current period to rise but had no further implications thereafter, then the policy-maker would have the relatively straightforward task of picking the preferred point along the inflation/unemployment trade-off. (The internal balance line would be interpreted as the level of demand corresponding to this point, which might not be precisely the same as the level corresponding to "full employment.") In truth, however, there are future periods to consider as well. The trade-off between output and inflation does not stay put over time, as Chapter 23 will show. If inflation is high this period, then the public—particularly workers—will enter the next period with higher expectations of inflation and higher wage demands, raising the level of inflation (for any given level of output) in the next period. Chapter 23 will show that such complications resulting from expectations, even aside from the problems of lags and uncertainty, offer a reason for policy-makers to reduce the frequency with which they adjust ("*fine-tune*," to use a pejorative word) their instrument settings in response to new developments in the economy. Indeed, some economists believe that government should abandon such discretionary policy-making altogether and instead should follow preset rules for monetary and fiscal policy.

The fourth difficulty for policy-makers in practice is that, even if a politician or economist feels confident of exactly what policy changes should be made, there are always formidable political constraints that must be overcome before enacting any changes. The government is not a unified, rational agent. Most politicians give at least some weight to their own selfish interests, and even those who might genuinely have the public welfare at heart will disagree over their interpretation of how to maximize that welfare. Most questions are decided more on the basis of simplistic slogans, bureaucratic politics, and arbitrary historical precedents than on the basis of sound economic logic. A prime example is the making of U.S. fiscal policy. Almost everyone involved believes that the federal budget deficit should be cut more rapidly than it has been, but because they disagree over what categories of spending should be cut and whether taxes should be raised (and because such specific changes are always politically unpopular), little has been done.

The Assignment Problem

Governments sometimes deal with the diversity of information and goals within the policy-making arena by decentralizing, parceling out responsibility for various policy targets to different agencies. One agency might be put in charge of trade policy, for example. The danger is that agencies might find themselves working at cross-purposes. In such a situation, each views the other as representing the sort of political obstacles to successful policy-making noted earlier.

We will now examine a very "stylized" (simplified) version of decentralization. The two agencies to be examined, the central bank and the treasury, possess the tools of monetary policy (either the interest rate or the money supply) and fiscal policy (either government spending or tax rates), respectively. This analysis will show that internal and external balance (*E* in Figure 22.5) can be reached if policy-makers act independently and without direct coordination. However, just which responsibility goes to which authority turns out to be important. That is, one policy goal can be assigned to each authority, as long as the assignments are made correctly. This is the same problem examined in Chapter 18, only now the two instruments are fiscal and monetary policy, whereas there they were fiscal policy and the exchange rate.

Figure 22.5 can be used to explore this possibility. Suppose, arbitrarily, that government policy-makers tell the central bank to pursue external balance. It follows the rule: Lower the interest rate when there is an external surplus, raise it when there is a deficit. To the treasury, responsible for fiscal policy, goes the instruction: Raise government spending when there is unemployment, cut it when there is inflationary pressure. Suppose that the country finds itself with the combination of deficit and potential inflation indicated by *A*. The central bank acts first, leaping into action by raising the interest rate so as to attain external balance at *C'*. That action mitigates inflationary pressure but does not eliminate it. The treasury therefore cuts government spending, bringing the economy to point *F* in Figure 22.5. The central bank now finds it must back off, as a surplus emerges, and lower the interest rate a bit at point *I*. Because inflation is revived by the interest-rate cut, the treasury keeps cutting government spending. Clearly, their separate actions are pulling the economy toward internal and external balance at *E*. This policy assignment appears to work.

Suppose the policy-makers had made the alternative assignment, telling the central bank to look after internal balance and the treasury to mind external balance. Start again from *A*, indicating inflation and an external deficit. The central bank girds itself to fight inflation, raising the interest rate and bringing the system to *C* on the *YY* schedule. What the treasury now observes, however, is not the initial deficit, but an external surplus, which it attacks by *raising* government expenditure. Here is the problem. If the treasury seeks external balance, the system reaches a point on *BB* directly east of *C*. Inflation is again unleashed, and the central bank hastens to raise the interest rate further. The point indicating the economy's actual state, rather than approaching *E*, proceeds northeast in zone III until some higher authority realizes that something is amiss and changes the policy assignments. What this example indicates is a quite general conclusion: Assigning each target to a single policy instrument can work, but the assignment must be right. The right assignment is determined by a rule of comparative advantage: *Give each target to the authority whose instrument has the relatively greater influence on it*. Figure 22.5 shows that monetary policy's comparative advantage under a fixed exchange rate lies in pursuing external balance. That is the whole reason why *BB* is flatter than *YY*. (Chapter 18.5 referred to the general rule as Mundell's principle of effective market classification.)[6]

---

[6] As we will see in the next section, monetary and fiscal policy have very different effects under floating exchange rates than under fixed rates. One implication is that the correct answer to the Assignment Problem is probably reversed. When exchange rate effects are taken into account, fiscal policy has a greater effect on the trade balance and monetary policy a smaller effect, so that fiscal policy should be assigned to external balance and monetary policy to internal balance. James Boughton, "Policy Assignment Strategies with Somewhat Flexible Exchange Rates," in B. Eichengreen, M. Miller, and R. Portes, eds., *Exchange Rate Regimes and Macroeconomic Policy*, (London: Centre for Economic Policy Research, 1989).

22.2 FISCAL AND MONETARY POLICY UNDER FLOATING EXCHANGE RATES

It has already been pointed out that equilibrium under fixed exchange rates often entails a balance of payments surplus or deficit, but that such disequilibria will eventually have to be corrected, if not by a deliberate change in government policy, then by an automatic mechanism of adjustment. In particular, if a country is running a balance of payments deficit, the central bank is losing reserves and will eventually have to allow the money supply to fall if it wishes to remain on a fixed exchange rate. We have already explored the implications of allowing money to flow out through the balance of payments. The alternative possibility is that, instead of abandoning the money supply that it had previously set, the central bank abandons the exchange rate. In other words, the central bank can allow the currency to depreciate until the balance of payments deficit is eliminated. This will happen automatically if the country is on a floating exchange rate regime to begin with, as are the United States and most large industrialized countries.[7] This section considers the effects of monetary and fiscal policy under floating exchange rates.

What makes this analysis different from that in Chapter 18, where we first examined floating rates, is that we have now introduced capital mobility. At the beginning of the chapter we saw how capital mobility means that when policy changes the interest rate, this has implications for the capital account and therefore for the balance of payments. If the central bank follows a regime of sterilized intervention, so as to keep both the exchange rate and money supply constant, then there are no further immediate implications for the level of income. However, the change in the balance of payments will itself have implications for the level of income when either the money supply is allowed to change (as in the monetary approach to the balance of payments, previously considered) or when the exchange rate is allowed to change (as under floating exchange rates, to be considered now). In each case, the effect on the balance of payments derived under fixed exchange rates holds the key to the effect on income under floating rates.

When the exchange rate is floating and the central bank does not intervene, the overall balance of payments, BP, is always zero. In algebraic terms, Equation 22.4 must hold continuously. In terms of the graphical apparatus derived previously, the economy must always be on the BP schedule. If a shock threatens to cause a move off it, the exchange rate will adjust automatically to shift the curve. As was already seen, a devaluation, because it stimulates net exports, shifts the BP curve to the right, and a revaluation of the currency shifts it to the left. Under floating rates, when the economy is at a position that threatens to lie off the BP curve, the currency will instantly depreciate or appreciate to the degree necessary to shift the curve to that position.

Recall that although the balance of payments is always zero, this does not mean that the trade balance is necessarily zero. At any point in the upper part of the BP curve, the interest rate is attracting a capital inflow that is financing a trade deficit. In the lower part of the curve, there is a capital outflow offsetting a trade surplus.

---

[7] Although most continental European countries maintain relatively fixed exchange rates vis-a-vis each other, as a unit they float against the dollar, yen, and Canadian dollar. Thus, the floating-rate model could be used to study any changes in monetary or fiscal policy that the European countries all enact *jointly*.

Fiscal Expansion and Capital Mobility Under Floating Rates

We will now consider a fiscal expansion, such as an increase in government expenditures or a cut in taxes. We will begin with the case of no capital movements and then progress to higher degrees of capital mobility, just as in the case of fixed exchange rates.

We saw in Figure 22.2(a) that when the fiscal expansion shifts the IS curve out and raises income,[8] the higher level of imports produces a balance of payments deficit. This is point A in Figure 22.6(a). A situation that under fixed exchange rates produces a balance of payments deficit, under floating exchange rates automatically produces a depreciation of the currency. The depreciation stimulates the $\overline{X} - \overline{M}$ component of the trade balance, which we know causes both the BP curve (Equation 22.5) and the IS curve (Equation 22.2) to shift to the right. We also know that depreciation shifts the BP curve to the right faster than the IS curve. This is fortunate, because, on the one hand, the economy is always at the intersection of the IS and LM curves and, on the other hand, the balance of payments will remain in deficit and the currency will have to keep depreciating as long as the economy is to the left of the BP curve. Eventually the depreciation will have shifted the BP curve sufficiently far to the right that it will catch up with the IS-LM intersection. Then all three curves will intersect at the same place, point B in Figure 22.6(a). Only there will the balance of payments be zero, as it must be under floating.

Because of the additional stimulus from depreciation, the fiscal expansion raises income by more under floating than under fixed exchange rates (B lies to the right of A). This is the same result obtained in Chapter 18 before the effect of the interest rate on expenditure was introduced.[9] It was described then as the result that floating exchange rates "bottle up" disturbances so that their full effect is felt in the country of origin.

What changes with the introduction of capital mobility? As Figure 22.2(b) showed, the higher interest rate now attracts a capital inflow. There is an improvement in the capital account that partially offsets the deterioration in the trade balance. If the degree of capital mobility is relatively low, the net effect is still to worsen the overall balance of payments under fixed exchange rates. Thus, the effect under floating rates is again to depreciate the currency. The resulting stimulus to net exports again shifts both the BP and IS curves rightward until the BP curve catches up and all three curves intersect at the same point. Figure 22.6(b) shows this as a movement from A to B. As in Figure 22.6(a), the stimulus to income is greater under floating than under fixed rates. Introducing capital mobility, however, has made a difference. The capital inflow means that the potential balance of payments deficit that would exist if the exchange rate were to remain unchanged is smaller, and so the size of the needed

---

[8] Recall from Chapter 18 that the increase in income at A is equal to the simple open economy multiplier, $\Delta\overline{G}/(s + m)$, minus an allowance for crowding out of investment by the higher interest rate.

[9] The effect on income is given by $\Delta\overline{G}/s$, minus an allowance for crowding out by the higher interest rate, the same as it would be in a closed economy. A comparison with the preceding footnote shows that the effect is greater under floating rates. In the event that money demand is highly elastic with respect to the interest rate, so that the LM curve is flat, income increases by the full amount of the rightward shift of the IS curve: $\Delta\overline{G}/(s + m)$ in the case of fixed rates, and $\Delta\overline{G}/s$ in the case of floating. The same would be true if the central bank were to follow a monetary policy of automatically accommodating changes in fiscal policy in such a way as to keep the interest rate unchanged.

FIGURE 22.6 Fiscal Expansion Under Floating Exchange Rates

A fiscal expansion shifts the *IS* curve to *IS'*, raising *Y* and *i* to *A*. (a) Without capital mobility, the trade deficit at *A* requires a depreciation, which stimulates net exports and thus further raises *Y* to *B*. (b) With low capital mobility, the balance of payments deficit is smaller at *A*, so the required depreciation and the further stimulus to *Y* at *B* are smaller. (c) With high capital mobility, the balance of payments is in surplus at *A*, so a small *appreciation* is required, which discourages net exports; thus the increase in *Y* at *B* is smaller than in the earlier cases.

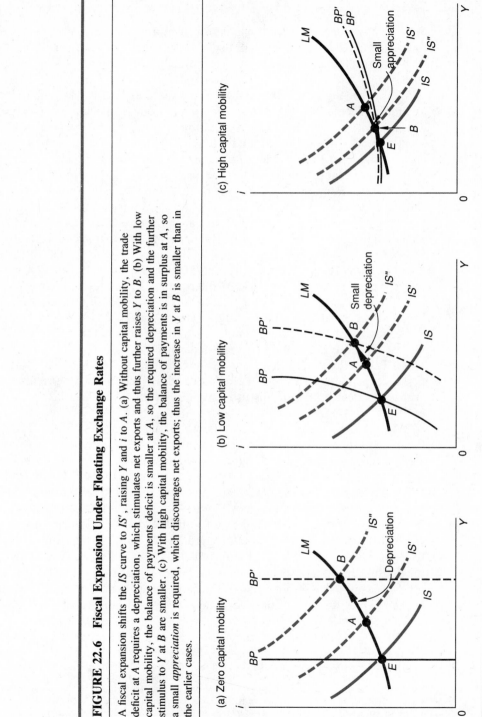

(a) Zero capital mobility

(b) Low capital mobility

(c) High capital mobility

depreciation is smaller. Thus, the rightward shift and the additional stimulus to output are not as great in Figure 22.6(b) as in 22.6(a).

With higher degrees of capital mobility comes the loss of *all* additional stimulus from floating rates. To see why, recall from Figure 22.2(c), represented by point *A* in Figure 22.6(c), that under conditions of high capital mobility, the improvement of the capital account was more than enough to offset the deterioration of the trade balance. Under fixed exchange rates, the overall balance of payments actually went into surplus. This means that under floating exchange rates, the currency will *appreciate* to clear the balance of payments, not depreciate. The effect is to discourage net exports rather than to encourage them. The *BP* and *IS* curves shift left rather than right. The curves keep shifting until the *BP* schedule catches up with the *IS-LM* intersection and all three curves meet at a point such as *B* in Figure 22.6(c). The fiscal expansion still increases income. However, the increase in income is not only less than it was under floating rates with no capital mobility, it is also less than it was under fixed exchange rates—because the foreign sector now enters negatively rather than positively.[10]

The finding that under a regime of floating exchange rates capital mobility reduces the effectiveness of fiscal policy is exactly the opposite of the case under a regime of fixed exchange rates. We saw in our discussion of the monetary approach to the balance of payments that the higher the degree of capital mobility, the faster money comes into the country through the balance of payments to augment the effect of the fiscal expansion on income.

At *B* the economy is running a continuing trade deficit, financed by the capital inflow attracted by the higher interest rate. This is an equilibrium situation. There is no automatic monetary mechanism of adjustment, because under floating exchange rates there are no changes in reserves, and so the question of whether the central bank sterilizes never even arises. (As much "money" flows in through the capital account surplus as flows out through the current account deficit.)

Effects of the U.S. Budget Deficit in the 1980s

The perfect illustration of this model is the great U.S. fiscal expansion undertaken by the Reagan Administration in the form of the 1981–1983 tax cuts and simultaneous increases in the defense spending. Between 1980 and 1985 there was an increase in the structural budget deficit equal to 3 percent of GNP. ("Structural" means that the increase in the deficit was not due to lower tax receipts arising from a fall in income, as happened in the 1981–1982 or 1990–1991 recessions.) As was mentioned previously, this fiscal expansion was unusual not only in its magnitude but also in that it was not at all accommodated by monetary policy. The Federal Reserve, having undertaken a commitment in 1979 to restrict monetary growth in order to fight inflation, allowed interest rates to rise sharply beginning in 1980. From 1979 to mid-1982, the short-

[10] How do we know that the fiscal expansion still has a positive effect on income despite the loss in net exports, under conditions of floating rates and high capital mobility? That is, how do we know that the three-curve intersection at *B* takes place to the right of the starting point, *E*? If the currency appreciation were so great that the *IS* curve shifted as far back to the left as *E*, then the balance of payments would pass into deficit, because *i* and *Y* would be unchanged, leaving only the negative effect of the appreciation. For the overall balance of payments to be in equilibrium, the appreciation has to stop while there is still some surplus left on the capital account, that is, with *i* higher than at the starting point.

term interest rate rose by 2 percent and the long-term interest rate by 5 percent. Just as the model predicts, the higher interest rates attracted a large capital inflow from abroad and caused a large appreciation of the dollar.

International investors care not only about nominal interest rates in various currencies but also about expectations as to how much the currency is going to be worth in the future. Chapter 24 will add expectations to the model. For now, it is important to realize that a domestic firm's decision whether or not to undertake investment in plant and equipment depends not on the nominal interest rate, but on the *real* interest rate, that is, the interest rate adjusted for expected inflation. Nominal interest rates began to decline in mid-1982, when the Federal Reserve began to ease up slightly on monetary growth (in response to the severity of the 1981–1982 recession and to the international debt crisis that had been in part precipitated by the earlier monetary contraction). Yet expected inflation was declining more rapidly. In other words, real interest rates remained high after 1982.[11] The increase in U.S. real interest rates helps explain why, despite the fact that the 1981 tax bill was especially favorable to corporate investment (and despite the strength of the 1983–1984 recovery), investment in the rest of the 1980s did not quite reattain the share of GNP that it had held in the 1970s. To introduce into the *IS* curve the effects of expected inflation and corporate taxation on investment, it would be necessary to redefine the vertical axis to show the complete after-tax real cost of funds to the firm, rather than the simple interest rate, *i*, that we have been using.

Between 1980 and 1984 the dollar appreciated by 58 percent against a weighted average of other currencies.[12] As we saw in the discussion of the J-curve in Chapter 17, a change in the exchange rate actually takes several years to have its effect on net exports. The U.S. trade deficit hit the then-record level of $67 billion in 1983, reached $113 billion in 1984, and continued to mount steadily thereafter. Imports, in particular, increased rapidly. Part of the increase in imports could be explained by the growth in income in these years, but more of it was due to the high value of the dollar that made other countries' goods cheaper than U.S. goods.[13] Both the income effect and the exchange rate effect are precisely what is predicted from a fiscal expansion in Figure 22.6(c).

There is a neat way of summing up the effects of a fiscal expansion under modern conditions: In addition to crowding out investment (and other components of ex-

---

[11] Real interest rates among other major industrialized countries rose also, but not by as much, on average, as in the United States. Various measures of the long-term real interest differential show a peak in 1984 of about 4 percent, as compared to approximately zero in 1980.

[12] This is the appreciation in nominal terms. The appreciation in real terms was 52 percent. (The source is the Federal Reserve Board's index with multilateral trade weights. CPIs are used for the real exchange rate.) The small difference between these numbers means that very little of the change in the exchange rate was offset by different changes in the countries' price levels. In other words, the "Keynesian assumption" appears justified: To analyze the effects of changes in policy, prices can be taken as given in the relatively short run.

[13] There were other factors behind the U.S. trade deficit as well. The countries of Latin America, which had previously been some of the best customers for U.S. exports, were hit by the international debt crisis in 1982. They were then forced to cut back sharply on their trade deficits, in fact turning them into trade surpluses to earn the foreign exchange to help service their debts. As a result, the United States lost $20 billion in net exports to Latin America between 1981 and 1983.

TABLE 22.1 Net Savings and Investment Flows as a Percentage of GNP (NIPA Basis)

	Net Private Domestic Savings (1)	State and Local Surplus (2)	Federal Deficit (3)	Net Domestic Savings Available for Domestic Investment: (1) + (2) − (3) (4)	Net Private Domestic Investment (5)	Net Domestic Savings Shortfall (5) − (4) = Net Capital Inflows (6)
1950–1959	7.5	−0.2	−0.1	7.8	7.5	−0.3
1960–1969	8.1	0.0	0.3	7.8	7.1	−0.7
1970–1979	8.1	0.8	1.7	7.2	6.9	−0.3
1980	6.4	1.0	2.2	5.2	4.9	−0.3
1981	6.6	1.1	2.1	5.6	5.5	−0.1
1982	5.5	1.1	4.6	2.0	2.0	0.0
1983	5.7	1.4	5.2	1.9	3.1	1.2
1984	6.8	1.7	4.5	4.0	6.6	2.6
1985	5.7	1.6	4.9	2.4	5.1	2.7
1986	5.3	1.4	4.8	1.9	5.0	3.4
1987	4.1	1.2	3.5	1.8	5.1	3.5
1988	4.6	1.0	3.0	2.6	4.8	2.4
1989	4.3	0.9	2.6	2.6	4.2	1.9
1990	4.6	0.5	3.0	2.1	3.8	1.5
1991	4.6	0.5	3.5	1.8	1.8	0.0

Source: Department of Commerce and author's calculations

penditure coming from the domestic sector) via higher interest rates, the fiscal expansion also crowds out net exports (expenditure coming from the international sector) via a higher value of the currency.

The general principle can be seen from the national saving identity, derived in Chapter 18:

$$S + T - G \equiv I + X - M$$

Private saving, S, plus public saving, $T - G$, is equal to investment in the stock of physical capital I, plus the accumulation of claims against foreigners through the trade balance, $X - M$. As a matter of accounting, this equation must hold at all times, regardless of how its components are determined and what happens to interest rates and exchange rates. Table 22.1 presents the relevant numbers for recent U.S. history. The federal budget deficit, shown in column 3, climbed to a plateau of about 5 percent of GNP during 1983–1986: $T - G$ in the national saving equation has been negative. The private saving rate (column 1) did not rise. Thus, there was barely enough private saving, S, to finance the budget deficit. In other words, total net national saving (shown in column 4) fell from over 7 percent of GNP in the 1970s, to 2 percent of GNP in the late 1980s.[14] This low level of domestically available funds is not enough to finance

[14] When the term "net" is applied to national saving, investment, or output, it means net of the depreciation of the capital stock. The country must devote a certain amount of saving and investment each year to replacing worn-out old machines and buildings before it can start increasing the size of the capital stock.

investment in plant and equipment, let alone to undertake any net lending overseas.

The national saving identity says that as a simple matter of arithmetic, when there is a fall in national saving, there must be a fall in investment, I, a fall in the trade balance, $X - M$, which is also an increase in borrowing from abroad, or some combination of the two. In a closed economy, all the burden of the crowding out caused by a fiscal expansion must fall on investment. This principle had some relevance for the United States in earlier decades and has some relevance for some other countries even today. However, as a consequence of the high degree of capital mobility in the United States in the 1980s, much of the burden of the crowding out instead fell on net exports,[15] as is seen in Table 22.1. Investment in the late 1980s averaged about 5 percent of GNP, down about 2 percentage points from level of the 1970s (though up from the depths of the recession years 1980–1982). This means that the 5 point fall in national saving was reflected partly as a fall in investment, but more as a net capital inflow.

A trade deficit, when viewed from its more flattering profile, is the same thing as a capital inflow. It makes sense that a decision by the government to run a deficit, that is, to borrow—if it is not offset by the actions of domestic residents—is reflected in a deficit for the country as a whole, that is, national borrowing from the rest of the world. Of the large quantities of treasury securities that the government has to sell to finance the budget deficit, the share sold directly to foreigners is still less than the share sold to domestic residents. In an economic sense, however, it is as if foreign investors are financing the U.S. budget deficit. It makes no difference whether foreigners lend money to Americans who then buy treasury securities or whether the foreigners buy the securities directly from the treasury. Alternatively, one could think of foreigners as financing U.S. investment in plant and equipment. This is investment that would otherwise be financed out of the U.S. pool of saving, if the budget deficit were not devouring so much of the available funds.

Imagine that the capital inflow had somehow been prevented. Imagine, for example, that the government had been willing and able to impose effective capital controls (which is unlikely). Then the trade deficit would not have deteriorated so much, because the dollar would not have appreciated so much in 1981–1985. This sounds like a favorable effect; but investment would have been at a lower level, because interest rates would have risen even more than they in fact did. The burden of crowding out simply would have been redistributed from net exports to investment. Those producers that rely on foreign customers would have been helped, but sectors sensitive to interest rates would have been hurt. Examples of industries sensitive to net foreign demand include agriculture, semiconductors, textiles, and scientific instruments. An example of an industry that is sensitive to interest rates is construction. Many industries, such as autos, aircraft, earth-moving equipment, and other capital goods, are sensitive to both, and so would lose either way.

---

[15] The last section of the appendix to this chapter discusses the "saving-retention" coefficient, which answers the question, "For a given exogenous change in national saving, how much is retained domestically, that is, reflected as a change in investment, rather than as a change in borrowing from abroad?"

Monetary Expansion and Capital Mobility under Floating Rates

We will now consider the effects of a monetary expansion, for progressively greater degrees of capital mobility. We have already seen what happens with a given exchange rate when an increase in the money supply shifts the *LM* curve to the right: The higher level of income leads to a trade deficit and also to a deficit in the overall balance of payments. The equilibrium was represented by point *M* in Figure 22.3(a), which becomes point *A* in Figure 22.7(a). When the experiment is translated to the case of floating rates, the currency must depreciate to eliminate the deficit. The depreciation stimulates net exports (relative to what they would be at point *A*, not necessarily relative to what they were at point *E*, before the expansion raised income and therefore imports). It thus shifts the *BP* curve and *IS* curve to the right, until all three curves intersect at the same point. With no capital mobility, this is point *B* in Figure 22.7(a). The monetary expansion stimulates income by more under floating exchange rates than under fixed exchange rates. (Point *B* lies to the right of *A*.)

What difference does the introduction of capital mobility make in this context? Figure 22.7(b) illustrates the case of low capital mobility. Again there is a deficit at a given exchange rate, point *A*, implying a depreciation, a rightward shift of the *BP* and *IS* curves, and further stimulus to income. The only difference arises from the capital outflow in response to the fall of the domestic interest rate below the foreign level. The overall balance of payments at point *B* in Figure 22.7(b) is larger than in Figure 22.7(a), where there was only a deficit on the *trade* account to contend with. This implies that the depreciation of the currency must be even greater to equilibrate the balance of payments. Thus, the stimulus to net exports, and therefore to income, is even greater. Indeed, the depreciation is sufficiently great that the trade balance is in surplus at *B* despite the increase in income. The surplus on the current account is just offset by the deficit on the capital account resulting because the interest rate at *B* is still lower than it was at the starting point, *E*. The "bottom line" is that capital mobility enhances the effectiveness of monetary policy. In addition to the usual route of stimulating investment and other components of domestic demand via lower interest rates, the expansion also stimulates foreign demand via a lower value for the currency.[16]

Now we progress to the case of high capital mobility in Figure 22.7(c). The story is similar. However, there is an even greater capital outflow in response to the same decline in the interest rate. Thus, the depreciation of the currency and the further stimulus to net exports, and therefore to income at *B*, are even greater than in the case of lower capital mobility. Notice that as a consequence of the high degree of capital mobility, the interest rate does not fall as far below the foreign interest rate as before. This means that the stimulus to investment is not as large as before. When

---

[16] This Mundell-Fleming result that a monetary expansion gives rise to a capital outflow (and corresponding current account surplus) is based on the assumption that capital flows depend only on interest rate differentials. When capital flows are allowed to depend also on exchange rate expectations, as in Chapter 24, this result need not hold.

FIGURE 22.7 Monetary Expansion under Floating Rates

A monetary expansion shifts the *LM* curve out to *LM'*, lowering *i* and raising *Y*. (a) Even without capital mobility, the trade deficit at *A* requires a depreciation, which further raises *Y* at *B*. (b) With some capital mobility, the balance of payments deficit is larger at *A*; this requires a larger depreciation, which raises *Y* even further at *B*. (c) With high capital mobility, the deficit at *A*, depreciation, and stimulus at *B* are all larger still.

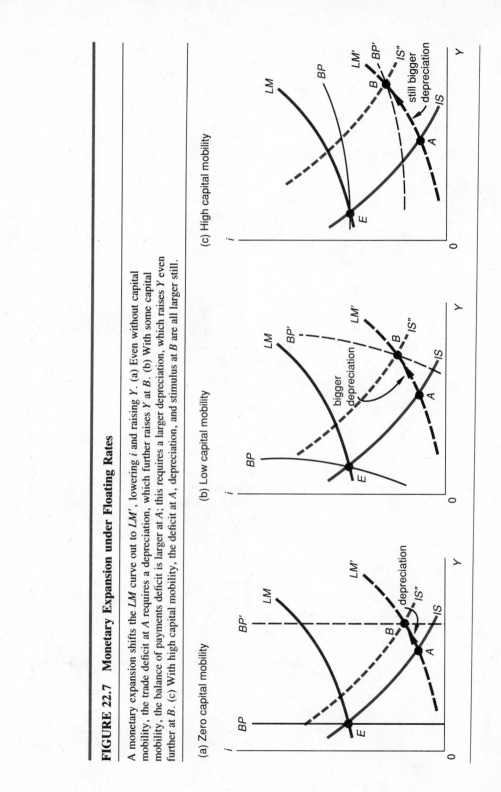

(a) Zero capital mobility

(b) Low capital mobility

(c) High capital mobility

capital mobility is sufficiently high, more of the stimulus comes from net exports than from domestic demand.[17]

The main result is that the effectiveness of monetary policy at changing output is enhanced the greater the degree of capital mobility. Notice that this is just the opposite of the result obtained from the monetary approach to the balance of payments under fixed exchange rates. When the central bank chooses to keep the exchange rate fixed, high capital mobility means that any given expansion in domestic credit simply flows out through the balance of payments that much faster. When the country chooses to keep the money supply fixed and instead to let the exchange rate adjust, high capital mobility means that any given expansion has an extra impact via the depreciation. This is one reason that a country where the financial markets become more developed and more integrated into world markets may opt to switch from a fixed exchange rate regime to a floating rate, assuming that it wishes to be able to pursue an independent monetary policy.

The results for monetary policy are also just the opposite of the results for fiscal policy. The key to the differences is the reaction of the interest rate. A monetary expansion operates by *lowering* the interest rate, causing capital to *flow out* of the country. This effect subtracts from the income expansion in the case of fixed rates but enhances it when the exchange rate is allowed to change. A fiscal expansion, on the other hand, operates by *raising* the interest rate, and attracting a capital *inflow*. Thus, the effects are the opposite of those achieved with monetary policy: They add to the income expansion in the case of fixed rates and subtract from it in the case of floating rates.

The way that changes in monetary policy operate in a modern floating-rate mobile-capital economy is illustrated by developments at the end of the 1970s in the United States. By 1979, public exasperation with inflation had become sufficiently great that there was something of a consensus that the top priority should be bringing inflation down, even if the cost might be a recession. The Federal Reserve Board under Chairman Paul Volcker tightened monetary policy. Interest rates shot up in 1980, and the contractionary effects in investment and other components of spending were soon felt in the 1980 and 1981–1982 recessions. The unemployment rate reached a postwar high in 1982. One reason why the recession was more severe than many expected (and why the inflation rate came down more rapidly than many expected) was the strong appreciation of the dollar that began in 1980. This chapter has already discussed the role of the fiscal expansion in driving up interest rates and the value of the dollar in the early 1980s. However, many observers think that the monetary contraction was the origin of the 1980–1982 phase of this process. As in the model just developed, a leftward shift of the LM curve raises interest rates, attracts capital from abroad, appreciates the currency, and worsens the trade balance. Thus, the brunt of the recession is borne by exchange-rate-sensitive industries as well as by interest-rate-sensitive industries.

---

[17] The rightward shifts of the BP and IS curves in Figure 22.7(c) are so great that one might wonder whether the interest rate, i, at B is still lower than at E. The answer is that it is. To see this, imagine what would happen if i remained at its original level. Then the capital account, KA, would still be at its original level, which implies that the trade balance, TB, would still be at its original level ($TB = -KA$). So would investment, I. Yet total output, Y, has increased, which cannot happen if there is no reason for any of its components, $C + I + G + X - M$, to increase. To stimulate I and $X - M$, i must be lower.

The expansion that began in 1983 eventually returned the economy to the same position in the business cycle as before the recession. Because its origin was a fiscal expansion, real interest rates remained high. Comparing 1985 to 1980, the net policy change was neither contraction nor expansion, but rather a shift in the *mix* of monetary and fiscal policy. The mid-1980s mix implied high real interest rates and a high real value for the dollar. As a consequence, the composition of GNP featured higher shares for C and G at the expense of lower shares for I and $X - M$.[18]

A similar sequence of events occurred in the United Kingdom. When Margaret Thatcher took office in 1979, she imposed tight monetary targets. The pound appreciated sharply (though this may have been due to an increase in North Sea oil wealth as much as to the tight money policy). British firms that had been dependent on export demand or that competed directly with imports, particularly in manufacturing, were hit very hard as a consequence of their loss in international competitiveness. The resulting decline in this sector was labeled "de-industrialization." Unemployment rose steadily (from 5 percent in 1979 to 12 percent in 1982), though, as in the United States, the benefit of lower inflation did eventually arrive. The point, again, is that exchange rate effects enhance the effects of changes in monetary policy, for better or for worse.[19]

22.3 POLICY UNDER PERFECT CAPITAL MOBILITY

Chapter 21 showed that transaction costs, capital controls, and other barriers that can separate international investors from the portfolios they wish to hold are close to negligible among most of the large industrialized countries. Thus the degree of capital mobility is not just high, but close to infinite. The parameter k in Equation 22.1, the responsiveness of capital flows to rates of return, is close to infinite. This case is the natural limit of the logical progression—zero, low, and high capital mobility—that we have been considering in this chapter. One advantage of studying the polar case of perfect capital mobility is that the relative effects of monetary policy, as compared to fiscal policy, are sharpened; the results stand out quite clearly, whereas in the case of partial capital mobility the graphs can be messy, as we have seen.

Recall that the slope of the BP curve is m/k. As k goes to infinity, the slope goes to zero. In other words, the BP curve is flat. The flat line is drawn at the level of the interest rate, i, that is equal to the world rate, i^*. If i were to rise above i^*, even for just an instant, the differential would immediately attract a very large capital inflow.

[18] Given total GNP, what would be the point in altering its composition through such a monetary/fiscal policy mix? An advantage is that the strong dollar, by lowering import prices, helped to bring inflation down faster than would otherwise have been the case. But there are a number of disadvantages, especially in terms of longer-run consequences. In the first place, what went up (the dollar) eventually had to come back down (for reasons that will be discussed in a later chapter); the likely consequence is that inflation would go back up again. Second, when investment is crowded out today, it means that the capital stock will be lower in the future, and so real growth is lower in the long run. Third, net exports are crowded out. This gives rise to strong protectionist pressures from the adversely affected sectors, which can have damaging effects on the efficiency of the economy. Furthermore, that the country runs a current account deficit means that it is borrowing from abroad. As a result, the country will be poorer in the future and at the mercy of foreign creditors.

[19] British macroeconomic policy in 1979–1981 is described by Willem Buiter and Marcus Miller in "Changing the Rules: Economic Consequences of the Thatcher Regime," *Brookings Papers on Economic Activity*, 2 (1983): 305–379.

Portfolio Effect
rearrange

All foreign investors would want to acquire the better-paying assets in the home country rather than those in their own country, while domestic residents would seek to borrow at the cheaper rate abroad. Such capital flows will arbitrage away the interest differential, that is, will keep it from opening up to begin with. Thus, another way of saying that k is infinite is to say that $i - i^*$ is always zero, as is clear from Equation 22.5.

Fixed Exchange Rates and Perfect Capital Mobility

We return briefly to the case of fixed rates, beginning with a fiscal expansion. In Figure 22.8(a) the *IS* curve once again shifts right. The increase in the demand for money drives up the interest rate to point *A* as usual, attracting a large capital inflow. More precisely, *if* the economy could remain at *A*, then the higher interest rate *would* attract a capital inflow, and the central bank would have to make the usual decision under fixed rates whether to sterilize it. The potential inflow, however, is so large that the central bank has no option. There is no limit to the quantity of foreign exchange it would have to buy up in return for domestic currency until it exhausted its holdings of domestic assets. (In the case of a fiscal contraction that lowers the interest rate, there is no limit to the quantity of foreign exchange that the central bank would have to supply in exchange for domestic currency until it exhausted its holdings of foreign assets.) If the central bank does not wish to abandon the exchange rate peg, it will have to abandon its money supply target: It must allow the inflow of reserves through the capital account to swell the domestic money supply. The increase in the money supply will shift the *LM* curve to the right, to *LM''* in Figure 22.8(a). The shift must be great enough that the intersection with the new *IS'* curve, at point *B*, is on the *BP* line. Only then will the interest rate, i, be back at the level i^*, as it must if the capital inflow is not to be infinite.

Income is much higher at point *B* than at *A*.[20] The case of perfect capital mobility is the limit of the progression of cases illustrated in Figures 22.2(a), 22.2(b), and 22.2(c). With high capital mobility, the effect of the fiscal expansion on income is supplemented by an increase in the money supply in the long run. With infinite capital mobility, the effect is even stronger in that (1) the money flows in instantaneously, whether the central bank attempts to sterilize it or not, and (2) the increase in the money supply is greater.

We now consider a monetary expansion. In Figure 22.8(c), the increase in the money supply shifts the *LM* curve rightward to *LM'* and drives down the interest rate. The lower interest rate at point *A* gives rise to a capital outflow. More precisely, the interest rate *would* fall if the economy could remain at point *A*. Yet there is no limit to the potential magnitude of the capital outflow. If the central bank tries to maintain both its exchange rate target and its new money supply target, it will rapidly exhaust its entire stock of foreign exchange reserves. If it chooses to stay with the

---

[20] Indeed, the increase in income is the full Keynesian multiplier effect, without any of the usual crowding out from a higher interest rate. An increase in government spending, $\Delta \overline{G}$, always shifts the *IS* curve to the right by $\Delta \overline{G}/(s + m)$. Usually the final effect on income is less because the economy is at a point like *A*. However, when capital mobility is so high that it prevents the interest rate from rising, income increases by the full amount of the rightward shift. In this case, international capital flows have the same effect as an automatically accommodating monetary policy.

FIGURE 22.8   Perfect Capital Mobility

When capital mobility ties i to the world interest rate, i^*, the BP schedule is flat. The potentially infinite capital inflow that would result from a fiscal expansion to A means that (a) under fixed rates, the reserve inflow must be large enough to shift the LM curve instantaneously all the way out to B, or (b) under floating rates, the appreciation must be large enough to return the IS curve all the way back to E. The potentially infinite capital outflow that would result from a monetary expansion means that (c) under fixed rates, the reserve outflow must be large enough to return the LM curve all the way back to E, or (d) under floating rates, the depreciation must be large enough to shift the IS curve all the way out to B.

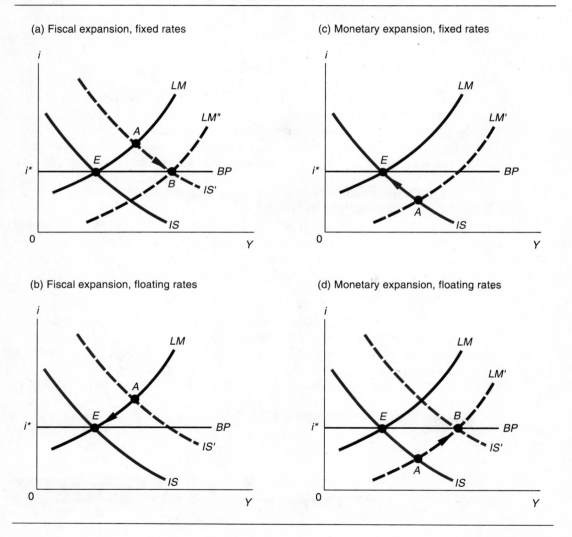

(a) Fiscal expansion, fixed rates

(c) Monetary expansion, fixed rates

(b) Fiscal expansion, floating rates

(d) Monetary expansion, floating rates

fixed exchange rate, it will be forced to give up its money supply target and allow the outflow of reserves through the capital account to reduce the money supply. The reduction in the money supply immediately shifts the LM curve back to the left until it returns to the original LM curve. Only when the money supply is back to its pre-expansion level at point E will the interest rate have returned to the world level; only then will domestic investors stop pumping capital out of the country. At point E there is no effect on income at all.

Again, this case is the limit in the progression illustrated in Figures 22.3(a), 22.3(b), and 22.3(c). Under the monetary approach to the balance of payments, any increase in the money supply eventually flows back out through the balance of payments, when the central bank decides to give up the attempt to sterilize the outflow, with the process proceeding more rapidly the higher the degree of capital mobility. In the case of perfect capital mobility, the central bank could not sterilize the outflow even if it wanted to and even in the short run. Thus, the expansion in income does not actually take place even in the short run. Point A is purely a hypothetical location.

Even though Figure 22.8(c) looks precisely the same after the monetary expansion as before, one detail has changed. Recall that the total money supply is given by international reserves plus domestic credit. When the central bank increased the money supply, it did so by increasing the supply of domestic credit. (In the United States, this would normally mean purchasing Treasury securities.) When the money flowed back out, it was international reserves that were lost. Thus, the *composition* of the monetary base has been permanently altered, as between domestic credit and international reserves.

Notice incidentally that besides being flat, the BP schedule has a subtly different interpretation under perfect capital mobility, as does its algebraic representation, Equation 22.5. When capital mobility is less than complete, the BP schedule is the set of points for which the balance of payments is zero. When capital mobility is infinite, however, the BP schedule is the set of points for which the balance of payments is neither plus infinity nor minus infinity. This is another way of saying that the economy must always be on the BP schedule. It also means that, *given* that the economy is on the schedule, neither the net capital flow nor the overall balance of payments can be determined. They will not necessarily be zero.

Our conclusions are quite striking. In a regime of fixed exchange rates, fiscal policy reaches its peak effectiveness under perfect capital mobility, but monetary policy *loses* all effectiveness under perfect capital mobility. In both cases, the key to the conclusion is that potentially infinite capital flows prevent the interest rate from deviating from the world level. In both cases, the IS curve alone determines the level of income; attempts to shift the LM curve by increasing domestic credit have no effect because the money simply flows out of the country as fast as it is created.

The Example of European Monetary Integration

There follows from our results a simple rule applicable to programs of economic integration like that currently being undertaken by the countries of Europe. *Of fixed exchange rates, financial openness, and monetary independence, a country can choose to have any two, but it cannot choose all three.* The European Monetary System was formed in 1979 by Germany, France, Italy, and other members of the European Economic Community seeking to stabilize their exchange rates. Initially, France and Italy retained a degree of ability to use monetary policy independently. This independence was not entirely inconsistent with exchange rate stability because they retained capital controls. In the late 1980s, as we have seen, France and Italy removed those controls. Simultaneously, they have sought to achieve greater exchange rate stability. Current plans call for renouncing exchange rate realignments (the discrete changes in the mid-point of the range that occurred periodically from 1979 to 1987), narrowing the margins (which have been at plus or minus $2\frac{1}{4}$ percent), and eventually adopting a single currency (the ECU) by 1999.

This combination of fixed exchange rates and financial integration will put European countries in the category of economy described by Figure 22.8(c). We have seen that under these conditions, with both the exchange rate and the interest rate tied down, monetary policy is powerless to affect the level of economic activity within the country. The lesson is that France, Italy, and the other individual countries of Europe had better be prepared politically for the loss of their monetary independence, or the plan for exchange rate fixity with full financial integration will not be successful.

European politicians find the principle of economic integration very attractive. In December 1991, an EC summit meeting at Maastricht in the Netherlands affirmed the members' political commitment to monetary integration. Within days of the summit, this commitment was sorely tested by a decision of the German central bank to raise interest rates. The Germans had their own reasons for tightening monetary policy (namely to head off their inflation, which had recently risen above French inflation for the first time in many years), but at a time of slowdown in worldwide economic growth, Germany's partners in the EMS would not have chosen to tighten monetary policy of their own volition and did not welcome the upward pressure that the German move placed on their interest rates. It remains to be seen whether individual European countries are truly ready politically to surrender monetary independence to the extent implied by the further moves toward integration that are planned.

Floating Exchange Rates and Perfect Capital Mobility

So far, the conclusion has been that when capital is perfectly mobile, the central bank has to abandon its money supply target *if* it does not wish to abandon its exchange rate target. What if the monetary authorities respond to the potentially limitless inflow of reserves (which comes, for example, with a fiscal expansion) by allowing the currency to appreciate? What if they respond to the potentially limitless outflow of reserves (which comes, for example, with a monetary expansion) by allowing the currency to depreciate? This is the case of floating exchange rates, with which we now conclude this taxonomy of cases. Floating rates allow the country to recapture its monetary independence despite perfect capital mobility. The *LM* curve will shift when the central bank deliberately decides to change monetary policy and *only* when it deliberately decides to do so.

Figure 22.8(b) illustrates the fiscal expansion. Again, the capital inflow that would be attracted by the higher interest rate at point *A* is infinite, but under floating rates, the currency instantly appreciates, reducing net exports and shifting the *IS* curve back to the left.[21] This is the same thing that happened with less-than-perfect capital mobility in Figure 22.6(c), but now the potential capital inflow and the appreciation of the currency are so large that the *IS* curve shifts all the way back to the starting

[21] As in the case of imperfect capital mobility, the appreciation causes the *BP* schedule, as well as the *IS* curve, to shift to the left. However, because the *BP* curve is flat, horizontal shifts make no difference.

point at E. This must be the case, so that the domestic interest rate does not exceed the world rate. It also means that there is no effect on income at all; fiscal policy loses all power under floating exchange rates. This is the ultimate extrapolation of the argument that under floating rates, the higher capital mobility, the lower the effectiveness of fiscal policy.

Even though Figure 22.8(c) looks the same after the fiscal expansion as before, it is not true that nothing at all has changed. The currency has appreciated in the meantime, which means that if the trade account was originally in balance, it is now in deficit. The trade deficit must be financed by a capital inflow for the overall balance of payments to be zero. Recall that when k is infinite, $i = i^*$ no longer implies that the capital account is necessarily zero. Rather, foreigners lend the amount necessary to finance the current account deficit. They are happy to do so, as long as the home country pays the going rate of return.

Even though total GNP has not changed, the *composition* of GNP has. The share going to net exports is smaller. The share going to government expenditure is larger—or, if the fiscal expansion took the form of a tax cut that increased households' disposable income, rather than an increase in government expenditure, then it is the share of GNP going to consumption that is larger. There is no crowding out of investment, because the interest rate has not risen. Even though crowding out caused by the fiscal expansion is 100 percent (i.e., there is no effect on total GNP), all the crowding out is now borne by the international sector.[22]

Finally, consider a monetary expansion under floating rates. When the LM curve shifts to LM', the capital outflow that would take place at point A is infinite. Yet the currency instantly depreciates, stimulating net exports, shifting the IS curve to the right, and adding to the expansion of income. This is also what happened with less-than-perfect capital mobility, but now the shift continues until the economy moves all the way to the original interest rate at point B. The effect of the monetary expansion on income is not only greater than it was under fixed exchange rates, it is also greater than it was under lesser degrees of capital mobility. Monetary policy reaches its peak effectiveness under floating rates and perfect capital mobility. One way of describing the result is in terms of the money market equilibrium condition, Equation 22.4. Normally, when there is an increase in the real money supply the interest rate falls so as to help increase the demand for money and restore equilibrium. Here, however, the interest rate is tied to the foreign interest rate; as a result, the increase in income must be so great that the increase in the transaction demand for money alone equals the increase in the money supply.

An implication is that the change in the exchange rate must be very large to generate the necessary increase in income, especially in the short run when the elasticities of export and import demand are low. This property of the model with perfect

---

[22] In practice, there are a number of reasons why even under modern conditions of highly integrated financial markets, most countries cannot borrow an unlimited amount at a given interest rate. (1) If the country is large, it will drive up the world interest rate, as we will see in Chapter 23. (2) If the currency is expected to depreciate in the future (perhaps because of a large accumulation of indebtedness to foreigners), foreign investors will demand a higher interest rate on domestic assets in compensation, as we will see in Chapter 24. (3) If foreigners are highly risk-averse and wish to diversify their portfolios, they may become reluctant to put an ever-increasing share of their wealth into domestic assets, as we will see in Chapter 25. Nevertheless, in the case of the U.S. fiscal expansion of the 1980s, the capital inflow from abroad was sufficiently large that there was very little crowding out of investment, as noted.

capital mobility is realistic, because exchange rates have been highly variable since the floating system began in 1973.

Besides the magnitude of the increase in income, a further striking result of perfect capital mobility is that the monetary expansion operates *entirely* via the international sector, that is, by depreciating the currency and stimulating net exports. *None* of the expansion comes from the usual domestic route, that is, by reducing the interest rate and stimulating investment.

To summarize the conclusions regarding perfect capital mobility, there is a neat symmetry in the results. Under fixed exchange rates, fiscal policy reaches its peak effectiveness, but monetary policy becomes completely powerless. Under floating exchange rates, by contrast, fiscal policy loses all power and it is monetary policy that reaches its peak effectiveness. Some of the results seem too strong to be taken literally. For example, it is hard to believe that a monetary expansion under floating rates has none of its effect via domestic demand. More generally, there is an obvious problem with the proposition that international capital flows force the domestic interest rate into continuous equality with the foreign interest rate. Interest rates are in fact observed to differ across countries. For example, the U.S. interest rate exceeded the German interest rate throughout the 1980s. The reverse was true in 1990–1992. How can such differentials exist if transaction costs, capital controls, and other barriers to the movement of capital across national boundaries are as low as was argued in Chapter 21? Why doesn't all the capital flow to the country paying the higher interest rate?

The answer is that when one country's interest rate is measured in dollars and the other's in, say, marks, investors will not treat the two interest rates as the same because of the likelihood of future changes in the exchange rate. If investors think that there is a danger that the dollar will depreciate in the future, then they will only be willing to hold dollar assets if the interest rate is higher than that on mark assets to compensate them for their threatened loss. Chapter 24 will introduce exchange rate expectations as a factor that enters investors' calculations in addition to interest rates. Some of our conclusions regarding the operation of monetary and fiscal policy will be modified.

Consider point *B* in Figure 22.7, where a monetary expansion has driven down both the interest rate and the value of domestic currency. We have argued that, in the absence of barriers to capital flows, this point is not an equilibrium because the domestic interest rate is lower than the foreign interest rate. This argument changes when allowance is made for investors' expectations of possible changes in the exchange rate. If investors have an expectation that domestic currency will appreciate in the future, then they may be happy at *B* holding domestic assets, despite the lower interest rate.

Why should they have an expectation of future appreciation? At *B* the currency has depreciated, perhaps considerably. If investors' expectation of the long-run or future exchange rate has not changed, then they will expect the currency to appreciate in the future because it is below that value now. Even if their expectation of the future exchange rate does change when the current rate changes, as long as it changes by less, then today's depreciation of the currency generates the expectation of a future appreciation back in the direction from which it came. If expectations are formed in this manner, then *B* can be an equilibrium after all. This makes the model developed here more realistic. The first implication of introducing expectations is that the domestic interest rate can lie below the world interest rate despite perfect capital mobility. The second is that some of the stimulus to output can come from domestic demand such as investment; it need not all come from net foreign demand such as exports. The third is that the exchange rate doesn't have to move quite as far as was previously thought, when higher output had to bear the entire burden of higher money demand.

An analogous point applies in the case of a fiscal expansion. Point B in Figure 22.6(c) could be an equilibrium, despite the fact that the interest rate is higher at home than abroad, provided investors hold the expectation that the domestic currency will depreciate in the future. Investors will indeed hold such an expectation after the currency has appreciated to get to B, provided that their expectation of the future level of the exchange rate does not change, or that it changes less than the contemporaneous level. If there is an expectation of future depreciation that is enough to compensate, then the domestic interest rate can lie above the world rate despite perfect capital mobility. A second realistic consequence is that there is now some crowding out of investment; net exports do not bear the entire burden of the crowding out, as they appeared to in Figure 22.8. A third is that total crowding out of other sectors by the fiscal expansion is less than 100 percent: There is some expansionary effect on aggregate GNP after all. A fourth implication is that the movement in the exchange rate need not be quite as large as when it had to shift the IS curve all the way back to E.

Chapter 24 will explore at greater length the determination of expectations and the role that this additional factor has in the determination of the exchange rate. The chapter will concentrate on the effects of changes in monetary policy, including not just the short-run effects on the exchange rate at a point like B in Figure 22.7 but also the effects then expected with the passage of time.[23] First, however, Chapter 23 considers what happens when the home country is large in world financial markets.

22.4 SUMMARY

This chapter showed the difference that international capital mobility in the modern world economy makes in regard to the important questions of policy-making, particularly the effects of monetary and fiscal policy. It turns out to make quite a difference.

The key assumption is that a country's capital account depends on the difference between its interest rate and foreign interest rates. We considered fixed exchange rates first. A monetary expansion leads to a balance of payments deficit, a loss in reserves, and consequently a loss over time of any expansionary effects on income as the money flows out of the country. In this case, capital mobility simply speeds up the process, as the money flows out not just through the trade account but also through the capital account. Though capital mobility changes the results in one direction in the

[23] We will see the effects of the monetary expansion as the price level adjusts over time. It will turn out that at point B in Figure 22.7, the expectation of future appreciation of the currency is precisely the correct one for investors to have. The situation is a little different for a fiscal expansion. Expected future adjustment of the price level is not sufficient for investors at point B in Figure 22.6(c) to hold an expectation of future depreciation. For that we would need to introduce expected future adjustment of the level of foreign indebtedness. Jacob Frenkel and Assaf Razin, "The Mundell-Fleming Model a Quarter Century Later: A Unified Exposition," *IMF Staff Papers*, 34(4) (December 1987): 567–620.

case of monetary policy (giving it a smaller effect on total GNP over time), it changes it in the opposite direction in the case of fiscal policy (giving it a larger effect over time). A fiscal expansion causes capital to flow into the country in response to a higher interest rate. If capital mobility is sufficiently high, then the overall balance of payments increases rather than decreases. Over time, reserves are gained rather than lost.

The implications are quite different under floating exchange rates. A monetary expansion causes a depreciation of the currency, which tends to stimulate the trade balance. The effect is greater, the higher the degree of capital mobility and thus the greater the capital outflow in response to the decline in the interest rate. When capital mobility is very high, a monetary expansion has a major effect on output, but the effect comes primarily through currency depreciation stimulating net foreign demand rather than through the traditional channel of a lower interest rate stimulating domestic demand.

Though capital mobility changes the results in one direction for the case of monetary policy (giving it a greater effect on total GNP), it changes it in the opposite direction in the case of fiscal policy (giving it a smaller effect). If capital mobility is high, the capital inflow attracted by a fiscal expansion causes the currency to appreciate, which in turn discourages net exports. The higher the degree of capital mobility is, the higher is the "crowding out" of the trade balance via a higher-valued currency—as opposed to the traditional crowding out of investment via a higher interest rate—and the smaller is the effect of the fiscal expansion on total GNP.

The switch in macroeconomic policy undertaken in the United States in the 1980s offers a good illustration of these principles. The government enacted a large fiscal expansion in the early 1980s, with the Federal Reserve keeping a firm rein on monetary policy. The result of this unprecedented shift in the monetary/fiscal policy mix was an increase in U.S. interest rates, a large capital inflow, an appreciation of the dollar (in the early 1980s), and an unprecedented U.S. trade deficit.

CHAPTER PROBLEMS

1. A country that maintains a fixed exchange rate suffers from unemployment and a balance of payments deficit. What combination of policies is appropriate?

2. A country imports wine, exports steel, and has a floating exchange rate. If it raises government spending on health care, increasing the budget deficit, how are the following four domestic interest groups affected: hospital workers, steel mills, wineries, and construction workers? How does your answer depend on the degree of international capital mobility?

3. This question refers to ten possible Keynesian small-country models.
   Interest rate fixed (e.g., accommodating monetary policy):
   (a) closed economy
   (b) open economy; fixed exchange rates
   (c) open economy; floating exchange rates
   Open economy: interest rate determined by IS-LM:
   (d) no capital mobility; fixed exchange rates; reserve flows sterilized
   (e) no capital mobility; fixed exchange rates; reserve flows not sterilized
   (f) no capital mobility; floating exchange rates
   (g) low capital mobility; floating exchange rates
   (h) high capital mobility; floating exchange rates

(i) perfect capital mobility; floating exchange rates

(j) perfect capital mobility; fixed exchange rates

The government increases expenditure. In each case, indicate under which of the two models there is a larger effect on income, and explain why (in a few words, or with a graph labeled with letters).

1) a vs. b   7) f vs. g

2) b vs. c   8) d vs. h

3) b vs. d   9) h vs. i

4) d vs. e   10) d vs. j

5) d vs. f   11) b vs. j

6) d vs. g

4. You are the Finance Minister of the country of Fuji which still has some capital controls in place. A large trading partner has undertaken a fiscal expansion, pushing its interest rate above yours and causing capital to flow from Fuji to the other country. (The interest rates are not equalized, because of the capital controls.) The authorities in the other country are unhappy with the fact that their currency has appreciated against yours and with the consequent trade deficit. They ask you to remove your capital controls, with the aim of helping their currency depreciate against yours and improving their trade balance. How do you respond?

Extra Credit

5. For this question, it will help to use linearized versions of Equations 22.2 and 22.3:

$$Y = [\overline{A} - bi + \overline{X} - \overline{M}]/(s + m)$$
$$M/P = KY - hi$$

a. A fiscal expansion is known to cause the currency to appreciate if the degree of capital mobility, k, is sufficiently high. What exactly is the necessary condition on k (in Equation 22.4) in terms of the other parameters?

b. Section 22.1 presented an economic argument as to why the YY schedule must be steeper than the BB schedule, as long as the degree of capital mobility, k, is greater than zero. The slope of the YY line is given by the increase in Y resulting from a fiscal expansion divided by the increase in Y given by a monetary expansion. The slope of the BB line is given by the decrease in BP resulting from a fiscal expansion divided by the decrease in BP resulting from a monetary expansion. Show that the ratio of the two slopes is greater than 1.

SUGGESTIONS FOR FURTHER READING

Branson, William. "Causes of Appreciation and Volatility of the Dollar," *The U.S. Dollar—Recent Developments, Outlook, and Policy Options.* (Federal Reserve Bank of Kansas City, 1985) pp. 33–53. Examines three hypotheses for the appreciation of the dollar after 1980, and favors the story of a U.S. fiscal expansion as in the model of this chapter (but with expectations, as in Chapter 24).

Cooper, Richard. "The U.S. Payments Deficit and the Strong Dollar: Policy Options," *The U.S. Dollar—Recent Developments, Outlook, and Policy Options.* (Federal Reserve Bank of

Kansas City, 1985) p. 157. Also discusses alternative explanations for the strength of the dollar in the early 1980s and the resulting trade deficit (most importantly the shift in the monetary/fiscal mix), and alternative policy responses.

Fleming, J. M. "Domestic Financial Policies under Fixed and under Floating Exchange Rates," *IMF Staff Papers* 9(3) (1962): 369–379. The complete Mundell-Fleming model succinctly developed.

Frankel, Jeffrey. "International Capital Flows and Domestic Economic Policies," in Martin Feldstein, ed.,*The United States in the World Economy*, (Chicago: University of Chicago Press 1988). Nontechnical analysis of the origins of the unprecedented U.S. inflow of capital in the 1980s, including the role of the budget deficit.

Mundell, Robert. "The International Disequilibrium System," *Kyklos* 14 (1961): 154–227. The original model under fixed exchange rates, including the role of nonsterilized reserve flows.

―――. "Capital Mobility and Stabilization Policy under Fixed and Flexible Exchange Rates," *Canadian Journal of Economics and Political Science* (November 1963): 475–485. The original model with perfect capital mobility.

Sachs, Jeffrey. "The Dollar and the Policy Mix: 1985," *Brookings Papers on Economic Activity*, 1 (1985): 117–197. The Reagan mix of an expansionary fiscal policy with a tight monetary policy and its effects, particularly in reducing inflation.

Swoboda, Alexander. "Equilibrium, Quasi-Equilibrium and Macroeconomic Policy under Fixed Exchange Rates," *Quarterly Journal of Economics* (February 1972): 162–171. A clear early explanation of the Mundell-Fleming model emphasizing the adjustment to reserve flows over time.

APPENDIX: THE THEORY OF INTERNATIONAL CAPITAL FLOWS

This chapter began with the assumption that capital flows from the low-interest-rate country to the high-interest-rate country. This assumption was used throughout the chapter (though by the end it was assumed that the degree of capital mobility was so high that interest rates are equalized). This appendix will show how the assumption is rooted in the economic theory of individual agents who optimize.

The procedure here will be that used to introduce the theory of international trade in Chapters 2 and 3: first taking supply as given and looking at trade that arises from differences in demand, and then introducing supply differences. Rather than discussing the supply and demand for goods, however, the discussion here will be concerned with the supply and demand for *bonds*.

Borrowing as Intertemporal Trade

This analysis is necessarily *intertemporal*, meaning that it concerns different periods in time. The purchase of a bond in the present period is the purchase of a claim to consumption in the future. Assume two periods: the present, period 0, and the future, period 1.

First consider an economy in which output in the two periods is fixed. Imagine, for example, a country where coconuts fall off the trees with no effort on the part of the population. Figure 22.A.1 shows the number of coconuts in period 0 on the horizontal axis and the number of coconuts in period 1 on the vertical axis. Point *A* indicates the number of coconuts that fall off the trees in the two periods.

Assume that it is possible to draw community indifference curves along which consumers

---

FIGURE 22.A.1   Borrowing from Abroad, with Fixed Output in Both Periods

The horizontal axis represents the current period, the vertical axis the future period. A represents given levels of output in the two periods. If the country is relatively impatient to consume, at B it can borrow to finance a relatively greater level of current consumption, C_0, at the expense of lower consumption, C_1, next period.

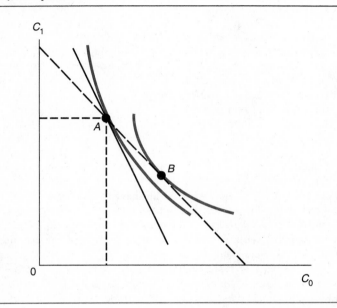

---

are indifferent between different combinations of the two kinds of consumption, in this case present and future consumption, C_0 and C_1. The slope of the indifference curve is called the intertemporal rate of substitution. It tells how many future coconuts the agent is willing to give up to get one more coconut this period. Thus, it reflects how impatient the agent is.

In autarky, where there is no possibility of trade between periods, the point of output A must also be the point of consumption. Point A is located on the graph in such a way that $C_1 > C_0$. There are more coconuts in the second period than in the first. (This is the usual case: Output, like the size of coconut trees, tends to grow over time.) The market price of C_0 in terms of C_1 is (the absolute value of) the slope of the indifference curve that passes through A. A solid line is drawn through A tangent to the indifference curve. As drawn, the slope is greater than 1 (in absolute value): Present consumption must be more expensive than future consumption in order to induce agents to wait for the next period, when more coconuts will be available.

Another way of expressing the slope is $1 + i$, where i is the market interest rate. Why is $1 + i$ the price of C_0 in terms of C_1? Because an individual saver can take $1 worth of coconuts, buy a one-period bond, receive back the principal plus interest next period, and then consume $(1 + i)$ worth of coconuts. The proposition that the marginal rate of substitution is greater than 1 is thus the same as the proposition that the interest rate i is greater than 0.

Now assume that the country is opened up to international financial markets, that it can borrow or lend at the going world interest rate. Suppose that the world interest rate, i^*, corresponds to the slope of the dotted line in Figure 22.A.1. It has been drawn less steep than the solid line, meaning that the world interest rate, i^*, is less than the domestic autarkic interest rate, i. The relative price of current consumption, while still greater than 1, is lower in the rest of the world. (Or the relative price of *future* consumption is *greater* in the rest of the world.) Foreign agents are less impatient than domestic agents, less anxious to consume today.

Domestic agents will take advantage of a lower interest rate abroad by borrowing. In terms of the figure, they will slide down the new relative price line to point *B*, where the line is tangent to a new indifference curve that represents a higher level of welfare. At point *B*, domestic agents are giving up some consumption in period 1 in exchange for more consumption in period 0. They gain from this arrangement because it assuages some of the impatience they feel at point *A*.

To illustrate with a key feature of the world economy in recent years, Japan is the perfect example of a country where people have a low rate of impatience: The Japanese have a high saving rate because they are willing to postpone consumption to the future even for a relatively low interest rate. The United States is the primary example of a country with a high rate of impatience: Americans (including the government) have a low national saving rate because they are reluctant to postpone spending, even for a relatively high interest rate.[24] In autarky, Japan would have a low interest rate and the United States a high one. When nations remove barriers to the international flow of capital (as the Japanese government did in the early 1980s), the Japanese lend and the Americans borrow.

We now consider the possibility that the quantities of coconuts produced in the two periods are not determined exogenously but are the outcome of an economic decision. In the illustration, the coconuts do not fall off the tree, but have to be picked. The decision as to how many to leave on the tree (or the decision as to how many trees to plant) is an *investment* decision, of the sort firms make when planning additions to factory capacity. Figure 22.A.2 draws a production-possibility frontier, showing the trade-off between coconuts harvested for sale this period and coconuts available next period.

The point *A* again represents autarky, determined where the indifference curve is tangent to the production-possibility frontier. Again, the graph is drawn so that the slope is relatively high at *A*. Again, the interest rate, *i*, in autarky exceeds the world interest rate, *i**, and the domestic country will borrow from abroad when it is opened up to international capital movements. Now, however, the international borrowing has two effects. The new one is that the country responds to the lower interest rate by increasing investment (planting more coconuts): Output takes place at point *B*, with a greater harvest in period 1 in exchange for a smaller harvest in period 0. The second effect is that, as before, the international borrowing allows the home country to reallocate some of its consumption from period 1 to period 0: Consumption takes place at point *C*, where consumption is higher than output in period 0 and lower than output in period 1.

To return to the example of the United States, the net capital inflow, since it began in 1982, has kept interest rates lower than they otherwise would be. The capital inflow thereby has both prevented U.S. investment from being crowded out as much as it would have otherwise been and allowed U.S. consumption to be higher than it would have otherwise been.

---

[24] If the rate of intertemporal substitution for a country like the United States is higher than for other countries, as at point *A* in the figure, this can be for either of two reasons. First, the high degree of impatience may be inherent in Americans' preferences: Their indifference curves might be steeper than the indifference curves of Japanese would be at the corresponding point in the graph. Second, even if the pattern of indifference curves is the same for all nationalities, if the U.S. economy is growing more rapidly than the Japanese economy, then the autarky point *A* will be located higher and farther to the left than it would be for the Japanese economy. Because all indifference curves are curved, it would then follow that the indifference curve at *A* would be steeper in the U.S. case. Either way, the slope of the solid line comes out higher (absolute value) than the slope of the dotted line that represents the rest of the world. (The fact that the saving rate and the rate of growth of the economy have both been so much higher in Japan than in the United States suggests strongly that the first of these two possible explanations for U.S. borrowing from Japan is the more applicable one.)

FIGURE 22.A.2   Borrowing from Abroad, with Investment

The possibility of physical investment means that there is a transformation frontier between output in the two periods. The country can divert resources to future production at B, and borrow more to finance current consumption at C, thereby realizing further welfare gains.

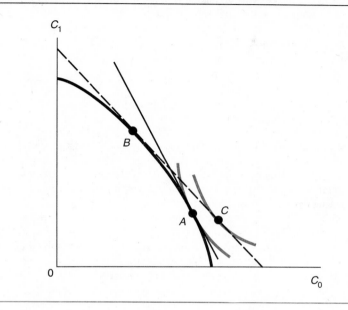

The "Debt-Neutrality" Proposition

This is perhaps the appropriate place to acknowledge a school of thought that is associated with the economist Robert Barro. The key proposition, known as "Ricardian equivalence," or "debt neutrality," states that changes in the government budget deficit have no effect on the economy. (This refers to changes in the deficit with government spending held constant, that is, to tax cuts such as those enacted in the United States in 1981–1983.) The argument runs as follows. A budget deficit implies that the government is accumulating debt. At some point in the future, the government will have to raise taxes to service or pay off that debt. If people can see far into the future, and if they intertemporally plan in an optimizing way like the consumers in Figures 22.A.1 and 22.A.2, then they will save more today, so that they or their children will have the money to pay the taxes in the future. Their spending will fall by the same amount as the budget deficit. On net, total national saving will be unchanged. The fiscal expansion will have no effect on total spending. It will not shift the *IS* curve out and thus will have none of the effects on income, the interest rate, the exchange rate, and the current account studied throughout the chapter.

Many economists, and most other observers as well, find it difficult to believe that households in reality look that far into the future when planning their consumption. A great many theoretical and econometric points have been scored on both sides of this debate. Yet perhaps the most compelling argument against the debt-neutrality proposition is precisely the massive U.S. experiment of the early 1980s. Many of those who supported the tax cuts and countered worries over the resulting budget deficits predicted that private saving would rise to offset the decline in public saving. What happened, however, was quite the reverse.

The federal budget deficit averaged less than 2 percent of GNP in the 1970s. It then rose sharply, to 5 percent of GNP in the mid-1980s, as is shown in Table 22.1. (The deficit then fell to 3 percent of GNP in the late 1980s before rising sharply in the 1990–1991 recession. The average for the decade was 3.8 percent of GNP.) Private saving as a share of GNP, far from rising to help finance the budget deficit, actually fell. As a result, the total level of net domestic saving, private plus public together, available to finance additions to the capital stock was down to about 2 percent of GNP by the late 1980s, compared to about 7 percent on average in the 1970s. If it had not been for the large-scale borrowing from abroad, investment would have had to have fallen sharply as a percentage of GNP. Events of the 1980s do not seem to have borne out the predictions of Ricardian equivalence.[25]

The "Saving-Retention" Coefficient and Measures of International Capital Mobility

If we take as an established event a fall in national saving, it is interesting to examine how the shortfall is divided between a net capital inflow—that is, a current account deficit—and a decline in investment. Alternatively, there is the more positive experiment of an increase in national saving as the result of a cut in government spending, an increase in taxes, or a rise in private saving. To what extent are the funds that are generated retained at home to finance additions to the capital stock, and to what extent do they instead go to reduce the capital inflow from abroad?

This question has been examined in a series of papers by Martin Feldstein and others inspired by him.[26] The name "saving-retention" coefficient will be used to describe the effect that an exogenous change in national saving (whether public, i.e., the budget deficit, or private) equal to 1 percent of GNP has on the country's investment, again as a percentage of GNP. The initial finding was that the coefficient for a cross-section of countries was about .9. Changes in national saving were reflected almost one-for-one as changes in investment. Feldstein considered this result surprising, in light of the existing consensus that the degree of international capital mobility was close to perfect. His logic was that perfect capital mobility implies that the domestic interest rate is tied to the foreign interest rate, as in Section 22.3. Thus, a fiscal expansion or other shortfall in national saving should be easily financed by borrowing from abroad, with no increase in the domestic interest rate and consequently no crowding out of investment. According to this logic, the saving-retention coefficient should have been zero![27]

The direct way to test statistically for capital mobility is to examine international differentials in interest rates and to see if arbitrage is able to drive them to zero. How should interest differentials be measured? We will continue to define international capital mobility as the absence of transaction costs, default risk, capital controls, risk of future capital controls, or other barriers to financial integration across political boundaries. Chapter 21 showed that

[25] A clear survey of issues regarding the theory of debt in the open economy is Douglas Purvis, "Public Sector Deficits, International Capital Movements, and the Domestic Economy," *Canadian Journal of Economics*, 18(4) (November 1985): 723–742.

[26] Martin Feldstein and Charles Horioka, "Domestic Saving and International Capital Flows," *Economic Journal* 90 (1980): 314–329. For definitions of international capital mobility and citations to other contributions to the literature, see Jeffrey Frankel, "Quantifying International Capital Mobility in the 1980s," in D. Bernheim and J. Shoven, eds., *National Saving and Economic Performance* (Chicago: University of Chicago Press, 1991).

[27] To compute the statistics correctly, it is important that the changes in national saving examined be exogenous. The estimate of the saving-retention coefficient will not be accurate if national saving and investments are highly correlated just because both are responding to some common factor. However, the coefficient appears to be high also for exogenous changes in government budgets or in private saving.

interest rate differentials covered on the forward exchange market can be used to test for perfect capital mobility in this sense. The covered differential is expressed as

$$i - i^* - fd \qquad (22.A.1)$$

where i is the domestic interest rate, i^* is the foreign interest rate, and fd is the forward discount on domestic currency. As we saw in Chapter 21, this measure of the interest differential has indeed been very small for most major industrialized countries since 1974, and especially in the 1980s.

A somewhat broader measure of the international differential is the difference in expected returns on the two countries' bonds, expressed in terms of a common currency but *not* covered for exchange rate risk on the forward exchange market. This is the *uncovered* interest differential,

$$i - i^* - \Delta s \qquad (22.A.2)$$

where Δs is the rate at which investors expect the domestic currency to depreciate against the foreign currency in the future. The uncovered differential is equal to the covered differential *plus* the exchange risk premium, defined as

$$rp = fd - \Delta s \qquad (22.A.3)$$

The risk premium is the extra expected return that investors demand in compensation for holding a currency that they perceive as riskier than others; it can be small if risk is not important (if uncertainty regarding the future exchange rate is not very large or if investors are not very risk-averse). In general, however, even if the covered differential, expression 22.A.1, is zero, the uncovered differential, 22.A.2, will not be zero because of the existence of the risk premium, Equation 22.A.3.[28]

A still broader measure of the international differential in rates of return is the *real* interest differential. It is the real interest rate, defined as the nominal interest rate adjusted for expected inflation, upon which investment in each country depends, not the nominal interest rate. The real interest differential is

$$(i - \Delta p^e) - (i^* - \Delta p^{*e}) \qquad (22.A.4)$$

where Δp^e and Δp^{*e} are defined as the domestic and foreign expected inflation rates, respectively. It is equal to the uncovered differential, Equation 22.A.2, *plus* expected real depreciation of the currency, defined as

$$\Delta s^e - \Delta p^e - (\Delta p^{*e}) \qquad (22.A.5)$$

If purchasing power parity held, then expected real depreciation would be zero and there would be no difference between Equations 22.A.4 and 22.A.2. However, as seen in Chapter 19, purchasing power parity does not in reality hold and expected real depreciation is not always zero. It follows that arbitrage could equalize interest rates across countries when they are expressed in a common currency, not only on a covered basis, but even on an uncovered basis, and yet real interest rates will not be equalized. The explanation has little to do with the integration of financial markets. Even without barriers to capital mobility, international portfolio investors have no incentive to respond to differentials in rates of return in different countries expressed in terms of purchasing power over the different countries' goods. The explanation has more to do with imperfect integration of *goods markets*, which allows expected real depreciation, Equation 22.A.5, to be nonzero and thus allows the real interest differential, Equation 22.A.4, to be nonzero.

The point is that, no matter how highly integrated financial markets are, a country's shortfall in national saving can drive its real interest rate above the world level—thus crowding out

---

[28] Chapter 25 will examine the exchange risk premium at greater length.

investment—to the extent that there is an expectation of future real depreciation of the currency. Even though covered interest differentials became very small in the 1980s, reflecting low political barriers to the movement of capital across national boundaries, currency variability remained very high.

Recent studies that update the Feldstein-Horioka statistics to include the 1980s have found a decline in the saving-retention coefficient below the .9 estimate of the 1960s and 1970s. This structural change was presumably a result of the continued reduction in Japan and elsewhere of barriers to international capital mobility in the 1980s. Yet the coefficient is still greater than 0. Return to Table 22.1 and the case examined at length in the chapter, which concerned the fall in U.S. national saving between the 1970s and the late 1980s. Although roughly two-thirds of this decline was financed by borrowing from abroad, suggesting a high degree of capital mobility, there was nonetheless some crowding out of investment as well.

This now familiar episode can be interpreted in terms of the Mundell-Fleming model (for example, point B in Figure 22.6(c), as interpreted at the very end of the chapter). The mix of tight monetary policy and loose fiscal policy in the United States shifted the IS curve to the right and the LM curve to the left; it was able to drive real interest rates above world levels and to inhibit investment. The real interest differential is entirely consistent with perfect capital mobility if one accepts that portfolio investors held expectations that the dollar would depreciate in the future.

Interdependence, Aggregate Supply, and Policy Coordination

Chapter 18 showed how floating exchange rates could insulate countries from each other's policy changes or from other disturbances. However, this insulation or independence held only under certain very special conditions—most important the absence of capital flows. This chapter will show that even with freely floating exchange rates, countries are in fact highly interdependent. What happens in the United States has important effects in Japan, or Europe, and vice versa.

Along the way other floating exchange rate results will be modified as well, such as the finding in Chapter 22 that fiscal policy was powerless in the presence of perfect capital mobility. This chapter will also explore the aggregate supply side of the economy in some detail. Yet the emphasis will be on the international transmission of disturbances through various routes. The fact that the world is so interdependent leads to a new topic: international macroeconomic policy coordination. National policy-makers may be able to do better by setting their policies cooperatively than they can when each acts independently. The chapter concludes by considering the formation of monetary unions and other ways that a country can commit itself to monetary discipline.

23.1 INTERNATIONAL TRANSMISSION OF DISTURBANCES UNDER FLOATING EXCHANGE RATES

Recall that under floating exchange rates, the overall balance of payments must sum to zero. We last considered the effect of one country's expansion on another country's economy in Chapter 18. At that point we were assuming that the net capital flow was zero. It followed that the exchange rate always adjusted automatically so as to ensure that the trade balance was zero. In a model in which the trade balance was the only channel through which one country's disturbances affected another's, floating exchange rates provided complete insulation, almost as if each country were a closed economy with no trade. In practice, substantial international synchronization of business cycles has continued since 1973 (world recession in 1974–1975, slow expansion in the late 1970s, more recession in 1980–1982, expansion again in 1983–1989, and worldwide slowdown in 1990–1992). The extent of synchronization seems to have exceeded that during the fixed exchange rate era, though this must be due in large part to the greater magnitude of commonly shared disturbances, especially supply shocks, since 1973.

This section examines the two major routes through which disturbances can penetrate through the insulation provided by floating exchange rates. The first is the presence of capital flows, introduced in Chapter 22, which allow international transmission via the trade balance. The second consists of various effects that exchange rate changes can have on national economies *other* than the effect through the trade balance.

Transmission via Capital Flows

Even when the exchange rate adjusts so that the overall sum of the trade balance plus capital account is zero, the existence of any kind of net capital flow implies that the trade balance is not zero. If one country goes into trade deficit, the change will be transmitted to the rest of the world as a trade surplus. A flow of capital from the surplus country to the deficit country finances the trade imbalance.

We now examine the two-country version of the Mundell-Fleming model of floating exchange rates introduced in Chapter 22 showing how monetary or fiscal expansion in one country is transmitted to the other. *Any* degree of capital mobility would be sufficient to establish transmission. Perfect capital mobility will be assumed here, however, in part because it gives a simpler model than partial capital mobility and in part because this assumption has accurately described the major industrialized countries in recent years. There will be no more modeling of the capital account as a finite flow response to a given interest rate differential.

The foreign country is modeled analogously to the home country. Call the home country the United States and the foreign country Europe. Figure 23.1 shows the two side by side. Recall that under perfect capital mobility, arbitrage equates the U.S. and European interest rates (omitting for now any expectation of future changes in the exchange rate): $i = i^*$. This means that the two points representing the two countries' equilibrium positions must lie on the same horizontal line. Otherwise, if one had a higher interest rate, there would be a potentially infinite demand for that country's assets, with potentially infinite borrowing in the low-interest-rate country. E and E^* represent the initial equilibrium points.

A U.S. fiscal expansion would shift the IS curve out to IS' if there were no change in the exchange rate. However, as in Chapter 22, the large capital inflow that would be attracted by the higher interest rate at point A causes the dollar to appreciate, worsening the U.S. trade balance and shifting the IS curve back to the left. Under perfect capital mobility, the appreciation of the dollar and the backward shift of the IS curve continue until the parity condition, $i = i^*$, is restored. Previous chapters have all taken i^* as exogenously fixed, with the implication that the equilibrium is back at the starting point, E. But i^* need not be exogenous, as we will now see.

FIGURE 23.1   Fiscal Expansion in a Two-Country Mundell-Fleming Model

Despite perfect capital mobility, the United States can drive up the interest rate if it is large in world capital markets. After a U.S. fiscal expansion (to A) causes the dollar to appreciate, the European IS^* curve shifts right as the U.S. IS curve shifts left. Equilibrium entails expansion both for the U.S. at B and Europe at B^*

(a) United States   (b) Europe

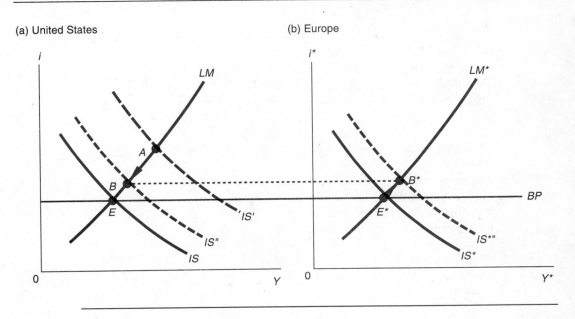

Saying that the dollar appreciates is the same as saying that the European currency depreciates. Saying that the U.S. trade balance worsens is the same as saying that the European trade balance improves. Therefore, as the U.S. IS curve shifts left, the European curve, IS^*, shifts right. The two curves will shift until their intersections with their respective LM curves occur at the same horizontal level: at points B and B^*, respectively. Only then are interest rates equalized. Each intersection lies on the country's BP curve, as floating rates imply it must, but the curve has shifted to a higher level.

Figure 23.1 shows how two of the (overly strong) results derived earlier must be modified. First, the insulation property of floating rates is undone by international capital mobility. Through the channel of the trade balance, the fiscal expansion is transmitted positively to Europe, as an increase in the demand for European output.

Furthermore, a property of fiscal expansion established in Chapter 22, that it is ineffective at raising domestic output under perfect capital mobility, is now also undone. Previously it was assumed that the home country was sufficiently small in world capital markets that it could take the foreign interest rate, i^*, as given. If the country is as large as the United States, however, then it is large enough to drive up interest rates everywhere in the world simultaneously. The fiscal expansion succeeds in raising i to the extent that it also raises i^*. Thus, it succeeds in raising Y to the extent that it also raises Y^* without violating equilibrium in the financial markets.

The large-country assumption restores effectiveness to fiscal policy despite perfect capital mobility.[1]

The U.S. fiscal expansion that generated U.S. recovery in 1983–1984 is a perfect illustration of international transmission. As was already noted, U.S. interest rates rose, attracting a capital inflow from abroad, and the dollar continued to appreciate against the European currencies and the yen. The U.S. trade deficit rose sharply, resulting in a corresponding improvement in trade balances in Europe, Japan, and almost everywhere else. The U.S. expansion thus did much to pull the rest of the world out of recession at the same time it did so domestically.

Another example is the 1990 increase in German spending in association with the absorption of the former East Germany. The higher spending drove up German interest rates, attracted a capital inflow, appreciated the mark, and in a short time changed a large German current account surplus into a deficit. Germany's trade balance loss was its trading partners' gain.

We next consider, in Figure 23.2, a U.S. monetary expansion. It would shift the LM curve out to LM' if there were no change in the exchange rate. However, as was explained previously, the large capital outflow induced by the lower interest rate at point A causes the dollar to depreciate, improving the U.S. trade balance (relative to what it would be at point A) and shifting the IS curve out to the right. Under perfect capital mobility, the dollar depreciation and the outward shift of the IS curve must continue until $i = i^*$ is restored. Previously i^* was taken as exogenously fixed, with the implication that the equilibrium was all the way out to point B in Figure 22.8(d). There was very strong stimulus to output, all coming from net foreign demand. This need no longer be the case, however. Saying that the dollar depreciates is the same as saying that the European currency appreciates. Saying that the U.S. trade balance improves is the same as saying the European trade balance worsens. Therefore, as the U.S. IS curve shifts right, the European curve, IS^*, shifts left. Again the two curves will shift until their intersections with their respective LM curves occur at the same horizontal level: at points B and B^*, respectively.

As with the fiscal expansion, two of the strong results derived earlier are overturned. First, the monetary expansion is transmitted abroad. However, the transmission is now negative, or perverse: European income *falls*, because of the lost net exports. As a result of lower transactions demand for money in Europe, i^* falls as well.

Because the U.S. monetary expansion succeeds in lowering i^*, it lowers i, as well: The United States is large in world financial markets, so it can drive down interest rates everywhere simultaneously. This allows the second new result. The monetary expansion does not cause as big a depreciation as in the small-country case of Chapter 22, so there is not as large a stimulus to net foreign demand. The lower interest rate means that some of the expansion will come from domestic demand. This is a more realistic result than when it appeared that all of the expansion had to come from a large increase in net foreign demand. The British monetary contraction that began

[1] It is the assumption of capital mobility, however, that restores transmission between countries, *regardless of their size*. Even if the home country is small, its fiscal expansion will have a positive dollar effect on the rest of the world that, though small as a proportion of foreign GNP, is significant relative to domestic GNP. Similarly, a fiscal expansion abroad will have a positive effect on the home country that is significant relative to the GNP. The original reference is Robert Mundell, "A Reply, Capital Mobility and Size," *Canadian Journal of Economics and Political Science*, 30 (1964): 421–431.

FIGURE 23.2   Monetary Expansion in a Two-Country Mundell-Fleming Model

---

After a U.S. monetary expansion (to A) causes the dollar to depreciate, the European IS^* curve shifts left as the U.S. IS curve shifts right. Equilibrium entails expansion for the U.S. at B but contraction for Europe at B^*.

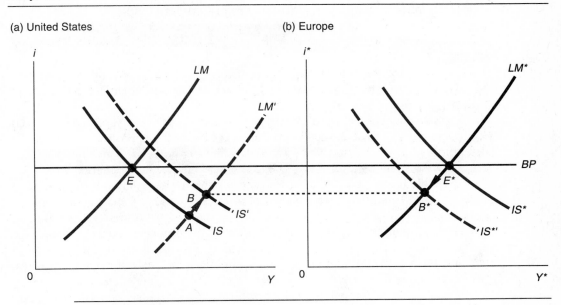

(a) United States

(b) Europe

---

in 1979 for example, though it did result in a subsequent loss of net exports as a result of the higher value of the currency, also resulted in a loss in domestic demand in construction and other sectors, as a result of the higher interest rates. The same is true of the U.S. monetary contraction of 1980–1982.

Transmission via (Non-Trade) Exchange Rate Effects

Whether or not there are international capital flows, and therefore nonzero trade balances, developments in one country can be transmitted to the other country's economy if the exchange rate has effects in addition to its effect on the trade balance. To begin with, an increase in the mark/dollar exchange rate will certainly be felt in Germany as an increase in the mark prices that Germans have to pay for imports. For there also to be an impact on German output requires some additional effect. Four possibilities are: effects on saving, money demand, prices of imported inputs, and wages. All four can result from higher import prices in Europe.

The effect on European saving is the Laursen-Metzler-Harberger effect, developed in the appendix to Chapter 18. A rise in the mark/dollar rate is an adverse shift in the terms of trade for European households: It is a fall in the purchasing power of a unit of European output over a basket of consumer goods that includes imports.

Europeans react as they would to any loss in real income, by reducing saving (for any given level of real income measured in *domestic* units) so as to smooth consumption over time. The higher level of expenditure raises real output and employment in Europe. If the increase in the mark/dollar rate originated in a U.S. fiscal expansion, then the rise in European output means that transmission is positive. If it originated in a U.S. monetary contraction, then the rise in European output means that transmission is inverse. In both cases, the Laursen-Metzler-Harberger effect reinforces the same pattern of transmission that we have just seen brought about by high capital mobility.

The next three possible exchange rate effects, however, go the other way. They are each reasons why an increase in the mark/dollar rate might lower output in Europe.

First is a possible effect via the demand for money.[2] Previous chapters have viewed P, the price level for domestically produced goods, as the appropriate variable for determining money demand. In the Mundell-Fleming model, P is fixed in the short run; thus the exchange rate does not enter the money demand equation. However, the CPI could be considered the appropriate variable for determining money demand as easily as P. If imports have a weight of α in the European CPI, then a 1 percent increase in the mark/dollar rate that raises European import prices by 1 percent will raise the CPI and reduce the real money supply by α percent. Thus, it will shift the LM curve to the left and have a contractionary effect on European output. If the dollar appreciation originated in a U.S. fiscal expansion, then the potential decrease in European output represents inverse transmission. If it originated in a U.S. monetary contraction, then it represents positive transmission. In either case, the effect via money demand is the opposite of the effect via the trade balance that appears in the standard Mundell-Fleming model. The contractionary effect in Europe was one of the arguments open to those Europeans who claimed that the U.S. policy mix of the early 1980s—tight money and a loose budget, resulting in a strong dollar—had adverse effects on European growth.

The aforementioned effects come via aggregate demand. There are two remaining effects, both of which come via aggregate supply rather than aggregate demand. If the price of oil or other imported inputs is set in dollars, then the increase in the mark/dollar rate will raise the price of the input for European firms. Finally, if European wages are indexed to the European CPI, then the increase in the mark/dollar rate will raise European wages relative to the price of goods produced in Europe. Either way, European firms find that their input costs have gone up relative to the price of the good they produce, which will cause them to cut back on output. The contractionary supply effects, like the contractionary demand effects, can reverse the transmission results of the Mundell-Fleming model and can also explain European displeasure with the strong dollar of the early 1980s. To understand fully aggregate supply effects requires a more detailed examination of the supply relationship than we have previously carried out. This is a convenient place at which to do it.

[2] William Branson and Willem Buiter, "Monetary and Fiscal Policy with Flexible Exchange Rates," in J. Bhandari and B. Putnam, eds., *Economic Interdependence and Flexible Exchange Rates* (Cambridge, MA: M.I.T. Press, 1983).

23.2 THE AGGREGATE SUPPLY RELATIONSHIP

Chapters 18 and 22 made the extreme Keynesian assumption that supply is infinitely elastic at a given price level. Chapters 19 and 20 made the extreme classical assumption that output is fixed at potential output. This section considers a more complete range of possible aggregate supply relationships, showing how fluctuations in demand are reflected in both output and prices.

To begin, we review the aggregate demand relationship familiar from introductory macroeconomics. Imagine that the price level rises for some reason (such as an oil price increase or other adverse supply shock). Then, for any given nominal money supply, M, the real money supply falls and the LM curve shifts left. There may be other contractionary effects as well. For example, holding the nominal exchange rate constant, an increase in the price level is a real appreciation that will reduce net export demand. In any case, the reduction in demand reduces output. This inverse relationship between P and Y is the downward-sloping AD curve drawn in Figure 23.3.

Now consider an exogenous increase in aggregate demand—for example, a monetary expansion. The AD curve shifts to the right. Equivalently, the curve shifts up. In fact, it can be determined precisely how much a 10 percent increase in the money supply shifts the curve vertically upward: 10 percent. Only if the increase in P were proportionate to the increase in M would Y be unchanged, because only then would M/P and the LM curve be unchanged. Therefore, for any given level of output on the aggregate supply curve, the corresponding price level is now found at a point 10 percent higher than before. That does not mean that 10 percent monetary expansion

---

FIGURE 23.3   The Aggregate Demand Curve and an Upward Shift

The AD curve slopes down because a higher P implies a lower real money supply, M/P, and therefore lower income, Y. A 10 percent increase in the money supply, M, shifts the AD curve up by 10 percent.

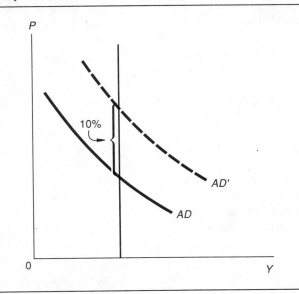

will in fact result in an immediate 10 percent increase in the price level. This depends on aggregate supply.

The aggregate supply relationship is less straightforward than the aggregate demand relationship. Five alternative aggregate supply relationships have been proposed by various economists: (1) frictionless neoclassical, (2) Keynesian, (3) Friedman-Phelps ("expectations-augmented"), (4) Lucas-Sargent-Barro ("new classical"), and (5) wage-indexation. Five may seem like a large number of alternative relationships to consider, but the following survey will place them all into a common overall framework.

The framework for these supply relationships is the following equation, which gives the level of output, Y, relative to potential output, $\overline{Y}$.

$$(Y/\overline{Y}) = (wP/W)^{\sigma} \tag{23.1}$$

The exponent σ is the elasticity of supply with respect to the price level, given the wage rate, W. In other words, it is the percentage increase in output that firms choose to supply when the price level goes up by 1 percent.

Equation 23.1 can be derived from the assumption that competitive firms choose employment so as to maximize profits. Figure 23.4(a) shows the firm's production function, giving output as a function of N, the number of workers employed. The slope, which is the marginal product of labor, is graphed in Figure 23.4(b). With the real wage on the vertical axis, this curve also represents the firm's demand for labor.[3] It slopes down because when the real wage falls, it pays firms to hire more workers. The additional workers produce more output to the extent it reduces the real wage. We thus have a very intuitive way to interpret Equation 23.1. When firms receive higher prices, relative to the cost of their variable input, the incentive provided by higher profits encourages them to produce more.

Frictionless Neoclassical Supply Relationship

In the absence of frictions in either prices or wages, labor will be fully employed and output will be fixed at potential output, $\overline{Y}$. This is the vertical aggregate supply relationship previously called "monetarist." It could be interpreted as the vertical line in Figure 23.3, if it is drawn at $Y = \overline{Y}$.

In terms of the general supply equation, the level of real wage, W/P, adjusts frictionlessly to equal w in Figure 23.4(b), so that the available labor force is fully employed (or, at least, is employed up to the natural rate of employment):

$$N = \overline{N}$$

It then follows, from the production function in Figure 23.4(a), that output, Y, is at the corresponding full-capacity level of output, Y. If in Figure 23.4(b) $W/P > w$, so that there is danger of excess supply of labor, then the wage rate falls instantly to increase the demand for labor. If $W/P < w$, so that there is danger of excess demand for labor, then the wage rate rises instantly to decrease the demand for labor and restore equilibrium. In short, the real wage adjusts so that labor demand equals labor

---

[3] The relationship among Y, N and W/P was explored in Figure 6.2. You are asked to show it more formally in Problem 5 at the end of the chapter.

FIGURE 23.4 The Demand for Labor

Firms' demand for labor, N, is a downward-sloping function of the real wage, W/P, because a profit-maximizing firm produces where the marginal product of labor, the slope of the firm's production function, is equal to the real wage.

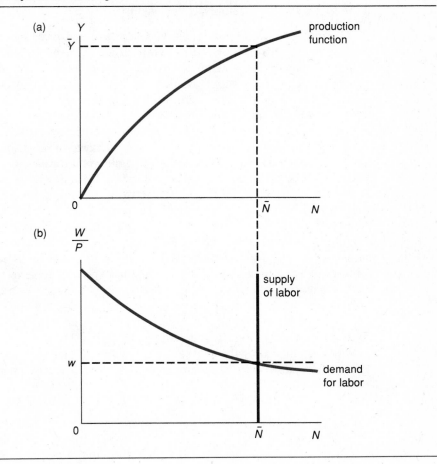

---

supply. This is why output is at the full-employment level irrespective of aggregate demand.

In the frictionless neoclassical model, any increase in aggregate demand goes entirely into prices and wages rather than into output of employment. A 10 percent monetary expansion, for example, simply raises W and P by 10 percent, as in Figure 23.3.

Those subscribing to the frictionless model—and thus believing that Y is always equal to $\overline{Y}$—recognize that output does change over time. However, they interpret all changes in Y as changes in $\overline{Y}$. The aggregate supply curve is still vertical, but its location often shifts. This view is known as "real business cycle theory." The changes in $\overline{Y}$ are attributed to changes in tastes and technology: supply shifts such as capital formation, technological change, or other changes in productivity, ϕ, and increases in the labor force, $\overline{N}$ (or in the natural rate of employment of a given labor force, due, for example, to "changes in workers' preference for leisure").[4]

Modified Keynesian Supply Relationship

The Keynesian view, of course, emphasizes wage and price rigidity, so that the aggregate supply curve is not vertical. Until now, we have been representing this view by the extreme opposite assumption, that the curve is horizontal: Firms simply set prices, $P = \overline{P}$, and then supply whatever output is demanded at that price. This may, in fact, be an adequate assumption to describe the *very* short run. To consider what happens in the slightly longer run, however, (for example, in the course of a year) means allowing the supply relationship to have some upward slope.

One convenient way of allowing the supply curve to have some upward slope is to allow goods prices to be flexible but to assume that wages, W, are predetermined. Wages may be set in contracts—for example, the outcome of bargaining between individual labor unions and firms or between a national labor federation and the government in some more centralized economies. Such contracts often last for longer than one year. They may build in future step increases in the wage rate; the important point for present purposes is that the path of W is preset and exogenous for the life of the contract. The contracts may even be implicit: Some employers (especially larger firms) establish a reputation for not trying to take advantage of their workers when the labor market is "slack" (i.e., by threatening to hire other workers at lower wages when there is a lot of unemployment) and the workers reciprocate by not taking advantage of the employer when the labor market is "tight" (i.e., by threatening to leave in order to get higher wages when there are a lot of unfilled vacancies).

Whatever the rationale, consider the wage set at some exogenous level, $W = \overline{W}$. Then the all-purpose supply relationship, Equation 23.1, becomes:

$$Y/\overline{Y} = (wP/\overline{W})^{\sigma} \qquad (23.2)$$

The curve is graphed in Figure 23.5. Say we start at the full employment point, A, where $P = \overline{W}/w$, so that $Y = \overline{Y}$. A monetary expansion or other increase in demand equal to 1 percent now goes partly into output and partly into prices, as at point B. Think of the expansion as raising the level of output chosen by firms *because* their product price, P, rises relative to the cost of their variable input, W: They choose to expand in response to the incentive of more lucrative profit margins. Equivalently, output and employment rise because the real wage has fallen.[5]

---

[4] International versions of the real business cycle approach include Richard Cantor and Nelson Mark, "The International Transmission of Real Business Cycles," *International Economic Review*, 29 (3) (August 1988): 493–507; and Alan Stockman, "Sectoral and National Aggregate Disturbances to Industrial Output in Seven European Countries," *Journal of Monetary Economics*, 21 (1988): 387–410.

[5] One possible problem with this model of supply—and with all of the other models discussed here, which assume firms to be always on their (short-run) neoclassical production functions—is that it implies that real wages and productivity are both countercyclical, that is, that they fall in economic booms and rise in recessions. The empirical evidence tends not to support this proposition. An alternative modeling approach to get an upward-sloping supply curve is to assume that prices are sticky in the very short run, but adjust partway within any given period in response to excess demand for goods.

FIGURE 23.5   Modified Keynesian Supply Curve

If the nominal wage is fixed at $\overline{W}$, then the aggregate supply curve slopes upward: An increase in the price level, P, in response to higher demand (e.g., at point B) reduces W/P and so encourages firms to raise Y. An adverse supply shift causes the curve to shift up to AS'.

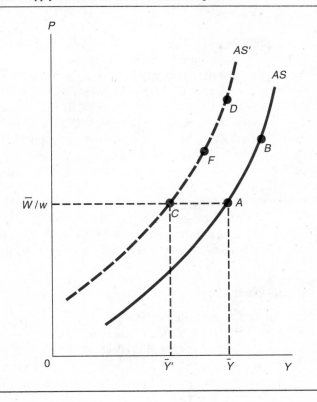

An adverse supply shock can be viewed as a fall in productivity, causing a fall in the potential output term in Equations 23.1 and 23.2 from $\overline{Y}$ to $\overline{Y}'$. A prime example is the 1973–1974 increase in world oil prices, which caused the 1974–1975 world recession. In the mid-1980s, world oil prices fell as sharply as they had risen in the preceding decade, causing an outward shift of aggregate supply and contributing importantly to the steady growth of the world economy in the 1980s. Another example, mentioned in Section 23.1, might be the increase in oil prices faced by a country whose currency has depreciated sharply against the dollar, like Germany in the early 1980s, or the decrease in oil prices faced by a country whose currency has appreciated sharply against the dollar, like Japan in the late 1980s.

An adverse supply shock shifts the aggregate supply curve left. What happens then depends on the aggregate demand policy the country chooses, which in turn depends on the country's priorities. If it wishes to avoid inflation even at the cost of a loss in output, it can restrict demand to keep the country at point C. This is essentially what Switzerland did in 1974. After a blip in inflation due to the oil price increase, price stability was immediately restored. The cost was a large recession, though most of the reduction in employment was suffered by "guest workers" from such southern European countries as Italy, Yugoslavia, and Turkey. The opposite extreme is to follow an expansionary demand policy to maintain the levels of output and employment at point D, even at the cost of a large increase in the price level. This was essentially the choice that Sweden made in 1974.[6] The intermediate possibility is to keep aggregate demand policy approximately unchanged, as at point F, suffering the adverse supply shift partly in the form of inflation and partly in the form of recession. This was the United States' policy in 1974.

The wage rate stays fixed only for the life of the contract. Notice that an increase in the wage rate will shift the aggregate supply curve up: It will take a proportionately higher P to call forth any given level of Y. If the increase in W is exogenous, for example, because of increased militancy by labor unions, then it is another example of a supply shock. W will also tend to rise endogenously—over time—if there has been an increase in demand leading to a tight labor market. A tight labor market means that unemployment is low, the number of job vacancies is unusually high, and many workers are working overtime; in other terms, $N > \overline{N}$. As W rises in response to the high demand for labor, the gradually shifting aggregate supply curve will cause P to rise as well.[7] Thus, an expansion of demand that raises prices only fractionally during the life of the contract will have a greater effect on prices thereafter. This point was neglected by Keynesians in the 1960s and leads to the next model.

Friedman-Phelps Supply Relationship

Milton Friedman and Edmund Phelps added expected inflation to the supply relationship toward the end of the 1960s. They pointed out that the wage rate, $\overline{W}$, set by workers and employers should reflect any inflation expected to take place during the life of the contract. They set $\overline{W} = wP^e$, where P^e represents the expected price level at the time the contract is signed. Substituting into Equation 23.2, the aggregate supply relationship becomes:

$$Y/\overline{Y} = (P/P^e)^\sigma \qquad (23.3)$$

The short-run AS curve always passes through the reference point ($P = P^e$ and $Y = \overline{Y}$), as is illustrated by point A in Figure 23.6. In other words, if the price level in a given period turns out to be what was expected, $P = P^e$, then the real wage will be at the correct level, w, to clear the labor market ($N = \overline{N}$), and the economy will be at full capacity ($Y = \overline{Y}$). If the price level turns out to be higher than expected, however, (for example, because of an unexpected monetary expansion) then Y will turn out higher than $\overline{Y}$; that is, the economy will turn out to be at some point along

---

[6] Sweden's attempt to expand its way out of the 1974–1975 recession resulted in large trade and budget deficits. A new political party came to power and reversed course by devaluing the Swedish krona in 1977. Sweden repeated the entire cycle after the second oil shock hit in 1979–1980.

[7] In an open economy, the rise in P may be especially rapid. A monetary expansion under floating exchange rates will cause the currency to depreciate and import prices to rise. Firms may pass on to consumers the higher prices they have to pay for oil and other imported inputs, in the same way that they pass on higher labor costs. Staff of the Federal Reserve Board estimate that a 10 percent devaluation of the dollar raises the price level by 1.5 percent over the next few years. The effect is certainly greater in smaller, more open countries.

FIGURE 23.6   Friedman-Phelps Supply Curve, in the Short and Long ⌐

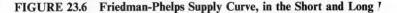

If the nominal wage is proportional to the expected price level, P^e, then AS a⸮
outward shift of demand to AD' raises output Y to B—but only in the short
update P^e to reflect the actual P; as a result W and P rise and Y falls back to⸮
output.

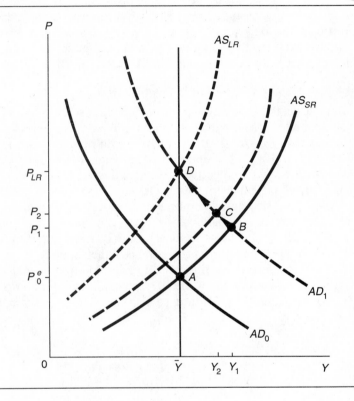

the upper portion of the AS curve. The reason firms decide to step up their level of
activity is the same as seen above: ex post, the real wage has fallen. If a monetary (or
other) expansion raises the price level unexpectedly ($P_1 > P_0^e$), then output will rise
($Y_1 > \overline{Y}$), again shown at point B. If the unexpected rise in the price level is 1 percent,
then by Equation 23.3 the rise in output is σ percent.

Along with the introduction of price expectations, the other half of the Friedman-
Phelps relationship is the proposition that expected inflation adjusts to actual inflation,
with the passage of time. In the second period, the AS curve still passes through the
reference point ($P = P^e$, $Y = \overline{Y}$), but because workers have raised their P^e in response
to the higher P observed in the previous period (P_1), this reference point is now higher
than it was before. It follows that the short-run curve has shifted up in the second
period. If demand remains at AD_1, there is a move to a point like C. More of the
higher level of aggregate demand takes the form of higher wages and prices (P_2), and
less takes the form of higher output (Y_2). It is again true in the second period that
the price level is higher than the expected level, P^e, which has two implications: (1)
Y is still above $\overline{Y}$, and (2) P^e will then have to rise still further, shifting the AS curve

up again in the third period. The logic is repeated in subsequent periods. As long as the economy is operating beyond normal full capacity, the price level keeps rising. The reason is that for Y to be greater than $\overline{Y}$, it must be true (by Equation 23.3) that the price level is higher than was expected in that period, from which it follows that workers will raise their expected price level further, and higher wages will be passed through to higher actual prices. This process of adjustment will continue until Y is restored to $\overline{Y}$, because Equation 23.3 shows that only then will $P^e = P$. In other words, in the long run the aggregate supply curve is vertical at $Y = \overline{Y}$. P, P^e, and W have all gone up by the same percentage as the money supply, so all real variables have returned to their original levels: M/P, P/P^e, W/P, and Y.

Lucas-Sargent-Barro Supply Relationship

Members of the "new classical" macroeconomic school, such as Robert Lucas, Thomas Sargent, and Robert Barro, adopted the Friedman-Phelps assumption that only unanticipated increases in the price level could raise Y above $\overline{Y}$. However, they carried further the idea that people are smart enough to adjust their expectations in an intelligent way. They objected to the idea that people could persistently underestimate (or overestimate) the price level for many consecutive periods. This reasoning led them to the conclusion that output could not exceed (or fall short of) potential output for many consecutive periods.

To understand the new classical model, consider first what would happen if people magically had "perfect foresight," that is, if they anticipated any increase in aggregate demand with precise accuracy. Then P^e would always equal P, thus Y would always equal $\overline{Y}$. In the period that the AD curve shifts up, the short-run AS curve shifts up by precisely the same distance, so that all intersections occur on the same vertical line (the same as point D in Figure 23.6, only it holds not just in the long run, but in the short run, as well).

Now we follow Lucas, Sargent, and Barro in making the assumption of "rational expectations," the phrase most often associated with this school of thought.[8] Expectations are said to be rational if the variable in question, in this case P, can differ from what was expected only by a random error term, ϵ:

$$P/P^e = 1 + \epsilon \tag{23.4}$$

When the expectational error, ϵ, is said to be random, this means that it is uncorrelated with all information available at the time the expectation was formed. The argument is that a rational worker will already have made use of such information in making his or her optimum forecast of the future price level. Sometimes ϵ will be positive and sometimes negative, but on average it will equal zero, in which case $P^e = P$.

Substituting Equation 23.4 into 23.3,

$$Y/\overline{Y} = (1 + \epsilon)^\sigma \tag{23.5}$$

---

[8] The name "new classical" is sometimes preferred, because the assumption of rational expectations means little in this context without the prior assumption that only unanticipated increases in the price level raise output.

We see that Y can sometimes deviate from $\overline{Y}$ (for example, when an unexpected monetary expansion raises P) but that this can only happen randomly, implying that the government cannot vary policy in any useful way. If monetary policy cannot have systematic effects, then it is of little use to the policy-maker. The government wants to be able to expand at certain times, such as when a recession threatens or prior to an election. Yet, if it follows systematic practices, the public will anticipate such expansions. If a recession threatens or an election approaches, P^e will go up just at the moment when the government expands. The result will be no change in P/P^e, and therefore no change in Y. Only random changes in policy can affect P/P^e, and therefore output, and they are not useful from the standpoint of policy-making.

In each of the four aggregate supply cases that we have considered so far, no special significance attaches to whether the economy is open or closed. An increase in demand for domestic goods, whether from the domestic side or the foreign side, simply goes into output or prices depending on what is assumed about the supply behavior of domestic firms. In the following case, however, a great deal depends on whether the economy is open or closed.

Indexed-Wages Supply Relationship

In some economies, particularly those with a past history of price instability, wages are automatically "indexed" to the price level. Whatever the increase in the price level during the life of the labor contract, the wage rate automatically increases by a corresponding amount, whether the increase in the price level was accurately foreseen or not. If the wage indexation is complete, then wages go up by the same percentage as the price level; in other words, a given real wage is assured. In the United States the indexation feature of a wage contract is known as a "COLA" or "Cost of Living Adjustment" clause, but these cover a relatively small fraction of the labor force, and the indexation to the CPI is usually less than 100 percent. Italy for years had its *scala mobile* ("moving stairway"), which automatically compensated much of the industrialized work force for any increases in the CPI. Chapter 20 noted that two middle-income countries, Brazil and Israel, went the furthest toward fully indexing their economies in the 1970s and early 1980s.

An important issue is the selection of the good or goods used in determining the price index to which the wage is tied. Consider what happens when wages are indexed only to the price of the domestically produced good, either because trade is not important to the economy or because the producers do not wish to accept the risk of having their wage bill fluctuate with import prices. The wage indexation equation is $W = \overline{w}P$, where $\overline{w}$ is the target real wage considered appropriate. Then Equation 23.1 becomes

$$(Y/\overline{Y}) = (w/\overline{w})^{\sigma} \tag{23.6}$$

Assuming that the target real wage is indeed the one that is appropriate to clear the labor market, $\overline{w} = w$, then the economy always operates at full employment: $N = \overline{N}$ and $Y = \overline{Y}$. When there is an increase in the money supply, it does not matter whether the increase was anticipated beforehand or not. The increase in the price level is automatically incorporated into wages by the indexation mechanism, so that there is no effect on real wages. While protecting real wages is the usual motivation behind wage indexation, there is also no effect on the demand for labor and other real magnitudes. Equation 23.6 states that output is the same regardless of the price level. In other words, indexation duplicates the vertical aggregate supply curve, though here it derives its verticality through a route quite different from the frictionless neoclassical model.

Is it a good idea for a country to adopt wage-indexation arrangements? First, they protect workers' incomes. Second, they help stabilize output and employment in the face of monetary disturbances and other disturbances to aggregate demand. Indexation automatically insulates the real economy from such disturbances.

There are also two good arguments against indexation, however. First, precisely because it makes any given level of inflation easier to live with, indexation can undermine the will to fight inflation.[9] For this reason, some high-inflation countries that undertook monetary stabilization plans in the mid-1980s reduced their degree of indexation. Italy, for example, decided to repeal the *scala mobile* law in 1984.

Second, indexation can be harmful in the face of supply disturbances. This possibility arises because the real wage frozen into the system, $\overline{w}$, may be the wrong one. Imagine that $\overline{w}$ is originally set at the level thought to guarantee employment at the natural rate, $N = \overline{N}$, but that there is subsequently an adverse shift in productivity—caused, for example, by an increase in the price of oil. Then the new real wage consistent with the natural rate of unemployment, called the "warranted" real wage, w, may turn out to be lower than $\overline{w}$. Because wage indexation prevents unemployment from lowering the real wage, there will now be unemployment above the natural rate. Furthermore, monetary or fiscal expansion won't help, because the problem is the real wage is frozen at the wrong level. (In terms of Equation 23.6, as long as $\overline{w}$ remains above the current w, then Y will be less than $\overline{Y}$.) Such a disequilibrium in the labor market is termed "classical unemployment," as opposed to "Keynesian unemployment."

Many European countries are thought to be characterized by wage-indexation and other forms of real wage rigidity to a greater extent than the United States. (In some, such as Germany, there is little in the way of formal indexation, but there is rather what might be called implicit indexation: a tacit understanding or "social compact" not to reduce real wages.) American labor markets in general operate more freely; furthermore, to the extent U.S. wages *are* rigid they are more likely to be rigid in *nominal* terms than in real terms.[10] It has been suggested that in the late 1970s the warranted real wage, w, fell behind the real wage actually embodied in European labor contracts, $\overline{w}$, and that this explains why European unemployment remained so high even long after the 1974–1975 recession. The United States increased employment by over 30 million jobs between 1974 and 1990, while Europe did not even begin to

[9] Stanley Fischer and Lawrence Summers, "Should Governments Learn to Live with Inflation?" *American Economic Review* 79 (2) (May 1989): 382–387.

[10] Japan represents yet a third arrangement. At large Japanese corporations, a substantial proportion of an employee's annual compensation takes the form of a semiannual bonus, the size of which varies depending in part on how profitable the year has been. Some observers believe that this form of "profit-sharing" keeps real wages in Japan close to the productivity of labor, and thus may account for the great stability in employment in that country.

add jobs until 1988. It has further been suggested that one reason why Germany has frequently resisted calls by the United States and some smaller countries for demand expansion is that the Germans believe that because of real wage rigidity the expansion would go entirely into prices and wages, and have no effect on output or employment.[11]

In practice, when wages are indexed, they are usually indexed to the CPI, representing the basket of goods consumed by the workers, rather than to the price of the product being produced. Thus, imports can affect indexation if they constitute a significant part of consumption. Assume, as we did earlier in the chapter, that the CPI gives a weight of α to imports and a weight of $(1 - \alpha)$ to domestically produced goods, and that the price of imports, P_M, varies proportionally with the exchange rate. Then a 1 percent increase in the mark/dollar rate raises the German CPI by α percent, even without any change in the price level, P, of goods produced in Germany. If wages are even partially indexed to the CPI, the nominal wage, W, will rise relative to P. Even though workers care about the CPI, firm managers care only about the product they are producing. They raise or lower their demand for labor depending on its marginal product and W/P, *the real wage expressed in terms of the product price*. If indexation to the CPI is complete, then even with no change in P, there will be an increase of α percent in W, and therefore in W/P. Figure 23.4(b) shows that the increase in the real wage in terms of the product price, P, lowers firms' demand for labor, because their profit margins are reduced. Figure 23.4(a) shows how the lower demand for labor translates into lower output; the aggregate supply curve shifts back. Output falls. Thus, a depreciation of the mark is contractionary for Europe.

If a German fiscal contraction is the original source of the increase in the mark/dollar rate, then the fall in German output provides an interesting result: Fiscal policy is an effective tool despite perfect capital mobility.[12] If a U.S. fiscal expansion is the original source of the increase in the mark/dollar rate, then the fall in German output indicates that the fiscal expansion has been transmitted inversely, as was noted at the end of Section 23.1.

Thus, changes in fiscal policy have real effects on an *open* indexed economy, even though they have no real effects on a *closed* indexed economy, because, when a change in fiscal policy changes the real exchange rate, the change in import prices opens up a gap between the CPI and the domestic-product price level, P. That is why even when wages are fully indexed to the CPI, a change in fiscal policy changes the real wage and has real effects.[13]

[11] Michael Bruno and Jeffrey Sachs, *Economics of Worldwide Stagflation* (Cambridge, MA: Harvard University Press, 1985), compare labor markets in Europe and the United States, and draw implications for macroeconomic policy in a global context. William Branson and Julio Rotemberg, "International Adjustment with Real Wage Rigidity," *European Economic Review* 13 (3) (May 1980): 309–342, like Sachs, argue that Europe has more real wage rigidity than the U.S. A dissenting view is held by Robert Gordon, "Back to the Future: European Unemployment Today Viewed from America in 1939," *Brookings Papers on Economic Activity*, 19 (1) (1988): 271–305.

[12] This chapter began by pointing out that in a large country a fiscal expansion affects output even if capital is perfectly mobile. The new result, however, is that if wages are indexed to the CPI, fiscal expansion also works even in a small country.

[13] Wage indexation was introduced into open-economy models by Victor Argy and Joanne Salop, "Price and Output Effects of Monetary and Fiscal Policy under Flexible Exchange Rates," *IMF Staff Papers*, 26 (1979): 224–256; F. R. Casas, "Efficient Macroeconomic Stabilization Policies under Floating Exchange Rates," *International Economic Review*, 16 (October 1975): 682–698; and Jeffrey Sachs, "Wages, Flexible Exchange Rates, and Macroeconomic Policy," *Quarterly Journal of Economics*, (1980): 731–747.

23.3 ECONOMETRIC MODELS OF THE
INTERDEPENDENT WORLD ECONOMY

Having looked at a bewildering variety of possible routes for transmission of monetary and fiscal policy, some positively affecting other countries' levels of economic activity, some affecting them negatively, we naturally might wonder which effects are likely to dominate in practice.

Economists have built a number of econometric models of the world macroeconomy, each including the major countries or blocs of countries. Often these models are quite large, in terms of the number of equations or the amount of work they require. Some of the models are built and maintained at private consulting firms, which make economic forecasts for corporate clients. Some are at agencies of national governments, or at multinational public institutions. Some are at universities.

The models also differ in their economic philosophies. Some are extremely Keynesian, showing little or no effect of a monetary expansion on prices. Others represent the "new classical" school of thought, featuring rational expectations and frictionless determination of wages and prices. Most adopt the intermediate synthesis view taken in this text. This still allows for tremendous divergence among the models, however. Even within the same overall model specification, different estimates of parameter values can have very different implications concerning issues such as whether international transmission is positive or negative.

The models are often used in simulations, in which they predict the effect of a given policy change (relative to some "baseline" predicted path for the world economy). It can be difficult to compare the results of two models, because the policy experiment being conducted may differ between the two. The simulation results from one model say that a Japanese fiscal expansion would appreciate the yen and those from another that it would depreciate the yen. One possibility is that the models truly differ, the first, for example, incorporating a high degree of capital mobility for Japan and the second a low degree. However, another possibility is that the first simulation is considering the experiment with the M1 money supply held constant, so that the fiscal expansion pushes the interest rate far up, while the second is holding something else constant (the monetary base, or even the interest rate itself), with the result that the fiscal expansion automatically leads to an accompanying increase in M1.

A project undertaken under the auspices of the Brookings Institution asked twelve leading international econometric models to perform simulations for some carefully specified macroeconomic policy experiments.[14] Tables 23.1 and 23.2 show the results in the second year after a fiscal expansion and a monetary expansion, respectively. The twelve models with their abbreviations are as follows: MCM—the Federal Reserve Board's Multi-Country Model; EC—the European Community Commission's COMPACT model; EPA—the Japanese Economic Planning Agency's model; LINK—Project Link, which put together the various models of national economies that had already been built in the respective countries; LIV—the Liverpool model of Patrick Minford, a "new classical" British economist who advised Prime Minister Margaret

[14] The model simulations are presented and evaluated in Ralph Bryant, Dale Henderson, Gerald Holtham, Peter Hooper, and Steven Symansky, eds., Washington: Brookings Institution, *Empirical Macroeconomics for Interdependent Economies*, 1988.

TABLE 23.1 Fiscal Policy: Simulation Effect in Second Year of Increase in Government Expenditure (1 Percent of GNP)

Fiscal Expansion in United States	Y	CPI	i	Currency Value	CA	CA*	i*	CPI*	Y*
		Effect in United States				Effect in Rest of OECD			
	(in percent)	(Pts.)	(in percent)	($b)	($b)	(Pts.)	(in percent)		
MCM	+1.8	+0.4	+1.7	+2.8	−16.5	+ 8.9	+0.4	+0.4	+0.7
EC[a]	+1.2	+0.6	+1.5	+0.6	−11.6	+ 6.6	+0.3	+0.2	+0.3
EPA[b]	+1.7	+0.9	+2.2	+1.9	−20.5	+ 9.3	+0.5	+0.3	+0.9
LINK	+1.2	+0.5	+0.2	−0.1	− 6.4	+ 1.9	NA	−0.0	+0.1
LIVERPOOL	+0.6	+0.2	+0.4	+1.0	− 7.0	+ 3.4	+0.1	+0.6	−0.0
MSG	+0.9	−0.1	+0.9	+3.2	−21.6	+22.7	+1.0	+0.5	+0.3
MINIMOD	+1.0	+0.3	+1.1	+1.0	− 8.5	+ 5.5	+0.2	+0.1	+0.3
OECD	+1.1	+0.6	+1.7	+0.4	−14.2	+11.4	+0.7	+0.3	+0.4
TAYLOR[c]	+0.6	+0.5	+0.3	+4.0	NA	NA	+0.2	+0.4	+0.4
WHARTON	+1.4	+0.3	+1.1	−2.1	−15.4	+ 5.3	+0.6	−0.1	+0.2
DRI	+2.1	+0.4	+1.6	+3.2	−22.0	+ 0.8	+0.4	+0.3	+0.7

Fiscal Expansion in Rest of OECD	Y	CPI	i	Currency Value	CA	CA*	i*	CPI*	Y*
		Effect in Rest of OECD				Effect in United States			
	(in percent)	(Pts.)	(in percent)	($b)	($b)	(Pts.)	(in percent)		
MCM	+1.4	+0.3	+0.6	+0.3	− 7.2	+ 7.9	+0.5	+0.2	+0.5
EC[a]	+1.3	+0.8	+0.4	−0.6	− 9.3	+ 3.0	+0.0	+0.1	+0.2
EPA[b]	+2.3	+0.7	+0.3	−0.7	−13.1	+ 4.7	+0.6	+0.3	+0.3
LINK	+1.2	+0.1	NA	−0.1	− 6.1	+ 6.3	+0.0	+0.0	+0.2
LIVERPOOL	+0.3	+0.8	+0.0	+3.3	−17.2	+11.9	+0.8	+3.1	−0.5
MSG	+1.1	+0.1	+1.4	+2.9	− 5.3	+10.5	+1.3	+0.6	+0.4
MINIMOD	+1.6	+0.2	+0.9	+0.6	− 2.2	+ 3.2	+0.3	+0.2	+0.1
OECD	+1.5	+0.7	+1.9	+0.9	− 6.9	+ 3.3	+0.3	+0.2	+0.1
TAYLOR[c]	+1.6	+1.2	+0.6	+2.7	NA	NA	+0.4	+0.9	+0.6
WHARTON	+3.2	−0.8	+0.8	−2.4	− 5.5	+ 4.7	+0.1	−0.0	+0.0

[a] Non-U.S. short-term interest rate NA; long-term rate reported instead.
[b] Non-U.S. current account refers to Japan, Germany, United Kingdom, and Canada.
[c] CPI NA. GNP deflator reported instead.

Thatcher; MSG—the McKibbon-Sachs Global model (which assumes rational expectations, but is otherwise somewhat Keynesian), built by Jeffrey Sachs of Harvard University and Warwick McKibbon of the Reserve Bank of Australia; MINIMOD—a smaller approximation of the MCM, built by Richard Haas and Paul Masson of the International Monetary Fund; VAR—estimates by Christopher Sims and Robert Litterman obtained by Vector AutoRegression (a technique that uses no economic theory, but merely looks for regular patterns in the data); OECD—the Interlink model built by staff members at the Organisation of Economic Cooperation and Development (an agency with a membership of twenty-four industrialized countries and a

TABLE 23.2   Monetary Policy: Simulation Effect in Second Year of Increase in Money Supply (4 percent)[a,b]

Monetary Expansion in United States	Y	CPI	i	Currency Value	CA	CA*	i*	CPI*	Y*
	Effect in United States					Effect in Rest of OECD			
	(in percent)		(Pts.)	(in percent)	($b)	($b)	(Pts.)	(in percent)	
MCM	+1.5	+0.4	−2.2	− 6.0	− 3.1	− 3.5	−0.5	−0.6	−0.7
EC[c]	+1.0	+0.8	−2.4	− 4.0	− 2.8	+ 1.2	−0.5	−0.4	+0.2
EPA[d]	+1.2	+1.0	−2.2	− 6.4	− 1.6	−10.1	−0.6	−0.5	−0.4
LINK	+1.0	−0.4	−1.4	− 2.3	− 5.9	+ 1.5	NA	−0.1	+0.1
LIVERPOOL	+0.1	+3.7	−0.3	− 3.9	−13.0	+ 0.1	−0.1	−0.0	−0.0
MSG	+0.3	+1.5	−0.8	− 2.0	+ 2.6	− 4.4	−1.2	−0.7	+0.4
MINIMOD	+1.0	+0.8	−1.8	− 5.7	+ 2.8	− 4.7	−0.1	−0.2	−0.2
VAR[e]	+3.0	+0.4	−1.9	−22.9	+ 4.9	+ 5.1	+0.3	+0.1	+0.4
OECD	+1.6	+0.7	−0.8	− 2.6	− 8.4	+ 3.1	−0.1	−0.1	+0.3
TAYLOR[e]	+0.6	+1.2	−0.4	− 4.9	NA	NA	−0.1	−0.2	−0.2
WHARTON	+0.7	+0.0	−2.1	− 1.0	− 5.1	+ 5.3	−1.3	−0.1	+0.4
DRI	+1.8	+0.4	−2.3	−14.6	− 1.4	+14.5	−1.1	−1.3	−0.6

Monetary Expansion in Rest of OECD	Y	CPI	i	Currency Value	CA	CA*	i*	CPI*	Y*
	Effect in Rest of OECD					Effect in United States			
	(in percent)		(Pts.)	(in percent)	($b)	($b)	(Pts.)	(in percent)	
MCM	+1.5	+0.6	−2.1	−5.4	+ 3.5	+ 0.1	−0.2	−0.2	−0.0
EC[c]	+0.8	+1.0	−1.0	−2.3	− 5.2	+ 1.9	+0.0	+0.1	+0.1
EPA[d]	+0.0	+0.0	−0.1	−0.1	− 0.1	+ 0.1	−0.0	−0.0	+0.0
LINK[f]	+0.8	−0.6	NA	−2.3	− 1.4	+ 3.5	+0.0	−0.0	+0.1
LIVERPOOL	+0.4	+2.8	−0.9	−8.4	+ 7.1	− 8.2	−1.1	−3.4	+1.6
MSG	+0.2	+1.5	−0.7	−1.4	−15.9	+12.0	−1.2	−0.6	+0.3
MINIMOD	+0.8	+0.2	−1.8	−4.8	+ 3.6	− 1.4	−0.6	−0.5	−0.3
VAR[c]	+0.7	−0.5	−3.0	−5.5	+ 5.2	−10.0	+0.6	−0.7	+1.2
OECD	+0.8	+0.3	−1.3	−2.1	− 1.6	+ 2.3	−0.2	+0.1	+0.1
TAYLOR[c]	+0.8	+0.7	−0.3	−3.5	NA	NA	−0.2	−0.5	−0.1
WHARTON	+0.2	−0.1	−0.8	+0.2	+ 2.6	+ 0.5	+0.0	+0.0	+0.0

[a] The increase in the money supply is phased in over four quarters.
[b] *Source:* Frankel and Rockett (1988).
[c] Non-U. S. short-term interest rate NA; long-term reported instead.
[d] Non-U. S. current account is Japan, Germany, United Kingdom, and Canada.
[e] CPI NA. GNP deflator reported instead.
[f] Appreciation of non-U. S. currency NA; depreciation of dollar reported instead.

Secretariat in Paris); TAYLOR—a rational expectations model built by John Taylor of Stanford University; WHARTON—a generally Keynesian model, originally built by Nobel Laureate Lawrence Klein of the University of Pennsylvania; and DRI—the model of Data Resources, Inc., a firm that sells economic forecasts to many corporations, as well as government agencies, from Lexington, Massachusetts.

The Results for Fiscal Policy

Table 23.1 summarizes the effects of a fiscal expansion, an increase in government spending equal to 1 percent of GNP, according to eleven of the models in the Brookings simulations. The variables shown are output, the consumer price index, the short-term interest rate, the exchange rate, and the current account. The first five columns show the variables in the region originating the fiscal expansion, the last four columns the foreign region.

As expected, the models all show a positive effect on output. The numbers in the first column can be read as fiscal multipliers.[15] They are mostly in the range of 1 to 2. Almost all the models show increases in the price level and the interest rate, from which follows some amount of crowding out of construction and other interest-sensitive sectors.

The main ambiguity in theory, as we saw in the preceding chapter, is whether the fiscal expansion causes the currency to appreciate: whether capital mobility is sufficiently high that the capital inflow attracted by higher interest rates is more than enough to finance the increased imports resulting from higher income. However, the eleven models in Table 23.1 show relatively little disagreement in practice. All but two show an appreciation of the dollar when the United States is the country initiating the fiscal expansion. This would not have been the case ten or twenty years ago; it reflects the high degree of capital mobility that had evolved by the 1980s.[16]

In almost all the models, the simulations show that fiscal expansion is transmitted positively to the foreign region. This is not surprising, because the current account worsens in the originating region and thus improves in the foreign region. The positive transmission does indicate, however, that the three possible contractionary effects of a currency depreciation (the ones studied in Section 23.1, via money demand, wages, or imported-input prices) either are not operating, or at least are not operating strongly enough to outweigh the increase in net export demand falling on the goods of the foreign region.

The Results for Monetary Policy

Table 23.2 summarizes the effects of a monetary expansion equal to 4 percent of the money supply (phased in over the first year). The simulations show more conflict among the models than do the results for a fiscal expansion. They all agree that the monetary expansion drives down the interest rate and thereby stimulates domestic income, and they generally agree that it depreciates the currency. Yet they divide almost evenly on the question whether the domestic trade balance improves, causing

---

[15] Because $(\Delta Y/Y)/(\Delta G/Y)$ is the same as $\Delta Y/\Delta G$.

[16] When the fiscal expansion originates in other countries, the appreciation of the currency is not as great as when the fiscal expansion originates in the United States. Indeed, there are four models that indicate a depreciation of the foreign currencies against the dollar. This largely reflects a belief that Japan and Europe are not as open financially as the United States (and perhaps also that the LM curve is steeper in the United States, so that interest rates tend to rise more easily than in the rest of the world).

the foreign trade balance to worsen and foreign income to decrease. That is, they disagree on whether international transmission is inverse.[17]

Many of the models say that the higher imports drawn in by higher income are more than enough to offset the effect of the exchange rate on the trade balance, with the result that the expansion is transmitted positively to the foreign region, rather than negatively. In large part, this comes from observing the effect in the second year after the change in policy. The full effect of the exchange rate on the trade balance is not felt until the third year or later. However, it is possible to sum up the results of all the models by saying that under floating exchange rates, one country's monetary expansion appears to have only small effects on other countries' incomes, because the income and exchange rate effects on the trade balance roughly cancel each other out.

23.4 INTERNATIONAL MACROECONOMIC POLICY COORDINATION

We have examined a wide variety of channels whereby policy changes in one country have effects in other countries.

The Institutions of International Cooperation

Policy-makers have become increasingly aware of the interdependence of national economies. They have established a number of institutions to facilitate discussion of economic issues that concern them all and to facilitate coordination of their policies. The International Monetary Fund conducts "surveillance" of the policies of the major industrialized countries, though its influence on them is inevitably far less than on the poorer indebted countries who have little choice but to listen to the Fund's advice. Each year the OECD sponsors meetings of cabinet ministers from its member countries, supported by regular meetings of the "Economic Policy Committee" and "Working Party 3," in addition to a plethora of other meetings of specialists from the member countries dealing with particular economic sectors. Central bankers from the Group of Ten industrialized countries meet regularly, often in association with the Bank for International Settlements.[18]

In 1975, at the suggestion of French Prime Minister Valéry Giscard d'Estaing, the heads of state of large industrialized economies met at Rambouillet, France. The purpose on that occasion was to ratify politically the movement from fixed exchange rates to floating exchange rates that market forces had imposed on the world monetary system a few years earlier. The Summit Meetings have continued each year since then, bringing together leaders from the group of seven largest industrialized countries, known as the G-7: the United States, Japan, Germany, France, the United Kingdom, Italy, and Canada. The most substantive G-7 Summit Meeting took place in Bonn,

[17] The Mundell-Fleming model says that this inverse transmission should occur. As we saw in the preceding chapter, the lower interest rate that results from a monetary expansion leads to a net capital outflow, which corresponds to a current account deficit abroad. However, the introduction of expectations into investors' asset preferences, as in Chapter 24, can reverse this effect.

[18] The BIS was originally set up after World War I to facilitate the reparations payments that appeared in the discussion of the transfer problem in Chapter 18. From its headquarters in Basel, Switzerland, the BIS continues to function as the central bankers' exclusive club.

Germany, in 1978. There Japan and Germany agreed to the U.S. plan for joint expansion, according to which the three countries would be the "locomotives" pulling the world economy out of the stagnation that had followed the 1974 oil shock. The U.S. motive behind the locomotive theory was the fear that if the United States continued to expand on its own, it would suffer an enlarged trade deficit.

In recent years, the earlier spirit of informal discussion has been lost and the G-7 Summit Meetings have become mammoth media events. Beginning in September 1985, the focus shifted—for the purpose of serious economic policy-making—to the regular meetings of the Finance Ministers. At the time, the membership was confined to the traditional G-5—the United States, Japan, Germany, France, and the United Kingdom—and the focus was on exchange rates. (The meeting took place at the Plaza Hotel in New York and produced the "Plaza Accord," under which the United States agreed to cooperate in bringing down the value of the dollar.) At the G-7 Summit Meeting the next year in Tokyo, the heads of state agreed to expand the membership of the G-5 Finance Ministers' meetings to include Canada and Italy, and to expand the list of "indicators" that the Ministers would focus on to ten variables, including real output, CPIs, and trade balances.

The Theory of Gains from International Policy Coordination

How should all these meetings and institutions be viewed? Are the meetings just media events, opportunities for the heads of state to escape domestic political difficulties and be seen on television looking statesmanlike? Are the institutions simply overpaid bureaucracies whose principal mission is the sampling of Continental cuisine? Although sometimes it might seem that way, there are some good arguments in favor of international cooperation.

There is an elegant theory of the economic gains from international macroeconomic policy coordination: Two or more countries will in general be better able to attain their economic objectives if they set their policies jointly than if they set them independently. The alternative, in which each country independently sets its own policies, taking the policies of the others as given, is called the noncooperative equilibrium, also termed the Nash equilibrium. (The appendix to Chapter 14 introduced the game theory term "Nash equilibrium," in a different context.)

There are a number of ways in which spillover effects among countries can render the noncooperative equilibrium unsatisfactory. Each defines a "game" between national policy-makers.

The game that comes up most often, particularly when the world is in recession due to inadequate demand, could be called "Exporting Unemployment." Consider two countries, the United States and Europe. Each must decide whether or not to

TABLE 23.3   The Game of "Exporting Unemployment"

	United States contracts	*United States expands*
Europe contracts	Recession in both countries; $TB = 0$	TB favors Europe
Europe expands	TB favors United States	Boom in both countries; $TB = 0$

TABLE 23.4   The Game of "Competitive Appreciation"

	United States Raises Interest Rate, i	United States Lowers Interest Rate, i
Europe raises i*	Recession in both; no change in exchange rate or CPI	Dollar depreciates; U.S. import prices and CPI go up; European CPI goes down
Europe lowers i*	Dollar appreciates; U.S. CPI goes down; European CPI goes up	Boom in both countries; no change in exchange rate or CPI

follow expansionary demand policies. Table 23.3 shows the four possible outcomes. If Europe has a trade balance objective, it will be reluctant to expand, for fear that the United States will be less expansionary and leave Europe with a trade deficit. Similarly, the United States will be reluctant to expand, for fear that Europe will be less expansionary and leave the United States with a trade deficit. The result is that each country will hold back its level of demand in an effort to improve its trade balance at its neighbor's expense. This policy is self-defeating when the countries try it simultaneously, plunging the world into a recession where everyone loses. This noncooperative equilibrium occurs in the first cell of the table.

A particular variety of the Exporting Unemployment game, called "Competitive Depreciation," arises when fiscal policy is the tool used and exchange rates are floating. Then each country has an especially strong temptation to contract, because a fiscal contraction will lower interest rates, cause its currency to depreciate, and provide further improvement in its trade balance at its neighbor's expense. (Recall "beggar-thy-neighbor" policies.)

The solution to the "Exporting Unemployment" problem is the "Locomotive Strategy": both countries should agree to expand simultaneously (whether by means of fiscal policy or by some combination of fiscal and monetary policy), so that output is higher everywhere with no change in the trade balance.[19] This was the logic behind the policy package adopted at the Bonn Summit of 1978.

Other games are possible as well. Under a system of floating exchange rates, one possibility is the game of "Competitive Appreciation" (the opposite of the "Competitive Depreciation" game). It is illustrated in Table 23.4. This game depends on the assumption that each country has as its ultimate objective, in addition to high output and employment, low inflation as measured by the CPI. It can, of course, be difficult to attain both of these objectives simultaneously, but there is a trick whereby a country can attain both objectives, to keep the overall CPI stable even if output is growing rapidly and thereby putting upward pressure on the prices of domestically produced goods. The trick is to appreciate the currency—for example, through a combination of tight monetary policy and loose fiscal policy that drives up interest rates and makes the country's assets attractive to international investors. The point is that the strong currency will reduce the prices of *imports*, when expressed in domestic currency. To

[19] The Supplement to this chapter presents the more complete analysis of the "Exporting Unemployment" game that is relevant when each country has a continuous range of macroeconomic expansion or contraction from which to choose, as opposed to the simple choice presented in Figure 23.3 (expand vs. contract).

the extent that imports have a share in the CPI, the overall inflation rate can be kept down, even if the prices of *domestic* goods are rising. Some economists have attributed such a motive to the U.S. government's adoption of its 1980s policy mix of tight money and loose fiscal policy.[20]

Notice, however, that this trick can only be brought about at the expense of the country's neighbors, by "exporting inflation." If the first country experiences an appreciation and downward pressure on its CPI, then its neighbors are experiencing depreciation and upward pressure on their CPIs. The noncooperative equilibrium again appears in the first cell of Table 23.4. Both countries are keeping interest rates high in unsuccessful attempts to appreciate their currency. The result is worldwide recession. The solution is that both agree simultaneously to lower interest rates. Then they can attain stronger economies with no adverse effect on their exchange rates or CPIs.

A more permanent solution to problems of competitive appreciation or depreciation would be for the countries to agree to a system of fixed exchange rates. Then the leaders do not have to get together to negotiate over specific macroeconomic policies. Perceptions that competitive depreciation had helped prolong the Great Depression of the 1930s were a major reason why the delegates to the Bretton Woods conference of 1944 chose a system of fixed exchange rates for the postwar international monetary system. In the language of the Articles of Agreement of the International Monetary Fund, the members agreed to refrain from manipulating their exchange rates to seek "unfair advantage."

Obstacles to Successful Coordination

If international policy coordination were really as easy as Tables 23.3 and 23.4 make it appear, it might seem odd that agreements do not take place more often than they do. There are a number of obstacles that make coordination difficult in practice. Even if the setting is as simple as we have laid out, there is first of all the problem of dividing the gains from cooperation between the two countries. In any "game" there is the possibility that both parties will bargain "tough," with the result that the potential gains are lost to both. Then there is the issue of enforcement of the agreement. The United States, knowing that Europe has set its money supply at the level agreed upon, may be tempted to reduce its own money supply because that will move it to higher levels of welfare. Of course, if the agreement were explicit, this deviation from it would constitute cheating. The gains would be at most short-run; when Europe realizes that America has broken the agreement, it too will change its policy settings, causing a return to the noncooperative state. Even if no automatic penalty is built in for cheating, America is not likely to decide to break the agreement if it is concerned that it would acquire an undesirable reputation as an untrustworthy party in potential future agreements.

A different difficulty arises from the fact that in the games described so far, policy-makers are maximizing their economic welfare only period by period. If coordination constitutes joint expansion, as in the locomotive game, then this will raise inflation

[20] Jeffrey Sachs, "The Dollar and Policy Mix: 1985," *Brookings Papers on Economic Activity* 1 (1985): 117–186.

in the current period. If the current period is the only one that matters, then the policy-makers will already have factored in the inflation correctly when mapping out their indifference curves. However, the expansion will also raise expected inflation in the next period, so workers will demand higher wages and there will be a higher level of actual inflation in the future for any given level of output, as we saw in Section 23.3. In such circumstances, coordinating period by period may actually reduce welfare in the long run.[21]

A final obstacle to successful macroeconomic policy coordination arises from uncertainty. So far we have assumed that policy-makers know precisely (1) what their proper objectives are (for example, what weight should be placed on full employment versus inflation), (2) where their economies are relative to the target optimums (the baseline forecast), and (3) what effect given changes in the policy instruments will have on the economy (the size of the multipliers in the correct model of the world macroeconomy). In reality, however, policy-makers are uncertain about each of the three. The third kind of uncertainty is illustrated in Table 23.2 by the disagreement among the major econometric models as to the effects of monetary policy. All three kinds of uncertainty make it difficult for each country in the bargaining process to know even what policy changes it should *want* its partners to make. A number of pessimistic conclusions emerge. Given differing perceptions, the policy-makers may not be able to agree on a coordination package; even if they do agree; the effects may be different from those anticipated.[22]

The standard German view of the joint expansion agreed upon at the 1978 Bonn Summit is that it turned out to have been undesirable because by the end of the decade the priority had shifted back to fighting inflation. One possible way to understand this view is to see it as an example of uncertainty about the baseline position of the economy relative to the optimum: The 1979 oil price increase associated with the crisis in Iran moved the world economy to a more inflationary position than had been anticipated at the time of the Summit. Another way to understand it is to see it as an example of disagreement over the correct model. In the model that the United States and some smaller countries have in mind, a monetary expansion can raise output and employment, whereas in the Germans' model, monetary expansion simply goes into prices. Conflicting perceptions as to how the economy works make international coordination difficult, as much today as in 1978.

Thus, the gains from international coordination are not as automatic as is suggested by the simple model illustrated here. The potential gains are still there, however. Many economists think that the world economy would improve if the United States agreed to make a more serious effort to reduce its budget deficit, in order to reduce the U.S. trade deficit, while Japan and others expanded their economies to promote

---

[21] The damage to inflation-fighting credibility is offered as an argument why countries might be better off renouncing coordination altogether, in Ken Rogoff, ''International Macroeconomic Policy Coordination May Be Counterproductive,'' *Journal of International Economics* 18 (February 1985): 199–217.

[22] Jeffrey Frankel and Katharine Rockett, ''International Macroeconomic Policy Coordination. When Policy-Makers Do Not Agree on the True Model,'' *American Economic Review* (June 1988): 318–340. Furthermore, even if the effects of coordination are as anticipated, the gains are generally estimated to be small, as was first shown by Gilles Oudiz and Jeffrey Sachs, ''Macroeconomic Policy Coordination among the Industrial Economies,'' *Brookings Papers on Economic Activity* 1 (1984): 1–64. The reason is that the magnitude of international transmission effects is estimated to be relatively small, as was noted in Section 23.3.

world growth. There are also other arguments in favor of cooperation defined more broadly to include, for example, the exchange of information among countries. Sometimes the international meetings help to give individual countries the clarity of vision, sense of purpose, and political momentum needed to accomplish tasks (like cutting budget deficits) that some leaders in the individual governments considered to be in their individual national interests all along but were unable to accomplish in isolation.

It is inevitable that national leaders will to an increasing extent have to work together, particularly in time of crisis. At the time of the stock market crash of October 19, 1987, the heads of the major countries' central banks together supplied needed liquidity and reassured the panicky financial markets. It is good that such policy-makers maintain steady contact and do not wait for a crisis to become acquainted.

23.5 ALTERNATIVE ANCHORS FOR A COUNTRY'S MONEY

The conclusion that emerges from the new classical view of policy-making is that if the government has some way of credibly committing to policies guaranteeing a zero inflation rate, it should do so. This conclusion is based on the argument that, in the long run, the supply relationship is vertical and, inevitably, $Y = \overline{Y}$, so policy-makers may as well give up on affecting output and concentrate on controlling inflation.

This may mean "tying their hands" in some way so that in the future they cannot follow expansionary policies even if they want to. Otherwise, they may be tempted in a particular period (such as an election year) to reap the short-run output and employment gains from expansion, knowing that the major inflationary costs will not be borne until the future. It may seem surprising that policy-makers can raise economic welfare by *giving up* the ability to use monetary policy freely. Yet Equation 23.3 shows that if the authorities make a credible commitment that convinces the public they will not be inflating in the future, the downward shift in P^e will mean that the country can enjoy a lower level of P for any given level of Y. A central bank that would like to constrain itself, so that in the future it can resist the political pressures and economic temptations of expansion, is like Odysseus in the Greek myth. As his ship was approaching the rocks from where the seductive Sirens lured weak-willed sailors to their doom, Odysseus had his sailors tie him to the mast. But how can a central bank make such a binding commitment?

Monetarists and Gold Bugs

A government can "tie its hands," committing to a near-zero inflation rate, by means of what is called a *nominal anchor*. This is a commitment to base monetary policy on some fixed nominal magnitude, thus eliminating the danger of runaway money growth and inflation. Two examples of nominal anchors are the money supply and the price of gold. The monetarists argue for a system under which the central bank rigidly commits to a fixed (low) rate of growth of the money supply. However, this prevents the monetary authorities from responding to future disturbances. For example, if there is an exogenous upward shift in the demand for money (shifting the *LM* curve to the left) and the central bank is constrained from accommodating it with an increase in the money supply, then it will cause an undesired deflation, perhaps a recession. Such velocity shocks have been especially severe since the mid-1970s. For this reason, the Federal Reserve Board abandoned its policy of pursuing targets for the M1 money supply a few years after adopting it in 1979.

Appendix B to Chapter 19 explored the gold standard of the nineteenth century. In recent years, "gold bugs" (including some visionaries who call themselves supply-siders) have argued for a return to a system under which the central bank rigidly commits to a fixed price of gold, standing ready to buy gold if its price threatens to fall and to sell gold if its price threatens to rise. The problem with such a system is that a shift in the demand for gold will be needlessly transmitted to the general economy, much like shifts in the demand for money.[23] Shifts in the demand for gold have been large in recent years. In both cases, committing monetary policy either to a fixed money growth rule or to a fixed price of gold, the disadvantage of allowing needless disturbances in the economy seem large.[24]

Optimum Currency Areas

A more practical proposal for some countries is to choose a fixed exchange rate as the nominal anchor. Many smaller countries peg their currencies to a major country's currency that is believed to be stable, partly as a way of resisting future temptations to expand. There is still the disadvantage of losing some independence, giving up the ability to respond to future disturbances with a different policy than that of the larger country. However, there are some other advantages to a fixed exchange rate, such as reducing the uncertainty facing importers and exporters.[25]

These advantages are particularly great for a small, open country, such as those discussed in Chapters 19 and 20. If traded goods with prices determined exogenously on world markets constitute a large proportion of the economy, then exchange rate uncertainty translates into a high degree of uncertainty in the economy's overall price level. Such an economy may be too small and too open to have an independently floating currency.

Even if prices of domestically produced goods are sticky, the arguments for fixed over floating exchange rates are stronger for a relatively more open country. In the Keynesian model of Chapter 18, variability under a fixed rate is lower when the marginal propensity to import is high.[26] A government that wants to be free to undertake discretionary changes in monetary policy, without regard to whether its trading partners necessarily wish to move in the same direction, can have bigger effects on the economy under floating rates. Under a fixed exchange rate, the tendency for an expansion to leak out through the balance of payments will be particularly high if the marginal propensity to import is high.

---

[23] There also exist more practical versions of this proposal, which see the authorities as pegging the price of a basket of commodities, rather than only gold.

[24] One promising proposal is to choose nominal GNP as the anchor to which policy-makers commit. Nominal GNP targeting has the advantage of insulating the economy from disturbances such as shifts in money demand and or in the demand for goods.

[25] Some empirical studies have found a negative effect of exchange rate uncertainty on the volume of trade since 1973. Peter Kenen and Dani Rodrik, "Measuring and Analyzing the Effect of Short-Term Volatility in Real Exchange Rates," *Review of Economics and Statistics*, 68 (February 1986).

[26] You were asked to figure out the relative stabilizing properties of fixed versus floating exchange rates in question 5 of the problems for Chapter 18.

In the case of a very small region or other economic unit, the argument is clear. Consider an American state (or a Canadian province, British county, etc.). In the limiting case think of a city or square block. Such an economic unit is clearly too small to have its own currency. Its residents would have to consult the day's exchange rate postings and go to the bank to convert currency every time they wanted to buy something in the next city or the next block. A unit this small should adopt the currency of a neighboring region with which it is highly integrated, thus forming a larger currency area. In other words, the unit does not constitute an *optimum currency area.*

An optimum currency area can be defined as a region for which it is optimal to have its own currency and its own monetary policy: *a region that is neither so small and open that it would be better off pegging its currency to a neighbor, nor so large that it would be better off splitting into subregions with different currencies.*[27]

Geographical regions within a country go beyond pegging their exchange rates to each other and literally use the same currency. The dollar bills issued by the Dallas Federal Reserve Bank are perfect substitutes for the dollar bills issued by the Boston Fed. Occasionally, sovereign nations also use other nation's currencies. Panama, for example, allows the U.S. dollar to circulate as legal tender. Botswana allows the South African rand to circulate similarly. A country may want the low inflation rate that would come from adopting a major trading partner's currency and yet want to retain its own currency—either for reasons of political pride[28] or to get the economic seignorage that comes with the right to print money. It can accomplish virtually the same nominal anchor gains by fixing its exchange rate vis-à-vis the major trading partner. If the exchange rate is truly and eternally fixed, then the difference is largely cosmetic. In practice, however, a country with its own currency, even if the exchange rate is declared fixed, is bound to change the exchange rate sooner or later.[29]

This is especially true in the case of a particular exchange rate arrangement that has become more popular among LDCs: pegging to a weighted basket of currencies instead of to just one. The theoretical advantage of the *basket peg* is that it stabilizes the effective exchange rate against a weighted average of trading partners, rather than just one. Central bankers, however, tend to find it a strong temptation to devalue a bit under a basket peg, especially when the weights in the basket have been kept secret.

---

[27] The phrase *optimum currency area* was coined by Robert Mundell, ''A Theory of Optimum Currency Areas,'' *American Economic Review* (November 1961): 509–517. He was thinking of openness in terms of labor (the degree of labor mobility across the region's borders versus within the region), rather than in terms of openness to trade. The idea of using the proportion of the economy composed of traded goods as the criterion for whether a region is large enough to have its own currency was suggested by Ronald McKinnon, "Optimum Currency Areas," *American Economic Review* 53 (September 1963): 717–724. The literature was surveyed by Edward Tower and Thomas Willett, "The Theory of Optimum Currency Areas and Exchange Rate Flexibility," *Special Papers in International Economics,* No. 11, Princeton University (1976).

[28] In 1983 the Israeli Finance Minister lost his job, in large part, for proposing that Israel adopt the U.S. dollar as its currency.

[29] Most Latin American countries, which remained pegged to the dollar in 1973, have devalued repeatedly since then. Former British colonies have long since given up their peg to the pound. The French-speaking countries of West and Central Africa have been the most steadfast in keeping their currencies pegged to that of a major country, France (largely because France grants them large subsidies to do so). Yet even the countries of the Central African franc area have considered devaluing against the French franc recently.

The Case of German Monetary Union

Some economists consider the German monetary union of 1990, in which the *Länder* of the former East Germany were joined to those of the former West Germany, to be an example of how *not* to go about forming a monetary union. It is not that the reunited Germany does not meet the criterion for an optimum currency area. As a result of the close cultural links within what used to be a single country, the extent of trade and labor mobility is rapidly returning to a high level—high enough to justify the adoption of a common currency. Especially important in the decision to undertake monetary union, as in other currency areas, was a political willingness for the more fortunate Western *Länder* to help out the less fortunate with large fiscal transfers.

The major mistake that the German government appears to have made was to miss its one and only chance to get the exchange rate right, between östmarks and deutschemarks, before the monetary union. Productivity among workers in the East is only a fraction of productivity in the West, and it will take time before the former acquire the human capital to close the gap. Wages must accurately reflect the differential in productivity if firms are to have adequate incentive to establish factories in the East and hire workers. The relatively easy way to accomplish this would have been to peg the exchange rate at a multiple, such as two östmarks per deutschemark. For political reasons, the German government pegged the exchange rate at one-to-one in 1990. (They considered that it would have been rude to suggest to the East Germans that they were less productive, notwithstanding that this was generally known to be true, and indeed was a major reason why the Easterners wanted to try the Western market system.) Unemployment in the East soared dramatically in the two years following the union. The cost of paying the unemployment benefits is now creating problems even for the powerhouse West German economy. If wages were perfectly flexible, then it would be immaterial at what rate the two currencies were unified, but this is clearly not the case (or wages in the East would have responded to the high unemployment rates by falling, which they have not done). The period of adjustment may be quite prolonged.

The European Monetary System

There is little point in even trying to impose exchange rate stability if the country is not politically ready to accept the loss of a certain amount of sovereignty in economic policy-making. An attempt to peg the exchange rate under such circumstances would fail as soon as a future disturbance forced the government to choose politically between the fixed exchange rate policy and an alternative such as counteracting an increase in unemployment.

Europe offers good examples of countries that may be politically ready to give up some sovereignty over economic policy for the sake of the advantages of exchange rate stability. Under the European Monetary System, members keep their currencies within margins of plus-or-minus 2.25 percent of each other, as was noted in the preceding chapter. (The margin is 6 percent in the cases of Spain, Britain and Portugal, who joined in 1989, 1990 and 1992, respectively.) One advantage of the system is that it provides a nominal anchor to the public's expectations regarding future monetary policy. Individual inflation-prone countries such as France, Italy, and some smaller countries can bring down their inflation rates by tying their currencies to the deutschemark and thereby tying their monetary policies to that of the Bundesbank, the tightly disciplined German monetary authority.[30] The other, more tangible, advantage of stabilizing exchange rates is the reduction in uncertainty facing importers, exporters, borrowers, lenders, and migrating workers, an advantage that is particularly important to a region seeking, in the 1990s, further integration of trade and factor movements.

In other words, the European countries may, when taken as a unit, constitute an optimum currency area. This was less true in the 1970s: The predecessor to the EMS, the "Snake,"[31] was less successful. Each time the French franc bumped up sharply against its limit in the Snake band, the French government would drop out of the agreement, rather than alter its policies. The EMS constituted a more serious attempt at stabilization of European exchange rates, and has been more successful since its inception in 1979. The most important test arose when the Socialist François Mitterrand first came to power in France in 1981 and tried to expand the French economy at a time when other European countries were not expanding theirs. The consequent balance of payments deficit and downward pressure on the French franc forced Mitterrand to choose between abandoning the expansionary policies and abandoning the exchange rate constraint. Partly for the sake of the EMS, he chose the former, and France has not looked back since.[32]

The balance in most countries throughout Western Europe appears to be slowly tipping toward a willingness to give up some economic sovereignty for the sake of monetary integration, as the result of both a steadily increasing degree of economic integration and a newly emerging European political consciousness. Given the dismantling of capital controls that most member countries had completed by 1992, the national authorities had better be prepared to lose almost *all* individual monetary autonomy to the EMS. (Recall the finding in Chapter 22 that monetary policy is powerless under perfect capital mobility and a fixed exchange rate.)[33]

In December 1991 leaders of the European Community agreed upon steps toward European Monetary Union. They agreed that a European Monetary Institute would be established on January 1, 1994, to coordinate monetary policy among members (as a prototype "EuroFed").[34] They also agreed that in order to join the Union later in the decade, each country must first meet four important tests. Its currency must

[30] Francesco Giavazzi and Marco Pagano, "The Advantage of Tying One's Hands: EMS Discipline and Central Bank Credibility," *European Economic Review* 32 (5)(1988): 1055–1088. Some authors, on the other hand, see from the evidence no sign that the costs (lost output) to a small European country of a program to reduce inflation are any lower when joining the EMS is part of the program. For the case of Ireland: Rudiger Dornbusch, "Credibility, Debt and Unemployment: Ireland's Failed Stabilization," *Economic Policy*, 1989.

[31] The system established in 1971 had the world's major currencies fluctuating within certain margins of each other and the European currencies fluctuating within a narrower band. The pattern that the movement of the European exchange rates made over time looked like a "snake within a tunnel."

[32] Jeffrey Sachs and Charles Wyplosz, "The Economic Consequences of Francois Mitterrand," *Economic Policy* 2 (1986): 261–313

[33] For more on the EMS, see Francesco Giavazzi and Alberto Giovannini, *Limiting Exchange Rate Flexibility: The European Monetary System* (Cambridge, Ma: M.I.T. Press, 1989). Susan Collins, "Inflation and the European Monetary System," in Francesco Giavazzi, Stefano Micossi, and Marcus Miller, eds., *The European Monetary System* (Cambridge, UK: Cambridge University Press 1988).

[34] Marcello de Cecco and Alberto Giovannini, eds., *European Central Bank?* (Cambridge, UK: Cambridge University Press, 1989). Daniel Cohen and Charles Wyplosz, "The European Monetary Union. An Agnostic Evaluation," in *Macroeconomic Policies in an Interdependent World*, Washington: International Monetary Fund, 1989. Matthew Canzoneri, Vittorio Grilli, and Paul Masson, eds., *Establishing a Central Bank: Issues in Europe and Lessons from the U.S.* (Cambridge, UK: Cambridge University Press, 1992).

have succeeded in remaining within the EMS band for two years; its inflation rate must be close to that of the three best-performing EC countries; the same must hold for its interest rates; and its budget deficit and debt must not exceed specified fractions of GDP. The signers of the agreement hope in this way to assure convergence of macroeconomic policies. At the time of the agreement, however, only three countries of the twelve met all four criteria. The open question is how many of the twelve are prepared to make the necessary sacrifices.

23.6 SUMMARY

This chapter showed that even with freely floating exchange rates, countries are interdependent. Only a small country can afford to ignore the effects its policy changes have on its trading partners, because for a large country some of the effects bounce back. This chapter extended the Mundell-Fleming model of Chapter 22 to large countries, and considered other extensions as well. The most important channel of transmission between countries is the trade balance; wherever there are net capital flows, there are nonzero trade balances. There are also other possible channels of transmission, in the form of effects that a change in the exchange rate has other than the effect through the trade balance. (These effects occur via saving, money demand, prices of imported inputs, and wages.) Econometric models suggest that the overall effect of a fiscal expansion in one country is the obvious one: There is an increase in the demand for the net exports of the other country. Thus the expansion is transmitted positively. The overall transmission effect of a monetary expansion appears to be small, however, as the income and exchange rate effects on the trade balance tend to cancel each other out.

This chapter also explored the aggregate supply side of the economy in some detail. It considered a number of alternative possible supply relationships that had different implications for the ability of monetary policy to affect domestic output. In the frictionless neoclassical model, an increase in the money supply has no effect on output and employment but rather goes proportionately into prices and wages. In the modified Keynesian model, the wage is fixed; it follows that an expansion succeeds in raising output to a degree (as in the simple Keynesian model of earlier chapters) but also raises the price level to a degree. Indeed, from the viewpoint of firms, the level of output they choose to supply increases *because* the price at which they can sell their goods rises relative to the wage. In the Friedman-Phelps model, workers subsequently raise their wage demands as they adjust their price expectations upward. In the long run, the aggregate supply curve becomes vertical, as in the frictionless neoclassical model, and the money supply increase has no effect on output. In the Lucas-Sargent-Barro model, the only effect that the government can have on output is the useless one of randomly changing the money supply in unexpected directions; for practical policy-making purposes, the aggregate supply curve is vertical even in the short run. Finally, with indexed wages, monetary policy again has no effect and the aggregate supply curve is vertical even in the short run. The fixed level of output can be the wrong one, however, if real wages fail to fall in the aftermath of a fall in productivity.

The fact that the world is interdependent leads to the topic of international macroeconomic policy coordination. National policy-makers may be able to do better by setting their policies cooperatively than they can in the (Nash) noncooperative equilibrium, where each acts independently. For example, in a worldwide recession, with each country afraid to expand its economy on its own for fear of a deterioration in its trade balance, there can be gains from general agreement to expand cooperatively.

The chapter concluded by considering the formation of monetary unions and other ways that a country can commit itself to monetary discipline. A commitment to monetary discipline via a nominal anchor offers a country the advantage that, by reducing workers' expectations of monetary expansion, it reduces wages and prices. For a country too small and too open to constitute an optimum currency area, the gains from pegging its currency to a neighbor's (acquiring a stable anchor to monetary policy as well as reducing exchange rate uncertainty) outweigh the loss of monetary independence. For large countries, the option of a fixed exchange rate is not generally practical. Alternative nominal anchors have been proposed, though the most prominent of these—fixing the rate of growth of the money supply and fixing the price of gold—have the major drawback that disturbances such as shifts in the demand for money or in the demand for gold can have large undesired impacts on the economy.

CHAPTER PROBLEMS

1. The country of Bretagne is holding its real money supply, M/P, constant, but the rest of the world is undertaking a monetary expansion that drives down interest rates in Bretagne as well. Which is greater: the stimulus to its economy from the lower interest rate or the loss of demand (net exports) when its currency appreciates against the rest of the world? (*Hint*: Consider the money market equilibrium condition.)

2. When the country of Euphoria adopts a combination of easy fiscal and tight monetary policy, and exchange rates are flexible, is a foreign country suffering from unemployment likely to be pleased with the consequences? a foreign country suffering from inflation? a foreign country with a large external debt denominated in the currency of Euphoria?

3. Equation 23.2 says that when there is an expansion of aggregate demand, the percentage increase in output equals σ times the percentage increase in P. If nominal GNP ($= PY$) goes up by 1 percent, what fraction of this takes the form of an increase in Y and what in P? If wages adjust over time, how do these fractions change?

Extra Credit

4. This problem concerns interdependence and the coordination of fiscal policy between two countries: Melanzane and Rigatoni.

   The country of Melanzane has two target variables: the domestic price level, p, and the exchange rate, s, in Melanzane-per-Rigatoni currency units (because the country wants to stabilize the two components of the CPI: domestic prices and import prices), both in log form. These target variables are affected both by the government spending of Melanzane, g_M as a percentage of GNP, and the government spending of its trading partner, Rigatoni, g_R as a percentage of GNP.

$$p = A + Cg_M + Fg_R$$
$$s = B + D(g_R - g_M)$$

a. In a standard Mundell-Fleming model, on what would the sign of D depend? What do most multicountry econometric models say about the signs of C, D, and F?

b. Assume that Melanzane wishes to reduce both s and p to zero. This could be the aftermath of an increase in oil prices that has raised A and B above zero. Solve for the optimal combination of g_M and g_R that would be preferred by Melanzane if it had its first choice. Assume that the signs of C, F, and D are as in a. What is the sign of $(g_M - g_R)$, that is, would Melanzane prefer that it cut spending more or that Rigatoni cut spending more? Why? Show the optimal point for Melanzane on a graph analogous to that in the Chapter Supplement.

c. If Melanzane seeks to minimize a quadratic loss function

$$L = p^2 + ws^2$$

where w is the weight placed on the exchange rate objective, derive its reaction function, giving g_M as a function of g_R. How will Melanzane react to a fiscal contraction by Rigatoni, if exchange rate effects are not very important (i.e., if D and w are low), and why? If they (D and w) are high?

d. Assume that Rigatoni has a similar objective function, with its prices determined analogously. Indicate on a graph what optimal combination of g_M and g_R would be preferred by Rigatoni, and its reaction function. Describe the Nash noncooperative equilibrium. What sort of cooperative bargain would raise economic welfare and why?

5. a. Let the production function be $Y = \phi N^\beta$, where N is the number of workers employed. What factors determine ϕ? If you know calculus, show that the marginal product of labor, dY/dN, can be expressed as

$$\beta \phi^{1/\beta} Y^{-(1-\beta)/\beta}$$

Why is the marginal product low when Y is high?

b. If firms maximize profits competitively, so that they choose the level of employment and output where the marginal product of labor is equal to the real wage, show how employment, N, can be expressed as a function of the real wage [i.e., derive an equation to describe Figure 23.4(b)]. Then show how output, Y, can be expressed as a function of the real wage. You have now derived Equation 23.1 from the text, $(Y/\overline{Y}) = (wP/W)^\sigma$. What must σ equal? If $\overline{Y} \equiv \phi \overline{N}^\beta$, what must w equal?

c. If an oil shock causes ϕ to fall, what must happen to W/P if full employment is to be maintained?

6. Assuming compete indexation, $\delta = 1$, it is shown in the supplement that the supply curve is given by Equation 23.S.5.

$$(Y/\overline{Y}) = (P/SP^*)^{\alpha\sigma}$$

Try to figure out whether a monetary expansion raises Y. If it does, what must happen to the real exchange rate? What would you expect to happen to the trade balance $X - M$? to the net capital inflow? to the interest rate? to investment demand, I? To total demand for domestic goods, $C + I + G + X - M$? What do you conclude about the effect on Y?

SUGGESTIONS FOR FURTHER READING

Akerlof, G., A. Rose, J. Yellen, and H. Hessenius. "East Germany in from the Cold: The Economic Aftermath of Currency Union," *Brookings Papers on Economic Activity* 1 (1991) 1–105. As some economists predicted, the terms of the German Monetary Union of June 30, 1990, have resulted in wages in the East that exceed labor productivity and, thus, in a sustained increase in unemployment.

Cooper, Richard. "Economic Interdependence and Coordination of Economic Policies," in Ronald Jones and Peter Kenen, eds., *Handbook in International Economics* Vol. 2 (Amsterdam: North Holland, 1985). A survey of interdependence and coordination from one of the first to explore the subject.

Eichengreen, Barry. "One Money for Europe: Lessons from the U.S. Currency Union," *Economic Policy* 10 (1990). Is economic integration in Europe high enough to constitute an optimum currency area? The United States offers a standard of comparison.

Fischer, Stanley. "International Macroeconomic Policy Coordination," in Martin Feldstein, ed., *International Policy Coordination*, (Chicago: University of Chicago Press, 1988). A relatively comprehensive, yet concise, survey of the rapidly growing literature, including some of the skeptics.

Funabashi, Yoichi. *Managing the Dollar: From the Plaza to the Louvre* (Washington: Institute of International Economics, 1988). A highly readable account of the G-5 and G-7 meetings of Finance Ministers from 1985 to 1987.

Kenen, Peter. *EMU After Maastricht* (Washington: Group of Thirty, 1992). A quick history and analysis of the plans for European Monetary Union that EC members agreed upon in December 1991.

Mussa, Michael. "Macroeconomic Interdependence and the Exchange Rate Regime," in Rudiger Dornbusch and Jacob Frenkel, eds., *International Economic Policy: Theory and Evidence*, (Baltimore: Johns Hopkins University Press, 1979) pp. 160–204. Surveys the two-country Mundell-Fleming model, including some of the transmission effects that were developed subsequently.

Oudiz, Gilles, and Jeffrey Sachs. "Macroeconomic Policy Coordination among the Industrial Economies," *Brookings Papers on Economic Activity* 1 (1984): 1–76. A readable introduction to international policy coordination, and the first serious attempt to quantify the gains.

Sachs, Jeffrey. "Real Wages and Unemployment in the OECD Countries." *Brookings Papers on Economic Activity* 1 (1983): 225–303. Updates the estimates in an earlier study of real wage rigidity in Europe as compared to the United States, and finds that the "wage gap" (the difference between the actual real wage and the warranted real wage) appeared to be even higher for major European countries in 1983 than it was in 1979.

Swoboda, Alexander, and Rudiger Dornbusch. "Adjustment Policy and Monetary Equlibrium in a Two-Country Model," in M. Connolly and A Swoboda, eds., *International Trade and Money* (London: George Allen and Unwin, 1973). A clear exposition of the two-country Mundell-Fleming model, using a graph with Y and Y^* on the axes, as in Figure 18.5

VI

The Determination of Exchange Rates in International Asset Markets

24

EXPECTATIONS, MONEY, AND THE DETERMINATION OF THE EXCHANGE RATE

At the end of Chapter 22, we adopted the assumption of perfect capital mobility, or perfect international integration of financial markets: There are no transaction costs, capital controls, or other barriers separating international investors from the portfolios they would like to hold. We will continue to maintain this assumption. Large quantities of capital are ready to move back and forth across national boundaries at will. Because investors adjust their portfolios instantaneously in response to changes in rates of return, exchange rates are volatile. The exchange rate is now the relative price of foreign versus domestic *assets*, rather than the relative price of foreign versus domestic *goods*. Thus, it is not surprising that exchange rates turn out to be as volatile as the prices of bonds, equities, gold, and other assets, in contrast to the much more stable national price levels. Refer back to Figure 19.6 for an illustration of this volatility.

In Chapter 22, the international portfolio investor's decision concerning what country's asset to hold depended only on interest rates. This chapter introduces an additional factor that enters investors' decision-making: expectations about future changes in exchange rates. It was reasonable to omit this factor when we were studying a fixed exchange rate, assuming that the rate had little likelihood of being changed; but under the modern floating rate system, investors are forced to wager on exchange rate movements every time they invest internationally.

24.1 INTEREST RATE PARITY CONDITIONS

If the dollar is expected to lose value in the future against the mark, then German investors will subtract the expected rate of dollar depreciation from the dollar interest rate when contemplating the purchase of U.S. assets. Similarly, U.S. investors will add the expected rate of mark appreciation to the mark interest rate when contemplating the purchase of German assets. If investors do not care about any factors other than the expected rates of return on the two countries' assets, then they will buy the asset with the higher expected return and sell the other, a process that continues until expected returns are equalized across countries. This means that the expected rate of depreciation of the domestic currency, Δs^e, will be equal to the nominal interest differential.

$$i - i^* = \Delta s^e \tag{24.1}$$

This condition is known as *uncovered interest parity.*

Uncovered interest parity is somewhat similar to *covered* interest parity, the arbitrage condition, Equation 21.2, introduced in Chapter 21:

$$i - i^* = fd \tag{24.2}$$

where *fd* is the forward discount. There is an important difference however. Any deviations from Equation 24.2 in the absence of transaction costs, capital controls, and so on, would mean that investors could risklessly make as much money as they wanted, simply by borrowing in the low-interest-rate country and lending in the other, covering on the forward exchange market. There would be no risk of capital losses (or gains), because the exchange risk is covered on the forward exchange market. It is very unlikely that such golden profit opportunities exist, and indeed, Chapter 21 showed that covered interest parity holds for most industrialized countries.

Uncovered interest parity is another matter. Here investors buying a foreign asset with an apparently high rate of return expose themselves to the risk that whatever is earned in interest will be wiped out by adverse movements in the exchange rate. Thus, uncovered interest parity is a stronger hypothesis than covered interest parity. It will hold only if investors treat domestic-currency and foreign-currency assets as similar—as *perfect substitutes*—in their portfolios. In particular, uncovered interest parity will hold only if exchange risk is not important to investors. (This would be the case if investors are relatively certain as to the future exchange rate, or alternatively if they are risk-neutral, that is, if they are unconcerned about risk.) Expected depreciation and exchange risk are the two factors that can separate domestic and foreign interest rates, even in the absence of barriers to international capital movement. This chapter considers only expected depreciation. Exchange risk will be considered in Chapter 25.[1]

We will be using Equation 24.1 throughout this chapter. It is important to clarify from the outset that the uncovered interest parity condition is not necessarily a statement about causality; it is not a model specifying the determination of interest rates. Equation 24.1 is an equilibrium condition. It is entirely consistent with the idea that the interest rate is determined to give equilibrium in the money market, as was assumed in previous chapters. This chapter simply adds Equation 24.1 as one of the equations that will have to be satisfied if investors are to be happy with the portfolios that they are holding.

---

[1] Note that if Equations 24.1 and 24.2 both hold, then we have $fd = \Delta s^e$. This is another way of saying that there is no exchange risk premium in the foreign exchange market. (Equation 22.A.3 defined the exchange risk premium. Chapter 25 will disuss it further.)

CM) + PS ≡ 1 Bond

24.2 THE MONETARIST MODEL WITH FLEXIBLE PRICES

Under the assumptions that (1) there are no transaction costs, government controls, or other barriers discouraging international trade in bonds, and (2) investors treat different countries' assets as perfect substitutes in their portfolios, it is as if there is only one type of bond in the world. Different countries' bonds can be aggregated together, as long as they all pay the same expected rate of return; investors will be indifferent to which country's bonds they hold. This is what is meant by assuming uncovered interest parity.

The first section of the chapter will also make some analogous assumptions about goods markets: (1) there are no transportation costs, government controls or other barriers discouraging international trade in goods, and (2) consumers' tastes are such that they treat different countries' goods as perfect substitutes. Thus, it is as if there is only one type of good in the world. Countries' goods can be aggregated together so long as their relative prices are fixed. This is what is meant by Purchasing Power Parity, the condition that was extensively covered in Chapter 19. That chapter distinguished between the *monetary* approach to the balance of payments, so named because it devotes special attention to international flows of money, and the *monetarist* model, which adds the assumption that prices are perfectly flexible so that goods and labor markets always clear. This chapter can be thought of as the monetary approach to the *exchange rate*, the floating-rate version of the model studied in Chapter 19 for the case of fixed rates. Only in the first section of this chapter do we add the assumption that goods prices are perfectly flexible, to get what might be called the monetarist model of the exchange rate.   = ONE Good

Why return to the assumption of price flexibility, given all the evidence against it reported earlier? First, the model in which there is only one good as well as one bond in the world is a conveniently simple starting point from which to begin the exploration of the complexities of modern exchange rate theory. Second, Purchasing Power Parity (PPP) is not a bad approximation for considering the very long run (or for considering other cases where there are large changes in money supplies, price levels, and exchange rates, as in hyperinflation). Section 24.3 will reintroduce short-run variation in the real exchange rate (due to monetary disturbances in the presence of sticky goods prices).

We first brought up the importance of exchange rate expectations at the end of the presentation of the Mundell-Fleming model in Chapter 22, which assumed that prices were fixed in the short run. The discussion there noted that investors might expect the exchange rate in the future to move from wherever it happened to be at the moment in the direction of long-run equilibrium. This is how Section 24.4 will model expectations. First, however, it will be helpful to have an idea of the long-run equilibrium toward which the exchange rate is expected to move. This is another reason for beginning here by studying the long-run equilibrium in which PPP holds.

We repeat the PPP assumption:

$$\bar{S} = P/P^* \tag{24.3}$$

Here $\bar{S}$ denotes the level of the exchange rate (the "spot" price of foreign exchange), P the domestic price level, and P^* the foreign price level. Placing a "bar" over the exchange rate indicates that—ultimately—the equation is taken seriously only in long-run equilibrium. $\bar{S}$ is on the left side here, because the focus is on how exchange rates are determined. This is in contrast to Chapter 19, which covered fixed exchange rates. There the domestic price level was determined by the exchange rate set by the government, so P was on the left side.

Equation 24.3 is incomplete as a theory of exchange rate determination, because it simply pushes back one step the question: What determines the price level?

The Exchange Rate as the Price of Money

The other essential equation in the monetary model of the exchange rate is the one that sets the real supply of money, M/P, equal to the real demand for money, L.

$$M/P = L(i, Y) \qquad (24.4)$$

As in the derivation of the LM curve (Equation 22.4), this equation assumes that the demand for money is a decreasing function of the interest rate, i, because people wish to hold less money when other assets pay a higher rate of return compared to money, but an increasing function of income, Y, because people have a greater need for money with which to undertake transactions when income is higher.[2] To treat the relationship as a theory of how the price level is determined, solve for P.

$$P = M/L(i, Y) \qquad (24.5)$$

It makes sense to think of the price level as being determined to set money demand equal to money supply, since prices are assumed perfectly flexible. Notice that a 10 percent increase in the money supply causes the price level to increase by 10 percent.

The supply and demand for money in the foreign country is modeled in precisely the same way.

$$P^* = M^*/L^*(i^*, Y^*) \qquad (24.6)$$

Now take the ratio of the two price-level equations, and substitute it into Equation 24.3.

$$\bar{S} = [M/L(i, Y)]/[M^*/L^*(i^*, Y^*)]$$
$$= [M/M^*]/[L(i, Y)/L^*(i^*, Y^*)] \qquad (24.7)$$

Equation 24.7 has a simple intuitive interpretation. The exchange rate is defined as the price of foreign currency in terms of domestic currency. Thus, we are now modeling it as the relative price of foreign money rather than the relative price of foreign goods. As such, it should be determined by the relative supply and demand for money. Notice that the foreign money supply, M^*, appears in the denominator. An increase in M^* will cause a decline in the price of foreign money—the exchange rate, $\bar{S}$—just as an increase in the supply of bananas causes a fall in the price of bananas. An increase in the demand for foreign money, L^*, will have the opposite

[2] It is possible to derive a money demand function from principles of optimization. Robert Lucas, "Interest Rates and Currency Prices in a Two-Country World." *Journal of Monetary Economics* 10 (1982): 335–360.

effect: an increase in the price of foreign money, just as an increase in the demand for bananas causes an increase in the price of bananas. The domestic money supply, M, is in the numerator. An increase in the domestic money supply causes an increase in the exchange rate, a depreciation of the currency. (This is the same result seen in previous chapters.) Finally, an increase in the domestic demand for money causes a decrease in the exchange rate.

The nature of the exchange rate's dependence on the money supplies is very simple: It is directly proportionate to M and inversely proportionate to M^*. When the domestic money supply increases by 10 percent relative to the foreign money supply, the exchange rate goes up by 10 percent, because the price level goes up by 10 percent. This is the property of *homogeneity* of nominal variables.

The money demand variables do not necessarily enter in as simply as the money supply variables. For convenience, however, we will adopt a simple functional form for the money demand function, in which the demand for money is proportional to real income in the same way as it is proportional to the price level.[3] Then Y and Y^* will determine the exchange rate in simple ratio form. We adopt the simplifying assumption that the interest rates enter in simple difference form:

$$\bar{S} = (M/M^*) \, L(i - i^*)/[Y/Y^*] \qquad (24.8)$$

The simpler functional form chosen for Equation 24.8 clarifies how the exchange rate depends on Y, Y^*, i, and i^*.[4] An increase in domestic real income, Y, has a negative effect on $\bar{S}$—that is, it causes the domestic currency to appreciate—and an increase in foreign income has the opposite effect. An increase in the interest differential, $i - i^*$, has a positive effect on $\bar{S}$—that is, it causes the domestic currency to depreciate.[5]

These effects are precisely the reverse of the effects that income and the interest rate appeared to have on the exchange rate in the Mundell-Fleming model in preceding chapters. The apparent contradictions merit some explanation.

Recall exchange rate determination in the Mundell-Fleming model. There an increase in income, Y, because it meant higher demand for imports and a deteriorated trade balance, required a depreciation of the currency.[6] Equation 24.8 implies the reverse relationship with Y. The difference is that this section assumes that prices are perfectly flexible and that Y is therefore always at the level of potential output, where all resources in the economy are fully employed. Think of Y having a bar over it (like $\bar{S}$) to indicate that it refers to potential output. In this context, if income increases, it is not because of expansionary monetary policy or any other kind of increase in demand, but because of "supply-side" factors such as higher level of national

[3] In other words, the demand for nominal money balances is proportional to nominal GNP, PY. This assumption holds, for example, in the monetarist model in which velocity, PY/M, is constant; but in that model, money demand does not depend on the interest rate.

[4] There is a particular functional form for $L(i, Y)$ that allows the interest rates to enter in simple difference form, as in Equation 24.8: the exponential function. The Chapter Supplement offers a formal presentation of the model in logs.

[5] Equation 24.8 could be applied to a context of fixed exchange rates as easily as to floating, or to a context in which the central bank intervenes in the foreign exchange market to some intermediate degree. (Lance Girton and Don Roper, "A Monetary Model of Exchange Market Pressure Applied to the Postwar Canadian Experience," *American Economic Review*, 67 (4 (September 1977): 537–548.)

[6] In Problem 4 at the end of the chapter, you are asked to solve the balance of payments equilibrium condition (Equation 22.4 S) for S.

resources or an improvement in economic efficiency. In other words, when prices are perfectly flexible, all changes in output are changes in potential output. When income increases because of such reasons, it is a sign of strength in the economy and tends to appreciate the currency because it raises the demand for money. For example, appreciation of the yen often can be attributed to rapid growth in the Japanese economy.

In the Mundell-Fleming model (with partial capital mobility), an increase in the interest differential, because it improved the capital account, required an appreciation of the currency. In Equation 24.8, on the other hand, an increase in the interest differential is associated with a depreciation of the currency. It is important to see the reason for the difference.

From the covered interest parity condition, Equation 24.2, the forward discount can be substituted in place of the interest differential. Furthermore, the uncovered interest parity condition, Equation 24.1, shows that the expected depreciation variable can be substituted in place of the interest differential. We can rewrite Equation 24.8 as follows:

$$\overline{S} = [M/M^*] \, L(\Delta s^e)/[Y/Y^*] \qquad (24.9)$$

An increase in the expected rate of depreciation of the currency, Δs^e, has a positive effect on today's exchange rate (it causes the currency to depreciate today). It is clear why: If investors expect the domestic currency to lose value over the coming period, they will choose to shift their portfolios out of that currency and into other assets, to protect themselves against the expected future losses. When they seek to shift out of the domestic currency, they drive down its price today ($\overline{S}$ rises). There is an important principle here: If expectations regarding what will happen in the future change, even if no other variables change today, then today's exchange rate will change. In this context, a high interest rate is not a sign of "strength" for a currency. Rather, it reflects expected future depreciation and is thus a sign of "weakness."[7] This is why a high (nominal) interest rate is not necessarily associated with a strong currency as it is in the Mundell-Fleming model.

So far, we have represented the rate-of-return variable (the opportunity cost of holding domestic money) of Equation 24.8 in three ways: as the interest rate differential, the forward discount, and the expected rate of depreciation. There is yet a fourth way to express the rate-of-return variable, and it will help clarify the first three expressions.

Equation 24.3 expressed purchasing power parity in terms of *levels*; but it can also be expressed in terms of *rates of change*:

$$\Delta \overline{s} = \Delta p - \Delta p^* \qquad (24.10)$$

---

[7] When investors shift their portfolios out of domestic money in response to expectations of depreciation, what do they shift into? They shift into either domestic or foreign bonds; it makes no difference which, because under the assumption of perfect substitutability, or uncovered interest parity, domestic and foreign bonds are essentially the same thing. In a different version of the model, the *currency substitution* model, people are thought to shift directly from domestic money to foreign money. However, unless they are planning on actually traveling to the foreign country to buy goods, there is in reality little reason for them to hold foreign money. To do so would be to voluntarily give up the interest that could be earned on foreign bonds. John Cuddington, "Currency Substitution, Capital Mobility and Money Demand," *Journal of International Money and Finance*, 1984.

where $\Delta \bar{s}$ is the percentage rate of change of the exchange rate in long-run equilibrium, Δp is the domestic inflation rate, and Δp^* is the foreign inflation rate. Equation 24.10 says that if the domestic inflation rate exceeds the foreign inflation rate, then the domestic currency depreciates at the rate of the inflation differential, in order to prevent the country's goods from becoming overpriced in world markets.[8]

If the exchange rate acts according to Equation 24.10, investors are presumably aware of this and form their expectations accordingly. Then expected depreciation is equal to the expected inflation differential.

$$\Delta s^e = \Delta p^e - \Delta p^{*e} \tag{24.11}$$

In other words, investors expect the domestic currency to lose value to the extent that they expect its purchasing power over goods to deteriorate at a faster rate than for the foreign currency.

Observe that if the interest differential is equal to the expected rate of depreciation (Equation 24.1, the uncovered interest parity condition) and the expected rate of depreciation is in turn equal to the expected inflation differential (Equation 24.11, PPP in rate-of-change form), then it follows that the interest differential is equal to the expected inflation differential.

$$i - i^* = \Delta p^e - \Delta p^{*e}$$

This can also be represented as the domestic *real* (that is, expected-inflation-adjusted) interest rate equal to the foreign real interest rate.

$$i - \Delta p^e = i^* - \Delta p^{*e}$$

This condition is called *real interest parity*.[9]

Using Equation 24.11, we can substitute the expected inflation differential into Equation 24.9.

$$\bar{S} = [M/M^*]L(\Delta p^e - \Delta p^{*e})/[Y/Y^*] \tag{24.12}$$

Now we see that investors will seek to shift out of a currency, thus causing it to depreciate, when it is expected to lose future value in the sense of a high expected rate of inflation.

Greece is an example of a country with a high rate of inflation, as compared to the United States. The Greek inflation differential has held consistently enough in the past that by now it is built into expectations, the interest differential, and the forward discount. Many LDCs, such as Brazil also have very high rates of inflation and currency depreciation which are reflected in very high interest rates. Switzerland

---

[8] Again, the empirical evidence in Chapter 19 showed that purchasing power parity is unlikely to hold in the short run. Remember, however, that the model in this section properly applies only to long-run exchange rate determination. The short-run deviations from the equation will be developed soon enough.

[9] Real interest parity could also be obtained through an alternative route: if the real interest rate in each country were tied to a technological constant, the marginal product of capital. In practice, however, real interest rates are observed to be neither constant over time nor equal across countries at a point in time. (Again, only as a description of the long run is the flexible-price view of the world that provides real interest parity meant to be taken literally.)

and Japan are examples of countries that are known to have low inflation rates, which have become similarly built into their economies. Thus, PPP states that the Greek drachma and Brazilian cruzeiro will depreciate over time, while the yen and Swiss franc will appreciate over time. The theory also states something stronger, however. It states that when there is a sudden increase in expected future inflation—for example, because a new, more expansionary head of the central bank is appointed— the currency depreciates suddenly, even before the price level has actually started to change.

Expectations of Money Growth

What determines the expected inflation rate? Many factors affect the inflation rate, especially in the short run. In the simple monetarist model, however, the rate of creation of money, exogenously set by the central bank, drives everything. This can be seen from the money market equilibrium condition, Equation 24.4. Remember that, because prices are perfectly flexible, income in the equation is tied to the exogenous level of potential output. Imagine that the inflation rate, though not zero, is in a "steady state," that is, is constant and has been fully incorporated into expectations and interest rates. It follows from Equation 24.4 that the given rate of increase of the price level presupposes a money growth rate of the same magnitude. If the money growth rate is exogenously set by the central bank, the inflation rate necessarily adjusts accordingly. The point can be made in terms of the *LM* curve used so extensively in the preceeding chapters: If the money growth rate were *not* fully reflected in the inflation rate, that is, if the real money supply were increasing, then the *LM* curve would be shifting to the right and real income would be increasing. For there to be a steady state, the ratio of the money supply to the price level must be constant.

What is the effect on the exchange rate of a permanent increase in the money growth rate of, say 1 percent per annum? The inflation rate goes up permanently by 1 percent per annum. As soon as the change is recognized by the public, expected depreciation and the interest rate go up by the same 1 percent and the demand for the currency falls. If the change is recognized at the same moment that it actually takes effect, as it will if the central bank announces the change in policy (and if the public has faith in such announcements), then the price of the currency falls instantaneously. Figure 24.1(a) shows this as a discrete upward jump in the exchange rate (and in the price level). This jump occurs even through the level of the money supply does not jump discretely, only its rate of growth. Thus, the percentage change in the exchange rate in any given interval of time can be greater than the percentage change in the money supply observed during that interval (particularly if the interval is short), if the change in the money supply is thought to signal a permanent change in the per annum money growth rate. This property has occasionally been called the "magnification effect."

An example where this framework, the monetary approach to the exchange rate, is thought to apply well is the case of hyperinflation. Hyperinflations occurred in a number of central European countries in the aftermath of World War I, including

FIGURE 24.1   The Effect of Changes in the Money Supply on the Equilibrium Exchange Rate

When the money supply jumps to a higher level, the equilibrium price level, P, and spot rate, S, jump in proportion, as in (b). When the money supply, M, grows at a faster rate, the equilibrium price level and spot rate grow at the same faster rate. In addition, there is a sudden drop in demand for the currency when investors discover the change, as in (a). If they learn that there will be an increase in M in the future, the drop in demand occurs today, as in (c).

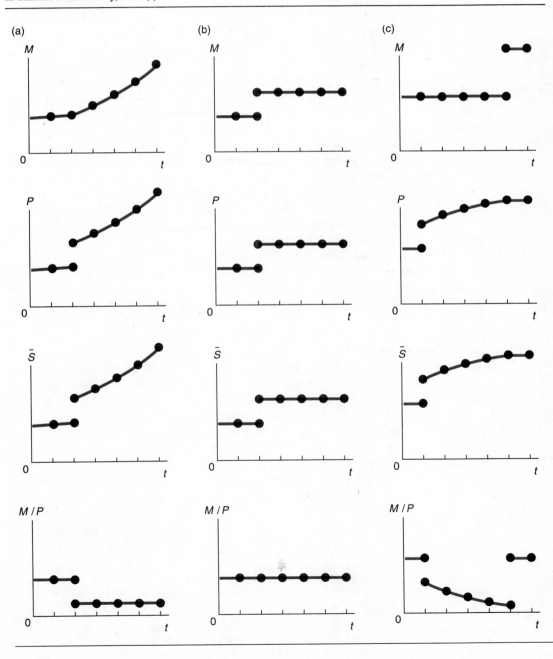

Germany, Russia, Austria, Poland, and Hungary. The German experience, from February 1920 to November 1923, has been extensively studied. In October 1923, the rate of money growth reached 1,300 percent *per month*. The inflation rate reached 29,586 percent per month. That is just over 20 percent per day; at that rate, the price level doubles in less than four days! Fascinating stories abound of what life was like under such conditions. Wages were paid twice a day so workers could shop at lunchtime before prices rose again. So much paper currency was needed to make simple purchases that a wheelbarrow might be needed to carry it to the store. It is said that one shopper left a wheelbarrow briefly, and found on returning that the wheelbarrow had been stolen ... but the currency had been left.

In October 1923 the rate of depreciation of the mark reached 29,957 percent per month. The price level and exchange rate were going up at roughly the same rate, that is, the real exchange rate had reached a "steady state." However, in the transition to this steady state, the price level (and exchange rate) had gone up more than the money supply: *real* money balances fell to a fraction (0.03) of their original level, as in the bottom panel of Figure 24.1(a). This reflects the fact that the real demand for the currency depends negatively on the rate at which it is expected to lose value. Thus, it is not quite true that in the monetarist model no change in a monetary variable can have an effect on any real variable (assuming that the level of real money balances is classified as a real variable). A change in the money growth *rate* has an effect on the level of real money balances.[10] Nevertheless, whether the change occurs in the level of the money supply or in its rate of change, there is still no effect on the real interest rate or real exchange rate.[11]

The case already considered, where people expect a constant growth rate of domestic money indefinitely into the future, is relatively easy to understand. In this case, the various versions of the rate of return on alternative assets—the expected inflation differential, nominal interest differential, forward discount, and expected rate of depreciation—are all equal to the expected money growth rate differential. The public's expectations as to the future path of the money supply in the long run, however, may not be accurately described by a single constant growth rate. Consider two alternatives.

First, what happens if the money supply is thought to follow a random walk? That is, although people know that the money supply will probably change, they think that it could go down as easily as up. At any point in time, the best forecast of the change in money supply is zero. As a matter of fact, there is indeed a great deal of "noise" in the monthly money supply numbers that are reported, for example, by the Federal Reserve. This means that when the central bank reports an increase in the money growth rate in a given month, the chances are good that the increase is purely transitory and does not signal a new, permanently higher money growth rate.

---

[10] This property (called a lack of "superneutrality") can exist in optimizing models. Lars Svensson "Currency Prices, Terms of Trade and Interest Rates: A General Equilibrium Asset-Pricing, Cash-in-Advance Approach," *Journal of International Economics* 18 (1985): 17–41.

[11] See Rudiger Dornbusch, "Lessons from the German Inflation Experience of the 1920s," in R. Dornbusch, S. Fischer, and J.Bossons, eds. *Macroeconomics and Finance: Essays in Honor of Franco Modigliani*, (Cambridge, MA: M.I.T. Press, 1987) 337–366. The seminal statement of the flexible-price version of the monetary approach to the exchange rate was made in the context of the German hyperinflation: Jacob Frenkel, "A Monetary Approach to the Exchange Rate: Doctrinal Aspects and Empirical Evidence," *Scandinavian Journal of Economics* (1976): 200–224. A classic study of money demand in interwar hyperinflation is Philip Cagan, "The Monetary Dynamics of Hyperinflation," in Milton Friedman, ed., *Studies in the Quantity Theory of Money* (Chicago: University of Chicago Press, 1956).

If the expected values of the future money supply changes are zero, then the expected inflation differential, expected depreciation rate, and interest rate differential are also zero.[12] The middle term disappears from the equations for $\bar{S}$ derived earlier. A 1 percent increase in the money supply, though it has a 1 percent effect on the price level and exchange rate, has no further effects. This case is illustrated in Figure 24.1(b) for a single change in the money supply. The exchange rate simply follows a random walk in lock step with the domestic money supply (relative to the foreign money supply). It is important to note that these are the only circumstances (random-walk money supplies, in a flexible-price monetary model) under which the exchange rate should theoretically be expected to follow a random walk. Most of the time there will be some reason to expect future depreciation (or appreciation) over a long horizon, as in a high- (or low-) inflation country.

What happens if the public suddenly raises its estimate of the probability that the money supply will be increased in four years (because the more expansionary of the two political parties will come to power in the next presidential election)? The case of an expected future increase in the money supply is illustrated in Figure 24.1(c). Four years from now, assuming that the anticipated increase in the money supply indeed materializes, the exchange rate will increase proportionately. It might seem that an event so far off in the future would have no effect on *today's* exchange rate. This supposition turns out to be incorrect, however, assuming that investors' expectations are rational. Under *rational expectations*, investors know the true model that determines the exchange rate and they form their expectations of the future exchange rate by taking the mathematical expectation, using all available information, including their knowledge of the true model. In other words, "expectations," meaning what investors anticipate, are now the same as "mathematical expectation," meaning the average realized value given all available information.[13]

A rational investor, in estimating how much the currency will be worth next period, will think farther ahead in the future than just one period. She will make the following calculation. She will realize that if it is known that the money supply and the exchange rate will increase in year 4, then in year 3 investors will shift their portfolios out of the domestic currency to protect themselves from the capital loss expected over the subsequent period. She will realize that, as a result, some of the depreciation will take place in year 3. However, if it can be foreseen that the currency will depreciate in year 3, then it can be foreseen that investors in year 2 will shift out of the domestic currency to protect themselves from the expected loss; some of the depreciation thus takes place in year 2. If the currency is expected to depreciate in year 2, by the same logic it will depreciate in year 1. Finally, if the domestic currency is expected to depreciate in year 1, then the rational investor living in the present will shift her portfolio out of it immediately. If *all* today's investors make this calculation, they will

[12] Any increase in money demand coming from growth in potential output is omitted here. If money demand increases, the currency can appreciate even without a change in the money supply. There also has long been a gradual downward trend in real money demand arising from innovation in banking. (For example, since the invention of automatic teller machines there has been less need to carry cash around.)

[13] Chapter 23 explained that workers who have rational expectations forecast the price level optimally, and determine their wage demands accordingly. Here investors who have rational expectations forecast the exchange rate optimally and determine their asset demands accordingly. In both cases, the individuals are assumed to have as much knowledge of the correct model of the economy, and as much up-to-date information on the economic variables, as the economists building the model.

cause the currency to depreciate today, even if the money supply is not expected to increase for four years.

In theory, if investors suddenly decided for some reason that the money supply was going to increase in the year 2000, or even in the year 3000, by the same logic there would be an effect on today's exchange rate. The effect on today's exchange rate is smaller, the farther into the future is the expected increase in the money supply. Future changes in the money supply are *discounted* back to the present. So, reassuringly, the anticipation of an increase in the money supply in the year 3000 would have a negligibly small effect on the exchange rate today.

24.3 TWO EXAMPLES OF THE IMPORTANCE OF EXPECTATIONS

The expectation regarding future changes in the exchange rate plays a key role, as we have seen. We further offer two specific illustrations of this point, while staying within the framework of the monetarist model.

Speculative Bubbles

Exchange rates are often alleged to fluctuate excessively, in the sense of "unnecessary" movement in the exchange rate that takes place even in the absence of any movement in fundamental macroeconomic variables such as the money supply. We have just seen that today's exchange rate can move in a given period without any movement in the money supply taking place in that period. This is not a valid example of excess variability, however, because such movements are caused by movements in expectations that are based in actual movements in the money supply, even if the latter do not take place in the same period. The question arises whether changes in expectations can occur, with no basis in fundamentals at all, that shift demand for the currency and thus cause the exchange rate to move.

Financial commentators have discussed the possibility of *speculative bubbles* ever since such classic historical episodes as the Dutch tulip bulb mania of the seventeenth century and the South Sea Company real estate bubble of the early eighteenth century, which even took in Sir Isaac Newton. In recent years, puzzling large movements in exchange rates have been identified as speculative bubbles by some. The final 20 percent appreciation of the dollar in the eight months preceding its peak in February 1985, for example, seems difficult to explain otherwise. (Refer to Figure 24.3(b).)

When the exchange rate is on a speculative bubble path, it wanders away from the equilibrium value dictated by macroeconomic fundamentals because of self-confirming expectations. Such a bubble would arise as follows. In period 0, speculators suddenly decide for some reason that the currency is going to depreciate in period 1. (For example, even without any good reason to expect a future change in fundamentals, speculators may form their expectations by simplistically extrapolating a recent blip in the exchange rate.) To protect themselves against the feared depreciation, they sell the currency and drive down its price in period 0. Is such behavior irrational? Not necessarily. The currency might actually turn out to depreciate in period 1, justifying their fears; it will do so if there is a fall in demand for it in period 1, which will happen if there is an expectation of further depreciation in period 2. Is it irrational to expect a depreciation in period 2? Not if there is a fall in demand for it in period 2 due to an expectation of depreciation in period 3. Similarly, it will be rational to

This is different than pushing based in macro fundamental Bno!

expect depreciation in period 3 if depreciation is also expected in period 4, and so forth. If there is an ultimate day of reckoning on which the value of the currency is known to be tied down to some specific value, this will prevent the speculative bubble from getting started. But without such a day of reckoning, there is nothing in the expectations logic that prevents the exchange rate from soaring indefinitely high, regardless of the economic fundamentals. While society in the aggregate will probably be harmed by such unnecessary movements, each individual speculator will feel constrained to go along with the herd because, given that everyone else is pushing the exchange rate up, he would lose money by trying to buck the trend alone.

macro coordinator

In practice, the exchange rate does not shoot off to infinity, that is, diverge indefinitely far from the long-run value implied by fundamentals. At most, it wanders away from fundamentals equilibrium for a short time before the bubble bursts. It is possible, however, that such bubbles do regularly form and subsequently burst, thus adding to the variability of floating exchange rates.[14] Some of those who believe that this phenomenon is important argue that a more interventionist policy on the part of the government might be able to reduce unnecessary volatility in the economy even without a change in monetary policy.[15]

Target Zones and the "Honeymoon Effect"

Some economists who dislike the high variability of floating exchange rates, but who recognize that fixed exchange rates are not a practical alternative for large industrialized countries, propose the adoption of a system of *target zones* for the dollar, yen, and European currencies, roughly analogous to the EMS. Under this system the countries involved would (1) agree on the fundamental equilibrium value of each exchange rate (subject to periodic review), (2) agree on fairly wide bands within which exchange rates wouuld be free to fluctuate, and (3) commit to alter monetary policies when exchange rates threatened to violate those bands. Critics of such schemes object that governments are not very good at choosing the correct fundamental equilibrium rates. Proponents respond that the private marketplace is even worse at it.[16]

[14] It might seem that as soon as investors accept that every speculative bubble will eventually burst, rational expectations would prevent them from ever starting in the first place. However, the theory of "stochastic" (as opposed to "deterministic") speculative bubbles shows that this need not be the case. It is easy to build in at each point in time a probability of the collapse of the bubble and the return of the currency in question to fundamentals equilibrium. If the probability of collapse of the currency during any given period is small, the rate of appreciation that is expected to hold in the event of non-collapse will be sufficient to presuade speculators to continue to hold the currency despite the possibility of collapse. (The assumption of rational expectations is satisfied if the interest differential is equal to the mathematically expected rate of appreciation of the foreign currency, i.e., the probability-weighted average of appreciation in the event that the bubble lasts another period and depreciation in the event that it collapses in the next period.) Olivier Blanchard, "Speculative Bubbles, Crashes and Rational Expectations," *Economics Letter* (1979): 387–389. Rudiger Dornbusch. "Equilibrium and Disequilibrium Exchange Rates," *Zeitschrift für Wirtschafts und Sozialwissenshaften*, 102 (6) (1982) reprinted in *Dollars, Debts and Deficits* (Cambridge, MA: M.I.T. Press, 1986).

[15] John Williamson and Marcus Miller, *Targets and Indicators: A Blueprint for the International Coordination of Economic Policy*, Policy Analyses in International Economics No. 22 (September 1987). On the other hand, analogous to the problem of speculative bubbles under floating exchange rates is the problem of speculative attacks under fixed rates. Robert Flood and Peter Garber, "Collapsing Exchange Rate Regimes: Some Linear Examples," *Journal of International Economics* (1984).

[16] John Williamson, "Target Zones and the Management of the Dollar," *Brookings Papers on Economic Activity*, 1 (1986): 165–174. See Jacob Frenkel and Morris Goldstein, "A Guide to Target Zones," *IMF Staff Papers* 33 (4) (December 1986).

Figure 24.2   The Target Zone

If expectations played no role, then the monetary authorities would have to intervene as soon as fundamentals had drifted as far as $\pm 2\frac{1}{4}$ percent, at D_1. But speculation helps reduce the range of variation of S.

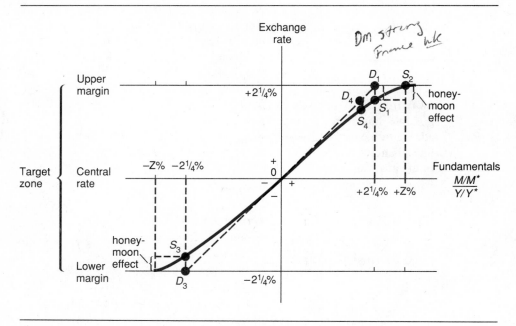

The recently developed theory of target zones shows—when the authorities are credibly committed to use monetary policy to stabilize the exchange rate within the announced bands—that speculation can help in this effort.[17] France and Germany announce that the franc/mark rate will be subject to specified margins around the central rate. What happens if, subsequently, French or German economic fundamentals drift in a particular direction and the exchange rate draws near to one of the proclaimed margins of the target zone?

The horizontal axis of Figure 24.2 measures economic fundamentals. Assume that the franc/mark rate is determined by the monetarist model, as represented by Equation 24.9, so that fundamentals are represented simply by $(M/M^*)/(Y/Y^*)$. The vertical axis measures the franc/mark exchange rate, S. Let us say that the exchange rate nears the upper margin, because real growth in Germany exceeds real growth in France. If the monetary authorities do not have a genuine commitment to the target zone arrangement, then there is nothing to stop the exchange rate from going right through the boundary. But let us assume that the authorities are in fact prepared to adjust monetary policy to keep the exchange rate inside the band. This means that the Bank of France is prepared to reduce French money growth to offset the decrease in the relative demand for francs.

[17] The theory is that of Paul Krugman, "Target Zones and Exchange Rate Dynamics," *Quarterly Journal of Economics* 106 (1991): 669–682.

(Banks!)

It might appear that as soon as the macroeconomic fundamentals reach the level of $2\frac{1}{4}$ percent above the central rate, where the diagonal line crosses the upper margin for S at point D_1, the Bank of France must step in to prevent the rate from breaching the limit. But we must remember that the exchange rate is determined not just by the current fundamentals $(M/M^*)/(Y/Y^*)$, but also by investor expectations Δs^e. When the exchange rate nears the upper margin, speculators are aware that it is much more likely in the future to move down rather than up, because the central bank will intervene against an upward movement. In other words, Δs^e is negative. Investors respond with a reduced demand for marks. The result is that, when fundamentals are at D_1, the equilibrium value of the exchange rate is at S_1. Thus speculation works to narrow the range of variation of the exchange rate, even before the authorities roll up their sleeves. The difference between the two points has been called the "honeymoon effect." Not until the fundamentals reach some more extreme limiting point, indicated in Figure 24.2 by "$+ Z\%$," will the exchange rate draw so close to the boundary of the target zone that the Bank of France is forced to intervene by reducing the money supply. This is point S_2.

The same honeymoon effect holds at the lower margin. If the fundamentals drift to $2\frac{1}{4}$ percent below the central rate, speculators know that a future increase is more likely than a future decrease and respond by increasing their demand for marks. They push the exchange rate up from point D_3 to point S_3. The honeymoon effect pushes other points off the diagonal line as well—for example, from D_4 to S_4, into a curve with a flattened "S" shape. The key point is that speculation helps narrow the range of variation. The "catch," once again, is that the authorities' commitment to intervene when necessary must be credible.

24.4 OVERSHOOTING AND THE REAL EXCHANGE RATE *(Sticky price MinEC!)*

The equation developed in Section 24.1 has a number of problems if it is intended as a complete theory. Chief among them is that it at best explains only movement in the *nominal* exchange rate. As a consequence of the flexible-price assumption, it cannot account for movement in the *real* exchange rate. Chapter 19 showed that the evidence is strongly against PPP, in other words, against a constant real exchange rate, in the short run. It appears that goods prices are in fact sticky, whether as a result of imperfect information, costs to changing prices, contracts, or inertia in consumer habits. As a result, disturbances in the nominal exchange rate are reflected as disturbances in the real exchange rate, which die out only very slowly over time. This was the justification for the constant-price assumption made in the Keynesian and Mundell-Fleming models (Chapters 18 and 22 respectively). Assuming that goods prices are literally constant is too extreme, however. The flexible-price monetary model went to the opposite extreme, and assumed that there are no barriers preventing goods prices from adjusting instantaneously. This section develops the sticky-price version of the monetary model. It is a realistic synthesis of the two extremes that turns out to be equivalent to the Mundell-Fleming model in the short run and the monetarist model in the long-run. The model is from a classic article by Rudiger Dornbusch.[18]

The effort to derive the long-run equilibrium exchange rate, $\overline{S}$, in the first half of

---

[18] "Expectations and Exchange Rate Dynamics," *Journal of Political Economy* (1976) 1161–1174.

the chapter has not been wasted. This section merely adds in short-run deviations of the exchange rate, S, from that equilibrium.

Related to the problem that real exchange rates are not constant is the problem that real interest rates also are not constant. National differences in nominal interest rates do not fully reflect differences in expected inflation rates. In the 1970s, there was a rough correspondence between major industrialized countries' interest rates and their inflation rates. The United Kingdom had the highest of the nominal interest rates, Switzerland the lowest, with Japan and Germany fairly low as well in the late 1970s. The United States was in between. Precisely the same ordering of countries applied to the inflation rates: Switzerland the lowest, followed by Germany and Japan, then the United States, and the United Kingdom the highest. There was also something of a correlation over time: Most countries experienced sharp increases in interest rates at the same time that inflation rates went up after 1973 (the time of the first worldwide oil price shock). Interest rates and inflation rates both came back down somewhat after 1975 and then both went back up again after 1979 (the time of the second oil price shock). Thus, the pattern of the 1970s was loosely consistent with the idea that nominal interest differentials reflect expected inflation differentials and expectations of currency depreciation. In other words, the pattern was consistent with the parity conditions that made Equations 23.8, 23.9. and 23.12 equivalent.

This pattern broke down after 1980. Nominal interest rates rose in all countries and came down only slowly after 1984, even though inflation began steadily declining in 1981. U.S. interest rates rose the farthest, even though inflation in the United States fell more rapidly than in Japan, Germany, and Switzerland. In other words, real interest differentials became large and highly variable in the 1980s.[19] For this reason, the model cannot remain in the simple form that assumes real interest parity. Variation in the real interest differential must be included as an additional factor in the model of variation in the real exchange rate.

We retain the assumption that expected returns are equalized across countries when expressed in common units: Not only are there no barriers that slow down portfolio adjustment, but investors treat domestic and foreign bonds as perfect substitutes in their portfolios.[20] Thus, uncovered interest parity holds as before.

$$i - i^* = \Delta s^e$$

Subtracting the expected inflation differential, $\Delta p^e - \Delta p^{*e}$, from both sides yields an analogous parity condition in real terms:

[19] One can sometimes come to different conclusions regarding real interest rates depending on the precise measure one uses for expected inflation. Apparent variation in real interests rates in the 1970s was small enough that some economists attributed it entirely to the problem of measurement, believing that ex ante real interest rates were in truth constant. But movements in the 1980s were so large, regardless of what measure one uses for expected inflation, that it is no longer possible to argue that real interest rates are constant. Real interest rates for the United States and an average of ten trading partners are shown in Figure 24.3(a).

[20] Saying that expected rates of returns are equalized across countries when expressed in common units is not the same as saying that real interest rates are equalized across countries. A country's real interest rate is the return on its bonds expressed in terms of purchasing power *over that country's goods*. An international investor has an incentive to arbitrage away any differentials in interest rates when expressed in a common currency, but there is no incentive to arbitrage away a differential between the U.S. rate of return expressed in terms of U.S. goods and the German rate of return expressed in terms of German goods. If PPP held, then the two calculations would be the same. However, this secion allows for the fact that PPP does not hold.

$$(i - \Delta p^e) - (i^* - \Delta p^{*e}) = \Delta s^e - \Delta p^e + \Delta p^{*e}$$

or

$$r - r^* = (\Delta s_{\text{real}})^e \tag{24.13}$$

where r and r^* are the domestic and foreign real interest rates, and $(\Delta s_{\text{real}})^e$ is the expected rate of change of the real exchange rate, SP^*/P, algebraically equal to the expected rate of the nominal exchange rate minus the expected inflation differential. Equation 24.13 shows that the differential in real interest rates is equal to the expected rate of real depreciation of the currency. Intuitively, if investors expect a country's currency to be depreciating in real terms, they will not be willing to hold its assets unless they are compensated by a higher real interest rate.

To take an example, in 1984 the U.S. real interest rate was above major trading partners' real interest rates, signaling that investors expected the dollar to depreciate in real terms in the future. (They turned out to be right.) To take a different example, Chile had very high real interest rates in the late 1970s, signaling in part that investors considered the government's attempt to peg the value of the currency at a high level to be unsustainable. (They too turned out to be right.)[21]

The next question is what determines expectations. It is always difficult to model expectations because it is difficult to know what goes on inside people's minds. Yet it is natural to suppose that, when the exchange rate is observed to deviate from the long-run equilibrium level, investors will expect it to move back in the direction of that equilibrium over time. For this purpose, we need to know what we mean by the long-run equilibrium. PPP is a good candidate for the long-run equilibrium. In fact, we used the assumption of PPP in the monetary model at the beginning of the chapter to represent the long-run equilibrium level of the exchange rate, $\bar{S}$.

Section 19.2 showed that after a disturbance, there is a slow but positive tendency for the real exchange rate to return toward PPP until the next disturbance comes along. The tendency to return to equilibrium is so slow—and new disturbances come along so often—that it is difficult to detect. When a sufficiently long time sample is examined, however, it is possible to detect a tendency for the exchange rate to eliminate as much as 30 percent of the existing gap per year. If this tendency to *regress* toward equilibrium exists in the real exchange rate, then investors are presumably aware of it. (This is another application of the idea that investors are rational.) Thus, investors are said to have *regressive expectations*:

$$\Delta s^e_{\text{real}} = - \theta(S - \bar{S})/\bar{S} \tag{24.14}$$

The equation says that when the currency is thought to be currently "overvalued," that is, to have a higher value than is given by long-run equilibrium, $\bar{S}$, investors will expect it to depreciate in the future; and when the currency is thought to be currently "undervalued," that is, to have a lower value than in long-run equilibrium, investors expect it to appreciate in the future. The parameter θ is the rate at which the real exchange rate is expected to regress toward its equilibrium.

---

[21] In the case of Argentina, the government attempted to have the nominal exchange rate depreciate along a gradual preannounced path. The table of preannounced exchange rates was called the "tablita." The fact that real interest rates were high again suggests that investors expected the currency not only to depreciate, but to depreciate at a rate faster than the inflation differential.

Before proceeding with Equation 24.14, it would be reassuring to have some evidence that this is, in fact, how expectations are formed. There are a number of surveys that periodically ask bankers, foreign exchange traders, economists, and other market participants their expectations regarding the exchange rate. While different survey respondents form their expectations in different ways, some systematic patterns are evident. After the dollar appreciated sharply above its PPP level in the early 1980s, the survey respondents reported an expectation that it would depreciate in the future. According to a survey conducted every six weeks by the *Financial Report* (a publication associated with the *Economist*), the median investor in 1984 expected the dollar to depreciate 10.0 percent over the following year, against an average of the mark, yen, pound, French franc, and Swiss franc.[22] Equation 24.14 turns out to fit these data well; the parameter θ is estimated at 0.2. It is often dangerous to put too much faith in responses to surveys. In this case, however, it is reassuring that the speed at which people seem to expect the exchange rate to regress to PPP is in the general range of estimates of the speed at which it in fact does regress to PPP.

We now combine Equations 24.13 and 24.14

$$r - r^* = - \theta(S - \overline{S})/\overline{S}$$

and solve for the exchange rate as a function of the real interest differential.

$$(S - \overline{S})/\overline{S} = - (1/\theta)(r - r^*) \tag{24.15}$$

Equation 24.15 says that when the domestic real interest rate exceeds the foreign rate, the value of the currency exceeds its long-run equilibrium value. Why?

Consider an increase in the Canadian real interest rate, for example, due to a monetary contraction. It quickly leads to an increase in international investors' demand for Canadian assets, causing the Canadian dollar to appreciate. When the currency appreciates above its long-run equilibrium value, investors expect that in the future it will have to come back down, because it is "overvalued." How much does the currency appreciate? Until it has gone far enough that the expectation of future depreciation back toward equilibrium is large enough to offset the interest differential. Only then will investors be willing to hold U.S. assets despite the fact that they do not pay as high an interest rate as Canadian assets. In other words, the overvaluation must be sufficiently large to offset the interest differential in the minds of investors. Loosely speaking, capital comes into the country and the currency appreciates until this condition is met. More precisely, the appreciation is simultaneous with the increase in the interest rate and the resulting increase in demand for domestic assets; no measurable net capital inflow need actually take place. (Recall that the exchange rate adjusts instantaneously so as to equate supply and demand.)

Notice from Equation 24.15 that if θ is large, then a given increase in the real interest differential will be associated with only a small appreciation of the currency,

---

[22] According to a survey conducted by American Express Banking Corporation in London, in 1984 the dollar was expected to depreciate against the five currencies at a rate of 8.5 percent over the following year. This is as contrasted with the average for the period 1976–1979, before the dollar appreciation had begun, when expected depreciation was − 0.2 percent. (Jeffrey Frankel and Kenneth Froot, "Using Survey Data to Test Standard Propositions Regarding Exchange Rate Expectations," *American Economic Review* (March 1987): 136.)

because this is sufficient to generate the necessary expectation of future depreciation. If the expected speed of adjustment is low, however, then the effect on the exchange rate can be large. For example, if θ is 0.2, then a .01 increase in the real interest rate causes a 5 percent (.01/0.2) appreciation of the currency.

Let us return to the example of the shift in U.S. monetary policy that took place in 1979. In the late 1970s, monetary policy was loose in the United States and the inflation rate was high. As a result, real interest rates became low, even below zero. (Although nominal interest rates were relatively high by historic standards, the inflation rate was just as high.) Figure 24.3(a) shows how low U.S. real interest rates were in the late 1970s. In this period the dollar depreciated to its lowest level of the floating-rate era. Then, in October 1979, the Federal Reserve Board under Chairman Paul Volcker dramatically shifted monetary policy to a tighter stance, to fight inflation. Interest rates rose sharply in early 1980, and the dollar appreciated in response to the increased attractiveness of U.S. assets. The nominal interest rate differential between the United States and its trading partners, approximately zero in the period 1976–1979, rose to about .03 in the period 1981–1982.

The real interest differential continued to rise through mid-1984, mostly in the form of declining expectations of U.S. inflation.[23] The rise was clearer for long-term interest rates, shown in Figure 24.3(a), than for short-term rates. Similar arguments apply, however. The increase in real rates of return made U.S. assets more attractive and caused the dollar to appreciate. Figure 24.3(b) shows how the real value of the dollar increased with the real interest differential. As of mid-1984, a real interest differential on ten-year bonds as large as 3 or 4 percent implied that investors expected the dollar to depreciate in real terms at a rate of at least 3 percent per year on average over the next ten years, or 30 percent altogether. If ten years is considered the appropriate length of time needed for the real exchange rate to return virtually all the way to its long-term equilibrium level, then this simple calculation suggests that investors considered the dollar to be about 30 percent above its long-run equilibrium (as compared to 20 percent *below* its long-run equilibrium in 1979). These numbers compare fairly well with the magnitude of the real appreciation of the dollar over this period, suggesting that there need not necessarily have been a change in the long-run equilibrium.[24]

In terms of the Mundell-Fleming graph, the U.S. economy in the mid-1980s could be represented as an *IS-LM* intersection at a real interest rate in excess of that prevailing in the rest of the world. The reason has been discussed before: a distorted mix of monetary and fiscal policy. Chapter 22 raised the question how a positive real interest differential like this could be consistent with perfect capital mobility. Now

---

[23] Roughly similar conclusions regarding the real interest rate hold whether expected inflation is measured by a distributed lag on actual inflation, by predictions of professional forecasters, or by a survey of international banks.

[24] The argument for looking at long-term real interest differentials to see how overvalued the market considers the exchange rate to be was developed by Peter Isard, ''An Accounting Framework and Some Issues for Modeling How Exchange Rates Respond to the News,'' in Jacob Frenkel, ed. *Exchange Rates and International Macroeconomics* (Chicago: University of Chicago Press, 1983). It was applied to the dollar in the Council of Economic Advisers' *Economic Report of the President*, 1984, Chapter 2.

FIGURE 24.3   U.S. and Foreign Real Interest Rates and the Exchange Rate

(a) The U.S. real interest rate was low in the late 1970s and high in the early 1980s, both absolutely and relative to Group of 10 trading partners. (b) The swings in the real interest differential usually coincide with swings in the value of the dollar.

(a) Nominal and real long term interest rates

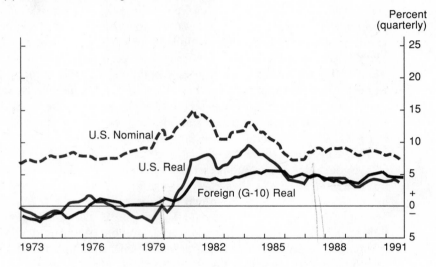

(b) The dollar and real interest rates

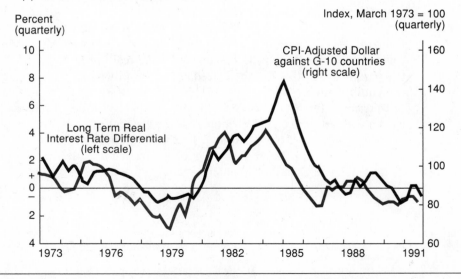

Source: Peter Hooper, Board of Governors of the Federal Reserve Systems, Washington, D.C.

we know the answer: Because the dollar had appreciated so far above its long-run equilibrium, there was an expectation of future dollar depreciation that was sufficient to offset the interest differential in investors' minds.

Long-Run Equilibrium

We have shown that the level of the exchange rate, S, relative to its long-run equilibrium, $\overline{S}$, is determined by the real interest differential, itself determined by such factors as monetary policy. If $\overline{S}$ is constant, for example, movement in S is entirely explained by movement in the real interest differential. In general, however, it is unlikely that the long-run equilibrium rate is constant. Even assuming that the long-run equilibrium *real* exchange rate is constant,[25] it cannot be assumed that the equilibrium *nominal* exchange rate, $\overline{S}$, is constant. Because it is a nominal magnitude like the price levels, it will follow a rising path over time in an economy with a high rate of money growth.

Section 24.2 used PPP to derive a model of the exchange rate. At that point we were operating under the assumption that prices were perfectly flexible, whereas we have recognized since then that they are in fact sticky. In the long run prices *are* flexible, however. Thus, PPP can be used to characterize long-run equilibrium. So, although Equation 24.12 no longer serves as a model of the moment-to-moment exchange rate, S, it now serves nicely as a model of the long-run equilibrium exchange rate, $\overline{S}$.

The next task is to see how the exchange rate moves from the short-run equilibrium to the long-run. The transition from short run to long run is illustrated in Figure 24.4, which shows the exchange rate on the horizontal axis and the price level on the vertical axis. The proportionality between $\overline{S}$ and P that holds in PPP equilibrium is graphed as an upward-sloping line. It is necessary to be on the PPP line only in the long run. This means that when the money supply goes up permanently by 10 percent and the price level eventually rises proportionately, the exchange rate too will eventually rise by the same 10 percent. This is a movement up along the PPP line, from point A to point B.[26]

Equation 24.15 indicates that in the long run in which the exchange rate is at its equilibrium level ($S = \overline{S}$), the real interest rate differential is zero ($r = r^*$). The explanation is that if there is no reason for investors to expect future depreciation of the

---

[25] The possibility that the long-run equilibrium real exchange rate might itself change cannot be ruled out. Japan is an example of a country that is often thought to have an upward trend in the long-run equilibrium real value of its currency. To take another example, it has been suggested that the long-run equilibrium real value of the dollar will be lower in the 1990s than it was in the 1970s, because the United States ran up over $700 billion in international debt in between, which requires a permanent improvement in the trade balance to earn the foreign exchange to service the debt. The same could be said of the currencies of many LDCs after they ran up large debts in the 1970s.

[26] Other experiments can be considered as well. If the level of output goes up permanently, as it does when the level of potential output goes up, then the higher demand for money implies that in long-run equilibrium the currency will appreciate proportionately, as in Equation 24.12. This is a movement to the left down the PPP line (lower P and lower S).

FIGURE 24.4   The Dornbusch Overshooting Diagram

An increase in the money supply, M, raises the price level, P, and spot rate, S, proportionately in the long run by PPP (at B). In the short run, however, P is tied down. As a result, S increases more than proportionately in the short run at C, that is, it overshoots its long-run equilibrium.

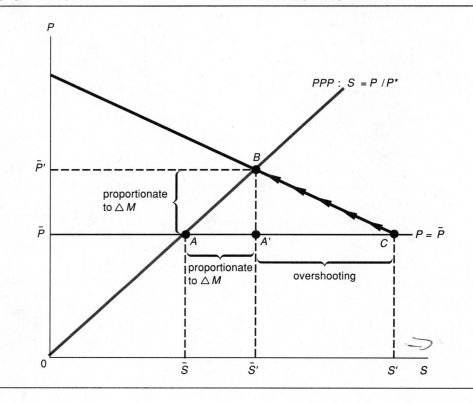

currency (in real terms), then they have no reason to require a (real) interest differential to be willing to hold the currency. This international equalization of real interest rates is similar to the real interest parity condition that followed from Equation 24.11 in Section 24.2, but now we see that it only holds in long-run equilibrium.

The Path from Short-Run Overshooting to Long-Run Equilibrium

What happens in the immediate aftermath of an increase in the money supply? It would clearly be wrong to assume that the economy will stay on the PPP line; goods markets do not adjust fast enough to guarantee this in the short run. The assumption that goods prices are sticky means that when the nominal money supply, M, increases by 10 percent, the real money supply, M/P, on impact, also increases by 10 percent, because prices do not move at all in the short run. (In terms of the Mundell-Fleming model, the LM curve shifts to the right.) Money market equilibrium (Equation 24.4) then requires that the monetary expansion will drive down the interest rate. The lower interest rate in the home country in turn causes international investors to head for the exits. The decline in demand for domestic assets causes the currency to depreciate.

We can figure the size of the depreciation. $\bar{S}$ alone increases by the same 10 percent as the money supply, but the total change in S is greater: Equation 24.15 says that $S/\bar{S}$ increases by $(1/\theta)$ times the fall in the interest rate.[27] Only when the currency has depreciated that far do investors have the necessary expectation of appreciation back toward the (new) long-run equilibrium that they must have if they are to hold domestic assets willingly despite the fact that these assets pay a lower rate of interest than foreign assets. We have just derived the now classic *overshooting* result of Rudiger Dornbusch: Even though the long-run equilibrium exchange rate increases by the same proportion as the money supply, the short-term equilibrium exchange rate increases more than proportionately.

Where is the economy now on Figure 24.4? In the short run, it cannot leave the horizontal latitude of the starting point, A, because P is tied down. S increases, which means a move to the right in the graph. How far? The economy moves farther than point A', because if it stopped there, S would have increased only by the same percentage as $\bar{S}$. S must increase by more than $\bar{S}$. Thus the economy moves, on impact, to a point like C.[28]

Establishing the short-run equilibrium, C, and the long-run equilibrium, B, prompts the next question: How do we get from here to there? At point C, there are several factors stimulating the demand for goods. First, the real interest rate has fallen, which should stimulate the domestic demand for capital goods, construction, and consumer durables. Second, the real value of the currency has fallen. Indeed, any point below, or to the right of, the PPP line is a point where domestic goods are cheaper than foreign goods. This should stimulate the demand for domestically produced tradable goods, such as the foreign demand for exports. The increased demand for goods will put upward pressure on prices. The price level will be somewhat higher after a little time has passed.

As the price level, P, slowly rises to higher levels, the real money supply, M/P, slowly declines to lower levels, though it is still higher than it was before the increase in M. (The LM curve slowly shifts back to the left.) As a result, the interest rate slowly rises, though it is still lower than the foreign interest rate. Equation 24.15 shows that as the interest rate rises, the currency appreciates back toward its long-run equilibrium; international investors no longer find domestic assets quite so

---

[27] The fall in the nominal rate is in turn $1/\mu$ times the increase in the money supply. where μ is the semi-elasticity of money demand with respect to the interest rate. (See the Chapter Supplement.)

If the monetary expansion raises the level of output, as it probably will, then the interest rate will not fall by as much as it would if the level of output were constant. As a result, the currency will not overshoot its long-run equilibrium by as much. Similarly, if the monetary expansion raises the expected inflation rate, then the real interest rate will not fall by as much as the nominal interest rate, and as a result the currency will not overshoot its long-run equilibrium by as much. But this does not qualitatively change the results described in the text. The algebra for these cases, and indeed for this entire section, can be found in Rudiger Dornbusch, "Expectations and Exchange Rate Dynamics," *Journal of Political Economy* (1976).

[28] Point C corresponds to point B in the Mundell-Fleming diagram, Figure 22.7, with the interest differential attributed to the expectation of future appreciation (rather than to imperfect capital mobility).

unattractive. Thus, as we move up in Figure 24.4 (higher P), we also move back to the left (lower S).[29]

The process continues as long as the real money supply is greater than it was before the monetary expansion, that is, as long as the real interest rate and real currency values are low, because the excess demand for goods causes prices to rise. When the price level has risen by the same proportion as the money supply, then the real money supply, real interest rate, and real exchange rate are all back to their original levels. Only then is there no excess demand for goods and no need for prices to continue rising. This long-run equilibrium is none other than point B, the PPP point at which all nominal magnitudes have increased by the same percentage. This illustrates a general principle that has recurred over several previous chapters: In the long run in which all real magnitudes have had time to return to their equilibrium values, all nominal magnitudes must change proportionately. Figure 24.5(a) shows how, after the initial overshooting caused by the increased in the level of the money supply, over time the real money supply and real interest rate gradually return to their original levels, and as a consequence the exchange rate gradually approaches its new equilibrium level.

Notice the correspondence between what investors at pont C thought would happen in the future and what actually happens. In the short-run overshooting equilibrium at C (when the price level had not yet had time to adjust to the increase in the money supply), investors thought that the currency would appreciate in the future because they have regressive expectations. We have just established that this is in fact what happens as the price level adjusts: S does indeed move in the direction of $\bar{S}$. If investors have rational expectations, then they know the complete model, and the rate at which they expect S to move toward $\bar{S}$ is precisely the rate at which it in fact turns out to do so. It is possible to think of rational expectations as a special case, however.

The model studied at the beginning of this chapter, where goods prices were perfectly flexible, can be viewed as a special case of the complete model, the case where the adjustment in goods markets is instantaneous. If the rate of change of prices is highly responsive to the excess demand for goods, then the system will move to point B very quickly. In the limit, the system will jump from A to B instantaneously. In that case, PPP always holds, $S = \bar{S}$, and Equation 24.12 constitutes a complete analysis of exchange rate determination. The Mundell-Fleming model can be viewed as the opposite extreme, where the speed of adjustment in goods markets is very slow.[30]

Exchange Rate Volatility

We have seen what happens in the aftermath of a single monetary disturbance. However, in practice, if one looks for the nominal exchange rate to follow the path of Figure 24.4 in the aftermath of an overshooting episode—a smooth return to long-run equilibrium—one is likely to be disappointed. In the real world, new disturbances

---

[29] The downward-sloping line connecting points B and C represents equilibrium in the asset markets, the relationship that must hold between P and S (via the interest rate, i) for the given money supply, M, to be willingly held.

[30] This discussion of overshooting has considered only changes in the level of the money supply. Changes in the expected growth rate of the money supply are considered in the appendix to this chapter. Analogous overshooting results appear as is illustrated in Figure 24.5(b).

FIGURE 24.5 Overshooting Effects of Changes in the Money Supply

(a)After a jump in the *level* of the money supply, P can only increase slowly. As a result, the real money supply, M/P, real interest differential, $r - r^*$, and spot rate, S, temporarily deviate from their long-run equilibriums. (b) An increase in the *rate of change* of the money supply causes similar deviations from long-run equilibrium, but now equilibrium is itself a moving target.

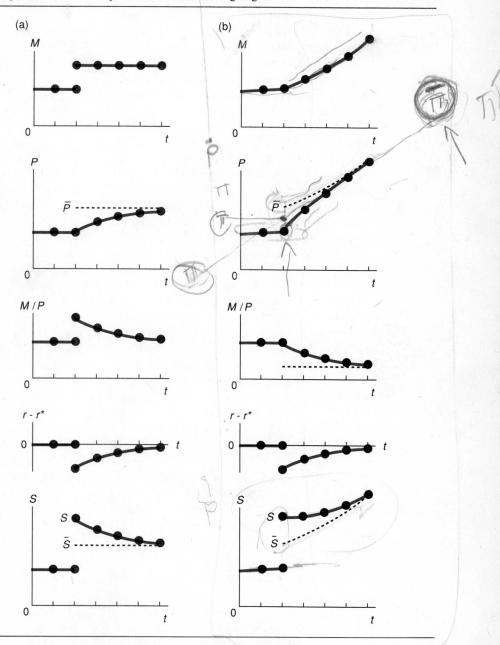

come along all the time, so that before the exchange rate has had time to return much of the way to its equilibrium, a new policy change in one direction or the other is likely to occur.[31] The effect on the exchange rate of any given monetary disturbance is as we have just seen, notwithstanding the possibility of future disturbances. When each new change in the money supply hits, the exchange rate changes more than proportionately; it then begins to move gradually back toward its long-run equilibrium until the next monetary disturbance comes along.

In practice, changes in the exchange rate are more variable than changes in the money supply or the price level. It is an attractive property of the overshooting model that it can explain this variability in exchange rates without having to bring in speculative bubbles or irrationality on the part of investors. The volatility of exchange rates in the model is a consequence of the fact that asset markets adjust instantaneously, while goods markets adjust slowly. If goods prices adjusted instantaneously, there would be no overshooting of the exchange rate. Exchange rate changes would be no more variable than changes in the money supply.

There is an analogy with a law of chemistry called Le Châtelier's Principle. When one variable in a physical system (such as the pressure or temperature of a gas) is constrained from changing in response to a disturbance (such as a change in its volume), one or more of the other variables in the system must change by more than it otherwise would, in order to compensate. Paul Samuelson first pointed out the possible application to economics: When one price is constrained from changing in response to a change in supply of a commodity, some other price must change by more in order to compensate. William Branson has pointed out the relevance for overshooting of the exchange rate: When the general price level is constrained from changing in response to a change in the money supply, the exchange rate changes more than proportionately to compensate.

Furthermore, the slower is the speed of adjustment (expected by investors), θ in Equation 24.14, the greater is the degree of overshooting.[32] This is because if the speed of exchange rate adjustment, θ is low, then for any given fall in the interest differential it takes a large undervaluation of the exchange rate to generate the necessary expectation of future appreciation equal to the interest differential. In terms of Figure 24.4, if θ is low, the asset market equilibrium line is flat and the exchange rate has to increase even farther than C before investors are willing to hold domestic assets. If the expected speed of adjustment is very high, on the other hand, then a movement just slightly beyond A', an increase in S just a little more than proportionate to the increase in the money supply, will be sufficient to satisfy investors.

Without knowing precisely the size of θ (or the other parameters in the monetary model), we cannot say that the observation that exchange rates are much more variable than money supplies necessarily means that exchange rates are "excessively variable." The variability may simply be the overshooting phenomenon in operation.

---

[31] For example, the dollar was still below its long-run equilibrium, in the aftermath of the easy monetary policy of the late 1970s, when the switch to a tighter monetary policy caused it to overshoot in the opposite direction in 1980–1982. Then, while the dollar was still above its long-run equilibrium, further increases in the real interest differential in 1983–1984 caused it to overshoot even farther on the upside, as can be seen in Figure 24.4. Refer back to Figure 19.5 for an idea of the frequency of disturbances to the real exchange rate in 119 years of U.S.-U.K. history.

[32] The greater is the speed of adjustment of goods prices, in turn, the greater is the expected speed of exchange rate adjustment, θ (assuming that expectations are rational).

24.5 TWO MORE EXAMPLES OF THE IMPORTANCE OF EXPECTATIONS

We have emphasized throughout this chapter the important role that expectations play in determining exchange rates in modern asset markets. We illustrate the point with two more examples.

The Example of Weekly Money Announcements

A clear illustration of the effect of changes in monetary expectations is the case of the weekly money announcements. Every Thursday, the Federal Reserve Board announces what the money stock was in the preceding week. In the early 1980s, the announcements were made at 4:10 P.M. on Friday afternoons and referred to the money stock nine days earlier. The financial markets looked forward to each week's announcement with both eagerness and trepidation. When the time drew near, trading slowed down and even stopped, as traders gathered around the newswire or computer terminal. When the announcement came out, prices in the various financial markets would jump in reaction, and trading would take off again. The most widely remarked reaction took place in the credit markets. When the Fed announced a money supply that was greater than observers had previously been expecting, interest rates would immediately jump up in reaction (or bond prices would jump down, which is another way of saying the same thing).[33] When the Fed announced a money supply that was smaller than had been expected, interest rates would fall in reaction.

What was the reason for these reactions? They might seem puzzling, considering that an increase in the money supply works to lower the interest rate rather than to raise it. The first thing to realize is that the interest rate movements on Thursday afternoons were not directly caused by the changes in the money supply themselves, which had taken place a week earlier, but rather by the effect of the new information on *expectations* as to future monetary policy.

According to the theory of efficient markets, it is only the *unanticipated* component of the announced change in the money supply that matters. If the announcement reports an increase no larger than had been previously expected, then there should be no effect on prices in the bond market, foreign-exchange market, or any other financial markets. Economics often refer to the importance of the "news," to signify that it is only the new information that matters.

There are two different explanations for a rise in the nominal interest rate in response to a money announcement: a rise in the expected inflation rate, or a rise in the real interest rate. The rise in the nominal interest rate could be due to a rise in the expected inflation rate if investors concluded from the announcement of an increase in the money supply that the Fed planned a faster rate of money growth in the future than had previously been expected. This is the case where investors do not put much credence in the money growth target that the Fed has announced for the year and interpret deviations of the money supply from the previously expected path as evidence

---

[33] Bond prices move inversely with the interest rate. If the interest rate is 10 percent, then a one-year treasury bill with a face value of $10,000 will have a price of about $9,000, so that investors who buy the treasury bill have the same rate of return as if they put their money into the bank and earned the interest. If the interest rate goes up, then the amount investors will be willing to pay for the treasury bill goes down.

that the Fed has changed its target. On the other hand, the rise in the nominal interest rate would be due to a rise in the real interest rate if investors interpret the announcement as a sign that the Fed will tighten monetary policy in the near future. This is a reasonable thing to expect the Fed to do if the increase in the money stock occurred for reasons beyond its control (for example, banks can expand credit to a certain degree, without there necessarily having been a change in Fed policy), and if it is seriously committed to keeping the money supply within its previously set target range. In other words, this is the case when the Fed's commitment to the preannounced target is credible to the financial markets.

How is it possible to tell, at any particular time, which of these is the real cause of an increase in the nominal interest rate? The foreign-exchange market provides the answer to this question. If there is an expectation of looser monetary policy and higher expected inflation, the exchange rate models predict that the dollar will fall on the news. Conversely, if there is an expectation of tighter monetary policy and a higher real interest rate, the dollar should rise on the news.

The evidence suggests that in the late 1970s, the Fed's money growth targets were not very credible. The dollar often fell in value immediately following announcements of money supplies that were greater than had been expected; investors worried about excessive money growth and the inflationary consequences.

After October 1979, however, when the Fed switched to a new set of operating procedures designed to set a firm course for the money supply with the aim of fighting inflation, the pattern of reaction to the weekly money announcements switched as well. In the early 1980s, there was a clear pattern in which both the interest rate and the dollar rose immediately in response to announced money stocks that were greater than expected. This suggests (1) that investors during this period expected the Fed to correct deviations from the target, (2) that investors believe that monetary contraction raises real interest rates, and (3) that higher real interest rates make U.S. assets more attractive and cause the dollar to appreciate, as in the overshooting model.[34]

The importance of the weekly money announcement diminished after October 1982, when the Federal Reserve started paying less attention to the money supply because innovations in the banking sector and other shifts in the demand for money had taken much of the meaning from M1 and the other traditional measures of monetary policy. By 1987, the Federal Reserve Board had stopped all pretense of setting M1 targets. As a result, interest rates and exchange rates no longer respond as strongly to the money announcements. However, there are still macroeconomic variables that provoke major reactions when announced. Following news suggesting strong economic growth, such as a decline in the unemployment rate or an increase in retail sales or durable goods orders, the dollar tends to appreciate. Investors figure, as in the monetary models, that higher domestic output raises the demand for domestic money.[35]

[34] Bradford Cornell, "Money Supply Announcements, Interest Rates, and Foreign Exchange," *Journal of International Money and Finance*, 1 (August 1982): 201–208. Charles Engel and Jeffrey Frankel, "Why Interest Rates React to Money Announcements: An Explanation from the Foreign Exchange Market," *Journal of Monetary Economics*, 13 (1984): 31–39.

[35] Gikas Hardouvelis, "Economic News, Exchange Rates and Interest Rates," *Journal of International Money and Finance*, 7 (1988).

Similarly, when there is an announcement of a better trade balance than had been expected, the dollar tends to appreciate.[36] The markets have paid more attention than ever to trade balance announcements in recent years. On October 14, 1987, the U.S. Commerce Department announced an August trade deficit that, though not quite as high as the peak earlier in the year, was higher than had been expected. Within minutes, investors responded in alarm; the dollar fell, interest rates rose, and the stock market plunged 95 points in one day (which, at the time, was a record). When the stock market fell another 508 points the following Monday, October 19, some observers pointed to the trade deficit announcement the week before as the bit of news that may have triggered the collapse.[37]

Is Speculation Stabilizing?

It might seem that overshooting is an example of what is called "destabilizing speculation," that investors, by freely buying and selling foreign exchange based on their expectations of changes in the exchange rate, make the exchange rate more variable than it would otherwise be. This is not the case, however. The overshooting model just developed illustrates the general principle that expectations are stabilizing rather than destabilizing, as long as an increase in the level of the exchange rate causes investors to reduce their expectations as to its future rate of change. (This is the case in regressive expectations, represented by Equation 24.14: S enters with a negative sign.) The reason is that if investors act on the basis of such expectations, they will be buying the currency when its value is low and selling when its value is high. This will raise the currency's price when it would otherwise be low and lower the price when it would otherwise be high. This type of speculation works to moderate the fluctuations that would otherwise occur in the exchange rate.

Investors, or "speculators," who buy low and sell high will also make a profit. This is why Milton Friedman (1953) argued that stabilizing speculators would prosper. Any speculators who were destabilizing would be buying high and selling low. They would lose money and thus soon be driven out of business.

It has sometimes been suggested that the government should try to discourage speculation—for example, by enacting capital controls or a tax on foreign exchange transactions, thereby returning the economy to a lower degree of international capital mobility. James Tobin has written that "we need to throw some sand in the well-greased wheels" of international financial markets through a small tax on all foreign exchange transactions.[38] If investors act on the basis of the type of stabilizing expectations studied here, Tobin's proposal to discourage speculation would increase

[36] Ked Hogan, Michael Melvin, and Dan Roberts, "Trade Balance News and Exchange Rates: Is There a Policy Signal?" *Journal of International Money and Finance* 10 (March 1991): S90–S99.

[37] The trade balance has no effect on the exchange rate in the model developed in this chapter (beyond the effect of any of the other components of GNP $= C + I + G + X - M$). This is a consequence of the assumption that when a country runs a trade deficit, the rest of the world is willing to lend it however much money it needs to finance its deficits—regardless of how much debt it has already incurred in the past—so long as it pays the world rate of interest. The next chapter introduces a role for the debt, so that the trade balance again matters for exchange rate determination.

[38] James Tobin, "A Proposal for International Monetary Reform," *Eastern Economic Journal*, 4 (3–4) (1978): 153–159. Similarly inclined is Rudiger Dornbusch, "Flexible Exchange Rates and Excess Capital Mobility," *Brookings Papers on Economic Activity*, 1 (1986): 209–226.

overshooting rather than reduce it, assuming that the new barrier to international capital flows were effective. If investors had to overcome a significant transaction cost in order to buy a foreign currency, then the exchange rate would have to drift even farther from its long-run equilibrium before the expectation of future appreciation was sufficiently great to inspire investors to buy it.

What, then, do proponents of such "anti-speculator" taxes have in mind? They have in mind that speculators do not form expectations in a stabilizing manner, such as is given by Equation 24.14. Rather, speculators may form their expectations by simply extrapolating past trends. Such forecasting rules are called *bandwagon expectations*: If investors actually act on the basis of them, they will jump on the bandwagon whenever the currency starts to move one direction or the other. In this case, they can create the sort of speculative bubbles described earlier. Investors buy when the currency is already high, thereby pushing it higher (until the bubble bursts); they sell the currency when it is already low, thereby pushing it lower. In such an environment, speculation would indeed increase exchange rate volatility.

Which expectations, stabilizing or destabilizing, prevail in practice? Under normal circumstances, when markets are functioning properly, economists believe that expectations are formed predominantly in a stabilizing manner. For example, during the period 1982–1984, because the dollar had risen above its PPP equilibrium, many forecasters expected it to depreciate in the future. Any investors who acted on the basis of such expectations, far from being the cause of the appreciation of the dollar, were selling dollars and thus dampening the price below what it would be otherwise.

There are times, however, when most market participants seem to lose sight of economic fundamentals and to extrapolate trends instead. As noted earlier, some observers have argued that July 1984 to February 1985 was such a period, with the final appreciation of the dollar up to its peak attributable to a speculative bubble rather than to fundamentals. Figure 24.4 does make it appear this way: The 1985 spike in the dollar appears to be the only major movement in the exchange rate that does not correspond to a movement in the real interest differential. In this view, the dollar did more than overshoot its long-run equilibrium; it overshot its short-run equilibrium as well.[39]

The view that the dollar was following a speculative bubble path by the end of 1984 would be sympathetic to the switch at the U.S. Treasury from a noninterventionist policy of "benign neglect" of the dollar under Secretary Donald Regan from 1981–1984, to a more activist policy under Secretary James Baker beginning in 1985. The switch was symbolized in September 1985 by the Plaza Accord, in which the finance ministers of the G-5 countries agreed to try to bring the dollar down. The dollar fell 4 percent the day the agreement was announced and continued to depreciate steadily thereafter. The Plaza was widely regarded as being a case of successful management of the exchange rate by policy-makers. Unfortunately, government officials are not always more skilled at identifying when the exchange rate has departed from fundamentals than are private investors.

---

[39] See Paul Krugman, "Is the Strong Dollar Sustainable?" *The U.S. Dollar–Recent Developments, Outlook, and Policy Options* (Kansas City: Federal Reserve Bank of Kansas City), pp. 103–133; and Stephen Marris, *Deficits and the Dollar: The World Economy at Risk*, Policy Analyses in International Economics (Washington: Institute for International Economics, 1985).

One thing to keep in mind is that the existence of a speculative bubble does not mean that it is easy for an investor to profit from it. The dollar in 1984 illustrates a point made in the discussion of speculative bubbles in Section 24.2. The knowledge that the bubble must eventually burst does not mean that investors can confidently expect to make money by moving into another currency (or "selling short"), because there is no telling how long the bubble will continue, and the investor who doesn't go along with the trend will lose money as long as it continues. This is what happened to all those in 1983 or 1984 who predicted the dollar depreciation too early.

24.6 SUMMARY

This chapter examined how monetary forces determine the exchange rate under a floating-rate system. This required introducing exchange rate expectations as a factor, in addition to interest rates, in determining investors' decisions regarding what assets to hold. Modern models of exchange rate determination share the property of perfect international capital mobility. If there is also perfect substitutability between domestic and foreign bonds, then uncovered interest parity holds: The interest differential must be just large enough to offset investors' expected depreciation of the domestic currency.

This chapter also introduced a flexible-price version of the monetary model, in which Purchasing Power Parity holds, which is relevant for long-run equilibrium. The resulting equation shows how the exchange rate, as the relative price of two currencies, is determined by the supply and demand for two currencies. It is useful for seeing how (1) an exogenous increase in real income raises the demand for money and thus causes the currency to appreciate, (2) an increase in the current level of the money supply causes an immediate proportionate depreciation of the currency in equilibrium, and (3) an increase in the expected future rate of growth of money and inflation causes an immediate depreciation of the equilibrium value of the currency.

These results pertain to long-run equilibrium. The rest of the chapter explained that the short-run equilibrium is characterized by overshooting. When the money supply increases, the currency immediately depreciates *more* than proportionately, that is, it depreciates by more than it will in the long run. This is a consequence of goods prices being sticky in the short run. The increase in the nominal money supply is an increase in the real money supply. It reduces the interest rate, causing investors to shift their demand to foreign assets and causing the domestic currency to depreciate. This much is similar to the effects of monetary expansion in the Mundell-Fleming model of Chapter 22. The new effect is that today's depreciation generates the expectation among investors that the currency will in the future have to appreciate back toward long-run equilibrium; this expectation of appreciation must be just sufficient to offset the interest differential for investors to be willing to hold domestic assets. Thus, when a loose monetary policy pushes the domestic real interest rate below the foreign real interest rate, it will also push the real value of the currency below its usual level.

Modern models of exchange rate determination share another property: They are designed to fit the empirically observed high variability of floating exchange rates. These models explain such variability in three respects. First, because the exchange rate is seen to be determined in financial markets, it can be as volatile as the prices of stocks, bonds, precious metals, and other assets. The expectation of a future loss in the value of the currency is enough to cause a large shift in demand and thus a large fall in the equilibrium value of the currency today. Second, when goods prices adjust slowly but asset markets adjust instantly, the exchange rate in the short run overshoots its long-run equilibrium. Third, when a speculative bubble gets started, the exchange rate can deviate even from the short-run equilibrium that is determined by the monetary fundamentals.

CHAPTER PROBLEMS

1. If there is a downward shift in the demand for dollars because of increased use of credit cards, what is the effect on the exchange rate?

2. a. If an investor were able to predict that a country's currency will appreciate in the future because of a slower inflation rate in that country than in others, does this mean that the investor can necessarily earn a higher return by holding that currency?
   b. What if the investor were able to predict that a currency will appreciate in the future because it has already overshot (downward) its long-run equilibrium?

3. Are the following three statements true or false?
   (i) If a country has a high interest rate, then its assets will be attractive to hold, and so the value of the currency will be high.
   (ii) If a country has a high interest rate, investors must expect that its currency will lose value in the future.
   (iii) If investors expect that a currency will lose value in the future, then they will have a low demand for it and it will have a low value today. Can you reconcile the three statements with each other? (*Hint*: It might help to distinguish *why* the interest rate is high.)

4. The following is the balance of payments equilibrium condition from the Mundell-Fleming model, Equation 22.4, with exports depending on the exchange rate, S, and foreign income, Y^*, and imports depending on Y. (All relationships here are assumed linear, and m and m^* are the marginal propensities to import.)

$$\chi S + m^* Y^* - mY + \overline{KA} + \kappa(i - i^*) = 0$$

   a. Turn this equation into a model of exchange rate determination by solving for S.
   b. What policies determine i?
   c. Explain why the signs on Y, Y^*, i, and i^* here differ from those in Equation 24.8.

SUGGESTIONS FOR FURTHER READING

Dornbusch, Rudiger. "Expectation and Exchange Rate Dynamics," *Journal of Political Economy* (December 1976). The classic paper on the overshooting of the exchange rate in response to a change in the money supply.

Frenkel, Jacob. "A Monetary Approach to the Exchange Rate: Doctrinal Aspects and Empirical Evidence," *Scandinavian Journal of Economic* (1976): 200–224. The original statement of the flexible-price version of the monetary approach to the exchange rate, with an application to the German hyperinflation.

Friedman, Milton. "The Case for Flexible Exchange Rates," in his *Essays in Positive Economics* (Chicago: University of Chicago Press, 1953). The arguments for floating, 20 years ahead of their time.

Mussa, Michael. "The Exchange Rate, the Balance of Payments, and Monetary and Fiscal Policy under a Regime of Controlled Floating," *Scandinavian Journal of Economics*, 78 (May 1976): 229–248. Shows how, in the monetary model with rational expectations, the exchange rate is the present discounted sum of future monetary conditions.

Obstfeld, Maurice, and Alan Stockman. "Exchange-Rate Dynamics," in, R. Jones and P. Kenen, eds. *Handbook of International Economics* (Amsterdam: Elsevier, 1985), pp. 917–977. A more theoretical survey of models of exchange rate determination.

Shafer, Jeffrey, and Bonnie Loopesko. "Floating Exchange Rates After Ten Years," *Brookings Papers on Economic Activity*, 1 (1983): 1–70. Another survey of models of exchange rate determination.

APPENDIX:
CHANGES IN THE EXPECTED MONEY GROWTH RATE IN THE OVERSHOOTING MODEL OF THE EXCHANGE RATE

Section 24.2, which ruled out variation in the real exchange rate for the model of $\bar{S}$, looked both at the effect of a one-time change in the level of the money supply and at the effect of a change in the expected future rate of growth of the money supply. When Section 24.4 allowed for the implications of sticky prices, it became clear that the exchange rate overshoots in response to a change in the *level* of the money supply. However, it is not yet clear what happens when there is a change in the future rate of growth of the money supply.[40]

It would be awkward to consider this experiment on a graph like Figure 24.4 because if the money supply is steadily increasing over time, then the long-run equilibrium variable, $\bar{S}$, is itself steadily increasing over time. However, the equations already derived can show the effects, provided $\bar{S}$ is given a time subscript, so that it can increase over time in steady-state equilibrium, at the same rate as the money supply. There are two distinct effects of an increase in the money growth rate, as with an increase in the level of the money supply: a purely nominal effect on $\bar{S}$, and an additional real, or overshooting, effect on S relative to $\bar{S}$, as Figure 24.5(b) illustrates.

In long-run equilibrium, the inflation rate is known to go up by the same amount as the money growth rate. Thus, the effect on $\bar{S}$ is precisely the one given by Equation 24.12: It goes up by the change in the expected inflation rate times the semi-elasticity of money demand with respect to the rate of return (μ in the chapter supplement). The explanation is that the higher rate of expected inflation will make the currency less attractive to hold.[41] The decrease in demand for real money balances will take the form of an increase in the price level and (by long-run PPP) in the exchange rate. Figure 24.5(b) shows how $\bar{P}$ and $\bar{S}$, represented by the dashed lines, shift up when the rate of growth of the money supply shifts up.

This much was true before allowing for variation in the real exchange rate. Now the overshooting effect, given by Equation 24.15, has been added. The higher expected inflation rate reduces the real interest rate, which sparks a capital outflow (i.e., international investors reduce their demand for domestic assets). As a result, the currency depreciates. It depreciates

---

[40] The effect of changes in the money growth rate in the Dornbusch overshooting model is shown in Jeffrey Frankel, "On the Mark: A Theory of Floating Exchange Rates Based on Real Interest Differentials," *American Economic Review* (1979); and Willem Buiter and Marcus Miller, "Real Exchange Rate Overshooting and the Output Cost of Bringing Down Inflation," *European Economic Review*, 18 (May/June 1982): 85–123.

[41] It is not necessarily assumed that the demand for money depends directly on the expected inflation rate. It is sufficient that it depends on the nominal interest rate, and that in the long run the expected inflation differential is built into the nominal differential.

by more than it will long-run equilibrium, so that there is an expectation of future real appreciation sufficient to offset the lower real interest differential. The effect of the fall in the real interest differential, even though it takes the form of an increase in the expected inflation rate with no necessary change in the nominal interest rate, is the same as when there is a reduction in the nominal interest rate with no change in the expected inflation rate. In both cases, the total effect on the current exchange rate, S, is simply the effect on $\bar{S}$ plus the overshooting effect on S relative to $\bar{S}$.

As before, the price level responds to excess demand for goods by rising over time toward its long-run equilibrium path. As it does, the real money supply and real interest rates return to their previous levels and the exchange rate returns to its long-run equilibrium path, $\bar{S}$.

25

EXCHANGE RATE FORECASTING AND RISK

Chapter 24 considered the macroeconomic determination of the exchange rate and explored the effects of monetary policy, particularly from the viewpoint of the monetary policy-maker. This chapter begins by looking at this issue from the viewpoint of the individual market participant, who must take the movements in the exchange rate as given.

25.1 FORECASTING THE SPOT EXCHANGE RATE

Those who forecast the exchange rate for a living quickly discover that the real world is less straightforward than the theory of exchange rate determination might make it appear. Chapter 24 assumed that everyone knew with confidence what the correct model was, except perhaps for a disagreement between the flexible-price version of the monetary model and the sticky-price version. The fact is, there are many conflicting approaches to forecasting. One consequence is that investors can disagree widely on their exchange rate forecasts.[1]

Forecasting Methods in Actual Use and Their Performance

As distressing as it is for economists to admit, many professional exchange rate forecasters do not base their forecasts on any model of money supplies or other fundamental economic variables, even simple ones. So-called "technical analysts" instead forecast by using computer techniques, or hand-drawn graphs in the case of more old-fashioned" chartists," to try to uncover trends in the exchange rate. One of

---

[1] In the *Economist Financial Report* survey, market participants' forecasts of the exchange rate at a 6-month horizon vary over a high-low range that averages 15.2 percent. [Jeffrey Frankel and Kenneth Froot, "Chartists, Fundamentalists, and Trading in the Foreign Exchange Market," *American Economic Review* 80 (2) (May 1990): 181–185.] The heterogeneity of expectations among Japanese market participants is documented by Takatoshi Ito, "Foreign Exchange Rate Expectations: Micro Survey Data," *American Economic Review* 80 (1990): 434–449.

the most popular rules calls for buying a currency whenever the short-term moving average (the average over the preceding week, for example) rises above the longer-term moving average (over the preceding month), and selling whenever the reverse happens. The "momentum" models call for buying when the current price exceeds the price that existed, for example, five days ago. Such techniques, in effect, forecast by extrapolating past trends and thus generally fall into the category of expectations that are destabilizing if acted upon by investors.[2] The same can be true of another forecasting approach called ARIMA (AutoRegressive Integrated Moving Average). A simple example of an ARIMA model is a prediction that if the spot rate went up 1 percent last week, then it will go up AR percent this week, where AR is the auto-regressive coefficient.

How well do all these techniques forecast the spot rate? The answer is "not well," if the criterion is to forecast with small errors. The generalization applies not just to economic fundamentals models, technical analysis, and ARIMA techniques, but to virtually any forecasting approach imaginable. This is because exchange rates are so volatile. Even spot traders who claim to be highly successful will admit that they lose money on many of their trades.[3]

We should not be surprised that a large proportion of the movement in the exchange rate cannot be forecast by any technique. Even if the spot rate behaved precisely as predicted by a model, such as the monetary equation of exchange rate determination developed earlier, one could not accurately forecast the future exchange rate without knowing the future values of the money supplies, income levels, and so on. If the exchange rate departs from the economic fundamentals because of a speculative bubble, then the forecast errors will be that much larger.

Professional forecasters intending to earn a return on their investment of time and expertise can, at best, hope to predict the direction of movement correctly slightly more than half the time or to forecast slightly better on average than others in the market. Thus, when testing the performance of the various techniques, we should keep in mind that we cannot hope to forecast a large proportion of the movement in the spot rate. A useful benchmark for comparison is the random walk. Forecasters would hope to be able to predict the future spot rate better than the current spot rate does.[4] In other words, though they should not be so ambitious as to hope to predict all or most of the movement in the exchange rate, neither should they be so unambitious as to expect to be able to predict *none* of the movement.

When Chapter 19 first introduced the concept of the random walk, it was noted that the real exchange rate has a tendency to return over time to the long-run

[2] There are probably as many methods of technical analysis as there are technical analysts, but most fit this description.

[3] Bear in mind that the percentage of traders who can truthfully expect to make money is not as high as it sounds when listening to them talk. For every winner there must be a loser. (There is a bit of a "sample selection" problem, however. If each month half the traders win and half lose, at random, and each month some of the ones who lose badly decide to abandon this line of work, then more than half the traders remaining in the sample at any time will truthfully be able to claim that they made money over the preceding month.)

[4] Recall from Chapter 24 that there is no theoretical reason to expect the exchange rate to follow a random walk. This point is often misunderstood. As Section 25.2 will show, if some component of changes in the spot rate—such as that reflected in the forward discount—were predictable, it would not violate the rational expectations hypothesis. The hypothesis says only that the economist should not be able to forecast easily a greater percentage of movement in the spot rate than the market can.

equilibrium dictated by Purchasing Power Parity. In other words, the principle of regression to PPP might be used to obtain a better predictor than the random walk. This information is of some benefit in predicting the spot rate over the long term. Thus, it might be used by a portfolio fund manager in deciding whether to buy (and hold) foreign securities or by a corporate executive in deciding whether to build a factory in a foreign country. The rule would be to invest in the country where the value of the currency is below its long-run PPP equilibrium, because the currency can be expected to rise again in the future. However, because the speed of regression to PPP is so slow and because large new disturbances come along so frequently, the information is not of much use in predicting the spot rate a few months or less into the future.

Richard Meese and Kenneth Rogoff studied the ability of a number of models to predict the exchange rate at horizons of several months. Included were the monetary model (both the flexible-price or "monetarist" version of Section 24.2 and the sticky-price version of Section 24.4) as well as the ARIMA model. Their finding was that at horizons of one, six, or twelve months into the future, all models are outperformed by the simple random walk. That is, a forecaster would be more successful using the current spot rate.[5] This was an extremely discouraging discovery for exchange rate modelers. In view of how frequently one hears of an econometric finding that the exchange rate (or GNP, or other macroeconomic variables) follows a random walk model, it is important to note that such outcomes are failures to find anything that explains movement in the exchange rate. Random walk results are useful because they remind economists of the extent of their ignorance; but they are not evidence in favor of a model, in any meaningful sense.

Others have found somewhat greater success by including the lagged value of the exchange rate in addition to the other variables on the right-hand side of the equation.[6] For a forecaster who must predict the future exchange rate, the conclusion seems to be as follows. It would be difficult to make any prediction using *only* information on macroeconomic variables such as the money supplies, income levels, interest rates, and inflation rates. There is more useful information in today's spot rate than in everything else combined. However, given that today's spot rate is known, the monetary model seems to contain additional information that is of some help in predicting the direction of future movement, especially at longer horizons. In short, the optimal predictor would use *both* the information contained in today's spot rate and the information contained in the monetary model. Evidently there must be important elements missing from the monetary equation of exchange rate determination, unobserved elements that behave much like a random walk and thus are picked up by the lagged spot rate. Possible missing elements include speculative bubbles and permanent shifts in the real exchange rate.

[5] "Empirical Exchange Rate Models of the Seventies: Do They Fit Out of Sample?" *Journal of International Economics* 14 (February 1983): 3–24; and "The Out-Of-Sample Failure of Empirical Exchange Rate Models: Sampling Error or Misspecification?" in Jacob Frenkel, ed., *Exchange Rates and International Macroeconomics* (Chicago: University of Chicago Press, 1983) 67–105. The monetary model does begin to perform slightly better when forecasting more than twelve months into the future.

[6] Wing Woo, "The Monetary Approach to Exchange Rate Determination Under Rational Expectations," *Journal of International Economics* 18 (1985): 1–16; V. S. Somanath, "Efficient Exchange Rate Forecasts: Lagged Models Better than the Random Walk," *Journal of International Money and Finance* 5 (1986): 195–220.

None of these studies includes models of technical analysis. Relatively few careful tests of the forecasting performance of technical analysis have been conducted. One such study recently reported the surprising finding that many of the trading rules, such as the moving average and momentum models, *were* effective at forecasting the dollar/deutschemark rate from April 1973 to October 1986, so by following these rules one could have made money (above and beyond transactions costs).[7]

One possible explanation of how a speculative bubble in the dollar—if that is what it was—might have begun in 1984 is that market investors had by then stopped listening to the forecasts issued by economists because their predictions that the dollar would depreciate back to equilibrium had repeatedly failed to materialize over the preceding two years, and most investors were instead relying on the forecasts of the technical analysts. *Euromoney* magazine use to run an annual review of foreign-exchange forecasting firms. Between 10 and 27 firms were reviewed. In 1978–1981 only one or two of the forecasting firms reported using models based on technical analysis; most relied on models based on economic fundamentals. By 1984, however, models based on economic fundamentals had fallen into such disfavor that none of the forecasting firms that revealed their approach would admit to relying on them exclusively. Most said their forecasts were based only on technical analysis.

Many of the technical analysts in the *Euromoney* review, and their customers, are only interested in very short-term horizons. The short-term focus of many market traders helps explain why they are not interested in longer-term economic fundamentals. Section 24.4 mentioned that exchange rate expectations measured by regular surveys of market participants' forecasts show a tendency to expect regression toward long-run equilibrium, as in Equation 24.14. This was at horizons of six months or one year. The Money Market Services International survey data instead show its respondents forming expectations at horizons of one week to one month by extrapolating recent trends. This seems to confirm that different techniques are used for long-term and short-term forecasting.[8]

Does the Forward Exchange Market Give an Unbiased Predictor?

Consider the owner of a small company involved in international trade who must guess what the exchange rate will be in three months to decide what currency a payment should be made in or what price to set for a product. The owner is bewildered by the proliferation of different exchange rate models and the knowledge that no single one performs particularly well. The owner also suspects that much relevant information comes out every day (for example, a speech by the Chairman of the Federal Reserve Board) not captured in any of the statistical models, and does not have the time or resources to monitor such news each day.

---

[7] Stephan Schulmeister and Michael Goldberg, "Noise Trading and the Efficiency of Financial Markets," in G. Luciani, ed., *Structural Change in the American Financial System*, (Rome: Centro di Studi Americani, 1989) pp. 117–164. A similar result was found earlier by S. H. Goodman, "Foreign Exchange Forecasting Techniques: Implications for Business and Policy," *Journal of Finance*, 34 (May 1979): 415–427.

[8] Jeffrey Frankel and Kenneth Froot, "Chartists, Fundamentalists and the Demand for Dollars," in A. Courakis and M. Taylor, eds., *Policy Issues for Interdependent Economies* (London: Macmillan, 1990). See also Charles Goodhart, "The Foreign Exchange Market: A Random Walk with a Dragging Anchor," *Economica*, 55 (November 1988): 437–460.

An easy strategy in such conditions is to use the three-month forward rate as the forecast of the future spot rate. (Chapter 21 introduced the forward exchange market.) What makes this strategy so easy is that it simply means looking up the forward rate in the newspaper.

Furthermore, this owner would not necessarily do any better than the forward rate by subscribing to a forecasting service or hiring a staff forecaster. All the useful information contained in the various models, along with the latest bits of news, will already be reflected in the forward rate if the *efficient markets hypothesis* holds. The efficient markets hypothesis is closely related to the rational expectations hypothesis.[9] It states that any excess profit opportunities in the financial markets based on publicly available information will be quickly eliminated. Imagine, for example, that it were possible to use an ARIMA model to forecast better than the forward rate. In such a circumstance many speculators would rush to take advantage of the profit opportunity. They would buy forward currency whenever the ARIMA model predicted a price higher than the forward rate, and vice versa; before long they would drive the forward rate into equality with the forecast of the model. Thus, whatever useful information there is in the ARIMA model should already be contained in the forward rate. The same applies to whatever useful information there is in technical analysis, in the monetary models, and in the day's news.

There have been a great many studies testing whether the forward market offers an unbiased predictor of the future spot rate.[10] "Unbiased" means there is no obvious alternative predictor that performs better on average. Consider the following equation, which relates the observed change in the spot rate to the change that the forward discount would have predicted ahead of time.

$$\Delta s_{t+1} = \alpha + \beta\, fd_t + \varepsilon_{t+1} \tag{25.1}$$

The subscripts denote time: fd_t is the one-month (for example) percentage forward discount (on the domestic currency) observed at the present time, and Δs_{t+1} is the percentage change in the exchange rate (the percentage depreciation of the domestic currency) that takes place over the coming month.

As is usual in econometrics, we proceed by specifying a hypothesis and then seeing if the data are favorable to it or unfavorable. In the present case, we are interested in the hypothesis that the forward discount is an unbiased predictor of the change in the exchange rate. This hypothesis, if true, implies in Equation 25.1 the condition $\beta = 1$. It might also include the condition $\alpha = 0$. Thus the hypothesis becomes:

$$\Delta s_{t+1} = fd_t + \varepsilon_{t+1} \tag{25.2}$$

[9] The efficient markets hypothesis not only requires that investors form their expectations rationally, it requires a second condition as well: that there are few transaction costs of other market imperfections that prevent investors from buying and selling freely on the basis of these expectations. This allows investors' expectations to be fully reflected in the marketplace. Under normal circumstances, this second condition is easily met in well-developed financial markets. The small size of transactions costs can be shown directly, as it was in chapter 21. (There are rare exceptions. On October 19, 1987, the day of the world stock market crash, the market mechanism broke down and it became difficult to transact at posted prices.)

[10] Surveys of this literature include: Robert Hodrick, *The Empirical Evidence on the Efficiency of Forward and Futures Foreign Exchange Markets.* Chur, Switzerland: Harwood Academic Publishers, 1988; Richard Levich, "On the Efficiency of Markets of Foreign Exchange," in R. Dornbusch and J. Frenkel, eds., *International Economic Policy* (Baltimore: Johns Hopkins, 1979) pp. 246–266.

The term ε is the error that investors make at predicting Δs. Under the efficient markets hypothesis, ε must be random, uncorrelated with any information available to investors at time t.[11]

The "unbiasedness" hypothesis actually consists of two hypotheses that are tested at the same time.

1. The *rational expectations hypothesis* is stated as

$$\Delta s_{t+1} = \Delta s_t^e + \varepsilon_{t+1} \tag{25.3}$$

In other words, the hypothesis is that investors predict the change in the exchange rate with an error term that is purely random. (Notice that the hypothesis does not claim that the prediction error is necessarily small, only that it is unbiased—equal to zero on average.)

2. The *zero exchange risk premium hypothesis* is stated as

$$fd_t - \Delta s_t^e = 0 \tag{25.4}$$

The exchange risk premium has been defined as the expression that appears on the left side of Equation 25.4 (in the appendix to Chapter 22, Equation 22.A.3). It will be zero if risk is not important to investors. This is because, if investors care only about expected rates of return and nothing else, then they will drive them into equality across currencies.

Check for yourself that Equations 25.3 and 25.4 together imply unbiasedness of the forward discount, Equation 25.2. It would be preferable to test the rational expectations hypothesis by itself. This is difficult, however, because it is difficult to observe investors' expectations. Instead, the two hypotheses are tested at the same time, by testing whether $\beta = 1$ in Equation 25.1. The major disadvantage of this strategy is that if it is decided that the data do not support $\beta = 1$, it is impossible to determine which of the two hypotheses fails to hold.

Of the many econometric studies performed on Equation 25.1 and others like it, most find that the data observed since 1973 in fact do not support the unbiasedness hypothesis. Typically, the estimate of β is not 1 but is significantly less. This indicates that the forward discount is a biased forecast of the future change in the spot rate. Some estimates put β in the vicinity of 1/2. This would mean that when the dollar sells at a forward discount of 4 percent per annum, the best guess is that it will depreciate at 2 percent per annum. (Similarly, if the dollar sells at a forward *premium* of 4 percent per annum, the best guess is that it will *appreciate* at 2 percent per annum.)

Many estimates put the coefficient even farther from 1, in the vicinity of 0. If β were 0, this would mean that, regardless of the forward market, the best guess for the future spot rate is today's spot rate—in other words, "no change." This is another "random-walk" finding, and is much in line with the findings of Meese and Rogoff described previously.

How should economists interpret such findings? One possibility is that speculators are simply bad forecasters, that the rational expectations hypothesis 1 does not hold.

---

[11] The logic is the same as for the ε term in Equation 23.5, which represented the error that workers make at predicting inflation. To repeat the logic, if there were information publicly available that people could use to improve their forecasts, they would have already used it.

One researcher, for example, interprets such findings as evidence that speculators are "overly excitable," that they have a false confidence in their ability to predict changes in the exchange rate. They would do better on average if they calmed down a bit, instead of always predicting that the exchange rate is about to shoot off in one direction or the other.[12]

Most economists, however, are extremely reluctant to accept this interpretation. They believe in hypothesis 1 on a priori grounds. The logic, once again, is that if it were so easy to make excess profits (on average), speculators would have already taken advantage of the opportunity. For this reason, most economists consider it more likely that the findings of bias are evidence against hypothesis 2—in other words, that the findings are evidence in favor of the existence of an exchange risk premium that separates the forward discount from investors' expectations of depreciation.[13]

25.2 THE ROLE OF EXCHANGE RISK

The Exchange Risk Premium

Under the risk-premium interpretation of the finding of bias (the finding of $\beta < 1$ in Equation 25.1), some positive part of the forward discount is a risk premium. Risk-averse investors will only take a large position in a currency that they perceive as risky if they are offered as compensation a higher expected rate of return than on other currencies. This can explain the difference between the forward discount and expected depreciation; it is the premium that the risk-averse investors demand in order to hold a risky currency.

The risk-premium interpretation says that when the pound is selling at a forward discount, it must be because investors consider the pound riskier to hold than other currencies, and they therefore demand extra compensation for holding it. This is perhaps most clearly shown by using the covered interest parity condition to substitute the nominal interest differential, $i - i^*$, in place of the forward discount, fd, obtaining the alternate (but equivalent) definition of the exchange risk premium:

$$rp_t \equiv i_t - i_t^* - \Delta s_t^e$$

Now it is readily apparent that if the risk premium on a particular currency is positive, then that means that investors are receiving a higher expected return to compensate

[12] John Bilson, "The Speculative Efficiency Hypothesis," *Journal of Business*, 54 (1981): 435–451. Another study that finds bias and interprets it as a failure of rational expectations is David Longworth, "Testing the Efficiency of the Canadian-U.S. Exchange Market Under the Assumption of No Risk Premium," *Journal of Finance*, 36 (1981): 43–49. Some direct evidence that the bias may indeed be attributable to Bilson's "overexcitability" is offered by Kenneth Froot and Jeffrey Frankel, "Forward Discount Bias: Is it an Exchange Risk Premium?" *Quarterly Journal of Economics*, (February 1989): 139–161; another direct test of expectations is Kathryn Dominguez, "Are Foreign Exchange Forecasts Rational? New Evidence from Survey Data," *Economics Letters*, 21 (1986): 277–282.

[13] Examples include Eugene Fama, "Forward and Spot Exchange Rates," *Journal of Monetary Economics*, 14 (1984): 319–338; Robert Hodrick and Sanjay Srivastava, "An Investigation of Risk and Return in Forward Foreign Exchange," *Journal of International Money and Finance*, 3 (1984): 5–30; David Hsieh, "Tests of Rational Expectations and No Risk Premium in Forward Exchange Markets," *Journal of International Economics*, 17 (1984): 173–184; and Roger Huang, "Some Alternative Tests of Forward Exchange Rates as Predictors of Future Spot Rates," *Journal of International Money and Finance*, 3 (1984): 157–167.

for holding assets in that currency. Consider the case of ''random-walk'' expectations $(\Delta s^e = 0)$, for example. A British interest differential of 4 percent signifies that speculators demand an expected return 4 percent higher than the expected return on other currencies before they are willing to take an "open" position in pounds. It is analogous to the premium that the stock market pays relative to bonds: The rate of return on stocks is on average significantly higher than the interest rate, with the difference being interpreted as the premium that investors require in order to bear the greater risk that attaches to stocks.[14]

It might seem that investors would find holding "foreign currency" in general to be risky, that foreign currency must pay a positive risk premium to compensate domestic investors for holding it. No such general rule can hold for all currencies, however. If one currency pays a positive risk premium, then the other pays a negative risk premium. Viewed from the vantage point of the global investor, the domestic currency could be the riskier one as easily as the foreign currency.

What Makes a Currency Risky?

Throughout the 1980s, the dollar sold at a forward discount against the mark and yen. As we would expect to follow by covered interest parity, dollar assets paid a higher interest rate than mark or yen assets. If the findings of bias are to be interpreted as evidence of a risk premium, it would follow that international investors in the 1980s must have perceived the U.S. dollar as riskier than the mark or yen.

What makes an investor perceive some currencies as more risky and others as less risky? There are essentially three factors that contribute to exchange risk. We are not including default risk and the risk of capital controls, which pertain to the identity of the issuer of a security, rather than to its currency of denomination.

First is the *variability* of the value of that currency, in terms of other currencies and in terms of purchasing power over goods (i.e., the variability of the price level).[15] The currency of a country with an unstable monetary policy, leading to a highly variable price level and exchange rate, is viewed as risky.

It is easy, but wrong, to slip into the habit of viewing dollars as completely safe. It is wrong because investors ultimately care about the *real* value of their wealth, its purchasing power over the goods they consume, not about the dollar value per se. It follows immediately that a foreign citizen will consider the dollar risky if its exchange rate vis-à-vis the foreign currency is uncertain. (We are assuming here that the foreign investor cares about purchasing power over goods produced in the foreign country. To the extent that the investor also consumes some American goods, the risk of holding dollars will be somewhat reduced.) The fact that the investor cares about purchasing power over goods also implies that even an American who consumes only

---

[14] It is easy to test Equation 25.1, with the interest differential, $i - i^*$, substituted for the forward discount, *fd*. Just as before, the results do not support the hypothesis of unbiasedness. Just as before, the finding of bias could be interpreted either as a bias in expectations or as a risk premium. Robert Cumby and Maurice Obstfeld, "Exchange Rate Expectations and Nominal Interest Differentials: A Test of the Fisher Hypothesis," *Journal of Finance*, 36 (1981): 697–703.

[15] By "variability" we mean the degree of uncertainty regarding the value of the currency next period. If an exchange rate were highly variable, but the movements were mostly predictable, then uncertainty would be low. In practice, however, exchange rate movements are mostly unpredictable. Therefore, uncertainty is almost the same as the measured variability in exchange rate changes.

American goods should consider the dollar as risky to the extent that dollar prices of goods are uncertain. This is inflation uncertainty. As we have seen, the price level is actually much less variable than the exchange rate. For this reason, Americans would probably not go too far wrong by viewing their own currency as safe. However, exceptions arise in small, very open economies (such as those studied in Chapter 19) and in economies with a high degree of monetary instability. Residents of Argentina, for example, should view foreign currency as less risky than their own.

We have been thinking of the potential holder of a foreign-currency asset as an individual consumer or household. What if it is a corporation? In theory, this should not make any difference. Corporations are owned by people (the shareholders), who consume goods just like everybody else. If the manager of the corporation operates in the shareholders' interest, then the outcome should be the same as if the shareholders were making the investment decisions themselves.

In practice, however, corporate behavior can and does deviate from this theoretical ideal. If corporate managers do not have confidence that stock market investors can see through all the complexities of modern finance and accounting, they may be reluctant to make an investment that does not "look good on the books" even if they believe it is in the true interest of the company. To take an example, in 1976, when the Financial Accounting Standards Board adopted a rule (FASB 8) requiring companies to translate their overseas earnings into dollars at the current exchange rate, many companies suddenly altered their behavior so as to reduce exposure in foreign currency. They knew that such exposure would show up on their annual reports as earnings that were highly variable in terms of dollars. They sought to hedge their foreign earnings—for example, by selling foreign exchange on the forward market.[16] While some hedging might always be prudent for a company with large overseas operations, in this case the change in corporate behavior in response to FASB 8 was a sign that managers did not think that their shareholders would see through the accounting rule change. Such managers may err in the direction of the simple rule that the domestic currency is safe and the foreign currency is risky.

The second factor that makes a currency appear risky from the viewpoint of an individual investor is related to the quantity of assets the investor already holds denominated in that currency. The principle of *portfolio diversification* states that investors can reduce the risk in their overall wealth by diversifying their portfolio among many different assets. Even if each of several currencies has the same degree of variability, investors will be less vulnerable if they hold some of each than if they "put all their eggs in one basket." This is because, assuming the movements of the various currencies are at least partly independent, it is very unlikely that all of them will sharply lose value at the same time. Usually some will go up and some down, and the overall return on the diversified portfolio will be much more stable than if the entire portfolio were allocated to just one of the assets.[17]

Thus, if investors already hold a large amount of franc bonds in their portfolio, they will consider it risky to acquire additional franc assets; it would be safer adding

---

[16] Patricia Revey, "Evolution and Growth of the United States Foreign Exchange Market," *Federal Reserve Bank of New York Quarterly Review*, 6 (Autumn 1981): 32–44. (Incidentally, the rule has since been abolished; the earnings reports of a multinational corporation need no longer show its overseas subsidiary's gains or losses from exchange rate changes.)

[17] The optimal degree of portfolio diversification is derived in the supplement to this chapter.

to their holdings of other assets, to remain well diversified. They will only be willing to accept additional franc assets if the return is sufficiently high to compensate for the risk of "going farther out on a limb," of being further exposed in francs.[18]

The third factor is the extent to which movement in the currency value is *correlated* with movement in the values of other assets that investors hold. "Correlation" refers to the tendency for both assets to go up at the same time and go down at the same time. If the currency is highly correlated with other assets that the investors already hold, then it should be viewed as risky. The Dutch guilder, for example, is highly correlated with the deutschemark (as is the Canadian dollar with the U.S. dollar). If the investors already hold many deutschemarks, then even if they hold no guilders they should realize that the prospect of acquiring some would add to their overall risk as much as would the acquisition of more deutschemarks. This is because the guilder offers little opportunity for diversification: When the deutschemark falls, the guilder will fall right along with it.[19] Conversely, if the currency has a low correlation with the other assets that investors already hold, they should view it as subtracting from their overall risk because it offers an opportunity for diversification.[20]

This is especially true if the correlation happens to be negative. The returns on gold and the dollar, for example, are negatively correlated with each other. In those months when the value of the dollar goes up, the price of gold goes down, and vice versa. Thus, even if the dollar and gold are each highly variable when considered alone, a portfolio that holds some of each will be less variable. In the limit, imagine that the two were perfectly negatively correlated: For every 1 percent that the dollar moved, the price of gold could be relied on to move 1 percent in the opposite direction. In this special case, a portfolio allocated half to dollars and half to gold would be completely safe. The return on the overall portfolio would be guaranteed beforehand, regardless of price fluctuations, because the returns on the two halves would cancel each other out.

We have now seen that, from the viewpoint of the individual investor, it is important to look at more than just the expected return when deciding whether to acquire a country's currency. It is also important to look at the risk of the asset, where the risk

---

[18] Consider another example, like the FASB 8 story, of how a corporation's behavior in practice can deviate from the theoretical ideal of diversification. Imagine that the New York office is highly exposed in yen and the London office is highly exposed in deutschemarks. The company in the aggregate may in fact be well diversified. Yet if each office does not know what the other is doing—or if each manager is more worried about the variability of his own performance, and the risk of being terminated if he suffers large losses, than he is about the "big picture"—then each may anxiously hedge or unload its holdings, even at a loss. As communications and computer technology and risk management techniques become more and more sophisticated, however, corporations get better and better at keeping track of changes in their global currency exposure and at responding appropriately. In this sense, actual corporate financial practices are becoming more like the theoretical ideal.

[19] Similarly, though a well-diversified portfolio would hold both stocks and bonds, the return on Dutch bonds is correlated with the return on Dutch stocks, so that an investor who already holds a lot of one should regard the other as risky. The return on a country's bonds is correlated with the return on its stocks and other assets, not just because of the exchange rate factor, but for another reason as well. If the country's economy turns out to do poorly, it may be reflected not only in its stock market but also in increased probability of default on bonds.

[20] Financial analysts speak of the "beta" of a stock or other security, which reflects the correlation of its return with the return on the overall portfolio of securities that the market holds. A security with a high beta is risky for investors; it should pay a high expected return to compensate them for holding it. (This is the lesson of what finance theorists call the Capital Asset Pricing Model.)

that a given asset would bring to the portfolio is determined by not only (1) uncertainty regarding its future value but also (2) the assets that the investor already holds and (3) the correlation of the return on the currency in question with the return on the other assets.

We have also seen that the existence of risk causes investors to view domestic and foreign bonds as imperfect substitutes, with the result that expected returns need not be equalized internationally. If we return to the issue of the determination of the exchange rate by aggregate behavior in the marketplace, it is now apparent that a condition assumed by the monetary models in Chapter 24, uncovered interest parity, need not hold. Thus, it seems that we must go back and modify the model of exchange rate determination.

25.3 PORTFOLIO-BALANCE EFFECTS ON THE EXCHANGE RATE

In the monetary models of Chapter 24, the stock of government debt had no effect on the exchange rate, only the stock of money. (Refer to Equation 24.8.) This section will examine possible effects of the stocks of debt and other non-money assets. To do so, it is necessary to introduce the portfolio-balance model.[21] To gain the insights provided by this new model, it is not necessary to jettison what was learned in Chapter 24. Rather, we are adding some possible effects in the foreign exchange market to what we have previously studied.[22]

Previous chapters assumed that investors were willing to absorb indefinitely large quantities of a country's bonds as long as the country was willing to pay the world interest rate. The quantity of bonds issued did not in itself necessarily have any effects on the financial markets. Now, however, we recognize that investors care, not just about expected return, but about risk as well. Investors will not willingly hold increasing quantities of a country's bonds at an unchanged interest rate. Individual investors can, of course, simply decide not to hold an asset denominated in a currency viewed as risky. (They could also decide to hold it but to sell the currency risk to somebody else on the forward exchange market.) In the aggregate, however, assets exist, and someone has to hold them. When the French government issues bonds, for example, even if the original buyer resells them or hedges the currency risk on the forward market, someone somewhere must end up with increased exposure in French

[21] Important early applications of the portfolio-balance model to the subject of floating exchange rates include William Branson, "Asset Markets and Relative Prices in Exchange Rate Determination," *Sozialwissenschaftliche Annalen* 1 (1977): 69–89; Stanley Black, "International Money Markets and Flexible Exchange Rates," *Studies in International Finance*, 32 (1973), Princeton University, Pentti Kouri, "The Exchange Rate and the Balance of Payments in the Short Run and in the Long Run: A Monetary Approach," *Scandinavian Journal of Economics*, 78 (2) (May 1976) and Carlos Rodriguez, "The Role of Trade Flows in Exchange Rate Determination: A Rational Expectations Approach," *Journal of Political Economys* 88 (6) (December 1980).

[22] If risk is indeed so important that uncovered interest parity, Equation 24.1, fails to hold, then it is easy to amend the equation of exchange rate determination (for example, Equation 24.15), by including alongside the interest differential an additional term for the exchange risk premium (or for its determinants, such as the stock of government bonds that the public must hold). An appraisal of the two classes of models, including a suggestion for synthesizing them, can be found in Jeffrey Frankel, "Tests of Monetary and Portfolio Balance Models of Exchange Rate Determination," in J. Bilson and R. Marston, eds., *Exchange Rate Theory and Practice* (Chicago: University of Chicago Press, 1984).

francs. Risk aversion on the part of investors thus implies that when governments change the supplies of bonds denominated in various currencies, it does have an effect in the financial markets, an effect on the equilibrium prices at which investors are willing to hold these assets.[23]

In the portfolio-balance approach, the exchange rate is viewed not simply as the relative price of domestic and foreign money supplies but as the relative price of bonds and other assets as well. The model allows us to study two new effects on the exchange rate: *sterilized foreign exchange intervention* by central banks and what we might call *satiation* of investor holdings of a country's assets.

Sterilized Foreign Exchange Intervention

Part IV of the text introduced intervention in the foreign exchange market—central bank purchases or sales of foreign currency in exchange for domestic currency. At that point the discussion focused on the system of fixed exchange rates, under which central banks are obligated to intervene as often as necessary to maintain the parity. The larger countries, of course, have operated under flexible exchange rates since 1973. Nevertheless, all central banks do intervene from time to time.

Chapter 19 discussed in particular the option of sterilizing intervention: offsetting it by central bank operations in the domestic open market so as to leave the overall money supply unchanged. Assume that the intervention consists of buying up dollar currency that private agents want to get rid of (and giving them yen in exchange), as it will if the aim is to increase the value of the dollar. In this case, sterilization involves following this up by buying dollar bonds from private agents (and giving them dollar currency in exchange), so as to restore the amount of dollar currency in the hands of the public to its original level. On those occasions when the Federal Reserve intervenes, it routinely and immediately sterilizes its intervention in this way.[24] The German Bundesbank and other central banks, however, do not sterilize quite as completely as the Fed does.

Chapter 22 showed that when perfect capital mobility ties the domestic interest rate to the foreign interest rate, successful sterilized intervention is impossible. If the Bundesbank were to try to support the deutschemark in the foreign exchange market without allowing the domestic money supply to fall, it would quickly find that for every mark it created through purchases of domestic bonds, it lost another mark of foreign exchange reserves. It would have to abandon the attempt to determine si-

---

[23] Two qualifications are needed. First, we have made the assumption here for simplicity that the governments denominate their bonds in their own currency. In practice, governments sometimes denominate their bonds in other currencies. Second, we are also ruling out Robert Barro's "Ricardian equivalence" (discussed in the appendix to Chapter 22). This is the proposition that for every franc of bonds that the French government sells to the public, French taxpayers feel an offsetting liability in the form of future taxes, with the result that behavior is unaffected. [If this proposition held, then it is possible that no investor would need to incur exposure to the exchange risk of holding francs. Jeffrey Frankel, "The Diversifiability of Exchange Risk," *Journal of International Economics*, 9 (August 1979).]

[24] Even though the Federal Reserve trading desk in New York sterilizes any foreign exchange intervention on the same day that it occurs, the Federal Reserve Open Market Committee that meets every six weeks or so in Washington does sometimes take the exchange rate into account when setting monetary policy (when giving the open market trading desk in New York its instructions for the target money supply, for example, over the subsequent six weeks).

multaneously the exchange rate and the money supply, or face rapid depletion of its foreign exchange reserves.

If investors treat domestic and foreign bonds as imperfect substitutes because of exchange risk (or for any other reason), then the possibility of successful sterilized intervention is resurrected. The reason is as follows. When the central bank has completed its sterilization, the supply of domestic money in the hands of the public has not changed (by the definition of sterilization) but the supply of domestic bonds in the hands of the public has decreased. In the monetary model, the supply of bonds had no effect. As was noted, only the supply of money had an effect. In the portfolio-balance model, however, the change in the supply of bonds does have an effect. The exchange rate is the relative price of dollar bonds as much as it is the relative price of dollar currency; it is determined by the supply of and demand for all assets (domestic versus foreign). Thus, a decrease in the supply of dollar assets can cause an increase in the price of dollar assets, that is, an appreciation of the dollar, even if the currency component has not changed.[25]

In the late 1970s, the European central banks (and the Bank of Japan) bought large quantities of dollars through intervention, in an effort to dampen the dollar depreciation under way. After 1980, when the dollar began to appreciate sharply, the Europeans and Japanese sold dollars, to dampen the appreciation. This strategy is called *leaning against the wind*: Central banks sell a currency when it is appreciating and buy when it is depreciating, to try to dampen the fluctuations.

Other central banks wanted the United States to join in the intervention operations, because they thought it would make them more effective. Among the seven largest industrialized countries, the French have generally been the most enthusiastic about foreign exchange intervention and the United States has been the most skeptical. At the Versailles Summit of 1982, the United States agreed to study the effectiveness of intervention, as a concession to the French. The report released the following year concluded that intervention that is sterilized does not have significant effects on exchange rates, except perhaps very briefly. It is believed that domestic and foreign bonds, although not literally perfect substitutes, are close enough that relatively little effect results from changes in their relative supply, especially on the scale that is relevant.[26]

In 1985, the U.S. Treasury, in response to an ever-worsening trade deficit and resultant protectionist fever in Congress, made an abrupt about-face. The Treasury's new-found support for coordinated foreign exchange intervention to bring the value of the dollar down produced the Plaza Accord. The day after the agreement was

[25] The decrease in the supply of domestic bonds should also cause the domestic interest rate to fall, to induce investors to hold a smaller share of their portfolio in the form of domestic bonds. As a consequence of imperfect substitutability, the domestic expected rate of return is no longer perfectly tied down to the world interest rate. For a good presentation of the results from the portfolio-balance model, see Dale Henderson, "Exchange Market Intervention Operations: Their Effects and their Role in Finance Policy," in J. Bilson and R. Marston, eds., *Exchange Rate Theory and Policy* (Chicago: University of Chicago Press, 1984).

[26] Dale Henderson and Stephanie Sampson, "Intervention in Foreign Exchange Markets: A Summary of Ten Staff Studies," *Federal Reserve Bulletin* 69 (November 1983): 830–836. Kenneth Rogoff, "On the Effects of Sterilized Intervention: An Analysis of Weekly Data," *Journal of Monetary Economics*, 14 (September 1984): 133–150.

announced (September 22), the dollar fell more than 4 percent. As has already been seen, the dollar depreciation continued over the next few years. Many observers consider this to have been a successful initiative on the part of the U.S. Treasury. Others believe that there were good reasons why the dollar would have come down anyway. However, even those who believe that intervention efforts like the one agreed upon at the Plaza are effective do not believe that the primary effect comes from the changed asset supplies that investors must absorb in their portfolios. These *portfolio effects* are still considered relatively small.

The major effect must come instead via investors' expectations regarding the future exchange rate. The 1985 announcement by the U.S. government that it now considered the dollar to be too high and wanted it to fall, for example, may have caused investors to expect a more expansionary monetary policy in the future.[27] As we saw in Chapter 24, even a small change in expectations can cause a relatively large change in demand for a currency and therefore in the exchange rate. This is why a major announcement by central bank governors or treasury secretaries can have a major effect even on a day when no intervention actually takes place, whereas intervention with no public announcement is likely to have little effect.

The Effect of Satiation in Holdings of a Country's Debt

The only way that the public's holdings of bonds (or money, for that matter) can change suddenly is through operations in the financial markets on the part of the central bank, such as the intervention operations just discussed. However, the public's holdings of bonds change steadily over time whenever a country borrows to finance deficits. The budget deficit is precisely the rate of change of the government debt in the hands of the public. In Chapter 22 we examined the effects of a fiscal expansion. One effect was a current account deficit financed by a capital inflow from abroad. However, we ignored any further effects of the stock of government debt that builds up over time via a budget deficit, or the stock of national indebtedness to foreigners that builds up over time via a current account deficit. The country illustrated in Figure 22.6 apparently could go on running a budget deficit and current account deficit forever.

In reality, a country that borrows must eventually pay back. What mechanism forces this result, if a profligate country is inclined to go on borrowing indefinitely? The portfolio-balance model says that investors will become increasingly reluctant to hold larger and larger quantities of a given country's bonds. The problem may be small under normal conditions, but if the magnitude of the debt becomes large enough, investors will eventually become *satiated* with their holdings. If investors are forced to absorb ever-greater quantities in their portfolios despite their reluctance, one of several outcomes must occur. First, the exchange value of the currency may fall. Recall the assumption that the debt is denominated in the currency of the issuing country. If the nominal quantity of the debt is increasing at 10 percent per year, then the exchange rate must also change at 10 percent per year, if international investors do

---

[27] This has been called the "signaling effect" of foreign exchange intervention: Michael Mussa, *The Role of Official Intervention*, Occasional Paper No. 6, New York: Group of Thirty, 1981. It operates via the effect of the expected rate of return on investors' demand for domestic versus foreign assets.

not allow that country's debt to grow as a share of their portfolios. This relationship between the supply of bonds and the exchange rate is the portfolio or *valuation effect*.

Until recently, there was some reason to believe that the portfolio-balance model might have only limited relevance for large industrialized countries. The United States, Japan, Germany, and the United Kingdom were all creditor countries who held foreign assets more than they issued liabilities to foreigners. It seemed that they could borrow large amounts at the world interest rate if they so chose. Smaller countries were more likely to find that their cost of borrowing rose with the amount borrowed. (This is especially true of LDCs.) However, as noted before, smaller countries usually borrow in foreign currency rather than in their own currency, so the portfolio-balance model in its simple form does not apply.[28]

The massive increase in U.S. borrowing from abroad in the 1980s, however, raised the question whether the world's investors might not become satiated with their holdings of dollars. The United States clearly continues to run current account deficits into the 1990s. It follows that the country will continue to borrow from abroad, one way or another, into the 1990s. This leaves unresolved the issue of the terms under which this borrowing will take place. If international investors at some point become reluctant to accept ever-large quantities of dollars into their portfolios, one of the following will result: an increase in U.S. interest rates to induce them to increase the share of their portfolios allocated to U.S. assets, a depreciation of the dollar to keep that share from rising, or some combination of these two.

25.4 SUMMARY

This chapter covered three topics regarding international finance under floating exchange rates: exchange rate forecasting, the exchange risk premium, and portfolio balance.

In practice, forecasters do not all use monetary models, such as the one developed in Chapter 24. Many use other approaches, including "technical analysis."

Even within the theory presented in Chapter 24, a large fraction of exchange rate changes should be unpredictable. However, the forecasting performance of exchange rate models is worse than it should be. Often it seems that the fraction of exchange rate changes that can be predicted is zero, that is, the exchange rate follows a random walk. At longer horizons, however, the exchange rate does tend to move in the direction of the equilibrium dictated by monetary fundamentals.

A popular way of forecasting the future spot rate is by using the forward rate. However, the "random-walk spot rate" characterization of other forecasting methods applies to the forward rate as well: Tests show that the forward discount is a biased forecaster, that greater accuracy could be achieved by placing more weight on the

---

[28] If a country's capital transactions with the rest of the world are all denominated in foreign currency rather than domestic, then the exchange rate is not the relative price of foreign and domestic assets and so cannot be determined by the valuation effect. However, it can still be determined by the need to pay back debt in the long run. An increase in foreign indebtedness will still cause the country's currency to depreciate; investors realize that a depreciation will be needed sooner or later to improve the trade balance and service the debt. Michael Dooley and Peter Isard, "The Role of the Current Account in Exchange Rate Determination: A Comment on Rodriguez," *Journal of Political Economy*, 90 (6) (December 1982): 1291–1294.

contemporaneous spot rate. One possible interpretation of this finding is a failure of rational expectations and of the efficient markets hypothesis. Most economists, however, interpret the finding of bias in the forward discount as evidence of an exchange risk premium.

An exchange risk premium arises when risk-averse investors look not only at the expected return in deciding whether to acquire a country's currency, but also at risk. The theory of portfolio diversification says that the risk that a given asset would bring to the investor's portfolio is determined not only by uncertainty regarding its future value but also by the asset quantities that the investor already holds and by the correlation of the return on the currency in question with the return on the other assets.

If investors treat domestic and foreign bonds as imperfect substitutes in their portfolios because of risk then the portfolio-balance model applies. This framework makes it possible to talk about two effects on the exchange rate that have previously been omitted. First is the effect of sterilized foreign exchange intervention. Second is the effect of investor satiation with holdings of a given country's bonds. Even though both effects probably exist, the degree of substitutability among countries' bonds is generally thought to be high enough that the effects are small.

CHAPTER PROBLEMS

1. You are the treasurer of a U.S. company that holds open positions (working balances or accounts payable) in foreign currencies. Your bank levies a small but appreciable charge for hedging these positions in the forward market. If you believe the foreign exchange market is efficient, and your company is neutral about risks, will you hedge? What if your company is risk-averse? What if your company also has obligations in foreign currencies (bills for imported inputs or employees' wages at foreign subsidiaries)? What if you think that the market sometimes is a poor forecaster of future exchange rates?

2. If the dollar is selling at a forward discount of 4 percent per annum and you think that the dollar is going to depreciate at 2 percent over the next year, should you "go long" in dollars, or "sell the dollar short"? (Assume that you are risk-neutral.)

3. The chapter supplement shows that when there are two assets that each have the same variance, V, the variance of the overall portfolio is given by $V(r) = x^2 V + (1 - x)^2 V$, where x and $(1 - x)$ are the shares of the portfolios allocated to the two assets, and the returns on the two are assumed to be independent.
   a. Calculate $V(r)$ for $x = 0, .4, .5, .6$ and 1.0.
   b. If you know calculus, differentiate $V(r)$ with respect to x, to find the allocation of the portfolio that minimizes risk.

Extra Credit

4. If you know how to use the mathematical expectation, show how to go from Equation 25.S.1 for the return on the portfolio (in the supplement),

$$r = xr^{DM} + (1 - x)r^{\$}$$

to Equation 25.S.3

$$V(r) = x^2 \, V(r^{DM}) + (1 - x)^2 \, V(r^{\$}) + x(1 - x)2\text{Cov}(r^{DM}, r^{\$})$$

You will need to use the definition of the vaiance of r,

$$V(r) = E(r - Er)^2$$

and the covariance,

$$\text{Cov}(r^{\text{DM}}, r^{\$}) = \text{E}[(r^{\text{DM}} - Er^{\text{DM}})(r^{\$} - Er^{\$})]$$

5. a. If you know calculus, show how to use Equations 25.S.3 and 25.S.4 in the derivative of the welfare function, Equation 25.S.6, to obtain the expression for the optimally diversified portfolio, x. (This derivation is carried out in the supplement for the special case where the dollar is viewed as completely safe, but now we want to see it applied to the more general case.)

    b. What is the optimal x if the real value of the dollar is completely certain? Why?

    c. What is x if the real value of the mark is completely certain? Why?

    d. Assuming that both the real values of the mark and yen are uncertain, what is x if the investor is infinitely risk-averse? (This is called the minimum-variance portfolio.) How do you think it might be affected by the share of German goods in the consumption basket of the investor in question? How might it be affected by uncertainty regarding the German inflation rate?

SUGGESTIONS FOR FURTHER READING

Backus, David. "Empirical Models of the Exchange Rate: Separating the Wheat from the Chaff," *Canadian Journal of Economics*, 17 (1984): 824–826. Tests of performance for a variety of models.

Froot, Kenneth, and Richard Thaler. "Anomalies: Foreign Exchange," *Journal of Economic Perspectives* 4(3)(Summer 1990): 179–192. How should we interpret findings that the forward rate is a biased predictor of future spot rates?

Goodhart, Charles. "The Foreign Exchange Market: A Random Walk with a Dragging Anchor," *Economica*, 55 (November 1988): 437–460.

Levich, Richard. "Empirical Studies of Exchange Rates: Price Behavior, Rate Determination, and Market Efficiency," in Ronald Jones and Peter Kenen, eds., *Handbook of International Economics*, 2 (Amsterdam: Elsevier Publishers, 1985). pp. 979–1040. Surveys econometric tests of the efficient markets hypothesis, international parity conditions, and exchange rate models.

Marston, Richard. "Exchange Rate Policy Reconsidered," in M. Feldstein, ed., *International Economic Cooperation*, (Chicago: University of Chicago Press, 1988). pp. 74–136. A good introduction to volatility, misalignment, intervention, and related issues.

Mussa, Michael. *The Role of Official Intervention*, Occasional Paper No. 6, New York: Group of Thirty, (1981). A review of intervention in the foreign exchange markets.

Rogoff, Kenneth. "On the Effects of Sterilized Foreign Exchange Intervention: An Analysis of Weekly Data," *Journal of Monetary Economics*, 14 (1984): 133–150. One of the studies that followed the 1982 decision at the Versailles Summit to have the G-7 central banks look into whether intervention is an effective tool.

Solnik, Bruno. "Why Not Diversify Internationally Rather than Domestically?" *Financial Analyst Journal*, (July 1974): 48–54. By adding foreign securities to the portfolio, investors can reduce their risk, for any given expected rate of return.

Supplements for Selected Chapters

—

SUPPLEMENT TO CHAPTER 2:
The Equations of Exchange Equilibrium

This supplement introduces the notation and structure of the formal models that will be developed in subsequent supplements.

For notation, D will refer to demands and x to production. Thus, D_F signifies the home country's demand for food, and x_C^* the foreign country's production of clothing. The asterisk symbolizes foreign variables, as in the text. The price of commodity j is denoted by p_j if a monetary unit of account is used for the home country, or p_j^* if the foreign country uses a different unit of account or if the foreign price differs. In the two-commodity, food and clothing example, the home country's prices are p_F and p_C. The relative price of food is p_F/p_C, and because this, the "terms of trade," is prominent in the real models of trade, the simple p (in the home country) and p^* (in the foreign country, if prices are different) will denote the terms of trade.

The use of equations in the text is not completely forsaken. For this reason, a different numbering scheme is required for the supplements. Thus, Equation 2.S.4 refers to the fourth equation in the supplement to Chapter 2.

This account of the exchange model will begin by stating prices in monetary units. The budget constraint for this model posits that for each country the value of aggregate demand must be restricted to, and equal to, the value of the endowment bundle. Thus:

$$p_C D_C + p_F D_F = p_C x_C + p_F x_F \qquad (2.S.1)$$

$$p_C^* D_C^* + p_F^* D_F^* = p_C^* x_C^* + p_F^* x_F^* \qquad (2.S.2)$$

Assume that in a trading context the home country will import food. Then rewrite these two equations to highlight, on the left-hand side, the country's demand for imports and, on the right-hand side, the corresponding supply of exports.

$$p_F(D_F - x_F) = p_C(x_C - D_C) \qquad (2.S.3)$$

$$p_C^*(D_C^* - x_C^*) = p_F^*(x_F^* - D_F^*) \qquad (2.S.4)$$

The importance of *relative* prices is brought out by dividing Equation 2.S.3 by p_C and Equation 2.S.4 by p_C^*. Furthermore, in a free-trade equilibrium with no barriers to costless movement of commodities between countries, relative prices in the two countries are brought into line so that

$$p(D_F - x_F) = (x_C - D_C) \qquad (2.S.5)$$

$$(D_C^* - x_C^*) = p(x_F^* - D_F^*) \qquad (2.S.6)$$

The symbol p represents the relative price of food.

Suppose the terms of trade, p, clear the world market for food. That is, the home country's excess demand, $(D_F - x_F)$, equals the foreign country's excess supply, $(x_F^* - D_F^*)$. In such a case it is obvious from Equations 2.S.5 and 2.S.6 that the world's clothing market must be cleared as well: $(D_C^* - x_C^*)$ will equal $(x_C - D_C)$.

One consequence of this phenomenon is that free-trade market equilibrium can be expressed by the statement that *either* world demand and supply are equal for food (as in Equation 2.S.7) or they are equal for clothing (as in Equation 2.S.8):

$$D_F + D_F^* = x_F + x_F^* \qquad\qquad (2.S.7)$$

$$D_C + D_C^* = x_C + x_C^* \qquad\qquad (2.S.8)$$

If the budget constraints in Equations 2.S.5 and 2.S.6 are always satisfied, Equation 2.S.7 implies Equation 2.S.8, or vice versa. Oddly enough, neither market-clearing equation is typically used in the literature of the pure theory of trade. Rather, they are replaced by the equivalent statement that in free-trade equilibrium the value of the home country's imports equals the value of the foreign country's imports. This balance of payments equilibrium condition, in Equation 2.S.9, follows from the two budget constraints, Equations 2.S.5 and 2.S.6, and either Equation 2.S.7 or 2.S.8.

$$p(D_F - x_F) = (D_C^* - x_C^*) \qquad\qquad (2.S.9)$$

This redundancy in stating equilibrium conditions is two-sided. On the one hand it reveals that the model is more simple than a mere scanning of equations might reveal: There is only one market, and if the world demand for clothing balances the world production at specified terms of trade, then the food market must be cleared as well. Furthermore, the value of each country's demand for imports would, at those market-clearing terms of trade, equal the other country's demand for imports. On the other hand, it implies that there are several ways to describe the same equilibrium: The food market is cleared, the clothing market is cleared, or the home country's demand for imports equals, in value, the foreign country's demand for imports. Saying the same thing in three different ways can be confusing.[1]

SUPPLEMENT TO CHAPTER 3:
Real Incomes, Production, Elasticities, and the Trade Pattern

This supplement begins by showing explicitly how to express changes in a community's level of real income. This is followed by a breakdown of the impact of price changes on demand into substitution and income effects. Production changes are also considered and an expression developed for the elasticity of a country's demand for imports. Finally, a general formal statement is made to show how trade according to comparative advantage leads to gains.

Changes in Real Incomes

Throughout, assume that a community's level of satisfaction or real income depends only on the bundle of commodities it consumes. For the two-commodity example this can be stated formally as

$$u = u(D_C, D_F)$$

[1] That they are the same should be kept in mind when Chapter 4 describes the conditions for market stability.

The symbol u represents some arbitrary index used to measure utility or the level of welfare. Differentiate this expression to obtain

$$du = \frac{\partial u}{\partial D_C} dD_C + \frac{\partial u}{\partial D_F} dD_F$$

which states that when the amounts consumed are altered, utility changes by an amount that depends on the marginal utility of a commodity (e.g., $\partial u/\partial D_F$ for food) multiplied by the change in the quantity of it consumed. The arbitrariness of the utility index can be removed by dividing both sides of this equation by the marginal utility of clothing.

$$\frac{du}{\partial u/\partial D_C} = dD_C + \frac{\partial u/\partial D_F}{\partial u/\partial D_C} dD_F$$

The left-hand term is positive only if utility has increased. Furthermore, it is a measure of the change in utility expressed in units of clothing (the "utils" cancel out). Call this change in real income in clothing units "dy." The right-hand side can be simplified by noticing that the coefficient of "dD_F" is the *marginal rate of substitution*, the amount of clothing that must be added to compensate for a loss of one unit of food along an indifference curve. In a market equilibrium, however, this amount corresponds to the relative price of food, p. Thus, Equation 3.S.1 can be derived as the basic expression for a change of real income.

$$dy = dD_C + pdD_F \tag{3.S.1}$$

It could almost be taken as a *definition* of real income changes—the sum of consumption changes with each such change weighted by the relative price of that commodity.

The budget constraint,

$$D_C + pD_F = x_C + px_F \tag{3.S.2}$$

reveals that the source of any change in real income must reside in either a change in the endowment bundle or a change in the terms of trade. To see this, differentiate Equation 3.S.2 to obtain

$$dD_C + pdD_F + D_F dp = dx_C + pdx_F + x_F dp$$

Subtract $D_F dp$ from both sides, and use Equation 3.S.1 for dy to obtain

$$dy = -(D_F - x_F)dp + (dx_C + pdx_F) \tag{3.S.3}$$

This basic expression for the change of real income in the home country provides the following breakdown.

1. The term $-(D_F - x_F)dp$ is the *terms-of-trade effect* encountered in Chapter 3. Assume the home country is a net importer of food, and let M denote $(D_F - x_F)$. If the terms of trade deteriorate for the home country, dp is positive and real income at home falls by Mdp, an amount proportional to the volume of imports.

2. The term $(dx_C + pdx_F)$, the price-weighted sum of any change in the home country's production bundle, enters directly into the measure of a change in real income.

This two-term breakdown of the influences on a nation's real income is absolutely basic for the applications to be considered in Chapter 4 and elsewhere in the text.

A Basic Production Relationship

The discussion of commodity exchange in Chapter 2 held constant the amount produced in each country as prices changed. This inflexibility in production response ensures that a change in prices results in a zero value for $(dx_C + pdx_F)$ in Equation 3.S.3 for the change of real incomes, because dx_C and dx_F are each zero. If, instead, production possibilities are shown by a bowed-out transformation schedule (as in Figure 3.1), a rise in food's relative price, p, would encourage food production and discourage clothing output. Nonetheless, for output movements along the transformation schedule,

$$dx_C + pdx_F = 0 \qquad\qquad (3.S.4)$$

The reason is simple: At a competitive equilibrium (e.g., point B in Figure 3.1) the absolute value of the slope of the transformation schedule, $-(dx_F/dx_C)$, must equal clothing's relative price, $(1/p)$.

Substitution and Income Effects

Chapter 3 suggested that any change in price has both a substitution and income effect on quantity demanded. The decomposition into these two effects can be expressed algebraically for small price changes, making use of Equation 3.S.3's expression for the change in real income, which is simplified by Equation 3.S.4's relationship among outputs.

The demand for any commodity depends on all prices and income. Alternatively, in a two-commodity model it depends on relative price, p, and real income, y.[1] For example, consider the home country's demand for food, written as in Equation 3.S.5.

$$D_F = D_F(p, y) \qquad\qquad (3.S.5)$$

Differentiate this with respect to food's relative price, p, to obtain

$$\frac{dD_F}{dp} = \frac{\partial D_F}{\partial p} + \frac{\partial D_F}{\partial y} \cdot \frac{dy}{dp}$$

The first term is the substitution effect of a price rise—as p rises food demand falls along an indifference curve. The second composite term shows the two aspects of the income effect described in the text. The term dy/dp shows how real income at home

---

[1] The change in real income, dy, has been defined by Equation 3.S.1. Mathematical liberties are taken here in using the symbol y for real income itself. However, this supplement only requires the expression for dy, as it only considers "small" changes in prices and demands.

has been affected by the rise in food's relative price. Equation 3.S.3 reveals that dy/dp is just $-(D_F - x_F)$, because any output response along the transformation curve has negligible impact on real incomes (by Equation 3.S.4). If food is imported, dy/dp is negative. The other term, $\partial D_F/\partial y$, expresses the change in demand for food as a consequence of a unit rise in incomes with prices constant. This is not a pure number, as D_F is measured in food units and y in clothing units. Therefore, define α_F as $p \cdot (\partial D_F/\partial y)$, the home country's marginal propensity to consume food. This is a pure number, between 0 and 1 if neither commodity is "inferior." Therefore, Equation 3.S.6 depicts the breakdown of dD_F/dp into substitution and income effects.

$$\frac{dD_F}{dp} = \frac{\partial D_F}{\partial p} - \frac{(D_F - x_F)}{p} \cdot \alpha_F \qquad (3.S.6)$$

This breakdown of demand shows the importance of the direction of trade. If food is imported at home, both income and substitution terms combine to reduce food demand as the relative price of food rises. However, if food were exported, the income effect of a rise in food's price would be positive, running counter to the substitution effect and, in some cases, resulting in more food being demanded locally.

The Hat Notation

It will often prove convenient to express the change in a variable, dx, as a fraction of the original value of that variable, x. A hat, "$\hat{\ }$", denotes this relative change. Thus, for any variable, x,

$$\hat{x} \equiv \frac{dx}{x}$$

The Elasticity of Demand for Imports

This discussion of the components of demand behavior can be added to a consideration of production changes to investigate the *elasticity of demand for imports*, ϵ, defined as

$$\epsilon \equiv -\frac{\hat{M}}{\hat{p}} \qquad (3.S.7)$$

where the minus sign is used to make ϵ a positive number. M, of course, refers to home imports of food,

$$M = D_F - x_F$$

We argued in the text that three ingredients are involved in the expression for ϵ, the elasticity of demand for imports. As we now show, ϵ can be expressed as the simple sum of (1) $\bar{\eta}$, the pure substitution elasticity of demand, (2) m, the marginal propensity to import, and (3) e, the elasticity of supply for import-competing production:

$$\epsilon = \bar{\eta} + m + e \qquad (3.S.8)$$

To see this, differentiate the expression for M and use hat notation:

$$-\frac{\hat{M}}{\hat{p}} = -\frac{D_F}{M} \cdot \frac{\hat{D}_F}{\hat{p}} + \frac{x_F}{M} \cdot \frac{\hat{x}_F}{\hat{p}}$$

The expression for

$$-\frac{D_F \hat{D}_F}{M \hat{p}}$$

follows readily from Equation 3.S.6. Let $\bar{\eta}$ represent the (negative of the) pure substitution term in demand,

$$\bar{\eta} \equiv \frac{p \partial D_F}{-M \partial p}$$

and m the marginal propensity to import, which is the marginal propensity to consume the imported good (food) at home, α_F. Finally, define the elasticity of import-competing production, e, as[2]

$$e \equiv \frac{p}{M} \cdot \frac{dx_F}{dp}$$

Combining yields the final breakdown for the elasticity of demand for imports, ϵ.

Comparative Advantage and the Gains from Trade

A basic line of argument reveals how competitive behavior leads to gains from international trade when countries take advantage of world markets to import commodities that are relatively inexpensive compared to autarky. In striving for generality, this discussion removes the two-commodity (food and clothing) limitation and considers a country originally consuming and producing many commodities before international trade. Let autarky market-clearing prices and quantities be indicated by the "0" superscript, so that before trade item-by-item

$$D_i^0 = x_i^0 \tag{3.S.9}$$

International trade frees a country from the necessity of providing all its own requirements; imposed instead is a balance of payments constraint that the overall value of consumption match that of national production. Letting the superscript "1" denote free-trade variables,

$$\Sigma p_i^1 D_i^1 = \Sigma p_i^1 x_i^1 \tag{3.S.10}$$

A country is considered to gain from international trade if in a trade equilibrium it chooses a consumption bundle, D^1, that (at free-trade prices, p^1) costs more to purchase than does the autarky bundle, D^0. Such a choice is taken to *reveal* a preference

---

[2] An equivalent expression for e is $\dfrac{\hat{X}}{\widehat{(1/p)}}$ with demands constant, which could be termed the elasticity of export supply. (X represents $x_C - D_C$ for the home country.)

for the consumption choice available with trade, since it is selected despite the higher price tag. That is, Inequality 3.S.11 represents a criterion for the gains from trade.

$$\text{Gains if } \Sigma p_i^1 D_i^1 > \Sigma p_i^1 D_i^0 \tag{3.S.11}$$

This criterion provides one of the two fundamental building blocks for the general argument. The other compares the aggregate value of production at a given set of prices with any alternative production pattern along a given production-possibilities schedule. The basic production relationship, Equation 3.S.4, states that a price line is tangent to the transformation curve at the point chosen. The bowed-out curvature of the transformation curve implies that should any other production combination have been chosen at the same prices, it would have a lower aggregate value. This statement holds for any number of commodities and any set of prices. In particular, at free trade prices, p^1, the value of production bundle x^1 is greater than that of autarky bundle x^0 at those same prices. That is,

$$\Sigma p_i^1 x_i^1 > \Sigma p_i^1 x_i^0 \tag{3.S.12}$$

These results provide the basis for two propositions. First, the production relationship shown in Inequality 3.S.12 is used to prove that Inequality 3.S.11 is indeed satisfied. Adding up the value (at free-trade prices) of autarky consumption and production from Equation 3.S.9,

$$\Sigma p_i^1 D_i^0 = \Sigma p_i^1 x_i^0$$

Now substitute this and Equation 3.S.10 into Inequality 3.S.12 to establish Inequality 3.S.11. Free trade leads to gains.

The second proposition concerns the pattern of trade according to comparative advantage that leads to these gains from trade. It generalizes the notion that to obtain gains when trading, a country should export those commodities produced relatively cheaply at home and import commodities that are relatively inexpensive on world markets. Since it is established that free trade leads to gains, at autarky prices the consumption bundle purchased with free trade must have been out of consumers' reach. They could not afford to purchase the superior bundle, D^1, or they would have done so. This implies that

$$\Sigma p_i^0 D_i^1 > \Sigma p_i^0 D_i^0 \tag{3.S.13}$$

As for production comparisons at autarky prices, the notion that at *any* given prices production responds to maximize the aggregate value of produced income leads to the following:

$$\Sigma p_i^0 x_i^1 < \Sigma p_i^0 x_i^0 \tag{3.S.14}$$

The logic is the same as that leading to Inequality 3.S.12, except that at free trade prices, p^1, the production bundle x^1 has greater value than x^0. Let E_i^1 be defined as imports of commodity i in the trade situation, $(D_i^1 - x_i^1)$. Because the right sides of Inequalities 3.S.13 and 3.S.14 are the same, subtraction reveals that

$$\Sigma p_i^0 E_i^1 > 0 \tag{3.S.15}$$

That is, if evaluated at autarky prices, imports on the aggregate exceed exports. At free-trade prices, of course, they must have the same value if trade is balanced.

$$\Sigma p_i^1 E_i^1 = 0 \tag{3.S.16}$$

(This restates Equation 3.S.10.)

The final step involves subtracting Inequality 3.S.15 from Equation 3.S.16 to obtain

$$\Sigma(p_i^1 - p_i^0)E_i^1 < 0 \tag{3.S.17}$$

This states that *on average* any commodity, i, imported with free trade has an autarky price, p_i^0, higher than its trade price, p_i^1. It is not possible to establish such a relationship item by item, but Inequality 3.S.17 shows that in the aggregate a country imports goods that are relatively cheaper with trade and exports goods that are relatively expensive.[3]

Finally, note that original Inequality 3.S.11, used to show gains from trade, is overly stringent. The exchange model of Chapter 2 established gains from trade, but with production fixed the value at trade prices of consumption with trade ($\Sigma p_i^1 D_i^1$) matches that of autarky consumption ($\Sigma p_i^1 D_i^0$); both consumption bundles lie on the same budget line in Figure 2.3.

The line of argument developed here is pursued in the supplement to Chapter 12 to consider situations in which tariffs or export taxes distort home from world prices.

SUPPLEMENT TO CHAPTER 4:
Stability and Comparative Statics in the Basic Trade Model

Stability in the two-commodity world trade model requires that an increase in the relative price of food reduces world excess demand for food. Conditions sufficient to guarantee stability can be derived and presented in two alternative, but equivalent, ways.

The Marshall-Lerner Stability Condition

This form of the condition concentrates on the elasticity of each country's demand for imports. World excess demand for food is the difference between the home country's excess demand, M, and the foreign country's intended exports of food. These intended food exports have a value equivalent to foreign import demand (for clothing). This value is M^*/p. (The division by p is to change from clothing units to food units.) Therefore, stability requires an increase in p to lower ($M - M^*/p$). That is, the condition for stability is

$$\frac{dM}{dp} < \frac{d(M^*/p)}{dp}$$

---

[3] To see why you should not expect an item-by-item correspondence, suppose that commodity 17 is slightly more expensive with trade than it is at home in autarky. Some major items of consumption that are good substitutes for commodity 17 might become even more expensive with trade, thus deflecting demand onto commodity 17. Additionally, or alternatively, resources could be drained away from commodity 17 towards other commodities which have risen in price with trade. The net result? Commodity 17 might end up as an import instead of an export.

This inequality can be slightly modified by (1) dividing the denominators of both sides by p to highlight the *relative* price change, dp/p. (A circumflex ("hat") denotes relative changes: dp/p is written as $\hat{p}$.) Then, (2) divide the numerator on the left-hand side by M and the numerator on the right-hand side by M^*/p (which equals M at the initial equilibrium). Making use of the hat notation for relative changes, the inequality becomes

$$\frac{M}{\hat{p}} < \frac{\widehat{(M^*/p)}}{\hat{p}} \tag{4.S.1}$$

By definition, the elasticity of home demand for imports along the offer curve is $\epsilon \equiv -\hat{M}/\hat{p}$, while foreign ϵ^* is $-\hat{M}^*/(1/p)$, which is equivalent to $\hat{M}^*/\hat{p}$.[1] Because Inequality 4.S.1 can be written as

$$\frac{\hat{M}}{\hat{p}} < \frac{\hat{M}^* - \hat{p}}{\hat{p}}$$

substituting for ϵ and ϵ^* yields

$$\epsilon + \epsilon^* > 1 \tag{4.S.2}$$

This is known as the *Marshall-Lerner condition for stability*. It suggests that in order for the market to be stable, offer curves cannot be too inelastic. The offer curves in Figure 3.A.1 intersect at stable equilibrium point Q. Note that at that point ϵ is less than 1 but ϵ^* exceeds unity, so that the Marshall-Lerner condition is obviously satisfied. To illustrate an unstable equilibrium, both offer curves must be inelastic. Instability requires the offer curves to cut each other in the direction opposite that shown in Figure 3.A.1, as at point Q in Figure 4.A.1.

An Alternative Form for the Stability Condition

Concentrate on the excess world demand curve for food, but generalize by assuming many countries in the trading world. Some will be food importers, others exporters. The condition for market stability is that the slope of the excess world demand curve for food be negative, or

$$\Sigma \frac{dD_F^i}{dp} - \Sigma \frac{dx_F^i}{dp} < 0$$

Multiply each term by $-p$, which also changes the direction of the inequality sign. Next, divide and multiply each term in the first sum by D_F^i, country i's demand for food, and each term in the second sum by x_F^i. Finally, divide all terms by total world demand (ΣD_F^i) or by the equivalent (in the neighborhood of equilibrium) total world supply (Σx_F^i). At this stage the condition for stability is

$$\Sigma \lambda_F^i \left\{ -\frac{p}{D_F^i} \frac{dD_F^i}{dp} \right\} + \Sigma \rho_F^i \left\{ \frac{p}{x_F^i} \frac{dx_F^i}{dp} \right\} > 0 \tag{4.S.3}$$

In Inequality 4.S.3 two sets of weights appear in the summations. λ_F^i is the fraction of total world food consumption represented by country i's demand, $D_F^i/\Sigma D_F^i$. Similarly, the ρ_F^i are production weights; ρ_F^i equals $x_F^i/\Sigma x_F^i$. The λ and the ρ sums each add to unity.

---

[1] The relative change in a ratio, such as $(\widehat{x/y})$, is the difference between the relative change in the numerator and denominator: $\hat{x} - \hat{y}$. Since "1" is a constant, $(\widehat{1/p})$ equals $-\hat{p}$.

The final step involves breaking down the demand elasticities into income and substitution terms and defining the appropriate supply elasticities. The breakdown of home food demand response to price was shown in Equation 3.S.6, repeated here for country i as Equation 4.S.4.

$$\frac{dD_F^i}{dp} = \frac{\partial D_F^i}{\partial p} - \frac{(D_F^i - x_F^i)}{p}\alpha_F^i \tag{4.S.4}$$

Multiply Equation 4.S.4 by $-p/D_F^i$ and define the pure substitution term, $-\dfrac{p}{D_F^i}\dfrac{\partial D_F^i}{\partial p}$, as $\overline{\omega}_F^i$, which must be positive.[2] This yields

$$-\frac{p}{D_F^i}\frac{dD_F^i}{dp} = \overline{\omega}_F^i + \frac{(D_F^i - x_F^i)}{D_F^i}\cdot\alpha_F^i \tag{4.S.5}$$

Similarly, define

$$\frac{p}{x_F^i}\frac{dx_F^i}{dp}$$

as e_F^i. This own-supply response to price must be positive.

Sweeping countries together, let S be defined as

$$S \equiv \Sigma\lambda_F^i\overline{\omega}_F^i + \Sigma\rho_F^ie_F^i$$

That is, S is the sum of two terms: The first is the positive-weighted average of each nation's substitution elasticity of demand, and the second is the weighted average of own-production elasticities. In similar fashion for income effects, let γ be defined as

$$\gamma \equiv \Sigma\,(\lambda_F^i - \rho_F^i)\alpha_F^i$$

Each country's marginal propensity to consume food, α_F^i, has as weight in γ the fraction of total world food production represented by that country's net *imports* of food. If country i exports food, $(\lambda_F^i - \rho_F^i)$ would be a negative fraction. Substituting these terms into Inequality 4.S.3 yields Inequality 4.S.6 as an alternative basic stability condition.

$$S + \gamma > 0 \tag{4.S.6}$$

This form of the stability condition is in some ways more revealing than the equivalent Marshall-Lerner expression, Inequality 4.S.2. Substitution effects both in consumption and production are contained in the term S and must be positive. Thus, high values help ensure stability. As the price of food rises, in every country consumers substitute away from demanding food and resources are attracted to food production. γ captures the effect of a rise in food's price in redistributing real incomes toward countries exporting food and away from food importers. If all countries share identical marginal propensities to consume food, α_F^i, γ must vanish and the market be stable.

---

[2] Note that for the home country importing F, $\overline{\omega}_F$ is smaller than the trade substitution elasticity, $\overline{\eta}$, defined in the supplement to Chapter 3. Indeed, $\overline{\omega}_F$ is (M/D_F) times $\overline{\eta}$. They would be equal only if no food were produced at home.

If, on average, food importers have a higher marginal propensity to consume food, γ would be positive and market stability thus guaranteed. Returning to the two-country case in which the home country imports food (denoted by M), we have

$$\gamma = \frac{M}{D_F + D_F^*}(\alpha_F - \alpha_F^*)$$

Thus, stability would be endangered if foreign food exporters had a higher α_F^* than home food importers. Note, however, that γ's absolute size tends to be small if the volume of trade is small relative to total world consumption. In such a case the market is apt to be stable regardless of taste differences.

Comparative Statics

This chapter discussed several comparative statics exercises involving changes in tastes, the composition of outputs, growth, and international transfers. The basic equilibrium relationship for all these exercises (except transfers) is the balance of payments condition (see also Equation 2.S.9),

$$pM = M^* \tag{4.S.7}$$

The method of comparative statics involves seeing how a disturbance to the market causes prices to change so as to restore the equilibrium relationship shown by Equation 4.S.7. That is, anything that causes imports in either country to change must bring about an equilibrating price response.

Proceed formally by differentiating Equation 4.S.7, making use of the hat notation for relative changes.

$$\hat{p} + \hat{M} = \hat{M}^* \tag{4.S.8}$$

Imports in either country respond to a change in the terms of trade—this is what the offer curves describe. In addition, a disturbance may *shift* one or more offer curves. Let the relative change in imports at home that would take place at *constant terms of trade* be denoted by $\hat{M}|_{\bar{p}}$. This is the shift in the home offer curve. Similarly, $\hat{M}^*|_{\bar{p}}$ denotes the relative shift in the foreign offer curve. Putting these two sources of import change together,

$$\hat{M} = -\varepsilon\hat{p} + \hat{M}|_{\bar{p}}$$

$$\hat{M}^* = \varepsilon^*\hat{p} + \hat{M}^*|_{\bar{p}} \tag{4.S.9}$$

Substitute these into Equation 4.S.8 and solve for the relative change in the terms of trade to get

$$\hat{p} = \frac{(\hat{M}|_{\bar{p}} - \hat{M}^*|_{\bar{p}})}{\Delta} \text{ where } \Delta \equiv \varepsilon + \varepsilon^* - 1 \tag{4.S.10}$$

This is a basic, and readily understandable, result. From the Marshall-Lerner stability expression, Inequality 4.S.2, the denominator, Δ, must be positive. This shows that the less sensitive imports are to price changes (small Δ), the more price must adjust to clear markets. Furthermore, the numerator of Equation 4.S.10 has a ready interpretation. It shows the relative increase in world excess demand for the home country's import commodity (food) at the initial prices. In other words, Equation 4.S.10 shows that the equilibrium relative price of food rises if the excess world demand curve for food shifts to the right and the market is stable.

In many applications of the basic trade model, the aim is to analyze how real incomes at home and abroad are affected. The expression for real income changes at home was developed in the supplement to Chapter 3. A slight rewriting of Equation 3.S.3 yields

$$dy = - pM \cdot \hat{p} + (dx_C + pdx_F) \qquad (4.S.11)$$

There is a terms-of-trade effect and a direct effect from production changes. Recall that for movements along the transformation curve, $(dx_C + pdx_F)$ equals zero. Therefore, the second part of dy in Equation 4.S.11 picks up the value of *shifts* in the transformation curve.

Now consider the following scenarios, in each of which there is a shock or disturbance to a pre-existing world trade equilibrium balancing home and foreign import demands. The first involves only a change in the *composition* of outputs at home, the next two applications involve *growth*, and the final scenario deals with the *transfer* problem. In each case focus on the change in the terms of trade and on the consequent effects on real incomes:

1. *A Change in the Composition of Home Outputs.* In this case assume that at constant prices food output rises ($dx_F > 0$), clothing output falls ($dx_C < 0$), but, at initial prices, there is no change in the value of aggregate production ($dx_C + pdx_F = 0$). This means that at the initial price there is no alteration in home demand for food importables (both price and income are constant at the initial price). Yet production rises, and this causes demand for imports to fall. $dM = - dx_F$. Abroad no changes take place at the initial prices. Substitution into Equation 4.S.10 reveals that

$$\hat{p} = - \frac{1}{M \cdot \Delta} dx_F \qquad (4.S.12)$$

With the terms of trade improving, so must real income at home. Equation 4.S.11 thus gives

$$dy = \frac{pdx_F}{\Delta} \qquad (4.S.13)$$

The more inelastic are world demands and supplies, the more successful would be a policy of substituting import-competing production, x_F, for exportables, x_C. This is a theme picked up by the tariff literature.

2. *Export-Led Growth.* Suppose growth is biased so that at initial prices only the output of exportables at home expands: $dx_C > 0$ but, at constant prices, $dx_F = 0$. No *shifts* in demand or supply take place abroad. At initial prices there is no change in production of food (importables), but because incomes expand (at *initial* prices), so

does demand. That is, $dM = dD_F$ and $dD_F = (m/p)(dx_C)$. Demand for food rises by an amount determined by the marginal propensity to import food, m, and the increase in initial incomes in food units, dx_C/p. Substituting into Equation 4.S.10 yields

$$\hat{p} = \frac{m}{pM \cdot \Delta} \, dx_C \tag{4.S.14}$$

The terms of trade have deteriorated and, by Equation 4.S.11, this deterioration offsets at least a part of the initial growth effect on real incomes.

$$dy = \left(\frac{\Delta - m}{\Delta}\right) dx_C \tag{4.S.15}$$

The expression in parentheses provides the condition for immiserizing growth. Stability ensures that Δ is positive, but if elasticities are nonetheless low, Δ may not exceed the home marginal propensity to import. In such a case, real incomes at home would fall despite output growth.

3. *Balanced Growth.* The kind of growth just discussed was quite biased—at initial prices only the home country's export good expanded, which ensures a deterioration in its terms of trade. Yet what about balanced growth? Suppose the home country's transformation schedule shifts outward uniformly at rate μ—both dx_C/x_C and dx_F/x_F equal μ at initial prices. Assume also that demand for both goods expands in a balanced fashion at initial prices. Then imports (at initial prices) must also expand at rate μ ($M|_{\hat{p}}$ equals μ). Substitute into Equation 4.S.10 to show that neutral growth must cause a deterioration in the terms of trade (assuming no growth abroad).

$$\hat{p} = \frac{\mu}{\Delta} \tag{4.S.16}$$

It proves convenient to express the change in real income (given in Equation 4.S.11) in relative terms. $\hat{y}$ is dy divided by initial income ($x_C + px_F$). That is,

$$\hat{y} = -\theta_M \hat{p} + \mu$$

where θ_M represents the share of imports in the national income and μ, of course, is the growth rate at initial prices. This expression is perfectly general. Substituting the terms-of-trade change shown by Equation 4.S.16 for the case of balanced growth yields

$$\hat{y} = \left(\frac{\Delta - \theta_M}{\Delta}\right) \mu \tag{4.S.17}$$

This result shows that even balanced growth can be immiserizing, for it does worsen the terms of trade. If elasticities are sufficiently low, their sum may not exceed unity by more than the share of imports in the national income. Equation 4.S.17 should be compared with Equation 4.S.15. Retaining the assumption that at constant prices growth in demand is proportional, the marginal propensity to import, m, is the same as the fraction of total income spent on importables. Unless production of importables is nonexistent, this must exceed the share of income represented by total imports, θ_M. Export-led growth is more apt to worsen real incomes than is balanced growth.

4. *The Transfer Problem*. Discussion of the transfer problem requires a bit more preparation. The basic equilibrium relationship set out in Equation 4.S.7 rests on the classical form of the budget constraint: In each country all earned income is spent. The transfer process has the home country spending less than its produced income by the amount of transfer (call it T in units of clothing), matched by an equal amount of excess spending (over earned income) abroad. This implies that the value of spending on imports at home must also be cut below the value of foreign imports by the amount of the transfer.[3] This is the following basic relationship.

$$pM = M^* - T \qquad\qquad (4.S.18)$$

Assume that initially there is no transfer ($T = 0$ initially). Differentiation of Equation 4.S.18 yields

$$\hat{p} + \hat{M} = \hat{M}^* - \frac{dT}{pM} \qquad\qquad (4.S.19)$$

Proceeding as before (in the development of Equation 4.S.10), the result is

$$\hat{p} = \frac{\left(\hat{M}|_{\bar{p}} - \hat{M}^*|_{\bar{p}} + \dfrac{dT}{pM} \right)}{\Delta} \qquad\qquad (4.S.20)$$

With a transfer of purchasing power there are no production changes at the initial terms of trade.[4] Demand for imports falls at home and rises abroad, however. That is, $\hat{M}|_{\bar{p}} = - mdT/pM$ and $\hat{M}^*|_{\bar{p}} = m^*dT/pM$. In other words, the impact of the direct redistribution of income on the terms of trade is shown by:

$$\hat{p} = \frac{-(m + m^* - 1)}{\Delta}\frac{dT}{pM} \qquad\qquad (4.S.21)$$

This expression confirms Chapter 4's statement that with transfer the terms of trade might go in either direction. Note that the numerator can also be written as $[(1 - m^*) - m]$ or, to use the earlier terminology, as $(\alpha_F^* - \alpha_F)$. Whether the real income transfer is a consequence of a change in the terms of trade (as in the stability expression, Inequality 4.S.6) or of a direct transfer of purchasing power (as in Equation 4.S.21), the same comparison between foreign α_F^* and home α_F, the marginal propensities to consume a particular commodity in the two countries, is required.

This supplement will conclude by confirming Chapter 4's argument that even if the terms of trade move in favor of the transferor, real income for the transferor cannot improve. The equivalent of Equation 4.S.11 for the transfer problem is[5]

---

[3] The home budget constraint becomes $D_C + pD_F = x_C + px_F - T$. Rewriting, $p(D_F - x_F) = (x_C - D_C) - T$. When markets clear, home intended exports equal foreign imports, M^*.

[4] Ignored here is the chapter's discussion of a possible transfer of real resources. A general treatment of the transfer problem, which includes possible supply reactions, is R. W. Jones, "Presumption and the Transfer Problem," *Journal of International Economics* (August 1975): 263–274, reprinted as Chapter 10 in his *International Trade: Essays in Theory* (Amsterdam: North-Holland, 1979).

[5] Here dy is interpreted as the change in current real consumption. Left out of this account is the possibility that the transfer represents a loan, which will in the future be repaid. Presumably this does not by itself lower "real income" for the transferor. Also left out of this account in the expression that follows is the possibility that trade involves other countries in addition to the transferor and transferee. In such a case a transfer welfare paradox is possible, wherein real income may improve for the transferor. For a general discussion of this issue, with references to the literature, see R. W. Jones, "Income Effects and Paradoxes in the Theory of International Trade," *Economic Journal* (June 1985): 330–344.

$$dy = -pM\hat{p} - dT$$

Direct substitution of $\hat{p}$ into this expression yields

$$dy = -\left\{\frac{\epsilon + \epsilon^* - (m + m^*)}{\Delta}\right\}dT$$

However, the supplement to Chapter 3 decomposed the elasticity of import demand (ϵ, and, by analogy, ϵ^*) into a substitution term in consumption ($\bar{\eta}$ and $\bar{\eta}^*$), a positive elasticity in production (e and e^*), and the import propensity (m and m^*). Therefore, with transfer the expression for dy can finally be given as follows:

$$dy = -\frac{\{\bar{\eta} + \bar{\eta}^* + e + e^*\}}{\Delta}dT \qquad (4.S.22)$$

Real income for the transferor must declne, as is demonstrated in Figure 4.5.

SUPPLEMENT TO CHAPTER 5:
Comparative Advantage and the Assignment Problem

Because the Ricardian trade model has such a simple production structure—each commodity produced only with labor at fixed coefficients—it is ideally suited to the analysis of production assignments in a world with many countries and commodities. The concept of the world transformation schedule, illustrated in Figure 5.4 for the two-country, two-commodity case, provides the focus for this discussion of comparative advantage in the more general case.

It is useful to consider a concrete example. Suppose the world consists of three countries: A (America), B (Britain), and C (Continental Europe). Furthermore, suppose only three commodities can be produced and consumed: corn (Co), linen (Lin), and cloth (Cl). Let the numbers in the following table show the invariant labor input-output coefficients in each country to produce a unit of each commodity.[1]

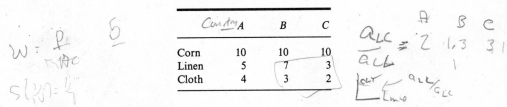

Country	A	B	C
Corn	10	10	10
Linen	5	7	3
Cloth	4	3	2

If only two commodities were to be produced, the techniques illustrated in Figure 5.4 for two countries could easily be extended to accommodate a third country. For example, if only corn and linen are produced, Figure 5.S.1 would show that the relatively most efficient producer of corn is Britain, followed by America and, last, Continental Europe, despite the fact that all three countries have the same absolute costs. Fig-

[1] This example, and much of the subsequent analysis, is found in R. W. Jones, "Comparative Advantage and the Theory of Tariffs: A Multi-Commodity, Multi-Country Model," *Review of Economic Studies* (June 1961) 161–175, and reprinted as Chapter 3 in his *International Trade: Essays in Theory* (Amsterdam: North-Holland, 1979). See also ibid., Chapter 18.

ure 5.S.1 arbitrarily assumes all countries have the same size labor force, an assumption that does not interfere with the analysis of *patterns* of specialization in production.

Panel (b) in Figure 5.S.1 summarizes much of what the two-dimensional transformation schedule in panel (a) shows. All countries produce linen at the left-hand linen origin. The lettering reveals that country *B* is the first country to release labor to produce corn, because it has the greatest comparative advantage in producing corn *relative to linen*. Country *A* is next in the line of comparative advantage—so that two-thirds across to the corn origin, countries *A* and *B* are completely specialized in corn and *C* in linen.

It is clear that adding one more country to a two-commodity analysis introduces no fresh difficulties, and a similar kind of ranking could display separately positions of comparative advantage in linen and cloth on the one hand and corn and cloth on the other. The information on bilateral cost ratios is computed from the table and summarized graphically in Figure 5.S.2. For example, if only cloth and linen are to be produced, and if two countries are to be assigned to produce linen and only one

---

FIGURE 5.S.1   The World Transformation Schedule: Three Countries

The world transformation schedule in the three-country, two-commodity version is a three-segment linear schedule bowed out from the origin. Information as to the pattern of specialization for countries *A*, *B*, *C* in linen and corn can be summarized in the one-dimensional line in panel (b).

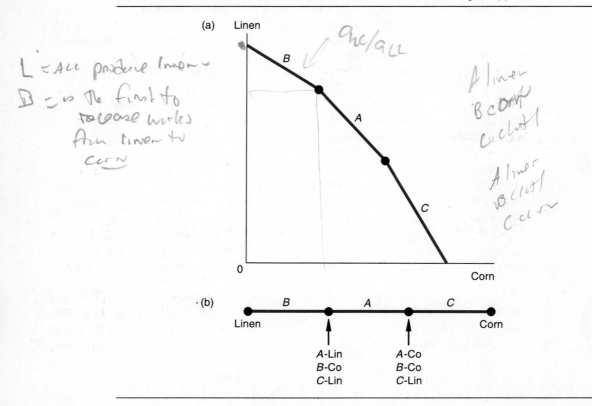

FIGURE 5.S.2 Bilateral Cost Rankings

Patterns of comparative advantage taking two commodities at a time are summarized below as in Figure 5.S.1(b).

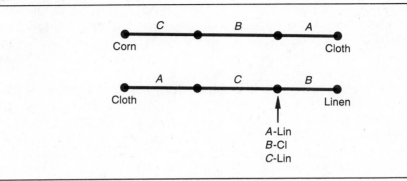

country to produce cloth, country B is selected as the cloth producer because its relative cost, $\frac{3}{7}$, is lower than either $\frac{2}{3}$ or $\frac{4}{5}$. Note that there are potentially three possible assignments that put one country in cloth and two in linen. Think of a *class* of assignments as a specification of the number of countries assigned to each commodity. In this example it was zero countries in corn, one in cloth, and two in linen. (There are five other classes of this type, e.g., zero countries in cloth, one in corn, and two in linen.) The doctrine of comparative advantage singles out the *efficient* assignment in each class.

Suppose all three commodities are to be produced, however. If each country were to be assigned a different commodity, which assignment pattern reflects comparative advantage? Look again at the table of cost figures. If only corn and linen were to be produced and only countries A and B involved, clearly B has a comparative advantage in corn and A in linen. Now add country C and the new commodity, cloth. Country C is in absolute terms the lowest-cost cloth producer. Therefore, consider this assignment: A in linen, B in corn, and C in cloth. As just noted, A has a comparative advantage in linen relative to corn compared with country B. Likewise, C has a comparative advantage in cloth relative to corn compared with B ($\frac{2}{10}$ is less than $\frac{3}{10}$). Finally, a bilateral comparison between countries A and C in linen and cloth shows that linen is produced relatively cheaply in A ($\frac{5}{4}$ is smaller than $\frac{3}{2}$). Yet this pattern of specialization is inefficient! There are six possible assignments in which all three commodities are produced, and the efficient one has corn produced by country A, cloth by country B, and linen by country C.

To confirm that this alternative assignment is indeed efficient, recall that the force of competition in world markets rules out inefficient production patterns. In a competitive equilibrium, any commodity actively produced in a country must have unit labor costs equal to price so that profits are bid away. Furthermore, if a country does not produce a commodity, unit labor costs must not be less than the world price of that commodity. As will now be shown, there is a range of world prices at which, simultaneously, country A can produce corn, country B cloth, and country C linen.

Because only relative prices matter, the price of corn is arbitrarily set at unity. If country A is to produce corn, the wage rate in country A must equal $\frac{1}{10}$. This, in turn, reveals that if country A were to attempt to produce linen, unit costs would equal $\frac{1}{2}$. Therefore, a competitive equilibrium in which country A does not produce linen must be one in which the world price of linen, p_{Lin}, is less than or equal to $\frac{1}{2}$. Figure 5.S.3 shows possible ranges for the world prices of linen and cloth (given the assumption that the price of corn is unity). Any value of p_{Lin} greater than $\frac{1}{2}$ is thus ruled out. Also, with a wage rage of $\frac{1}{10}$ the unit cost of producing cloth in A would be $\frac{2}{5}$, and this cannot fall short of the world price of cloth.

Now consider country B, which has been assigned to cloth production. The wage rate in country B depends on the price of cloth, and will equal $\frac{1}{3} p_{Cl}$. Therefore, if B were to attempt to produce corn, the cost per unit would be 10 times the wage rate, which must not fall short of the price of corn (which equals unity by assumption). That is, $\frac{10}{3} p_{Cl}$ must be ≥ 1, which puts a lower bound on the price of cloth. Similarly, unit costs in B for linen production would equal $\left(\frac{7}{3}\right) p_{Cl}$, which must be greater than or equal to the world price of linen. That is, any acceptable p_{Lin} must lie below the ray from the origin whose equation is $p_{Lin} = \frac{7}{3} p_{Cl}$. Finally, consider the required comparison in country C between the unit costs of corn and cloth and world prices. C is assigned to linen, so that the wage rate in C equals one-third the world price of linen. Its unit costs in corn would then be $\frac{10}{3}$ times the price of linen, so that $\frac{10}{3} p_{Lin}$ must exceed unity to avoid C being a potentially profitable location for corn pro-

FIGURE 5.S.3   Price Possibilities

If the price of corn is unity, any price combination for linen and cloth in the shaded area satisfies the competitive profit conditions when A produces corn, B cloth, and C linen.

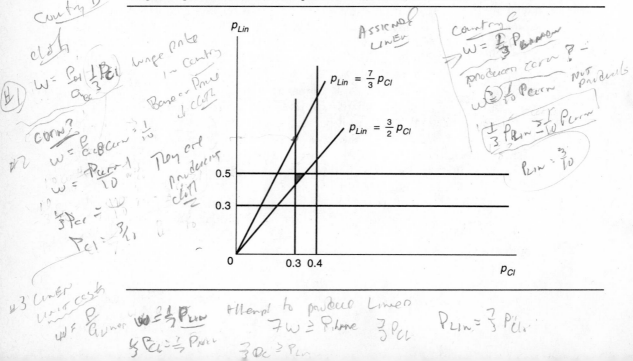

FIGURE 5.S.4   Assignments Along the World Transformation Surface

Along the ridges, one country's labor force is being reallocated between two of the three commodities.

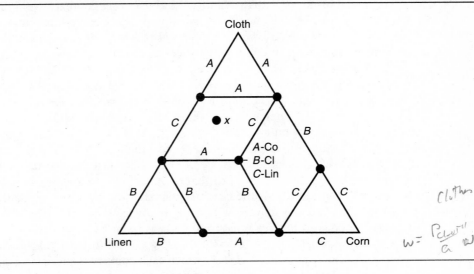

duction. As well, unit costs for cloth in C would be two times the wage rate in C, or $\frac{2}{3}$ times the price of linen. This cost figure must not fall short of the price of cloth, which means p_{Lin} must exceed $\frac{3}{2}$ times the price of cloth.

The shaded area in Figure 5.S.3 shows combinations of prices of linen and cloth, relative to a unit price for corn, at which competition allows America to produce corn, Britain to produce cloth, and, simultaneously, Continental Europe to produce linen. Of the six assignments in the *class* for which each country produces a commodity distinct from the other two, this one is the only efficient one. There is *no* set of free-trade prices that would tolerate the others (e.g., A in linen, B in corn, and C in cloth as originally suggested). This information is necessary in drawing the full world transformation surface. Such a surface would be three-dimensional, but a two-dimensional representation of the assignments can be made, just as panel (b) of Figure 5.S.1 contained in one dimension the information about assignments captured in panel (a)'s transformation locus.

Figure 5.S.4 shows the efficient assignment pattern along the world transformation surface.[2] The bottom edge of the triangle corresponds to panel (b) of Figure 5.S.1, while the side edges replicate the assignment patterns in Figure 5.S.2. In constructing the shape of the surface it was necessary to go through the previous analysis in search of the efficient assignment for the interior point where all three commodities are produced and each country is specialized. Figure 5.S.4 suggests that the transformation surface is made up of planar elements, ridges, and points. Points correspond to

---

[2] The technique of reducing a three-dimensional surface to a two-dimensional pattern of assignments was pioneered by Lionel McKenzie in "Specialization and Efficiency in World Production," *Review of Economic Studies*, (June 1954): 165–180.

positions in which all countries are completely specialized, and once the efficient assignment in each class of complete specializations is determined, the entire surface can be mapped out. Start at the linen corner, where all countries are producing linen. The cost figures suggest that country B has a strong comparative *dis*advantage in linen production, so that should the world wish to consume small amounts of either cloth or corn (or both), it is country B's labor that is first freed up from its assignment to linen. Indeed, relative commodity prices in the lower left-hand triangle in Figure 5.S.4 are given solely by comparative labor costs in country B. Thus, if the price of corn is unity, the price of linen would be $\frac{7}{10}$ and of cloth $\frac{3}{10}$. The lower left-hand triangle exactly replicates country B's planar transformation surface. At a point such as x, country B is completely specialized in cloth, while country A produces both linen and corn and country C produces linen and cloth. Thus, country A's technology determines the linen/corn relative price ($\frac{1}{2}$) and country C's labor costs determine that the relative price of linen to cloth is $\frac{3}{2}$. Along a ridge just one country is incompletely specialized to two commodities, so that one relative price is fixed and the other free to vary (within bounds). At the interior point showing complete specializations, both relative prices are free to vary within the bounds set by the three adjacent planes; this corresponds to relative prices in the shaded area of Figure 5.S.3.

There is a simple general rule for locating the assignment that is efficient in its *class*. Reconsider the interior class in which each country is specialized completely to a different commodity. In the efficient specialization A was assigned corn, B cloth, and C linen so that in symbols,

$$w^A a^A_{Co} = p_{Co}$$

$$w^B a^B_{Cl} = p_{Cl}$$

$$w^C a^C_{Lin} = p_{Lin}$$

where w^i is country i's wage rate and a^i_j is country i's labor cost of producing a unit of commodity j. In addition,

$$w^A a^A_{Lin} \geq p_{Lin}$$

$$w^B a^B_{Co} \geq p_{Co}$$

$$w^C a^C_{Cl} \geq p_{Cl}$$

since otherwise some country would have an unexploited profitable production possibility. Multiply the three equalities to get

$$w^A w^B w^C a^A_{Co} a^B_{Cl} a^C_{Lin} = p_{Co} p_{Cl} p_{Lin}$$

Multiply the three inequalities to obtain

$$w^A w^B w^C a^A_{Lin} a^B_{Co} a^C_{Cl} \geq p_{Co} p_{Cl} p_{Lin}$$

A comparison now reveals that if the assignment A-Co, B-Cl, C-Lin was the efficient member of its class, the product $a^A_{Co} a^B_{Cl} a^C_{Lin}$ must not exceed $a^A_{Lin} a^B_{Co} a^C_{Cl}$. According to the table, the first product is 90, while the second is 100. The general rule is that the assignment pattern that *minimizes the product of labor coefficients* among all assignments in its class is the efficient optimal assignment. No other assignment patterns in that class can ever be supported in a free trade equilibrium.[3] This is the generalization of the Ricardian law of comparative advantage that in the two-commodity, two-country case was cast in terms of cost ratios.[4]

As a final observation note that the doctrine of comparative advantage does not state what a country will produce. The actual production pattern depends largely upon demand. Instead, comparative advantage points out production patterns that are ruled out by free trade. In the 3×3 numerical example there are 3^3 or 27 possible complete specialization assignments of countries to commodities. Of these, 17 are inefficient and would never be observed in a free-trade world. The remaining 10 are the ones shown in Figure 5.S.4. The fraction of inefficient production patterns ruled out by the austere pressures of competition and free trade rises drastically as the number of countries and commodities expands.[5]

SUPPLEMENT TO CHAPTER 6:
The Specific-Factors Model of Production

This supplement provides a formal analytic treatment of the model of production described in Chapter 6. The community produces two commodities, clothing and food. Labor (L) and capital (K) are combined to produce clothing. The input requirements *per unit* output of clothing are denoted by a_{LC} and a_{KC}. Labor is also used to produce food, in cooperation with land (T). Thus, the per-unit output requirements in the food sector are a_{LF} and a_{TF}. Capital and land are each used specifically only in one sector, whereas labor is mobile between sectors.

The Distribution of Income

Pure competition is assumed to prevail, assuring that commodity prices (p_C and p_F) reflect units costs of production. These costs, in turn, depend in part on the input mix used in production (the a_{ij}'s) and in part on factor prices. The wage rate is denoted by w, and the amount that must be paid per unit rental on capital is given by r_K and the rental on land by r_T. The competitive profit conditions are thus summarized as follows.

$$a_{LC}w + a_{KC}r_K = p_C \tag{6.S.1}$$

$$a_{LF}w + a_{TF}r_T = p_F \tag{6.S.2}$$

Techniques of production are chosen so as to minimize the costs of producing a unit of output in the face of prevailing factor prices. To see what this entails, consider

---

[3] Thus, in Figure 5.4, the home country may produce food, for example, at point J, or the foreign country may produce clothing, but with free trade it is impossible for both home food production and foreign clothing production to exist simultaneously.

[4] In Equation 5.2, cross multiplying converts the comparative advantage criterion in terms of the minimum product of labor coefficients.

[5] For further discussion, see R. W. Jones, *International Trade: Essays in Theory* (Amsterdam: North-Holland, 1979), Chapter 18.

the clothing sector. The assumption of constant returns to scale implies that the *unit isoquant* captures all there is to know about techniques of production. At the point of cost minimization, the iso-cost line (with slope given by (minus) the ratio of factor prices, $-w/r_K$) is tangent to the unit isoquant (with slope da_{KC}/da_{LC}). That is, cost minimization entails that

$$w\,da_{LC} + r_K\,da_{KC} = 0$$

Once again it proves convenient to write these changes in *relative* terms (denoted by the hat, "^"). Thus, $\hat{a}_{LC}$ is da_{LC}/a_{LC}. Also, write the factor *distributive shares* as θ_{LC} and θ_{KC}, respectively, where, for example, θ_{LC} is wa_{LC}/p_C. Therefore, in the clothing sector cost minimization entails

$$\theta_{LC}\hat{a}_{LC} + \theta_{KC}\hat{a}_{KC} = 0 \qquad (6.S.3)$$

Similarly, in the food sector,

$$\theta_{LF}\hat{a}_{LF} + \theta_{TF}\hat{a}_{TF} = 0 \qquad (6.S.4)$$

Each of these expressions states that if labor is used more intensively, less of the specific factor need be used along the unit isoquant. The left-hand side in Equations 6.S.3 and 6.S.4 shows, for each industry, the relative change in unit costs involved in substituting one input for another. At a point of cost minimization this change must be zero: All cost reductions have already been taken at the minimum cost point.

It is now possible to confirm Chapter 6's argument that each commodity price change is flanked by the changes in the returns to productive factors used in that industry. Differentiate Equations 6.S.1 and 6.S.2, put into relative terms, and simplify by using Equations 6.S.3 and 6.S.4 to obtain

$$\theta_{LC}\hat{w} + \theta_{KC}\hat{r}_K = \hat{p}_C \qquad (6.S.5)$$

$$\theta_{LF}\hat{w} + \theta_{TF}\hat{r}_T = \hat{p}_F \qquad (6.S.6)$$

Thus, each commodity price change must be a weighted average of factor price changes, with the weights given by distributive shares—reflections of the importance of each factor in unit costs. Suppose now that commodity prices are disturbed, that clothing's price rises while the price of food remains unchanged. Equations 6.S.5 and 6.S.6 then suggest that some factor's return will rise relatively by more than p_C has, while some other factor's return will absolutely fall (since $\hat{p}_F = 0$). As is easily shown, capitalists are the clear gainers and landlords the losers. This is established by first showing that the wage rate must rise, but not as much, relatively, as the price of clothing.

The wage rate is determined by the condition that the labor force be fully employed. The clothing sector's demand for labor is written as $a_{LC}x_C$, where x_C shows the scale of output. Output is restricted by the availability of capital, however. If a_{KC} denotes the quantity of capital used per unit and if K units of capital are all the economy possesses, clothing output must be given by

$$x_C = \frac{K}{a_{KC}}$$

Therefore, the clothing sector's labor demand can be written as $a_{LC}/a_{KC} \cdot K$. In similar fashion the food sector's demand for labor must be $a_{LF}/a_{TF} \cdot T$. Thus, the following is the statement that all the economy's labor force is fully employed.

$$\frac{a_{LC}}{a_{KC}} \cdot K + \frac{a_{LF}}{a_{TF}} \cdot T = L \tag{6.S.7}$$

Differentiate this, assuming now that K and T remain constant but L may change, to obtain

$$\lambda_{LC}(\hat{a}_{LC} - \hat{a}_{KC}) + \lambda_{LF}(\hat{a}_{LF} - \hat{a}_{TF}) = \hat{L} \tag{6.S.8}$$

where the λ's correspond to the fraction of the economy's labor force used in each sector.

To proceed, reconsider the relationship between the wage rate and the value of labor's marginal product in each sector. These must be equal. Figure 6.S.1 illustrates how the quantity of labor used per unit of capital (a_{LC}/a_{KC}) depends inversely on the real wage in the clothing sector (w/p_C). (For a given clothing price this curve is the same as that drawn in Figure 6.4, reading from right to left.) The curve shows

---

FIGURE 6.S.1   The Elasticity of Labor's Marginal Product

A drop in the real wage from OA to OB would encourage labor to be used more intensively—an increase in the labor-capital ratio from OA' to OB'. The elasticity of labor's marginal product in clothing, γ_{LC}, is defined as $-(\hat{a}_{LC} - \hat{a}_{KC})$ divided by $(\hat{w} - \hat{p}_C)$.

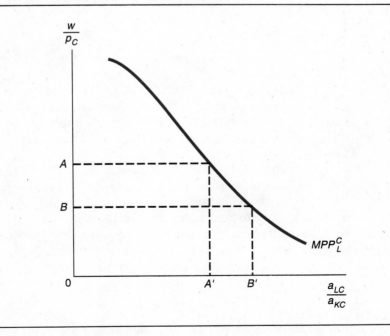

---

the marginal physical product of labor in clothing. Define the *elasticity* of labor's marginal product curve, γ_{LC}, as

$$\gamma_{LC} \equiv -\frac{(\hat{a}_{LC} - \hat{a}_{KC})}{(\hat{w} - \hat{p}_C)} \qquad (6.S.9)$$

Similarly, in the food industry,

$$\gamma_{LF} \equiv -\frac{(\hat{a}_{LF} - \hat{a}_{TF})}{(\hat{w} - \hat{p}_F)} \qquad (6.S.10)$$

These concepts are crucial. Substitute the expressions for the elasticities, γ_{LC} and γ_{LF}, into Equation 6.S.8 to obtain

$$\lambda_{LC}\gamma_{LC}(\hat{w} - \hat{p}_C) + \lambda_{LF}\gamma_{LF}(\hat{w} - \hat{p}_F) = -\hat{L} \qquad (6.S.11)$$

Solving explicitly for the change in the wage rate in terms of the commodity price changes and any change in the labor force,

$$\hat{w} = \beta_C\hat{p}_C + \beta_F\hat{p}_F - \frac{1}{\gamma}\hat{L} \qquad (6.S.12)$$

where

$$\beta_C \equiv \lambda_{LC}\frac{\gamma_{LC}}{\gamma}$$

$$\beta_F \equiv \lambda_{LF}\frac{\gamma_{LF}}{\gamma}$$

and

$$\gamma \equiv \lambda_{LC}\gamma_{LC} + \lambda_{LF}\gamma_{LF}$$

γ_{LC} and γ_{LF} are the elasticities of labor's marginal product curve in each sector, and γ is the economy-wide weighted average of these two elasticities. γ directly provides the answer to the following question: If commodity prices are constant and the wage rate rises by 1 percent, by what percentage will the entire economy's demand for labor fall? If γ is large, the answer is that the economy's demand for labor would be reduced by a relatively large amount. Conversely, Equation 6.S.12 shows that a given increase in the labor force would, at constant commodity prices, reduce the wage rate, but not by very much if γ is large. The β coefficients, which add to unity, reveal the power of each separate commodity price to influence the wage rate. At constant overall factor endowments, the wage rate change is trapped between (i.e., is a positive weighted average of) the commodity price changes. Therefore, if clothing's relative price rises ($\hat{p}_C > \hat{p}_F$), this relationship, coupled with Equations 6.S.5 and 6.S.6, establishes that

$$\hat{r}_K > \hat{p}_C > \hat{w} > \hat{p}_F > \hat{r}_T$$

The specific factors are most radically affected by price changes. The mobile factor (labor) finds its return rising in terms of one sector and falling in terms of the other.

The algebraic demonstration supplements the diagrammatic illustration of a price change in Figure 6.4.

The expression for each β coefficient in Equation 6.S.12 allows a further refinement. Consider only β_C, the relative effect of an increase in clothing's price on the wage rate. This coefficient was explicitly defined in Equation 6.S.12, but rewrite it as

$$\beta_C = \theta_C \cdot \frac{\lambda_{LC}}{\theta_C} \cdot \frac{\gamma_{LC}}{\gamma}$$

Reading from right to left, the term γ_{LC}/γ can be considered the *relative* degree of substitutability of the demand for labor in the clothing sector—a comparison of γ_{LC} with the economy-wide average, γ. Call this term s_C. Next is the expression (λ_{LC}/θ_C), where θ_C denotes the share of clothing production in the national income, $p_C x_C/(p_C x_C + p_F x_F)$. This expression also reflects a "relative" for the clothing industry; it is a measure of *relative labor intensity* for clothing. The concept of relative factor intensity in a two-factor setting comes into its own in Chapter 7 and the supplement to Chapter 7. Here it is used to compare λ_{LC}, the fraction of the labor force used in clothing, with θ_C, the fraction of the economy's entire input base used in clothing. (Thus, if λ_{LC}/θ_C were unity, clothing would neither be labor-intensive nor labor-unintensive.) Call this term i_C. Then β_C is the product of three terms:

$$\beta_C = \theta_C \cdot i_C \cdot s_C$$

That is, a price rise in clothing has a more severe impact on the wage rate (1) the more elastic is the demand for labor in clothing compared with the economy-wide average (i.e., the higher is s_C), (2) the more labor-intensive is the clothing sector (i.e., the higher is i_C), and (3) the more important is production of clothing as a fraction of national income produced (i.e., the higher is θ_C).[1]

Outputs, Prices, and Factor Endowments

Outputs respond to changes in relative prices along the transformation schedule. Outputs also respond to changes in factor endowments (at constant commodity prices). Chapter 6 showed how an ample supply of capital lends a presumption that relatively much clothing is produced. By contrast, plentiful land encourages food production. Now endowments of capital and land are kept constant but the implication for outputs (and thus for positions of comparative advantage) of changes in labor abundance are explored.

If, as assumed, the total capital stock is kept fixed, clothing output can expand only by using capital less intensively. Similarly, because x_F equals (T/a_{TF}), food output can change only if a_{TF} is altered, given that overall land is fixed in supply. Combining shows that

$$\hat{x}_C - \hat{x}_F = \hat{a}_{TF} - \hat{a}_{KC} \tag{6.S.13}$$

[1] This decomposition is discussed and applied in R. W. Jones, "Co-movements in Relative Commodity Prices and International Capital Flows: A Simple Model," *Economic Inquiry* (January 1989): 131–141. An application to the question of the effect of tariffs on real wages in the specific-factors model is found in R. Ruffin and R. Jones, "Protection and Real Wages: The Neoclassical Ambiguity," *Journal of Economic Theory* (April 1977): 337–348.

The ingredients are at hand to solve separately for $\hat{a}_{TF}$ and $\hat{a}_{KC}$. From Equations 6.S.4 and 6.S.10,

$$\hat{a}_{TF} = \theta_{LF}\gamma_{LF}(\hat{w} - \hat{p}_F)$$

Similarly, Equations 6.S.3 and 6.S.9 can be solved for $\hat{a}_{KC}$:

$$\hat{a}_{KC} = \theta_{LC}\gamma_{LC}(\hat{w} - \hat{p}_C)$$

The change in the wage rate is provided by Equation 6.S.12, so that Equation 6.S.13 can be written as

$$\hat{x}_C - \hat{x}_F = \sigma_s(\hat{p}_C - \hat{p}_F) + \frac{1}{\gamma}(\theta_{LC}\gamma_{LC} - \theta_{LF}\gamma_{LF})\hat{L} \qquad (6.S.14)$$

where

$$\sigma_S \equiv \theta_{LF}\gamma_{LF}\beta_C + \theta_{LC}\gamma_{LC}\beta_F > 0$$

The effect of a change in relative commodity prices on relative outputs along the transformation schedule (i.e., for given factor endowments) is captured by the positive term σ_S, the elasticity of supply of relative outputs. This is generally larger the greater are the elasticities of labor's marginal product curves in the two sectors.[2] The coefficient of $\hat{L}$ reveals that two distinct features of the technology determine the composition of output. As the labor supply expands (at given terms of trade), clothing output will tend to expand more than does the food sector if the elasticity of labor's marginal product is higher in clothing (i.e., if $\gamma_{LC} > \gamma > \gamma_{LF}$). This is one feature. However, the comparison of labor's distributive shares, θ_{LC} and θ_{LF}, is also important. The clothing sector tends to expand relative to food if θ_{LC} exceeds θ_{LF}. As the supplement to Chapter 7 reveals, this comparison of distributive shares is a comparison of *relative labor intensity* in the two sectors.[3] In the Heckscher-Ohlin model in Chapter 7, these factor intensity comparisons assume critical importance.

SUPPLEMENT TO CHAPTER 7:
The Two-Sector Heckscher-Ohlin Model

The two-sector Heckscher-Ohlin model of production assumes each of two outputs (clothing, food) is produced in a constant-returns-to-scale competitive setting with the use of two primary inputs (labor, capital). The productive factors are each homogeneous and mobile between sectors. Prices are flexible and both inputs are fully employed.

$$a_{LC}x_C + a_{LF}x_F = L \qquad (7.S.1)$$

$$a_{KC}x_C + a_{KF}x_F = K \qquad (7.S.2)$$

---

[2] The supplement to Chapter 7 compares this expression for σ_S with the comparable elasticity in the Heckscher-Ohlin model by making further simplifying assumptions.

[3] With reference to the definition of the relative degree of substitutability, s_C (and s_F for the food sector), on the one hand, and i_C (and i_F) for relative labor intensities, the coefficient of $\hat{L}$ in Equation 6.S.14 can also be written as $\theta_L[i_C \cdot s_C - i_F \cdot s_F]$, where θ_L is labor's distributive share in the national income. Thus, as the labor force expands at constant commodity prices, clothing output is apt to rise relatively more than food output to the extent that clothing is labor intensive and has a relatively high elasticity of demand for labor.

Furthermore, unit costs in each sector are equated to the prevailing commodity price (if output is positive):

$$a_{LC}w + a_{KC}r = p_C \tag{7.S.3}$$

$$a_{LF}w + a_{KF}r = p_F \tag{7.S.4}$$

Again, w refers to the wage rate, and now the common return to capital in the economy is denoted by r.

Equations of Change: Prices

As in the specific-factors model of Chapter 6, techniques of production are chosen so as to minimize unit costs. This condition implies Equations 7.S.5 and 7.S.6: The distributive-share weighted average of changes in input-output coefficients along the unit isoquant in each industry must vanish near the cost-minimization point.[1]

$$\theta_{LC}\hat{a}_{LC} + \theta_{KC}\hat{a}_{KC} = 0 \tag{7.S.5}$$

$$\theta_{LF}\hat{a}_{LF} + \theta_{KF}\hat{a}_{KF} = 0 \tag{7.S.6}$$

These relationships are crucial, for they suggest that differentiating Equations 7.S.3 and 7.S.4 totally yields

$$\theta_{LC}\hat{w} + \theta_{KC}\hat{r} = \hat{p}_C \tag{7.S.7}$$

$$\theta_{LF}\hat{w} + \theta_{KF}\hat{r} = \hat{p}_F \tag{7.S.8}$$

These conditions state that in each industry the distributive-share weighted average of factor-price changes equals the relative commodity price change. They correspond to Equations 6.S.5 and 6.S.6 for the specific-factors model. Yet now more can be said: This pair of equations links the commodity price changes ($\hat{p}_C$, $\hat{p}_F$) to the pair of factor-price changes ($\hat{w}$, $\hat{r}$). Factor prices are determined *uniquely* by commodity prices as long as both commodities are produced, and assuming the techniques used in clothing and food differ.

This qualification about techniques refers to the capital/labor ratio employed in the two sectors. As in the text, assume that food always is produced with a higher capital/labor ratio than clothing. This comparison must then be revealed in a ranking of distributive shares. Specifically, labor's distributive share in labor-intensive clothing, θ_{LC}, must exceed that in capital-intensive food, θ_{LF}. To see this, compute the determinant of coefficients in Equations 7.S.7 and 7.S.8. Call this determinant $|\theta|$. By definition,

$$|\theta| \equiv \theta_{LC}\theta_{KF} - \theta_{LF}\theta_{KC}$$

Substitute the formal definition of each distributive share (e.g., θ_{LC} is wa_{LC}/p_C) to obtain

$$|\theta| = \frac{wr}{p_C p_F}(a_{LC}a_{KF} - a_{LF}a_{KC})$$

---

[1] This states that an iso-cost line is tangent to the unit isoquant. Details are provided in the supplement to Chapter 6.

Therefore, $|\theta|$ is positive if clothing is labor intensive. However, since distributive shares in any industry add to unity, θ_{KF} is just $1 - \theta_{LF}$ and θ_{KC} is $1 - \theta_{LC}$. Therefore, $|\theta|$ can be written as

$$|\theta| = \theta_{LC} - \theta_{LF}$$

The relationships shown by Equations 7.S.7 and 7.S.8 underlie the shape of the curve in Figure 7.6. Subtract Equation 7.S.8 from Equation 7.S.7 to obtain

$$|\theta| \cdot (\hat{w} - \hat{r}) = (\hat{p}_C - \hat{p}_F) \qquad (7.\text{S}.9)$$

Thus, an increase in labor-intensive clothing's relative price must raise the wage/rent ratio by a magnified amount. Even more can be said: If $\hat{p}_C$ is greater than $\hat{p}_F$ and clothing is labor intensive,

$$\hat{w} > \hat{p}_C > \hat{p}_F > \hat{r}$$

The factor-price changes are magnified reflections of the commodity price changes. The *Stopler-Samuelson theorem* asserts that an increase in labor-intensive clothing's price (with food price constant) must unambiguously raise the *real wage*. This follows directly from this chain of inequalities.

If two countries share the same technology and produce both goods in common, free trade in commodities will not only equate commodity prices, it will also result in *factor price equalization*. Simply treat the variables in Equations 7.S.7 and 7.S.8 as relative differences between countries. Thus, if $\hat{p}_C = \hat{p}_F = 0$ with free trade, so must $\hat{w}$ and $\hat{r}$ be zero.

The Factor-Price Frontier

An isoquant in the food sector displays minimal combinations of capital and labor required to produce a prescribed quantity of food. *Dual* to this is a schedule, the unit-cost curve, showing, for a given price of food, the combinations of wage rates and rentals on capital that will lead to unit cost of production equal to price. The outer locus of such a curve and a similar unit-cost curve for the clothing sector is called the *factor-price frontier* and is illustrated in Figure 7.S.1 by the heavily shaded curve.

Cost-minimization by firms leads to techniques where the slopes of isoquants are set equal to the ratio of factor prices (e.g., point A and B in Figure 7.1). By contrast, such cost-minimization leads to points on the unit cost curves where slopes equal capital/labor ratios. For example, if wages and rents are shown by point B in Figure 7.S.1, the slope of food's unit-cost curve, C_F, at B equals the ratio of capital to labor used by the food sector, a_{KF}/a_{LF}, at those factor prices. Alternatively phrased, the elasticity of the unit-cost curve (at B) equals the ratio of distributive shares. The proof is direct: Set $\hat{p}_F$ equal to zero in Equation 7.S.8.

For the given set of food and clothing prices, could factor prices be given by a point such as D in Figure 7.S.1? If they were, unit costs would equal price in the clothing sector (since D lies on clothing's unit-cost curve), but costs would fall short of price in the food industry (D lies below the food unit-cost curve). Such a shortfall of cost below price could not persist in a competitive equilibrium. At these given commodity prices a country could produce *both* goods in a competitive equilibrium

---

FIGURE 7.S.1   The Factor-Price Frontier

At initial given prices for clothing (and food) the unit-cost curve $C_C(C_F)$ shows combinations of wages and rents that lead to unit costs of clothing (food) production equal to $P_C(P_F)$. The blue curve with a kink at A is the factor-price frontier. A country can produce both commodities only if its capital/labor endowment ratio lies between the right and left slopes of the frontier at kink-point A. An increase in clothing's price leads to new dotted C'_C unit-cost curve for clothing. If the country is incompletely specialized, wages rise by relatively more and rentals fall.

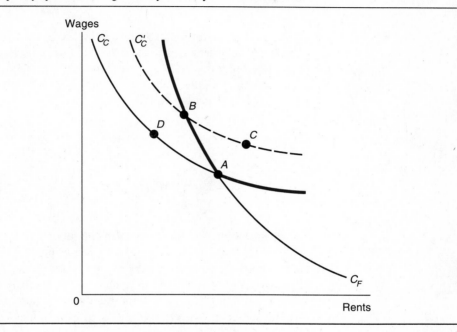

only if its factor prices are shown at point A in Figure 7.S.1. This requires that such a country have an endowment capital/labor ratio greater than that required in clothing (the absolute slope of clothing's curve at A) and less than that in food (the slope of food's curve at A). If its endowment ratio lies outside this range, but the country faces these same prices for food and clothing, it will be forced to specialize in one of the commodities and its factor prices will not be shown by point A. Thus, a country whose endowment capital/labor ratio is given by the (absolute value of the) slope of the factor-price frontier at B specializes in food; laborers and capitalists receive wages and rents shown by B.

The dotted curve in Figure 7.S.1 shows the result of a 15 percent increase in the world price of clothing. That is, (AC/OA) is 15 percent. The new factor-price frontier has its kink at B instead of A. For a country incompletely specialized both at B and A (i.e., whose endowment capital/labor ratio is lower than the slope of food's unit cost curve at A but higher than the slope of clothing's curve at B), such a price change clearly lowers rents and raises wages by a magnified amount. This corresponds to the earlier ranking.

Equations of Change: Outputs

The pair of full-employment equations suggests that outputs respond both to factor-endowment changes and to changes in intensity of techniques. Differentiate Equations 7.S.1 and 7.S.2 totally, and let λ_{ij} refer to the fraction of the total supply of factor i that is employed in commodity j.

$$\lambda_{LC}\hat{x}_C + \lambda_{LF}\hat{x}_F = \hat{L} - (\lambda_{LC}\hat{a}_{LC} + \lambda_{LF}\hat{a}_{LF}) \tag{7.S.10}$$

$$\lambda_{KC}\hat{x}_C + \lambda_{KF}\hat{x}_F = \hat{K} - (\lambda_{KC}\hat{a}_{KC} + \lambda_{KF}\hat{a}_{KF}) \tag{7.S.11}$$

Each equation points out the limitation on outputs provided by the overall endowment of the factor, as well as the intensity with which that factor is used. Consider the changed techniques in clothing: $\hat{a}_{LC}$ and $\hat{a}_{KC}$. Equation 7.S.5 provided one relationship between these two changes. Another follows from the *definition* of the *elasticity of substitution* between labor and capital in the clothing sector.[2]

$$\sigma_C \equiv \frac{\hat{a}_{KC} - \hat{a}_{LC}}{\hat{w} - \hat{r}} \tag{7.S.12}$$

Solve Equations 7.S.5 and 7.S.12 to obtain

$$\hat{a}_{LC} = -\theta_{KC}\sigma_C(\hat{w} - \hat{r}) \tag{7.S.13}$$
$$\hat{a}_{KC} = \theta_{LC}\sigma_C(\hat{w} - \hat{r})$$

Comparable solutions are obtained for changes in the labor and capital coefficients in the food sector—merely replace C with F in the subscripts of Equation 7.S.13.

With these solutions now in hand, reconsider expressions such as $(\lambda_{LC}\hat{a}_{LC} + \lambda_{LF}\hat{a}_{LF})$, which shows for the economy as a whole how much of an increase or reduction in labor is required at unchanged outputs. Suppose the wage/rent ratio rises. Both industries will economize on labor. Thus, Equations 7.S.10 and 7.S.11 can be rewritten as

$$\lambda_{LC}\hat{x}_C + \lambda_{LF}\hat{x}_F = \hat{L} + \delta_L(\hat{w} - \hat{r}) \tag{7.S.14}$$

$$\lambda_{KC}\hat{x}_C + \lambda_{KF}\hat{x}_F = \hat{K} - \delta_K(\hat{w} - \hat{r}) \tag{7.S.15}$$

where

$$\delta_L \equiv \lambda_{LC}\theta_{KC}\sigma_C + \lambda_{LF}\theta_{KF}\sigma_F$$
$$\delta_K \equiv \lambda_{KC}\theta_{LC}\sigma_C + \lambda_{KF}\theta_{LF}\sigma_F$$

Subtract Equation 7.S.15 from Equation 7.S.14 and let

$$|\lambda| \equiv \lambda_{LC} - \lambda_{KC}$$

Then

$$(\hat{x}_C - \hat{x}_F) = \frac{1}{|\lambda|}(\hat{L} - \hat{K}) + \frac{(\delta_L + \delta_K)}{|\lambda|}(\hat{w} - \hat{r}) \tag{7.S.16}$$

---

[2] You may wonder how the elasticity of substitution, σ_C, is related to the elasticity of labor's marginal product in clothing, γ_{LC}, defined in Equation 6.S.9. Because $(\hat{w} - \hat{p}_C)$ is equal to $\theta_{KC}(\hat{w} - \hat{r})$, from Equation 7.S.7 or 6.S.5, γ_{LC} equals σ_C divided by θ_{KC}

If clothing is labor intensive, $|\lambda|$ is a positive fraction.[3] Finally, substitute the link between factor and commodity prices provided by Equation 7.S.9 to obtain

$$(\hat{x}_C - \hat{x}_F) = \frac{1}{|\lambda|}(\hat{L} - \hat{K}) + \sigma_S(\hat{p}_C - \hat{p}_F) \qquad (7.S.17)$$

where

$$\sigma_S \equiv \frac{\delta_L + \delta_K}{|\lambda||\theta|} > 0$$

Several features of the two-sector production model are revealed by Equation 7.S.17. First, note that σ_S must be positive, since δ_L and δ_K are each positive and $|\lambda|$ and $|\theta|$ must have the same sign. If, as is assumed, clothing is labor intensive, both $|\lambda|$ and $|\theta|$ are positive. If clothing were capital intensive, each would be negative, making the product $|\lambda||\theta|$ positive once again. σ_S denotes the elasticity of supply along the bowed-out transformation curve. Figure 7.5 confirms the rising supply curve that reflects increasing opportunity costs of production—a positive σ_S. Second, note that at constant prices the coefficient of $(\hat{L} - \hat{K})$ in Equation 7.S.17 reveals how the transformation schedule shifts as factor endowments change. It confirms that in Figure 7.5 the home country's relative supply of clothing lies to the right of the foreign country's curve if, as assumed, the home country is relatively labor abundant and clothing is labor intensive. Indeed, Equation 7.S.17 confirms the magnification effect of uneven growth of factor endowments on outputs if the terms of trade are constant. If $\hat{L}$ exceeds $\hat{K}$,

$$\hat{x}_C > \hat{L} > \hat{K} > \hat{x}_F$$

If only labor expands, one output must actually fall—the Rybczynski result.[4]

Output Responses to Price Changes: Sector-Specific and Heckscher-Ohlin Models

Outputs are more responsive to price signals in the Heckscher-Ohlin model than in the specific-factor model because all factors are mobile between sectors. This was a comparison discussed in the appendix to Chapter 7 and graphically revealed in the envelope property of the Heckscher-Ohlin TT curve in Figure 7.A.2. The following discussion will probe more deeply into each model's expression for the elasticity of supply along the transformation curve, σ_s, to point out the basic similarity and the basic difference between models.[5]

In the Heckscher-Ohlin model the elasticity of supply with respect to prices was shown by σ_S in Equation 7.S.17. δ_L and δ_K each contain a blend of information on

---

[3] $|\lambda|$ is clearly the determinant of coefficients in Equations 7.S.14 and 7.S.15. The argument is similar to the one used in discussing $|\theta|$.

[4] See the reference in footnote 3 of Chapter 7. This supplement is based on R. W. Jones, "The Structure of Simple General Equilibrium Models," *Journal of Political Economy*, 73 (December 1965): 557–572, reprinted in his *International Trade: Essays in Theory* (Amsterdam: North-Holland, 1979).

[5] More details of this comparison are provided in Chapter 7 of R. W. Jones, *International Trade: Essays in Theory* (Amsterdam: North-Holland, 1979).

the degree of factor substitutability in the two sectors, σ_C and σ_F. Thus, σ_S can be rewritten as

$$\sigma_S = \frac{Q_C \sigma_C + Q_F \sigma_F}{|\lambda||\theta|} \qquad (7.S.18)$$

where

$$Q_C \equiv \theta_{LC}\lambda_{KC} + \theta_{KC}\lambda_{LC}$$
$$Q_F \equiv \theta_{LF}\lambda_{KF} + \theta_{KF}\lambda_{LF}$$

Clearly, σ_S is larger the larger is either sector's elasticity of factor substitution. To simplify, suppose $\sigma_C = \sigma_F = \sigma$. Furthermore, note that

$$Q_C + Q_F + |\lambda||\theta| = 1$$

Therefore, in the Heckscher-Ohlin model the assumption of common degree of factor substitutability in each sector leads to the following as the expression for σ_S:

$$\sigma_S = \frac{1 - |\lambda||\theta|}{|\lambda||\theta|}\sigma \qquad (7.S.19)$$

Two features of the model lead to elastic responses of outputs along the transformation schedule: first, a high degree of factor substitutability in each sector (σ), and second, fairly similar factor proportions, as shown by low values for $|\lambda||\theta|$. If factor proportions were identical, $|\lambda||\theta|$ would equal zero. If, by contrast, labor were used only in one sector and capital in the other, $|\lambda||\theta|$ would equal 1, and σ_S would be zero.

In the sector-specific model, the expression for σ_S was given in Equation 6.S.14. The elasticities of labor's marginal product curves, γ_{Lj}, are related to the elasticity of factor substitution.[6] Thus, γ_{LC} equals σ_C/θ_{KC} and γ_{LF} equals σ_F/θ_{TF}. As in the Heckscher-Ohlin case, simplify by assuming a common value for $\sigma = \sigma_C = \sigma_F$, since intersectoral differences between σ_C and σ_F do little to change the value of σ_S (in either model). Furthermore, simplify by equating labor shares between sectors. The rationale here is that the Heckscher-Ohlin model focuses upon the difference between factor intensities in the two sectors and assumes the *same* degree of factor mobility between sectors. (It assumes that labor and capital are each perfectly mobile between sectors.) By contrast, the sector-specific model focuses upon the different degree of factor mobility between sectors (labor perfectly mobile, capital—or land—completely immobile). It seems fair, therefore, to allow the same degree of labor intensity between the two sectors, as captured by θ_{LC} and θ_{LF}. Thus, the share of the specific factor in each industry is the same. Let θ_S denote the common value of θ_{KC} and θ_{TF}.

These simplifications allow σ_S for the sector-specific model in Equation 6.S.14 to be rewritten as

$$\sigma_S = \frac{1 - \theta_S}{\theta_S}\sigma \qquad (7.S.20)$$

A comparison with Equation 7.S.19 for the Heckscher-Ohlin model reveals (1) the

---

[6] See footnote 2.

common role in the two models played by the elasticity of factor substitution, σ, and (2) the focus in the sector-specific model on the importance of sector specificity as captured by θ_S, the share in the national income of specific factors. A greater degree of factor specificity implies a lower value for σ_S, precisely as, in the Heckscher-Ohlin model, a greater disparity in factor proportions implies a low σ_S. Each model is designed to focus upon a different feature of the technology, with somewhat analogous results in terms of the response of outputs to prices.

SUPPLEMENT TO CHAPTER 10:
Foreign Investment, "Brain Drain,"
and the Distribution of Income

The concept of the factor price frontier was introduced in the supplement to Chapter 7. Here it is applied to the following situation: Suppose two countries produce exactly the same commodity and have access to the same technology, but with the rate of return to capital, r^*, higher in the capital-scarce foreign country than is local r in the high-wage home country. Furthermore, suppose some quantity of home capital, $\overline{K}$, is attracted by the higher rate abroad and leaves in the form of foreign investment. What can be said about (1) the gain to the capital that moves, (2) the gain or loss to the bundle of factors left behind in the home country, and (3) the gain or loss to the original factors located abroad?

Figure 10.S.1 illustrates a bowed-in factor-price frontier for these two economies sharing the same technology and producing the same commodity. The supplement to Chapter 7 showed that the slope of the frontier at any point is the ratio of factor supplies employed by an economy with prevailing factor prices shown by such a point. For example, if W_0^* represents initial foreign wage rate and return to capital, the slope at W_0^* is (minus) L^*/K^*, the ratio of foreign labor and capital endowments. Furthermore, the horizontal intercept of the line tangent at W_0^* is output produced abroad, Q_0^*, per unit of the foreign labor force. The proof: The intercept is the sum of (1) w_0^*, and (2) r_0^* divided by the slope, L^*/K^*. This yields Q_0^*/L^*.

With this interpretation of slope and intercepts at hand, it becomes an easy task to measure real income gains and losses for various groups. In particular, suppose some home capital, amount $\overline{K}$, moves to the foreign country, where r_0^* is the original rate of return. This serves to lower the labor/capital ratio in use abroad; the (absolute value of the) slope of the common frontier at W_1^* is $L^*/(K^* + \overline{K})$. The foreign return has fallen from r_0^* to r_1^*, but the home capital that has gone abroad gains in total by $(r_1^* - r_0)\overline{K}$.

Foreign residents gain by such a move. Although foreign capitalists see their return lowered (from r_0^* to r_1^*), the foreign wage rate rises so that the original foreign inhabitants have net gain. This was the argument put forth in Section 10.2. To illustrate with the use of the factor-price frontier, draw a line through W_1^* with the same slope as the tangent at W_0^*, the slope representing the labor/capital ratio of *foreign* owned factors. The new horizontal intercept, OA, reflects the higher output per unit of the foreign labor force available to foreign-owned factors *after* home-owned $\overline{K}$ gets paid. (The level of output *produced* abroad, per foreign worker, would be the still higher horizontal intercept of the tangent at W_1^*.)

FIGURE 10.S.1   The Factor-Price Frontier and Income Distribution

The bowed-in curve shows possible wage and return to capital combinations for countries with a given technology. A movement of capital from the high-wage home country to the foreign country changes factor prices at home from W_0 to W_1 and abroad from W_0^* to W_1^*. Foreigners benefit, while those left behind at home lose by an amount BC per unit of home labor. However, the gains to home capital employed abroad (amount $(r_1^* - r_0)$ per unit of capital) exceed this loss.

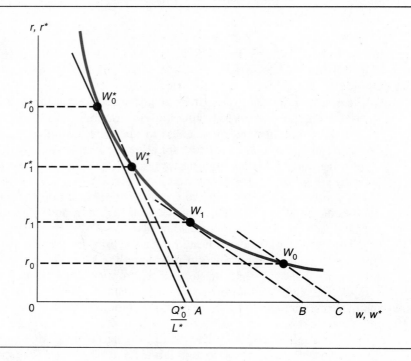

Such an outflow of capital from the home country must *harm* the real income of those left behind at home. Let these factors be denoted by L and K. The departure of capital lowers wages at home and raises the return to capital. This is represented by the move from W_0 to W_1, with the slope at W_1 equal to (minus) L/K, the ratio of factors employed at home after the departure of $\overline{K}$ abroad. [The slope at W_0 was minus $L/(K + \overline{K})$.] Initially, with factor prices shown by W_0, this "left-behind" group, (L, K), earned output per laborer shown by intercept OC. After the departure of $\overline{K}$, output per laborer for this same group is reduced to intercept OB. This is Section 10.2's argument put into reverse.

There are two groups of nationals of the home country: $\overline{K}$, the group of capitalists who have gained by moving abroad, and (L, K), the group of laborers and capitalists left behind who, as a group, have lost. Can anything be said about the welfare of both groups taken together? Yes. The gain to the first group is

$$(r_1^* - r_0)\overline{K}$$

The net gain to the group remaining behind is

$$(r_1 - r_0)K + (w_1 - w_0)L$$

a negative amount representing a loss. The sum of these two amounts is

$$(r_1^* - r_1)\overline{K} + [(r_1 - r_0)(K + \overline{K}) + (w_1 - w_0)L]$$

The first term is positive, showing that part of the gain to foreign investors represented by the gap between foreign return, r_1^*, and the home return, r_1, that prevails after foreign investment. The second, bracketed term would be represented in Figure 10.S.1 if two lines are drawn: the tangent line at W_0, and a line with the same slope, the ratio of original home factors $L/(K + \overline{K})$, passing through W_1. The latter has a higher value for its horizontal intercept, and the gap separating the two intercepts is the positive value of the second, bracketed term. On net this foreign investment has benefited both home nationals and foreign nationals.

The same kind of argument could be used if, instead of home capital flowing abroad, foreign labor is attracted by higher-paying job possibilities in the home country. Such a "brain drain" from abroad would lower welfare for the group remaining behind in the foreign country, although it would be of benefit to migrants and also to home residents. This discrepancy in the fates of those who leave and those who remain behind has prompted proposals whereby migrants get taxed to compensate the losing group. The preceding demonstration has shown that such compensation can be arranged so that both groups can benefit.

SUPPLEMENT TO CHAPTER 11:
Real Incomes, Prices, and the Tariff

Real Incomes and the Optimum Tariff

Recall from the supplement to Chapter 3 the basic expression for the change in the home country's level of real income, dy, in terms of the domestic price-weighted sum of consumption changes. This was Equation 3.S.1, reproduced here.

$$dy = dD_C + p\,dD_F \tag{11.S.1}$$

This expression needs no modification in the case of tariffs, for it rests on the simple notion that real income depends only upon the quantities of each commodity consumed and the relative valuation at the margin of one commodity in terms of another, as reflected in the *domestic* relative price of food, p.

The home country's budget constraint indicates the source of a change in real incomes. With a tariff, however, the budget constraint can be written in terms either of domestic or world prices. It is instructive to look at each in turn.

In terms of domestic prices, aggregate spending at home, $D_C + pD_F$, is limited to the value of income, which is derived both from income earned in producing commodities, $x_C + px_F$, and from the proceeds of the tariff revenue. In the case of *ad valorem* tariffs, revenue depends on the home country's quantity of food imports, M, the foreign relative price of imports, p^*, and the tariff rate, t, and is the product of these three terms:

$$D_C + pD_F = x_C + px_F + tp^*M \tag{11.S.2}$$

Figure 11.3 illustrates this form of the budget constraint with all items measured in food units instead of clothing units. With posttariff consumption at J, the aggregate value of incomes at domestic prices is OE, the value of incomes earned in production is shown by OC, and CE is the tariff revenue.

Consider, now, a small change in the tariff rate. This change leads to changes in prices, the consumption bundle, and production so that

$$dD_C + pdD_F + D_F dp = dx_C + pdx_F + x_F dp + d(tp^*M)$$

Shift $D_F dp$ to the right-hand side to obtain

$$(dD_C + pdD_F) = -Mdp + (dx_C + pdx_F) + d(tp^*M) \tag{11.S.3}$$

Note that the left-hand side is, by the definition given in Equation 11.S.1, the increase in the home country's real income, dy. Furthermore, the expression $dx_C + pdx_F$ on the right-hand side must vanish, because the slope of the transformation schedule, dx_F/dx_C, must equal the negative of clothing's relative *domestic* price, $1/p$.[1] Thus, Equation 11.S.3 can be simplified as

$$dy = -Mdp + d(tp^*M) \tag{11.S.4}$$

That is, the sources of any real income gain to the home country are to be found in (1) a change in the domestic relative price of imports, dp, where any decrease in this price will raise real incomes at home by a factor given by the volume of imports, M, and (2) any increase in the tariff revenue, $d(tp^*M)$.

This provides one decomposition of real income changes, highlighting *domestic* prices and tariff revenue. An alternative, but equivalent expression, one emphasizing *world* prices (the terms of trade), is more frequently used in the literature. Expenditure and income are related by world prices. The domestic relative price of food, p, is given by $(1 + t)p^*$, and substituting this quantity into Equation 11.S.2, noticing that M is given by excess food demand, $D_F - x_F$, results in

$$D_C + p^*D_F = x_C + p^*x_F \tag{11.S.5}$$

This equation states that at *world* prices the value of the home country's consumption bundle exactly equals the value of its production bundle. This equality is illustrated in Figure 11.3 by the fact that the posttariff consumption bundle, J, and production bundle, B, both lie on line 4, whose slope, $-(1/p^*)$, indicates the world terms of trade. Differentiate 11.S.5 to obtain

$$dD_C + p^*dD_F = -Mdp^* + (dx_C + p^*dx_F)$$

Add and subtract pdD_F on the left-hand side and pdx_F on the right-hand side. This yields

---

[1] See the supplement to Chapter 3 for a more complete account.

$$(dD_C + pdD_F) + (p^* - p)dD_F = -Mdp^* + (dx_C + pdx_F) + (p^* - p)dx_F$$

As was already explained, $dD_C + pdD_F$ is the definition of the increase in real income at home, and $dx_C + pdx_F$ vanishes if resources are allocated at the optimal point along the transformation schedule. Because the change in imports, dM, it equal to $dD_F - dx_F$, the entire expression reduces to

$$dy = -Mdp^* + (p - p^*)dM \qquad (11.S.6)$$

It is difficult to overestimate the importance of the breakdown represented by Equation 11.S.6 in understanding the welfare significance of tariffs. The first term, $-Mdp^*$, is the terms-of-trade effect, now stated in terms of world prices. Any policy that depresses the relative price at which the home country can purchase its imports in the world market will favorably affect welfare at home by an amount proportional to the volume of imports. If trade is impeded, however, as it will be if a tariff exists, the second term, $(p - p^*)dM$, must also be taken into account. $p - p^*$ is the tariff wedge—it is the discrepancy (tp^*) between the relative domestic price of imports and the world price of imports. This second term indicates that any increase in the home country's level of imports must increase real income if the cost of obtaining imports in the world market (as shown by p^*) falls short of the relative value of imports in the local market (as shown by p). Any policy pursued by the home country that restricts imports entails welfare loss if a tariff wedge has raised the domestic (relative) price of imports over the world level. This loss is directly proportional to the extent of the tariff rate.

Figure 11.S.1 is designed to illustrate the possible balance between the terms-of-trade effect and the volume-of-trade effect when a large country increases an already existing tariff rate. Let production in the large country remain fixed at A throughout. The country imports food at initial world prices shown by line 1, with consumption point B revealing a higher relative domestic price of food behind the tariff wall. The country now raises the tariff on food imports and, since it is a large country, succeeds in improving the terms of trade to line 2. Suppose the tariff raises the domestic relative price of food. The new consumption point would then lie southeast of ray OBC along line 2. If it lies in stretch CD, imports rise and both the terms-of-trade effect and volume-of-trade effect in (11.S.6) are positive. If the new consumption point lies in range DE, the volume of trade falls but the improvement in the terms of trade is relatively more important so dy in (11.S.6) is positive. Finally, if the new consumption point lies in the EA range of line 2, the reduction in import demand at the higher relative domestic price causes the second term in (11.S.6) to outweigh the favorable terms-of-trade effect, and real income falls.

We are now in a position to develop a formula for the *optimum tariff rate*. In Equation (11.S.6) the expression for dy can be set equal to zero if we are considering small variations in the tariff rate around the optimal rate that maximizes real income. (In Figure 11.5 $dy = 0$ at the optimal tariff rate t_0.) Replace $(p - p^*)$ by the equivalent expression, tp^*:

$$Mdp^* = tp^*dM$$

Dividing both sides by p^*M, and recalling the use of the "hat" notation to express

FIGURE 11.S.1   An Increase in the Tariff

The country produces at A and initially consumes at B, with world terms of trade shown by line 1 and an initial tariff on food imports. An increase in the tariff improves the world terms of trade (to line 2) and raises the relative domestic price of food. The new equilibrium thus lies between C and A on line 2, and real incomes may or may not improve, depending on the relative strengths of the (beneficial) terms-of-trade effect and the volume-of-trade effect.

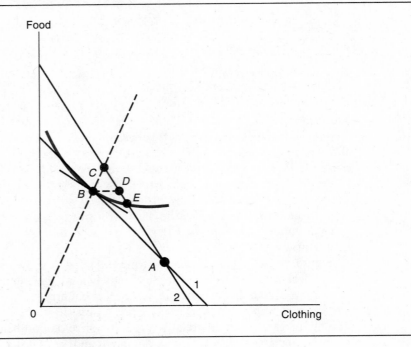

relative changes (e.g., $\hat{M}$ is defined as dM/M), the optimal tariff can be expressed as

$$t = \frac{1}{\hat{M}/\hat{p}^*} \tag{11.S.7}$$

The foreign offer curve remains stationary. Therefore, if $\hat{M}$, the relative change in the home country's import demand, could be linked to $\hat{M}^*$, the relative change in foreign import demand, the expression for the optimal tariff given by Equation 11.S.7 could be translated into an expression involving ε^*, the elasticity of import demand along the foreign offer curve.

The relationship between M and M^* is simple—it is given by the equilibrium condition 11.S.8, which states that at world prices the value of the home country's imports is equated to the value of foreign imports (or home country exports).

$$p^*M = M^* \tag{11.S.8}$$

Taking relative changes in Equation 11.S.8 yields

$$\hat{p}^* + \hat{M} = \hat{M}^* \qquad (11.S.9)$$

Therefore $\hat{M}/\hat{p}^*$ equals $\hat{M}^*/\hat{p}^* - 1$. But $\hat{M}^*/\hat{p}^*$ is merely the definition of ϵ^*, the elasticity of the foreign country's demand for imports along its offer curve.[2] This shows that the formula for the optimum tariff given in Equation 11.S.7 can be rewritten as

$$t = \frac{1}{\epsilon^* - 1} \qquad (11.S.10)$$

This formula needs to be interpreted carefully. It seems to state that if the foreign offer curve is inelastic, ($\epsilon^* < 1$), the tariff should be negative. This interpretation of the relationships underlying the formula would be incorrect. Reconsider Equation 11.S.6. If the foreign offer curve is inelastic, an increase in the tariff would cause home imports to rise. The terms of trade improve for the home country, and with ϵ^* less than 1, foreigners offer more food for export. (See the discussion in the appendix to Chapter 11.) On both counts dy in Equation 11.S.6 must be positive. The home country should raise its tariff until it reaches the elastic stretch of the foreign offer curve. Only then will a favorable movement in the terms of trade be countered by an unfavorable cutback in the volume of imports.

The Impact of Tariffs on World and Domestic Prices

Tariffs create wedges between domestic import prices and world prices. A natural presumption is that the imposition of a tariff drives up the price of imports at home relative to other goods while it depresses the world price. As we shall see, this may not always follow. What is required is an explicit solution for each of these price changes and a sharp distinction drawn between shifts of demand curves and movements along demand curves.

Equation 11.S.9 revealed the equations of change that can be utilized in solving for the change in world prices, $\hat{p}^*$. The change in foreign imports, $\hat{M}^*$, is captured by movements along the foreign offer curve, since our tariff does not cause their demand curve to shift. Thus:

$$\hat{M}^* = \epsilon^* \hat{p}^* \qquad (11.S.11)$$

The expression for $\hat{M}$ is more complicated. A change in the tariff rate shifts the home country's offer curve. Therefore, $\hat{M}$ will exhibit a mixture of such a shift and a move along the home country's offer curve. Specifically, this is shown as $M = M(p^*, t)$ and decomposing the rate of change as follows:

$$\hat{M} = -\epsilon \hat{p}^* + \beta dt \qquad (11.S.12)$$

where β, defined literally as $1/M \cdot \partial M/\partial t$, is the shift in the home country's offer curve at given world terms of trade. One of the primary objectives is to develop an explicit

---

[2] This elasticity formulation was introduced in Chapter 3. Because $1/p^*$ is the relative price of the foreign country's import (clothing), ϵ^* is defined as *minus* $\hat{M}^*$ divided by $1/\widehat{p^*}$, which is equivalent to *plus* $\hat{M}^*/\hat{p}^*$.

expression for β to guarantee that it is negative. Figure 11.4 showed that an increase in t would reduce imports at given world terms of trade.

Substituting Equation 11.S.11 for $\hat{M}^*$ and Equation 11.S.12 for $\hat{M}$ into Equation 11.S.9 yields the following solution for the effect of a tariff on world terms of trade.

$$\hat{p}^* = \frac{1}{\Delta} \beta dt \qquad (11.S.13)$$

where

$$\Delta = \epsilon + \epsilon^* - 1$$

The expression Δ captures the Marshall-Lerner condition for market stability discussed in the supplement to Chapter 4. Assuming the market to be stable, the sum of import-demand elasticities must exceed unity, and Δ must therefore be positive. Thus, if the home country's offer curve shifts inward (β negative), the world relative price of our import falls.

Home prices are linked to foreign prices by the tariff rate: $p = (1 + t)p^*$. Taking relative changes in these terms and equating yields

$$\hat{p} = \hat{p}^* + dt \qquad (11.S.14)$$

With the solution for the terms-of-trade change, $\hat{p}^*$, given by Equation 11.S.13 the next step is to substitute to obtain the solution for the change in the relative domestic price of imports, $\hat{p}$.

$$\hat{p} = \frac{1}{\Delta} (\Delta + \beta) dt \qquad (11.S.15)$$

Although Δ is positive, this discussion has maintained (and will subsequently prove) that β is negative. This argument underscores the doubts expressed in the text concerning whether an increase in t must protect the import-competing industry.

Elasticity and Shift of the Home Offer Curve

To simplify matters at this stage assume that initially there is free trade so that the initial value of t is zero.[3] The forces at work along the home country's offer curve were displayed in Equation 3.S.8 for the home elasticity of import demand:

$$\epsilon = \bar{\eta} + e + m$$

An improvement in the terms of trade encourages imports by (1) causing consumers to *substitute* toward the now cheaper imports ($\bar{\eta}$), (2) causing resources to be allocated away from now cheaper import-competing goods toward exports (e), and (3) raising real incomes, with part of the gain spilling over to importables (m).

The *shift* in the home offer curve reveals the forces encouraging a reduced volume of imports *at the initial terms of trade* as the tariff is raised. The hike in t at initial p^* raises domestic p and thus reduces imports via a substitution effect in consumption, $\bar{\eta}$, and a substitution effect in production, e. However, since the terms of trade are

---

[3] A more general treatment is provided in R. W. Jones, "Tariffs and Trade in General Equilibrium: Comment," *American Economic Review*, 59 (June 1969): 418–424.

unchanged, so is real income, so the (m) term in ϵ is missing from the shift. The reason: Since trade is initially free ($p^* = p$ initially), the expression for real income changes reduces to the terms-of-trade effect:

$$dy = -M dp^*$$

That is, the *shift* in the offer curve is shown by (11.S.16):

$$\beta = -(\bar{\eta} + e) \qquad\qquad (11.S.16)$$

The Metzler Tariff Paradox

It is now possible to develop an explicit criterion for the paradoxical case in which a tariff so depresses the terms of trade that the relative domestic price of imports falls as well. Substitute the expression for β in Equation 11.S.16 into the expression for $\hat{p}$ in Equation 11.S.15 to obtain

$$\hat{p} = \frac{1}{\Delta}(\epsilon + \epsilon^* - 1 - \bar{\eta} - e)dt$$

Given the breakdown of home ϵ, the solution for $\hat{p}$ is

$$\hat{p} = \frac{1}{\Delta}(\epsilon^* + m - 1)dt \qquad\qquad (11.S.17)$$

The argument in Chapter 11 suggested that a tariff could fail to protect if the foreign import demand elasticity, ϵ^*, were sufficiently small. Equation 11.S.17 reveals that the critical value for this elasticity is $(1 - m)$ or, more simply, the country's propensity to consume its export commodity.

The appendix to Chapter 11 shows, in Figure 11.A.2, an offer-curve diagram in which the Metzler tariff paradox may hold. The razor's-edge case in which the income-consumption curve is tangent at Q to the foreign offer curve, $O_T R^*$, corresponds to ϵ^* being equal to $(1 - m)$ in Equation 11.S.17.

SUPPLEMENT TO CHAPTER 12:
Tariffs, Growth, and Welfare

This supplement continues the algebraic analysis of tariffs initiated in the supplement to Chapter 11. It provides a formal proof of the fact that the maximum-revenue tariff rate exceeds the optimal rate. For a given degree of protection, a criterion is developed relating growth to welfare changes. Finally, a broader analysis of the tariff, making use of matrix algebra, allows an easy overview of the question of gains from trade and commerical policy.

The Maximum-Revenue Tariff

The supplement to Chapter 11 expressed the home country's budget constraint in terms of domestic prices (see Equation 11.S.2). When differentiated, this expression led to an expression for the change in real income, in terms of the change in the domestic price ratio and the tariff revenue. This was Equation 11.S.4, reproduced here.

$$dy = -Mdp + d(tp^*M) \qquad (12.S.1)$$

Consider this expression in conjunction with Figure 12.1. The optimal tariff rate is t_0, and the optimal tariff formula (Equation 11.S.10) showed that near t_0 the foreign offer curve must be elastic. This means that the tariff must be "protective" in the sense of raising p with a small further increase in t. Thus, the $-Mdp$ term in Equation 12.S.1 is negative in the neighborhood of the optimum tariff, where dy equals zero. As a consequence, $d(tp^*M)$ must be positive. That is, at rate t_0 in Figure 12.1 the curve plotting the tariff revenue against the tariff rate must be positively sloped. Tariff revenue reaches a maximum at the higher rate, t_2.

Growth with Protection

The supplement to Chapter 4 analyzed the possibility of *immiserizing growth*—a situation in which expansion of a country's production of exportables during the growth process causes such a deterioration in the terms of trade that the community's welfare actually falls. Concerns about worsening terms of trade have sometimes been cited in support of protection for import-competing commodities. Such protection tends to erode the potential welfare gains from growth for a small country.

Examine here the case of a country with fixed tariff rates and given world prices. For some reason (growth of resources, improvement in technology) the country's transformation schedule shifts outward so that at the fixed domestic prices (given world prices adjusted for fixed tariff rates) aggregate output expands. The budget constraint is shown by

$$D_C + p^*D_F = x_C + p^*x_F \qquad (12.S.2)$$

(This repeats Equation 11.S.5.) Differentiation leads to

$$dD_C + p^*dD_F = dx_C + p^*dx_F \qquad (12.S.3)$$

Note that there is no terms-of-trade effect because p^* is assumed constant. Add and subtract pdD_F on the left-hand side.

$$(dD_C + pdD_F) + (p^* - p)dD_F = (dx_C + p^*dx_F)$$

The first expression in parentheses is, of course, the change in home real income, dy. The change in home consumption of food, dD_F, can only be explained by income effects because domestic prices are constant. That is, with the home country's marginal propensity to import food denoted by m,

$$dD_F = \frac{m}{p}\, dy$$

The fraction $(p^* - p)/p$ is minus $t/(1 + t)$ so that

$$\left(1 - m\,\frac{t}{1 + t}\right)dy = (dx_C + p^*dx_F) \qquad (12.S.4)$$

This expression provides the criterion with which to judge growth in a protected economy. Real income gains are registered only if growth results in a greater aggregate production *evaluated at world prices*. This may seem paradoxical. The criterion for judging an increase in welfare is to measure consumption changes at *domestic prices*, yet production changes should be evaluated at world prices because world prices measure the trade-off between production and consumption (see Equation 12.S.2). Figure 12.4 illustrated how various possibilities of output expansion from point A— points D, B, C, or E, all showing a 25 percent gain in output at domestic prices— resulted in different real income gains. For point E the value of output actually fell at world prices.

Tariffs, Gains from Trade, and Welfare: A General Analysis

Turn, now, to a different question: How can welfare or real income of an economy be compared in two situations, in which prices, quantities traded, and trade restrictions may differ by more than "a small amount"? There is no restriction on the number of commodities produced or consumed at home or abroad. For notation, x is the vector of quantities produced at home, D is the vector of quantities demanded or consumed, p is the vector of prices ruling in the home country, and p^* is the vector of prices ruling abroad.[1] Not all commodities need be produced at home, so that in the vector $x = (x_1, x_2, \ldots, x_n)$ some entries may be zero. Similarly, not all commodities produced need be demanded locally, so that in the vector $D = (D_1, D_2, \ldots, D_n)$ some entries may also be zero. The two situations to be compared are denoted by a single prime and a double prime. Thus, in the initial situation home prices are given by the vector $p' = (p'_1, p'_2, \ldots, p'_n)$. This vector may or may not represent a situation in which some international trade takes place. In the second situation prices have altered at home to $p'' = (p''_1, p''_2, \ldots, p''_n)$. Let the vector E represent the home country's set of *excess demands*.

$$E \equiv D - x$$

An element E_i, in the vector E is positive if commodity i is imported at home, negative if i is exported, and zero if high transport costs or tariffs result in no international exchange of the ith commodity.

The basic criterion by which welfare in the double-prime situation is contrasted to welfare in the single-prime situation involves a comparison of the value of aggregate demand in each, when the prices used for the evaluation are in both instances those of the double-prime situation. Thus, welfare is deemed to have risen if

$$p''D'' - p''D' > 0 \tag{12.S.5}$$

This inequality states that if the initial bundle of goods consumed, D', could have been purchased in the double-prime situation, the community is assumed to have increased its real income.

This assumption is illustrated for the two-commodity case in Figure 12.S.1. The fact that the consumption bundle in the single-prime situation, D', lies below the line showing prices in the double-prime situation (and supporting demand, D'') is taken

---

[1] The analysis in this section rests heavily upon Michihiro Ohyama, "Trade and Welfare in General Equilibrium," *Keio Economic Studies* (1972): 37–73.

FIGURE 12.S.1   The Welfare Criterion for Two Commodities

Two alternative consumption bundles are illustrated: D' and D''. The prices ruling when D'' is consumed are shown by line p''. The welfare criterion whereby situation double-prime is superior to situation single-prime is shown by the fact that D' lies below line p'', which means $p''D'' - p''D' > 0$.

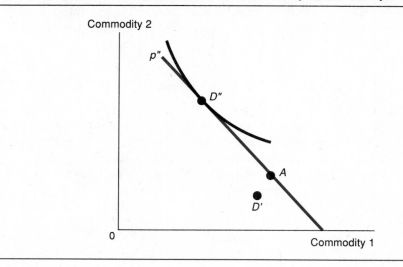

as a sufficient criterion for establishing that point D'' represents a higher level of welfare. Clearly, if indifference curves do not intersect, point D' must lie on a lower indifference curve than point D''.

The vector of excess demands equals the vector of total demands minus the vector of production. Turn this equation around to state that demand equals excess demand *plus* production. Making this substitution for both the single-prime and the double-prime situations in the improvement in welfare criterion, Inequality 12.S.5, yields the following inequality as an equivalent expression.

$$p''(E'' - E') + p''(x'' - x') > 0 \qquad (12.S.6)$$

Prices at home in the double-prime situation will differ from prices abroad for any traded commodity that is subject to a tariff, an export tax, or a subsidy in the home country. Let the matrix T'' represent these taxes and/or trade subsidies. T'' is a *diagonal matrix*, all of whose elements are zero except the diagonal terms. What does the entry t_i'' represent? This depends on whether commodity i is imported (E_i positive), in which case a positive t_i'' represents a tariff and a negative t_i'' an import subsidy, or exported (E_i negative), in which case an export tax is a negative t_i'' and an export subsidy a positive t_i''. In short, $t_i'' p_i^{*''} E_i''$ is positive if the government collects tax revenue and negative if the government is subsidizing a trade flow. For any commodity, i,

$$p_i'' = (1 + t_i'')p_i^{*''}$$

where $p_i^{*''}$ is the world price of commodity i. This can be summarized in matrix notation by making use of the identity matrix, I, whose off-diagonal elements are all zero, and with 1's all along the diagonal.

$$p'' = (I + T'')p*''$$ (12.S.7)

The home country's budget constraint states that the value at world prices of aggregate excess demand is zero, both for the double-prime and single-prime situations.

$$p*''E'' = 0$$ (12.S.8)
$$p*'E' = 0$$ (12.S.9)

Furthermore, if the single-prime situation refers to the pretrade situation at home, each element of the vector E' would have to equal zero, because in equilibrium local demand would have to be balanced by local sources of supply.

All the ingredients are now at hand to transform the welfare criterion, Inequality 12.S.6, into an explicit listing of the sources of an improvement in real incomes. To proceed merely substitute the relationship shown in Equation 12.S.7 between domestic and world prices into the first term in Inequality 12.S. 6.

$$p''(E'' - E') = (I + T'')p*''(E'' - E')$$

This expression, in turn, equals

$$p*''E'' - p*''E' + T''p*''(E'' - E')$$

Notice, however, that by 12.S.8, $p*''E''$ vanishes. This statement of the budget constraint at world prices applies as well to the single-prime situation (shown by Equation 12.S.9), and thus allows $p*'E'$ (equal to zero) to be added to the expression. Thus rewritten, the expression becomes

$$-(p*'' - p*')E' + T''p*''(E'' - E')$$

Substitute this expression for $p''(E'' - E')$ back into Inequality 12.S.6 to obtain the basic welfare criterion.

$$-(p*'' - p*')E' + T''p*''(E'' - E') + p''(x'' - x') > 0$$ (12.S.10)

Each of the three terms in this inequality should be familiar from the preceding discussion.

1. The term $-(p*'' - p*')E'$ is the terms-of-trade effect. If the two primed situations represent different trading equilibria very close to each other, and if only one relative price (because only two commodities) exists, it is shown by the $-Mdp*$ term in Equation 11.S.6. The general expression states that the community's welfare improves to the extent that the world price falls for any commodity imported ($E_i' > 0$), or rises for any commodity exported ($E_i' < 0$).

2. The term $T''p*''(E'' - E')$ measures the change in the volume of trade for all commodities for which domestic prices, p'', differ from world prices, $p*''$. The term $T''p*''$ is the tariff wedge. Returning again to the case in which only two commodities are traded, and the two situations are very close to each other, we see that this term reduces to the $(p - p*)dM$ term in Equation 11.S.6. It states in general that real income is improved if the level of imports rises for any commodity worth more at home (as indicted by p'') than it costs to obtain in world markets (as indicated by $p*''$).

3. The term $p''(x'' - x')$ must in any case be greater than or equal to zero. It shows the change in real income attributable to the change in production. In the absence of distortions, x'' is the point on the transformation schedule that maximizes the value of output at domestic prices when these are given by p''. Therefore, the value of any other production possibility, say x', at these prices p'' must be less. If the single-prime and double-prime situations are very close together in the two-commodity model, this term reduces to $dx_C + pdx_F$. As was argued in Chapter 3 and subsequently, this reduction approaches zero as an expression of the equality between the domestic price ratio and the slope of the transformation schedule.

This line of reasoning has been useful in comparing two states of trade, differing from each other in prices—perhaps as a result of changes in tariffs. It is also useful in comparing a state of trade (in the double-prime situation) with the pretrade situation. In such a case each element in the vector E' goes to zero. The welfare criterion, Inequality 12.S.10, then assumes the special form

$$T''p^{*''}E'' + p''(x'' - x') > 0 \qquad\qquad (12.S.11)$$

Because the production term, $p''(x'' - x')$, must be nonnegative, as was just argued, this criterion yields a powerful result. Suppose that a complex mixture of tariffs and trade subsidies exists. Is the community better off than with no trade? The question needs to be raised because an export subsidy by itself can reduce welfare at home— this is akin to giving something away. The term $T''p^{*''}E''$ represents the net tariff-and-subsidy revenue to the home government. The criterion reveals that regardless of the pattern of subsidies, if this net revenue is positive, trade must be superior to no trade.[2] Note that it is *sufficient* for the double-prime situation to represent an improvement that the net revenue be positive. However, even if net revenue is negative, it is possible for D'' to be preferred to D'.

This result, that trade distorted by the presence of trade taxes and subsidies is nonetheless superior to autarky as long as the net tariff revenue is positive, is illustrated in Figure 12.S.2. The tax-distorted consumption equilibrium at point G is similar to that illustrated in Figure 11.3's standard depiction of the effect of a tariff on real incomes. Prices lines labeled P show a higher relative domestic price for importables than does price line P^*, which reflects world prices. Behind the tax barriers, producers select point A and consumers choose G; these points have equal value at world prices, but the value of the consumption bundle at domestic prices exceeds the value of production by the amount of the net tariff revenue. Key to the argument that distorted trade with positive net tariff revenue is superior to autarky is the comparison between consumption point N, which would be selected if domestic price line P indicated world prices (so that tariff revenue were zero) and autarky bundle H. If the country were offered terms of trade P, differing from autarky prices (the slope at H), the country would gain. If, in addition, consumers were provided a boost to their disposable incomes in the form of a positive net tariff revenue, real incomes (at G) would rise even further. Indeed, even if on net the budget line were reduced slightly below

[2] This result is derived in M. Ohyama, "Trade and Welfare in General Equilibrium," *Keio Economic Studies* 9 (1972): 37–73.

FIGURE 12.S.2   Positive Tax Revenue Leads to Gains

Domestic prices represented by the P lines, are distorted from world prices, shown by the P^* line. Production is at A, consumption at G. N is superior to autarky bundle H, as is G, as long as net tariff revenue is positive.

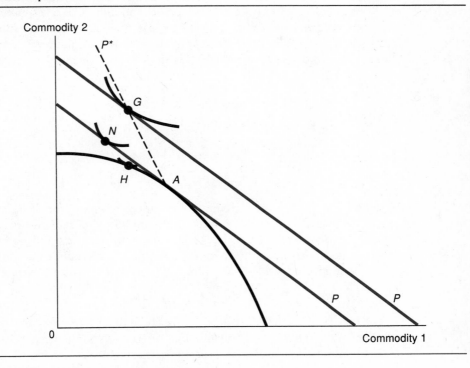

line NA, reflecting a small negative tax revenue (subsidies exceeding taxes), trade might be preferable to autarky, but a sufficient condition for distorted trade to lead to gains over autarky is a positive value for net tariff revenue.

SUPPLEMENT TO CHAPTER 13:
Imperfect Competition, Trade Restrictions, and Welfare

The supplement to Chapter 11 developed an expression for the way in which a country's aggregate real income is affected by changes in levels of protection when markets are perfectly competitive. The basic statement was contained in Equation 11.S.6, which showed how an increase in the rate of protection might aid by improving a country's *terms of trade* (lowering p^*, the relative world price of imports), but most likely at the expense of lowering the *volume of trade* (a negative dM) in a situation in which protection has raised the domestic price of imports, p, above the world price, p^*. The domestic price reflects the value to the home country of obtaining another unit of imports, whereas the foreign price indicates the real cost of obtaining another unit of imports. When elements of imperfect competition characterize home markets for importables or exportables, the breakdown of real income changes for competitive markets shown in Equation 11.S.6 needs to be supplemented to take into account the fact that any change in the economy's composition of outputs also affects aggregate welfare.

A useful starting point in the analysis is the statement that, when evaluated at world prices, the economy's aggregate consumption bundle must match the value of aggregate production. (The rationale: At world prices the value of exports equals the value of imports under the assumption that trade is balanced.) Returning to the standard two-commodity model, this is the relationship shown in Equation 11.S.5, reproduced here.

$$D_C + p^*D_F = x_C + p^*x_F \tag{13.S.1}$$

Proceeding as in the supplement to Chapter 11, total differentiation of both sides and a subsequent addition and subtraction of pdD_F from the left-hand side and pdx_F from the right-hand side yields

$$(dD_C + pdD_F) + (p^* - p)dD_F = -Mdp^* + (dx_C + pdx_F) + (p^* - p)dx_F$$

As in previous discussions, the country is assumed to import food (M). The expression can be simplified, as the change in the economy's level of real income, dy, is the first expression, $(dD_C + pdD_F)$, and the wedge separating foreign and home food prices, $(p^* - p)$, multiplied by the changes in consumption, dD_F, and local production, dx_F, can be combined to yield

$$dy = -Mdp^* + (p - p^*)dM + (dx_C + pdx_F) \tag{13.S.2}$$

The first two terms of Equation 13.S.2 are familiar from the tariff analysis in the supplement to Chapter 11, corresponding respectively to the term-of-trade effect and the volume-of-trade effect. Of course, a tariff that improves the terms of trade usually does so at the expense of a cutback in imports. The optimal rate of tariff in the absence of monopoly pricing involves a trade-off between the terms-of-trade effect and the volume-of-trade effect. In a competitive market setting, the final term, $(dx_C + pdx_F)$, vanishes. However, if competition locally is less than perfect, prices do not reflect the ratio of marginal costs. Let c denote the ratio of the marginal cost of producing food to the marginal cost of producing clothing, that is, the marginal opportunity cost of producing food (much as p denotes the relative domestic price of food). The term $(dx_C + cdx_F)$ equals zero, since the slope of the transformation schedule indicates, in general, marginal opportunity costs. Therefore, Equation 13.S.2 can be written as

$$dy = -Mdp^* + (p - p^*)dM + (p - c)dx_F \tag{13.S.3}$$

The last term in this equation reveals that if markets are imperfectly competitive at home, even small changes in the composition of output have welfare consequences. This exposes the basis for *industrial policy* in managing a nation's commercial policy instruments. Suppose, for example, that a local monopoly in producing food has caused its price to exceed marginal costs. Consider a tariff initially set at a rate that would be optimal for a *competitive* economy—i.e., a rate for which any further increase in the tariff would cause a volume-of-trade loss just balancing the terms-of-trade gain. Equation 13.S.3 suggests that if competition is less than perfect in the import-competing food sector, a further increase in the tariff rate would still contribute positively to national welfare because it would encourage a reallocation of resources towards producing more of the importable (food)—the value of food locally, p, exceeds its marginal cost of production, c. Tariff policy thus may have further dimension—it provides a second-best means of encouraging output in a sector in which the existence of monopoly power has curtailed output below the competitively optimal level.

Figure 13.1 showed an initial equilibrium at point B or B' on the transformation curve when food production is characterized by local monopolistic behavior. (The clothing sector is competitive, with price equal to marginal cost.) With the domestic price of food exceeding marginal cost, the budget line showing domestic prices at B or B' is flatter than the transformation schedule, so any policy encouraging a real-location of resources in favor of food production tends to raise national income.

Suppose, instead, that some element of local monopoly control exists in the export sector (clothing), so that at an initial free-trade equilibrium the relative domestic price of food falls short of its relative marginal cost. If the country can improve its terms of trade with a tariff, Equation 13.S.3 reveals that the temptation to pursue a pro-tectionist policy is limited both by the volume-of-trade effect once the tariff is suffi-ciently high and by the deleterious effect on welfare of an expansion in the competitive import-competing sector (food). If the volume of trade is somewhat limited (small value of M), and if the discrepancy between relative food price, p, and cost, c, is relatively large in absolute value (p lies below c if clothing is the monopolistic sector), the country may find free trade a better policy than any tariff level despite the forgone terms-of-trade improvement.

Expressions such as Equation 13.S.3 are useful in appraising the welfare conse-quences of the use of various instruments of commercial policy. In some cases, sim-plifications of the expression are allowed or modifications required. For example, suppose a small country has no influence on its terms of trade—then the first term in Equation 13.S.3 vanishes. If an import quota has been imposed and is binding, a loosening up of quota restrictions directly raises welfare as the volume of allowed imports rises. In such a setting the domestic price of food will fall as foreign sources supply a larger share of the home market, and this encourages local demand (a welfare gain). Since the change in imports equals the change in demand less the change in local supply, the last two terms in Equation 13.S.3 can be rewritten as

$$(p - p^*)dD_F + (p^* - c)dx_F$$

Thus, a loosening of quota restrictions encourages demand, which raises welfare but cuts back on local production. Of crucial relevance in appraising the consequences of such a cut is the relationship between the *world* price of food and local marginal costs. Even if domestic price exceeds marginal cost (with a local imperfectly competitive food industry), if world price is lower than marginal cost, the cutback in food pro-duction further improves welfare.

Finally, note the modifications required if the country has restricted imports with VERs (Voluntary Export Restrictions urged on foreign suppliers) instead of quotas. In such a case the home country receives none of the revenue represented by the gap between home and foreign prices. This implies that the first term in Equation 13.S.3 should be replaced by $(-Mdp)$, since p represents the price the country must pay to foreigners when VERs are imposed, and the second term, $(p - p^*)dM$, is deleted since the spread between home and foreign prices no longer accrues to the home government. One immediate consequence for a small, open economy in a competitive setting (so that p^* remains constant and the last term in Equation 14.S.3 can be ignored): Reductions in levels of protection must raise real incomes whether imports have been restricted by quotas or VERs. Reductions in import quotas lead to positive values for $(p - p^*)dM$; reductions in VERs lower the domestic price of importables and thus lead to positive values of $(-Mdp)$.

SUPPLEMENT TO CHAPTER 17:
Proof of the Marshall-Lerner Condition

For notational simplicity the normalization $P = P^* = 1$ will be adopted in the proof of this proposition. Then the trade balance expressed in foreign currency is

$$TB^* = (1/E)X_D(E) - M_D(E)$$

Differentiate with respect to E.

$$dTB^*/dE = -(1/E^2)X + (1/E)dX_D/dE - dM_D/dE$$

Multiply by E^2/X. This quantity is positive if

$$-1 + (E/X)dX_D/dE - (E^2/X)dM_D/dE > 0$$

Using the definitions of the elasticities,

$$\epsilon_X \equiv (dX_D/dE)E/X \qquad \epsilon_M = -(dM_D/dE)E/M$$

the condition becomes

$$-1 + \epsilon_X + (EM/X)\epsilon_M > 0$$

Starting from a position of balanced trade, $EM = X$, the equation reduces to the Marshall-Lerner condition that was asserted in Chapter 17.

SUPPLEMENT TO CHAPTER 19:
The Monetarist Two-Country Model
of the Balance of Payments

Chapter 19 assumed that the home country's money supply is too small to affect substantially the world money supply or world price level. When international reserves are flowing out through a balance of payments deficit, the rest of the world is running a balance of payments surplus. However, it was assumed that the reserve inflow is just a drop in the ocean so far as the rest of the world is concerned. This supplement relaxes the small-country assumption and moves to a two-country world. A domestic monetary expansion will succeed in raising the price level in the world to the extent that it raises the world money supply.

Determination of the Balance of Payments in the Two Countries

We model the foreign country just as we modeled the domestic country in the chapter. The rate of increase of the foreign money supply, foreign hoarding, H^*, is related to the foreign excess demand for money. The foreign excess demand for money is, in turn, an increasing function of foreign nominal income, or of the foreign price level with foreign real income determined at $\overline{Y}^*$ by exogenous supply factors, and a decreasing function of the foreign money supply M^*.

$$H^* \equiv \dot{M}^* = \delta K \overline{Y}^* P^* - \delta M^* \tag{19.S.1}$$

(For convenience it has been assumed that the same values of δ and K apply to the foreign country that applied to the domestic country.) We multiply through by the exchange rate in order to work in terms of domestic currency.

$$EH^* = \delta K \overline{Y}^* P - \delta E M^* \tag{19.S.2}$$

Here we have applied PPP $(P = EP^*)$. Equation 19.S.2 represents the foreign payments surplus measured in domestic currency. Its negative is the domestic payments surplus measured in domestic currency:

$$BP = -EH^* = -\delta K \overline{Y}^* P + \delta E M^* \tag{19.S.3}$$

This is a second equation describing the balance of payments, in addition to Equation 19.5. It represents, for a given foreign money supply M^*, a negative dependence of the domestic balance of payments on the price level. An increase in the domestic price level under fixed exchange rates is an increase in the world price level. As far as the foreign country is concerned, it raises the foreign demand for money leading to a foreign payment surplus, which is a domestic payments deficit.

The downward-sloping $BP = -EH^*$ schedule, Equation 19.S.3, is shown in Figure 19.S.1 on the same axes as the upward-sloping $BP = H$ schedule, Equation 19.5. Since both equations must hold, short-run equilibrium is given by the intersection of the two schedules, at point A initially.

Determination of the World Price Level

It is possible to solve the two simultaneous equations for the world price level, expressed in domestic currency.

$$\delta K \overline{Y} P - \delta M = \delta K \overline{Y}^* P + \delta E M^*$$
$$P = \frac{M + E M^*}{K(\overline{Y} + \overline{Y}^*)} \tag{19.S.4}$$

The numerator is the total world money supply measured in domestic currency (i.e., with the exchange rate used to evaluate the foreign money supply). Planet Earth considered in the aggregate is, after all, a closed economy, so it makes sense that the world price level should be proportionate to the world money supply. Equation 19.S.4 is shown in Figure 19.S.1 as a horizontal line at the price level P.

FIGURE 19.S.1   Monetary Expansion in the Monetarist Two-Country Model

---

A monetary expansion of 1 percent will raise the world price level by λ percent, where λ is the domestic country's fraction of the world's money supply. As with a small country (where $\lambda = 0$), the expansion shifts the H schedule left, leading to a temporary excess supply of money and balance of payments deficit.

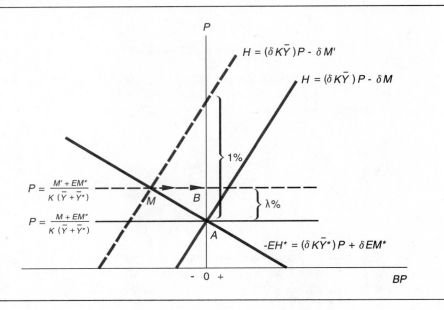

The Effect of an Increase in One Country's Money Supply

As in the chapter, we consider two policy changes: a monetary expansion and a devaluation.

An increase in the domestic money supply shifts the country's H schedule to the left by $\delta\Delta M$, precisely the same as in the small-country model: An excess supply of money leads to dishoarding. The H schedule also can be viewed as shifting vertically upward by the same proportion as the increase in the money supply: If the price level were for some reason to increase by the same proportion as the money supply, the excess supply of money would remain at zero. When the country was small the world price level was unchanged, but now it is recognized that the monetary expansion will raise the world price level to the extent that the domestic country is large.

Define the domestic country's share in the world money supply.

$$\lambda \equiv M/(M + EM^*)$$

A 1 percent increase in the domestic money supply is a λ percent increase in the world money supply. As shown in Equation 19.S.4, it raises the world price level by λ percent, whether that is measured in terms of domestic currency (P) or foreign (P^*). In Figure 19.S.1, the monetary expansion shifts up not only the domestic H line but the price level line as well. This means that the money demand function must be evaluated at a higher price level, at point M. Under the previous small-country case, in which λ

was negligible and so the price level shifted up negligibly, there was an increase in the money supply of, say, 1 percent, with no increase in money demand. Now there is a 1 percent increase in the money supply with a λ percent increase in money demand. There is still an excess supply of money (equal to $1 - \lambda$ percent of the original money supply), and therefore a balance of payments deficit, but they are not as large as in the small-country case.

What is happening in the foreign country? Its money supply has not changed, but it is faced with a λ percent increase in the price level. Therefore, its demand for money goes up by λ percent. It has an excess demand for money (equal to λ percent of its money supply) that is the counterpart of the domestic country's excess supply of money, causing a balance of payments surplus that is the counterpart of the domestic country's balance of payments deficit.

Over time, the domestic country loses gold to the foreign country. Under the nonsterilization assumption, the domestic money supply falls and the foreign money supply rises. The domestic H schedule shifts right and the *negative* foreign schedule, $-EH^*$, shifts right as well. The economy follows a sequence of intersections, moving rightward from M along the new price level line. The transfer of money from the home country to the foreign country gradually alleviates the excess demand in the foreign country. Long-run equilibrium is reached when both countries return to a zero balance of payments, at point B. There the supply of money equals the demand for money in both countries. Since the price level has risen by λ percent in both countries and the demand for money is proportional to the price level, this can only mean that the supply of money has increased by λ percent in both countries. The world money supply has increased by λ percent; in the short run the expansion took place entirely in the domestic country, but in the long run it is distributed equiproportionately across both countries.

It is instructive to graph directly the distribution of the world money supply between the two countries, as in Figure 19.S.2. Balance of payments equilibrium, which holds in the long run, is given by the equality of money supply and money demand in each country.

$$M = K\overline{Y}P$$
$$M^* = K\overline{Y}^*P^*$$

The ratio is:

$$M/M^* = (K\overline{Y}P)/(K\overline{Y}^*P^*) = (\overline{Y}/\overline{Y}^*)E \qquad (19.S.5)$$

Thus, for a given exchange rate, the world money supply in the long run is distributed in a given ratio, which gives the slope of the $BP = 0$ line in the figure. Points above this line represent excess supply of money and a payments deficit for the home country. The reverse holds for points below the line. At a moment in time the distribution of the world money supply between the two countries is a point on a line labeled WMS, with slope equal to $-E$. The initial equilibrium occurs at point A, where the world money supply is distributed according to the ratio in Equation 19.S.5. If gold were somehow forceably redistributed from the foreign to the home country, it would just flow back over time, each E dollars' worth of gold translating into one unit of foreign currency, until in the long run the economy returned to the $BP = 0$ line.

FIGURE 19.S.2   Redistribution of World Money Supply Following a Monetary Expansion

After the domestic country's money supply, M, increases 1 percent, it has an excess supply of money of $1 - \lambda$ percent (equal to its balance of payments deficit) and the foreign country has an excess demand for money of λ percent (equal to its balance of payments surplus). Over time, reserves flow out of the domestic country and into the foreign country until the distribution has been equalized.

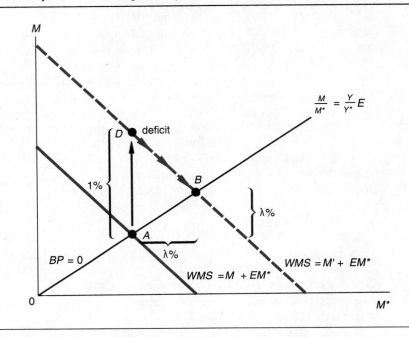

Now suppose the domestic money supply is increased 1 percent. The *WMS* line shifts vertically up 1 percent. At the moment of impact M^* is unchanged and M increases 1 percent; there is a jump from the old equilibrium at A, vertically up to D. This point lies above the $BP = 0$ line and so represents a domestic deficit. Over time, reserves are redistributed from the home country to the foreign country. In the long run the economy returns to the $BP = 0$ line at the new equilibrium point B, where M and M^* are each λ percent higher than before the disturbance.

The Effect of a Devaluation by One Country

Now, consider a devaluation of 1 percent. If it is operating under the gold standard, then the country increases the price of gold by 1 percent; with the other country pegged to gold, this increases the exchange rate, E, between the two currencies by 1 percent. The increase in E shifts the foreign EM^* schedule $BP = -\delta K \overline{Y}^* P + \delta E M^*$ to the right, as in Figure 19.S.3. This also can be viewed as a shift upward of 1 percent: If the domestic price level were for some reason to increase by the same proportion as the exchange rate, the foreign price level would be unchanged and foreign hoarding would remain at zero. The move is from A to D, the intersection of the domestic hoarding schedule with the new foreign hoarding schedule.

FIGURE 19.S.3   Devaluation in the Monetarist Two-Country Model

An increase in E of 1 percent will raise the price level P by $1 - \lambda$ percent when expressed in domestic currency, leading to an excess demand for money of $1 - \lambda$ percent and a corresponding balance of payments surplus ($BP > 0$ at D). Over time, money flows into the country and balance is restored ($BP = 0$ at B).

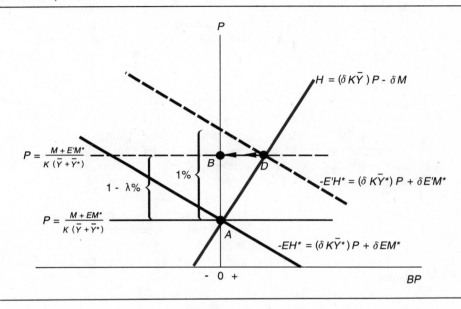

At D the price level, P, has shifted up. This is evident from Equation 19.S.4. The increase in E raises the value of the foreign money supply when expressed in domestic currency and thus raises the world price level when expressed in domestic currency. When E goes up by 1 percent, P goes up by $(1 - \lambda)$ percent, the fraction of the world money supply represented by foreign money.

If we are interested in P^*, the world price level when expressed in foreign currency, we divide Equation 18.11 through by the exchange rate.

$$P^* = \frac{M/E + M^*}{K(\overline{Y} + \overline{Y}^*)}$$

The increase in E reduces the value of the domestic money when expressed in foreign currency and thus reduces the world price level when expressed in foreign currency. When E goes up by 1 percent, P^* goes down by λ percent, the fraction of the world money supply represented by domestic money. When policy experiments under a fixed exchange rate were considered, effects on the foreign price level matched perfectly effects on the domestic price level because of PPP. Obviously, this is not the case when the exchange rate changes.

Adding the rise in the domestic price level to the decline in the foreign price level provides a check that the relative price level does change by precisely the change in the exchange rate, as expected from PPP.

$$(1 - \lambda)\% + \lambda\% = 1\%$$

The devaluing country is like a boat that uses a pole to push off from a larger boat. The change in their relative position depends only on the length of the pole (1 percent), but both boats move, and the change in each of their *absolute* positions depends on their relative size. If they are of equal size ($\lambda = 1/2$), they will each move equally far. In general, the smaller boat will move farther. In the limit ($\lambda = 0$), if a rowboat pushes off from an ocean liner, it can be assumed, for practical purposes, that the larger boat does not move at all and the smaller boat absorbs the entire change. This limiting case describes the small-country model in which the world price level was taken as given.

The chain of effects can be picked up from the increase in the domestic price level visible in Figure 18.A.3. The higher price level implies higher demand for domestic money. At the unchanged supply of domestic money there is excess demand: positive hoarding and a balance of payments surplus. Thus, the foreign country must be running a balance of payments deficit. A deficit is indeed what follows from the decrease in the foreign price level just noted: The demand for foreign money also decreases, leading to excess supply, and a payments deficit.

The home country gains reserves through its surplus. Under the nonsterilization assumption, the domestic money supply increases over time. As it does, the domestic H schedule shifts to the left. Meanwhile, the foreign country is losing reserves through its deficit. The foreign money supply decreases over time, shifting the foreign hoarding schedule, $-EH^*$, to the left. The point of intersection moves to the left along the new P line. The transfer of money gradually alleviates the excess demand for money in the home country and the excess supply abroad. In the long run, there is a return to equilibrium at point B, where both countries are happy with their money supplies and so the balance of payments is again zero.

SUPPLEMENT TO CHAPTER 23:
Real Wage Indexation

This supplement considers what happens when wages are indexed (either partially or completely) to the CPI:

$$W = \overline{w}\text{CPI}^\delta \qquad\qquad (23.\text{S}.1)$$

where δ is the degree of indexation. (If $\delta = 1$, then indexation is complete and the real wage—expressed in terms of the CPI—is fixed at the target level: $W/\text{CPI} = \overline{w}$.)

From Equation 23.1, the supply relationship is now

$$(Y/\overline{Y}) = (wP/\overline{w}\text{CPI}^\delta)^\sigma \qquad\qquad (23.\text{S}.2)$$

Assume that the target real wage, $\overline{w}$, is appropriately set to the warranted real wage, w, the one consistent with full employment. Also assume an open economy in which imports have a weight of α in the CPI.

$$\text{CPI} = (SP^*)^\alpha P^{1-\alpha} \qquad\qquad (23.\text{S}.3)$$

where the price of imports is given by the exchange rate, S, times the foreign price level, P^*. Substituting Equation 23.S.3 in Equation 23.S.2, the general supply relationship is

$$(Y/\overline{Y}) = [P/(SP^*)^{\alpha\delta}P^{(1-\alpha)\delta}]^{\sigma} \qquad (23.S.4)$$

For simplicity, consider the case where indexation is complete: $\delta = 1$. Then the supply relationship is

$$(Y/\overline{Y}) = (P/SP^*)^{\alpha\sigma} \qquad (23.S.5)$$

We readily see that real depreciation is contractionary, not expansionary as in a nonindexed economy. A 1 percent decrease in P/SP^* reduces output by $(\alpha\sigma)$ percent. The reason, as explained in the text, is that a real depreciation that leaves W/CPI unchanged necessarily raises W/P when it raises W. The result is that changes in fiscal policy have real effects. A domestic fiscal expansion that causes a real appreciation due to high capital mobility raises domestic output, Y. Notice that if imports are not important ($\alpha = 0$), there is little effect on Y.

Now consider international transmission in a two-country model. We model the foreign country just like the domestic country.

$$(Y^*/\overline{Y}^*) = (SP^*/P)^{\alpha^*\sigma^*} \qquad (23.S.6)$$

Looking at Equations 23.S.5 and 23.S.6 together reveals a remarkable property. The only circumstance that allows an increase in domestic output—a decrease in the real exchange rate SP^*/P—is also the only circumstance that allows a decrease in foreign output. Y and Y^* can vary from their potential output levels, but to the extent output goes up in one country it must go down in the other! A fiscal expansion in the foreign country, which raises foreign output to the extent it raises SP^*/P, reduces domestic output to the same extent. The only scope for variation in the real wage comes from real variation in the real exchange rate. This is why what goes up in one country goes down in the other. This is an extreme case of inverse transmission of policy.

What about monetary policy? While it remains true that any policy that changes the real exchange rate changes output, a monetary expansion in a completely indexed economy does not succeed in changing the real exchange rate. Rather, a 10 percent increase in the money supply raises S and P proportionately, with no real effects in either country, assuming indexation is complete ($\delta = 1$).[1]

The Locomotive Theory

Table 23.3 illustrates the game of Exporting Unemployment for the simple case where each country faces a simple choice of "expand" or "contract." Here we present the complete analysis with a continuous range of policy options.[2]

___

[1] This point is explored in problem 6 in the chapter problems. (Monetary policy can have effects on an economy with incomplete indexation: $\delta < 1$.) Wage indexation was introduced into two-country open-economy models by Victor Argy and Joanne Salop, "Monetary and Fiscal Expansion in a Two Country World under Flexible Exchange Rates," International Monetary Fund, (May 1979).

[2] The two seminal references in the application of game theory to coordination are: Matthew Canzoneri and Jo Anna Gray, "Monetary Policy Games and the Consequences of Non-Cooperative Behavior," *International Economic Review*, 26 (1985) 547–564. Koichi Hamada, *The Political Economy of International Monetary Interdependence* (Cambridge, MA: M.I.T. Press, 1985).

Assume that America and Europe seek to attain two objectives, internal balance, $Y = \overline{Y}$, and external balance, $TB = 0$, and that each has only one policy instrument, the money supply, M.[3] Figure 23.S.1 shows how the two countries set their monetary policies, with Europe's money supply, M_E, on the horizontal axis and America's, M_A, on the vertical axis.

First consider the problem from the U.S. point of view. There is some combination of the two money supplies that is optimal from the American viewpoint, represented by point A. A is in the lower right area, indicating that America would prefer that the other country do the expanding, enabling America to run a trade surplus while maintaining high output.[4] Of course, the other country will not in general set its money supply at the level desired. How should America set M_A, if it has to take M_E as given? Radiating out from A are a series of concentric indifference curves representing successive levels of American economic welfare farther and farther from the optimum. For any given level of M_E, America should choose the level of M_A that brings it to the highest indifference curve possible; this will be the point where the vertical line corresponding to M_E is tangent to an indifference curve. Thus, tracing out the set of points where America's indifference curves run vertically will trace out its *reaction line*, which shows how it will set its money supply as a function of Europe's. This is half the story.

Now consider the problem from Europe's viewpoint. Europe's optimum is the point E, located in the upper left area, indicating that Europe, too, would prefer that its trading partner be the one to expand. Successive indifference curves radiate out from E. How should Europe set M_E, if it takes M_A as given? To get as close to the optimum as possible, it should choose the point where the horizontal line corresponding to M_A is tangent to one of its indifference curves. Thus, tracing out the set of points where Europe's indifference curves run horizontally will trace out Europe's reaction line, which shows how it will set its money supply as a function of America's.

The state without coordination is the Nash noncooperative equilibrium, defined as the point at which each country is setting its money supply at the optimal level given what the other country is doing. It is represented by point N in Figure 23.S.1, where the two reaction lines intersect. It is now clear why the noncooperative point is suboptimal. There is a package of policy changes that will leave both countries better off. As the diagram has been drawn, the Pareto-superior package consists of joint expansion by the two countries, moving in the northeastward direction. This illustrates the locomotive theory, that is, each country is afraid to expand on its own

---

[3] We do the theory with two targets and one instrument, to keep it simple. We could introduce additional policy targets for each country, such as the exchange rate or the CPI. We could also introduce additional policy instruments for each country, such as fiscal policy. But one point to keep in mind is that if each country has as many independent policy instruments as policy targets, then it can obtain its optimum regardless what the other country does. (Think back to our diagram of internal and external balance in the preceding chapter.) In this case, a change in American policy has an effect in Europe if European policy-makers do not change their policy settings, but it is an effect that they can fully offset if they choose, without cooperation from the United States. Issues of conflict and coordination arise if each country has more targets than it has independent instruments, the usual case.

[4] We will assume for purposes of discussing Figure 23.S.1 that a monetary expansion in one country has a positive effect on the other country's trade balance and income, even though this is only true in some of the models shown in Table 23.2. Otherwise, the curves might look different.

FIGURE 23.S.1   The Gains from International Monetary Coordination

Each country's reaction function indicates how it would set its money supply if it took the other's as given. The Nash noncooperative equilibrium occurs at N. In this case, cooperation would take the form of both countries agreeing to joint monetary expansion. Higher welfare is attained at a cooperative point such as B.

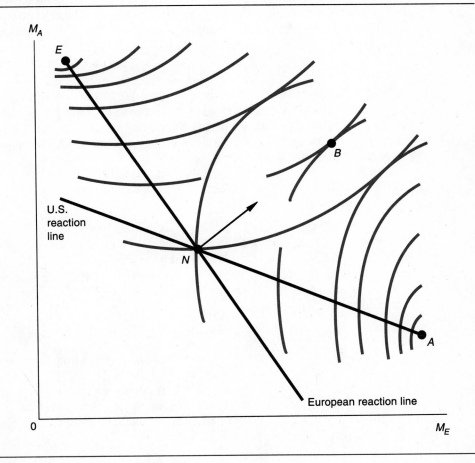

---

for fear of adverse trade balance consequences. (The figure could just as easily have been drawn so that coordination dictated some other combination of policy changes.) This package obviously raises welfare in both countries, because it moves both to higher indifference curves. Ideally they will agree to a bargain that is Pareto optimal—such as point B where the indifference curves are tangent—that is, a bargain that maximizes some weighted sum of the two countries' welfares as an omniscient world social planner would do. Any point in the "lens"-shaped area (the area bounded by the two indifference curves that run through point N) will entail gains from cooperation for both countries.

SUPPLEMENT TO CHAPTER 24:
The Flexible-Price Monetary Model of
the Exchange Rate

This first part of the supplement presents formally the complete model described in Section 24.1: the monetary approach to exchange rate determination with perfectly flexible goods prices.[1] Logarithms will be used so that equations that would otherwise be multiplicative come out linear (additive) instead. The PPP equation (Equation 24.3) thus becomes

$$s_t = p_t - p_t^* \quad \text{% change}$$
(24.S.1)

where s_t is the log of the exchange rate, p_t is the log of the domestic price level, and p_t^* is the log of the foreign price level. (The equation implies that the percentage change of the exchange rate is equal to the percentage change of the domestic price level minus the percentage change of the foreign price level.) The money demand equations (Equations 24.4 and 24.6) become

$$m_t - p_t = y_t - \mu i_t$$
(24.S.2)
$$m_t^* - p_t^* = y_t^* - \mu i_t^*$$
(24.S.3)

where m_t and m_t^* are the logs of the countries' money supplies, y_t and y_t^* are the logs of their income levels, and μ is the semi-elasticity of money demand with respect to the interest rate. (For simplicity, this parameter is assumed to be the same in both countries. Also, the elasticity of money demand with respect to income has been assumed equal to 1, as in the text.) Combining the three equations gives the equation of exchange rate determination:

$$s_t = (m_t - m_t^*) - (y_t - y_t^*) + \mu(i_t - i_t^*)$$
(24.S.4)

This is just the logarithmic version of Equation 24.8; indeed, it furnishes the justification for entering the interest rates in difference form in the text. It is easy to see how a 1 percent increase in the domestic money supply causes a 1 percent depreciation of the domestic currency and how anything that causes an increase in the demand for domestic money (a rise in income or fall in the interest rate) has the opposite effect.

The uncovered interest parity condition is

$$i_t - i_t^* = \Delta s_t^e$$

Substitute into Equation 24.S.4 to get the logarithmic version of Equation 24.9.

$$s_t = (m_t - m_t^*) - (y_t - y_t^*) + \mu(\Delta s_t^e)$$
(24.S.5)

If the currency is expected to depreciate over the coming period ($\Delta s_t^e > 0$), the result is a low demand for the currency today and a high exchange rate. Under rational expectations, it is possible to substitute the rationally expected future exchange rate,

[1] See Michael Mussa, "The Exchange Rate, the Balance of Payments, and Monetary and Fiscal Policy under a Regime of Controlled Floating," and other papers, in Jacob Frenkel and Harry Johnson, eds., *The Economics of Exchange Rates* (Reading, MA: Addison-Wesley, 1978).

$E_t s_{t+1}$ (conditional on information available at time t), in place of the investors' expected rate, s_t^e.

$$s_t = \tilde{m}_t + \mu(E_t s_{t+1} - s_t) \qquad (24.S.6)$$

where for ease of notation $\tilde{m} \equiv (m_t - m_t^*) - (y_t - y_t^*)$. The equation can be solved for the current exchange rate, which in Equation 24.S.6 appears on both sides.

$$s_t = \frac{1}{1+\mu}\tilde{m}_t + \frac{\mu}{1+\mu}E_t s_{t+1} \qquad (24.S.7)$$

This equation shows clearly how a change in expectations can cause today's exchange rate to change even in the absence of any change in today's macroeconomic fundamentals.

What determines the expected value of next period's exchange rate? Equation 24.S.7 itself; move it one period into the future and then take the expectation.

$$s_{t+1} = \frac{1}{1+\mu}\tilde{m}_{t+1} + \frac{\mu}{1+\mu}E_{t+1}s_{t+2}$$

$$E_t s_{t+1} = \frac{1}{1+\mu}E_t\tilde{m}_{t+1} + \frac{\mu}{1+\mu}E_t s_{t+2} \qquad (24.S.8)$$

Equation 24.S.8 can be substituted into Equation 24.S.7 to get today's exchange rate as a function of two-period-ahead expectations.

$$s_t = \frac{1}{1+\mu}\tilde{m}_t + \frac{\mu}{1+\mu}\frac{1}{1+\mu}E_t\tilde{m}_{t+1} + \left(\frac{\mu}{1+\mu}\right)^2 E_t s_{t+2} \qquad (24.S.9)$$

Pushing the expectation one step further into the future may not seem very helpful, except that the process can be repeated.

$$E_t s_{t+2} = \frac{1}{1+\mu}E_t\tilde{m}_{t+2} + \frac{\mu}{1+\mu}E_t s_{t+3} \qquad (24.S.10)$$

Substitute Equation 24.S.10 into Equation 24.S.9 and continue iteratively to get the following infinite series:

$$s_t = \frac{1}{1+\mu}\left[\tilde{m}_t + \frac{\mu}{1+\mu}E_t\tilde{m}_{t+1} + \left(\frac{\mu}{1+\mu}\right)^2 E_t\tilde{m}_{t+2} \right.$$
$$\left. + \left(\frac{\mu}{1+\mu}\right)^3 E_t\tilde{m}_{t+3} + \cdots\right] \qquad (24.S.11)$$

It is now clear that the entire expected future path of the relative money supply matters for determining today's exchange rate. The sum of the series is not infinite (assuming the money process itself is not explosive) because each stage multiplies by a factor $\mu/(1+\mu)$ less than 1. Today's exchange rate can be considered as a "present discounted sum" of future money supplies. We will use Equation 24.S.11 for three experiments which were also considered in the text. First, what happens if people suddenly decide today that the money supply will be increased by 1 percent at some point T periods into the future? It is immediately clear from Equation 24.S.11 that today's exchange rate will increase by $[1/(1 + \mu)][\mu/(1 + \mu)]^T$ percent. The chapter explained why: Forward-looking investors realize that the currency will lose value in the future, so they seek to shift out of it today. This is the case illustrated in Figure 24.1(c).

Second, what happens if the current money supply goes up by 1 percent? It depends how the expectations of future money supplies are affected. If the change in the current money supply is purely transitory (i.e., if the level is expected to go back down next period), then the current exchange rate goes up by $1/(1 + \mu)$ percent. The current depreciation is less than proportionate because speculators increase their demand for the currency in the knowledge that it will be gaining value over the *coming* period, thus partly offsetting the effect of the increase in supply. What if all the future money supplies are expected to be higher by the same 1 percent as the current money supply? This will be the case if the money supply is thought to follow a random walk. (The increase in the level of the expected money supply is permanent, but the increase in the growth rate is transitory.) When $\Delta \tilde{m}_t = \Delta E_t \tilde{m}_{t+1} = \Delta E_t \tilde{m}_{t+2} = \cdots$, then Equation 24.S.11 becomes the sum of a geometric series.[2]

$$\Delta s_t = \frac{1}{1 + \mu} \left[1 + \frac{\mu}{1 + \mu} + \frac{\mu}{1 + \mu} + \cdots \right] \Delta \tilde{m}_t$$

$$= \frac{1}{1 + \mu} \left[\frac{1}{1 - (\mu/1 + \mu)} \right] \Delta \tilde{m}_t = \Delta \tilde{m}_t \qquad (24.S.12)$$

In other words, the exchange rate goes up by the same 1 percent as the relative money supply. This is the case illustrated in Figure 24.1(b). When the money supplies follow random walks, the exchange rate moves in proportionate lockstep.

Finally, consider the case where the money supply is expected to rise at a new steady-state growth rate of 1 percent per annum (relative to the foreign money supply and to the countries' real incomes). Then for any period T years in the future, the money supply is expected to be T percent higher. The answer, though we omit its derivation from Equation 24.S.11, is that the effect on today's exchange rate is a depreciation of μ percent. The depreciation occurs at the moment that investors revise their expectation of the money growth rate, as is illustrated in Figure 24.1(a). Subsequently, if the money supply does indeed grow at a 1 percent faster rate, as expected, then the exchange rate increases at a 1 percent faster rate from then on. Equation 24.S.5 clearly shows that a 1 percent increase in the rate of expected depreciation causes a μ percent depreciation today.

Recall that μ is the semi-elasticity of money demand with respect to the rate of return on alternative assets. It has been estimated to be roughly in the range of 2 to 5. John Bilson, for example, obtained an estimate for the long-run semi-elasticity of 2.3, for the mark/pound exchange rate.[3] This estimate implies that when news about faster money growth raises the expected inflation rate by 1.0 percent per annum, the immediate impact on the equilibrium exchange rate is a depreciation of 2.3 percent (even before taking into account any overshooting, of the type discussed in Section 24.4 and the chapter appendix).

---

[2] Recall that the sum of a geometric series is 1 over the quantity 1 minus the factor that multiplies each term to get the next.

[3] John Bilson, ''Rational Expectations and the Exchange Rate,'' in Jacob Frenkel and Harry Johnson, eds., *The Economics of Exchange Rates* (Reading, MA: Addison-Wesley, 1978), p. 92.

The Overshooting Model of the Exchange Rate

We can continue to use logs to represent the monetary model when goods prices are sticky. The assumption that expected real depreciation is formed regressively is written,

$$\Delta s^e_{\text{real}} = -\theta(s - \bar{s}) \qquad (24.S.13)$$

Expected real depreciation is set equal to the real interest differential by international equalization of expected rates of return. Then, solving for the exchange rate shows how the percentage "undervaluation" is related to the real interest differential:

$$s - \bar{s} = -(1/\theta)(r - r^*) \qquad (24.S.14)$$

Equation 24.S.14 describes the magnitude of overshooting relative to long-run equilibrium. An increase in the real interest rate makes domestic assets more attractive and causes the currency to appreciate.

An increase in the level of the money supply causes a proportionate increase in the long-run equilibrium exchange rate, as we know from the earlier monetarist model, and in addition causes the exchange rate to overshoot. The magnitude of the overshooting is $1/\theta$ times the decrease in the interest rate (by Equation 24.S.14), which in turn is μ times the percentage increase in the money supply (by Equation 24.S.2). Thus a 1 percent increase in the money supply has a total initial impact on the exchange rate of $[1 + (1/\mu\theta)]$ percent.

SUPPLEMENT TO CHAPTER 25:
The Optimally Diversified Portfolio

This supplement develops the theory of optimal portfolio diversification described in Chapter 25.[1] To simplify, assume that there are only two assets, marks and dollars. The problem is how investors should allocate their portfolios between these two assets.

Use x to denote the share of the portfolio that investors decide to allocate to marks and $(1 - x)$ to dollars. The ex post real rate of return on the investors' total portfolio, r, is given by

$$r = xr^{DM} + (1 - x)r^{\$} \qquad (25.S.1)$$

where r^{DM} is the ex post real return on deutschemarks and $r^{\$}$ is the ex post real return on dollars. The investors care about two things: the mean or average return on their overall portfolio (they want it to be high) and the risk or uncertainty in their overall

---

[1] Some of the papers that spell out optimal diversification of the international portfolio in more detail are: Michael Adler and Bernard Dumas, "International Portfolio Choice and Corporation Finance: A Survey," *Journal of Finance* 38, (1983): 925–984; Rudiger Dornbusch, "Exchange Risk and the Macroeconomics of Exchange Rate Determination," in R. Hawkins, R. Levich, and C. Wihlborg, eds., *The Internationalization of Financial Markets and National Economic Policy*, (Greenwich: JAI Press, 1983); Jeffrey Frankel, "In Search of the Exchange Risk Premium: A Six-Currency Test Assuming *Mean-Variance Optimization*," *Journal of International Money and Finance* 1, (December 1982); and Pentti Kouri and Jorge Braga de Macedo, "Exchange Rates and the International Adjustment Process," *Brookings Papers on Economic Activity*, 1978, 1, pp. 111–130.

portfolio (they want it to be low). The average return is measured by the statistical concept of the *expected value*, represented by E; the expected return on the portfolio is given by

$$E(r) = xE(r^{DM}) + (1 - x)E(r^\$) \qquad (25.S.2)$$

(The E passes right through the x and $1 - x$; the expected value of half of the Dow Jones index is equal to half the expected value of the Dow Jones index.) The risk is measured by the statistical concept of the *variance*, represented by V. Basic properties of the variance can be used to show how the variance of the overall portfolio depends on the allocation share, x, and on the individual variances.[2]

$$V(r) = x^2V(r^{DM}) + (1 - x)^2V(r^\$) + x(1 - x)\,2\mathrm{Cov}(r^{DM}, r^\$) \qquad (25.S.3)$$

The last term represents the covariance, which reflects the correlation between the return on marks and the return on dollars. One lesson to be drawn from Equation 25.S.3 is that overall risk, $V(r)$, will be greater if the two returns are highly correlated. Chapter 25 mentioned that investors are happy if they can hold a pair of assets that have a low correlation.

Consider first the case where the two currencies happen to have the same variances: $V(r^{DM}) = V(r^\$) \equiv \overline{V}$. Is the overall risk in the portfolio the same regardless of the allocation x, because each asset has the same variance? The answer is no. Diversification among assets allows investors to reduce their risk.[3] If $x = 1$ (the portfolio is allocated entirely to marks), then $V(r) = \overline{V}[= V(r^{DM})]$; and if $x = 0$ (the portfolio is allocated entirely to dollars), then $V(r) = \overline{V}[= V(r^\$)]$; but if x is anything in between $V(r)$ is lower than $\overline{V}$. This is an example of the gains from diversification.[4] Risk-averse investors will not put all their portfolio into marks, even if the expected return on marks is greater than the expected return on dollars.

Now take the case where the dollar is considered completely safe. This will be the case if the investors are American residents seeking to minimize the risk of their position expressed in terms of dollars (either because they consume only U.S. goods with prices predetermined in dollars or because they represent a corporation seeking to minimize variability in terms of dollars for accounting reasons). The returns expressed in dollars are given by $r^\$ = i^\$$ (the U.S. interest rate) and $r^{DM} = i^{DM} + \Delta s$ (the German nominal interest rate plus the rate of appreciation of the mark against the dollar), respectively. The interest rates are already determined at the time the investors make their decision; this means that their variances are zero. Only the change in the

---

[2] The variance of r is defined as $E(r - Er)^2$. If this concept is unfamiliar, notice that it indicates how far away (by the square of the distance) r is from Er on average. Two properties are needed to derive Equation 25.S.3: The variance of x times a random variable is equal to x^2 times the variance of the variable, and the variance of the sum of two variables is equal to the sum of the variances of the two variables plus 2 times the covariance.

[3] The one exception arises where the returns on the two securities are perfectly correlated. In that case, it is not possible to reduce risk at all by diversification, because holding one is just like holding the other. [Exercise: Find $V(r)$ in Equation 25.S.3 when $\mathrm{cov}(r^{DM}, r^\$) = V(r^{DM}) = V(r^\$)$. Does it depend on x?]

[4] Assume for simplicity that the covariance is zero. Then $V(r) = x^2\overline{V} + (1 - x)^2\overline{V}$. The variance of the overall portfolio is minimized by setting $x = \frac{1}{2}$. You are asked to show this in Problem 3 at the end of Chapter 25.

spot rate is uncertain. Equation 25.S.2 for the mean becomes

$$E(r) = x(i^{DM} + E\Delta s) + (1 - x)(i^\$) \tag{25.S.4}$$

Equation 25.S.3 for the variance reduces to

$$V(r) = x^2 V(\Delta s) \tag{25.S.5}$$

The expressions for the mean and variance can be used to see how investors will choose x. If they are extremely risk-averse, caring little for expected returns and seeking only to minimize variance, then they will choose $x = 0$ because that way they can attain $V(r) = 0$. In other words, they will hold no marks at all, only dollars. This makes sense because of the assumption that they view the dollar as entirely safe.

In general, however, investors will care about both the mean and variance. Assume that they seek to maximize a function, W, of the mean and variance $W[E(r), V(r)]$. To choose the value of x that maximizes welfare, differentiate W with respect to x,

$$dW/dx = [dW/dE(r)][dE(r)/dx] + [dW/dV(r)][dV(r)/dx] \tag{25.S.6}$$

and substitute derivatives of the mean from Equation 25.S.4 and the variance from Equation 25.S.5.

$$dW/dx = [dW/dE(r)][i^{DM} + E\Delta s - i^\$] + [dW/dV(r)][2xV(\Delta s)]$$

Finally, set the derivative equal to zero, and solve for x to find the investors' optimal portfolio allocation.

$$x = \frac{[i^{DM} + E\Delta s - i^\$]}{\{[-dW/dV(r)]/[2dW/dE(r)]\}V(\Delta s)} \tag{25.S.7}$$

The expression inside the curly brackets measures how much the investors dislike risk relative to how much they like expected gains. It is often known as the coefficient of relative risk aversion, and so is denoted here by $\text{RRA} \equiv \{[-dW/dV(r)]/[2dW/dE(r)]\}$. Recall also the definition of the risk premium on marks.

$$rp \equiv [i^{DM} + E\Delta s - i^\$]$$

Thus, the expression for the optimal portfolio can be written more compactly.

$$x = rp/[\text{RRA } V(\Delta s)] \tag{25.S.8}$$

This equation states that the share of the portfolio allocated to marks (x) depends (1) positively on the expected rate of return relative to dollars (rp), (2) inversely on the coefficient of relative risk aversion (RRA), and (3) inversely on the variance of the change in the exchange rate. Notice again that if the investors are highly risk-averse (RRA is large), then they will hold few marks. What happens if the investors do not mind risk at all? They are said to be risk-neutral. When $\text{RRA} = 0$, the denominator is zero. Of course, x cannot be infinite, but the investors are infinitely responsive to expected rates of return. This is the case when marks and dollars are perfect substitutes.

The consequences are seen more clearly by inverting Equation 25.S.8.

$$rp = [\text{RRA } V(\Delta s)]x \tag{25.S.9}$$

Now it is clear that if investors have zero risk-aversion, then their infinite sensitivity to expected returns ensures that the risk premium is zero. The same holds if there is no uncertainty regarding the future exchange rate: $V(\Delta s) = 0$. In general, however, with nonzero risk and nonzero risk-aversion, the risk premium should also be nonzero. Notice, finally, that if x, the share of the portfolio consisting of marks, increases (for example, because the German government issues more bonds, which someone in the market must hold), then rp increases: Marks have to pay a higher expected return to induce investors to hold them.

Index